A POLITICAL AND ECONOMIC DICTIONARY OF CENTRAL AND SOUTH-EASTERN EUROPE

A POLITICAL AND ECONOMIC DICTIONARY OF CENTRAL AND SOUTH-EASTERN EUROPE

Roger East, Catherine Jagger and
Carolyn Postgate

FIRST EDITION

Routledge
Taylor & Francis Group

LONDON AND NEW YORK

First edition 2010

© Cambridge International Reference on Current Affairs (CIRCA) Ltd, 2010

Compiled and typeset by Cambridge International Reference on Current Affairs (CIRCA) Ltd, Cambridge, England

Published by Routledge, Albert House, 1–4 Singer Street, London EC2A 4BQ, United Kingdom
(Routledge is an imprint of the Taylor & Francis Group, an **informa** business)

ISBN 978-185743-359-3

Printed and bound in Great Britain by MPG Books, Bodmin, Cornwall

FOREWORD

A POLITICAL AND ECONOMIC DICTIONARY OF CENTRAL AND SOUTH-EASTERN EUROPE is being published for the first time as a separate entity from *A Political and Economic Dictionary of Eastern Europe*, the first edition of which covered the region as a whole.

The structure and organization of government, politics, production, international relations and trade across Europe has been reshaped dramatically in the past two decades. Since the collapse of communism, even the simplest maps of the continent's constituent countries from the Baltic to the Balkans, have had to be redrawn many times over. We have also had to rethink some of our broader concepts of the political geography of the continent. No longer is the default division that of East and West, along the political/military fault line of the furthest reach of Soviet domination. An older idea of Central Europe has, to some extent, recrystallized, and indeed been incorporated within the expanded membership of the European Union (EU), whose boundaries have also extended further to the south and east.

This book, *A Political and Economic Dictionary of Central and South-Eastern Europe,* accordingly covers the three Baltic States, four other former communist countries—the Czech Republic, Hungary, Poland and Slovakia—for which the term Central Europe is both historically appropriate and geographically accurate, and all of the Balkan States. The inclusion of Greece and Cyprus rounds out this geographical grouping. Among these countries, only Albania and most of the ex-Yugoslav countries have yet to realize the ambition of joining the EU.

Readers might note that a separate volume, *A Political and Economic Dictionary of Eastern Europe*, the second edition of which was published in 2007, covers the Russian Federation (although much of this vast country is obviously Asian rather than European), and those European countries which once formed part of the original Soviet Union, namely Belarus, Ukraine, Moldova, and the trans-Caucasian republics of Georgia, Armenia and Azerbaijan.

Although there can be no 'ideal time' to try to capture the shape of the contemporary political and economic situation in any region of the world, there is a powerful case for trying to establish an overview based on up-to-date information, and this is an objective that this book seeks to serve.

Entries in the dictionary are designed to stand on their own in providing definitions and essential facts, with coverage of recent developments and, where appropriate, full contact details. The broad scope of the dictionary includes political groups, institutions, main government leaders and prominent individuals, financial and trade bodies, religious organizations, ethnic groups, regions, geographical areas and principal cities, as well as essential terms and concepts, flashpoints, and other entries as appropriate.

There is extensive cross-referencing between entries, indicated by the simple and widely familiar device of using a bold typeface for those words or entities that have their own coverage. There is also a listing, by country, of the entries relevant to that country (p. 509), and a comprehensive index of personal names (p. 517).

The longest individual entries in this book are those for the region's 19 individual countries, giving a succinct structural description and historical survey to place recent events in context. The country entries are followed in each case by entries on that country's economy, again combining up-to-date basic data with a short overview and a focus on recent issues and developments.

Cambridge, May 2010

ACKNOWLEDGEMENTS

The editors gratefully acknowledge the assistance received with the compilation of this book from many of the organizations listed in it. We are also greatly indebted to the staff of Cambridge International Reference on Current Affairs (CIRCA) Ltd for their painstaking work in collecting and revising data, and to the *Europa World Year Book* which has been used extensively for the cross-checking of detailed factual information. (See www.europaworld. com.)

Special thanks go to Alan J. Day for his work in compiling the basic texts for the Cyprus and Greece entries in the current volume.

We also wish to acknowledge the assistance of national statistical offices, government departments and diplomatic missions, as well as the following publications as invaluable sources of statistical information for the present volume: the United Nations Population Fund's *The State of the World Population*, the World Bank's *World Bank Atlas* and *World Development Indicators*, the International Monetary Fund's *Direction of Trade Statistics Yearbook*, the Inter-Parliamentary Union's Parline Database, the International Institute for Strategic Studies' *The Military Balance* and CIRCA's *People in Power*.

CONTENTS

INTERNATIONAL TELEPHONE CODES

Central and South-Eastern Europe

Albania +355
Bosnia and Herzegovina +387
Bulgaria +359
Croatia +385
Cyprus +357
Czech Republic +420
Estonia +372
Greece +30
Hungary +36
Kosovo +381
Latvia +371
Lithuania +370
Macedonia, former Yugoslav Republic +389
Montenegro +382
Poland +48
Romania +40
Serbia +381
Slovakia +421
Slovenia +386

(The Turkish Republic of Northern Cyprus is accessed through Turkey's code +90 followed by 392.)

Other countries hosting relevant international organizations

Austria +43
Belgium +32
China, People's Republic +86
Finland +358
France +33

Iran +98
Italy +39
Netherlands +31
Norway +47
Saudi Arabia +966
Sweden +46
Switzerland +41
Turkey +90
United Kingdom +44
United States of America +1

ABBREVIATIONS

Used in addresses

Al.	aleja (alley, avenue)
Ave	avenue
bd, blvd, Bul., bulv.	boulevard (avenue)
BP	Boite Postale (Post Box)
c/o	care of
CP	Case Postale (Post Box)
Gen.	General
pl.	place (square)
POB	Post Office Box
pr.	prospect (avenue)
St	strada (street)
Str.	strada (street)
u., ut.	utca (street)
ul.	ulica/ulitsa (street)
vul.	vulitsa (street)

Miscellaneous

b/d	barrels per day
c.	circa
CEO	chief executive officer
Chair.	chairman/woman
EU	European Union
GDP	gross domestic product
GNP	gross national product
IMF	International Monetary Fund
m.	million
NATO	North Atlantic Treaty Organization
PPP	purchasing power parity
UN	United Nations

A

Abrene question

A territorial dispute between the Russian Federation and **Latvia** over the Abrene region along their common border. The 1920 Treaty of **Rīga** assigned the Abrene region to Latvia, but in the border reconstruction undertaken by the **Soviet** authorities towards the end of the Second World War, Abrene and its environs were absorbed wholesale into Russia, then becoming known as Pytalovo. Continuing dissent was muted due to the totalitarian nature of the Soviet state. Upon independence the Latvian authorities did not officially drop their claim to the district, setting out their case in a 1992 resolution, but the matter was not taken further.

Wording for a border treaty recognizing the *de facto* border between Russia and Latvia was formulated in 1997, but it was not until 2005 that both countries declared their agreement to sign this treaty, following Latvia's membership of the **North Atlantic Treaty Organization** and the **European Union**. Even then there was a hold-up just before the signing ceremony, when Latvia attempted to add a reference to the 1920 treaty, and Russia thereupon refused to sign the document at all. A further two years of wrangling finally ended with the Latvian **Parliament**'s approval of the signing of the treaty without the contentious reference.

Adriatic Charter

Charter signed in Washington, DC, on 2 May 2003, originally by **Albania**, **Croatia** and **Macedonia** to advance their integration into the **North Atlantic Treaty Organization** (NATO). These countries had formerly been part of the 10-member **Vilnius Group**. Two more countries, **Montenegro** and **Bosnia and Herzegovina**, joined the charter on 4 December 2008, while Albania and Croatia left on accession to NATO on 1 April 2009.

Aegean Macedonia *see* **Macedonian question**.

Agency for Restructuring and Privatization

Government agency in **Slovenia**.
   Director: Mira Puc.
   Address: Kotnikova 28, 1000 Ljubljana.
   Telephone: (1) 1326030.
   Fax: (1) 1316011.
   E-mail: webmaster@arspip.si
   Internet: www.arspip.si

AIDS
(acquired immunodeficiency syndrome)

Discussion of the impact of AIDS in **central** and **south-eastern Europe** has generally focused on the poorer sections of society, and particularly on drug users. The prevalence of HIV (human immunodeficiency virus, the virus responsible for AIDS) varies across the region. The situation is worst in **Estonia**, where UN figures for 2007 recorded that 1.3% of adults aged 15–49 were infected with HIV, a total of around 10,000 people. The level is 0.8% in **Latvia**, though the rate of infection in neither country is accelerating. In 2006 the number of newly diagnosed HIV infections was highest in **Poland** (750), Estonia (504), Turkey (290) and **Romania** (180). The fact that the epidemic has its roots among the socially excluded—drug users, sex workers and homosexuals—has made raising awareness, and prompting government action, disproportionately difficult.

AINA *see* **Albanian Independent News Agency**.

AKEL *see* **Progressive Party for the Working People**.

AKP *see* **National Agency for Privatization**.

Albania
Republika e Shqipërisë

An independent republic located in south-eastern Europe on the western coast of the **Balkan** peninsula, bounded by Montenegro to the north, Kosovo to the north-east, Macedonia to the east, Greece to the south, and the Ionian and Adriatic Seas to the west. Administratively, Albania is divided into 12 counties (qarqe—also called prefectures), 36 districts (rrethe), 65 municipalities and 309 communes.

Area: 27,398 sq. km; *capital*: **Tirana**; *population*: 3.2m. (2009 estimate), comprising ethnic **Albanians** c.95%, Greeks c.3%, others c.2%; *official language*: Albanian; *religion*: Muslim c.70%, Albanian **Orthodox** c.20%, **Roman Catholic** c.10%.

The supreme organ of government is the unicameral **People's Assembly** (Kuvendi Popullor) of at least 140 members elected for a four-year term. The Assembly elects the President as Head of State for a five-year term (once renewable) and also approves the Prime Minister designated by the President.

History: Albania was under Ottoman Turkish rule for five centuries from c.1400. Following an early revolt, conversion to Islam was widespread, often enforced, and the region had a majority Muslim population by the 18th century. Turkish repression and Albania's mountain-enclosed isolation inhibited the emergence of a nationalist movement until the 1870s. Independence was declared in November 1912 during the Balkan Wars and recognized internationally virtually within Albania's present-day borders under the 1913 Treaty of Bucharest. Thus Epirus was divided between Albania and **Greece** (*see* **Epirus question**), Albanian-majority **Kosovo** was confirmed as part of **Serbia**, and substantial ethnic Albanian minority populations were incorporated within both **Macedonia** and **Montenegro**.

A brief period of democratic rule after the First World War was ended in 1924 by the autocratic rule of a conservative Albanian chieftain who proclaimed himself King Zog in 1928 (*see* **Albanian royal family**). King Zog was deposed by the Italian invasion of April 1939. Italian occupation was followed during the Second World War by the launching of an abortive Italian attack on Greece, German military intervention in 1941 and the creation of a **Greater Albania** entity under Italian protection. Following Italy's exit from the war in 1943, communist-led Albanian partisans backed by the Allies expelled the Germans in mid-1944.

A People's Republic was established in January 1946 under the leadership of what became the Albanian Party of Labour (PPSh). Over the next four decades Albania pursued a rigidly Stalinist line. It was aligned with the **Soviet Union** until the early 1960s and then with the People's Republic of China until the late 1970s, after which it maintained an isolationist stance. A cult of personality surrounded long-term PPSh leader Enver **Hoxha**. He died in April 1985. His successor as party leader, Ramiz Alia, who was also Head of State from November 1982, oversaw a limited improvement in relations with the West including the ending of the technical state of war between Albania and Greece in 1987.

Albania's isolation did not leave it entirely unaffected by the turbulent events of 1989 as communist regimes collapsed elsewhere in **eastern Europe**. The Alia regime agreed to the formation of opposition parties in December 1990. Multi-party elections in March–April 1991 were won by the PPSh, which in June was renamed the **Socialist Party of Albania** (PSSh). A coalition Government headed by the PSSh gave way in December 1991 to Albania's first non-Marxist administration since the Second World War. Further elections in March 1992 were won by the centrist **Democratic**

3

Party of Albania (PDSh), whereupon Alia resigned as President and was succeeded by Sali **Berisha**. The latter appointed Aleksander Meksi (PDSh) as Prime Minister, heading a coalition that included two smaller parties.

Under a controversial 'genocide' law barring former communists from public life until 2002, some 70 opposition candidates, mostly PSSh members, were excluded from legislative elections held in May–June 1996, with the result that the opposition boycotted the second round of voting. In polling adjudged by international observers to have been riddled with malpractice, the PDSh obtained a large majority but nevertheless brought two smaller parties into the new Government. Opposition protest actions were compounded from early 1997 by popular outrage at the collapse of several **'pyramid' investment schemes**, amid allegations of government connivance in the frauds. Widespread anarchy and the establishment of rebel control in the south continued despite the declaration of a state of emergency and the formation in March 1997 of a broad-based Government of Reconciliation under Bashkim Fino of the PSSh. From April, on the initiative of the **Organization for Security and Co-operation in Europe** (OSCE), a 6,000-strong Italian-led multinational protection force was deployed in Albania with UN approval. The force helped to restore a measure of public order before it withdrew in August, although without reducing the exodus of large numbers of Albanians seeking illegal entry to Italy and other western European countries.

People's Assembly elections in June–July 1997, described as relatively fair by observers, resulted in a heavy defeat for the PDSh and the return of the former communists to government. The PSSh won 101 seats, with 52.8% of the vote, whereas the PDSh as the second-largest party won only 29 seats. Berisha resigned as President immediately after the elections, whereupon the Assembly elected Rexhep Meidani (PSSh) as his successor unopposed. The new President appointed a coalition headed by Fatos Nano (PSSh) and including four smaller parties, the Social Democratic Party of Albania (PSDSh), the Human Rights Union Party (PBDNj), the Party of the Democratic Alliance (PAD) and the Albanian Agrarian Party (PASh).

Further instability in September 1998 resulted in Nano being replaced as Prime Minister by Pandeli Majko (PSSh), who at 31 became Europe's youngest Head of Government, heading a coalition of the same five parties. The country's first post-communist Constitution was approved by 93.5% of those voting in a referendum held on 22 November 1998, although the PDSh rejected the new text and claimed that the turnout had been well below the official figure of just over 50%.

Having failed to dislodge Nano's grip on the PSSh leadership, Majko resigned as Prime Minister in October 1999 and was succeeded by Ilir Meta (PSSh), who continued the existing five-party coalition. Controversial cabinet changes in July 2000 provoked a further temporary boycott of parliament by the PDSh, which accused the Meta Government of fostering corruption and smuggling. Nevertheless, in local elections in October the PSSh made major advances, notably winning control of Tirana, hitherto a PDSh stronghold.

Legislative elections held on 24 June 2001 resulted in another clear majority for the PSSh, which won 73 of the 140 seats with 42% of the vote. The Union for Victory coalition, headed by the PDSh, won 46 (36.8% of the vote), the New Democrat Party (PDR) six (5.1%), the PSDSh four (3.6%), the PBDNj three (2.6%), the PASh three (2.6%), the PAD three (2.5%) and non-partisans two.

Despite relative approval for the 2001 poll from international election observers, the PDSh condemned it as 'farcical'. From the opening of the new legislature in September 2001 the party and its coalition partners refused to take up their seats for several months.

Meta was re-elected Prime Minister at the head of a 'non-partisan' cabinet. However, the PSSh Government soon ran into internal difficulties. Party Chairman Nano blocked the appointment of Ministers in a reshuffle in late 2001, accusing Meta and his team of corruption and ultimately forcing the resignation of four Ministers in December. On 29 January 2002 Meta resigned, and Majko was nominated on seven February to head a Government that included supporters from each of the two PSSh factions. This took office on 22 February, and the following month the opposition ended its parliamentary boycott.

Nano had to set aside his presidential ambitions, the PSSh recognizing that his candidacy was too divisive to achieve the required three-fifths majority in view of the adamant hostility of the PDSh. Instead Gen. (retd) Alfred Moisiu was nominated as a compromise candidate; he was elected by the People's Assembly on 24 June with 97 votes out of 140, and took office a month later on 24 July. The following day Majko resigned as Prime Minister, and Nano was appointed in his place, again heading a Government containing both his supporters and Meta's. This Government lasted for a year, but in July 2003 Meta and one of his close allies resigned. Meta then obstructed the appointment of replacements, and by November the number of unfilled ministerial vacancies had risen to four. Moisiu insisted on Nano filling the posts, so he negotiated a Coalition for Integration with the PSDSh, PBDNj, PAD, the Environmentalist Agrarian Party (PAA—successor to the APA) and the Social Democracy Party of Albania (PDSSh—a splinter from the PSDSh), and a new Government was approved on 29 December.

Meta left the PSSh in September 2004, and formed the Socialist Movement for Integration (LSI). Several PSSh members defected to the new party, causing the PSSh to lose its majority in the People's Assembly.

At the 3 July 2005 People's Assembly election the PDSh won 56 seats, the PSSh won 42 seats and the National Front, led by the Republican Party of Albania (PRSh), won 18 seats. The PSDSh won seven seats, the LSI won five seats, the PAA won four seats, the PAD won three seats, the PDSSh won two seats, as did the PBDNj, while the final seat went to an independent. Final results were not released until the beginning of September, giving a total of 80 seats to the PDSh and its allies, as opposed to 60 for the PSSh and its allies. On 2 September PDSh leader Berisha was nominated as Prime Minister, and a Government of the PDSh, PRSh, New Democrat

Party, PAA and PBDNj was approved on 10 September. (In July 2006 the Christian Democratic Party of Albania also joined the Government.) Meanwhile, Nano had resigned as Chair of the PSSh, succeeded by Mayor of Tirana Edi Rama in October.

In 2007 the PDSh nominated Bamir **Topi** to be the next President, without consulting the opposition. The PSSh boycotted the repeated ballots, leaving Topi just short of the three-fifths of the vote required to secure election. Only at the fourth attempt (of a constitutionally possible five before the People's Assembly would have had to be dissolved) did five PSSh and two PAD deputies break the boycott to end the stalemate. Topi was sworn in four days later, on 24 July.

Electoral reform in 2008 ended the system of 100 constituency seats and 40 seats allocated by proportional representation in the People's Assembly, in favour of a full proportional representation system. Also the majority required in a presidential election was reduced from three-fifths of Assembly votes to a simple majority of 50%. Smaller parties complained that the full PR system would unduly disadvantage them. In the run-up to the June 2009 elections, the PBDNj left the Government to join the PSSh's electoral coalition.

Latest elections: At the 28 June 2009 People's Assembly election, the PDSh-led Alliance for Changes won 70 seats and 46.9% of the vote (PDSh 68; PRSh one; Party for Justice and Integration one; 13 others including PAA none). The PSSh-led Unification for Changes won 66 seats and 45.3% of the vote (PSSh 65; PBDNj one; three others including PSDSh none). The Socialist Alliance, led by the LSI, won the remaining four seats (with 5.6% of the vote). International observers declared that the election process was making progress toward European democratic standards.

Recent developments: One seat short of a majority, the PDSh-led Alliance found itself looking for a coalition partner from among its left-wing opponents. Berisha negotiated a coalition with the LSI, and his new cabinet was approved by the People's Assembly on 16 September.

International relations and defence: Albania's transition to multi-party democracy in 1990–91 facilitated a transformation of its external relations. Admitted to what became the OSCE in 1991, Albania joined NATO's **Partnership for Peace** in 1994 and the **Council of Europe** in 1995. It is also a member of the **Organization of the Black Sea Economic Co-operation** and the **Central European Initiative**. As a predominantly Muslim country, Albania joined the **Organisation of the Islamic Conference** (OIC) in 1992, confirming its membership in December 1998 after some uncertainty earlier in the year.

Relations with **Yugoslavia** deteriorated from mid-1998 over the treatment of ethnic Albanians in the Serbian-ruled province of Kosovo. The Albanian Government accordingly gave full support to the air-strikes launched against Yugoslavia by the **North Atlantic Treaty Organization** (NATO) in March 1999 and welcomed the agreement in June under which Yugoslav forces were obliged to withdraw from Kosovo and the province placed under an effective NATO protectorate. NATO subsequently deployed Albania Force (AFOR) to help Albania cope with the influx of refugees from Kosovo, this mission being succeeded by an Italian-led force in September 1999. That year, Albania received a NATO Membership Action Plan, and a decade later it acceded to the organization on 1 April 2009.

Signalling its European aspirations, Albania in April 2000 signed Council of Europe instruments confirming the country's formal abolition of the death penalty. Negotiations for a Stabilization and Association Agreement (SAA) with the **European Union** (EU) began in January 2003, but the Agreement was not signed until June 2006, due to delays over lack of progress with implementing judicial and police reforms. The SAA entered into force on 1 April 2009, and at the end of that month Albania made a formal application for EU membership.

Always a staunch supporter of the ethnic Albanian community in Kosovo, Albania was one of the first countries to recognize the province's declaration of independence from Serbia on 17 February 2008.

Albania's defence budget for 2008 amounted to some US $254m., equivalent to about 1.9% of GDP. The size of the armed forces in 2010 was some 14,000 personnel. The armed forces became fully professional from 1 January 2010.

Albania, economy

One of the least developed economies in Europe. The movement of people, materials and goods is hampered by the country's mainly mountainous terrain, and communications problems are compounded by poor infrastructure.

GNP: US $12,057m. (2008); *GNP per capita*: $3,840 (2008); *GDP at PPP*: $24,251m. (2008); *GDP per capita at PPP*: $7,700 (2008); *real GDP growth*: 0.7% (2009 estimate); *exports*: $1,353m. (2008); *imports*: $5,229m. (2008); *currency*: lek (plural: lekë; US $1 = L93.63 in mid-2009); *unemployment*: 12.7% (2009); *government deficit as a percentage of GDP*: 6.9% (2009); *inflation*: 1.7% (2009).

In 2006 agriculture, hunting and forestry contributed 20% of GDP, industry 25% and services 55%. Some 58% of the workforce is engaged in agriculture, 14% in industry and 28% in services.

Some 21% of the land is arable, 20% permanent pasture and crops, and 38% forest or woodland. The main crops are wheat, maize, watermelons, potatoes, tomatoes and grapes; livestock raising, dairy farming and forestry are also important.

The main mineral resources are chromium ore (of which Albania is one of the world's largest producers) and copper; there are also reserves of oil estimated at 165m. barrels. The main industries are food-processing, textiles, metal-working, building materials, wood processing and oil refining. The main energy source is hydroelectric power.

Albania's main exports by value are textiles and footwear (which accounted for 48.4% of the total), construction materials, metals, and mineral fuels and electricity. Principal imports are machinery equipment and spare parts, mineral fuels and electricity. In 2008 Italy took 62% of Albanian exports, **Greece** 9% and **Serbia** 8%; altogether, 80% of exports go to the EU, which is the source of 61% of imports, mainly from Italy (27%) and Greece (15%), while 7% come from the People's Republic of China. Remittances from **Albanians** abroad make an important contribution (equalling 9.6% of GDP in 2008), as does financial and other aid from overseas donors.

The last decade of the 20th century was an especially turbulent one for Albania's economy. The end of communist rule in 1990 and the subsequent efforts to convert to a market economy caused severe dislocation and virtual economic collapse in 1991–92. GDP fell by 40% a year and hyperinflation became a real threat. Assisted by extensive financial and technical aid from the West, aggregate growth resumed in 1993 (from a very low base), averaging 9% a year in 1993–96, and industrial production grew in 1995 (by 7%) for the first time since the collapse of communism. However, in the election year of 1996 the Government lacked sufficient resolve to maintain stabilization policies, and inflationary pressures were renewed as a result. The problems were compounded in 1997 by the collapse of **'pyramid' investment schemes** in which large numbers of Albanians had invested their savings. The resultant panic, popular uprising and anarchy contributed to an 8% fall in GDP in 1997. This was recovered in 1998 on the strength of a new economic restructuring programme. The hostilities over **Kosovo** in 1999, however, and the resultant influx of ethnic Albanian refugees, caused particular economic problems. International aid helped to defray the resultant costs, and by the end of 1999 inflation and the budget deficit were under control. GDP growth reached 7% in 2001. However, unemployment remained high, at 17% officially (and probably over 30% actually).

The increasing stability of the early 2000s attracted foreign banks into Albania, and the consequent rise in mortgage availability helped fuel growth in the construction sector. Overall economic growth was sustained with GDP increases averaging around 6% a year between 2003 and 2007, while inflation remained between 2% and 3%. Improvements in telecommunications and transport infrastructure helped facilitate this growth, but much remains to be done, particularly in the beleaguered energy sector. Reforms in tax collection and property laws have improved economic governance, but the size of the informal economy remains a major issue; the **International Monetary Fund** (IMF) estimates that it still amounts to half the total GDP, and tackling corruption and improving transparency are key to attracting more foreign investment.

In 2006 the IMF and **World Bank** approved funds totalling over US $220m. to combat poverty and unemployment, stimulate economic growth and strengthen the financial system. Also that year, the Government signed a Stabilization and Association Agreement with the EU. It entered into force in December, establishing duty-free trade for 90% of agricultural and industrial products.

The trade deficit remains a problem, with imports exceeding exports to the tune of 26% of GDP in 2008. Apart from this, the economy performed well that year, with

GDP growth rising to 6.8%, and it has been relatively sheltered from the global economic downturn, with little effect on the domestic banking sector. Small positive growth was achieved in 2009 (0.7% estimated), though drops were seen in exports and in the level of remittances from Albanians abroad, particularly Greece and Italy.

The shift away from state ownership, which dominated the entire economy under communist rule, effectively began with the transfer of most agricultural land into private ownership in 1992, followed by the privatization of small and medium-sized industrial concerns in 1993–94 and, theoretically, large enterprises from 1995. A new banking law introduced in 1996 ended state control of the banks and redefined the role of the central **Bank of Albania**, while legislation was also introduced to protect foreign investors. However, privatization in the late 1990s was marked by erratic timetabling, pervasive corruption and chronic mismanagement. A significant step in the establishment of a better ordered process was the sale of the country's Savings Bank in 2004, by which time the private sector accounted for around 75% of GDP. In mid-2007 some 80% of the state-owned telecommunications company, Albtelecom, was divested to a consortium of two Turkish companies.

Albanian Centre for Foreign Investment Promotion

Government-sponsored body founded in 1993, charged with promoting foreign investment in **Albania** and providing practical assistance to investors.
   Director: Estela Dashi.
   Address: Bulevardi Gjergj Fishta, P. Shallvare, Tirana.
   Telephone: (4) 252976.
   Fax: (4) 222341.
   E-mail: info@anih.com.al
   Internet: www.anih.com.al

Albanian Independent News Agency (AINA)
Agjensia e Lajmevetë Pavarura Shqiptare

Independent news agency founded in 1996.
   Director: Zenel Çeliku.
   Address: Rruga 4 Deshmorët Vila 80, Tirana.
   Telephone: (4) 241727.
   Fax: (4) 230094.
   E-mail: aina@abissnet.com.al
   Internet: www.tirfaxnews.com

Albanian royal family

A short-lived monarchy of the period between the two World Wars, deposed in 1939 but seven decades later still seeking a restoration. Albanian chieftain Ahmet Zogu ended a brief post-First World War period of democracy in 1924, declaring himself King Zog in 1928. He was ousted by the Italian invasion in April 1939, the crown passing to King Victor Emmanuel of Italy. Although Zog nominally resumed the throne in 1944, the post-Second World War communist regime proclaimed a People's Republic in 1946, whereupon Zog lived in exile until his death in April 1961. His only son, Leka I Zogu, settled in South Africa in the 1970s, being given diplomatic immunity by the apartheid-era Government. He maintained a claim to the Albanian throne, backed by the small **Movement of Legality Party** (PLL).

Following the end of communist rule, Leka Zogu briefly attended the PLL's 50th anniversary celebrations in Albania in November 1993, before being asked to leave by the authorities. He returned in April 1997 'to share the suffering' of the Albanian people, successfully calling for a referendum on whether the monarchy should be restored. This took place simultaneously with the July 1997 parliamentary elections, and produced a 66.7% majority in favour of continued republican status, but the PLL claimed that the vote had been rigged. During the campaign Leka Zogu held a rally of armed supporters, and he was later convicted *in absentia* of trying to organize a coup attempt. He was pardoned in 2002 and invited to return to Albania to live. Leka has now withdrawn from public life, but his son, Prince Leka II, works for the Albanian Ministry of Foreign Affairs.

Albanian Telegraphic Agency (ATA)
Agjencia Telegrafike Shqiptare—ATSh

Albania's state-owned news agency, which professes an independent editorial line, with correspondents in most main Albanian towns and also in **Kosovo**. Originally founded in 1929, ATA is proud of its role in reporting to the world about anti-fascist resistance during the Second World War, but less proud that, together with Radio Tirana, it was one of the sole sources of information about Albania in the communist era, with coverage notorious for its promotion of the cult of personality surrounding Enver **Hoxha**.

Director General: Artur Zheji.
Address: Bul. Zhan D'Ark 23, Tirana.
Telephone: (4) 235584.
Fax: (4) 234230.
E-mail: atsh@albnet.net
Internet: www.ata-al.net

Albanians

An Indo-European people living within, and dispersed in significant numbers beyond, the present-day borders of **Albania**. The Albanians migrated to the **Balkans** in about 1000 BC to the region later named Illyria (Illyricum) and annexed by the Romans. Albanians therefore claim descent from the ancient Illyrians and stress that their history as a distinct ethnic group long predates that of the surrounding **Slavic peoples**. Their regional distinctness was accentuated by five centuries of Ottoman Turkish rule from c.1400, during which most Albanians were converted to Islam, whereas the Slavs and **Greeks** remained Christian. All religious observance in Albania was banned under communist rule, but in the post-communist era many ethnic Albanians have rediscovered their Muslim heritage. Although the Albanians are essentially a homogeneous people, there have been periodic strains between two distinct dialect groups, the dominant Tosk in the south and lowlands and the Gheg in the north.

The borders of independent Albania established in 1913 left substantial numbers of ethnic Albanians in other countries, notably in **Kosovo**, **Macedonia** and **Montenegro**, and in the **Epirus** region of Greece. The creation of a **Greater Albania** has therefore been a feature of Albanian nationalist aspirations, the aim being to acquire adjoining areas containing an ethnic Albanian majority.

Figures for the numbers of ethnic Albanians outside present-day Albanian borders are mostly speculative; the US Census in 2000 listed 113,661 people of Albanian descent; in 2001 there were 443,550 Albanian emigrants in Greece, in 2006 there were 348,813 in Italy. The majority ethnic Albanian population of neighbouring Kosovo is usually put at 1.5m., while 400,000 ethnic Albanians are thought to reside in Macedonia. In the 2003 census there were 31,163 in Montenegro.

Alliance of Democrats

A loose international grouping of mainly centrist political parties, international organizations and individuals, founded in 2005. Several European countries have a political party that is a member, including **Cyprus**, **Czech Republic**, **Lithuania**, **Serbia** and **Slovakia**.

Co-Chairs: François Bayrou, Francesco Rutelli, Ellen Tauscher.
Address: Via di Sant' Andrea delle Fratte 16, 00187 Rome, Italy.
Telephone: (6) 69532367.
Fax: (6) 69532206.
E-mail: info@allianceofdemocrats.org
Internet: www.allianceofdemocrats.org

Alliance of Independent Social Democrats
Savez Nezavisnih Socijaldemokrata (SNSD)

A centre-left political formation in **Bosnia and Herzegovina**, which belongs to the **Socialist International** and commands a significant level of support in the **Serb** community. Founded in March 1996 as the Party of Independent Social Democrats (SNSD), it contested the post-**Dayton** elections in September 1996 as part of the moderate People's Alliance for Peace and Progress. It won two **Serb Republic** (RS) Assembly seats in November 1997, following which party leader Milorad **Dodik** became RS Prime Minister in January 1998, heading a non-partisan administration. In the September 1998 elections the SNSD backed the successful Socialist Party of the Serb Republic candidate for the Serb seat on the union collective presidency, while the party increased its representation in the RS Assembly to six seats. In early 1999 Dodik, with Western support, resisted efforts by RS President Nikola Poplasen of the ultra-nationalist Serbian Radical Party (SRS) to replace him as Prime Minister, withdrawing his resignation when the UN **High Representative** dismissed Poplasen. In the November 2000 elections, however, Dodik came a poor second in the contest for the RS presidency, winning only 26% of the vote and being defeated by hard-liner Mirko Šarović of the SRS. Although the SNSD improved its representation in the RS Assembly to 11 seats (and also won one in the **Muslim-Croat Federation** lower house), Dodik was succeeded as RS Prime Minister by Mladen Ivanić of the **Party of Democratic Progress** (PDP).

In May 2002 the SNSD merged with the Democratic Socialist Party, and changed to its present name, retaining the SNSD acronym. At the elections the following October it finished second in the RS Assembly with 19 seats, seven behind the leading party, while it won three seats (10.1% of the vote) in the all-Bosnia lower house and one seat in the Federation lower house. In early 2006, it forced a no-confidence vote against the RS Government and, when this succeeded, Dodik was nominated to head the new administration.

At the October 2006 elections, SNSD candidate Nebojša **Radmanović** won the Serb seat on the union Presidency with 53.3% of the vote, while in the RS Milan Jelić of the SNSD won the presidency with 48.8% of the vote. In the RS Assembly the SNSD ended just short of a clear majority, securing 41 seats in the 83-seat chamber, and in the all-Bosnia lower house it won seven seats (with 19.1% of the vote). Nikola **Špirić** of the SNSD became union Prime Minister in January 2007, while Dodik remained as RS Prime Minister.

Miroslav Lajčák took over as UN High Representative in July 2007, and in October he announced measures for reforming parliamentary and government decision-making procedures, including new regulations to prevent representatives of one ethnic group from obstructing the adoption of legislation. Serb politicians, including Dodik, threatened to boycott institutions if they were imposed, and on 1 November Špirić resigned the union premiership in protest. However, at the end of

November the Serbs ended resistance to the legislation. On 11 December Dodik announced that six of the parties in the union Assembly supported Špirić's renomination as union Prime Minister, which was approved by the Assembly on 28 December. An unchanged Council of Ministers was approved on 28 February 2008.

Meanwhile, RS President Jelić died of a heart attack in September 2007. Rajko **Kuzmanović** (also SNSD) was elected as his successor on 9 December. At his inauguration on 28 December, he stated his opposition to any further transfer of powers to central government from the entities.

Leadership: Milorad Dodik (Chair.).
Address: 5 Petra Kocića, Banja Luka 78000.
Telephone: (51) 318492.
Fax: (51) 318495.
E-mail: snsd@snsd.org
Internet: www.snsd.org

ANA *see* **Athens News Agency**.

Ansip, Andrus

Prime Minister of **Estonia**.

Andrus Ansip heads a minority Government of his own centre-right **Estonian Reform Party** (ER) and the **Union of Pro Patria and Res Publica** (IRL). A chemist and engineer at Tartu State University, he chaired various business and investment ventures, before becoming a popular Mayor of Tartu. He first took office as Prime Minister on 13 April 2005.

Born on 1 October 1956 in Tartu, he graduated in 1979 in organic chemistry from the University of Tartu (then known as Tartu State University). He remained at the university as an engineer until 1987, except for a period of military service. He then studied at the Estonian Academy of Agriculture before heading out into industry. A business management course at York University in Toronto, Canada, helped him join several management boards in the 1990s, including Rahvabank (People's Bank), Radio Tartu Ltd, Fundmanager Ltd and Livonia Privatization IF. In 1998 he was elected Mayor of Tartu, a post he held for six years. In 2004 he was appointed Minister of Economic Affairs and Communications in a coalition Government of the Union for the Republic—Res Publica, the ER and the Estonian People's Union (ERL).

When this Government fell in March 2005, Ansip himself formed a new government—having become the leader of ER following the appointment of party founder Siim Kallas as Estonia's European Union Commissioner. His coalition included the Estonian Centre Party (Kesk) and the ERL.

The ER's strong performance at the March 2007 election ushered in a second term for Ansip as Prime Minister. On this occasion his main coalition partner was the IRL. The inclusion of the **Social Democratic Party** (SDE) gave his Government a parliamentary majority for its first two years, but in May 2009 he dismissed its SDE members as a result of their protests against employment law reforms. Thereafter he continued in office as head of a minority ER–IRL Government.

Andrus Ansip is married to Anu Ansip, and speaks Estonian, English, Russian and conversational German.

Address: Office of the Prime Minister, Stenbock House, Rahukohtu 3, Tallinn
          15161.
Telephone: 6935555.
Fax: 6935554.
E-mail: valitsus@rk.ee
Internet: www.peaminister.ee

APIU *see* **Trade and Investment Promotion Agency**.

ARIS *see* **Romanian Agency for Foreign Investment**.

ARN *see* **Enterprise Restructuring Agency**.

Assembly (Croatia)
Sabor

The unicameral legislature of **Croatia**, the House being known as the House of Representatives (Zastupnički Dom). It currently has 153 members (increased from 127 to at most 160 under a law of October 1999), directly elected for a four-year term. In the enlarged House, 140 deputies are elected in 10 constituencies, eight elected by ethnic minorities, and a variable number (not more than 15) chosen to represent Croatians abroad (five in the 2007 elections). The Assembly was formerly bicameral, with an upper House of Counties (Županijski Dom). The then lower House of Representatives voted in late March 2001, however, to abolish the House of Counties after the expiry of its mandate in May 2001. The last elections were held on 25 November 2007.

Address: Zastupnički Dom, Hrvatski Sabor, Trg sv. Marka 6–7, 10000 Zagreb.
Telephone: (1) 4569222.
Fax: (1) 6303018.
E-mail: sabor@sabor.hr
Internet: www.sabor.hr

Assembly (Macedonia)
Sobranie

The unicameral legislature of **Macedonia**. It has 120 members, directly elected for a four-year term. The last elections were held on 1 June 2008, with re-runs in nearly 200 constituencies on 15 June.

Address: Sobranie, 11 Oktomvri b.b., 1000 Skopje.
Telephone: (2) 3112255.
Fax: (2) 3237947.
E-mail: sobranie@sobranie.mk
Internet: www.sobranie.mk

Assembly of Kosova
Kuvendi i Kosovës (Albanian); *Skupština Kosova* (Serbian)

The unicameral legislature of **Kosovo**. It has 120 members. Directly elected members hold 100 seats, 10 seats are reserved for Serbians, and 10 more for other minorities. All members are elected for a four-year term. The last elections were held on 17 November 2007.

Address: Rruga Nëna Tereze p.n., 10000 Pristina.
Telephone: 38211186.
Fax: 38211188.
E-mail: mail@ks-gov.net
Internet: www.kuvendikosoves.org

Assembly of the Republic of Montenegro
Skupština Republike Crne Gore

The unicameral legislature of **Montenegro**. It has 81 members, elected for a four-year term, five of whom are elected from the ethnic Albanian community. The last elections were held on 29 March 2009.

Address: Bulevar Svetog Petra Cetinjskog 10, 81000 Podgorica.
Telephone: (20) 241083.
Fax: (20) 242192.
E-mail: generalni.sekretar@skupstina.me
Internet: www.skupstina.me

Association of Lithuanian Chambers of Commerce, Industry and Crafts

Lietuvos Prekybos, Pramonės ir Amatų ru mų Asociacija

The principal organization in **Lithuania** for promoting business contacts, both internally and externally, in the post-communist era. Founded in 1992.
President: Darius Mockus.
Address: J-Tumo Vaižganto 9/1–63A, Vilnius 01108.
Telephone: (5) 2612102.
Fax: (5) 2612112.
E-mail: info@chambers.lt
Internet: www.chambers.lt

ATA *see* **Albanian Telegraphic Agency**.

Athens

The capital city of **Greece**, situated in the Attica region. *Population*: 789,166 (city, 2001 census), 3.8m (metropolitan, including suburbs, 2001 census). Athens, which has a 3,000-year history, is today the political, business and cultural hub of Greece. In the fifth and fourth centuries BC it was the centre for arts, philosophy and education, and the birthplace of western democracy. The Acropolis, with its classical temples and monuments, still dominates the city. In 1896 the city was host to the first modern-day Olympic Games, which returned there in summer 2004. Nikitas Kaklamanis became the 50th mayor of Athens in 2007, following the first female mayor of Athens, Dora Bakoyannis. The modern port of Piraeus, once separate, is now a suburb of Athens, and is an important trade centre for Mediterranean shipping.

Athens Chamber of Commerce and Industry

The principal organization in **Greece** for promoting business contacts, both internally and externally. Founded in 1919.
President: Dracoulis Foundoukakos.
Address: Odos Akademias 7, 106 71 Athens.
Telephone: (210) 3625342.
Fax: (210) 3618810.
E-mail: info@acci.gr
Internet: www.acci.gr

Athens News Agency (ANA)

Founded in 1895, ANA has correspondents in all the leading capitals of the world and towns throughout Greece.

Managing Director: Nikolas Voulelis.
General Director: Andreas Christodoulides.
Address: Odos Tsoha 36, 115 21 Athens.
Telephone: (210) 6400560.
Fax: (210) 6400581.
E-mail: ape@ana.gr
Internet: www.ana.gr

Athens Stock Exchange

Founded in 1876. In March 2010 there were 79 members.
President: Panayotis Alexakis.
Chairman: Spyridon Capralos.
Address: Odos Sophokleous 10, 105 59 Athens.
Telephone: (210) 3366800.
Fax: (210) 3311975.
E-mail: webmaster@ase.gr
Internet: www.ase.gr

Auschwitz-Birkenau
Oświęcim-Brzezinka

The infamous German Nazi concentration camp near the city of Katowice in south-west **Poland**. A memorial to the Holocaust, known as the Museum of Martyrdom, was established in 1946 on the site of the Auschwitz camp and the much larger Birkenau site where the majority of people were gassed. Most of Birkenau, including the gas chambers, was destroyed by German troops before they fled in 1945.

As one of the largest of the many concentration camps, Auschwitz-Birkenau is perhaps the most potent symbol of the genocide of European **Jews**. However, the Polish authorities have stressed that the memorial should not be seen as solely commemorating the Jewish victims. The first inmates of the camp, established in 1940 initially for the detention of political prisoners, were Polish political opponents of the Nazi regime. There was a long controversy from the mid-1980s over the establishment of a Polish Carmelite convent, in a building that was once a storehouse for the poisonous Zyklon B gas. Jewish groups protested that the 'Christianization' of the site was inappropriate and insulting to the memory of the camp's overwhelmingly more numerous Jewish victims. (It has been estimated that 1.6m. people died there, of

17

whom 1.35m. were Jews.) The last nuns left the convent in the mid-1990s but there was renewed controversy over the erection of a large number of wooden crosses for Christian victims of the Nazis, near the museum and visible from within the compound. The smaller crosses were removed in 1999, but the large Papal cross that had been erected in 1979 at the time of Pope John Paul II's mass at Auschwitz remains in situ.

The Polish Ministry of Culture requested in 2006 that UNESCO officially rename Auschwitz Concentration Camp, to emphasize that Germans rather than Poles were responsible for the deaths at the 'Polish death camp' as it was commonly referred to. In 2007 the World Heritage Committee announced the name would change to Auschwitz-Birkenau German Nazi Concentration and Extermination Camp (1940–45).

Authority for the Capitalization of State Assets
Autoritatea pentru Valorificarea Activelor Statului (AVAS)

The successor organization to the State Ownership Fund in **Romania**, AVAS was created by the merger of the Banking Assets Resolution Agency (AVAB) and the Authority for Privatization and Management of State Ownership (APAPS).

General Director: Giliola Ciorteanu (acting).
Address: Str. Capt. A. Şerbănescu 50, 715151 Bucharest 1.
Telephone: (21) 3036122.
Fax: (21) 3036521.
E-mail: infopublic@avas.gov.ro
Internet: www.avas.gov.ro

AVAS *see* **Authority for the Capitalization of State Assets**.

B

Bajnai, Gordon

Prime Minister of **Hungary** (2009–10).

Independent businessman Gordon Bajnai was chosen as Prime Minister in April 2009 to manage Hungary's severe economic crisis caused by the global credit crunch. At that time, he had been serving as Economy Minister in the **Hungarian Socialist Party** (MSzP) Government of his old friend Ferenc Gyurcsány. He will be replaced in late May 2010, following the **National Assembly** election in April.

Born on 5 March 1968 in Szeged, Gordon György Bajnai graduated in international relations from the Budapest University of Economic Sciences in 1991. Brief stints with the Creditum financial consultancy, as an intern at the **European Bank for Reconstruction and Development** in London and then with EUROCORP International Finance plc, ended with him joining CA IB Securities as managing director in 1995. Five years later he became CEO of the Wallis investment company, and was also a board member for several other companies. He was named Young Manager of the Year in 2003 by the Hungarian Federation of Industrialists.

His first government role came in June 2006 when he was appointed as Government Commissioner for Development Policy at the National Development Agency. A year later he joined the cabinet as Minister of Local Government and Regional Development, switching in May 2008 to the National Development and Economy portfolio. The global credit crunch hit Hungary hard that year and, with the economy shrinking and the forint plummeting, unpopular Prime Minister Gyurcsány came under intense pressure to step down. He nominated Bajnai as his successor, charged with managing the crisis until elections due in spring 2010. Bajnai took office on 14 April 2009 and immediately announced drastic cuts in wages, pensions and social services.

Address: Office of the Prime Minister, V. Kossuth Lajos tér 4, 1055 Budapest.
Telephone: (1) 4413000.
Fax: (1) 4413050.
E-mail: lakossag@meh.hu
Internet: www.meh.hu

Balkan Stability Pact *see* **Stability Pact for South-Eastern Europe**.

Balkans

The south-east peninsula of Europe. The name derives from the Turkish for mountain and the area is traversed by various mountain chains, particularly in the west. The Balkans stretch south from the Pannonian plain (mainly in **Hungary**) to the northern highlands of **Greece**, and from the Italian Alps in the west to the Ukrainian plain in the east. Politically, the name Balkans is commonly used as a collective term for the countries of the region: **Albania**, **Bosnia and Herzegovina**, **Bulgaria**, **Croatia**, Greece, **Kosovo**, **Macedonia**, Moldova, **Montenegro**, **Romania**, **Serbia** and **Slovenia**. The region's collective history has often set these countries apart from the rest of Europe, from the Ottoman domination of the 14th to 19th centuries, at least until the communist-dominated post-1945 period. More recently the Balkans have suffered some of the continent's most bitter wars, pitting diverse yet often closely-related ethnic groups and various religions against one another. The fragmentation of previously homogeneous groups, particularly the south **Slavs**, has spawned the concept of Balkanization.

Baltic Council of Ministers (BCM)

An institution for facilitating co-operation between the Governments of **Estonia**, **Latvia** and **Lithuania**. It was formally established in its present structure, as an intergovernmental ministerial body, in June 1994, following an initiative by the Council of the Baltic States (an organization set up in 1990 which dissolved itself after handing over its mission to the Baltic Council of Ministers and the inter-parliamentary Baltic Assembly). Reforms completed in 2003 improved co-operation between the BCM and the Assembly. The Baltic Council of Ministers' main areas of activity are foreign policy, justice, the environment, education and science. The chairmanship rotates on an annual basis. Latvia holds the chairmanship in 2010, to be followed by Lithuania and then Estonia.

> *E-mail*: bmn@mfa.ee
> *Internet*: www.vm.ee/?q=en/node/4096

Baltic Marine Environment Protection Commission
(or Helsinki Commission, HELCOM)

The main regional organization co-ordinating environmental protection efforts in the Baltic and seeking to combat pollution of the Baltic. Its original Helsinki Convention, signed in 1974 by the then seven Baltic coastal states and entering into force on

3 May 1980, marked the first time ever that all the sources of pollution around an entire sea were made subject to a single convention. In the light of political changes, and developments in international environmental and maritime law, a new convention was signed in 1992 by all the states bordering on the Baltic Sea and by the European Community. After ratification this new convention entered into force on 17 January 2000. It covers the whole of the Baltic Sea area, including inland water, and also commits its signatories to take measures in the whole catchment area of the Baltic Sea to reduce land-based pollution. A new Baltic Sea Action Plan to reduce pollution and reverse the degradation of the marine environment was adopted at the HELCOM Ministerial Meeting on 15 November 2007.The chairmanship of the Commission rotates on a biennial basis; Russia has held the position since 1 July 2008.

Members: Denmark, **Estonia**, **European Union**, Finland, Germany, **Latvia**, **Lithuania**, **Poland**, Russian Federation and Sweden.

Chair: Igor Ivanovich Maydanov.

Address: Katajanokanlaituri 6в, 00160 Helsinki, Finland.

Telephone: (207) 412649.

Fax: (207) 412645.

E-mail: helcom@helcom.fi

Internet: www.helcom.fi

Baltic News Service (BNS)

The Baltic News Service is the largest news agency in the **Baltic States**. Founded in 1990, its staff of 160 distributes around 1,000 news items in five languages every day.

Chief Executive: George Shabad.

Address: Pärnu mnt. 105, Tallinn 15043.

Telephone: 6108800.

Fax: 6108811.

E-mail: bns@bns.ee

Internet: www.bns.ee

Baltic States

The three countries—**Estonia, Latvia** and **Lithuania**—along the eastern shore of the Baltic Sea. Although ethnically, linguistically and culturally very distinct, these three territories have had a common history facing German, Swedish and ultimately Russian encroachment. In particular the Baltic States were grouped together as the first three countries to break free from the **Soviet Union** in 1991 and the only three to emerge with relatively stable and prosperous economies. As such, they occupy a unique place on the European political map, squashed between the aspirations of **central Europe**, the political hegemony of the Russian Federation and the economic success of Scandinavia. All three have now forged greater ties with the West, including membership of the **North Atlantic Treaty Organization** and the **European Union**—thereby causing concern in the neighbouring Russian Federation and straining regional relations.

Banja Luka

A city in the north of **Bosnia and Herzegovina** and the capital of the **Serb Republic** (RS). *Population*: 224,647 (2004 estimate). An ancient settlement dating from pre-Roman times, Banja Luka rose to significance during the Ottoman occupation of Bosnia from the 14th century. When an international conference placed Bosnia and Herzegovina under Austro-Hungarian rule from 1878, the **Hungarians** made the city a regional administrative centre. Rebuilt after massive destruction in an earthquake on 27 October 1969, it was home to an evenly mixed population of **Serbs**, **Croats** and **Bosniaks** before the Bosnian civil war (1992–95) and had one of Bosnia's largest communities of those who preferred to define their nationality as **Yugoslav**. However, in the very first year of fighting Banja Luka became a focus for Serb nationalists and the Bosniak population was driven out wholesale, their properties seized and given to ethnic Serbs. In 1993 the Croats became the subject of Serb aggression and were also 'encouraged' to leave, swapping homes in many cases with ethnic Serbs driven out of the **Krajina** region of **Croatia**. Finally in 1995, during the climax of the Croatian–Bosnian Serb conflict, the remaining Croats were forcibly exiled. Completing the city's **'ethnic cleansing'**, the empty homes were soon filled with ethnic Serbs from the Krajina and areas of Bosnia under control of the **Muslim-Croat Federation**. Now 90% of the city's people are ethnically Serb. Tensions remained high for several years, as was shown in 2001 when an international delegation attending a ceremony to rebuild the city's mosques was trapped in a community centre by violent Serb demonstrators.

The surrounding region is home to almost half of the population of the RS and is an important centre for the republic's economy. The major activities in the city are the metallurgy and electrical industries while production of timber products is vital to the nearby rural districts.

Bank for International Settlements (BIS)

One of the institutions of the international financial and monetary system, originally founded pursuant to The Hague Agreements of 1930 to promote co-operation among national Central Banks and to provide additional facilities for international finance operations. As of 2010, the Central Banks of 55 countries and Hong Kong, together with the European Central Bank, were entitled to attend and vote at general meetings, held annually in late June/early July.

Members: Of the countries of **central** and **south-eastern Europe, Bosnia and Herzegovina, Bulgaria, Croatia,** the **Czech Republic, Estonia, Greece, Hungary, Latvia, Lithuania, Macedonia, Poland, Romania, Serbia, Slovakia** and **Slovenia** participate and hold shares in the BIS.
Chair of the Board: Christian Noyer.
General Manager: Jaime Caruana.
Address: Centralbahnplatz 2, 4002 Basel, Switzerland.
Telephone: (61) 2808080.
Fax: (61) 2809100.
E-mail: email@bis.org
Internet: www.bis.org

Bank of Albania
Banka e Shqipërisë

The central bank founded in 1992 in the context of the post-communist Government's commitment to the creation of a market economy. The Bank's principal statutory objective is to achieve and maintain price stability, its basic tasks being (i) to run the country's monetary and exchange-rate policies; (ii) to supervise and regulate the banking system; (iii) to hold and manage official foreign reserves; (iv) to act as banker to the Government; and (v) to promote the smooth operation of the payments system. As of December 2006, the Bank held reserves of −740.0m. lekë.
Governor: Ardian Fullani.
Address: Sheshi Skënderbej 1, Tirana.
Telephone: (4) 222152.
Fax: (4) 223558.
E-mail: public@bankofalbania.org
Internet: www.bankofalbania.org

Bank of Estonia
Eesti Pank

The central bank in **Estonia,** originally founded in 1919 by the Provisional Government. It was restructured in 1927 to implement League of Nations monetary reforms. The kroon, declared sole legal tender in 1928, was devalued by 35% in 1933 and fixed to sterling. The Bank was nationalized in 1940 as the Estonian Republican Office of the State Bank of the **Soviet Union** (known as the Gemeinschaftsbank Estland in 1941–44, under German occupation). Re-established in 1990 by the Estonian republic, the Bank was fully recognized in 1991 under the presidency of Siim Kallas. Under legislation in 1993, the board consists of the President and eight members appointed by the **State Assembly** for a five-year term. The 1998 board fixed the kroon against the euro. As of December 2007, the Bank held reserves of 3,348.3m. kroons.

President: Andres Lipstok.
Address: Estonia pst. 13, Tallinn 15095.
Telephone: 6680719.
Fax: 6680954.
E-mail: info@epbe.ee
Internet: www.bankofestonia.info

Bank of Greece

The central bank and state bank of issue of **Greece**. Established in 1927, the Bank began operations on 14 May 1928, under the first Governor Alexandros Diomidis. The Bank is a member of the European System of Central Banks. As of December 2007, the Bank held reserves of 685.8m. euros.

Governor: Nicholas Garganas.
Address: Leoforos E. Venizelos 21, 102 50 Athens.
Telephone: (210) 3201111.
Fax: (210) 3232239.
E-mail: secretariat@bankofgreece.gr
Internet: www.bankofgreece.gr

Bank of Latvia
Lativijas Banka

The central bank of **Latvia**, originally founded in 1922. Nationalized in 1940 as the Latvian Republican Office of the State Bank of the **Soviet Union**, it was transferred to the jurisdiction of the German Rīga State Credit Bank from 1941 until its return to the Soviet monetary system in 1944. The Bank was re-established in 1990 by the Latvian republic and restored to Central Bank status after independence in 1991. The Governor, appointed by **Parliament**, chairs the six-member board. As of December 2007, the Bank held reserves of 94.0m. lats.

Governor: Ilmārs Rimšēvičs.
Address: K. Valdemāra iela 2A, Rīga 1050.
Telephone: 67022300.
Fax: 67022420.
E-mail: info@bank.lv
Internet: www.bank.lv

Bank of Lithuania
Lietuvos Bankas

The central bank of **Lithuania**, originally established in 1922, following Lithuania's independence. It was nationalized in 1940, under the authority of the **Soviet Union** Gosbank. The Bank was re-established by the Lithuanian republic in 1990 and restored to Central Bank status after independence in 1991. As of December 2007, the Bank held reserves of 632.2m. litai.

Chair. of Board: Reinoldijus Šarkinas.
Address: Gedimino pr. 6, Vilnius 01103.
Telephone: (5) 2680029.
Fax: (5) 2628124.
E-mail: info@lb.lt
Internet: www.lb.lt

Bank of Slovenia
Banka Slovenije

The central bank of **Slovenia**. The Bank was established from the remains of the **Yugoslav**-era republican National Bank of Slovenia in June 1991 as one of the institutions needed by a state in the process of becoming independent. As a modern Central Bank, it controls monetary policy and regulates the banking industry. It is independent of the Government. The euro became legal tender in Slovenia on 1 January 2007. As of December 2007, the Bank held reserves of 799.9m. euros.

Governor: Marko Kranjec.
Address: Slovenska 35, 1505 Ljubljana.
Telephone: (1) 4719000.
Fax: (1) 2515516.
E-mail: bsl@bsi.si
Internet: www.bsi.si

Băsescu, Traian

President of **Romania**. Traian Băsescu was an officer in the Romanian merchant navy who entered politics only in the post-communist era. A former Mayor of the capital **Bucharest**, he was elected to his first term as President in December 2004 and narrowly secured a second term five years later. He is regarded as a thick-skinned populist with a pro-Western bent who is willing to undertake controversial reforms.

Traian Băsescu was born on 4 November 1951 in Basarabi, a small town in south-eastern Romania near the port city of Constanța. He graduated from the Navy Institute in Constanța in 1976 and joined the merchant navy, working for the state-owned shipping company Navrom. From 1981 to 1987 he captained the country's flagship oil tanker Biruinta before heading the Navrom Agency office in Antwerp, Belgium.

Though a member of the Communist Party, Băsescu did not seriously enter politics until after the Romanian revolution of December 1989. He first joined the National Salvation Front, then on its demise joined the Democratic Party (PD—which later merged to become the **Democratic Liberal Party**, PD-L). He served as Minister of Transport from 1991 to 1992 as a PD representative in the coalition Government of Theodor Stolojan, and held the post again in the succession of Governments from 1996 until 2000; that year he was narrowly elected Mayor of Bucharest, and a year later took over as PD President. He was re-elected as Mayor with a larger majority in 2004. Băsescu is credited with ridding the city of its packs of stray dogs and improving its infrastructure.

When Stolojan withdrew from the 2004 presidential election, Băsescu stood on behalf of the Justice and Truth Alliance (ADA), formed by the PD and Stolojan's **National Liberal Party** (PNL). In an unexpected result, he won the presidential run-off on 12 December. On taking office on 20 December, Băsescu was required to suspend his party membership, and Emil **Boc** succeeded him as party leader.

In the early months of 2007 tensions rose between President Băsescu and PNL Prime Minister Călin Popescu-Tăriceanu, reaching a head at the start of April when Băsescu's PD was ejected from the ruling coalition. On 19 April Parliament backed a motion to suspend Băsescu on grounds of unconstitutional conduct. Senate Chair Vacaroiu became interim President. However, in a national referendum on 19 May Băsescu's removal from office was opposed by three-quarters of voters. He was reinstated four days later.

The first round of the presidential election in November saw Băsescu lead with 32.4%, ahead of **Social Democratic Party** leader Mircea Dan Geoană with 31.2%. The presidential run-off on 6 December proved to be ever so close, with official results giving Băsescu 50.33% of the vote—a margin of just over 70,000 votes. With over 138,000 votes having been deemed as invalid, the PSD called for the result to be annulled. Instead the Constitutional Court decided that the invalid votes should be recounted; only around 2,000 votes were validated, and so the result was upheld.

Address: Office of the President, Cotroceni Palace, blvd Geniului 1–3, 060116
      Bucharest 6.
Telephone: (21) 4100581.
Fax: (21) 4103858.
E-mail: procetatean@presidency.ro
Internet: www.presidency.ro

Basic Agreement *see* **Erdut Agreement**.

BCM *see* **Baltic Council of Ministers**.

BCPB *see* **Bratislava Stock Exchange**.

Belgrade

The capital of **Serbia**, situated at the confluence of the Danube and Sava rivers. *Population*: 1.6m. (2002 census). The name *Beograd* literally means white fortress in Serbian, a reference to the ancient fortified settlement on the site, and testimony to the city's strategic importance. Belgrade changed hands between various groups in the **Balkans** until 1284 when it came under the control of the **Serbs**, who made it their capital in 1440.

As Serbia emerged from centuries under Ottoman rule, Belgrade began growing rapidly, particularly after 1920 when it was made the capital of the new Yugoslav kingdom. A process of industrialization and the increase in the city's importance drew thousands of people from the surrounding rural areas. Under communist rule Belgrade was established as a major centre for mechanical engineering and light industry. It was the largest commercial centre for Yugoslavia and the focal point of that country's transport connections, a regional role that it is seeking to re-establish after the upheavals of the 1990s during which the Yugoslav state was dismembered by conflict. Damage caused to the city during the 1999 **North Atlantic Treaty Organization** (NATO) bombing campaign seriously affected the local economy but work has been under way to reconstruct the battered infrastructure since the fall of Slobodan **Milošević** in 2000.

The population is mainly ethnically Serb although there are significant numbers of **Croats** and Montenegrins (*see* **Montenegro**). The city is also home to one of the biggest Chinese communities in the Balkans, encouraged by close ties between Yugoslavia and the People's Republic of China during the Milošević era.

Belgrade Stock Exchange
Beogradska berza (BB)

The principal stock exchange in **Serbia**, based in **Belgrade**. The original bourse was established in 1894 but was closed down in the 1950s by the communist regime. It reopened as the Yugoslav Capital Market in 1989 and was transformed into the BB in 1992. Total turnover for 2009 equalled 442m. euros. In March 2010 there were 76 members trading on the BB.

Chair.: Gordana Dostanić.
Address: Omladinskih Brigada 1, POB 50, 11070 Belgrade.
Telephone: (11) 3117297.
Fax: (11) 3117304.
E-mail: marketing@belex.co.rs
Internet: www.belex.rs

Berisha, Sali

Prime Minister of **Albania**.

Sali Berisha, a professor of cardiology, was a prominent voice calling for reform in Albania in the late 1980s as communism began to collapse around the world. He is the long-term leader of the **Democratic Party of Albania** (PDSh), and became Albania's first non-communist head of state in 1992. After a long period in opposition after 1997, the PDSh regained power in 2005, with Berisha appointed Prime Minister on 2 September.

Born on 15 October 1944, he studied medicine at the University of Tirana, graduating in 1967. Specializing in cardiology, he worked at Tirana General Hospital, while also becoming first assistant professor, and then in 1989 a full professor, at the university.

Around this time, Berisha was becoming known as a leading proponent of reform in Albanian politics, calling for liberalization, multi-party democracy, freedom of speech and the establishment of a market economy. At the first congress of the PDSh in February 1991 he was elected as the new party's Chairman. The party secured 39% of the vote at the Assembly elections the following month, making it the main opposition movement to the ruling Labour Party. It briefly joined in a broad Government but quit in December, and called for early elections. These were won convincingly by the PDSh in March 1992, and Berisha was elected by the People's Assembly as President of Albania on 8 April, in succession to the former communist leader Ramiz Alia.

During Berisha's presidency, Albania underwent political and economic transformation, privatizing land and businesses, liberalizing prices, ending international isolation and improving rights and freedoms. However, the collapse of several **'pyramid' investment schemes**, amid allegations of government connivance in the frauds, provoked widespread anarchy and rebels seized control in the south.

Unsurprisingly, the 1997 elections brought a heavy defeat to the PDSh. Berisha stepped down from the presidency, resumed the chairmanship of the PDSh and led it into opposition for two terms. It reclaimed power at the July 2005 election, and on 2 September Berisha was nominated as Prime Minister, a position he retained after the PDSh again won, in the June 2009 election.

Sali Berisha is married to Liri Rama and they have a son and a daughter. He speaks English, French, Italian and Russian.

Address: Office of the Prime Minister, Bulevardi Dëshmorët e Kombit, 1000 Tirana.

Telephone: (4) 250474.

Fax: (4) 237501.

E-mail: kryeministri@km.gov.al

Internet: www.albgovt.gov.al

Bessarabia question

A historical territorial dispute between **Romania** and Russia, arising from the artificial division of the Romanian principality of Moldavia between Romania and Russia in the 1812 Treaty of Bucharest. Resurrecting the medieval title Bessarabia for the eastern half of Moldavia, between the Rivers Prut and Dnester, the tsarist authorities attempted to distance the ethnic **Romanian** population from their connections with the state of Romania, and thus foster a separate sense of Bessarabian identity. The division, however, laid the foundation for Romanian claims to the area, and for conflict with future Russian Governments.

With the rise of the **Soviet Union** the Bessarabia question was aggressively revisited. The temporary reunification of Bessarabia and Romania during the inter-war years (1918–39) flew in the face of Soviet insistence that Bessarabia remained an integral part of the Soviet Union. With the onset of hostilities at the start of the Second World War the Romanian Government conceded the Soviet annexation of Bessarabia. The Moldavian Soviet Socialist Republic (already created east of the Dnester to substantiate Russia's claims) was redrawn to include part of Bessarabia and thus to cover the area of what is now Moldova. On the other hand southern and northern Bessarabia, known as Bukovina (*see* **Bukovina question**), were ceded to the Ukrainian Soviet Socialist Republic. A programme of russification of the Bessarabian Romanians resulted in the creation of a Moldovan identity, based on communist social policies and the use of the **Cyrillic alphabet**. The authorities also encouraged the influx of non-Romanians.

The collapse of the Soviet Union in 1991 unleashed a wave of pro-Romanian sentiment in Moldova and reignited the Bessarabia question, which the pre-1989 Romanian communist regime had preferred to leave dormant. Political parties on both sides of the Prut called for the reunification of the Moldavian lands, despite initial hesitation in Romania. Claims to the southern and northern districts were not included. However, attempts to move towards unification led to uprisings in the non-Romanian/Moldovan areas of Moldova, known as Transdnestria and Gagauzia, in the same year. By the mid-1990s the concept of unification was irrevocably entwined with the idea of the division of Moldova and was thus popularly rejected by the Moldovan people. Aspirations for unification remain dormant for the time being and the notion of Bessarabia seems defunct.

BIS *see* **Bank for International Settlements**.

BISA *see* **Bulgarian Industrial Association**.

BNR *see* **National Bank of Romania**.

BNS *see* **Baltic News Service**.

Boc, Emil

Prime Minister of **Romania**. Former Mayor of Cluj-Napoca, the largest city in **Transylvania**, and leader of the **Democratic Liberal Party** (PD-L), Boc took office as Prime Minister on 22 December 2008.

Emil Boc was born on 6 September 1966 in Răchiţele in Transylvania. In 1991 he graduated from the Faculty of History and Philosophy of Babeş-Bolyai University in Cluj-Napoca, then studied law (and was called to the Cluj Bar in 1996) and received a doctorate in political sciences and political philosophy in 2000. During the 1990s he also had short periods of study abroad, in the United Kingdom, USA and Belgium.

In 2000 he was elected to the House of Deputies (lower house of **Parliament**) representing the Democratic Party (PD). From 2001 he was Vice-Chairman of the House's Legal Committee, and from 2003 was Vice-Chairman of the Committee responsible for revising the Constitution. That year he also became the leader of the PD parliamentary group and joined the party's executive presidency.

In June 2004 Boc secured election as Mayor of Cluj-Napoca. Following the inauguration of Traian Băsescu as President of Romania, Boc succeeded him as PD President. When the PD merged with the Liberal Democratic Party in 2007, Boc was named leader of the new PD-L.

In the 2008 local elections Boc secured re-election as Mayor of Cluj-Napoca. His party went on to win the November legislative elections. Theodor Stolojan of the PD-L was initially nominated as Prime Minister, but he resigned the mandate within days, and Boc was nominated in his place. On 18 December a coalition Government between the PD-L and the **Social Democratic Party** (PSD) was approved by Parliament, and Boc took office four days later; he resigned as Mayor on 4 January 2009.

His coalition did not last long, however, the PSD ministers resigning on 1 October 2009 in protest over the dismissal three days earlier of the Minister of the Interior, and Boc's Government was defeated in a vote of no confidence 12 days later. Political impasse ensued, amid which Băsescu secured a second term in a controversial election; during this time Boc remained as acting Prime Minister. Finally, on 17 December, Băsescu again nominated Boc to head the Government. His new coalition comprised the PD-L and the **Hungarian Democratic Union of Romania** (UDMR), with five independents also included in the cabinet, and was approved by Parliament on 23 December.

Emil is married to Oana, and they have two daughters. He speaks English and French.

Address: Office of the Prime Minister, Piaţa Victoriei 1, 71201 Bucharest 1.
Telephone: (21) 3143400.
Fax: (21) 3139846.
E-mail: drp@guv.ro
Internet: www.guv.ro

Bohemia

One of the two ancient states which in combination form the modern **Czech Republic**, the other being **Moravia**. Making up the north-western two-thirds of the republic, with its traditional capital in **Prague**, Bohemia has long been a vital **central European** state. Bismarck, the architect of **German** unification in the 19th century, famously summed up the state's strategic importance when he said 'He who controls Bohemia, controls Europe.'

Bohemia takes its name from the ancient Celtic tribe of the Boii, which inhabited the region before the arrival of the **Czechs** in the fifth and sixth centuries. The Bohemian kingdom became a powerful regional force under the aegis of the Holy Roman Empire between the 12th and 13th centuries. After sporadic revolts inspired by **Protestant** Hussite or nationalistic sentiments, the region was fully absorbed into the Habsburg Empire in 1620. Within the empire it was stripped of its authority over the surrounding territory and obliged to convert to **Roman Catholicism**. By the time of the creation of **Czechoslovakia** in 1918, the industrial development concentrated in Bohemia had made it the country's economic as well as political centre. In 1949 the communist authorities stripped Bohemia of its separate administrative status.

Borisov, Boiko

Prime Minister of **Bulgaria**. A former firefighter and bodyguard, Borisov was Mayor of Sofia prior to his appointment as Prime Minister on 27 July 2009.

Boiko Metodiev Borisov was born on 13 June 1959 in Bankya, now a suburb of **Sofia**. He trained as a firefighter, and from 1985 taught at the Ministry of the Interior's Higher Institute of Officer Training and Research. Five years later he left the Ministry and founded IPON-1, which became one of the largest security companies in Bulgaria; Borisov became a member of the International Association of Personal Protection Agents and worked as bodyguard to Todor **Zhivkov** and Simeon II among others.

In 2001 he rejoined the Ministry of Interior as Secretary-General, and gained promotion to Lieutenant-General. In November 2005 he was elected to the first of two terms as Mayor of Sofia. In May 2007 he founded the centre-right **Citizens for European Development of Bulgaria** (GERB), though his position as Mayor prevented him from chairing the new party. It performed well in municipal elections later that year, which included Borisov's re-election.

After GERB won the legislative elections in July 2009, Borisov formed a minority Government supported by small right-wing parties. In January 2010 he became the official leader of GERB.

Borisov lives with Tsvetelina Borislavova, and has one daughter from his former marriage. He has also coached the Bulgarian karate team.

Address: Office of the Prime Minister, 1 Dondukov blvd, Sofia 1194.
Telephone: (2) 9402770.
Fax: (2) 9802056.
E-mail: gis@government.bg
Internet: www.government.bg

Bosnia and Herzegovina
Bosna i Hercegovina

An independent republic located in south-eastern Europe in the **Balkan** peninsula, bounded by Montenegro to the south-east, Serbia to the east and Croatia to the north, west and south, with a narrow land corridor to the Adriatic Sea. Within its recognized international borders, the country is divided into two main entities: a joint **Muslim-Croat Federation** (Federacija Bosne i Hercegovine, FBiH) covering about 51% of the territory, and a **Serb Republic** (Republika Srpska, RS) covering about 49%. Administratively, the Federation is subdivided into 10 cantons and 84 municipalities, while the Serb Republic has 63 municipalities. In addition, on the boundary between them but not part of either, the north-eastern town of **Brčko** was established as a neutral self-governing district in 2000, under the sovereignty of the state Government.

Area: 51,209 sq. km; *capital*: **Sarajevo**; *population*: 3.8m. (2009 estimate), comprising **Muslims/Bosniaks** 43.7%, **Serbs** 31.4%, **Croats** 17.3%, others 7.6%; *official languages*: Bosnian, Serbian and Croatian; *religion*: Muslim 40%, **Orthodox** 31%, **Roman Catholic** 15%, other 14%.

Bosnia and Herzegovina's current government structures were created by the 1995 **Dayton Agreement** which ended three years of civil war (see below). The central state Government is responsible for foreign, economic and fiscal policy. Executive power lies with an elected three-member rotating Presidency (one representative from each of the Muslim, Serb and Croat communities, each of whom serves a four-year term including two eight-month periods as Chair) and a Council of Ministers headed by a Prime Minister (who may not be from the same community as the current Chair of the Presidency). Legislative authority rests with a bicameral **Parliamentary Assembly** (Parlamentarna Skupština). This consists of a 42-member House of Representatives (Predstavnički Dom/Zastupnički Dom) directly elected for a four-year term (28 from the Muslim-Croat Federation and 14 from the Serb Republic) and a 15-member House of Peoples (Dom Naroda), elected indirectly by the legislatures of the two entities (10 from the Federation and five from the Serb Republic).

The separate entities also have their own assemblies and executives. In the case of the Federation, the Assembly (Skupština) comprises a House of Representatives (Predstavnički/Zastupnički Dom Federacije) with 98 directly elected members, and a 58-member House of Peoples (Dom Naroda Federacije), elected on an ethnic basis, in both cases for a four-year term. The Federation's President and Vice-President are chosen by the Bosniak and Croat members of its House of Peoples, and a Second Vice-President by its Serb members. The President nominates the FBiH Council of Ministers for endorsement by the legislature. There are also 10 cantonal assemblies.

The Serb Republic's legislature, also bicameral, comprises a People's Assembly (Narodna Skupština) with 83 members directly elected, and a Council of Peoples (Vijeće Naroda), whose members (eight Bosniaks, eight Croats, eight Serbs and four others) are chosen by the People's Assembly. Both houses have a four-year term, and the RS President is also directly elected for a four-year term.

History: Once a part of the Roman Empire, Bosnia and Herzegovina was settled by **Slavic** tribes during the seventh century. In the 11th–12th centuries it was under **Hungarian** authority, before gaining independence around 1200. In 1463 the territory was conquered by the Turks; it remained a province of the Islamic Ottoman Empire for over 400 years, during which time a distinctive Bosnian Muslim culture took form within a multi-ethnic population. At an international congress in 1878, Bosnia and Herzegovina was placed under Austro-Hungarian administration. Formal annexation by Austria-Hungary in 1908 embittered **Serbia** (which had aspirations towards a **Greater Serbia** in the **Balkans**); this hostility climaxed in the assassination in 1914 of the heir to the Austro-Hungarian throne by a Serb nationalist, precipitating the start of the First World War. In 1918 Bosnia and Herzegovina became part of the newly-formed Kingdom of Serbs, Croats and Slovenes (known as **Yugoslavia** from 1929).

During 1941–45 the territory was under Nazi occupation, within a fascist-controlled puppet-state of **Croatia**. At the end of the Second World War it came under communist rule as one of six constituent republics (with Serbia, Croatia, **Montenegro**, **Macedonia** and **Slovenia**) of the **Socialist Federal Republic of Yugoslavia**, under Marshal **Tito** until his death in 1980.

On the collapse of communism in **eastern Europe** from 1989, Yugoslavia's political structure could not contain increasing nationalism and rivalry among the republics. Slovenia and Croatia seceded in 1991, provoking conflict with Serbia. In March 1992, following a referendum, the republican Government of Bosnia and Herzegovina also declared independence. Despite international recognition, this was opposed vehemently by Bosnian Serb nationalists, precipitating a savage civil war between the ethnic communities in which Croatia and rump Yugoslavia (Serbia and Montenegro) were also closely involved. During 1992 Serb nationalist forces, with the help of the largely Serbian Yugoslav army, gained control of about 70% of Bosnian territory. Under the leadership of Radovan **Karadžić**, they declared their own Serb Republic in Serb-controlled areas and pursued a campaign of '**ethnic cleansing**'. Bosnian Croats, aided by Croatia, similarly declared a new republic in the Croat-controlled area of the country, before joining the mainly Muslim government forces in a new Muslim-Croat Federation in March 1994 (under a power-sharing agreement brokered by the USA). Fighting between Muslim-Croat forces and Bosnian Serbs continued through 1994 and 1995, galvanizing international efforts through the **Contact Group** (Russian Federation, USA, United Kingdom, France and Germany), the United Nations and the **North Atlantic Treaty Organization** (NATO) to bring about a settlement. An estimated 250,000 people were killed in the conflict, over 200,000 injured and 13,000 permanently disabled.

The Dayton Agreement, a US-sponsored peace accord between the warring parties, was agreed in Dayton, Ohio, in November 1995. This preserved Bosnia and Herzegovina as a sovereign state, with a central republican Government and bicameral Parliamentary Assembly, while dividing it territorially between the Muslim-Croat Federation and the Serb Republic. NATO-led peacekeeping forces have since overseen the implementation of the military requirements of the agreement, initially as the Implementation Force (IFOR) and from December 1996 as the **Stabilization Force** (SFOR), while an **Office of the High Representative** created by the UN Security Council has supervised the civilian aspects of the accord.

The first pan-Bosnian presidential and Assembly elections, held in September 1996 under the terms of the Dayton accord, were dominated by three main nationalist parties—the (Muslim) **Party of Democratic Action** (SDA), the **Serbian Democratic Party** (SDS) and the **Croatian Democratic Union** (HDZ)—mirroring the ethnic divisions in the country. At the executive level, Alija Izetbegović of the SDA became the first Chairman of the new rotating Presidency following his election together with Momčilo Krajišnik (SDS) and Krešimir Zubak (HDZ), while the two posts of Co-Prime Minister went to Haris **Silajdžić** of the moderate Muslim **Party for Bosnia and Herzegovina** (SBiH) and Boro Bosić (SDS). In the RS, Biljana Plavšić of the SDS was re-elected President (having replaced indicted war criminal Karadžić in 1995). The Western-backed Plavšić quickly came into conflict with Karadžić, who secured her expulsion from the SDS in July 1997 after she had dissolved the SDS-dominated RS Assembly. In further RS elections in November 1997, SDS strength was eroded by Plavšić's new Serbian People's Alliance (SNS). As a result, Plavšić was able to appoint a 'non-partisan' Government headed by Milorad **Dodik** of the moderate **Party of Independent Social Democrats** (SNSD).

In nationwide elections in September 1998, Izetbegović was re-elected as the Muslim candidate for the union Presidency with 86.8% of the Muslim vote (and 31% nationally), along with hard-line Croat nationalist Ante Jelavić of the HDZ, who took 52.9% of the Croat vote (and 11.5% nationally) and moderate Serb Zivko Radišić of the Socialist Party of the Serb Republic (SPRS), who won 51.2% of the Serb vote (and 21.8% nationally) standing for the Sloga (Unity) alliance. At the legislative level, there was a decrease in support for nationalist parties in the all-Bosnia and Federation lower houses, so that moderate Serb Svetozar Mihajlović of the SNS joined Silajdžić as union Co-Prime Minister. Polling in the RS, in contrast, resulted in Plavšić being defeated in the presidential contest by Nikola Poplasen of the ultra-nationalist Serbian Radical Party (SRS) with the backing of the SDS. (Plavšić was subsequently indicted by the **International Criminal Tribunal for the former Yugoslavia** (ICTY), which in 2003 sentenced her to 11 years' imprisonment for crimes against humanity.) Poplasen then tried to replace Dodik as RS Prime Minister, but was himself dismissed in March 1999 by the UN High Representative Carlos Westendorp (the chief overseer of the Dayton accords) for 'abuse of power'. At the same time, an international arbitration tribunal ruled that the disputed town of Brčko (strategically linking the eastern and western sections of the Serb entity) should become a neutral district shared by Bosnia's two halves, further enflaming Serb opinion.

While the political impasse continued in the RS, further progress towards depoliticization at the union level was made in June 2000 with the appointment of Spasoje Tusevljak (a non-party Serb) as sole Prime Minister, although with misgivings in the SDA and HDZ and among Western Governments because of his former links with Karadžić and the rump Yugoslavia. In October 2000 Izetbegović retired from the collective Presidency on grounds of age and was succeeded by Halid Genjac of the SDA. The chairmanship of the collective Presidency then passed to Radišić, meaning that—under the Dayton rule that this post and the union premiership could not be held by the same ethnic group—Martin Raguž of the HDZ was installed as union Prime Minister in place of Tusevljak.

Further elections in November 2000 produced a major advance for the multi-ethnic **Social Democratic Party of Bosnia and Herzegovina** (SDPBiH) in the all-Bosnia and Federation legislatures, although Serb nationalist parties remained dominant in the RS. In the all-Bosnia lower house the SDPBiH won nine seats (with 19.0% of the vote nationally), the SDA eight (18.8%), the SDS six (17.8%), the HDZ five (11.4%), the SBiH five (11.4%), the moderate Serb **Party of Democratic Progress** (PDP) two (6.4%) and seven other parties one seat each.

The results for the Federation lower house were: SDA 38 seats (26.8% of the vote), SDPBiH 37 (26.1%), HDZ 25 (17.5%), SBiH 21 (14.9%) and 13 other parties took the remaining 19 seats. The nationalist parties boycotted the presidential elections that followed in February 2001. These resulted in the election of two moderates to the bi-partisan body, President Karlo Filipović (SDPBiH and Croat) and Vice-President Safet Halilović (SBiH and Bosniak). (Halilović took over as President from 1 January 2002.)

The November 2000 electoral advance of the moderate parties in the all-Bosnia and Federation legislatures resulted in tension between the new Alliance for Change (of moderate parties) and union Prime Minister Raguž (of the Croat nationalist HDZ). The outcome was the replacement of Raguž in February 2001 by Bozidar Matić (a Croat member of the SDPBiH), heading the first all-Bosnia Government not dominated by nationalists.

In the Muslim-Croat Federation, three months passed between the elections and the final approval of a moderate Government headed by Alija Behman of the SDPBiH on 12 March 2001. His administration immediately faced a major new crisis when the HDZ reacted to the loss of the union premiership by declaring a revived separate Croat state based in **Mostar** and led by Jelavić and Raguž. UN High Representative Wolfgang Petritsch thereupon used his powers to dismiss Jelavić from the union collective Presidency, amid urgent UN and other efforts to preserve the structure created under the Dayton Agreement.

The departure of Jelavić from the union Presidency broke the stranglehold of the ethnic-nationalist parties; the moderate Alliance for Change provided two new members—who joined Radišić, the incumbent Chair—Jozo Križanović (SDPBiH and Croat; assumed the rotating chairmanship of the Presidency in June 2001) and Beriz Belkić (SBiH and Bosniak; assumed the chairmanship in February 2002).

Meanwhile in the November 2000 elections for the RS presidency, incumbent Vice-President Mirko Šarović of the SRS, who had remained in office despite the dismissal of Poplasen in March 1999, dismayed Western Governments by achieving a comfortable victory over Dodik of the SNSD, taking 53% of the vote with backing from the SDS. In the RS Assembly elections the SDS received reciprocal SRS backing, enabling the party to recover its numerical dominance by winning 31 of the 83 seats on a 36.1% vote share. The SNSD and PDP each took 11 seats, the SDA six, the SBiH, SDPBiH, SPRS and Democratic Socialist Party four each, and five other parties took the remaining eight seats. Hard-line President Šarović sought to accommodate moderate forces by appointing eminent economist Mladen Ivanić of the PDP as Prime Minister in January 2001, heading a 'non-partisan' coalition Government which included the SPRS, a Muslim and a representative of the SDS. Ivanić responded to Western criticism by arguing that political stability required the inclusion of the SDS and by decreeing that his Ministers should not act as party representatives.

In June 2001, the failure of the union parliament to adopt key electoral laws, necessary to conduct polls independent of the UN, prompted union Prime Minister Matić to resign. He was replaced the following month by Foreign Minister Zlatko Lagumdžija. The electoral laws were finally passed in August, and were widely praised, although the **Organization for Security and Co-operation in Europe** (OSCE) condemned a clause banning voters from electing candidates from outside their own ethnic group in presidential elections. Tensions with the HDZ had calmed sufficiently by November for the party to end its eight-month boycott of the legislature. In March 2002, after the union Presidency had rotated, Dragan Mikerević of the PDP was appointed to succeed Lagumdžija as all-Bosnia Prime Minister. Later in March Petritsch pressed for agreement on the adoption of constitutional reforms (implemented in April) to ensure representation of Serbs, Croats and Bosniaks at all levels of government throughout the country; in particular this established the second legislative chamber, the Council of Peoples, in the RS.

The main nationalist parties (SDA, HDZ, SDS) performed well at the October 2002 elections, their candidates taking all three Presidency seats: Sulejman Tihić (Bosniak) won with 37.3% of the vote, Mirko Šarović (Serb) won with 35.5% and Dragan Čović (Croat) won with 61.5%. In the simultaneous all-Bosnia lower house election the SDA won 10 seats (with 23.7% of the national vote), the SBiH was second with six seats (12% of the vote), the SDS, SDPBiH, and coalition of the HDZ and Croatian Christian Democrats each won five seats (15.2%, 11.8% and 10.1% respectively), the SNSD won three seats (10.1%), the PDP retained its two seats (4.7%) and six other parties won one seat each. In December the UN High Representative (now Lord Ashdown) strengthened the powers of the state Government by proposing the creation of all-Bosnia ministries of security and justice and giving the post of union Prime Minister a four-year term instead of the rotation system. Adnan Terzić of the SDA was nominated to this position in January 2003, and his Government included the three main nationalist parties as well as representatives of the moderate PDP and SBiH.

In the Federation lower house (now reduced from 140 members to 98 members), the SDA won 32 seats, the HDZ-led coalition won 16 seats, the SDPBiH and SBiH each won 15, and 14 smaller parties took the remaining 20 seats. In January 2003 the house elected a new Federation President, Croat Niko Lozančić, along with the two new joint Vice-President posts (Bosniak and Serb). The appointment of Ahmet Hadžipašić as Federation Prime Minister was approved in February.

In the RS Assembly, the SDS won 26 seats, the SNSD won 19, the PDP nine, the SDA six, the SBiH and SRS four each, and nine smaller parties took the remaining 15 seats. SDS candidate Dragan Čavić secured the RS presidency. He nominated outgoing union Prime Minister Mikerević (PDP) as RS Prime Minister.

On 2 April 2003 Šarović resigned from the union Presidency, which he had been chairing, after being implicated in two scandals involving illicit exports to Iraq and alleged espionage activities by the RS military. Borislav Paravać, also SDS, was nominated to replace him eight days later.

During 2004 Lord Ashdown pushed through measures in an attempt to reform the national security structure and dismissed several Serb officials over the failure to apprehend Karadžić. In November the RS Government finally issued an official apology for the Srebrenica massacre.

Čović was removed from the union Presidency by Lord Ashdown in March 2005, after being charged with corruption during his term as Federation Minister of Finance. Ivo Miro Jović became the new Croat member of the union Presidency in May.

Meanwhile, Mikerević had resigned as RS Prime Minister on 17 December 2004, and Pero Bukejlović (SDS) replaced him on 17 February 2005. However, towards the end of the year the PDP withdrew its support for the RS Government, but Bukejlović refused to resign and was forced out by a vote of no confidence in January 2006. SNSD leader Dodik headed the new administration of the SNSD, PDP and SDA, which took office on 28 February. In April the RS rejected a package of constitutional amendments that had been agreed by the principal parties at union level.

Latest elections: The moderate parties fought back at the October 2006 elections, retaking all three seats on the union Presidency: Silajdžić (SBiH) regained the Bosniak seat with 62.8% of the vote, Nebojša **Radmanović** (SNSD) won the Serb seat with 53.3%, and Željko **Komšić** (SDPBiH) won the Croat seat with 39.6%. In the simultaneous all-Bosnia lower house election the SDA won nine seats (with 16.9% of the vote nationally), the SBiH eight (15.5%), the SNSD seven (19.1%), the SDPBiH won five (10.2%), three seats went to both the SDS and the coalition of the HDZ and Croatian National Union (HNZ), two to the Croats Together (HZ) coalition headed by the HDZ 1990 (an offshoot from the HDZ), and five other parties won one seat each. Nikola **Špirić** of the SNSD was nominated as union Prime Minister on 3 January 2007 and confirmed on 11 January. His Government comprised the SNSD, SDA, SBiH, HDZ and HDZ 1990.

In the Federation lower house, the SDA dropped to 28 seats, the SBiH increased to 24, the SDPBiH to 17, and the HDZ-led coalition halved its representation to just eight seats. Croat Unity took seven seats and six smaller parties took the remaining 14 seats. Borjana **Krišto** (HDZ) was subsequently elected President, and took office on 22 February 2007. A new Government led by Nedžad Branković (SDA) was approved on 22 March, but it was immediately suspended by the UN High Representative (now Christian Schwarz-Schilling) as his office had not yet approved all the proposed Ministers. On 30 March the Government, with a replacement Interior Minister, was again approved by the Federation parliament.

In the 83-member RS Assembly, the SNSD ended just short of a clear majority, securing 41 seats, while the SDS dropped to 17 seats, the PDP won eight, the SBiH and Democratic People's Alliance of the Serb Republic four each, the SDA and SPRS three each, the SRS two and the SDPBiH one. Milan Jelić of the SNSD won the RS presidency with 48.8% of the vote, replacing Čavić, who polled 29.4%. Jelić was inaugurated on 9 November, pledging to eradicate corruption and crime. He retained Dodik as Prime Minister.

Recent developments: Miroslav Lajčák took over as UN High Representative in July 2007, and in October he announced measures for reforming parliamentary and government decision-making procedures, including new regulations to prevent representatives of one ethnic group from obstructing the adoption of legislation. Serb politicians, including Dodik, threatened to boycott institutions if they were imposed, and on 1 November Špirić resigned the union premiership in protest. However, at the end of November the Serbs ended resistance to the legislation. On 11 December Dodik announced that six of the parties in the union Assembly supported Špirić's renomination as union Prime Minister, which was approved by the Assembly on 28 December. An unchanged Council of Ministers was approved on 28 February 2008.

Meanwhile, RS President Jelić died of a heart attack in September 2007. Rajko **Kuzmanović** (also SNSD) was elected as his successor on 9 December. At his inauguration on 28 December, he stated his opposition to any further transfer of powers to central government from the entities.

In July 2008 Serbia announced the surprise discovery and arrest of Karadžić in **Belgrade**. This was welcomed by the international community, which increased pressure on the RS to co-operate with the ICTY on finding Gen. Ratko Mladić, the main war crimes indictee still at large.

Federation Prime Minister Branković resigned on 27 May 2009, after being charged with misappropriation of funds while he was CEO of Energoinvest; Mustafa **Mujezinović** (also SDA) was nominated to replace him on 11 June, and approved two weeks later.

Arguments over constitutional reform continued through 2009, with rising ethno-nationalist tensions raising fears that partition might be the eventual outcome. In late 2009 the UN Security Council extended the mandate of the 2,000-strong EU peacekeeping force (**EUFOR**) for another year. Meanwhile the Peace Implementation Council (the group of 55 countries and organizations sponsoring and directing the peace and reforms implementation process in Bosnia) was forced to conclude that the country remained too dysfunctional to allow a reduction in the powers of the UN High Representative (currently Valentin **Inzko**). Plans to reduce this role to that of an EU Special Representative were accordingly placed on hold.

International relations and defence: Bosnia and Herzegovina was recognized as an independent state by the **European Union** (EU) and the USA in April 1992 and admitted to UN membership in May 1992. It is a member of the OSCE (which has supervised the country's post-Dayton elections to date) and the **Central European Initiative**, and has guest status at the **Council of Europe**. It also has observer status at the **Organisation of the Islamic Conference**. In December 2006 Bosnia and Herzegovina joined NATO's **Partnership for Peace** programme, the first step towards its ambition for full NATO membership. Two years later it joined the **Adriatic Charter** to advance its case for accession.

Discussions with the EU on a Stability and Association Agreement (SAA) opened in November 2005. Police reforms became a major stumbling block, but agreement was finally reached for a proposal that satisfied the EU criteria in late 2007, allowing the SAA to be initialled on 4 December and signed six months later, after parliamentary approval of implementation of the reforms.

The Bosnian Serbs blocked Bosnian recognition of **Kosovo**'s secession from Serbia in February 2008. Moreover, the RS Assembly immediately adopted a resolution declaring that the RS had the right to secede from Bosnia and Herzegovina if most UN and EU member nations were to recognize Kosovo's independence.

The defence budget of the all-Bosnia Government was US $244m. in 2008, equivalent to about 1.3% of GDP. The entities' separate armed forces were merged by January 2006 into a single professional army. The size of the armed forces at the start of 2010 was some 11,000 personnel.

Bosnia and Herzegovina, economy

The economic problems of a relatively underdeveloped region within the former Yugoslavia were hugely increased by three years of civil war following independence in 1992. The economy remains in transition to a market system, although much progress has been made towards recovery under post-war reconstruction programmes, largely financed by the international community. The economies of the two entities, the **Muslim-Croat Federation** and the **Serb Republic** (RS), have become separate in many respects, so that economic indicators for the overall country can mask wide internal discrepancies.

GNP: US $17,000m. (2008); *GNP per capita*: $4,510 (2008); *GDP at PPP*: $31,656m. (2008); *GDP per capita at PPP*: $8,400 (2008); *real GDP growth*: −3.0% (2009 estimate); *exports*: $5,064m. (2008); *imports*: $12,282m. (2008); *currency*: convertible marka pegged to euro (plural: maraka; US $1 = BKM1.39 in mid-2009); *unemployment*: 24% (2009); *government deficit as a percentage of GDP*: 5% (2009); *inflation*: 0.9% (2009).

In 2007 agriculture, forestry and fishing contributed 10% of GDP, industry 25% and services 65%. Around 20% of the workforce is engaged in agriculture, 33% in industry and 47% in services.

About 14% of land is arable, 5% under permanent crops, 20% permanent pasture and 39% forests and woodlands. The main crops are wheat, maize, tobacco, fruit and vegetables; animal husbandry is also significant.

Mineral resources include copper, zinc, lead and gold, as well as some coal (lignite) and iron ore. The manufacturing sector is based largely on the processing of iron ore, non-ferrous metals, coal, and wood and paper products.

The main exports are wood and paper products and iron and steel, while the principal imports are food products and electric power. In 2008 **Croatia** took 17% of Bosnia and Herzegovina's exports, the other main destinations being **Serbia** (15%) and Germany (14%). The main sources of imports were Croatia (17%), Germany (12%) and Serbia (11%). A large trade deficit is covered principally through foreign aid and a significant inflow of remittances from overseas (which were equivalent to over 20% of GDP in 2007).

Within a virtually landlocked territory, Bosnia and Herzegovina as a republic in the **Socialist Federal Republic of Yugoslavia** was relatively less developed than the other republics, with inefficient agriculture (almost all in private hands on small farms) and a stagnant, though diversified, state-owned industrial sector that included military construction and armaments manufacturing as well as other branches of metallurgical and electrical/engineering industries. The civil war destroyed much of the country's infrastructure and severely disrupted economic life. Whereas total GDP in 1990 had been US $11,000m. and annual income per head $2,400, by 1995 GDP had plummeted to $2,000m. and per head income to an estimated $500, with much economic activity taking place in the 'black' market. The industrial sector, which in 1991 had accounted for over 40% of GDP, had shrunk by 1996 to 23% (with an estimated 80% fall in production and with unemployment reaching 80%) and a decade later was still only 25%.

Since 1995 major reconstruction progress has been achieved (although almost entirely in the Federation). The **World Bank** estimated real growth in GDP in the immediate post-war years at 69% in 1996, 35% in 1997, 13% in 1998 and 10% in 1999 (the slowdown in 1999 being partly attributable to the crisis in **Kosovo**). A major step was taken in June 1998 when a new currency went into circulation, with a currency board arrangement and with the external value for the new marka guaranteed through being pegged to the German currency (and from 1999 the euro) for an initial six-year period. By the end of the decade transport, telecommunications, power, water and education services had been restored to close to pre-war levels of availability and unemployment had been reduced to around 40%. Fiscal discipline had also been imposed, with the budget deficit falling from 5% of GDP in 1998 to 1.3% in 1999 and inflation from 5% to nil. Nevertheless, the economic situation remained precarious (especially in the RS), in view of continued reliance on external support and slow progress on achieving structural reforms and market liberalization.

During 2002 the UN **High Representative** imposed a series of economic regulations, with the ultimate aim of unifying the telecommunications, banking, and tax and customs administration sectors throughout the country, as a prerequisite for eventual membership of the **European Union** (EU). Macroeconomic indicators continued to improve steadily: GDP grew by over 6% in 2004, dipped to below 4% in 2005 and then reached almost 7% in 2006–07. Talks officially began on a Stabilization and Association Agreement (SAA) with the EU in November 2005, and a single-rate value-added tax came into effect in January 2006. Bosnia and Herzegovina joined the **Central European Free Trade Agreement** (CEFTA) in September 2007 and signed the SAA on 16 June 2008.

Inflation has remained low, except for spikes in 2006 and 2008, which has helped maintain the stability of the marka. The **International Monetary Fund** has commended the country's post-conflict reconstruction, noting a rise in real wages of 44% in 2000–07, increased international reserves and a largely privatized banking system (which from 2001 attracted foreign banks, which now account for over 80% ownership of the sector). An increase in credit availability was driving domestic consumption, though lending reduced in late 2008 as the global financial crisis spread. GDP growth slowed to 5.5% in 2008 and the economy entered recession in 2009, not helped by a fall in foreign remittances. Bosnia and Herzegovina negotiated an IMF stand-by arrangement to help reduce government spending and strengthen tax collection. The official unemployment rate remains high at 23%, though informal employment in the 'black' economy in reality reduces this figure.

Key goals are further EU integration, accession to the **World Trade Organization** and development of the private sector. Reversing the pattern of the late 1990s, it has been the RS that has made more economic progress in recent years than the Federation, as it benefits from a more unified administrative structure, strong links with the fast-recovering **Serbian economy** and greater foreign direct investment.

Because of the civil war no privatization took place in the first years of independence. In April 1999 the first **voucher privatization** was undertaken (mainly in the Federation), but rigid labour laws and corruption have slowed the process. The public sector remains large, accounting for some 50% of GDP in 2007. While the RS authorities proceeded with their privatization programme during 2008, the Federation Government only reached consensus on major privatization projects in February 2009. The limited privatization that has occurred has led to some improvements in efficiency of those sectors.

Bosniaks

A title adopted by the Muslim **Slav** population, proportionately the largest, of **Bosnia and Herzegovina** to distinguish themselves from the ethnically identical, but Christian, **Croat** and **Serb** populations. The Bosniaks are the descendants of south Slavs, mostly originally **Orthodox Christians**, who converted to **Islam** during Bosnia's incorporation into the Ottoman Empire (1463–1878). Sharing their overlords' religious faith gave the Bosniaks an opportunity to attain positions of responsibility in the Ottoman administration. After 1918, once included in what was to become **Yugoslavia**, the Muslim community in Bosnia failed to identify itself as a separate ethnic group until the late 1960s. Eventually the Muslims were granted 'nation' status by the communist authorities. By the 1970s they were the republic's largest ethnic group and a clear separate identity appeared.

This fuelled tensions in Bosnia and Herzegovina, which exploded in the country's civil war in 1992–95. Whereas Bosniaks had once occupied areas across the country, after 1995 they were concentrated in the **Muslim-Croat Federation**, having been all but wiped out in Serb- and Croat-dominated areas through deliberate campaigns of '**ethnic cleansing**'. Mosques were destroyed and Muslims forced from their homes in these areas. Although work was undertaken from 2000 to rebuild the mosques and invite Bosniaks back to their original homes, progress has been slow.

The persecution served to strengthen the Bosnian Muslims' identity, and the adoption of the Bosniak title legitimized the idea of a distinct ethnic group. Bosnian is recognized as one of the country's official languages despite its great similarity to Serbian and Croatian. Like Croatian, it uses the Latin alphabet. Bosniak 'nationalist' interests are represented by the **Party of Democratic Action**, although other Muslims support the multi-ethnic **Social Democratic Party of Bosnia and Herzegovina**.

BQK *see* **Central Bank of the Republic of Kosovo**.

Bratislava

The capital city of **Slovakia**, situated in the far west of the country on the banks of the River Danube. *Population*: 424,200 (2007 estimate). The city was known as Pozsony under its prolonged domination by the neighbouring kingdom of **Hungary**, for which it served as the capital from 1526 until 1784. Its dominating castle also served until 1811 as the residence of the Habsburg royal family, to whom the city was known by its German name of Pressburg. The city's infrastructure and economic importance made it the natural choice for the capital of the Slovak Republic within **Czechoslovakia** in 1919 and it remained in this role when an independent **Slovakia** emerged in 1993. Bratislava's modest community of **Jews** was completely destroyed in the Holocaust and the Jewish quarter was bulldozed to make way for the Bridge of the Slovak National Uprising.

Bratislava Stock Exchange
Burza Cenných Papierov v Bratislave a.s. (BCPB)

Officially founded in **Slovakia** in 1991, the BCPB first began trading in April 1993. Trading in foreign securities began in July 1997. In 2008 it had 19 members, and a total market capitalization of 620,487,029,994 koruny.

Director General: Mária Hurajová.
Address: Vysoká 17, POB 151, 814 99 Bratislava.
Telephone: (2) 49236111.
Fax: (2) 49236103.
E-mail: info@bsse.sk
Internet: www.bsse.sk

Brčko

Town in north-eastern **Bosnia and Herzegovina**, on the Sava river which runs along the border with **Croatia**. At the end of the Bosnian war, following the **Dayton Agreement** of November 1995, control of the town was divided between the different Bosnian ethnic groups. However, owing to the strategic sensitivity of its geographical position—as both a part of the narrow Posavina Corridor between the eastern and northern sections of the **Serb Republic** (RS), and an important north-south link between the **Muslim-Croat Federation** and north-eastern Croatia—the final status and governance of the town became the subject of arbitration by an international tribunal. Both the Federation and the RS pressed for exclusive control of the area, but the international tribunal decided in March 1999 that the pre-war Brčko municipality would become a self-governing 'neutral district', subject to Bosnian sovereignty and the authority of the Bosnian central institutions.

BSE (Bulgaria) *see* **Bulgarian Stock Exchange**.

BSE (Hungary) *see* **Budapest Stock Exchange**.

BSEC *see* **Organization of the Black Sea Economic Co-operation**.

BSP *see* **Bulgarian Socialist Party**.

BTA *see* **Bulgarian Telegraph Agency**.

Bucharest

The capital city of **Romania**, situated in the centre of the Wallachian plain north of the Danube river. *Population*: 2m. (2009 estimate). The city was first fortified by the infamous Romanian prince Vlad the Impaler (believed to be the historical figure behind Count Dracula) in 1459. However, it was under Ottoman suzerainty that Bucharest gained in importance. It was made the administrative centre of **Wallachia** in 1659. During the 19th century it functioned as the focus for Romanian nationalism. Bucharest-based movements helped topple the Greek Phanariote dynasty in 1821 and led to the unification of Wallachia and Moldavia (*see* **Bessarabia question**) in 1859. Three years later the city was proclaimed the capital of the unified Romanian state.

The growth of Romania after independence in 1878 was reflected in the expansion of Bucharest. Under communist rule its architecture was dominated by prestige projects. The dictator Nicolae **Ceauşescu** left particularly drastic marks upon it, most notoriously by tearing down 10,000 hectares of the old city to make way for his grandiose House of the People. Economic activity is varied including production of consumer goods and vehicles.

Bucharest Stock Exchange
Bursa de Valori Bucureşti (BVB)

The principal stock exchange in **Romania**, trading mainly in government bonds. Reopened officially in July 1995 after the communist period, it began trading in November that year. It is managed by its members and 24 securities companies that form the Stock Exchange Association. In 2007 there were 54 companies and five sectorial investment funds trading on the BVB, compared with about 6,000 listed on the less stringently-regulated RASDAQ market, which began operations in October 1995, to give all companies from the Mass Privatization Programme the possibility of being listed on an organized market.

President: Stere Farmache.
Address: 14th Floor, bd Carol I 34–36, 020922 Bucharest 2.
Telephone: (21) 3079500.
Fax: (21) 3079519.
E-mail: bvb@bvb.ro
Internet: www.bvb.ro

Budapest

The capital city of **Hungary** situated in the north of the country on the River Danube, which divides the historically separate entities of Buda and Pest. *Population*: 1.7m. (2003 estimate). Budapest as a single city only came about in 1873 when the fortified town of Buda, located on the river's west bank, was amalgamated with the economically vibrant Pest to the east. Since then it has been the capital of Hungary and as such has become the economic and cultural heart of the country, with good transport connections to the rest of **central Europe** and the **Balkans**. It was also the central stage for the country's major political events in the 20th century including the invasion of Soviet tanks in 1956 and the re-emergence of democracy in 1989.

Economic activity centres on heavy industry in the city itself, as lighter industries have gradually spread out around the country. The services sector is also significant.

Budapest Stock Exchange
Budapesti Értéktőzsde (BSE)

Originally founded in **Hungary** in 1864, the exchange reopened after the communist period on 21 June 1990. Partly owned by a consortium of banks in Hungary and Austria, in March 2010 it had 37 members.

Chair.: Attila Szalay-Berzeviczy.
Address: Andrássy út. 93, 1062 Budapest.
Telephone: (1) 4296857.
Fax: (1) 4296899.
E-mail: info@bse.hu
Internet: www.bse.hu

Bukovina question

A dispute between **Romania** and Ukraine over the Bukovina region, which was rather arbitrarily divided between the two at the end of the Second World War. The northern part of Bukovina had, under Austrian suzerainty, become home to a large Ukrainian (Ruthenian) population and is contiguous with the similarly-populated regions of Transcarpathia and eastern **Galicia**. At the end of the Second World War the **Soviet** authorities incorporated it into the Ukrainian Soviet Socialist Republic. Owing to unclear instructions at the time, the cession included the principally Romanian town of Herta. The region is now known as the Chernovtsy oblast (region). The southern region of Bukovina is traditionally the cradle of Moldavian civilization (*see* **Bessarabia question**) and was consequently incorporated into Romania's Moldavian region. Romanian nationalists have long cherished the aspiration of obtaining the return of northern Bukovina, especially Herta. However, since the normalization of relations between Romania and Ukraine after 1991 the claim has not been pursued.

Bulgaria
Republika Bulgaria

An independent republic located in **south-eastern Europe** on the eastern coast of the **Balkan** peninsula, bounded by Romania to the north, Serbia and Macedonia to the west, Greece and Turkey to the south, and the Black Sea to the east. Administratively, Bulgaria is divided into 28 regions (obruzi), and 209 municipalities.

Area: 110,994 sq. km; *capital*: **Sofia**; *population*: 7.5m (2009 estimate), comprising **Bulgarians** 83.9%, **Turks** 9.4%, **Roma** 4.7%, other 2%; *official language*: Bulgarian; *religion*: **Bulgarian Orthodox** 82.6%, Muslim 12.2%, other Christian 1.2%, other 4%

The President is directly elected (with a Vice-President) for a five-year term and nominates the Prime Minister, who in turn nominates the Council of Ministers. Legislative authority is vested in the unicameral **National Assembly** (Narodno Sabranie) whose 240 members are elected for a four-year term; 31 of them are directly elected in constituencies under the first-past-the-post system, while 209 are directly elected under a system of proportional representation from party lists, subject to a minimum requirement of 4% of votes cast.

History: The Bulgars founded their first state in the seventh century and were a powerful nation until subjugated by the Byzantine Empire in the 11th century. A second Bulgarian state was established in the 12th century, but was conquered by the Ottoman Turks towards the end of the 14th century and remained a province of the Ottoman Empire for the next 500 years. The 1878 Congress of Berlin, concluding a Russo-Turkish war, recognized an autonomous principality of Bulgaria under Turkish sovereignty. In 1908 the Government adopted the Constitution of a monarchy and Bulgaria was proclaimed an independent kingdom under Tsar Ferdinand I (*see* **Bulgarian royal family**). Ferdinand abdicated in 1918 following Bulgaria's defeat alongside Germany in the First World War, as a result of which Bulgaria was obliged to cede the Black Sea coastal region of Southern **Dobruja** to **Romania** under the 1919 Treaty of **Neuilly**. Ferdinand's successor, Boris III, reigned until his death in 1943, establishing a virtual dictatorship from 1934. He was succeeded by his infant son, Simeon II. During the Second World War Bulgaria was again allied with Germany before it was occupied by Soviet forces in September 1944 and a coalition Fatherland Front Government, dominated by the Communist Party of Bulgaria (BKP), set up. A referendum held in 1946 formally deposed the Tsar and the following year a new Soviet-style Constitution abolished all opposition parties and established a People's Republic. The 1947 Treaty of Paris formally restored Southern Dobruja to Bulgaria.

The post-war period was dominated by the BKP under the leadership of Todor **Zhivkov**, who maintained Bulgaria as one of the **Soviet Union**'s most loyal satellites. After 35 years in power, Zhivkov was eventually forced to resign in November 1989 in the face of mounting economic problems and the influence of the democratization movements sweeping other **eastern European** countries. Under his immediate successor, Petur Mladenov, the BKP was obliged to relinquish its constitutional monopoly of power and to hold multi-party elections, prior to which it renamed itself the **Bulgarian Socialist Party** (BSP). Against the odds and amid allegations of corruption, the BSP narrowly won the elections in June 1990. Political instability ensued, with mass demonstrations and strikes, until the formation the following December of a multi-party administration which undertook to implement a programme of economic and political reform. A new Constitution was adopted in July 1991, enshrining democracy and commitment to a free-market economy. In the October 1991 legislative elections the right-of-centre Union of Democratic Forces (SDS) defeated the BSP by a narrow four-seat margin to form the first non-communist Government, with Filip Dimitrov as Prime Minister. In January 1992 the incumbent President, Zhelyu Zhelev (SDS), was re-elected for five years in the country's first popular presidential election.

The immediate post-communist years were marked by political fragility in Bulgaria. No single party held a clear mandate to govern, nor was there any obvious consensus between them about how to tackle the mounting economic problems because of the pressure of vested interests. Prime Minister Dimitrov's administration collapsed at the end of 1992, and the subsequent Government of non-party technocrats led by Lyuben Berov resigned in September 1994. Early legislative elections held in December 1994 returned a BSP-led alliance with an overall majority of seats in the National Assembly, capitalizing on the economic discontent in the country. Zhan Videnov of the BSP was appointed Prime Minister. This Government dismissed the heads of state television and radio within six months of taking office, creating intense suspicion of the BSP's political agenda. However, it was the inability to manage the extreme crisis in the financial sector in 1996, caused by the collapse in the banking system and in the value of the currency, which did most to undermine public confidence in the administration. Zhelev was defeated in the October–November 1996 presidential election by Petar Stoyanov of the SDS. Videnov resigned as Prime Minister and BSP party leader in December 1996, and in February 1997 the new President overcame BSP resistance to the installation of a caretaker Government and the calling of early legislative elections for April. This poll was won by the SDS-led United Democratic Forces (ODS) alliance which gained an overall majority of 137 seats in the National Assembly, leaving the BSP once again in opposition, with only 58 seats for their Democratic Left alliance. The Union for National Salvation, headed by the mainly ethnic Turkish **Movement for Rights and Freedoms** (DPS), won 19 seats, the Euro-Left Coalition 14 and the Bulgarian Business Bloc (subsequently renamed the Georgi Ganchev Bloc) 12.

Installed as SDS Prime Minister in May 1997, Ivan Kostov headed a strongly-mandated Government that moved quickly to restore economic and social stability after the crisis of 1996 and early 1997 (*see* **Bulgaria, economy**). In December 1998 Bulgaria formally abolished capital punishment. Despite periodic tensions in the ruling ODS alliance and the surfacing of corruption allegations against certain ministers in 2000, the Government retained its command of the Assembly for the four-year parliamentary term, largely untroubled by various efforts by the BSP to construct a viable opposition alliance for the 2001 elections.

However, more opposition materialized from a somewhat unexpected quarter. The former child-king, Simeon II, now a successful businessman based in Spain, had made a number of attempts to return to Bulgaria and was finally able to take up residence in early 2001, after which he formed the National Movement Simeon II (NDS II). The non-party movement rapidly gained popularity, drawing support from voters weary of the established party system, and from disaffected members of the ruling SDS.

By the time of legislative elections in June the NDS II posed a very credible threat to the Government. It won exactly half of the 240 seats, securing 42.7% of the popular vote. The ODS (including the SDS, the Bulgarian Agrarian People's Union (BZNS), the Bulgarian Social Democratic Party (BSDP), the Democratic Party (DP) and the National Movement for Rights and Freedoms) won 51 seats (with 18.2% of the vote), the **Coalition for Bulgaria** (KzB—headed by the BSP and including the Communist Party of Bulgaria among other factions) won 48 (17.1%) and the DPS 21 (7.5%).

Despite initially suggesting he would remain outside the cabinet, ex-Tsar Simeon II, now known as Simeon Saxecoburggotski, was appointed Prime Minister on 15 July 2001. He turned to the DPS to create a working majority in the Assembly— marking the first time the DPS had been given a role in government. Saxecoburggotski's high popularity rating and personal endorsement of the candidacy of incumbent President Stoyanov in presidential elections in November 2001 was insufficient to save the SDS stalwart; Stoyanov was defeated in the second round. The BSP candidate Georgi **Purvanov** garnered 54% of the vote against Stoyanov's 45.9%, suggesting a trend back towards the left among the electorate.

The next few years were full of controversial political issues, including agreement with the **European Union** (EU) for the future closure of the third and fourth reactors at the Kozloduy nuclear plant, changes to privatization regulations, and efforts to reform the judiciary and to combat organized crime. Saxecoburggotski's Government faced, and survived, six votes of no confidence during its term, caused either by its lack of progress on the problems or too much intervention. Its popularity gradually fell, and several Assembly members left the NDS II, though the coalition retained a slim majority.

In the June 2005 election the BSP-led KzB emerged as the largest bloc with 82 seats (and 34% of the vote), though well short of a majority. The ruling NDS II won 53 seats (21.8% of the vote), while its coalition partner, the DPS, increased its share to 34 seats (14.1%). The new far-right National Union Attack won 21 seats (8.9%), the ODS won 20 seats (8.4%), the Democrats for a Strong Bulgaria (DSB—a recent splinter from the SDS, led by Kostov) won 17 seats (7.1%) and the Bulgarian People's Union (BNS—an alliance led by the BZNS) won 13 seats (5.7%).

BSP leader Sergey Stanishev was nominated as Prime Minister in mid-July, but later that month his proposed cabinet, involving a coalition with the DPS, was rejected by the Assembly. Saxecoburggotski, as head of the second-placed party, was given the next mandate, but he in his turn struggled to form a coalition. With pressure mounting for a government to take office in order to carry though the reforms needed to achieve EU membership, a broad coalition cabinet headed by Stanishev and comprising members of the BSP, NDS II, DPS and an independent took office in mid-August.

Incumbent President Parvanov easily secured re-election in October 2006: he garnered 64% in the first round, only failing to win outright due to a below 50% turnout, so faced second-placed Volen Siderov of Attack (as the National Union Attack had now been renamed) in the run-off, beating him by 75.8% to 24.2%.

The May 2007 European elections saw the rise of the new centre-right **Citizens for European Development of Bulgaria** (GERB), and municipal elections later that year resulted in GERB winning most of the key mayoralties, including re-election for its leader Boiko **Borisov** as Mayor of Sofia.

In April 2009 the electoral law was amended to introduce a constituency-based system for the election of 31 of the 240 members of the Assembly, while the remaining 209 members would continue to be elected by proportional representation from party lists.

Latest elections: In the July 2009 elections GERB won 116 seats (including 26 of the constituency-based seats), just short of a majority in the Assembly, with 39.7% of the vote. The BSP-led KzB won just 40 seats (with 17.7% of the vote), the DPS won 38 seats, including the other five constituency seats (14.5% of the vote), Attack won 21 seats (9.4%), the Blue Coalition (SK—an alliance of centre-right parties including the SDS and DSB) won 15 seats (6.8%) and Order, Lawfulness, Justice (RZS) won 10 seats (4.1%). The NDS II—renamed since 2007 as the National Movement for Stability and Progress—failed to pass the 4% threshold to secure Assembly seats. (A February 2010 ruling from the Constitutional Court on electoral violations adjusted the results to give GERB 117 seats and the DPS 37 seats, and required the replacement of two Assembly members from the SK and RZS.)

Recent developments: After the election, Borisov announced that he would form a minority Government with backing in the National Assembly from Attack, the SK and the RZS. His new Government was approved by the Assembly on 27 July. He promised that his priorities would be to tackle crime and corruption and to reverse the economic downturn.

International relations and defence: Bulgaria is a member of the United Nations, the **Organization for Security and Co-operation in Europe**, the **Council of Europe**, the **Central European Initiative**, the **Danube Commission** and the **Organization of the Black Sea Economic Co-operation**. While participating in

NATO's **Partnership for Peace** programme, Bulgaria allowed NATO aircraft to use Bulgarian airspace during the **Kosovo** conflict with **Yugoslavia** in 1999. It became a full member of NATO in March 2004.

In December 1999 the EU placed Bulgaria on its official list of prospective new members, and an offer of membership was made in April 2005. It was approved by the National Assembly the following month, and Bulgaria acceded (along with Romania) on 1 January 2007. Bulgaria plans to implement the EU's Schengen Agreement, allowing free movement of citizens within the zone's borders, in 2011. It is unlikely to join the **eurozone** before 2013 (*see* **Bulgaria, economy**).

At the regional level, Bulgaria in February 1999 signed a declaration with **Macedonia** settling a longstanding language dispute that arose when Bulgaria refused to recognize Macedonian as a language separate from Bulgarian. The agreement also resolved potential territorial disputes that had threatened to prevent both countries from joining NATO. Bulgaria's relations with Turkey also improved in the late 1990s, following the sharp tensions caused by the programme of 'Bulgarianization' (forced assimilation) in the last months of the communist regime in 1989 and the resultant mass exodus of ethnic Turks to Turkey. In March 1999 Bulgaria, Turkey and Romania agreed to set up a free-trade zone. Bulgaria's recognition in March 2008 of **Kosovo**'s independence has strained relations with **Serbia**, though later that year the two countries, together with Romania, signed an agreement on co-operation in combating cross-border crime. Bulgaria has also agreed several energy projects with Russia, but a dispute between Russia and Ukraine in early 2009 that led to power supplies to Bulgaria being cut off has prompted Bulgaria to also look for other solutions to its energy supply.

Bulgaria's defence budget for 2008 amounted to some US $1,315m., equivalent to about 2.6% of GDP. The size of the armed forces in 2010 was some 35,000 personnel, including those serving under compulsory conscription of nine months, while reservists numbered an estimated 303,000. Bulgaria supported the US-led military campaign in Iraq in 2003, and troops remained in Iraq until December 2008.

Bulgaria, economy

A formerly centrally-planned economy whose initially halting transition to a market system accelerated after 1997. It joined the **European Union** (EU) a decade later. One of the poorest EU members, Bulgaria was badly affected in 2009 by the global downturn.

GNP: US $41,830m. (2008); *GNP per capita*: $5,490 (2008); *GDP at PPP*: $94,476m. (2008); *GDP per capita at PPP*: $12,400 (2008); *real GDP growth*: –6.5% (2009 estimate); *exports*: $22,587m. (2008); *imports*: $37,369m. (2008); *currency*: lev, pegged to euro (US $1 = L1.39 in mid-2009); *unemployment*: 8.1% (end 2009); *government deficit as a percentage of GDP*: 0.7%; *inflation*: 2.7% (2009).

In 2007 industry accounted for 32% of GDP, agriculture for 6% and services for 62%. Around 7% of the workforce is engaged in agriculture, 36% in industry and 57% in services.

Some 37% of the land is arable, 2% under permanent crops, 16% permanent pasture and 35% forests and woodland. The main crops are grain, oilseed, vegetables, fruit (including grapes for wine) and tobacco, and there is also animal husbandry.

The principal mineral resources are bauxite, copper, manganese, lead and zinc. Bulgaria does have some coal, although mostly lignite and brown coal. The main industries are machine-building and metal-working, food processing, chemicals, textiles, construction materials, and ferrous and non-ferrous metals. Bulgaria's own resources account for just over half of its energy requirements (including substantial generation of electricity by nuclear power, accounting for 43% of consumption, and some hydroelectricity generation) and there are small hydrocarbon reserves.

Bulgaria's main exports are metals (including iron and steel), petroleum products, clothing and footwear, and machines and equipment. The principal imports are crude petroleum and natural gas, machines and equipment, vehicles, textiles, and ores. In 2008 **Greece** took 10% of exports, followed by Germany and Turkey (9% each), while Germany supplied 13% of imports, followed by Italy (9%) and Ukraine (8%).

Although traditionally an agricultural country, Bulgaria underwent a considerable programme of industrialization after the Second World War. Already in decline prior to the end of communist rule in 1989–90, the Bulgarian economy continued to suffer in the early 1990s, as lack of political stability meant that necessary decisions were frequently postponed. Industrial and agricultural output dropped sharply, there were serious trade and balance-of-payments deficits, and by 1996 foreign exchange reserves had fallen to US $446m. (covering only one month's imports). The problems were exacerbated by the reluctance of the post-1994 Government headed by the (ex-communist) **Bulgarian Socialist Party** to pursue pro-market and liberalization reforms, in the interests of preserving social stability. The result in late 1996 was a major banking and financial crisis, featuring a massive depreciation of the external value of the lev and hyperinflation that spiralled to over 200% a month in early 1997 and to 580% for the full year. GDP contracted by some 10% in 1996, with devastating effects on social conditions.

The situation was retrieved by the centre-right Government of the Union of Democratic Forces elected in April 1997, following which structural and other economic reforms were vigorously reactivated and macroeconomic discipline was imposed. With the support of the **International Monetary Fund** (IMF) and other international donors, a currency board was established in July 1997 and the lev was pegged to the Deutsche Mark (and to the euro from the beginning of 1999). Real GDP growth of 3.5% was achieved in 1998, while the inflation rate was dramatically reduced to only 1%. Further recovery in 1999 was hampered by the damaging economic impact of the **Kosovo** crisis on Bulgaria; GDP growth fell back to 2.4% and inflation revived to 6%. The reform programme was continued, however, and was boosted in December 1999 when the Government achieved its aim of securing acceptance of Bulgaria as a designated candidate for EU membership, to assist which it had joined the **Central European Free Trade Area** (CEFTA) at the beginning of the year. GDP growth recovered to between 4% and 5% in 2000–03, although inflation rose briefly to 10% before dropping back to 2% by 2003.

Prime Minister Simeon Saxecoburggotski's Government (2001–05) brought down unemployment, which had risen to 18% by the end of 2000, restructured the country's foreign debt and continued a programme of economic reforms to reduce taxes, cut corruption and attract more foreign investment. In 2002 the European Commission deemed Bulgaria to be a 'functioning market economy'.

In 2006 Bulgaria attracted the highest levels of foreign direct investment as a share of GDP in **eastern Europe**, and these continued following EU accession at the beginning of 2007. The already rising budget surplus was stimulated further by the introduction of a lower corporate tax rate of 10% in 2007. This was followed in 2008 by a 10% flat rate for personal income. These measures helped to cut labour costs and reduce the size of the informal economy.

GDP growth in 2008 exceeded 6% for the fifth consecutive year, though inflation also rose from its average of 7% to 12%. However, in July 2008 the EU withheld funds worth millions of euros from Bulgaria—the first time this had happened to a EU member state—due to lack of progress with reforming the judiciary and combating corruption. By 2009 contractions in export demand and foreign investment due to the global economic downturn had pushed the economy into recession, with unemployment and household debt rising. While the downturn had been expected to hit Bulgaria less hard than some of the other eastern EU members, its fixed exchange rate made it harder to keep its exports competitive on the world market, and its reputation for corruption made it more difficult to attract external support from international financial agencies.

Bulgaria was expected to join the **eurozone** on 1 January 2013, although some analysts now believe that this is unlikely before 2015; it must first be part of the Exchange Rate Mechanism II (which it is expected to join soon) for a minimum of two years. It does already meet most of the convergence criteria due to its low budget deficit and its currency being pegged to the euro.

The privatization process in post-communist Bulgaria, although slow to get under way (and plagued by rampant corruption in the early stages), accelerated in the late 1990s. The post-1997 Government completed the privatization of nearly all agricultural land (mostly restored to former owners) and also introduced a free-market structure by abolishing food price subsidies and by privatizing most of the food industry. Privatization of the industrial sector was relaunched with urgency in 1998, resulting in the sell-off of 80% of former state-owned asset value by the end of 1999. The Government also instituted a programme of isolation and liquidation of unviable industrial enterprises. By the end of 2000 well over 90% of the former state-owned industrial sector was actually or imminently under private ownership. The

Saxecoburggotski Government pressed ahead with long-delayed plans to privatize some of the remaining major state monopolies. The Bulgarian Telecommunications Company was privatized in 2005, and Bulgaria Air a year later.

Bulgarian Chamber of Commerce and Industry

The principal organization in **Bulgaria** for promoting business contacts, both internally and externally, in the post-communist era. Originally founded in 1895.

President: Bojidar Bojinov.
Address: Iskar Street 9, Sofia 1058.
Telephone: (2) 9872631.
Fax: (2) 9873209.
E-mail: bcci@bcci.org
Internet: www.bcci.bg

Bulgarian Industrial Association (BISA)

BISA assists economic enterprises in **Bulgaria** with promotion and foreign contacts, analyses the economic situation, formulates policies for legislative and commercial projects, assists the development of small and medium-sized firms and organizes privatization and investment operations. Founded in 1980.

Chair. and President: Bojidar Danev.
Address: Alabin St 16–20, Sofia 1000.
Telephone: (2) 9320911.
Fax: (2) 9872604.
E-mail: office@bia-bg.com
Internet: www.bia-bg.com

Bulgarian National Bank
Bulgarska Narodna Banka (BNB)

The central bank of **Bulgaria**. A Bulgarian Central Bank was first created in 1879 after the country's emergence from the rule of the Ottoman Empire, and the Bulgarian lev was first put into circulation in note form by the Bank in 1885. In 1991 a two-tier banking system was enforced, remodelling the BNB as an independent, modern Central Bank in the post-communist era. The country was struck by hyperinflation in the winter of 1996–97 before the BNB fixed the lev to the Deutsche Mark. In 1998 the Bank began issuing its own lev notes for the first time since 1948 and the currency was devalued by a factor of 1,000 the following year. As at December 2007, the BNB had reserves of 2,608.8m. lev.

Governor: Ivan Iskrov.
Address: Aleksandur Battenberg Sq. 1, Sofia 1000.
Telephone: (2) 91451203.
Fax: (2) 9802425.
E-mail: press_office@bnbank.org
Internet: www.bnb.bg

Bulgarian royal family—Saxe-Coburg-Gotha dynasty

The family which gave rise to the hereditary monarchs of **Bulgaria** from 1908 to 1946. Drawn from the German Duchy of Saxe-Coburg-Gotha, the dynasty was founded by Prince Ferdinand of Bulgaria who proclaimed himself King (Tsar) Ferdinand I in 1908. The last reigning monarch was Simeon II who succeeded as King in 1943 at the age of six, and who was forced to abdicate three years later after a dubious communist-organized referendum ruled in favour of a republic. He made a dramatic return to political prominence in 2001 as the inspiration behind a newly-formed **National Movement Simeon II** that achieved a striking victory in legislative elections in June of that year. Under the name Simeon **Saxecoburggotski**, the ex-King was Prime Minister of Bulgaria from July 2001 until August 2005; he never dropped his claim to the throne but maintained that his political agenda did not include a return to monarchy. The heir apparent is his eldest son Kardam, Prince of Tirnovo.

Bulgarian Socialist Party
Balgarska Sotsialisticheska Partiya (BSP)

A left-wing political party in Bulgaria, currently in opposition, which leads the **Coalition for Bulgaria** (KzB). It is a member of the **Socialist International**.

The successor to the former ruling Bulgarian Communist Party (BKP), dating from April 1990 when the BKP changed its name and embraced democratic socialism. The BKP had traced its descent from the Bulgarian Social Democratic Party (BSDP), founded in 1891, but really dated from 1919, when the pro-Bolshevik BSDP faction became a founder member of the Third International (Comintern). It later organized armed opposition to right-wing regimes of the inter-war period and renamed itself the Workers' Party in 1927, before it was banned in 1934. For the following decade the party was based in Moscow, where many of its exiled leaders were executed in Stalin's purges. During the Second World War the party played a leading role in resistance to the pro-German Bulgarian regime in power until 1944, its activities being directed by Georgi Dimitrov, Bulgarian Secretary-General of the Comintern. In September 1944 the communist-dominated Fatherland Front, including left-wing agrarians and social democrats, took power in Sofia, assisted by the advancing Red

Army. In the post-war period the communists consolidated their position, Dimitrov becoming Prime Minister after the October 1946 elections and a People's Republic being declared in December 1947. In 1948 the rump of the old BSDP was merged with the Workers' Party, the resultant formation adopting the BKP rubric and effectively becoming the sole ruling party, although the Bulgarian Agrarian People's Union (BZNS) remained a nominally independent component of the Front.

On Dimitrov's death in 1949 the BKP leadership passed to Vulko Chervenkov, but he was replaced in 1954 by Todor **Zhivkov** after being accused of fostering a personality cult. Under Zhivkov's long rule Bulgaria remained closely aligned with the **Soviet Union** and participated in the 1968 Soviet-led intervention in **Czechoslovakia** (*see* **Prague Spring**). At the 13th BKP congress in April 1986 Zhivkov announced a reform programme reflecting the Gorbachev *glasnost* and *perestroika* initiatives in the Soviet Union; but reform proved difficult to accomplish because of party in-fighting. Amid the rapid collapse of European communism in late 1989, Zhivkov was replaced as BKP leader and Head of State by Petur Mladenov, who initiated a purge of Zhivkov supporters. The BKP's 'leading role' in society and the state was terminated under constitutional amendments enacted in January 1990, following which an extraordinary party congress renounced 'democratic centralism' and opted for a 'socially-orientated market economy'. The party leadership passed to Aleksandur Lilov (a prominent BKP reformer of the Zhivkov era), with Mladenov remaining Head of State.

Paradoxically, the BKP was obliged to form the first openly all-communist Government in Bulgaria's history in February 1990, when the BZNS opted to go into opposition and the new pro-democracy Union of Democratic Forces (SDS) refused to join a national unity coalition. In April 1990, following a ballot of party members, the BKP officially renamed itself the BSP, which in multi-party elections in June resisted the post-communist **eastern European** trend by being returned to power with 211 of the then 400 **National Assembly** seats. In July 1990, however, Mladenov resigned as Head of State, after disclosures about his role in the suppression of anti-Government demonstrations in December 1989. He was succeeded by SDS leader Zhelyu Zhelev in August, while in December 1990 the BSP also vacated the premiership, although it remained the largest component in an uneasy coalition with the SDS and the BZNS.

The adoption of a new democratic Constitution in July 1991 was followed by political dissension over the BSP's attitude to the August coup attempt by hard-liners in Moscow, seen by many as initially supportive. In further elections in October 1991 the BSP was allied with eight small parties and organizations on a platform of preserving the 'Bulgarian spirit and culture', but was narrowly defeated by the SDS. It therefore went into opposition for the first time since 1944. At a party congress in December 1991, Lilov was replaced as leader by Zhan Videnov, who advocated a 'modern left socialist party' and easily defeated the candidate of the reformist social democrats, Georgi Pirinski. The BSP also suffered a narrow defeat in the direct presidential election held in January 1992, its preferred candidate securing 46.5% of the second-round vote.

In September 1992 the decision of the (ethnic Turkish) **Movement for Rights and Freedoms** (DPS) to withdraw support from the SDS minority Government enabled the BSP to reassert its influence. A 'Government of experts' headed by Lyuben Berov (non-party), appointed in December, was backed by most BSP deputies. Thereafter, as the Government achieved a degree of stability by not hurrying privatization and deregulation of the economy, the BSP was content to avoid direct governmental responsibility during a period of transition, while relying on its establishment network and the party's strength in the Assembly to influence decision-making. By mid-1993 the BSP was again the largest Assembly party, owing to the steady erosion of SDS affiliation, although the BSP also experienced defections in this period.

On the resignation of the Berov Government in September 1994, the BSP declined the opportunity to form a new administration, preferring early elections. These were held in December, the BSP being allied principally with factions of the BZNS and the Ecoglasnost Political Club. The outcome was an overall Assembly majority of 125 seats for the BSP-led list and the formation of a coalition Government in January 1995 under the premiership of Videnov, committed to a socially-orientated market economy and integration into European institutions. It made little progress on either front, however, and so faced a renewed challenge from the SDS in the 1996 presidential elections. Aiming to attract centrist support, the BSP nominated Pirinski (by now Foreign Minister) as its candidate, but he was ruled ineligible because he had been born in the USA. The BSP replacement was Culture Minister Ivan Marazov, who ran under the Together for Bulgaria label but who was defeated by Petar Stoyanov (SDS) in the second voting round in early November on a 60:40 split.

Videnov quickly resigned as both Prime Minister and BSP Chairman, being replaced in the latter capacity by Georgi **Purvanov** in December 1996. After initial resistance by the BSP, Stoyanov was able to install a caretaker administration and to call early Assembly elections in April 1997. The BSP ran as leader of the Democratic Left alliance (again including BZNS and Ecoglasnost factions) but was heavily defeated by the SDS-led United Democratic Forces, the BSP alliance being reduced to 58 seats.

In opposition, the BSP in December 1998 formed the Social Democracy Union with other left-wing forces, while also establishing an alliance with the Euro-Left Coalition with a view to broadening its popular base for the 2001 Assembly elections. In mid-2000 the pro-BSP faction of the BZNS broke into two groups, the main one withdrawing from the alliance in opposition to the BSP's support for membership of **NATO** and the **European Union**. In January 2001 the BSP launched yet another alliance of left-wing parties, this time called the New Left, which was committed to 'the values of modern social democracy and the European left'.

Heading into the 2001 elections the BSP formed the current KzB coalition, uniting left-of-centre parties in the face of dwindling support for the ruling SDS-led coalition.

However, it was also up against the overwhelmingly popular National Movement Simeon II (NDS II). The KzB gained just 17% of the vote (48 seats) but was invited into a broad-based coalition by the NDS II Prime Minister, Simeon Saxecoburggotski, along with the DPS. The BSP was awarded two cabinet positions in the initial Government. Purvanov proved the party's continuing political effectiveness when he surprised political analysts by winning presidential elections in November 2001. He was inaugurated on 22 January 2002, having already stepped down as party leader. Sergey Stanishev was elected as the new party leader.

In the June 2005 election the KzB emerged as the largest bloc with 82 seats (and 34% of the vote), though well short of a majority. BSP leader went on to head a cross-party Government from August, after his first proposed cabinet of the KzB and DPS had been rejected by the Assembly.

The KzB won just 40 seats (with 17.7% of the vote) at the July 2009 election, and went into opposition to a Government led by the centre-right **Citizens for European Development of Bulgaria**.

Leadership: Sergey Stanishev (Chair.).
Address: 20 Pozitano Street, 1000 Sofia.
Telephone: (2) 8107200.
Fax: (2) 9812185.
E-mail: bsp@bsp.bg
Internet:www.bsp.bg

Bulgarian Stock Exchange (BSE)

The successor, launched in October 1997, to the suspended First Bulgarian Stock Exchange (FBSE). The FBSE had been inaugurated in November 1991 but was suspended in October 1996 owing to new regulations from the Securities and Stock Exchange Commission. Since 2007 the BSE is 44% owned by the Bulgarian Government. Total market capitalization in June 2008 was US $18,300m. The BSE is managed by a Board of Directors and the Chief Executive Officer.

Chair.: Viktor Papazov.
Address: ul. Triushi 10, Sofia 1303.
Telephone: (2) 9370934.
Fax: (2) 9370946.
E-mail: bse@bse-sofia.bg
Internet: www.bse-sofia.bg

Bulgarian Telegraph Agency
Bulgarska Telegrafna Agentsia (BTA)

Bulgaria's main and official news agency, originally set up in 1898. BTA is now regulated under legislation dating from June 1994 which designates it as an 'autonomous national news organization' with a Director General elected by the Bulgarian **National Assembly**. It has its own network of reporters in major towns throughout the country.

Director General: Maksim Minchev.
Address: Bul. Tzarigradsko 49, Sofia 1024.
Telephone: (2) 926242.
Fax: (2) 9862289.
E-mail: bta@bta.bg
Internet: www.bta.bg

Bulgarian Turks

A community of 746,664 ethnic Turks (2001 census) in **Bulgaria**, concentrated in the traditional tobacco-growing regions in the southern Arda basin and north-eastern **Dobruja**. In 2001 they constituted 9.4% of the total population. It is largely accepted that the Bulgarian Turks arrived in Bulgaria during the era of the Ottoman Empire, between the 14th and 19th centuries. However, some scholars have attempted to prove that they were either ethnic **Bulgarians** who adopted the Turkish language and Islam under Ottoman suzerainty, or the descendants of much earlier **Turkic** migrants from central Asia.

After Bulgaria became autonomous under Turkish sovereignty in 1878, the Bulgarian Turks had their own Turkish-language schools and retained their own cultural identity. This situation continued within the independent Bulgaria to the extent that even in 1946 half of all Bulgarian Turks could not understand Bulgarian. Although initially this situation was tolerated by the post-war communist authorities, a strenuous policy of Bulgarianization was implemented after 1958. Over the next 30 years Turkish schools were shut, Turkish was dropped from the curriculum and Turkish newspapers were closed down; by 1985 the Government forced the adoption of **Slavic** names and outlawed the use of Turkish in public. The policy led to violent resistance, imprisonments and killings. A mass exodus of Turks to Turkey began in June 1989, actively encouraged through intimidation and confiscation of property. Although 350,000 fled within two months, 130,000 had returned by January 1990 as the Bulgarian communist regime liberalized.

Between 1990 and 1992 Bulgarian Turks were rehabilitated into Bulgarian society. Arabic and Islamic names were readmitted and Turkish-language media flourished. However, the decline of the country's tobacco industry has hit the Turkish community particularly badly and large numbers continue to emigrate to Turkey. This demographic downturn has eroded the traditional support base of the **Movement for Rights and Freedoms** (DPS), forcing it to seek greater links with the minority **Pomak** community.

Bulgarians

A modern people of south-eastern Europe, usually considered south **Slavic**. The Bulgars, from whom their name is derived, actually originated as a Turkic tribe from central Asia, who settled in the seventh century in what is now Ukraine, where they established a Great Bulgarian Empire. On the disintegration of this empire a group of Bulgars migrated south and west into the southern **Balkans** where they merged with the earlier immigrant Slavs, and to a lesser extent with local **Vlachs**, to form the modern Bulgarian people. As such, they are considered most closely related to the neighbouring **Macedonians**; indeed it is sometimes said there is no discernible ethnic difference between Bulgarians and Macedonians. The further advance of the Bulgarians into what is now **Macedonia** in the ninth century led to their adoption of Christianity, the spread of the Slavic Macedonian language and ultimately the spread of the **Cyrillic alphabet**.

Outside Bulgaria itself, there are some 480,000 Bulgarians in **Turkey**, and over 200,000 Bulgarians concentrated in the Odessa region of Ukraine, with whom the Bulgarian Government has striven to forge links. The third-largest group outside Bulgaria consists of around 93,000 who live in Spain; 84,000 live in Moldova, and form a majority in the rural southern Taraclia district, where they have sought some regional autonomy.

BVB *see* **Bucharest Stock Exchange**.

C

Camera Deputaţilor
(House of Deputies)

The lower house of the **Parliament of Romania**.

CAN *see* **Cyprus News Agency**.

Catholicism *see* **Roman Catholic Church**.

CBCG *see* **Central Bank of Montenegro**.

CBSS *see* **Council of the Baltic Sea States**.

CDI *see* **Centrist Democrat International**.

Ceauşescu, Nicolae

Communist leader in **Romania** from 1965 until the violent overthrow of his dictatorial regime in December 1989, and Head of State for all but two of those years. Born in 1918, he began his political life as a teenage communist activist from a peasant family, and was imprisoned under King Carol and again by the pro-Nazi Iron Guard during the war. Associated closely with Gheorghe Gheorghiu-Dej's nationalist group in the communist party, he succeeded his mentor as General Secretary in 1965, and played the patriotic card riskily but successfully. Besides maintaining contacts with the People's Republic of China and Israel, he condemned the **Warsaw Pact**'s 1968 invasion of **Czechoslovakia**, and declared all-out resistance to the threat of Romania suffering the same fate. Although he kept Romania within the Warsaw Pact, he offered Western Governments the possibility of an intermediary, and enjoyed the attention and foreign honours that he (and his high-profile wife Elena) received in return. His economic schemes were geared to notions of Romania's grandeur, and a pride in what modern man could do to his environment, but his lifestyle was remote from the hardship that such policies entailed for ordinary people. The Ceauşescu nepotism was unpopular in the upper echelons of the party, but strict censorship and a pervasive personality cult stifled dissenting voices as he proclaimed his rule to be the 'golden age'. He seemed genuinely astonished to encounter protest and even hatred from his people in December 1989, when he and Elena were overthrown, captured and shot. Some national-communist politicians have since called for Ceauşescu's rehabilitation as a national hero who protected Romania from **Soviet** domination.

CEFTA *see* **Central European Free Trade Area.**

CEI *see* **Central European Initiative.**

Central Bank of Bosnia and Herzegovina
Centralna Banka Bosne i Hercegovine

The central bank of **Bosnia and Herzegovina** with sole authority for the country's currency and monetary policy since it began operations in 1997. It replaced the National Bank of Bosnia and Herzegovina and the National Bank of the Republika Srpska. It does not grant credits, or lend capital to private or governmental concerns, and is not a lender of last resort to the banking system. As of December 2008, the Bank held reserves of 474.2m. KM (convertible marks).

Governor: Kemal Kozarić.
Address: 25 Maršala Tita, 71000 Sarajevo.
Telephone: (33) 278222.
Fax: (33) 215094.
E-mail: contact@cbbh.ba
Internet: www.cbbh.gov.ba

Central Bank of Cyprus

The central bank of **Cyprus**, founded in 1963, and fully independent of government control since July 2002. As of December 2008, the Bank had reserves of 31.8m. euros.

Governor: Christodoulos Christodoulou.
Address: POB 25529, 80 Kennedy Ave, 1076 Nicosia.
Telephone: 22714100.
Fax: 22378153.
E-mail: cbcinfo@centralbank.gov.cy
Internet: www.centralbank.gov.cy

Central Bank of Montenegro
Centralna Banka Crne Gore (CBCG)

The central bank of **Montenegro**, established in 2001. As of December 2007, the Bank held reserves of 41.9m. euros.
> *Governor*: Ljubisa Krgović.
> *Address*: Bul. Petra Cetinjskog 6, 81000 Podgorica.
> *Telephone*: (20) 403191.
> *Fax*: (20) 664140.
> *E-mail*: info@cb-cg.org
> *Internet*: www.cb-mn.org

Central Bank of the Republic of Kosovo
Banka Qendror e Republikës së Kosovës (BQK)

The central bank of **Kosovo**, successor to the Banking and Payments Authority of Kosovo. Founded in 2006, CBAK has authority to license, supervise and regulate financial institutions in Kosovo. As of December 2008, the Bank held total assets of 1,113.2m. euros.
> *Chair.*: Gazmend Luboteni.
> *Address*: Garibaldi 33, Pristina.
> *Telephone*: (381) 222055.
> *Fax*: (381) 243763.
> *E-mail*: publicrelations@cbak-kos.org
> *Internet*: www.bqk-kos.org

Central Europe

An ill-defined term used generally of the countries between the Baltic and Adriatic Seas, and in its adjectival form to describe historic cities such as Prague and Vienna. Changing borders and geopolitical configurations in the area have confused the usage of terms such as central Europe, and indeed eastern and western Europe. **Eastern Europe** would have been generally taken to include East Germany during the communist period, whereas reunified Germany after 1990 would now be considered an integral part of western Europe. In intellectual terms central Europe existed in the 1990s as a transitional zone somewhere between the liberal economies of the 'West', with their apparent security, prosperity and established democratic pluralism, and the largely authoritarian and struggling states of the 'East'—the former **Soviet Union** and the **Balkans**—with their so-called 'economies in transition'. In this sense, to become 'central European' was an aspiration, and suggested a greater suitability for entry into the Western-dominated world economy, particularly the **European Union**. This loose use of the term was most frequently applied to the **Baltic States**, **Poland**, the **Czech Republic**, **Hungary** and **Slovenia**. However, this was by no means definitive, and by varying political, cultural and geographic criteria Austria, **Croatia**, **Slovakia** and even parts of Germany and Italy could be considered central European.

Central European Free Trade Area (CEFTA)

A grouping to promote trade and co-operation between its member countries. CEFTA was originally founded in 1992 (coming into effect from 1993) between the **Visegrád Group** of countries: **Czech Republic**, **Hungary**, **Poland** and **Slovakia**. A fifth member, **Slovenia**, joined at the beginning of 1997, followed in July by **Romania** and in January 1999 by **Bulgaria**. All these countries have since joined the EU, at which point they left CEFTA (the first five in May 2004 and the last two in January 2007). Meanwhile, **Croatia** had joined CEFTA in 2003 and **Macedonia** joined in 2006. In December 2006 a new Agreement was signed between Croatia, Macedonia, **Albania**, **Bosnia and Herzegovina**, Moldova, **Montenegro**, **Serbia** and **UNMIK** (on behalf of **Kosovo**) to enlarge CEFTA. Ratification was completed by September 2007.

CEFTA's Secretariat was set up in Brussels in September 2008. Decisions are adopted within the Joint Committee, whose members are the ministers of CEFTA countries with jurisdiction over foreign economic relations. The chairmanship of the Joint Committee rotates annually; Serbia holds the chairmanship for 2010, to be followed by Kosovo in 2011 and Albania in 2012.

Director of the Secretariat: Renata Vitez.
Address: CEFTA Secretariat, Rue Joseph II 12–16, 1000 Brussels, Belgium.
Telephone: (2) 2291011.
Fax: (2) 2291019.
E-mail: cefta@cefta.int
Internet: www.cefta2006.com

Central European Initiative (CEI)

A sub-regional co-operation initiative in **central** and **eastern Europe**, which originated in 1989 as the Pentagonale group (Austria, **Czechoslovakia**, Italy, **Hungary**, **Yugoslavia**). It became Hexagonale with the admission of **Poland** in July 1991, and adopted its present name in March 1992. It aimed to encourage regional and bilateral co-operation, working within the **Organization for Security and Co-operation in Europe** (OSCE), and to assist in the preparation process for **European Union** (EU) membership. Since the accession of five CEI member states to the EU in 2004 and two more in 2007, the CEI's focus has shifted to its non-EU member states. The presidency rotates annually between its members in alphabetical order; in 2010 it is being held by Montenegro.

Members: 18 eastern and central European countries: **Albania**, Austria, Belarus, **Bosnia and Herzegovina**, **Bulgaria**, **Croatia**, **Czech Republic**, **Hungary**, Italy, **Macedonia**, Moldova, **Montenegro**, **Poland**, **Romania**, **Serbia**, **Slovakia**, **Slovenia**, Ukraine.
Leadership: Gerhard Pfanzelter (Secretary-General).
Address: CEI Executive Secretariat, Via Genova 9, 34121 Trieste, Italy.
Telephone: (040) 7786777.
Fax: (040) 7786766.
E-mail: cei-es@cei-es.org
Internet: www.ceinet.org

Centrist Democrat International (CDI)

An organization founded in 1961 as the Christian Democrat World Union as a platform for the co-operation of political parties of Christian Social inspiration. It has changed its name several times, also having been called the Christian Democrat International and the Christian Democrat and People's Parties International.

Members: Over 100 parties worldwide, including parties in **Albania**, **Bosnia and Herzegovina**, **Bulgaria**, **Croatia**, **Cyprus**, **Czech Republic**, **Estonia**, **Greece**, **Hungary**, **Kosovo**, **Lithuania**, **Romania**, **Serbia** (observer party only), **Slovakia** and **Slovenia**.
President: Pier Ferdinando Casini.
Address: rue d'Arlon 67, 1040 Brussels, Belgium.
Telephone: (2) 2854160.
Fax: (2) 2854166.

CERN *see* **European Organization for Nuclear Research**.

CFE *see* **Conventional Forces in Europe**.

Chamber of Commerce and Industry of Romania and the Municipality of Bucharest

The principal organization in **Romania** for promoting business contacts, both internally and externally, in the post-communist era. Originally founded in 1868.
President: Gheorghe Cojocaru.
Address: blvd Octavian Goga 2, Bucharest 3.
Telephone: (21) 3229536.
Fax: (21) 3229542.
E-mail: ccir@ccir.ro
Internet: www.ccir.ro

Chamber of Commerce and Industry of Slovenia

The principal organization in **Slovenia** for promoting business contacts, both internally and externally, in the post-communist era.

President: Samo Hribar Milić.
Address: Dimičeva 13, 1504 Ljubljana.
Telephone: (1) 5898000.
Fax: (1) 5898100.
E-mail: info@gzs.si
Internet: www.gzs.si

Chamber of Commerce of Bosnia and Herzegovina

The principal organization in **Bosnia and Herzegovina** for promoting business contacts, both internally and externally, in the post-communist era.

President: Milan Lovrić.
Address: Branislava Đurđeva 10, Sarajevo 71000.
Telephone: (33) 663631.
Fax: (33) 663632.
E-mail: cis@komorabih.com
Internet: www.komorabih.com

Chamber of Commerce of Montenegro
Privredna Komora Crne Gore

The principal organization in **Montenegro** for promoting business contacts, both internally and externally, in the post-communist era.

President: Vojin Đukanović.
Address: Novaka Miloševa 29, 81000 Podgorica.
Telephone: (20) 230545.
Fax: (20) 230493.
E-mail: pkcg@pkcg.org
Internet: www.pkcg.org

Chamber of Commerce of Serbia
Privredna Komora Srbije

The principal organization in **Serbia** for promoting business contacts, both internally and externally, in the post-communist era. Founded in 1990.

President: Radoslav Veselinović.
Address: Resavska 13–15, 11000 Belgrade.

65

Telephone: (11) 3300900.
Fax: (11) 3230949.
E-mail: pksrbije@pks.co.rs
Internet: www.pks.co.rs

Chamber of Deputies
Poslanecká Sněmovna

The lower house of **Parliament** of the **Czech Republic**.

Chamber of Industry and Trade for Foreign Investors
Izba Przemysłowo-Handlowa Inwestorów Zagranicznych

A private-sector body promoting economic and business contacts; effectively
Poland's main externally-orientated chamber of commerce.
President: Zdzisław Jagodziński.
Address: ul. Pańska 73, 00834 Warsaw.
Telephone: (22) 3147575.
Fax: (22) 3147576.
E-mail: biuro@iphiz.com.pl
Internet: www.iphiz.com.pl

Charter 77

A document drawn up by dissidents in **Czechoslovakia** in 1977, which called for the
liberalization and democratization of the communist regime, and spawned a human
rights movement by the same name. Charter 77 served as a focal point for the
intellectual opposition in Czechoslovakia, and several of its signatories, including
Václav **Havel**, emerged as leading political figures in and after the '**velvet
revolution**' of 1989. Charter 77 was disbanded in 1992, having 'completed its
historical role'.

Chetniks

The name originally given to the **Serb** nationalist and royalist guerrillas, led by Draza
Mihailović, who fought in **Yugoslavia** during the Second World War both against the
German and Italian occupation forces and against the rival communist **Yugoslav**
Partisans led by **Tito**. The term, which carries associations from this period of Serb
atrocities against other Yugoslav nationalities, has more recently been applied to Serb
militias fighting **Bosniaks** and **Croats** in the Bosnian civil war in the early 1990s.

Christian Democratic People's Party
Kereszténydemokrata Néppárt (KDNP)

A centre-right political party in Hungary, in opposition prior to the April 2010 **National Assembly** election. Refounded in 1989, the KDNP claims to be a successor to the anti-communist, **Roman Catholic**-based Democratic People's Party that was prominent in opposition in the immediate post-Second World War period. In 1990 it won 21 seats in the **National Assembly** election, with 6.5% of the vote, and joined a centre-right Government under József Antall of the **Hungarian Democratic Forum** (MDF). The KDNP slightly improved on its position in 1994 with 22 seats and 7% of the vote. However, the resounding defeat of the MDF at this election by the resurgent former communist **Hungarian Socialist Party** (MSzP) resulted in a left-wing Government, with the KDNP in opposition. György Giczy was elected as KDNP Chairman the following year.

By 1997 the party faced internal dissension over an increasing association with extreme nationalists, in particular the far-right Hungarian Justice and Life Party. The parliamentary caucus disbanded, half of its deputies allying with the Federation of Young Democrats–Hungarian Civic Party (FiDeSz–MPP). As a result, the KDNP only won 2.6% of the vote in the 1998 election, falling below the threshold for representation in the new Assembly.

Giczy resigned from the party leadership in June 2001, and Tivadar Bartók was elected to succeed him. In November 2001, the KDNP joined a new Centre Party alliance, with the Green Democrats, Hungarian Democratic People's Party and the Third Side of Hungary. However, the alliance only secured 3.9% of the vote at the 2002 election, so the KDNP remained outside the Assembly for another term.

In 2005 the KDNP signed an election co-operation agreement with the main opposition **Federation of Young Democrats–Hungarian Civic Alliance** (FiDeSz–MPSz). At the April 2006 election, the alliance failed to unseat the ruling MSzP–SzDSz coalition, securing 164 seats with 42.5% of the vote (141 seats for FiDeSz–MPSz and 23 for the KDNP). The two parties agreed to form separate parliamentary blocs in opposition, but work together under a Solidarity Union.

The two parties allied again for the April 2010 election, and secured an overall majority, with 262 seats in the 386-seat chamber and 52.7% of the vote. FiDeSz leader Viktor **Orbán** was nominated as Prime Minister, to take office in late May, and designated KDNP leader Zsolt Semjén as one of three Deputy Prime Ministers.

Leadership: Zsolt Semjén (Chair.).
Address: István utca 44, 1078 Budapest.
Telephone and fax: (1) 4890878.
E-mail: elnok@kdnp.hu
Internet: www.kdnp.hu

Christian Democratic Union–Czechoslovak People's Party
Křesťanská a Demokratická Unie–Československá Strana Lidová
(KDU–ČSL)

A **Roman Catholic**-orientated centrist party in the **Czech Republic**, affiliated to the **Centrist Democrat International**. The KDU–ČSL is descended from the main inter-war Catholic party, which was represented in several Governments in **Czechoslovakia** until its dissolution in late 1938.

Revived as a component of the communist-dominated National Front in 1945, the then Czechoslovak People's Party (ČSL) was allowed to continue in existence as a Front party after the communists took sole power in 1948. On the collapse of communist rule in late 1989, the ČSL became an independent pro-democracy formation and joined a broad-based coalition Government appointed in December 1989. The party contested the elections of June 1990 in an alliance called the Christian Democratic Union (KDU), which won nine of the 101 Czech seats in the federal lower house and was included in the post-1990 Czech coalition Government. Following the departure of the Christian Democratic Party (KDS) to form an alliance with the new **Civic Democratic Party** (ODS), in April 1992 the remaining constituents officially became the KDU–ČSL, which in the June 1992 elections won 15 seats in the Czech National Council (with 6.3% of the vote). The party became a member of the ODS-led Czech coalition Government that took the republic to separate independence in January 1993. However, the party's residual preference for the federation with Slovakia was apparent in the retention of Czechoslovak in its combined title.

Following the separation, the KDU–ČSL came out in favour of a free enterprise system and Czech membership of Western economic and security structures. In late 1995 its parliamentary party was strengthened by the defection to it of five KDS deputies opposed to their party's decision to merge with the ODS. In the mid-1996 elections to the lower house of **Parliament** the KDU–ČSL won 18 seats on a vote share of 8.1% and was included in another ODS-led Government, now with minority status. Growing political and economic troubles in 1997 impelled the KDU–ČSL and the other junior coalition party to withdraw in November 1997, causing the Government's resignation, following which the party was represented in a transitional administration pending new elections.

In the early lower house elections in June 1998 the KDU–ČSL improved to 20 lower house seats and 9% of the vote, but went into opposition to a minority Government headed by the **Czech Social Democratic Party** (ČSSD). In June 1999 long-time party Chairman Josef Lux was succeeded by Jan Kasal, who took the KDU–ČSL into an opposition Coalition of Four with the Freedom Union (US), Democratic Union (DEU) and Civic Democratic Alliance. In the November 2000 partial Senate elections the KDU–ČSL advanced strongly within the opposition alliance, becoming the second-largest party with 21 of the 81 seats. In January 2001

KDU–ČSL Deputy Chairman Cyril Svoboda was unexpectedly elected leader of the Coalition of Four, ahead of the party's official candidate Jaroslav Kopriva, and went on to take the chairmanship of KDU–ČSL in May 2001. Later that year the US and DEU merged, and by February 2002 the Coalition of Four had been dissolved.

The KDU–ČSL subsequently formed a further grouping with the US–DEU, known as the Coalition, to contest the June 2002 election. It won 31 seats and 14.3% of the vote, the fourth and smallest bloc in the house. The KDU–ČSL itself increased its position to 22 seats, while the US–DEU declined from 19 seats to nine. Vladimír Špidla, leader of the victorious ČSSD, invited both Coalition parties into Government, forming a 101-seat bloc—just large enough to hold a majority in the 200-seat house. (The Coalition grouping was not utilized in further elections.)

When Špidla resigned as Prime Minister in mid-2004, following a ČSSD leadership vote that underlined his loss of popularity, the KDU–ČSL remained in Government under the new Prime Minister Stanislav Gross. However, when allegations emerged against Gross in early 2005 of financial impropriety, the KDU–ČSL demanded his resignation—and when this was not forthcoming the party left the Government in late March. Gross eventually resigned a month later, and the KDU–ČSL agreed in May to rejoin the Government now headed by Jiří Paroubek.

At the June 2006 election the KDU–ČSL won just 13 seats (with 7.2% of the vote). The ODS, which had won the poll, signed a coalition agreement with the KDU–ČSL and the **Green Party** (SZ) to form a Government, but the bloc controlled exactly 100 of the 200 seats, and no members of the ČSSD or **Communist Party of Bohemia and Moravia** (KSČM) were prepared to cast their vote in support of approving the Government in the lower house. Impasse resulted, during which Miroslav Kalousek (who had held the KDU–ČSL leadership since 2003) began negotiations with the ČSSD towards formation of a minority government backed by the KSČM. Many party members were horrified at the prospect of alignment with the communists, and Kalousek was forced to withdraw and resign the party leadership. Kasal became acting party leader, until the election of Jiří Čunek in December. Meanwhile government negotiations had been continuing, and eventually in January the original coalition of the ODS, KDU–ČSL and SZ was approved in the lower house. Čunek was appointed Deputy Prime Minister and Minister of Regional Development, Kalousek became Finance Minister, and the KDU–ČSL also held three other portfolios.

Čunek himself resigned from his post as Deputy Prime Minister in November 2007 over the reopening of a corruption probe against him. His controversial reappointment the following April, after he was acquitted of the charges, almost caused the SZ to quit the Government. At the October 2008 Senate partial elections the KDU–ČSL dropped from 10 seats to seven.

Mirek Topolánek's Government was defeated in a vote of no confidence in the Chamber of Deputies on 24 March 2009. On 6 April Jan **Fischer**, head of the Czech Statistical Office and of no political party, was nominated to be interim Prime

Minister; Fischer took office on 8 May with a caretaker non-partisan cabinet comprising members nominated by the ODS, ČSSD and SZ, but not the KDU–ČSL. At the end of that month Čunek was replaced as party Chairman by Cyril Svoboda, from the left wing of the party; this precipitated Kalousek and the right wing of the party to break away to form TOP 09.

Leadership: Cyril Svoboda (Chair.).
Address: Karlovo nám. 5, 12801 Prague 2.
Telephone: (2) 26205111.
Fax: (2) 26205100.
E-mail: info@kdu.cz
Internet: www.kdu.cz

Christofias, Dimitris

President of **Cyprus**. Christofias was General Secretary of the communist **Progressive Party for the Working People** (AKEL) for two decades from 1988. Since taking office as President on 28 February 2008, he has taken part in numerous inter-communal talks in an attempt to resolve the Cyprus problem.

Christofias was born on 29 August 1946 in Dhikomo, Kyrenia, in what is now part of the self-proclaimed **Turkish Republic of Northern Cyprus** (TRNC). At 18 he joined AKEL's youth movement, the United Democratic Youth Organization (EDON), and went to Moscow's Institute of Social Sciences to study history, then earning a doctorate from the Academy of Social Sciences of the **Soviet Union**. In Moscow he met his wife Elsi Chiratou; they have two daughters and one son.

Returning to Cyprus in 1974, he became Central Organizational Secretary for EDON, having already been voted on to its Central Council in 1969. In 1977 he was elected EDON General Secretary, a position he held for the next decade. Meanwhile he also began to rise up the hierarchy within AKEL itself, elected to the Central Committee in 1982, the Political Bureau of the Central Committee in 1986 and the Secretariat of the Central Committee a year later. When AKEL General Secretary Ezekias Papaioannou died on 10 April 1988 Christofias became acting General Secretary, and was elected to the post 12 days later.

He entered the House of Representatives in 1991, re-elected in the subsequent three elections, and from 2001 was Speaker of the House. He also became a member of the National Council, advising the President on the Cyprus problem.

In the February 2008 presidential election Christofias secured 33.3% of the vote, just behind Ioannis Kasoulidis of the opposition **Democratic Rally** on 33.5%; incumbent President Tassos Papadopoulos was a close third with 31.8%. In the run-off Christofias won by 53.4% to 46.6%. He was inaugurated on 28 February, becoming the first communist head of state of a **European Union** member country.

Christofias promised to push forward with reunification negotiations with the TRNC, and held his first meeting with TRNC President Mehmet Ali **Talat** just three weeks later. Direct, UN-backed negotiations began in early September. Christofias stepped down as AKEL General Secretary in December 2008.

Christofias speaks English and Russian.

Address: Office of the President, Presidential Palace, Dem. Severis Avenue, 1400 Nicosia.

Telephone: (22) 867400.

Fax: (22) 663799.

E-mail: info@presidency.gov.cy

Internet: www.presidency.gov.cy

CISCO *see* **Cyprus Investment and Securities Corporation Ltd**.

Citizens for European Development of Bulgaria
Grazhdani za evropeysko razvitie na Balgariya (GERB)

A centre-right political party in Bulgaria, currently heading the Government. Founded in December 2006 by Mayor of Sofia Boiko **Borisov**, it was formally chaired by his close associate Tsvetan Tsvetanov as Bulgarian law prohibits mayors from holding other offices.

At its first electoral contest in the May 2007 European elections it secured five of the 18 mandates, and in municipal elections later that year it won most of the key mayoralties, including the re-election of Borisov in Sofia.

In the July 2009 elections GERB won 116 seats, just short of a majority, with 39.7% of the vote. (A February 2010 ruling from the Constitutional Court on electoral violations adjusted the results to give GERB 117 seats.) After the election, Borisov formed a minority Government with backing in the National Assembly from small right-wing parties.

In January 2010 Borisov took over from Tsvetanov as the official leader of the party.

Leadership: Boiko Borisov (Chair.).

Address: 17th Floor, NDK Administration Bldg, 1 Bulgaria Square, 1000 Sofia.

Telephone: (2) 4901313.

Fax: (2) 4900979.

E-mail: info@gerb.bg

Internet: www.gerb.bg

Civic Democratic Party
Občanská Demokratická Strana (ODS)

The leading centre-right political formation in the **Czech Republic**, affiliated to the **International Democrat Union**. It was founded in February 1991 as a result of a split in the original pro-democracy **Civic Forum**.

Under the leadership of Federal Finance Minister Václav **Klaus** the ODS quickly built a strong organization and concluded an electoral alliance with the Christian Democratic Party (KDS). In the June 1992 elections the ODS/KDS combination became the leading formation both at federal level and in the Czech National Council. The resultant Czech-Slovak federal coalition was headed by Jan Stráský (ODS), while Klaus preferred to take the Czech premiership at the head of a coalition which included the KDS and the **Christian Democratic Union–Czechoslovak People's Party** (KDU–ČSL).

The ODS-led Government moved swiftly to implement the party's economic reform programme, including wholesale privatization of the state sector, especially in the Czech Lands. However, the party's main immediate concern was the constitutional question and, in particular, the gulf between the Slovak demand for sovereignty within a federation and the Czech Government's view that preservation of the federation only made sense if it had a real role. The outcome was a formal separation as from the beginning of 1993, when the Czech coalition headed by the ODS became the Government of the independent Czech Republic, with Klaus as Prime Minister. In January 1993 Václav **Havel** was elected President of the new Republic on the proposal of the ODS and its government allies.

In November 1995 the ODS voted in favour of a formal merger with the KDS (under the ODS party name), although the decision of half of the 10-strong KDS parliamentary party to join the KDU–ČSL rather than the ODS reduced the impact of the merger. The ODS lost ground in the mid-1996 elections to the Chamber of Deputies (lower house of the **Parliament**), winning only 68 seats on a 29.6% vote share. Klaus was nevertheless reappointed Prime Minister of a further centre-right coalition, now with minority status and dependent on the qualified external support of the **Czech Social Democratic Party** (ČSSD). Mounting difficulties in 1997, including a major financial crisis in May and allegations that the ODS had accepted illegal funding, led to the resignation of the Klaus Government in November.

Although Havel secured parliamentary re-election as President in January 1998 on the proposal of the ODS, divisions in the party resulted in the creation of the breakaway Freedom Union (US) and a sharp decline in ODS membership. In early lower house elections in June 1998 the ODS slipped to 63 seats and 27.7% of the vote, being overtaken by the ČSSD. It opted thereafter to give external support to the resultant ČSSD minority Government, thus ending its previous centre-right alliance.

Support for the ODS declined further at the June 2002 elections, totalling only 24.5% of the vote and securing the party 58 seats. The ČSSD formed a majority coalition, leaving the ODS to head the opposition. Klaus resigned the party leadership later that year, succeeded by Mirek Topolánek, and stood in the presidential election that began in January 2003. Several inconclusive rounds of balloting dragged on past the expiry of outgoing President Hável's term. Eventually Klaus won the poll on 28 February and was inaugurated on 7 March.

The ODS made substantial gains in the local elections and partial Senate elections in October–November 2004, but as the 2006 Chamber of Deputies' election approached the ČSSD was recovering in opinion poll ratings. In the event the ODS secured a narrow victory with 81 seats (35.4% of the vote), just ahead of the ČSSD with 74 seats. Klaus nominated Topolánek to form a Government, and by 26 June he had signed a coalition agreement with the KDU–ČSL and the **Green Party** (SZ), but these three parties only controlled a total of 100 seats in the Chamber of Deputies— one short of an overall majority. An impasse resulted and several months passed without the Government being approved. In mid-August success in electing a Speaker permitted the official appointment of Topolánek as Prime Minister. On 4 September Klaus eventually approved a minority ODS Government, but this only survived a month before losing a confidence vote. Topolánek then resigned. Partial Senate elections in October resulted in the ODS holding 41 seats in the 81-member chamber—the first time since the Senate's creation in 1996 that any party had secured a majority. This success boosted the ODS's position, and in November Topolánek was redesignated as Prime Minister. He presented a further ODS coalition with the KDU–ČSL and the SZ, which Klaus eventually accepted in early January 2007. The abstention of two ČSSD deputies allowed the coalition to gain parliamentary support later that month.

Presidential elections in early 2008 were again protracted, with Klaus eventually defeating ČSSD candidate Jan Svejnar to secure a second term in office. At the partial Senate elections in October, the ODS fell back to 35 seats, losing its majority in that chamber.

Topolánek's Government was defeated in a vote of no confidence in the Chamber of Deputies on 24 March 2009. Coalition party leaders on 6 April nominated Jan **Fischer**, head of the Czech Statistical Office and of no political party, to be interim Prime Minister; Fischer took office on 8 May with a caretaker non-partisan cabinet comprising members nominated by the ODS, ČSSD and SZ.

Leadership: Mirek Topolánek (Chair.).

Address: Polygon House, Doudlebská 1699/5, 140 00 Prague 4.

Telephone: (2) 34707111.

Fax: (2) 34707103.

E-mail: hk@ods.cz

Internet: www.ods.cz

Civic Forum
Občanská Fórum (OF)

The Czech-dominated pro-democracy movement launched in **Czechoslovakia** in November 1989 by various anti-communist groups, notably the **Charter 77** movement, under the acknowledged leadership of dissident playwright Václav **Havel**. Together with its Slovak counterpart **Public Against Violence**, it brought about the '**velvet revolution**', quickly forcing the then regime to give up sole state power. In December 1989 Havel was elected President by a Federal Assembly still dominated by communists, while the OF itself triumphed in the Czech Lands in the June 1990 Czechoslovak elections. It then entered a federal coalition Government with other pro-democracy parties and headed the Czech Government. In October 1990 Federal Finance Minister Václav **Klaus** was elected as the first official Chairman of the OF, but internal divisions resulted in February 1991 in Klaus and his supporters formally launching the **Civic Democratic Party**.

Civic Platform
Platforma Obywatelska (PO)

A centre-right political formation in **Poland**, which heads the ruling coalition Government formed in November 2007. The PO is affiliated to the **Centrist Democrat International**. Launched in January 2001, its principal founders were Maciej Plazyński, Marshal (Speaker) of the Sejm (lower house of the **National Assembly**) and hitherto a member of the then ruling Solidarity Electoral Action (AWS); Donald Tusk, Deputy Speaker of the Senat (upper house) and hitherto a member of the Freedom Union (UW); and independent politician Andrzej Olechowski, who had come second in the 2000 presidential election with 17.3% of the vote. Declaring its basic aim as being to prevent the **Democratic Left Alliance** (SLD) from regaining power in the autumn 2001 parliamentary elections, the new formation quickly attracted substantial support from within both the UW and the AWS. The PO was the second-placed party in the 2001 Sejm elections, winning 65 seats (and 12.7% of the vote), but a long way behind the SLD-led coalition. In the Senat elections PO candidates stood as part of the Blok Senat 2001, which won 15 seats. During the subsequent parliamentary term, both Olechowski and Plazyński left the PO, leaving Tusk as party leader.

At the September 2005 election the PO was the second-placed party with 24% of the vote, 133 Sejm seats and 34 Senat seats. It was widely expected to form a coalition with the victorious **Law and Justice** (PiS), led by the Kaczyński twins, but after a month of talks (parallel to a tight presidential election between Tusk and Lech **Kaczyński**, which Tusk led in the first round but lost in the run-off) the demands of the PO were refused by the PiS, which instead took office with a minority Government supported (and later joined) by small far-right, nationalist parties.

When this Government collapsed in August 2007, early elections were called for October. A surge of support for the PO left it just short of an outright majority in the Sejm, with 209 seats and 41.5% of the vote. It also secured 60 of 100 seats in the Senat. Tusk formed a coalition Government in November 2007 with the centrist **Polish People's Party** (PSL).

In early 2010 Bronisław **Komorowski**, Marshal of the Sejm since 2007, was nominated as the PO's candidate for the presidential election due by October. In light of President Kaczyński's death in April, however, an early election was scheduled for 20 June 2010, and meanwhile Komorowski (as Marshal) became acting President.

Leadership: Donald Tusk (Chair.).
Address: ul. Andersa 21, Warsaw 00-159.
Telephone: (22) 6357879.
Fax: (22) 6357641.
E-mail: poczta@platforma.org
Internet: www.platforma.org

CMEA *see* **Council for Mutual Economic Assistance**.

ČNB *see* **Czech National Bank**.

Coalition for a European Montenegro
Koalicija za Europsku Crnu Goru (KECG)

The ruling coalition in **Montenegro**. The first coalition formed under this name, ahead of the September 2006 **Assembly** election, comprised the **Democratic Party of Socialists of Montenegro** (DPSCG) and the Social Democratic Party of Montenegro (SDPCG), which had already been working together in various coalition agreements for eight years, plus the Croat Civic Initiative. At the 2009 election the Bosniak Party was also included in the alliance.

Coalition for Bulgaria
Koalicija za Balgarija (KzB)

A centre-left coalition of political parties in **Bulgaria**, currently in opposition. It is led by the **Bulgarian Socialist Party** (BSP), and currently includes the Party of Bulgarian Social Democrats, the Communist Party of Bulgaria (KPB), the Bulgarian Agrarian National Union–Alexander Stambolijski (BZNS–AS), the Movement for Social Humanism, the Roma Party and New Zora.

First formed to contest the 2001 **National Assembly** election, the KzB then comprised the BSP, the BZNS–AS, the KPB, the Political Movement 'Social

Democrats' (PDSD), the United Labour Bloc (OBT), the Alliance for Social Liberal Progress (ASLP) and the Civil Union 'Roma'. It won 48 seats (with 17.1% of the vote), making it the third-largest bloc behind the National Movement Simeon II and the United Right Forces.

The OBT and ASLP left the KzB ahead of the 2005 elections, and the Green Party of Bulgaria and Movement for Social Humanism joined. In the June election the KzB emerged as the largest bloc with 82 seats (and 34% of the vote), though well short of a majority. The BSP went on to head a cross-party Government from August, after the first proposed cabinet of the KzB and **Movement for Rights and Freedoms** had been rejected by the Assembly.

The KzB won just 40 seats (with 17.7% of the vote) at the July 2009 election, and went into opposition to a Government led by the centre-right **Citizens for European Development of Bulgaria**.

Internet: www.zabulgaria.org

Coalition of the Left of Movements and Ecology
Synaspismos tis Aristeras ton Kinimaton kai tis Oikologias (Synaspismos or SYN)

A radical left-wing party in **Greece**. Synaspismos was created in 1989 as the Coalition for Left and Progress, an alliance of the orthodox **Communist Party of Greece** (KKE) 'exterior', the Greek Left Party (EAR) and smaller leftist groups. The EAR had been launched in 1987 by the majority wing of the KKE 'interior', itself founded in 1968 by resident Communists opposed to the pro-Soviet orthodoxy of the then exiled leadership of the KKE.

Synaspismos polled strongly in the June 1989 elections, winning 28 seats out of 300. However, the decision of the Synaspismos leadership to join a temporary coalition Government with the conservative **New Democracy** (ND) generated rank-and-file unrest, with the result that the alliance fell back to 21 seats in the November 1989 elections. The subsequent participation of Synaspismos in another temporary coalition, this time with ND and the **Pan-Hellenic Socialist Movement** (PASOK), was also controversial, and the alliance slipped again in the April 1990 elections, to 19 seats. In 1991 the orthodox faction regained control of the KKE 'exterior', which withdrew from Synaspismos. In opposition to an ND Government, Synaspismos endeavoured to transform itself into a unified party, to which end the EAR was dissolved in 1992. However, the local organizational strength of the KKE (now the sole Communist Party) proved decisive in the 1993 general election victory of PASOK, in which Synaspismos failed to win representation, whereas the KKE won nine seats.

Benefiting from disenchantment among some PASOK voters with the incumbent Government, Synaspismos returned to Parliament after the 1996 elections, winning 10 seats. But the party slipped to six seats with 3.2% of the vote in the April 2000 elections. In June 2003 Synaspismos changed its name to the Coalition of the Left of Movements and Ecology to broaden its appeal, and fought the March 2004 election at the head of the **Coalition of the Radical Left** (SYRIZA), but it made no real advance, retaining six seats on a 3.3% vote share. Having led the party for a decade, Nicos Constantopoulos was succeeded in December 2004 by Alekos Alavanos, a Marxist economist.

Popular discontent with PASOK, and SYRIZA's own expansion, helped it rise to 14 seats (5% of the vote) at the 2007 election. Alavanos stepped down as Chairman for personal reasons in 2009, and was succeeded by Alexis Tsipras, who at 33 became the youngest person ever to lead a Greek political party. His popularity helped SYRIZA to retain 13 of its seats (4.6% of the vote) at the early elections in October 2009.

Leadership: Alexis Tsipras (Chair.).
Address: Plateia Eleftherias 1, 10553 Athens.
Telephone: (210) 3378400.
Fax: (210) 3219914.
E-mail: intrelations@syn.gr
Internet: www.syn.gr

Coalition of the Radical Left
Synaspismos Rizospastikis Aristeras (SYRIZA)

A political alliance formed in **Greece** in January 2004, led by the **Coalition of the Left of Movements and Ecology** (Synaspismos) and also including several leftist groups and independent activists. At the March 2004 Parliament election SYRIZA won 3.3% of the vote and six seats (all in fact won by Synaspismos). Prior to the 2007 election, the Democratic Social Movement and other small parties joined SYRIZA. This expansion, coupled with popular discontent with PASOK, helped SYRIZA to win 14 seats (5% of the vote). It retained 13 seats (4.6% of the vote) at the election of October 2009.

Leader: Alexis Tsipras (Chairman of Synaspismos).
Address: Odos Valtetsiou 39, 10681 Athens.
Telephone: (210) 3829910.
Fax: (210) 3829911.
E-mail: info@syriza.gr
Internet: www.syriza.gr

Cold War

A phrase in common usage from 1947, describing the protracted period of post-Second World War antagonism between the communist bloc, particularly the **Soviet Union**, and the West, led by the USA. Sir Winston Churchill's March 1946 speech at Fulton in Missouri, USA, when he warned of the threat of Soviet expansion and of an 'iron curtain' falling across Europe, and the subsequent Soviet imposition of communism in east-central Europe, are usually offered as starting points of the Cold War. The two blocs fought a vigorous propaganda battle in which each sought to discredit its rival and to gain prestige for itself. The balance of terror that followed the Soviet Union's development of the atomic bomb led the blocs to avoid direct military conflict, although there were several dangerous confrontations. Much conflict took place by proxy: one bloc funded and trained indigenous military groups to engage opposing forces when it appeared that the rival bloc was likely to extend its sphere of influence, for instance in Afghanistan. The Cold War forced the two blocs to maintain their readiness for a possible 'hot war'; the expense of the resulting arms race eventually helped to bankrupt the Soviet Union. The appointment in 1985 of Mikhail Gorbachev as General Secretary of the Communist Party of the Soviet Union marked the beginning of a rapprochement with the West, which was confirmed with the Soviet decision in 1989 not to intervene when the communist regimes in **eastern Europe** were collapsing. Three of the clearest symbols of the ending of the Cold War were the beginning of work on 2 May 1989 to dismantle the 'iron curtain' barrier between **Hungary** and Austria, the opening in November 1989 of the Berlin Wall and the final dissolution in 1991 of the **Warsaw Pact**—the military alliance between the former communist-bloc countries.

Comecon *see* **Council for Mutual Economic Assistance**.

Communist Party of Bohemia and Moravia
Komunistická Strana Čech a Moravy (KSČM)

A left-wing party in the **Czech Republic**, founded under its present name in March 1990, which is directly descended from the former ruling Communist Party of Czechoslovakia (KSČ). Out of government since 1990, it remains part of the parliamentary opposition, although facing some calls for it to be banned.

The KSČ was founded in 1921 by the pro-Bolshevik wing of the **Czech Social Democratic Party** (ČSSD) and was the only **eastern European** communist party to retain legal status in the 1930s, under the leadership of Klement Gottwald. It was eventually banned, as a gesture of appeasement to Nazi Germany, its leaders mostly taking refuge in Moscow. They returned at the end of the Second World War in the wake of the Red Army as the dominant element of a National Front of democratic parties and in the 1946 elections became the largest party in the Czech Lands and the second strongest in **Slovakia**. Gottwald became Prime Minister and a government crisis of February 1948 enabled the KSČ to assume sole power, although most other Front parties were allowed to remain in existence in a subservient role throughout the subsequent 40 years of communist rule.

Purges of the KSČ leadership in 1951 in the wake of the Soviet–Yugoslav breach led to show trials and the execution of 11 prominent communists in 1952. Among the victims was Rudolf Slánský, who had succeeded Gottwald as party leader when the latter became President in 1948. Following Gottwald's sudden death in 1953, Antonín Novotný was elected to the revived post of party leader and later became President. Nikita Khrushchev's denunciation of Stalin in 1956 resulted in the rehabilitation of most of those executed in **Czechoslovakia** in 1952 and also of those imprisoned in that era, including Gustáv **Husák**. Pressure for political reform grew in the 1960s within and outside the party. In January 1968 Novotný was replaced as KSČ leader by Alexander **Dubček**, hitherto Slovak party leader, and as President by Gen. Ludvík Svoboda.

In the short-lived '**Prague Spring**', the KSČ central committee in April 1968 elected a new presidium dominated by reformers and promised democratization of the government system (although not multi-partyism), freedom of assembly, the press, foreign travel and religion, curbs on the security police (**StB**), rehabilitation of previous purge victims, and autonomy for Slovakia. This 'socialism with a human face' alarmed the Soviet leadership and its **Warsaw Pact** satellites. Increasing pressure on the Prague reformers culminated in the military occupation of Czechoslovakia in August 1968 by forces of the **Soviet Union**, East Germany, **Poland**, **Hungary** and **Bulgaria**, on the grounds that they had been invited in by KSČ leaders, including Husák, who believed that the reform movement was out of control. Dubček and his immediate supporters were taken to Moscow as prisoners. They were quickly released on the insistence of President Svoboda, but the reform movement was effectively over. After anti-Soviet riots in early 1969, Husák replaced Dubček as party leader and initiated a major purge of reformist elements, those expelled from the party including Dubček himself.

Over the following two decades Husák combined rigorous pro-Soviet orthodoxy with a measure of economic liberalization. Having become President in 1975, Husák held both this post and his party position until in December 1987 he surrendered the party leadership to Miloš Jakeš, another political hard-liner. Meanwhile, the impact of the post-1985 Gorbachev reform programme in the Soviet Union was beginning to be felt in Czechoslovakia. In the event, the communist regime crumbled with remarkable rapidity following the opening of the Berlin Wall in early November 1989, amid an upsurge of massive popular protest. At the end of November Jakeš was replaced as KSČ leader by Karel Urbánek and the following month Husák resigned as President. Shortly before he stepped down he had attempted to assuage the demand for far-reaching change by swearing in the first Government with a non-communist majority for over four decades, although it was led by a KSČ member.

The Federal Assembly, still dominated by KSČ deputies, elected Dubček as its new Chairman and went on to vote in the dissident playwright Václav **Havel** as State President in succession to Husák. In late December 1989 an extraordinary KSČ congress elected Ladislav Adamec to the new post of party Chairman and issued a public apology for the party's past actions.

The Czech component of the KSČ responded to events by relaunching itself as the KSČM in March 1990, with Jiří Svoboda as leader and with a socialist rather than a Marxist-Leninist orientation. In the June 1990 multi-party elections, the Czech communists took second place in the Czech National Council, winning 32 of the 200 seats, and were also runners-up in the Czech balloting for the Federal Assembly, winning 15 of the 101 Czech federal lower house seats. The communists then went into opposition for the first time since 1945, amid a continuing exodus of party members.

In October 1990 the KSČM declared itself independent of the federal KSČ, shortly before the passage of a law requiring the KSČ to surrender its assets to the Government. In mid-1991 the KSČ was officially dissolved, but both the KSČM and its Slovak counterpart remained 'Czechoslovak' in orientation, i.e. opposing the break-up of the federation.

In the June 1992 elections the KSČM headed the Left Bloc, which won 35 of the 200 Czech National Council seats (with 14.1% of the vote) as well as 19 of the 99 Czech seats in the federal lower house and 15 of the 75 Czech seats in the upper house. Still in opposition, the KSČM mounted ultimately abortive resistance to the dissolution of the federation. Following the creation of the independent Czech Republic in January 1993, the party experienced much internal strife, including the resignation of Svoboda as leader over the rejection of his proposal to drop 'Communist' from the title. He was replaced in June 1993 by the conservative Miroslav Grebeníček, whose election precipitated the creation of two breakaway parties by the end of the year, to which the KSČM lost the majority of its deputies elected in 1992.

The KSČM nevertheless retained substantial core membership and organizational strength, as well as significant support for its advocacy of a 'socialist market economy' based on economic democracy and co-operatives, and for its opposition to membership of the **North Atlantic Treaty Organization** (NATO) and to absorption into the 'German sphere of influence'. In the mid-1996 elections to the **Parliament** it took 10.3% of the national vote and 22 lower house seats, effectively becoming the main opposition to a further coalition headed by the centre-right **Civic Democratic Party** (ODS), given that the Social Democrats (ČSSD) gave the new Government qualified support. In April 1998 the KSČM joined the far-right Republicans in voting 'against' in the decisive parliamentary vote in favour of NATO membership. In the early June 1998 elections the KSČM advanced marginally to 24 lower house seats on an 11% vote share, remaining in opposition, now to a minority Government of the ČSSD supported by a so-called 'opposition agreement' with the ODS.

In regional elections in November 2000 the KSČM advanced strongly to take 21% of the vote, and the party also performed better at the 2002 lower house election, winning 41 seats with 18.5% of the vote. This again made it the third-largest party.

In October 2005 Grebeníček stood down after 12 years as party Chairman. He was succeeded by Vojtěch Filip, and the party hoped that the new face at the helm would revitalize the party's falling popularity. However, at the June 2006 elections the KSČM won only 26 seats with 12.8% of the vote. It again finished as the third-largest party. Following the Senate partial elections later that year the KSČM controlled three seats in the upper house, a position that remained unchanged after the 2008 partial election.

Early in 2008 the Ministry of the Interior succeeded in banning the KSČM's youth movement, the official reason being its goal of collective ownership of the means of production; however, the Supreme Administrative Court overturned the ban in September 2009. Meanwhile, in October 2008 the Senate called on the Government to request a ban on the KSČM itself, on the grounds that its Constitution, which enshrines Marxist-Leninist principles, does not explicitly renounce the use of violence. However, the request has not yet been put before the Supreme Administrative Court.

Leadership: Vojtěch Filip (Chair.).

Address: Politických vězňů 9, 110 00 Prague 1.

Telephone: (2) 2897111.

Fax: (2) 2897207.

E-mail: info@kscm.cz

Internet: www.kscm.cz

Communist Party of Greece
Kommounistiko Komma Elladas (KKE)

An orthodox Marxist-Leninist party in **Greece**. Long known as the KKE 'exterior' because many of its activists were forced into exile after the Second World War, the party is directly descended from the Socialist Workers' Party of Greece (SEKE) founded in 1918, which joined the Communist International (Comintern) in 1924 and changed its name to KKE. The party secured its first parliamentary representation in 1926 and in 1936 held the balance of power between the Monarchists and the Liberals, the resultant deadlock provoking a military coup in 1936, following which all parties were banned. During the Second World War popular resistance to the occupying Axis powers was organized by the Communists in the National Liberation Front (EAM) and the guerrilla Greek People's Liberation Army (ELAS). Following the liberation, however, ELAS was suppressed by British (and later US) troops after civil war had broken out between the Communists and centre-right forces favouring restoration of the monarchy. The KKE was banned in 1947 and by 1949 had been defeated, its leadership and thousands of members fleeing to Communist-ruled countries.

The banned KKE became the dominant force within the legal United Democratic Left (EDA), which won 79 seats in 1958, before falling back to 22 in 1964. In 1967–74 the KKE took a leading role in the opposition to the Greek military junta, but factional conflict between the exiled party and Communist forces in Greece culminated in the latter forming an 'interior' KKE in 1968. Legalized after the fall of the junta, the KKE 'exterior' contested the 1974 elections as part of the EDA, which also included the 'interior' Communists, winning five of the EDA's eight seats. Standing on its own in subsequent elections, the KKE 'exterior' advanced to 11 seats in 1977 and to 13 in 1981. Its overtures for representation in the new Government of the **Pan-Hellenic Socialist Movement** (PASOK) were rejected, although tens of thousands of KKE supporters, exiled since the late 1940s, were allowed to return to Greece.

In the 1985 elections the KKE 'exterior' won 12 seats. The party's 12th congress in 1987 called for a new left-wing alliance, the eventual result being what later became the **Coalition of the Left of Movements and Ecology** (Synaspismos), including the KKE 'interior', which won 28 seats in the June 1989 elections. However, the subsequent participation of Synaspismos in two temporary Governments, the first with the conservative **New Democracy** (ND) and the second with ND and PASOK (after further elections in November 1989), generated unrest in the KKE 'exterior'. The party remained in Synaspismos for the 1990 elections, in which the alliance fell back to 19 seats. However, the 13th congress in 1991 resulted in the party's orthodox wing gaining control and the election as leader of Aleka Papariga, who took the party out of Synaspismos.

The KKE (now having dropped the 'exterior' descriptor) retained significant support in the 1993 elections, winning nine seats, whereas Synaspismos obtained none. In the 1996 elections the KKE advanced to 11 seats, which it retained in 2000 with 5.5% of the vote. In the March 2004 elections it advanced to 12 seats (out of 300) on a 5.9% vote share. In September 2007 it rose to 22 seats (8.2% of the vote), and in the early election in October 2009 won 21 seats (7.5%).

Leadership: Aleka Papariga (General Secretary).
Address: Leoforos Irakliou 145, 14231 Athens.
Telephone: (210) 2592111.
Fax: (210) 2592298.
E-mail: cpg@int.kke.gr
Internet: inter.kke.gr

Conflict Prevention Centre (CPC)

One of the two main departments of the **Organization for Security and Co-operation in Europe** (OSCE). The Centre was established in Vienna, Austria, in March 1991, following the decision of a summit meeting the previous November. Its main function is to support the OSCE Chairman-in-Office in the implementation of OSCE policies, in particular the monitoring of field activities and co-operation with other international bodies.

Director: Herbert Salber.
Address: Wallnerstrasse 6, 1010 Vienna, Austria.
Telephone: (1) 51436122.
Fax: (1) 51436996.
E-mail: pm-cpc@osce.org
Internet: www.osce.org/cpc

Conservative Party
Partidul Conservator (PC)

A centre-right political party in **Romania**, currently in opposition. It is the successor of the centrist Humanist Party of Romania (PUR), founded in 1991 by former media magnate Dan Voiculescu to promote a political 'third way'—entrepreneurial capitalism.

The PUR contested the November 2000 elections as part of the Social Democratic Pole of Romania (PDSR) which emerged as the largest bloc in **Parliament**. The PUR was awarded one ministerial position in Adrian Năstase's minority PDSR Government, requesting the formation of a Ministry of Small and Medium-sized Enterprises to further its political ideals. When the cabinet was restructured in June 2003 and this Ministry was subsumed into the Ministry of Economy, the PUR ended its co-operation with the Government.

For the November 2004 elections, the PUR again joined with the Social Democrats (now known as the **Social Democratic Party**—PSD) to form a National Alliance (UN). The UN won a plurality of parliamentary seats: 132 in the 332-member House of Deputies (including 19 for the PUR) and 57 seats in the Senate (11 for the PUR). However, Năstase failed to win the presidential election, and the PUR found itself controlling the balance of power in Parliament. It abandoned its former partner and joined a centre-right Government with the **National Liberal Party**, Democratic Party and **Hungarian Democratic Union of Romania**. A PUR Minister of State was appointed to co-ordinate the activities of ministries involved in improving the business climate and encouraging small and medium-sized enterprises.

In May 2005 the PUR changed its name to the Conservative Party, to reflect the gradual trend that the party's policies had followed towards a more centre-right stance. In February 2006 it absorbed the Romanian National Unity Party. In June that year Voiculescu was nominated to be Deputy Prime Minister, but it was then revealed that official records confirmed him as an informant for the Securitate during the Communist era, despite Voiculescu having frequently denied such allegations. His appointment was blocked, and in December the PC withdrew from the Government, leaving it in a minority position.

In 2007, after the PC failed to win any seats in the European Parliament elections, Voiculescu stood down as party President and was succeeded by Daniela Popa, although Voicelescu remained a driving force behind the party. The PC contested the 2008 local and legislative elections again in coalition with the PSD: the PC won four House seats and one Senate seat in its own right, and the alliance finished as the second-largest bloc. However, it was not included in the coalition Government that was formed between the **Democratic Liberal Party** (successor to the PD) and the PSD.

At the 2009 presidential election the PC backed the ultimately unsuccessful candidacy of PSD leader Mircea Dan Geoană. In February 2010 Popa stepped down as PC President and Daniel Constantin was elected as her successor.

Leadership: Daniel Constantin (President).

Address: Str. Muzeul Zambaccian 17, Bucharest 1.

Telephone: (31) 4251100.

Fax: (21) 2304776.

E-mail: secretariat@partidulconservator.ro

Internet: www.partidulconservator.ro

Contact Group (for the former Yugoslavia)

An unofficial collection of six countries (France, Germany, Italy, Russian Federation, United Kingdom and USA). It was formed in April 1994 (at which point it comprised five countries—Italy joining in 1996) to co-ordinate US-**European Union**-Russian policy regarding the warring nations of the former **Socialist Federal Republic of Yugoslavia**. Following the signing of the final **Dayton Agreement**, which ended the war in **Bosnia and Herzegovina** in 1995, the Contact Group assumed responsibilities for overseeing the implementation of the Agreement. The Group has continued to apply international pressure in the region to attain security, most notably calling for sanctions and paving the way for air strikes by **North Atlantic Treaty Organization** (NATO) forces against **Yugoslavia** over the crisis in **Kosovo** in 1999, and raising concern over the ethnic crisis in **Macedonia** in 2001. Since then it has been involved in talks to determine the final status of Kosovo.

Conventional Forces in Europe
(or CFE Treaty)

A key disarmament agreement at the end of the **Cold War**, signed in November 1990 by the member states of the **North Atlantic Treaty Organization** (NATO) and of the **Warsaw Pact**. The Treaty limits non-nuclear air and ground armaments in the signatory countries. It was negotiated within the framework of the Conference on Security and Co-operation in Europe (CSCE—*see* **Organization for Security and Co-operation in Europe**) and signed at a CSCE summit meeting in Paris. In 2007, the Russian Federation, unhappy over NATO expansion and US plans for central European bases for its missile defence shield, suspended its participation in the treaty.

Corporate Supervision and Privatization

Departments I–V in the Ministry of the Treasury of **Poland**. The departments oversee indirect privatizations of state enterprises and companies.
Director (Dept I): Janusz Radomski.
Director (Dept II): Małgorzata Dobczyńska.
Director (Dept III): Michał Lehmann.
Director (Dept IV): Paweł Pacholski.
Director (Dept V): Anna Mańk.
Address: Ministry of the Treasury, ul. Krucza 36, 00522 Warsaw.
Telephone: (22) 6959000.
Fax: (22) 6213361.
Internet: www.msp.gov.pl

Council for Mutual Economic Assistance (CMEA or Comecon)

The now defunct structure (known more colloquially as Comecon) established in 1949 during the Stalin era, within which the centrally-planned economies of the so-called Soviet-bloc countries were co-ordinated. In 1971 the organization moved on from its co-ordination phase to a so-called integration phase, with the adoption of a Comprehensive Programme for the Further Extension and Improvement of Co-operation and the Further Development of Socialist Economic Integration.

Significant growth in mutual trade among member countries was recorded until a generalized slump in the 1980s. Following the collapse of communism in Europe in 1989–91 the CMEA was disbanded, leaving a legacy of problems for member countries. Their economies, having been structured over decades to fulfil specific roles within the CMEA, could suddenly count on neither the resources on which they had come to depend from other member countries (such as gas from the **Soviet**

Union, at costs not reflecting the world market) nor the market for their output, particularly in heavy industry.

Members of the CMEA at the time it was disbanded in 1991 were **Bulgaria**, Cuba, **Czechoslovakia**, East Germany, **Hungary**, Mongolia, **Poland**, **Romania**, **Soviet Union** and Viet Nam. A form of associate status in the organization was specified for **Yugoslavia** in a 1964 agreement. **Albania** was a member until 1961 (when it ceased participating, although without formally revoking its membership). The People's Republic of China and to some extent the Democratic People's Republic of Korea (known as North Korea) also participated with observer status until 1961.

Council of Europe

A regional organization originally founded in May 1949 with 10 members in western Europe, which has now been expanded continent-wide. Its objectives are promoting regional unity and social progress, and upholding the principles of parliamentary democracy, respect for human rights and the rule of law. It has a Committee of Ministers and a Parliamentary Assembly, which elects its Secretary-General. The chairmanship of the Council rotates every six months; it passed to Switzerland in November 2009.

The **European Court of Human Rights**, established in 1959 in Strasbourg, France, is part of the activities of the Council of Europe, overseeing the implementation of the Convention for the Protection of Human Rights and Fundamental Freedoms (usually known as the European Convention on Human Rights). Council member countries are required to adhere to the Convention, which should entail among other things the abolition of the death penalty.

Members: 47 European countries, including **Albania, Bosnia and Herzegovina, Bulgaria, Croatia, Cyprus, Czech Republic, Estonia, Greece, Hungary, Kosovo, Latvia, Lithuania, Macedonia, Montenegro, Poland, Romania, Serbia, Slovakia** and **Slovenia**.

Secretary-General: Thorbjørn Jagland.
Address: Avenue de l'Europe, 67075 Strasbourg Cédex, France.
Telephone: (3) 88412000.
Fax: (3) 88412754.
E-mail: infopoint@coe.int
Internet: www.coe.int

Council of the Baltic Sea States (CBSS)

A regional forum, meeting usually annually since 1992 at the level of foreign ministers (with summit meetings for heads of government on a biennial basis since 1996). It has a broad remit to promote democracy, greater regional unity and economic development. The Council was established in 1992 under the Copenhagen Declaration, the outcome of a meeting held in the Danish capital in March of that year. A permanent International Secretariat was inaugurated on 20 October 1998 and is located in Stockholm, Sweden. The chairmanship of the CBSS rotates annually on 1 July. In 2009/10 it passed to Lithuania, to be followed by Norway.

Members: Denmark, **Estonia**, Finland, Germany, Iceland, **Latvia**, **Lithuania**, Norway, **Poland**, Russian Federation and Sweden. The European Commission (of the **European Union**) is also represented in its own right.

Director General of the Secretariat: Gabriele Kötschau.

Address: CBSS Secretariat, Strömsborg, POB 2010, 103 11 Stockholm, Sweden.

Telephone: (8) 4401920.

Fax: (8) 4401944.

E-mail: cbss@cbss.org

Internet: www.cbss.st

Council of the Baltic States *see* **Baltic Council of Ministers**.

Cour permanente d'arbitrage *or* **CPA** *see* **Permanent Court of Arbitration**.

CPC *see* **Conflict Prevention Centre**.

Croatia
Republika Hrvatska

An independent republic located in south-eastern Europe on the western coast of the **Balkan** peninsula, part of the former **Yugoslavia** until 1991 and bordered by Slovenia and Hungary to the north, Serbia to the east, Bosnia and Herzegovina to the south-east, Montenegro to the south and the Adriatic Sea to the west. The country is divided administratively into 20 counties and the City of **Zagreb**, 424 municipalities and 123 towns.

Area: 56,594 sq. km; *capital*: Zagreb; *population*: 4.4m. (2009 estimate), comprising roughly **Croats** 89.6%, **Serbs** 4.5%, others 5.9% (based on 2001 census); *official language*: Croatian; *religion*: **Roman Catholic** 87.8%, **Orthodox** 4.4%, Muslim 1.3%, **Protestant** 0.4%, others 6.1%.

Constitutional amendments which obtained parliamentary approval in November 2000 moved Croatia from a presidential form of government to a parliamentary model, with the Prime Minister and cabinet accountable solely to the legislature, which could only be dissolved by the President on its own recommendation. The

President retained substantial powers in the spheres of foreign and security policy, however, and continued to be directly elected. Legislative authority is vested in what is now a unicameral **Assembly** (Sabor), containing a House of Representatives (Zastupnički Dom), elected for a four-year term. It has up to 160 members (currently 153), of whom 140 are elected by proportional representation from multi-member constituencies, up to 15 (currently five) elected to represent Croatians abroad and eight to represent ethnic minorities whose share of the population is at least 8%. Until 2001 there was also an upper house, the House of Districts (Županijski Dom) with 63 elective members, plus a further five appointed by the President.

History: Croatia was part of the Roman Empire for several centuries before settlement of the area by **Slavic** migrations beginning in the sixth century (the original home of the Slavic Croats is generally believed to be present-day Ukraine). By the 10th century, an independent and Christian Croat kingdom (including parts of modern **Bosnia and Herzegovina**) had been established. In 1102 Croatia, retaining its autonomy, entered into an enduring dynastic union with the kingdom of **Hungary**. The Hungarians were defeated by the invading Turks in 1526, after which much of Croatia fell under Ottoman rule. The rest of the territory was absorbed into the Habsburg Empire, and a military frontier, peopled largely by ethnic Serbs, developed along the border between the Habsburg and Ottoman Turkish dominions. By the end of the 17th century all of present-day Croatia was under Habsburg rule, becoming in 1867 part of the Hungarian-ruled half of the empire.

Following Austria-Hungary's disintegration at the end of the First World War, Croatia joined other south Slav territories in an uneasy union within the Kingdom of Serbs, Croats and Slovenes (renamed Yugoslavia in 1929). In 1941 Germany invaded Yugoslavia and encouraged the creation of a separate Croatian state (including Bosnia and Herzegovina and part of present-day **Serbia**) controlled by a fascist dictatorship sympathetic to the Nazis. At the end of the Second World War, Croatia came under communist rule as one of six constituent republics (with Bosnia and Herzegovina, Serbia, **Slovenia**, **Macedonia** and **Montenegro**) of the **Socialist Federal Republic of Yugoslavia**. However, it consistently sought greater autonomy within a federal structure that became increasingly dysfunctional after the death of President **Tito** in 1980.

The collapse of communism at the end of the 1980s led to the election in 1990 of a nationalist Croatian Government under Franjo **Tudjman** of the **Croatian Democratic Union** (HDZ). This Government's declaration of independence in June 1991 sparked insurrection by the ethnic Serb minority within the Croatian republic, who carved out autonomous regions with the military help of the Serb-dominated Federal Yugoslav Army. A six-month war subsided in January 1992 with a UN-brokered ceasefire and the deployment of UN peacekeeping forces in the Serb-controlled areas (**Krajina** and **Slavonia**). Croatian policy towards the concurrent eruption of ethnic conflict in neighbouring Bosnia and Herzegovina veered from an initial alliance with the Muslim-dominated Government against Bosnian Serb nationalism, to military support (from early 1993) for Bosnian Croat separatism, and then to acceptance in March 1994, under pressure from the USA, of a **Muslim-Croat Federation**. In mid-1995 most Serb-held territory in Croatia, with the exception of eastern Slavonia, was recovered in an advance by Croatian forces (leading to a mass exodus of ethnic Serbs). Under the **Erdut Agreement** of November 1995 (complementing the **Dayton Agreement** for Bosnia and Herzegovina), a transitional UN administration was established in eastern Slavonia, leading to the eventual reintegration of the enclave into Croatia in January 1998.

Meanwhile, the HDZ had retained an overall majority in parliamentary elections in October 1995 and Tudjman had been re-elected as President in June 1997 with 61.4% of the vote, although the ballot was criticized as unfair by the **Organization for Security and Co-operation in Europe** (OSCE). In April 1997 the HDZ won a majority of 42 seats in elections to the 63-member House of Districts. In November 1997 the legislature approved constitutional amendments which prohibited the re-establishment of a union of Yugoslav states.

In the late 1990s growing popular discontent with economic and social conditions was accompanied by increasing disarray within the ruling HDZ, as Tudjman slowly succumbed to cancer. His death in December 1999 precipitated parliamentary and presidential elections which marked the end of a decade of HDZ supremacy.

Elections to the House of Representatives in early January 2000 were won by a centre-left alliance of the **Social Democratic Party of Croatia** (SDP), the **Croatian Social-Liberal Party** (HSLS) and two small regional parties. The alliance won 71 of the 151 seats and 38.7% of the vote, while the HDZ retained only 46 seats (with 26.7%), and most of the rest (25 seats) went to a United List alliance of the **Croatian Peasants' Party** (HSS), the Istrian Democratic Assembly (IDS), the Croatian People's Party (HNS) and the Liberal Party (LS, now merged with the HSLS). In presidential elections in late January and early February, however, Dražen Budiša of the HSLS (also backed by the SDP) trailed in second place on the first round and was easily defeated in the run-off by Stipe Mesić of the HNS, who won by 56% to 44%.

As leader of the dominant party within the centre-left alliance, Ivica Račan of the SDP became Prime Minister in January 2000, heading a coalition with not only the HSLS but also the United List parties (although the IDS later left this coalition, in protest over the Government's revocation of a law adopting Italian as an official language in **Istria**). Račan set as his two main policy goals the reduction of unemployment and the integration of Croatia into European/Western institutions.

Constitutional reform was also on the agenda. Under a compromise accord between the Government and President Mesić, the Assembly in November 2000 adopted constitutional amendments curtailing presidential powers and establishing Croatia as a parliamentary democracy. In March 2001 the Assembly voted to abolish the upper House of Districts, which took effect on the expiry of that house's term in May.

The greatest threat to the Government's cohesion was the issue of its continued co-operation with the **International Criminal Tribunal for the former Yugoslavia**. Račan's administration survived a vote of no confidence over this in mid-2001, despite the brief withdrawal of HSLS participation in his Government. HSLS support wavered again in February 2002, but was eventually withdrawn in July of that year over a different issue, the parliamentary approval of an agreement on joint ownership of the Krško nuclear power installation in Slovenia. Račan resigned on 5 July, but was reappointed five days later; his new Government was announced on 28 July and approved by the House two days later.

The voters punished both Račan's SDP and, even more severely, his fractious erstwhile HSLS allies, at the November 2003 parliamentary elections. A coalition of the SDP, IDS, Party of Liberal Democrats (Libra–SLD, splinter of the HSLS) and LS won 43 seats (34 SDP, four IDS, three Libra, two LS) with 22.6% of the vote, while the HSLS in alliance with the Democratic Centre (DC, splinter of the HDZ) ended up with just three seats. The HDZ regained its position as the largest bloc, though short of a majority with 66 seats (and 33.9% of the vote). To form a government, HDZ leader Ivo Sanader negotiated coalition agreements with the fourth-placed HSS (with 10 seats in the House) and the rump HSLS and DC, and obtained the support of several other deputies. The new Government, principally comprising HDZ members, was approved on 23 December.

Co-operation with the ICTY continued to be a troublesome issue for the Government, and its EU membership talks were stalled because of its slow progress in extraditing key suspects. The last of these, Gen. (retd) Ante Gotovina, was finally apprehended in the Canary Islands, Spain, in December 2005; his arrest removed the main obstacle to the country's NATO and EU membership.

At the January 2005 presidential election Mesić stood for a second term. Although he just failed to secure outright election in the first round, with 48.9% of the vote, his personal popularity was sufficient to ensure his convincing victory in the run-off, defeating the HDZ candidate Jadranka **Kosor** by 65.9% to 34.1%.

The DC withdrew its support for Sanader's Government in February 2006, after its leader Škare Ožbolt was dismissed as Minister of Justice.

Latest elections: Elections to the House of Representatives on 25 November 2007 were dominated by the ruling HDZ and a resurgent SDP, its popularity restored by its period in opposition. The HDZ remained the largest party, again with 66 seats, though with a slightly larger share of the vote (36.6%). The SDP increased its share considerably to 56 seats (31.2% of the vote). The Green–Yellow Coalition of the HSS, HSLS and other parties secured eight seats (six HSS, two HSLS) with 6.5% of the vote, the **Croatian People's Party—Liberal Democrats** (merger of HNS and Libra) won seven seats (6.8% of the vote), the IDS won three seats (1.5%), the Croatian Democratic Assembly of Slavonia and Baranja (HDSSB) won three (1.8%), and one seat was won by each of the Croatian Party of Pensioners (HSU—in alliance with the Democratic Party of Pensioners—DSU, securing together 4.1% of the vote) and the Croatian Party of Rights (HSP—3.5%), plus the eight seats secured by ethnic minority communities (three for the Independent Democratic Serbian Party—SDSS). The alliance of the Democratic Centre (DC) and Green Party–Green Alternative (ZS–ZA) won 7.4% of the votes, but secured no seats in the House.

Recent developments: After several weeks of negotiations, Sanader formed a new Government in early January 2008, comprising members of the HDZ, HSS, HSLS and SDSS, and with support from four of the other five ethnic minority representatives. Croatia's official recognition of Kosovo's independence in March 2008 almost caused the SDSS to withdraw from the Government.

When Sanader announced on 1 July 2009 that he was quitting politics, he recommended Kosor as his successor. She was nominated on 3 July, and took office three days later, becoming Croatia's first female Prime Minister.

At the 2009–10 presidential election Ivo **Josipović** of the SDP led the first round on 27 December with 32.4%. His nearest rival, Milan Bandić, won 14.8% standing as an independent, having been expelled from the SDP the previous month for announcing that he would stand against Josipović. These two went forward to the run-off on 10 January. Josipović won by 60.3% to 39.7% and took office on 18 February.

International relations and defence: Croatia's independent status received international recognition in early 1992 and the country was admitted to the United Nations in May of that year. It is a member of the **Council of Europe**, the OSCE and the **Central European Initiative**. Aspirations towards integration in Western institutions, notably the **European Union** (EU) and the **North Atlantic Treaty Organization** (NATO), were boosted by the end of HDZ rule in January 2000, following which Croatia joined NATO's **Partnership for Peace** programme in May 2000 and was admitted to the **World Trade Organization** in July. Full NATO membership was achieved on 1 April 2009, and progress towards EU accession held out the prospect of membership in 2011, though a border dispute with Slovenia (over the maritime border in the Bay of Piran) was blocking the final stages of talks in 2009–10.

In November 2000 Croatia hosted the first summit conference of the EU and **Balkan** states in Zagreb. Some progress has been made in normalizing relations with the other former Yugoslav republics, although two border issues remain unresolved: the maritime border with Slovenia in the Bay of Piran, and the issue of sovereignty over the **Prevlaka peninsula** on the Croatia–Montenegro border, which has been placed before the **International Court of Justice** for resolution. Croatia's recognition of Kosovan independence angered Serbia. Croatia also has a pending genocide suit against Serbia, although it has said it will back Serbia's bid to join the EU.

Croatia's defence budget for 2008 amounted to some US $1,090m., equivalent to about 1.6% of GDP. The size of the armed forces in 2010 was some 19,000 personnel, while reservists numbered an estimated 21,000. Conscription (formerly of six months) was phased out on 1 January 2009.

Croatia, economy

Once one of the two most prosperous former federal republics of the **Socialist Federal Republic of Yugoslavia** (second only to **Slovenia**), Croatia was beset in the 1990s by post-communist transition problems compounded by involvement in regional conflict. Tourism has driven economic growth since 2000, but a still over-sized state sector and ailing subsidized industries are restricting the country's competitiveness.

GNP: US $60,192m. (2008); *GNP per capita*: $13,570 (2008); *GDP at PPP*: $84,621m. (2008); *GDP per capita at PPP*: $19,100 (2008); *real GDP growth*: –5.2% (2009 estimate); *exports*: $14,112m. (2008); *imports*: $30,728m. (2008); *currency*: kuna (plural: kuna; US $1 = K5.19 in mid-2009); *unemployment*: 10.9% (end 2009); *government deficit as a percentage of GDP*: 2.9% (2009); *inflation*: 2.8% (2009).

In 2007 industry accounted for 30% of GDP, agriculture for 7% and services for 63%. Around 6% of the workforce is engaged in agriculture, 31% in industry and 63% in services.

Some 21% of the land is arable (though much was severely affected during the 1991–95 hostilities), 2% is under permanent crops, 20% permanent pasture and 38% forests and woodland. The principal crops are maize, sugar beet, grapes, wheat and potatoes, and there is animal husbandry and dairy farming as well as fishing on Croatia's lengthy Adriatic Sea coast.

The main mineral resources are petroleum, coal, natural gas, bauxite and low-grade iron ore. The principal industrial sectors are machine tools, aluminium, chemicals and plastics, textiles, shipbuilding and petroleum.

Croatia's main exports are manufactures, chemicals and capital goods, while principal imports are capital goods, fuel and energy and food items. The main destinations of Croatia's exports in 2008 were Italy (19%), **Bosnia and Herzegovina** (15%) and Germany (11%), while the main sources of imports were Italy (17%), Germany (13%) and the Russian Federation (10%).

Prior to the dissolution of the former **Yugoslavia** in 1991–92, Croatia had an economic position within the federation well above average among the republics and was relatively industrialized. The ethnic and factional disturbances following secession caused severe material destruction, damage to arable land, communications disruption and the virtual suspension of the country's tourist industry, while the movement of refugees also resulted in serious economic problems. Over the period 1989–93 GDP declined in real terms at an average of just over 10% a year. Hyperinflation, which had fallen to about 120% in 1991, shot up in the following two years to over 1,500% in 1993, while unemployment rose officially to over 20% and in reality was probably significantly higher.

In 1993 Croatia instituted a comprehensive economic stabilization plan, under which a new currency was introduced in 1994 and the inflation rate dropped sharply to around 5% per year in 1995–99. The plan also yielded buoyant GDP growth rising to 6.5% in 1997, although a subsequent slowdown saw the growth rate drop back to 2.5% in 1998 and to –0.3% in 1999, when confidence was damaged by a major bank corruption scandal.

GDP growth revived to around 3% in 2000 as tourism in particular rebounded, though unemployment was still running at 21%. The new **Social Democratic Party** (SDP) Government improved relations with the West, and financial aid and foreign investment increased. A Stabilization and Association Agreement with the **European Union** (EU) entered into force in February 2005. Growth averaged around 5% in 2001–07 and unemployment steadily declined, but external debt rose, reaching 85% of GDP. Tourism underpinned a surplus in the balance of trade in services, but imports of goods continued to greatly exceed exports.

Inflation rose in 2008 and economic performance was weaker as the global financial crisis began to affect Croatia, while the EU pressed for greater efforts to combat organized crime and reform the judiciary and public administration. Sharp drops in consumer spending and in tourism receipts in 2009, coupled with low export competitiveness, caused GDP to contract by 5%, while foreign debt grew to 95% of GDP.

The high level of state participation in the economy and the provision of subsidies to large loss-making industries such as shipbuilding pushes government expenditure above 40% of GDP, the highest level in the region. Croatia is under pressure to increase its competitiveness by reducing subsidies, reforming public services, encouraging new business start-ups and improving the skills of its workforce.

Privatization in post-communist Croatia began slowly. Although most of the country's 2,600 small and medium-sized state-owned companies had been transferred into the private sector by the end of 1998, little progress was made under the **Tudjman** regime in privatizing large enterprises in sectors such as oil, electricity, the railways and telecommunications. The subsequent SDP Government relaunched the process, partly to assist with its aim of eliminating the fiscal deficit and also in the framework of Croatia's accession to the **World Trade Organization** in July 2000. A review of the privatization process in 2001 showed that many state-owned companies had been sold off at below true value to politically-connected buyers. In 2003 the privatization process stalled again, as it proved relatively difficult to sell the remaining share holdings of the **Croatian Privatization Fund** (HFP). The **Croatian Democratic Union** Government that took office in 2004 attempted to regain the momentum of privatization, and in 2007 three large metal plants were privatized. However, by the end of 2008 the HFP still owned a majority share in just under 100 companies, and a minority share in a further 800 companies. In May of that year the Government announced plans to privatize the shipyards, a major icon of state ownership in Croatia.

Croatian Chamber of Economy
Hrvatska Gospodarska Komora (HGK)

The principal organization in **Croatia** for promoting business contacts, both internally and externally, in the post-communist era.
   President: Nadan Vidošević.
   Address: Rooseveltov trg 2, 10000 Zagreb.
   Telephone: (1) 4561555.
   Fax: (1) 4828380.
   E-mail: hgk@hgk.hr
   Internet: www.hgk.hr

Croatian Defence Force
Hrvatske Obrambene Snage (HOS)

A paramilitary group once active in **Croatia** and with connections to similar groups in neighbouring **Bosnia and Herzegovina**. The HOS, effectively the armed wing of the far-right **Croatian Party of Rights** (HSP), was founded along with its parent party in 1990. The guerrillas gained popularity among local **Croats** in the frontline areas (*see* **Krajina**) and were credited with putting up a more credible defence against local ethnic **Serb** militias than the regular Croatian army. Following the country's independence in 1991, the Government moved to dilute the HOS and began absorbing its armed units into the army under the pretext of not permitting the existence of private armies. Like the HSP, the group lost popularity as the country attained post-conflict stability.

Croatian Democratic Union (Bosnia and Herzegovina)
Hrvatska Demokratska Zajednica (HDZ)

The dominant political party of the ethnic **Croat** population of **Bosnia and Herzegovina**, of nationalist orientation. The HDZ was launched in August 1990, partly on the initiative of the then ruling **Croatian Democratic Union of Croatia**. In the pre-independence Assembly elections of late 1990 it took most of the ethnic Croat vote, electing the two guaranteed Croat members of the then seven-member collegial presidency. It joined a post-election coalition Government with the main **Muslim** and **Serb** parties, but strains developed over the Bosnian Croats' ambivalence on whether there should be an independent state of Bosnia and Herzegovina.

The party effectively withdrew from the central Government in 1992 and in August 1993 spearheaded the proclamation of the Croatian Republic of **Herceg-Bosna** in the Croat-populated south-western region, with its own assembly at Grude. A change of policy in Zagreb, however, resulted in HDZ participation in the March 1994 agreement to set up a **Muslim-Croat Federation** of Bosnia and Herzegovina in the territory not under Bosnian Serb control, and in the replacement of hard-liner Mate Boban as HDZ leader by the more moderate Krešimir Zubak, who became Federation President in May 1994. After long resistance by hard-line Croats, Zubak in August 1996 signed an agreement for the abolition of Herceg-Bosna and full Croat participation in the Federation. In the first post-**Dayton** elections (September 1996), Zubak was elected as the Croat member of the union collective Presidency with overwhelming support from Croat voters, while the HDZ won seven of 42 seats in the all-Bosnia House of Representatives (lower house of the **Parliamentary Assembly**) and 35 of 140 in the Federation lower house. In March 1997 Zubak was succeeded as Federation President by Vladimir Soljić of the HDZ.

The election of Croat nationalist Ante Jelavić as HDZ Chairman in May 1998 precipitated the exit of Zubak and his supporters, who formed the New Croatian Initiative (NHI), while the **Organisation for Security and Co-operation in Europe** banned some HDZ candidates from running in the September 1998 elections because of their close links with Croatia. Nevertheless, the HDZ remained dominant among Croat voters, Jelavić being elected as the Croat member of the union collective Presidency with 53% of the Croat vote (and 11.5% nationally), although the party's representation slipped to six seats in the all-Bosnia lower house and to 28 in the Federation lower house.

In June 1999 Jelavić began an eight-month term in the rotating chairmanship of the union collective Presidency, declaring as his priorities Bosnia and Herzegovina's admission to the **European Union**, the **Council of Europe** and the **World Trade Organization**. However, a poor HDZ performance in local elections in April 2000 exacerbated internal divisions, which became public in July at an HDZ congress which re-elected Jelavić to the chairmanship, and also adopted new statutes making the party formally independent of the Croatian HDZ. In elections for five Vice-Chairmen, the congress declined to return moderate Foreign Minister Jadranko Prlić, who in September resigned from the party, claiming that Jelavić was wedded to 'obsolete political methods'.

In October 2000 Martin Raguž of the HDZ became union Prime Minister in succession to Spasoje Tusevljak, a non-party Serb (who could not remain in office because the accession of Zivko Radišić of the Socialist Party of the Serb Republic to the chairmanship of the union's collective Presidency on the retirement of Alija Izetbegović of the **Party of Democratic Action** would have meant that the both posts were held by the same ethnic group, a situation not permitted under the Dayton Agreement). In the November 2000 legislative elections, the HDZ slipped to five seats in the union lower house and to 25 in the Federation lower house, while moderate parties gained ground in both legislatures. The consequence was the replacement of Raguž in early 2001 by a Croat member of the **Social Democratic Party of Bosnia and Herzegovina**, heading the first all-Bosnia Government not dominated by nationalists. The reaction of the HDZ the following month was the declaration of a revived separate Croat state based in **Mostar**, whereupon the UN **High Representative** dismissed Jelavić from the union collective Presidency, amid urgent UN and other efforts to preserve the structure created under the Dayton Agreement. The party eventually backed down and, in November, ended an eight-month boycott of the Parliamentary Assembly.

The nationalist parties performed well at the October 2002 elections, with HDZ candidate Dragan Čović convincingly winning the Croat seat on the union Presidency with 61.5%. In the simultaneous all-Bosnia lower house election a coalition of the HDZ and Croatian Christian Democrats won five seats (10.1% of the vote), while in the Federation lower house (now reduced from 140 members to 98 members), a larger HDZ-led coalition that also included the Croatian National Union (HNZ) won 16 seats. In January 2003 the Federation lower house elected HDZ Vice-President Niko Lozančić as Federation President.

Čović was removed from the union Presidency in March 2005, after being charged with corruption during his term as Federation Minister of Finance. Ivo Miro Jović succeeded him in May. Nevertheless Čović was elected HDZ President in June in a close-fought election against party rival Božo Ljubić. Ten months later Ljubić, Raguž and their supporters broke away from the HDZ and formed the HDZ 1990. This split had a significant impact at the October 2006 elections: Jović and Ljubić split the nationalist vote for the Croat seat on the all-Bosnia Presidency, which was won by moderate Željko **Komšić**, while in the all-Bosnia lower house the coalition of the HDZ and HNZ won just three seats and in the Federation lower house halved its representation to eight seats. However, the HDZ was included in the union-level Government of Nikola **Špirić** of the **Alliance of Independent Social Democrats** (SNSD) that took office in January 2007. In the Federation, Borjana **Krišto** (HDZ) was subsequently elected President, and took office on 22 February 2007.

Leadership: Dragan Čović (Chair.).
Address: bb Kneza Domagoja, Mostar Zapad.
Telephone: (36) 314686.
Fax: (36) 322799.
E-mail: hdzbih@hdzbih.org
Internet: www.hdzbih.org

Croatian Democratic Union (Croatia)
Hrvatska Demokratska Zajednica (HDZ)

A nationalist party of Christian orientation which took **Croatia** to independence in 1991 but lost power with a heavy electoral defeat a month after the death of founder Franjo **Tudjman** in December 1999. Repositioning itself as less stridently right-wing, the party recovered ground and returned to government after the 2003 election, and currently remains at the head of the ruling coalition. It is a member of **Centrist Democrat International** and the **International Democrat Union**.

Founded in mid-1989 in opposition to the then communist regime of the **Socialist Federal Republic of Yugoslavia**, the HDZ was joined by many of the elite of the Yugoslav regime, although Tudjman himself, a history professor with a military background, had been a prominent dissident in the 1970s and 1980s. Contesting the 1990 multi-party elections on a pro-autonomy platform, the HDZ won a landslide parliamentary majority, by virtue of which Tudjman was elected President in May 1990 by vote of the deputies. The HDZ Government secured a 94% pro-independence vote in a referendum in May 1991 and declared Croatia's independence the following month. In further elections in August 1992, the HDZ retained an overall parliamentary majority in the lower house of the **Assembly** and Tudjman was directly re-elected President with 56.7% of the popular vote.

Thereafter, the HDZ Government was riven by dissension about how to deal with the civil war in neighbouring **Bosnia and Herzegovina**. Also controversial was its maintenance of much of the panoply of central economic control. In October 1993 a special HDZ congress approved a new party programme espousing Christian democracy, describing the HDZ as the guarantor of Croatian independence and defining the liberation of **Serb**-held Croatian territory as the Government's most important task. In February 1994 President Tudjman publicly apologized for having, in an earlier book, doubted the veracity of received accounts of the Nazi extermination of **Jews** during the Second World War. The following month he also apologized for the role of the pro-German Ustaša regime in the extermination.

In April 1994 the HDZ was weakened by the breakaway of a moderate faction which favoured alliance with the **Muslims** of Bosnia and Herzegovina against the **Serbs** and also objected to Tudjman's dictatorial tendencies. Nevertheless, boosted by **Croat** military successes against the Serbs, the HDZ retained an overall majority in lower house elections in October 1995, winning 75 out of 127 seats with a vote share of 45.2%. The party also retained its majority in the upper house of the Assembly in April 1997, while in June 1997 Tudjman was re-elected President with 61.4% of the vote.

In the late 1990s the HDZ displayed evidence of internal dissension between hard-liners and moderates as Tudjman became increasingly ill, amid rising popular discontent with economic and social conditions. Following Tudjman's death in December 1999, the HDZ was heavily defeated in Assembly elections in early January 2000, retaining only 40 of the 151 seats (with 26.7% of the proportional vote) and going into opposition to a centre-left Government headed by the **Social Democratic Party of Croatia**. In subsequent presidential elections, moreover, outgoing Deputy Premier and Foreign Minister Mate Granić of the HDZ, despite resigning his party offices on the eve of polling, was eliminated in the first round in late January 2000, taking third place with 22.5% of the vote.

Ousted from government, the HDZ experienced an exodus of leading members, including Granić in March 2000, as new evidence emerged of corruption in the Tudjman regime. (Granić then co-founded the right-wing Democratic Centre party.) In April 2000 the HDZ presidency was conferred on Ivo Sanader, a moderate, who declared his aim of restoring the party's public image. In November 2000 HDZ deputies unsuccessfully opposed the conversion of Croatia into a parliamentary democracy. The trials of former Croat army commanders at the **International Criminal Tribunal for the former Yugoslavia** provoked mass rallies in Croatia, which were attended by the HDZ, though Sanader was careful to distance the party from extremist protests. Politically as well he steered the party away from its historic nationalist rhetoric to more centre-right policies. HDZ approval for these changes was confirmed in 2002 when Sanader overcame a challenge from Ivić Pašalić, Tudjman's former adviser, for the party leadership.

In the November 2003 parliamentary elections the HDZ regained its position as the largest bloc, though short of a majority with 66 seats (and 33.9% of the vote). Sanader negotiated coalition agreements with the **Croatian Peasants' Party** (HSS—with 10 seats) and the **Croatian Social-Liberal Party** (HSLS) and Democratic Centre (which together controlled three seats), and obtained the support of several other deputies, in order to command a narrow parliamentary majority. On 23 December a new Government, principally comprising HDZ members, was approved. Sanader's main policies continued the path towards EU membership, though co-operation with the ICTY remained a difficult issue. At the January 2005 presidential election HDZ candidate Jadranka **Kosor** faced incumbent Stipe Mesić in the run-off, but Mesić won easily with 65.9% to 34.1%.

At elections to the House of Representatives on 25 November 2007 the HDZ remained the largest party, again with 66 seats, though with a slightly larger share of the vote (36.6%). After several weeks of negotiations, Sanader formed a new Government in early January 2008, comprising members of the HDZ, HSS, HSLS and Independent Democratic Serbian Party (SDSS), and with support from four of the other five ethnic minority representatives.

Sanader made the surprise announcement on 1 July 2009 that he was quitting politics. He recommended his deputy Kosor as his successor. She was nominated on 3 July, secured the presidency of the HDZ the following day, and took office on 6 July.

HDZ candidate Andrija Hebrang was eliminated in the first round of the presidential election in December 2009, having finished third with 12% of the vote.

Leadership: Jadranka Kosor (Chair.).
Address: 4 Trg Žrtava Fašizma 4, 10000 Zagreb.
Telephone: (1) 4553000.
Fax: (1) 4552600.
E-mail: hdz@hdz.hr
Internet: www.hdz.hr

Croatian National Bank
Hrvatska Narodna Banka (HNB)

The central bank of **Croatia**. The HNB was established as Croatia's central issuing bank in December 1990. The Yugoslav dinar was replaced by a Croatian dinar in 1991 and the Croatian kuna replaced the latter as the sole legal tender in May 1994. As of December 2007, the HNB had reserves of 3,566.6m. kuna.

Governor: Željko Rohatinski.
Address: Trg Hrvatskih Velikana 3, 10002 Zagreb.
Telephone: (1) 4564555.
Fax: (1) 4550726.
E-mail: info@hnb.hr
Internet: www.hnb.hr

Croatian Peasants' Party
Hrvatska Seljačka Stranka (HSS)

A middle-ranking formation in **Croatia** which has participated in post-independence governments, including the current coalition. The HSS is descended from a co-operative party founded in 1904, which became a standard-bearer of **Croat** nationalism in inter-war **Yugoslavia** but was suppressed by the wartime pro-Nazi Ustaša regime in Croatia. Revived in November 1989 and committed to pacifism, local democracy, privatization and rural co-operatives, the HSS won three seats in the August 1992 elections to the lower house of the **Assembly** and five in the February 1993 upper house balloting. It then joined a coalition with the then ruling **Croatian Democratic Union** (HDZ) until the end of 1994.

In the October 1995 lower house elections the HSS won 10 seats as part of the opposition United List (ZL) alliance. For the January 2000 lower house elections it maintained the ZL, which then included the **Istrian Democratic Assembly**, the **Liberal Party** and the **Croatian People's Party** (HNS). The HSS took 16 of the 25 seats won by the alliance and obtained two portfolios (including agriculture) in the new centre-left coalition Government headed by the **Social Democratic Party of Croatia**. In presidential elections in January–February 2000 the HSS backed the successful candidacy of Stipe Mesić of the HNS (and supported his candidacy for re-election in 2005).

At the 2003 elections the HSS finished in fourth place with 10 seats (and 7.2% of the vote), in a poll won by the resurgent HDZ. This time it joined an HDZ-led coalition Government, which included parties across much of the political spectrum.

The HSS contested the 2007 elections as part of the Green–Yellow Coalition with the **Croatian Social-Liberal Party** (HSLS) and three small regional parties, securing just eight seats (six HSS, two HSLS) with 6.5% of the vote. The HDZ, which remained the largest party, again included the HSS in its governing coalition.

Leadership: Josip Friščić (President).
Address: ul. Kralja Zvonimirova 17, 10000 Zagreb.
Telephone: (1) 4553624.
Fax: (1) 4553631.
E-mail: hss@hss.hr
Internet: www.hss.hr

Croatian People's Party—Liberal Democrats
Hrvatska Narodna Stranka—Liberalni Demokrati (HNS–LD)

A centre-left liberal party in **Croatia** whose candidate Stipe Mesić held the national presidency from 2000 to 2010, although the party has not been part of Croatia's coalition governments since 2003. The Croatian People's Party (HNS) was founded in 1990, although its core leadership had formed a dissident group since the attempt in 1970–71 to liberalize the then ruling **League of Communists** of Croatia within the **Socialist Federal Republic of Yugoslavia**. Drawing some support from ethnic **Serbs** as well as **Croats**, the party advocates 'modernity' in political and economic structures, private enterprise, regionalism and membership of the **European Union** and the **North Atlantic Treaty Organization**. In the August 1992 elections to the lower house of the **Assembly** it won six seats, while its Chairman came third in the concurrent presidential contest with 6% of the national vote. For the October 1995 lower house elections the HNS was part of the United List (ZL) alliance, winning two seats in its own right.

The HNS retained two lower house seats in the January 2000 Assembly elections, again standing as part of the ZL, which then included the **Croatian Peasants' Party**, the **Istrian Democratic Assembly** and the Liberal Party. HNS leader Radimir Čačić was appointed as Minister of Public Works, Construction and Reconstruction in the new centre-left Government headed by the **Social Democratic Party of Croatia**. The party's profile was raised by the election of its Vice-Chairman, Stipe Mesić, as President of Croatia in the January–February 2000 presidential elections, in which he stood as the HNS/ZL candidate. Against most initial forecasts, Mesić led in the first round with 41.1% of the vote and triumphed in the second with 56%. In April 2000 Vesna Pusić was elected as party leader.

At the November 2003 election the HNS led an alliance with two regional parties, which secured 8% of the vote and 11 seats (10 HNS), making it the third-largest bloc. However, the right-wing **Croatian Democratic Union** (HDZ) formed the new Government and the HNS returned to opposition.

Mesić stood for a second term in the January 2005 presidential elections, backed by the HNS and seven other parties. He just failed to secure victory in the first round, with 48.9% of the vote, so he had to face HDZ candidate Jadranka **Kosor** in the run-off, which he won easily with 65.9% to 34.1%.

In February 2005 the HNS merged with the Party of Liberal Democrats (Libra–SLD), which had splintered from the **Croatian Social-Liberal Party** in 2002. At the November 2007 election the HNS–LD won seven seats, with 6.8% of the vote. It remained in opposition to an HDZ-led coalition. Čačić resumed the party leadership in April 2008.

Pusić stood as the HNS–LD candidate in the first round of the presidential election in December 2009, finishing fifth with 7% of the vote.

Leadership: Radimir Čačić (Chair.).
Address: Kneza Mislava 8, 10000 Zagreb.
Telephone: (1) 4629111.
Fax: (1) 4629110.
E-mail: hns@hns.hr
Internet: www.hns.hr

Croatian Privatization Fund
Hrvatski fond za privatizaciju (HFP)

Founded in 1994 by a merger of the Croatian Fund for Development and the Restructuring and Development Agency.

President: Damir Ostović.
Address: Ivana Lučića 6, 10000 Zagreb.
E-mail: hfp@hfp.hr
Internet: www.hfp.hr

Croatian Social-Liberal Party
Hrvatska Socijalno-Liberalna Stranka (HSLS)

A mainstream centre-right liberal party in **Croatia** founded in 1989, which came to government office in January 2000 and is part of the current ruling coalition. It is a member of **Liberal International**. Having made little impact in the 1990 pre-independence elections, the HSLS became the second-strongest party in the lower house elections to the **Assembly** in August 1992, winning 14 seats, while its Chairman Dražen Budiša took second place in the simultaneous presidential contest with 21.9% of the vote. In the February 1993 upper house elections, the party won 16 of the 63 elective seats. Opposed to the Government of the **Croatian Democratic Union** (HDZ), the HSLS participated in an opposition boycott of the Assembly from May to September 1994. In the October 1995 lower house elections the party took 11.6% of the vote and 12 seats, confirming its status as the strongest single opposition party. In the June 1997 presidential elections, the then HSLS Chairman Vlado Gotovać came third with 17.6% of the vote (later leaving the HSLS to found the Liberal Party (LS), at which point Budiša regained the leadership of the HSLS).

For the January 2000 Assembly elections, the HSLS was allied with the **Social Democratic Party of Croatia** (SDP), together with two small regional formations, and won 24 seats in the anti-HDZ victory. It took six portfolios in the resultant six-party coalition Government, headed by the SDP under Ivica Račan. In the presidential elections three weeks later HSLS Chairman Budiša, backed by the SDP, took second place in the first round with 27.7% of the vote and therefore contested the second round in early February, when he won 44% but was defeated by Stipe Mesić, candidate of the **Croatian People's Party** (HNS).

In July 2001 the Government's continued co-operation with the **International Criminal Tribunal for the former Yugoslavia** (ICTY) provoked a crisis in the coalition, with Budiša spearheading dissent within the HSLS. Four HSLS members quit the cabinet, but after the Government won a vote of confidence in the Assembly, Budiša was forced to resign from the party leadership and the ministers resumed their posts. Jozo Radoš became acting party Chair. In February 2002 Budiša was re-elected party leader, and soon First Deputy Prime Minister, Goran Granić, and a further two HSLS ministers were removed from the Government; it was reported that Budiša questioned their loyalty to the party, owing to their failure to support his apparent opposition to co-operation with the ICTY. The remaining three HSLS members in the Government subsequently tendered their resignations to demonstrate disagreement with the party leadership. In early March, following lengthy discussions, the coalition parties in the Government reached agreement on a cabinet reorganization. Budiša became First Deputy Prime Minister, while Granić (henceforth an independent) and three of the HSLS representatives were reappointed to the Government. In early July 2002 Budiša finally withdrew the HSLS from the government coalition, after an agreement on joint ownership of the Krško nuclear power installation in Slovenia was ratified in the Assembly, despite the opposition of 17 of the HSLS's 23 deputies. Disagreeing with Budiša's attempts to bring down the Government, a faction of his party broke away and formed the Party of Liberal Democrats (Libra–SLD), which gave its support to Račan, enabling him to form a new Government without the HSLS.

In the run-up to the 2003 election Budiša formed an alliance with the new right-wing Democratic Centre (DC), which had splintered from the HDZ. However, this bloc performed very badly in the November election, winning only three seats (two HSLS, one DC) and 4% of the vote. Budiša, who failed to retain his own seat, resigned as party leader, and was replaced by Ivan Čehok. Despite the party's poor electoral showing, the HDZ invited the HSLS to join a four-party coalition with a narrow parliamentary majority.

The HSLS fielded its own candidate Đurđa Adlešič in the 2005 presidential elections; she came fourth with 2.7% of the vote. In early 2006 the Liberal Party (which had splintered from the HSLS in 1997) re-merged with the HSLS; Adlešič was elected leader of this reunited party.

At the 2007 elections the HSLS was part of the Green–Yellow Coalition with the **Croatian Peasants' Party** (HSS) and three small regional parties, securing just eight seats (six HSS, two HSLS) with 6.5% of the vote. The HDZ, which remained the largest party, again included the HSLS in its governing coalition.

Adlešič stepped down as HSLS President in November 2009, and Darinko Kosor was elected as her successor.

Leadership: Darinko Kosor (President).
Address: 17/I Trg Nikole Šubića Zrinskog, 10000 Zagreb.
Telephone: (1) 4810401.
Fax: (1) 4810404.
E-mail: hsls@hsls.hr
Internet: www.hsls.hr

Croats

A south **Slavic people** dominant in **Croatia** and **Herzegovina**. Having arrived in the western **Balkans** in the Slavic migration of the seventh century, the Croats converted to **Roman Catholicism** under the suzerainty of the **Hungarian** kingdom. Ethnically and linguistically the Croats are almost identical to their neighbours the **Bosniaks** in **Bosnia and Herzegovina**, and the **Serbs** in **Yugoslavia** and Bosnia. The major distinction between the Croats and other south Slavs is their Catholic faith and the use of the Latin alphabet to transcribe their (Croatian) language.

Around 20% of Croats, roughly 750,000, live in Bosnia and Herzegovina where they constitute around 17% of the total population, mostly in the southern Herzegovina region. Communities living in what became the **Serb Republic** within Bosnia were subject to discrimination and policies of '**ethnic cleansing**' during the Bosnian War (1992–95). Although calls for the union of Bosnian Croat communities with Croatia proper were effectively extinguished in the **Dayton Agreement** of November 1995, calls for greater ethnic autonomy came to the fore in a provocative, if short-lived, declaration of Croat self-determination in March 2001 (*see* **Herceg-Bosna**).

Csángós

A minority **Roman Catholic** ethnic group resident in Moldavia (eastern **Romania**). The Csángós are generally accepted to be a community of ethnic **Hungarians** who arrived in modern Romania in the Middle Ages. There are an estimated 60,000–70,000 Csángó language speakers in Romania today, but in the 2002 census only 1,370 people declared themselves to be Csangos. However, the Romanian authorities are keen to see them as 'Hungarianized' Romanians. They have maintained a separate status owing to their strong adherence to Catholicism within their dominantly

Orthodox Christian host country, and through the use of their language, which is seen as an ancient dialect of Hungarian. Csángó culture is proudly rooted in folk traditions but is perceived to be under threat as there is no established means of preserving the language and customs in Moldavia, unlike in neighbouring **Transylvania** where there is a well-established Hungarian community. As a result, the European Council pledged in November 2001 to investigate and protect the minority.

ČSSD *see* **Czech Social Democratic Party**.

ČTK *see* **Czech News Agency**.

CTP-BG *see* **Republican Turkish Party–United Forces**.

Cvetković, Mirko

Prime Minister of **Serbia**.

Mirko Cvetković trained as an economist, and worked as a financial adviser prior to joining the Government as a privatization specialist. He is a member of the pro-European **Democratic Party** (DS) and has been Prime Minister of Serbia since July 2008.

Born in Zajecar on 16 August 1950, he studied economics at the University of Belgrade, completing first his degree, then his master's and finally his doctorate. He worked at the Mining Institute, then at the Economics Institute, before becoming a financial adviser for CES MECON. During the 1980s he was also an external consultant for the World Bank on projects in Pakistan, India and Turkey and for the UN Development Programme in Somalia.

In January 2001 he was appointed Deputy Minister of Economy and Privatization in the first post-**Milošević** Government. In 2003 he was appointed Director of the Privatization Agency and in 2005 became a special adviser to the Intercon consulting agency.

When the DS returned to Government in May 2007, he was appointed Minister of Finance, and when fresh elections were held a year later he was nominated to head the new Government, taking office on 7 July 2008.

Cvetković is married, with two children, and is a fluent speaker of English.

Address: Office of the Prime Minister, Nemanjina 11, 11000 Belgrade.
Telephone: (11) 3617719.
Fax: (11) 3617609.
E-mail: predsednikvladesrbije@srbija.sr.gov.rs
Internet: www.srbija.sr.gov.rs

Cyprus
Kypriaki Dimokratia (Greek); *Kibris Cumhuriyeti* (Turkish)

An independent island republic in the eastern Mediterranean, with mainland Turkey its nearest neighbour to the north and Syria and Lebanon to the east. Cyprus has been partitioned since 1974 into areas controlled by the Greek Cypriot Government and the self-proclaimed **Turkish Republic of Northern Cyprus** (TRNC). The island is divided administratively into six districts, of which Larnaca, Limassol, Paphos and part of **Nicosia** are in the Greek Cypriot area, whereas Famagusta, Kyrenia and northern Nicosia are in the TRNC. There are also two British sovereign base areas (SBAs), Akrotiri and Dhekelia, covering 256 sq km. Except where stated, the data below refer to the Greek Cypriot area.

Area: 5,896 sq km (total area of the island is 9,251 sq km, of which TRNC 3,355 sq km); *capital*: Nicosia/Lefkoşa; *population*: 871,000 (2009 estimate), consisting of **Greeks** 95%, Turks 2%, others 3%; *official languages*: Greek and Turkish; *religion*: Eastern **Orthodox** Christian 95%, **Muslim** 2%, others 3%.

Under the 1960 Constitution, the Republic of Cyprus has an executive President, who is directly elected for a five-year term, by compulsory universal suffrage of those aged 18 and over, and who appoints the Council of Ministers. Legislative authority is vested in a unicameral House of Representatives (Vouli Antiprosópon in Greek, Temsilciler Meclisi in Turkish), which theoretically has 80 members elected for a five-year term by proportional representation, 56 by the Greek Cypriot community and 24 by the **Turkish Cypriots**. Since 1963, however, the Turkish Cypriot community has refused to participate in these arrangements. Three further representatives are elected by the Armenian, Maronite and Latin religious communities and have a consultative role in the House.

History: Colonized by a succession of mainland empires from the 15th century BC, Cyprus came under Roman rule in 58 BC and continued with what became known as the Byzantine Empire in AD 395. Held by King Richard the Lionheart of England in the late 12th century and then ruled by French feudal lords, Cyprus was annexed by Venice in 1489. Conquest by the Ottoman Turks in 1571 ushered in three centuries of Muslim rule, during which the island's Greek inhabitants were joined by substantial numbers of Turks. Declining Ottoman power, the Russian threat and the opening of the Suez Canal impelled the United Kingdom, with the endorsement of the 1878 Congress of Berlin, to make Cyprus a British protectorate. When Turkey joined the Central Powers in the First World War, the United Kingdom annexed the island (1914) and in 1915 offered to cede it to **Greece** in return for a Greek declaration of war, which was not forthcoming. When Greece entered the war in 1917, the offer was not repeated. British sovereignty over Cyprus was recognized by Greece and Turkey under the 1923 Treaty of Lausanne and the island became a Crown Colony in 1925.

The Greek Cypriots' demand for *enosis* (union with Greece) gathered strength after the Second World War, led politically from 1950 by Archbishop **Makarios III** and militarily by the National Organization of Cypriot Struggle (EOKA), which waged an anti-British terrorist campaign from 1955. Amid growing violence, Makarios was exiled in 1956. He returned in triumph in 1959, after the United Kingdom, Greece and Turkey had agreed that Cyprus would become an independent republic within the Commonwealth with a power-sharing political structure as between Greek Cypriots and Turkish Cypriots. It was also agreed that the United Kingdom, Greece and Turkey would be guarantor powers and that the United Kingdom would retain sovereignty over its military bases at Akrotiri and Dhekelia. In December 1959 Makarios was elected as the first President of Cyprus and the Turkish Cypriot leader, Fazil Kutchuk, as Vice-President, following which the Republic of Cyprus became formally independent in August 1960.

The power-sharing arrangements quickly broke down amid growing inter-communal conflict, which caused the Turkish Cypriots to withdraw from the House of Representatives and the Council of Ministers in late 1963. The following year a UN force (UNFICYP) was deployed to keep peace between the two communities. In 1968 the Turkish Cypriots set up an 'autonomous administration' in the north, of which Rauf **Denktaş** became the leader. Among the Greek Cypriots, dissension between Makarios supporters and pro-*enosis* hard-liners culminated in July 1974 in a coup by Greek-born army officers backed by the military regime then in power in **Athens**. Makarios was forced to flee and Nicos Sampson, a former EOKA leader, was installed as President. Claiming to be acting as a guarantor under the 1959 agreement, Turkey launched a large-scale military invasion, its forces rapidly taking control of the northern two-fifths of Cyprus, from which about 200,000 Greek Cypriots fled to the south, while 40,000 Turkish Cypriots moved to the north. Sampson resigned after only a week, whereupon Glafcos Clerides (the House Speaker) became acting President until Makarios returned in December 1974.

The division of Cyprus resulting from the Turkish invasion hardened into an effective partition on the ceasefire **Green Line**. A Turkish Federated State of Cyprus declared in the north in 1975 under the presidency of Denktaş was converted into the 'independent' TRNC in 1983. It obtained recognition only from Turkey, which maintained some 40,000 troops in the north. Makarios died in 1977 and was succeeded as President by Spyros Kyprianou of the **Democratic Party** (DIKO). He was replaced in 1988 by businessman George Vassiliou, an independent backed by the powerful left-wing communist **Progressive Party for the Working People** (AKEL). Several initiatives to achieve a settlement foundered under Vassiliou's presidency, with the Turkish Cypriots insisting on 'self-determination' and the Greek Cypriots calling for implementation of UN resolutions supporting the maintenance of Cyprus as a single sovereignty. In the 1993 Greek Cypriot presidential elections, Vassiliou was unexpectedly defeated by Clerides, now leading the **Democratic Rally** (DISY), who went on to win a second term in 1998. Over his decade in office further efforts to unblock the inter-communal logjam failed.

Presidential elections in February 2003 resulted in a first-round victory for Tassos Papadopoulos (DIKO), who was backed by AKEL and the **Movement of Social Democrats EDEK** and received 51.5% of the vote against 38.8% for Clerides and 9.7% for eight other candidates. Papadopoulos strongly opposed a new settlement plan tabled by UN Secretary-General Kofi Annan, which envisaged the creation of a federal United Cyprus Republic consisting of two 'constituent states', on the grounds that it would solidify the island's division to the disadvantage of the Greek Cypriots. The signature by the Greek Cypriot Government in April 2003 of a treaty with the **European Union** (EU) providing for the accession of Cyprus in May 2004 gave a new dimension to the island's division. Claiming that the Greek Cypriots had no right to act for the TRNC vis-à-vis the EU, the Turkish Cypriot authorities responded in late April by relaxing restrictions on the movement of people across the Green Line, enabling large numbers from each community to visit the other side. However, hopes that such contact would expedite a political settlement were disappointed in March 2004 when the two sides reached another deadlock in talks in Bürgenstock, Switzerland. Annan therefore presented the fifth version of his plan directly to the Cypriot people in simultaneous referendums in April 2004. The Turkish Cypriots delivered a 64.9% vote in favour, but 75.8% of Greek Cypriot voters followed the recommendation of Papadopoulos by rejecting the plan. Accordingly, the accession of Cyprus to the EU in May 2004 applied only to the area under the control of the Greek Cypriot Government, with the application of EU regulations suspended in the Turkish Cypriot area pending a settlement.

The final departure of Denktaş as Turkish Cypriot leader in April 2005 and his replacement by the more moderate Mehmet Ali **Talat** gave rise to new hopes of a settlement. However, with the UN refusing to get involved again until there were real prospects of an agreement, not until July 2006 did Papadopoulos and Talat agree to resume bicommunal talks, and then only at preparatory technical level.

Latest elections: Elections for the 56 Greek Cypriot seats in the House of Representatives in May 2006 resulted in AKEL, the strongest formation in the ruling DIKO-AKEL-EDEK coalition, losing its position as the largest single party. It took 18 seats with 31.2% of the vote, while the main opposition DISY also won 18 seats with 30.3%. DIKO advanced to 11 seats (17.9%) and EDEK to five (8.9%), with the new European Party (EVROKO) winning three (5.7%) and the Ecological and Environmental Movement retaining one (1.9%).

In July 2007 AKEL withdrew from the ruling coalition in order to field a separate candidate in the February 2008 presidential election. In the first round Ioannis Kasoulidis, a DISY member of the European Parliament, led with 33.5% of the vote, just ahead of AKEL General Secretary Dimitris **Christofias** with 33.3% of the vote, with incumbent President Tassos Papadopoulos, backed by DIKO and EDEK, coming a close third with 31.8%. In the run-off DIKO and EDEK supported Christofias, who won by 53.4% to 46.6%.

Recent developments: Christofias was inaugurated on 28 February 2008, becoming the first communist head of state in an EU member country. He appointed an AKEL-DIKO-EDEK Council of Ministers the following day. He promised to push forward with reunification negotiations with the TRNC, and held his first meeting with Talat just three weeks later. Direct, UN-backed negotiations began in early September. Although a deal has yet to be made despite more than 60 meetings, both leaders profess to remain fully committed to finding a lasting settlement to the island's problems. EDEK, however, having always opposed Christofias's relatively conciliatory approach to reunification, finally decided to withdraw from the Government in February 2010. Meanwhile, the political configuration was also changing in the TRNC, with the hard-line National Unity Party (UBP), which has opposed reunification, winning the April 2009 TRNC Assembly elections and then the April 2010 presidential election.

International relations and defence: Having been admitted to the UN and the Commonwealth at independence in 1960, Cyprus subsequently joined the **Council of Europe** and the **Organization for Security and Co-operation in Europe**. A long quest by the Government for admission to the EU was successful in May 2004, although Greek Cypriot opposition blocked a federal solution that could have allowed the simultaneous accession of the TRNC-administered area. Cyprus subsequently withdrew from the Non-Aligned Movement, of which it had been a founder member in 1961. Cyprus joined the **eurozone** on 1 January 2008 (*see* **Cyprus, economy**). Cyprus has not yet implemented the EU's Schengen Agreement, allowing free movement of citizens within the zone's borders, due to the ongoing dispute with the TRNC.

The cornerstone of bilateral relations is Cyprus' close alliance with Greece. There has also traditionally been a strong relationship with Russia, maintained in part to balance the perceived bias of the USA and the United Kingdom towards Turkey. Cyprus also aspires to be a bridge between Europe and the Muslim Near East.

The Greek Cypriot Government's defence budget was some US $537m. in 2008, equivalent to about 2.2% of GDP. The National Guard consists of land, sea and air forces, the bulk of its 10,000 personnel coming from compulsory conscription of 24 months. The commander of the National Guard is customarily a serving officer from Greece, which itself maintains a permanent military contingent in Cyprus.

Cyprus, economy

A free-market economy in a country politically divided since 1974, with the Greek Cypriot area prospering within the **European Union** (EU) since 2004, whereas the **Turkish Republic of Northern Cyprus** (TRNC) has lagged far behind. The figures and data below refer to Greek Cypriot Cyprus.

GNP: US $21,539m. (2008); *GNP per capita*: $24,940 (2008); *GDP at PPP*: $22,721m. (2008); *GDP per capita at PPP*: $29,900 (2008); *real GDP growth*: –0.5% (2009 estimate); *exports*: $1,721m. (2008); *imports*: $10,848m. (2008); *currency*: euro (US $1 = €0.7129 in mid-2009), but the TRNC uses the Turkish lira (US $1 = TL1.536 in mid-2009); *unemployment*: 6.2% (end 2009); *government deficit as a percentage of GDP*: 6.1% (2009); *inflation*: 0.4% (2009).

In 2007 industry accounted for 19% of GDP, agriculture 2% and services 79%. Around 23% of the workforce is engaged in industry, 4% in agriculture and 73% in services.

Although most of the island's grain-producing land and citrus groves are located in the TRNC, about 27% of the Greek Cypriot area is utilized for agriculture. The main crops are cereals, citrus fruits, potatoes, olives and grapes. Livestock and dairying are also important, Cyprus being particularly notable for its unique halloumi cheese.

Mineral resources are limited to low-value deposits such as sand and gravel, although there are hopes of reviving the ancient copper mining industry, while preliminary surveys have shown that hydrocarbon reserves exist in the Cypriot sector of the continental shelf to the south of the island. Industrial output includes clothing and footwear, paper products, building materials and metal products. The services sector is dominated by finance and banking and by tourism, which provided 28% of GDP in 2007.

The main exports are machinery and transport equipment, citrus fruits, potatoes, pharmaceuticals, cement, clothing and cigarettes, while imports are led by consumer goods, petroleum and lubricants, machinery and transport equipment. The main destinations of Cyprus's exports in 2008 were **Greece** (19%), the United Kingdom (10%) and Germany (5%), while the main sources of imports were Greece (17%), Italy (11%) and the United Kingdom (9%).

The division of Cyprus as a result of the 1974 Turkish invasion, which left the bulk of the island's economic resources in the north, resulted in a sharp drop in Greek Cypriot living standards. The Greek Cypriot area recovered quickly, however, experiencing an economic boom in the late 1970s and solid if uneven growth in the 1980s and 1990s, as diversification into services, offshore banking and package-holiday tourism proceeded apace, taking the Greek Cypriot area far ahead of the TRNC in terms of economic prosperity. In 1988 Cyprus entered into a customs union with what became the EU and applied for full membership in 1990. Economic policy was thereafter dictated by the difficult task of adapting to EU standards and criteria. This effort resulted in the accession of Cyprus on 1 May 2004. However, in the absence of a political settlement, application of the EU *acquis communautaire* was suspended in the Turkish Cypriot area and the potential economic benefits of a reunified island deferred. The opening of the internal line of division, known as the **Green Line**, to free movement of people since April 2003 has not been accompanied by any substantial growth in intra-island trade, despite EU regulations intended to facilitate it.

Aiming to join the **eurozone**, the Government in June 2004 introduced austerity measures designed to bring Cyprus into compliance with the Maastricht convergence criteria. These succeeded in reducing the budget deficit to 4.2% of GDP in 2004 (from 6.3% in 2003), enabling the Cyprus pound to be admitted to the Exchange Rate Mechanism II in April 2005 as the transitional stage. Adoption of the euro was achieved on 1 January 2008.

GDP growth averaged around 4% in 2004–07, and inflation and unemployment remained low. In 2008 the expected financial benefits of joining the eurozone (increased exports and foreign investment) were diminished by the onset of the global downturn, which particularly hit the tourism and financial services sectors. The economy contracted slightly in 2009, and unemployment rose, although still remaining one of the lowest rates in the EU. Public finances were in fairly good shape, with an almost balanced budget and relatively low public debt (just under 50% of GDP in 2008).

Cyprus Chamber of Commerce and Industry

The principal organization in **Cyprus** for promoting business contacts, both internally and externally. Founded in 1927, it has 8,000 members and 120 affiliated trade associations.

President: Vassilis Rologis.
Address: POB 21455, 38 Grivas Dhigenis Ave, 1509 Nicosia.
Telephone: 22889800.
Fax: 22669048.
E-mail: chamber@ccci.org.cy
Internet: www.ccci.org.cy

Cyprus Investment and Securities Corporation Ltd (CISCO)

Founded in 1982 to promote the development of capital markets. It offers brokerage services, fund management and investment banking, and is a member of Bank of Cyprus Group.

Chair.: Vassilis Rologis.
Address: POB 20597, 1660 Nicosia.
Telephone: 22881700.
Fax: 22338800.
E-mail: info@cisco.bankofcyprus.com
Internet: www.cisco-online.com.cy

Cyprus News Agency (CNA)

The national news agency in **Cyprus**, officially established in 1976. In 1989, the **House of Representatives** approved legislation providing for the operation of the Cyprus News Agency as a 'semi-governmental' news organization with full editorial independence. CNA is governed by a seven-member Board of Directors comprising established media professionals.

Acting Director: George Penintaex.
Address: 7 Kastorias Street, 2002 Strovolos, Nicosia.
Telephone: 22556009.
Fax: 22556103.
E-mail: director@cna.org.cy
Internet: www.cna.org.cy

Cyprus Stock Exchange

Official trading commenced in March 1996. There were 24 members and 127 companies listed in March 2010.

Chair.: Giorgos Koufaris.
Address: POB 25427, Kampou Street, IMC Strovolos, 1309 Nicosia.
Telephone: 22712300.
Fax: 22570308.
E-mail: info@cse.com.cy
Internet: www.cse.com.cy

Cyrillic alphabet

The script used to transcribe eastern and southern **Slavic** languages as well as some non-Slavic tongues. It was first created in the ninth century by the Byzantine monks St Cyril and St Methodius, when they were dispatched to Moravia to help convert the local Slavic people to Christianity. The monks adapted their native Greek alphabet specifically for the use of the Slavic tribes, enabling the production of a Slavic liturgy. The script was reformed over the centuries with a final deletion of Greek-specific characters in 1918. The adoption of Cyrillic became linked to the **Orthodox Christian** Church, and its use remains a clear point of distinction between the **Roman Catholic** Slavs, who use Latin script, and their Orthodox neighbours (although the Romanian Orthodox used the Latin script). In the most significant cases, the difference has become the focus for nationalists in Moldova and has delineated major ethnic divisions in the former **Yugoslavia**. In **south-eastern Europe**, **Bulgaria**, **Macedonia** and **Serbia** use the Cyrillic script. In **Bosnia and Herzegovina** it is the official script in the **Serb Republic** and a joint official script elsewhere. It is also used in **Montenegro** and **Kosovo,** with Serb minorities, and in parts of **Albania** with large **Macedonian** minorities. When Bulgaria joined the **European Union** (EU) in 2007, Cyrillic became the EU's third official alphabet.

Czech National Bank
Česká národní banka (ČNB)

The central bank of the **Czech Republic**. The ČNB was formed in 1993 as a result of the need to divide the activities of the former State Bank of **Czechoslovakia** into its Czech and Slovak elements. It is independent of the Government and aims to control the national currency, the koruny. It is the central authority on monetary policy, legislation and foreign exchange permission. It also supervises the banking industry in general. As of December 2007, the ČNB had reserves of –147,391m. koruny.

Governor: Zdeněk Tůma.
Address: Na Příkopě 28, 11503 Prague 1.
Telephone: (2) 24411111.
Fax: (2) 224412404.
E-mail: info@cnb.cz
Internet: www.cnb.cz

Czech News Agency
Česká tisková kancelář (ČTK)

The national news agency of the **Czech Republic**, a public corporation with a supervisory council elected by the Chamber of Deputies (lower house of **Parliament**). The ČTK was established in its current form in 1992, and has been required to finance itself without a budget from the Government since 1996.

General Director: Milan Stibral.
Address: Opletalova 5–7, 11144 Prague 1.
Telephone: (2) 22098111.
Fax: (2) 24220553.
E-mail: ctk@mail.ctk.cz
Internet: www.ctk-online.cz

Czech Republic
Česká Republika

An independent landlocked republic in **central Europe**, bounded to the north-east by Poland, to the north-west and west by Germany, to the south by Austria and to the south-east by Slovakia. Administratively, it is divided into 14 regions (kraje).

Area: 78,868 sq km; *capital*: **Prague**; *population*: 10.4m. (2009 estimate), comprising **Czechs** 94.1%, **Slovaks** 1.9%, **Poles** 0.5%, **Germans** 0.4%, **Roma** 0.1%, others 3%; *official language*: Czech; *religion*: **Roman Catholic** 26.8%, **Protestant** 2.5%, other 11.7%, atheist 59%.

Legislative authority is vested in the bicameral **Parliament** (Parlament), consisting of a 200-member lower house, the Chamber of Deputies (Poslanecká Sněmovna), and an 81-member upper chamber, the Senate (Senát). The Chamber of Deputies is elected for a four-year term by a system of proportional representation applied to party lists winning at least 5% of the popular vote. Senate members are elected for a six-year term by popular vote from single-member constituencies, with one-third coming up for renewal every two years. The Head of State is the President, who is elected for a five-year term (renewable once only) by both houses of the legislature jointly. Executive power is held by the Prime Minister, who is appointed by the President. The Council of Ministers is also appointed by the President after nomination by the Prime Minister.

History: The region was settled by **Slavic** tribes from the fifth century. In the ninth century the Great Moravian Empire (*see* **Bohemia**, **Moravia** *and* **Slovakia**) was established. Moravia was conquered by the Magyars (**Hungarians**) before becoming a fief of Bohemia in 1029 (Bohemia itself having become an independent margravate in the late 10th century). In 1526 Bohemia came under the rule of the Habsburg dynasty. It was fully integrated from 1620 into the Austrian (subsequently Austro-Hungarian) Empire. In September 1919 the Treaty of St Germain recognized the new Republic of **Czechoslovakia**, proclaimed in 1918 and consisting of Bohemia, Moravia, and Slovakia. The 'tail' of Ruthenia was added from **Hungary** under the 1920 Treaty of **Trianon**.

Presidents Tomás Masaryk (elected in 1918) and Edvard Beneš (elected in 1935) maintained the young democracy between the wars until ethnic tensions increased. The Slovaks resented the dominance of Czech power in the political life of the state, while, more importantly, the German minority, influenced by the rise of Nazism, embraced extreme nationalism. Under the 1938 Munich Agreement, Czechoslovakia was forced to accept the annexation by Germany of its (German-speaking) **Sudetenland** border territories. The following year Nazi forces invaded the weakened state, establishing Bohemia and Moravia as a German protectorate and Slovakia as a self-governing puppet state.

After Soviet forces had liberated the country in 1945, the pre-1938 Czechoslovak state was re-established, although Ruthenia was ceded to the **Soviet Union** and the ethnic German population of the Sudetenland was expelled. In legislative elections in 1946, the Communist Party of Czechoslovakia (KSČ) won 38% of the vote and became the dominant political party. Two years later the communists gained full control and declared a 'people's democracy' in the Soviet style of government. In 1968, following the political repression of the post-war years, KSČ leader Alexander **Dubček** introduced a programme of political and economic liberalization known as the '**Prague Spring**'. This was perceived by the Soviet Union as a threat to stability, and **Warsaw Pact** forces consequently invaded Czechoslovakia to restore the orthodox line. Czech dissidence continued, however, reflected most notably in the **Charter 77** human rights movement.

In 1989, encouraged by democratization movements elsewhere in **central** and **eastern Europe**, anti-Government demonstrations in Czechoslovakia forced the communists to relinquish their monopoly of power, in what was dubbed the '**velvet revolution**'. By the end of 1989 a new Government with a non-communist majority, including members of the **Civic Forum** (OF) coalition of Czech opposition groups, had been formed, and Gustáv **Husák** (KSČ leader in 1969–87) had been replaced as State President by Václav **Havel**, a prominent writer and long-time dissident. The historic KSČ was proscribed in mid-1991, but by then its Czech component had become the **Communist Party of Bohemia and Moravia** (KSČM).

Political liberalization in Czechoslovakia was paralleled by the emergence of a strong Slovak nationalist movement seeking independence for Slovakia as a sovereign state. The creation of separate Czech and Slovak entities was agreed during 1992 and took effect in January 1993 with the dissolution of the Czechoslovak federation (the so-called '**velvet divorce**'). Havel was subsequently elected President of the new Republic (having previously resigned as Head of State of Czechoslovakia in 1992).

In mid-1996, in the first post-separation elections to the Czech Chamber of Deputies, the incumbent centre-right Government headed by the **Civic Democratic Party** (ODS) under the leadership of Václav **Klaus** was returned to power but without an overall majority, having obtained a combined total of 99 of the 200 seats. It therefore concluded an external support arrangement with the **Czech Social Democratic Party** (ČSSD), which had won 61 seats. In 1997 the Klaus Government faced mounting difficulties, including a major financial crisis in May and allegations of illegal funding against the ODS. The withdrawal of the two small coalition parties impelled Klaus to resign in November 1997. A mainly 'technocratic' Government was installed under a non-party Prime Minister, after the ČSSD had secured an agreement that early elections would be held. In January 1998 Havel was re-elected as President for a second term (and subsequently underwent further surgery for a serious medical condition).

Polling in June 1998 for the Chamber of Deputies resulted in the ČSSD becoming the largest party with 74 seats (32% of the vote), just ahead of the ODS with 63. In July a ČSSD minority Government was formed under the premiership of Miloš Zeman, who secured a pledge of external support from Klaus and the ODS. Zeman agreed to continue his predecessor's pro-market policies, but the presence of several former communists among his ministers raised question marks about the Government's commitment to reform, as the economic situation deteriorated in 1999 and little progress was made against financial corruption. The so-called 'opposition agreement' between the ČSSD and the ODS continued to underpin the Government into 2002, but was increasingly questioned in both parties, especially after both suffered major reverses in the November 2000 partial Senate elections.

In the June 2002 Chamber of Deputies election the ČSSD remained the largest party, though slightly reducing its position to 70 seats (30.2% of the vote). The ODS also slipped to 58 seats, while the main gainer was the third-placed KSČM, rising from 24 to 41 seats. Incumbent Deputy Prime Minister Vladimír Špidla, who had taken over from Zeman as ČSSD leader in April 2001, formed a new Government by mid-July, comprising the ČSSD and the fourth-placed Coalition (an alliance of the **Christian Democratic Union–Czechoslovak People's Party** (KDU–ČSL) and the Freedom Union–Democratic Union, which controlled 31 seats).

Presidential elections to find a successor for Havel began in January 2003, but had not succeeded by the time his term expired. Eventually, on 28 February, Klaus was elected, defeating the ruling party's candidate; he took office on 7 March.

A poor performance by the ČSSD in the country's first European Parliament elections in May 2004 led to a vote of confidence in Špidla's party leadership. While the votes against him were not sufficient to oust him, they did amount to a majority (three-fifths were required for removal)—and so in late June he offered his resignation as ČSSD leader and Prime Minister. In August his deputy Stanislav Gross was appointed to head the new Government, but this change of leadership failed to save the party from an overwhelming defeat in the local elections and Senate partial elections in the autumn. Allegations of financial impropriety emerged against Gross in early 2005, but he retained the support of the ČSSD. However, the KDU– ČSL withdrew from his Government, leaving it in a minority. Pressure on Gross mounted, and he eventually resigned on 25 April, being succeeded by ČSSD deputy leader Jiří Paroubek. This change of Prime Minister soon brought the KDU–ČSL back into the ruling coalition.

Latest elections: In the June 2006 election to the Chamber of Deputies the ODS became the largest party with 81 seats (with 35.4% of the vote). The ČSSD was just behind with 74 seats (32.3%), then the KSČM with 26 (12.8%), the KDU–ČSL with 13 (7.2%) and the **Green Party** (SZ) with six (6.3%). No other parties passed the 5% vote threshold to secure representation. Following the 2006 Senate partial elections, the standings were: ODS 41, ČSSD 12, KDU–ČSL 11 (including one independent) and other parties 18. This was the first time since the Senate's creation in 1996 that any party had secured a majority in the 81-seat chamber.

Recent developments: Mirek Topolánek of the ODS was invited to form a Government, and by 26 June 2006 he had signed a coalition agreement with the KDU–ČSL and the SZ, but these parties only controlled 100 seats in the Chamber of Deputies—one short of a majority. An impasse resulted and several months passed without the Government being approved. In mid-August success in electing a Speaker permitted the official appointment of Topolánek as Prime Minister. On 4 September President Klaus eventually approved a minority ODS Government, but this only survived a month before losing a confidence vote: Topolánek resigned. In November he was redesignated as Prime Minister, and presented a further ODS coalition with the KDU–ČSL and the SZ. Klaus initially refused to accept this, but agreed to it in early January 2007. The abstention of two ČSSD deputies allowed the coalition to gain parliamentary support later that month.

Presidential elections in early 2008 were again protracted, with Klaus eventually defeating ČSSD candidate Jan Svejnar to secure a second term in office. The next set of Senate partial elections took place in October, after which the standings were: ODS 35, ČSSD 29, KDU–ČSL seven and other parties and independents 10.

Topolánek's Government was defeated in a vote of no confidence in the Chamber of Deputies on 24 March 2009. He immediately offered his resignation and on 28 March agreed with the opposition ČSSD that early elections should be held in October 2009. Coalition party leaders on 6 April nominated Jan **Fischer**, head of the Czech Statistical Office and of no political party, to be interim Prime Minister; Fischer took office on 8 May with a caretaker non-partisan cabinet comprising members nominated by the ODS, ČSSD and SZ. A Constitutional Court ruling subsequently forced the abandonment of the planned early elections, leaving the existing chamber to complete its full term not expiring until June 2010.

International relations and defence: The Czech Republic, as a new sovereign state, was admitted to the United Nations in 1993 and also joined the **Organization for Security and Co-operation in Europe**, the **Council of Europe**, the **Central European Initiative** and the **Central European Free Trade Area**, as well as the **Organisation for Economic Co-operation and Development** and the **World Trade Organization**. Having acceded to the **Partnership for Peace** programme in 1994, the Czech Republic became a full member of **NATO** (together with Hungary and **Poland**) in March 1999. Following its 1996 application for membership of the **European Union** (EU), the Czech Republic opened formal accession negotiations with the EU in March 1998, after the contentious issue of compensation for expelled Sudetenland Germans had been put aside in March 1997. An offer of membership was made in December 2002, in a major wave of EU expansion. It was supported by referendum in June 2003, and the Czech Republic acceded on 1 May 2004. In December 2007 the Czech Republic also joined the EU's Schengen Agreement, allowing free movement of citizens within the zone's borders. It is unlikely to join the **eurozone** before 2015 (*see* **Czech Republic, economy**).

A lengthy dispute with Slovakia over the division of assets of the former federation was finally resolved in May 2000, while later that year serious strains with Austria over a controversial new Czech nuclear plant at Temelín were eased, after the Government agreed to meet the recommendations of an EU safety assessment.

The Czech Republic's defence budget for 2008 amounted to some US \$3,165m., equivalent to about 1.5% of GDP. The size of the armed forces in 2010 was some 18,000 personnel; it has been a professional force since 2005.

Czech Republic, economy

Despite the strong industrial traditions of its **Bohemia** region in particular, and the country's apparently impressive initial progress in the transition from communist-era state control to a free-market system, the Czech Republic made only a slow and partial recovery from the economic problems that beset it in the latter part of the 1990s, and has struggled to find a route out of the more recent recession. It joined the **European Union** (EU) in 2004, but has not yet adopted the euro.

GNP: US $173,154m. (2008); *GNP per capita*: $16,600 (2008); *GDP at PPP*: $257,696m. (2008); *GDP per capita at PPP*: $24,700 (2008); *real GDP growth*: –2.2% (2009 estimate); *exports*: $145,921m. (2008); *imports*: $141,593m. (2008); *currency*: koruna (plural: koruny; US $1 = K18.5 in mid-2009); *unemployment*: 8.2% (end 2009); *government deficit as a percentage of GDP*: 6% (2009); *inflation*: 1.0% (2009).

In the Czech Republic, industry contributed 38% of GDP in 2007, agriculture 3% and services 59%. Around 40% of the workforce is engaged in industry, the highest proportion in the region; 4% work in agriculture and 56% in services.

Some 41% of the land is arable, 2% under permanent crops, 11% permanent pasture and 34% forests and woodland. The main crops are grain, potatoes, sugar beet, hops and fruit, while pigs, cattle and poultry are raised and forests are exploited.

The main mineral resources include both hard coal and soft coal (lignite). The principal industries are ferrous metallurgy, machinery and equipment, coal, motor industries and armaments. Tourism is an important element in the services sector. About 30% of energy requirements are provided through nuclear power generation.

Although landlocked, the Czech Republic's location on a strategic trans-European communications crossroads gives it a natural role as a centre of inter-regional trade. Its main exports are machinery and transport equipment, other manufactured goods and chemicals. Principal imports are machinery and transport equipment, other manufactured goods, chemicals and mineral fuels. The main destinations of the Czech Republic's exports in 2008 were Germany (30%), **Slovakia** (9%) and **Poland** (6%), while the main sources of imports were Germany (27%), the People's Republic of China (9%) and the Russian Federation (6%).

The Czech Republic emerged from the January 1993 division of **Czechoslovakia** stronger than **Slovakia** economically. Despite damaging new barriers to Czech-Slovak trade, by the end of 1995 the Czech economy was regarded as a success story of post-communist transition, with low inflation and unemployment rates combined with GDP growth of 6% in 1995 and apparent speedy progress towards a market economy. As a mark of the transformation, the Czech Republic in 1995 became the first post-communist state to be admitted to the **Organisation for Economic Co-operation and Development** (OECD) of the rich developed countries.

Privatization had started under the Czechoslovak regime, using an innovative system under which vouchers for prospective share ownership were issued to citizens (*see* **voucher privatization**). Almost all small and medium-sized enterprises passed into private ownership, while in 1995 the Government announced that certain major enterprises were also to be privatized, although the state would retain holdings. Pervasive domestic corruption tarnished the privatization process, however, with the result that economic efficiency was by no means enhanced. The post-1998 Government relaunched the process, which was extended to the banking sector. In 1999 a number of struggling Czech-owned companies were taken back into temporary state control. A new restructuring agency took over loans made by state-owned banks and sought foreign buyers for the companies.

Meanwhile, macroeconomic performance had begun to falter in 1996, as Western investment and weak corporate governance fuelled inflation and undermined the current account, so that the existing fixed exchange rate system became unmanageable. A crisis in May 1997, partly brought on by the Asian financial collapse, forced the Government to adopt a managed float of the previously pegged koruna and effectively to devalue the currency by 10%–12%. GDP growth was under 1% in 1997, when the position was worsened by massive floods over a third of the country, following which GDP contracted by 2.3% in 1998, as inflation rose to 13% and unemployment to over 8%.

GDP contracted further in 1999, by 0.5%, but inflation was reduced to 2.5%. Modest recovery then began, with annual GDP growth of around 2% in 2000–02, although unemployment remained high at around 9% and the budget deficit rose. At accession to the EU in May 2004, the deficit, equivalent to 5.6% of GDP in 2003, was the highest of any member state. The budget deficit was brought down to 1.9% of GDP by 2007 and below 1% in 2008, but rose in 2009 as the global downturn impacted economic activity and therefore tax revenues. This placed the Czech economy outside the convergence criteria for joining the **eurozone**, so the 2010 target for entry to the Exchange Rate Mechanism II has been postponed. It needs to be part of that mechanism for a minimum of two years before adopting the euro, which is now not expected before 2015.

Meanwhile, the strong koruna was helping to control inflation, and the banking sector was relatively healthy (the Czech Republic is one of the few OECD countries that has not had to recapitalize its banks), but global downturn nevertheless saw the overall economy shrink in the grip of recession, hit by a combination of reduced demand for its exports in the euro area, and reduced availability of credit domestically. Unemployment has risen, with rates particularly high in the coal and steel producing regions of Northern **Moravia** and Northern Bohemia. The economy is expected to stay in recession until demand for its exports recovers in Germany and other western European markets.

Czech Social Democratic Party
Česká Strana Sociálně Demokratická (ČSSD)

The leading left-wing party in the **Czech Republic**, a member party of the **Socialist International**. Founded in 1878 as an autonomous section of the Austrian labour movement, the ČSSD became an independent party in 1911. Following the creation of **Czechoslovakia** after the First World War, it won a quarter of the vote in the 1920 elections but was weakened by the exodus of its pro-Bolshevik wing in 1921. In 1938 the party was obliged to become part of the newly-created National Labour Party under the post-Munich system of 'authoritarian democracy'. When Hitler moved on to the further dismantling of Czechoslovakia in March 1939, the party went underground and was a member of the Government-in-exile in London during the Second World War. It participated in the post-war communist-dominated National Front but came under mounting pressure from the communists, who used the state security apparatus in a campaign to eliminate their main political rivals. In a political crisis in February 1948 the ČSSD was forced to merge with the Communist Party, and thereafter maintained its separate existence only in exile.

Following the collapse of communist rule in late 1989, the ČSSD was officially re-established in Czechoslovakia in March 1990, aspiring at that stage to be a 'Czechoslovak' party appealing to both **Czechs** and **Slovaks**. It failed to secure representation in the June 1990 elections, after which its Czech and Slovak wings in effect became separate parties, although 'Czechoslovak' remained its official descriptor. In the June 1992 elections the ČSSD won 16 seats in the 200-member Czech National Council and also secured representation in the Czech sections of both federal houses. It then mounted strong opposition to the proposed '**velvet divorce**' between Czechs and Slovaks, arguing in favour of a 'confederal union', but eventually accepting the inevitability of the separation. At its first post-separation congress in February 1993, the party formally renamed itself the Czech SSD and elected a new leadership under Miloš Zeman, who declared his aim as being to provide a left-wing alternative to the neo-conservatism of the Government led by the **Civic Democratic Party** (ODS), while at the same time ruling out co-operation with the **Communist Party of Bohemia and Moravia**.

The ČSSD made a major advance in the 1996 **Parliament** elections, winning 61 of the 200 Chamber of Deputies seats on a 26.4% vote share and becoming the second-strongest party. It opted to give qualified external support to a new centre-right coalition headed by the ODS, on the basis that privatization of the transport and energy sectors would be halted and that a Social Democrat would become Chairman (or Speaker) of the new lower house. Following the resignation of the Government in November 1997, the ČSSD became the largest party in early elections in June 1998, winning 74 of the lower house seats with 32.3% of the vote. Zeman therefore formed a minority ČSSD Government, which was given external support by the ODS under a so-called 'opposition agreement'.

119

In March 1999 the Zeman Government took the Czech Republic into the **North Atlantic Treaty Organization** (NATO) and in December secured official candidate status for **European Union** accession. It also continued the previous Government's pro-market liberalization policies, although a deteriorating economic situation eroded its support, as did allegations of illicit ČSSD funding.

In partial Senate elections in November 2000 the ČSSD won only one seat (its representation in the 81-member upper chamber falling to 15), while in simultaneous regional elections its vote slumped to 14.7%.

With Zeman having given notice that he would stand down as party leader before the elections due in 2002, his heir apparent, Deputy Chairman Vladimír Špidla, distanced himself from the accord with the ODS, advocating that the ČSSD should be 'free and without commitment' in the next electoral contest. Špidla was duly elected Chairman of the party on 7 April 2001.

At the June 2002 election the ČSSD remained the largest party, winning 70 seats and 30.2% of the vote. Špidla was duly invited to form a Government, and by mid-July he had reached agreement with the fourth-placed Coalition (an alliance of the **Christian Democratic Union–Czechoslovak People's Party** (KDU–ČSL) and the Freedom Union–Democratic Union, which controlled 31 seats).

Presidential elections to find a successor for Václav **Havel** began in January 2003, but had not succeeded by the time his term expired. Eventually, on 28 February, ODS candidate Václav **Klaus** was elected, defeating the Government's candidate, Jan Sokol.

A poor performance by the ČSSD in the country's first European Parliament elections in May 2004 led to a vote of confidence in Špidla's party leadership. He lost the vote 103:78, but a three-fifths majority was required to succeed in ousting him. However, this evident lack of support forced him to offer his resignation in late June from both the ČSSD leadership and post of Prime Minister. In August his deputy Stanislav Gross, who had become acting party leader, was appointed to head the new Government, but this change of leadership failed to save the party from an overwhelming defeat in the local elections and Senate partial elections in the autumn.

Allegations of financial impropriety emerged against Gross in early 2005, but he retained support within his party and was re-elected as party leader in March. However, the KDU–ČSL withdrew from the Government, leaving it in a minority. Pressure on Gross mounted, and he eventually resigned as Prime Minister on 25 April, succeeded by ČSSD deputy leader Jiří Paroubek. This change of Prime Minister soon brought the KDU–ČSL back into coalition.

Gross remained as party leader until September when Bohuslav Sobotka took over in an acting capacity. Then in May 2006 the party elected Paroubek to lead it into the June elections. Support for the ČSSD was rallying, but it managed only second place in the poll with 74 seats (32.3% of the vote), behind the ODS on 81 seats (35.4%). Political impasse ensued as the new Chamber of Deputies was equally divided between right-wing and left-wing blocs, so ODS leader Mirek Topolánek found it impossible to secure parliamentary support for a government. While this drama was playing itself out, the ODS gained control of the Senate at the October–November partial elections, with the ČSSD holding 12 seats. This strengthened Topolánek's position, and in early 2007 two ČSSD deputies agreed to abstain from the Chamber's vote on Topolánek's coalition in order to end the crisis.

Presidential elections in January–February 2008 were again protracted, with ČSSD candidate Jan Svejnar eventually losing to incumbent President Klaus. In the next set of Senate partial elections in October of that year, the ČSSD won 23 of the 27 seats being contested, improving its position to hold a total of 29 seats, and causing the ODS to lose its majority in the chamber.

Topolánek's Government was defeated in a vote of no confidence in the Chamber of Deputies on 24 March 2009. He immediately offered his resignation and on 28 March agreed with the opposition ČSSD that early elections should be held in October 2009.

Coalition party leaders on 6 April nominated Jan **Fischer**, head of the Czech Statistical Office and of no political party, to be interim Prime Minister; Fischer took office on 8 May with a caretaker non-partisan cabinet comprising members nominated by the ODS, ČSSD and SZ. A Constitutional Court ruling subsequently forced the abandonment of the planned early elections, leaving the existing Chamber to complete its full term in June 2010.

Leadership: Jiří Paroubek (Chair.).
Address: Lidový dům, Hybernská 7, 110 00 Prague 1.
Telephone: (2) 96522111.
Fax: (2) 96522237.
E-mail: info@socdem.cz
Internet: www.cssd.cz

CzechInvest
Česká Agentura pro Zahraniční Investice

Foreign investment agency in the **Czech Republic**. Founded in 1992.
Director: Tomáš Hruda.
Address: Štěpánská 15, 12000 Prague 2.
Telephone: (2) 96342500.
Fax: (2) 96342502.
E-mail: agentura@czechinvest.com
Internet: www.czechinvest.com

Czechoslovakia

A former unified state which divided formally into the **Czech Republic** and **Slovakia** on 1 January 1993. Czechoslovakia was first created as one of the successor states to the Habsburg Empire in November 1918 and was officially recognized by the international community in the Treaty of St Germain in September 1919. Containing the industrially important regions of **Bohemia** and **Moravia**, Czechoslovakia, with its capital at **Prague**, had an apparently bright future. However, ethnic tensions between the **Czechs, Slovaks** and other minorities (chiefly **Germans** and **Hungarians**) were exacerbated by the new centralized state. These rifts were successfully exploited by nationalist Governments in neighbouring Germany and **Hungary**. Its integrity fatally compromised by the Munich Agreement in 1938 (*see* **Sudetenland**), whereby Germany was allowed to annexe swathes of its territory, Czechoslovakia was reduced to a rump entity before and during the Second World War, under Nazi rule apart from a nominally independent Slovak collaborationist regime.

In 1945 a reconstituted Czechoslovakia (minus the 'tail' of Ruthenia which had been added from Hungarian territory under the 1920 Treaty of **Trianon**) became one of the key frontier states between western and **eastern Europe** (*see* **Potsdam Agreements** and **Yalta Agreements**). Under communist government from 1947, it attempted an experiment in liberalization—the **Prague Spring** of 1968—which was crushed by **Soviet**-led military intervention, but in 1989 the old regime was swept aside by one of the more dramatic of that year's wave of pro-democracy movements, a democratic Czechoslovakia emerging from what became known as the '**velvet revolution**'. Despite a federal-style Constitution, tensions between the Czech Lands and Slovakia quickly emerged thereafter, leading to the so-called '**velvet divorce**' and the final separation of the two modern states.

Czechs

A west **Slavic people** dominant in the modern **Czech Republic**. The Czechs had replaced the local Celtic and **German** tribes of **Bohemia** and **Moravia** by the fifth to sixth century and established the two respective kingdoms in following centuries. Like the other neighbouring west Slavs (**Slovaks** and **Poles**) the Czechs are traditionally **Roman Catholic** and use the Latin script to transcribe their language, which is very similar to Polish and almost identical to Slovak. As the most westerly of all Slavic states, the Czechs have perhaps the most 'western' identity of all the Slavs, and consider themselves very much to be a **central European** people. Tensions between Czechs and Slovaks, with whom they shared the state of **Czechoslovakia** after 1919, gained free expression after the collapse of communism and prompted the '**velvet divorce**' which left each with a separate state in 1993. Small communities of ethnic Czechs live throughout **eastern Europe**.

D

Dalmatia

The Adriatic coast of **Croatia** extending from Rijeka in the north to the **Prevlaka peninsula** in the south. The thin coastal strip, with its many nearby islands, is agriculturally rich and scenically beautiful. Separated from the **Balkan** hinterland by the Dinaric Alps, it has had a history distinct from that of the inland regions. Originally inhabited by Illyrians, Dalmatia felt the tread of over 30 different conquerors up to the 15th century when the area fell under the sway of the Venetian trading empire. It was part of the Habsburg Empire, apart from a nine-year period when it formed the coastal region of the Napoleonic Illyrian Provinces (1805–14), and was directly ruled from Vienna from 1879 to 1918. Under the post-1918 European peace settlement Dalmatia was reunited with the Croatian district of **Slavonia** and formed an integral part of Croatia within what was later named **Yugoslavia**.

Noted for the cultivation of vines and olives, Dalmatia also contains some rich deposits of bauxite and limestone, and the major tourist destinations of Split and **Dubrovnik** (although the vibrant tourist industry was greatly set back by the wars of the early 1990s). There are also some shipyards at Split and hydroelectric plants along the course of some of the fast-flowing Dalmatian rivers.

Danube Commission

A body set up in 1948 to supervise the implementation of the Convention on the Regime of Navigation on the River Danube. The Commission holds annual sessions, approves projects for river maintenance and supervises a uniform system of traffic regulations on the whole navigable portion of the Danube and on river inspection.

Members: Austria, **Bulgaria**, **Croatia**, Germany, **Hungary**, Moldova, **Romania**, Russian Federation, **Serbia**, **Slovakia** and Ukraine.
President: Aleksandr Tolkatch.
Director General: István Valkár.
Address: Benczúr utca 25, 1068 Budapest, Hungary.

> *Telephone*: (1) 4618010.
> *Fax*: (1) 3521839.
> *E-mail*: secretariat@danubecom-intern.org
> *Internet*: www.danubecommission.org

Danzig *see* **Gdańsk**.

Dayton Agreement

The November 1995 Agreement to end the conflict in **Bosnia and Herzegovina**. The Agreement, signed formally the following month in Paris, was named after the US town of Dayton, Ohio, where the so-called 'proximity talks' took place after the 5 October ceasefire. Its signatories were representatives of the Republic of Bosnia and Herzegovina (but not of the Bosnian **Serb** side in the war), the Republic of **Croatia** and the Federal Republic of **Yugoslavia** (FRY). It was witnessed by representatives of the **Contact Group** nations—the USA, the United Kingdom, France, Germany and the Russian Federation—and the **European Union** Special Negotiator.

The Dayton Peace Agreement consisted of a General Framework for Peace in Bosnia and Herzegovina (a brief document in which the signatories agreed to respect each other's sovereignty and to settle disputes by peaceful means, and under which the FRY and the Republic of Bosnia and Herzegovina recognized one another) and 11 annexes on the detailed issues. These included: the withdrawal of forces and the involvement of the multinational military Implementation Force (IFOR—*see* **Stabilization Force**); the definition of the boundary within Bosnia between the **Muslim-Croat Federation** and the **Serb Republic**; the arrangement of elections according to a prescribed timetable; the adoption of the new Constitution of Bosnia and Herzegovina; provisions on human rights and the right of return for refugees; and the creation of the **Office of the High Representative** to co-ordinate and facilitate civilian aspects of the peace settlement.

Democrat Party
Demokrat Parti (DP)

A nationalist **Turkish Cypriot** party in the self-proclaimed **Turkish Republic of Northern Cyprus** (TRNC), currently in opposition.

The DP was formed in 1992 by a dissident faction of the **National Unity Party** (UBP) favouring a somewhat more conciliatory line in inter-communal talks than the hard-line UBP leadership, and was joined by TRNC President Rauf **Denktaş**, previously a UBP member. In the 1993 Assembly elections, the DP came close to supplanting the UBP as the leading party, winning 15 of the 50 seats and taking the leadership of a majority coalition Government with the Republican Turkish Party (CTP, later renamed as **Republican Turkish Party–United Forces**, CTP-BG). In May 1996 the DP leadership was taken by Serdar Denktaş, son of the TRNC President, following which the DP formed a coalition with the UBP in which Serdar Denktaş became Deputy Prime Minister. In the 1998 Assembly elections the DP slipped to 13 seats and went into opposition until June 2001, when it joined another coalition with the UBP. In April 2003 the UBP-DP Government took the historic decision to allow freedom of movement across the ceasefire line.

Assembly elections in December 2003 reduced the DP to seven seats. Ending its coalition with the UBP, it entered instead a coalition with the CTP-BG committed to the accession of a reunified Cyprus to the **European Union** (EU). However, although Turkish Cypriot voters overwhelmingly approved a UN settlement plan in April 2004, its rejection by the **Greek Cypriots** meant that the occupied area was excluded from the EU when Cyprus joined in May 2004. In the wake of this debacle, early Assembly elections in February 2005 saw the DP slip to six seats (with 13.5% of the vote), but it continued as the junior coalition partner of the CTP-BG. In presidential polling in April 2005, to elect a successor to Rauf Denktaş, DP candidate Mustafa Arabacioglu came third with 13.2% of the vote.

Strains in the coalition, with the DP uneasy over the CTP-BG's conciliatory line on the reunification issue, resulted in the Government's collapse in September 2006 and the replacement of the DP as the CTP-BG's coalition partner by the new Freedom and Reform Party (ÖRP). DP leader Serdar Denktaş accused Turkey of orchestrating the change. His party's ouster from government meant that no Denktaş was in office for the first time since the creation of the breakaway Turkish Cypriot entity.

The DP won just five seats (with 10.7% of the vote) in the April 2009 TRNC Assembly elections.

Leadership: Serdar Denktaş (Chair.).
Address: 13/A Hasane İlgaz Street, Lefkoşa/Nicosia.
Telephone: +90-392-2287089.
Fax: +90-392-2287130.
E-mail: basin@demokratparti.net
Internet: www.demokratparti.net

Democratic League of Kosovo
Lidhja Demokratike e Kosovës (LDK)

A centre-right political party in **Kosovo**, currently in government, and a member of the **Centrist Democrat International**. The LDK succeeded the Democratic Alliance of Kosovo (DSK) in 2000 as the main ethnic **Albanian** party in **Yugoslavia/Serbia**, advocating independent status for the province of Kosovo.

The DSK was formed in 1989 after the Serbian Government ended Kosovo's autonomous status, thus provoking widespread ethnic Albanian protest against Serb rule. Calling for a negotiated settlement and officially opposing armed struggle, the DSK won a majority of seats in provincial assembly elections organized by Albanians in May 1992, with its leader Ibrahim Rugova being declared the 'President of Kosovo'. However, the elections were declared illegal by the Serbian and federal authorities and the Assembly was prevented from holding its inaugural session. Subsequent Serbian and federal elections were boycotted by the DSK.

Although Rugova and the DSK won large majorities in further presidential and assembly elections organized illegally in Kosovo in March 1998, he and his party appeared to be marginalized as conflict in the province intensified and the **Kosovo Liberation Army** (UÇK) came to the fore. Rugova continued to support a negotiated settlement, attracting criticism from ethnic Albanians when he appeared on television with President Slobodan **Milošević** in April 1999 (possibly under duress), soon after the start of the **North Atlantic Treaty Organization** bombardment of Serbia. He was also censured for departing to Italy for the rest of the conflict.

Following the withdrawal of Serb forces from Kosovo in June 1999 and Rugova's return a month later, the DSK recovered its status as the principal political representative of Kosovar Albanians. In August 1999 it joined the Kosovo Transitional Council set up by the new UN administration, thereafter working with the UN to promote inter-ethnic peace and reconciliation. On 1 February 2000 Rugova's alternative Government recognized the authority of the UN Interim Administration Mission in Kosovo (**UNMIK**). In October the party, renamed as the LDK, welcomed the ousting of the Milošević regime, although the successor Government of the **Democratic Opposition of Serbia** (DOS) was also resolutely opposed to independence for Kosovo. In municipal elections in Kosovo in the same month, the LDK obtained 58% of the vote and won control of 21 of the 30 municipalities at issue. Its success, however, was not welcomed by pro-independence groups, which launched a brief violent backlash that included the assassination of a close aide to Rugova in November. Tensions were quickly calmed but the party registered a slight drop in support in elections for the UN-sponsored regional Assembly a year later. It did nevertheless emerge as the largest single party, winning 47 seats and 46% of the vote. Rugova immediately angered the international community by making open calls after the LDK victory for the full independence of Kosovo. Repeated attempts in the Assembly to elect Rugova as President failed as the other parties boycotted the proceedings. Eventually inter-party negotiations enabled his election on 4 March 2002, while a power-sharing Government with the **Democratic Party of Kosovo** (PDK) was formed.

At the 23 October 2004 Assembly election, the LDK retained its 47 seats (with 45.4% of the vote) and remained the largest party. It formed a minority Government with the third-placed Alliance for the Future of Kosovo. Rugova was re-elected as President in December, but just over a year later, on 21 January 2006, he died of lung cancer. The LDK nominated Fatmir **Sejdiu** to succeed him, and the Assembly elected him unopposed on 10 February. Rugova's death caused a shift in the dynamics within the LDK. After Assembly Speaker Nexhat Daci and Deputy Prime Minister Adem Salihaj were removed from office in February and replaced by Sejdiu's supporters, a rift opened within the party between the two factions, and the vacant party leadership remained unfilled until December. Sejdiu won the eventual leadership contest, and in January 2007 Daci and his supporters left the LDK to form the Democratic League of Dardania.

This split, and the formation of a pro-business New Kosovo Alliance, greatly damaged the LDK's prospects ahead of the November 2007 Assembly elections. The party emerged in second place with just 25 seats and 22.6% of the vote. However, it negotiated to join the coalition of the winning PDK, and Sejdiu was re-elected by the Assembly as President in December. Two months later, the Government unilaterally declared Kosovo's independence.

Leadership: Fatmir Sejdiu (Chair.).
Address: Kompleksi Qafa, 10000 Pristina
Telephone: (38) 242242.
Fax: (38) 245305.
E-mail: ldk@ldk-kosova.eu
Internet: www.ldk-kosova.eu

Democratic Left Alliance
Sojusz Lewicy Demokratycznej (SLD)

The principal left-wing party in **Poland**, currently in opposition, descended from communist-era formations but now of democratic socialist orientation and affiliated to the **Socialist International**. The SLD was created prior to the 1991 elections as an alliance of Social Democracy of the Polish Republic (SdRP), the direct successor of the former ruling (communist) Polish United Workers' Party, and the All-Poland Alliance of Trade Unions (OPZZ), which was derived from the official federation of the communist era. Having won 60 seats in the Sejm (lower house of the **National Assembly**) in 1991, the SLD became the largest party in the September 1993 elections, with 171 seats and 20.4% of the vote, and formed a coalition Government with the **Polish People's Party** (PSL).

The PSL held the premiership until February 1995, when Józef Oleksy of the SLD/SdRP took the post. The then SdRP leader, Aleksander Kwaśniewski, was the successful SLD candidate in the November 1995 presidential elections, narrowly defeating incumbent Lech **Wałęsa** with the support of over 30 other groupings. In February 1996 Oleksy was replaced as Prime Minister by Włodzimierz Cimoszewicz, an adherent of the SLD but not of any of its constituent parts.

In the September 1997 parliamentary elections the SLD increased its share of the vote to 27.1%, but its lower house representation fell to 164 seats, well below the total achieved by the new centre-right Solidarity Electoral Action (AWS). The SLD therefore went into opposition, taking some consolation from a strong performance in local elections in October 1998, when its 32% vote share gave it control of nine of the country's 16 voivodships.

Having supported Poland's accession to the **North Atlantic Treaty Organization** (NATO) in March 1999, the SLD formally established itself as a unitary party two months later, this being followed by the dissolution of the SdRP in June. At the first congress of the new SLD in December 1999, former Interior Minister Leszek **Miller** was elected Chairman and the party undertook to support pro-market reforms but in a way that would soften their impact on the population. The party also reiterated its strong support for Polish accession to the **European Union** (EU).

Benefiting from the unpopularity of the AWS-led Government, the SLD secured the re-election of Kwaśniewski in presidential elections in October 2000, his outright first-round victory being achieved with 54% of the vote. The SLD went on to achieve a massive victory in legislative elections on 23 September 2001 in partnership with the Labour Union (UP), collectively securing 216 seats in the 460-seat Sejm. Miller was nominated as Prime Minister and again formed a coalition Government with the PSL, along with the UP.

In March 2003 Miller ejected the PSL after it refused to support his Government's tax plans. The resultant minority Government struggled on, gaining the support of the Peasant Democratic Party (until January 2004) though even this left it 13 seats short of a majority in the Sejm. Internal divisions within the SLD forced Miller to announce in January 2004 that he would step down as party leader, but remain as Prime Minister to focus on EU accession, scheduled for 1 May. At the party congress in March Krzysztof Janik was elected as Chairman. None the less, in late March more than 20 SLD deputies, led by Marek Borowski, announced their defection to form **Polish Social Democracy** (SDPL); subsequently, Miller announced that he would resign as Prime Minister on 2 May, the day after Poland's EU accession. Former Finance Minister Marek Belka, an independent, was nominated to succeed him, heading a Government of SLD/UP members and independents, with support from the SDPL. The Sejm initially rejected Belka's nomination on 14 May, raising the possibility that early elections would be needed, but it endorsed him at a second nomination vote on 24 June.

In December 2004 Józef Oleksy was elected Chairman of the SLD. Janik and his supporters responded by announcing that they would form an opposition faction within the party. Meanwhile, Oleksy was accused of having concealed his collaboration with the communist-era military intelligence services. In February 2005 Deputy Prime Minister and Economy Minister Jerzy Hausner resigned from the SLD, and announced plans for a new centrist **Democratic Party** (PD). In May Wojciech Olejniczak replaced Oleksy as Chairman of the SLD.

Prime Minister Belka remained in office until the September 2005 elections, despite the difficulties of minority rule, and the internal divisions of the SLD: he offered his resignation to President Kwaśniewski in May 2005, but it was refused.

Unsurprisingly the SLD was defeated at the September 2005 election by the ascendant centre-right parties. It finished in fourth place, with 11% of the vote, 55 Sejm seats and no seats in the Senat (upper house). It went into opposition, and in September 2006 formed a centre-left alliance **Left and Democrats** (LiD) with the SDPL, UP and PD, initially just to contest local elections. In early 2007 a common policy programme was devised, and the SLD candidates in the early legislative elections held in October 2007 stood under the LiD banner. The alliance achieved 13% of the vote, but only 53 Sejm seats (40 of which were SLD or SLD-affiliated candidates). The SLD questioned whether in fact it would have scored better standing alone. Over the next few months, policy differences strained relations with the PD, and in March 2008 Olejniczak, who had formerly been staunchly in favour of the LiD alliance, announced that the SLD would no longer co-operate with the PD. This, coupled with tensions between the SLD and its splinter SDPL, led to the dissolution of the LiD shortly thereafter, though the 40 SLD-affiliated Sejm members and two of the SDPL Sejm members remained in alliance as The Left. Olejniczak's actions were perhaps an attempt to reassert his leadership of the SLD, but nevertheless at the May–June party congress LiD-sceptic Grzegorz Napieralski defeated Olejniczak in the election for party Chairman.

Leadership: Grzegorz Napieralski (Chair.).
Address: ul. Rozbrat 44A, 00-419 Warsaw.
Telephone: (22) 6210341.
Fax: (22) 6216069.
E-mail: rk@sld.org.pl
Internet: www.sld.org.pl

Democratic Liberal Party
Partidul Democrat-Liberal (PD-L)

A centre-right political party in **Romania**, formed on 15 December 2007 by the merger of the Democratic Party (PD) and the smaller Liberal Democratic Party (PLD). It became the largest party in both chambers of **Parliament** at the November 2008 election, and heads the ruling coalition.

The Democratic Party was historically a centre-left party, descended from the less successful of two factions that emerged within the National Salvation Front (FSN) after it assumed power following the overthrow of the **Ceauşescu** regime in December 1989. Most FSN leaders had previously been members of the communist **nomenklatura**. Having won landslide victories in the 1990 presidential and parliamentary elections, however, the FSN became divided between those favouring rapid transition to a market economy and President Ion Iliescu's more cautious approach. In March 1991 an FSN conference, against the vote of the Iliescu faction, approved radical free-market reforms tabled by the then Prime Minister Petre Roman. When Roman was re-elected FSN leader in March 1992 (having vacated the premiership the previous October), the Iliescu faction broke away to form a new left-wing party which later became the core of the Social Democracy Party of Romania (PDSR). The rump pro-market FSN fared badly in the autumn 1992 presidential election, obtaining only 4.8% for its candidate, but in the simultaneous parliamentary elections it won 43 seats in the House of Deputies (lower house of Parliament) on a vote share of over 10%. The following year it adopted Democratic Party as a prefix in its title and quickly became known as the PD.

The PD contested the November 1996 elections within the Social Democratic Union (USD) alliance with the Romanian Social Democratic Party (PSDR), Roman coming third in the presidential contest with 20.5% of the vote and the PD again winning 43 House seats in its own right. The PD joined the subsequent coalition Government headed by the centre-right Christian Democratic National Peasants' Party (PNȚCD) as the leading component of the Democratic Convention of Romania (CDR), left it in February 1998 and rejoined it two months later when a new Prime Minister was appointed, but continued thereafter to have strained relations with the other coalition parties.

Whereas the PSDR opted to join Iliescu's PDSR in the Social Democratic Pole of Romania for the November–December 2000 elections and was therefore on the winning side, the PD was damaged by its participation in a deeply unpopular Government. Roman sank to sixth place, winning less than 3% of the vote, in the first round of the presidential contest, whereupon the PD backed Iliescu in his second-round victory over the leader of the far-right Greater Romania Party. In the House elections the PD avoided the wipe-out experienced by the CDR parties, but was reduced to 31 seats and 7% of the vote. It thereafter gave qualified external support to a PDSR minority Government, while becoming preoccupied with an internal power struggle between Roman and his would-be successors. Mayor of **Bucharest** Traian **Băsescu** became the new PD leader in May 2001, and Roman eventually broke away from the party in 2003.

In the run-up to the November 2004 elections, the PD joined with the **National Liberal Party** (PNL) to form the Justice and Truth Alliance (ADA). It finished in second place with 112 seats in the House of Deputies (64 PNL, 48 PD—with 31.5% of the vote), and 49 seats in the Senate (31.8% of the vote). Băsescu stood as ADA candidate in the presidential election, winning 33.9% in the first round, and then overtaking incumbent Social Democrat Prime Minister Adrian Năstase in the second round with 51.2% to Năstase's 48.8%. On taking office, Băsescu was required to suspend his party membership, and Emil **Boc** succeeded him as party leader. Băsescu nominated PNL President Călin Popescu-Tăriceanu as Prime Minister, and he succeeded in negotiating a coalition Government between his PNL, the PD, the

Hungarian Democratic Union of Romania (UDMR) and the Humanist Party of Romania (PUR), even though the latter had contested the election in alliance with the **Social Democratic Party** (PSD). In the early months of 2007 tensions rose between President Băsescu and Prime Minister Popescu-Tăriceanu, reaching a head at the start of April when the PD was ejected from the ruling coalition.

Meanwhile, Boc had led the PD towards a more centrist political stance, favouring pro-market economic policies. In December 2007 it merged with Theodor Stolojan's Liberal Democratic Party, which had splintered from the PNL in 2006. The new centre-right party was named the Democratic Liberal Party. In the November 2008 elections, it won 115 seats in the House of Deputies (with 32.4% of the vote), just one more seat than the alliance of the PSD and the **Conservative Party** (PC—formerly known as the PUR), which actually had won a slightly larger 33.1% of the vote. In the simultaneous Senate election the PD-L won 51 of the 137 seats (33.6% of the vote).

On 10 December Stolojan was nominated as Prime Minister, but he resigned the mandate within days, and Boc was nominated in his place. On 18 December Parliament approved a coalition Government between the PD-L and the PSD, which took office four days later.

The withdrawal of the PSD on 1 October 2009 in protest over the dismissal three days earlier of its Interior Minister led to the Government's defeat in a confidence vote 12 days later. Lucian Croitoru, a politically independent economist, and Liviu Negoita of the PD-L were each in turn nominated to form a cabinet but both were unsuccessful, and on 17 December Boc was again nominated as Prime Minister. His new Government was a coalition of the PD-L and the UDMR, with five independents also included, and was approved by Parliament on 23 December.

Leadership: Emil Boc (President).
Address: Aleea Modrogan 1, 011825 Bucharest 1.
Telephone: (21) 2303701.
Fax: (21) 2301625.
E-mail: office@pd.ro
Internet: www.pd-l.ro

Democratic Opposition of Serbia
Demokratska Opozicija Srbije (DOS)

The broad alliance of parties in the **Yugoslav** republic of **Serbia** which defeated the **Milošević** regime in the 2000 elections. The DOS was launched in early 2000 in the wake of the 1999 **Kosovo** crisis as a broad-based alliance of parties and groups seeking the removal of Slobodan Milošević from power and an end to the dominance of his **Socialist Party of Serbia** (SPS). The alliance eventually embraced 19 parties and organizations, including the nationalist **Democratic Party** (DS) and **Democratic Party of Serbia** (DSS), the radical liberal Civic Alliance of Serbia (GSS), the pro-business New Democracy (ND), the centrist Christian Democratic Party of Serbia and Democratic Centre, the centre-left Social Democratic Union and Social Democracy, four parties representing ethnic **Hungarians** in **Vojvodina** and the **Muslim**/ethnic **Albanian** Party of Democratic Action (SDA).

The DOS candidate for the September 2000 federal presidential elections was Vojislav **Koštunica** of the DSS, regarded as the most right-wing of the alliance components. Despite widespread intimidation and vote-rigging, Koštunica was widely believed to have obtained an outright first-round victory over Milošević. Attempts by the regime to resist the democratic verdict prompted a DOS-orchestrated national uprising, which forced Milošević to hand over power in early October. Concurrent Federal Assembly elections, regarded by observers as equally flawed, resulted officially in the DOS alliance winning 58 of the 138 seats in the lower house.

Inaugurated as Federal President, Koštunica appointed Zoran Žižić of the **Socialist People's Party of Montenegro** (SNPCG) as Federal Prime Minister, heading a transitional Government which consisted mainly of DOS representatives. In elections to the Serbian **National Assembly** in December 2000, the DOS alliance displayed its true popular support by winning 176 of the 250 seats with a 64.1% vote share. A new Serbian Government appointed in January 2001 was headed by DS leader Zoran Ðinđić and included representatives of all of the main DOS components.

The coming to power of the DOS and Koštunica was warmly welcomed by the international community, although the new President made it clear that his administration would be nationalist in orientation, notably in that it would resist any move to detach Kosovo from Serbia and would not co-operate with the **International Criminal Tribunal for the former Yugoslavia** (ICTY) in its pursuit of Yugoslavs indicted for alleged crimes, including Milošević. He also came out strongly in favour of maintenance of Serbia's federation with **Montenegro** and against the latter's moves towards independence.

Despite being in government, the alliance continued to use the DOS appellation pending a possible decision to adopt a more appropriate title and/or to create a unitary movement. Meanwhile, the component parties and organizations all maintained their individual identities and structures. This loose framework proved increasingly fragile, with clashes between the constitutionally weak Koštunica and the reform-minded Ðinđić, sparked by the latter's unilateral decision to extradite Milošević in June 2001. The DOS only narrowly voted to remain intact at an internal vote held in August, but lost the support of the DSS, which withdrew from the Serbian Government on 17 August, claiming disappointment at the Government's record on fighting crime. Disputes between DOS factions continued, not helped by ongoing pressure from the USA for greater co-operation with the ICTY, and in June 2002 the DSS boycotted the Serbian National Assembly after 21 of its deputies were expelled. It was soon also expelled from the DOS coalition. In November 2003 two small parties withdrew from the DOS coalition, causing it to lose its majority in the Serbian National Assembly. This brought the coalition to the end of its workable life, and it soon broke up.

Democratic Party (Cyprus)
Dimokratiko Komma (DIKO)

A centre-right **Greek Cypriot** party in **Cyprus**, currently in the ruling coalition. DIKO was founded in 1976 as the Democratic Front, which supported President **Makarios**'s struggle against the Turkish occupation of northern Cyprus. It became the largest party in the 1976 parliamentary elections, in an alliance which included the (left-wing) **Progressive Party for the Working People** (AKEL) and what later became the **Movement of Social Democrats EDEK**. Having succeeded Makarios as President on the latter's death in 1977, DIKO leader Spyros Kyprianou was elected unopposed in his own right in 1978 and re-elected in 1983. Meanwhile, DIKO had been weakened by defections and its parliamentary representation had slumped in the 1981 elections. It recovered in 1985, but since 1991 it has been the third party behind AKEL and the conservative **Democratic Rally** (DISY).

Kyprianou failed to obtain a third presidential term in 1988, following which DIKO mounted strong opposition to the policies of the new AKEL-endorsed independent President, George Vassiliou. It was strengthened in 1989 when it absorbed the small Centre Union led by Tassos Papadopoulos, subsequently forming a tactical alliance with EDEK to oppose the 1992 UN plan for Cyprus on the grounds that it formalized the island's partition. In the 1993 presidential elections, DIKO and EDEK presented a joint candidate, Paschalis Paschalides, who was eliminated in the first round. In the second, DIKO backed Glafcos Clerides (DISY), who won a narrow victory over Vassiliou and included DIKO in the new Government.

The 1998 presidential elections occasioned serious divisions within DIKO, which officially joined with AKEL to back the independent candidacy of George Iacovou, who was narrowly defeated in the second round by Clerides. DIKO dissidents were included in the new Government. In October 2000 Kyprianou was succeeded as DIKO leader by Papadopoulos, an outspoken critic of the Government's conduct of UN-sponsored talks on Cyprus. He was the surprise outright victor of the February 2003 presidential elections, winning 51.5% in the first round as the joint candidate of DIKO, AKEL and EDEK, which formed the new coalition Government. A speedy success was the signature in April 2003 of a treaty with the **European Union** (EU) providing for accession in May 2004. Thereafter, Papadopoulos and DIKO led opposition to a UN plan for a Cyprus settlement in advance of EU accession, securing the support of 75.8% of Greek Cypriot voters in a referendum in April 2004. In parliamentary elections in May 2006, DIKO advanced from nine to 11 seats out of 56 with 17.9% of the vote. Having stood down as DIKO leader, Papadopoulos was succeeded in October 2006 by Marios Karoyian.

Papadopoulos failed in his bid for re-election as President in February 2008, finishing a close third in the first round with 31.8% of the vote. In the run-off DIKO supported the successful candidacy of AKEL General Secretary Dimitris **Christofias**, and the party was then included in Christofias's new Government.

Leadership: Marios Karoyian (President).
Address: 50 Grivas Dhigenis Ave, PO Box 23979, 1080 Nicosia.
Telephone: (22) 873800.
Fax: (22) 873801.
E-mail: diko@diko.org.cy
Internet: www.diko.org.cy

Democratic Party (Poland)
Partia Demokratyczna (PD)

A liberal centrist political party in **Poland**, currently in opposition, which contested the 2007 election as part of the **Left and Democrats** (LiD) alliance. The PD was founded in May 2005 by former Prime Minister Tadeusz Mazowiecki, Jerzy Hausner, formerly of the **Democratic Left Alliance** (SLD), and Władysław Frasyniuk, Chairman of the Freedom Union (UW). It is the legal successor to the UW.

The UW had itself been founded in 1994 by the merger of the Democratic Union (UD, created to support Mazowiecki's unsuccessful presidential candidacy in 1990) and the smaller pro-privatization Liberal Democratic Congress (KLD), founded in 1990 under the leadership of journalist Donald **Tusk**. The UW candidate Jacek Kuron came third in the 1995 presidential elections and the party advanced to 13.4% and 60 seats in the Sejm (lower house) in the 1997 legislative elections, opting (after some hesitation) to join a centre-right coalition Government headed by Solidarity Electoral Action (AWS). The UW left this Government in June 2000, however, as its leader Balcerowicz's reform proposals as Finance Minister were rejected by the more populist elements of the AWS. The UW did not present a candidate in the October 2000 presidential election. In December 2000 Balcerowicz was appointed as President of the **National Bank of Poland** and was succeeded as UW Chairman by former Foreign Minister Bronisław Geremek. In January 2001 the UW was weakened when Tusk and other prominent centrist politicians formed the **Civic Platform** (PO), which was joined by a substantial number of UW members. The UW's fortunes slipped further as the PO soaked up its electoral support. The UW received only 3.1% of the vote in the September 2001 legislative elections, falling below the 5% threshold for representation in the Sejm (lower house). Geremek resigned as UW Chairman soon after this defeat and was replaced by Władysław Frasyniuk.

The formation of the PD was based on an agreement in February 2005 between Frasyniuk, Mazowiecki and Hausner, who agreed that it should be a centrist party with a pro-market and pro-European platform. The party held its first congress in May 2005. There were rumours at this time that Prime Minister Marek Belka, the non-party head of the SLD minority Government, was considering joining the new party. However, it only won 2.5% of the vote at the September election, failing to reach the 5% threshold for representation in the Sejm. Following this defeat, Janusz

Onyszkiewicz, Vice-President of the European Parliament, was elected as party Chairman at the second congress in March 2006, replacing Frasyniuk.

In September 2006 the PD joined the centre-left LiD alliance with the SLD, SDPL and UP, initially just to contest local elections. In early 2007 a common policy programme was devised, and the PD candidates in the early legislative elections held in October 2007 stood under the LiD banner. The alliance achieved 13% of the vote, and 53 Sejm seats (three of which were PD or PD-affiliated candidates). The uneasy collaboration of the centrist PD with centre-left and left-wing parties was a key factor in the LiD's dissolution in March–April 2008.

Leadership: Janusz Onyszkiewicz (Chair.).
Address: ul. Marszałkowska 77/79, 00-683 Warsaw.
Telephone: (22) 3355800.
Fax: (22) 3355817.
E-mail: sekretariat@demokraci.pl
Internet: www.demokraci.pl

Democratic Party (Serbia)
Demokratska Stranka (DS)

A pro-European social-democratic political party in **Serbia**, currently holding the presidency and heading the Government, and a member of the **Socialist International**. Founded in 1990 as **Serbia**'s first opposition party under the leadership of prominent academic Dragoljub Mićunović, the DS adopted a right-wing nationalistic programme and advocated Serbian intervention in support of Serb separatists in **Bosnia and Herzegovina**. Nevertheless, its even more ultra-nationalist wing broke away in 1992 to form the **Democratic Party of Serbia** (DSS). Having won five lower house seats in **Yugoslavia**'s December 1992 Federal Assembly elections, the DS advanced to 29 seats in the Serbian **National Assembly** elections in December 1993. Abandoning for the time being its opposition stance, it then joined a coalition Government headed by Slobodan **Milošević**'s **Socialist Party of Serbia** (SPS). In January 1994 Mićunović was succeeded as DS Chairman by Zoran Đinđić, then Mayor of **Belgrade**.

The DS reverted to opposition in 1996, joining the Zajedno (Together) alliance with the DSS, the Serbian Renewal Movement (SPO) and the Civic Alliance of Serbia, which won only 22 lower house seats in the November 1996 federal Yugoslav elections. The alliance collapsed in mid-1997 when Đinđić refused to back the SPO leader as opposition candidate for the Serbian presidency, the SPO retaliating by helping to eject the DS leader from the Belgrade mayoralty. The DS then boycotted the Serbian National Assembly elections in September 1997 in protest against media manipulation by the Milošević regime.

In late 1998 the DS joined a new opposition grouping called the Alliance for Change, which formed the core of the anti-Milošević **Democratic Opposition of Serbia** (DOS) alliance launched in January 2000. The eventual victory of the DOS candidate, Vojislav **Koštunica** of the DSS, in the September 2000 federal presidential elections resulted in DS representatives joining the Federal Government. Moreover, following a landslide DOS victory in Serbian National Assembly elections in December 2000, Đinđić was appointed Prime Minister of the Serbian Government in January 2001.

On 12 March 2003 Đinđić was assassinated, and fellow DS-member Zoran Živković succeeded him as Prime Minister six days later. In November the DOS coalition lost its majority in the Serbian National Assembly and broke up; early elections were called. A DS-led coalition won 37 seats (12.6%), putting it in third place behind the **Serbian Radical Party** (SRS) and Koštunica's DSS-led coalition. It did not join the Government formed by Koštunica.

In June 2004 the new DS leader Boris **Tadić** won the Serbian presidential election, defeating SRS candidate Tomislav Nikolić in the run-off.

Following the secession of Montenegro in June 2006, Tadić called early elections for January 2007. This time the DS won 64 seats (22.7%). Although the SRS headed the poll, the DS as the second-largest party played a key role in lengthy coalition talks to find a formula to keep the radicals out of power. Its participation in a Government led by Koštunica as Prime Minister, as eventually agreed on 11 May, could not mask the deteriorating relations between Tadić (whose key priority was Serbia's accession to the EU) and Koštunica (whose key priority was to retain the UN-administered province of **Kosovo** as part of Serbia). In the 2008 presidential election run-off, Koštunica refused to back Tadić against SRS leader Nikolić, but Tadić emerged with 50.3% of the vote, and was inaugurated for a second term on 15 February. Kosovo seceded two days later.

On 8 March 2008 Koštunica resigned and early elections were called for May. The DS-led coalition **For a European Serbia—Boris Tadić** (ZES), with its pro-European appeal boosted by the signature on 29 April of a Stabilization and Association Agreement with the EU, won 102 seats with 38.4% of the vote. On 28 June Tadić nominated Mirko **Cvetković** of the DS as Prime Minister. His new Council of Ministers, a coalition of the ZES, SPS, Party of United Pensioners of Serbia and some minority parties, was approved by the Assembly on 7 July 2008.

Leadership Boris Tadić (President).

Address: Krunska 69, 11000 Belgrade.

Telephone: (11) 3443003.

Fax: (11) 2444864.

E-mail: info@ds.org.rs

Internet: www.ds.org.rs

Democratic Party of Albania
Partia Demokratike e Shqipërisë (PDSh)

The main centre-right pro-market political party in **Albania**, heading the current Government, and a member of the **International Democrat Union** and the **Centrist Democrat International**. Founded in December 1990 and based primarily in northern Albania, the PDSh was the first authorized opposition party to emerge in the post-communist era. It was descended from a movement of dissident intellectuals seeking to undermine communist rule from within. Led by cardiologist Sali Berisha, the PDSh won 75 of 250 **People's Assembly** seats in the March–April 1991 elections, subsequently joining a 'non-partisan' Government with the **Socialist Party of Albania** (PSSh). Complaining about the slow pace of reform, the PDSh withdrew from this Government in December 1991. Its breakthrough to political dominance came shortly thereafter, when the party won 92 out of 140 Assembly seats in the March 1992 election, with 62.8% of the first-round vote. The following month Berisha was elected President of Albania (and was succeeded as PDSh Chairman by Eduard Selami), whereupon Aleksander Meksi of the PDSh became Prime Minister in a coalition with the small **Social Democratic Party of Albania** (PSDSh).

The rejection in November 1994 of a draft constitution proposed by the PDSh-led coalition was accompanied by charges that Berisha was seeking to increase presidential powers at the expense of the People's Assembly. At a special PDSh conference in March 1995 Selami was deposed from the chairmanship, having opposed Berisha's plan to hold another constitutional referendum. In March 1996 the pro-Berisha Tritan Shehu was appointed PDSh Chairman, while a month later Selami and a group of supporters were ousted from the party's national council. In the controversial People's Assembly elections of May–June 1996 the PDSh won 122 of the 140 seats, but the descent into near anarchy and north–south conflict early in 1997 forced the PDSh to surrender the premiership to the PSSh in March. In new People's Assembly elections in June–July 1997 the PDSh slumped to 29 seats out of 155 (and 25.7% of the vote), whereupon Berisha vacated the presidency and the party went into opposition to a Government led by Fatos Nano of the PSSh.

The shooting of a PDSh deputy by a PSSh member in September 1997 provoked a PDSh boycott of the Assembly which was to last, with short intervals of participation, for nearly two years. The murder of prominent PDSh deputy Azem Hajdari in September 1998 produced a new crisis in which Berisha and the PDSh were accused of attempting a coup in **Tirana**. The resignation of Nano at the end of September was welcomed by Berisha, who gave qualified support to the new Government of Pandeli Majko (PSSh). New strains developed over the PDSh boycott of a constitutional referendum in November 1998 and its rejection of the result on the grounds of low turnout. However, from March 1999 the PDSh gave general backing to the Government's line on the **NATO–Yugoslavia** hostilities over **Kosovo**, and in July it called off its latest boycott of the Assembly.

In September 1999 the then PDSh parliamentary leader Genc Pollo called on the centre-right opposition parties to unite under PDSh leadership. At a party congress the following month, however, Pollo failed to unseat Berisha, who was re-elected PDSh Chairman unopposed following a purge of moderate members of the party executive. The moderates subsequently regrouped within the party as the Democratic Alternative, which attracted the support of eight PDSh parliamentary deputies. Tensions within the party between Berisha and Pollo came to a head in February 2001 when Pollo created a splinter party, which became the New Democrat Party (PDR) and contested the June elections on a separate ticket.

The PDSh had suffered major reverses in local elections in October 2000, winning only a third of the vote and losing control of Tirana to the PSSh. It improved its share of the vote at the June 2001 elections, however, receiving 46 seats at the head of the Union for Victory coalition, despite the existence of the splinter PD. The PDSh hotly contested the final results, declaring them 'farcical' and beginning a boycott of the People's Assembly that lasted for several months.

At the 3 July 2005 People's Assembly election the PDSh won 56 seats, while its allies secured a further 24 seats, giving Berisha control of 80 out of 140 seats. On 2 September he was nominated as Prime Minister, and a Government of the PDSh, the Republican Party of Albania (PRSh), the PDR, the Environmentalist Agrarian Party (PAA) and the Human Rights Union Party (PBDNj) was approved on 10 September. (In July 2006 the Christian Democratic Party of Albania also joined the Government.)

In 2007 the PDSh nominated Bamir **Topi** to be the next President, without consulting the opposition. The PSSh boycotted the repeated ballots, leaving Topi just short of the three-fifths of the vote required to secure election. Only at the fourth attempt (of a constitutionally possible five before the People's Assembly would have had to be dissolved) did a few Assembly members break the boycott to end the stalemate. Topi was sworn in four days later, on 24 July.

At the 28 June 2009 People's Assembly election, the PDSh-led Alliance for Changes won 70 seats and 46.9% of the vote (PDSh 68; PRSh one; Party for Justice and Integration one; 13 others including PAA none). One seat short of a majority, the PDSh-led Alliance found itself looking for a coalition partner from among its left-wing opponents. Berisha negotiated a coalition with the Socialist Movement for Integration (LSI), and his new cabinet was approved by the People's Assembly on 16 September.

Leadership: Sali Berisha (Chair.).
Address: Rruga Punëtorët e Rilindjes, 1001 Tirana.
Telephone: (4) 2228091.
Fax: (4) 2223525.
E-mail: info@pd.al
Internet: www.pd.al

Democratic Party of Kosovo
Partia Demokratike e Kosovës (PDK)

A centre-left political party in **Kosovo**, currently in government. The PDK emerged from the political wing of the **Kosovo Liberation Army** (UÇK) in September– October 1999, offering a more radical agenda than the existing main ethnic **Albanian** party, the **Democratic League of Kosovo** (LDK), but pursuing the same ultimate goal of independence for the province of Kosovo from **Yugoslavia/Serbia**.

In March 1999 UÇK leader Hashim **Thaçi** had been appointed 'Prime Minister' of the UÇK's provisional Government. He formed the new party a few months later (initially called the Party of Democratic Progress in Kosovo until May 2000), and in February 2000 the provisional Government was disbanded, Thaçi instead recognizing the authority of the UN Interim Administration Mission in Kosovo (**UNMIK**).

The PDK's first participation in the political process was at municipal elections in October 2000, when it achieved a 27% vote share and gained control of six of the 30 municipalities at issue. Its popularity remained stable the following year when it won 25.7% of the vote (and 26 seats) in the November 2001 elections for the UN-sponsored **Assembly**. With the leading LDK unable to negotiate a coalition with any of its rivals, agreement was reached in March to form a power-sharing Government with LDK leader Ibrahim Rugova as President and Bajram Rexhepi of the PDK as Prime Minister.

At the October 2004 Assembly election, the PDK share of the vote rose to 28.9% and it won 30 seats, but it lost its role in government as the LDK formed a coalition with the Alliance for the Future of Kosovo. However, at the November 2007 election, the PDK overtook the LDK, winning 37 seats (with 34.3% of the vote). The two parties formed the expected, if uncomfortable, grand coalition in January 2008, with PDK leader Hashim Thaçi becoming Prime Minister. He issued Kosovo's declaration of independence from Serbia the following month.

Leadership: Hashim Thaçi (Chair.).
Address: Rruga Nënë Terezë 20, 10000 Pristina.
Telephone: (44) 156774.
E-mail: pdk@pdk-ks.org
Internet:. www.pdk-ks.org

Democratic Party of Serbia
Demokratska Stranka Srbije (DSS)

A nationalist, centre-right political party in **Serbia**, currently in opposition, and member of the **International Democrat Union** and the **Alliance of Democrats**. It first entered federal government in **Yugoslavia** upon the fall of Slobodan **Milošević** in late 2000 as a leading component of the **Democratic Opposition of Serbia** (DOS), and featured in various Yugoslav and Serbian coalition governments until 2008.

Founded in 1992 by a right-wing faction of the **Democratic Party** (DS), the DSS contested the December 1992 **Federal Assembly** elections as part of the DEPOS opposition alliance, which won 20 lower house seats. In the December 1993 Serbian **National Assembly** elections, the DSS won seven seats in its own right, remaining in opposition. It subsequently joined the Zajedno (Together) alliance with the DS, the Serbian Renewal Movement (SPO) and the Civic Alliance of Serbia, which won 22 lower house seats in the November 1996 federal elections. The party joined the DS in boycotting the Serbian National Assembly elections in September 1997 in protest against media manipulation by the **Milošević** regime.

In late 1998 the DSS joined a new opposition grouping called the Alliance for Change, which formed the core of the anti-Milošević DOS alliance launched in January 2000. The eventual victory of DSS founder and DOS candidate Vojislav **Koštunica** in the September 2000 federal presidential elections resulted in DSS representatives joining the Federal Government. Following a landslide DOS victory in Serbian National Assembly elections in December 2000, the DSS was strongly represented in the resultant Serbian Government headed by the DS Chairman, Zoran Đinđić. However, clashes between Koštunica and Đinđić drove a wedge between the DSS and the DS, prompting the DSS to withdraw from the Serbian Government altogether on 17 August 2001, officially in protest at the Government's failure to tackle rising crime levels. Disputes between DOS factions continued, not helped by ongoing pressure from the USA for greater co-operation with the International Criminal Tribunal for the former Yugoslavia, and in June 2002 the DSS boycotted the Serbian National Assembly after 21 of its deputies were expelled. It was soon also expelled from the DOS coalition.

The DSS contested early elections for the Serbian National Assembly in December 2003 in coalition with the People's Democratic Party, the Serbian Liberal Party and the Serbian Democratic Party. This DSS-led coalition finished second with 53 seats (on 17.7% of the vote), behind the ultra-nationalist **Serbian Radical Party** (SRS). A general desire to keep the SRS from power enabled Koštunica to form a minority coalition of his DSS with **G17 Plus**, the SPO, and New Serbia (NS), with external support—surprisingly—from the pro-Milošević **Socialist Party of Serbia**. Koštunica became Prime Minister at the head of the new Government on 3 March 2004.

At the January 2007 elections, a few months after Montenegro had left the union with Serbia, the DSS in alliance with NS fell back to 47 seats (on 16.6% of the vote), making it the third-largest bloc in the Serbian National Assembly. Again an anti-SRS coalition was formed, this time by the DS, DSS, NS and G17 Plus, and retaining Koštunica as Prime Minister. However, tensions rose in the coming months between President Boris **Tadić** (of the DS) and Koštunica over relations with the **European Union** (EU), encompassing the level of co-operation with the **International Criminal Tribunal for the former Yugoslavia** (ICTY), the speed of EU accession talks, and the attitude toward the UN-administered province of Kosovo. Koštunica resigned on 8 March 2008 and early elections were called.

At the May 2008 elections the DSS-NS alliance finished in a poor third place, with only 30 seats (and 11.6% of the vote). Neither party joined the new DS-led Government.

Leadership: Vojislav Koštunica (Chair.).
Address: Pariska 13, 11000 Belgrade.
Telephone: (11) 3204719.
Fax: (11) 3204743.
E-mail: info@dss.rs
Internet: www.dss.rs

Democratic Party of Slovenian Pensioners
Demokratična Stranka Upokojencev Slovenije (DeSUS)

A centrist party in **Slovenia**, currently part of the ruling coalition, which defends the rights of the elderly generally and pensioners in particular, and opposes any privatization of pension arrangements. Also known as the Grey Panthers, the DeSUS was part of the (ex-communist) United List of Social Democrats (ZLSD) in the 1992 **National Assembly** elections. It contested those of 1996 independently, winning five seats with 4.3% of the vote, and joining the subsequent coalition Government headed by **Liberal Democracy of Slovenia** (LDS). In the October 2000 elections, the party slipped to four seats (while improving to 5.2% of the vote), but was included in a new ruling coalition headed by the LDS. DeSUS fielded its own candidate, Anton Bebler, in the 2002 presidential election, but he finished seventh with 1.8% of the vote. At the October 2004 Assembly election DeSUS again won four seats (4% of the vote), this time joining a coalition Government headed by the centre-right **Slovenian Democratic Party** (SDS). In the 2007 presidential election, DeSUS did not join the other ruling coalition parties in backing independent candidate Lojze Peterle but instead backed another independent, Danilo **Türk**, who defeated Peterle in the run-off. DeSUS improved to seven seats (7.5% of the vote) at the September 2008 Assembly election, and remained in Government, this time headed by the **Social Democrats**, as the ZLSD was now known.

Leadership: Karl Viktor Erjavec (President).
Address: Kersnikova 6, 1000 Ljubljana.
Telephone: (1) 4397350.
Fax: (1) 4314113.
E-mail: desus@siol.net
Internet: www.desus.si

Democratic Party of Socialists of Montenegro
Demokratska Partija Socijalista Crne Gore (DPSCG)

The leading political party in **Montenegro**, heading the ruling coalition Government, and a member of the **Socialist International**. It is the direct successor to the **League of Communists** of Montenegro (SKCG).

The DPSCG, which changed its name from SKCG in 1991, was until the late 1990s in favour of the federation with **Serbia**. The party obtained an overall majority in the Montenegrin **Assembly** in December 1992, also winning 17 lower house seats in simultaneous Federal Assembly elections and joining a coalition Government led by the **Socialist Party of Serbia** (SPS) of Slobodan **Milošević**. The following month its then leader Momir Bulatović was elected President of Montenegro. The DPSCG retained its Montenegrin Assembly majority in November 1996, when it also advanced to 20 federal lower house seats.

Increasing internal opposition to Bulatović for his pro-Federation stance culminated in October 1997 in his narrow defeat by Prime Minister Milo **Đukanović** in Montenegrin presidential elections in which both ran as DPSCG candidates. Đukanović also became undisputed DPSCG Chairman, while Bulatović launched the breakaway **Socialist People's Party of Montenegro** (SNPCG). Now advocating greater independence for Montenegro, the DPSCG contested the May 1998 Montenegrin Assembly elections at the head of the For a Better Life alliance, with the People's Party (NS) and the Social Democratic Party of Montenegro (SDPCG—which has remained in all subsequent DPSCG-led electoral alliances). The coalition won 42 out of 78 seats and therefore formed a new Government with Filip Vujanović as Prime Minister.

Relations between the DPSCG and the Milošević regime deteriorated during the 1998–99 **Kosovo** crisis, with the Montenegrin Government receiving strong Western backing for its proposal for loose 'association' with Serbia. When Milošević enacted constitutional amendments in July 2000 that were seen as reducing Montenegrin powers in the Federation, the DPSCG came out in favour of full separation and boycotted the September 2000 federal elections, in which Milošević and the SPS were defeated by the **Democratic Opposition of Serbia** (DOS).

At elections to the Montenegrin Assembly held in April 2001, the DPSCG headed an alliance of pro-independence parties called The Victory is Montenegro's, emerging as the largest bloc with 36 seats (and 42% of the vote); the overall pro-separation vote was only 5,000 greater than the vote against.

Short of an overall majority and failing to reach a coalition agreement with the pro-independence Liberal Alliance of Montenegro (LSCG), the DPSCG-led bloc opted to form a minority Government with parliamentary support from the LSCG. However, the closeness of the election and the fact that the new Government in **Belgrade** was as opposed to the break-up of the **Yugoslav** Federation as its predecessor—and now enjoyed Western support—raised major question marks over whether the DPSCG would pursue the independence objective. On 14 March 2002 Đukanović signed a framework agreement providing for the establishment of a State Union of Serbia and Montenegro, with Montenegro retaining the right to refer the issue of independence to a referendum after a period of three years. The accord took effect on 4 February 2003.

Since the LSCG was hostile to this new Union even as a temporary arrangement, Đukanović had to seek a mandate at fresh elections in which, on 20 October 2002, the DPSCG-led Democratic List for a European Montenegro secured a majority of 39 out of 75 seats (with 47.3% of the vote). Đukanović then resigned as President on 5 November in order to be nominated as Prime Minister, in which capacity he formed a Government which was approved on 8 January 2003. Two attempts to hold a presidential election, in December 2002 and February 2003, were invalidated by low turnout after the SNPCG and LSCG boycotted the poll. The Assembly then voted to remove the turnout condition for future elections, and on 11 May former Prime Minister Vujanović of the DPSCG secured the presidency with 64% of the vote.

Once the prescribed three-year waiting period had elapsed, the independence referendum had been held and independence duly declared on 3 June 2006, Montenegro's first post-independence elections on 10 September 2006 returned the DPSCG-led **Coalition for a European Montenegro** to power with 41 out of 81 seats (and 48.6% of the vote). Đukanović, who had announced that he would not remain as Prime Minister (although he would remain leader of the DPSCG), favoured Finance Minister Igor Lukšić as his successor, but a compromise was agreed with another senior party leader, Svetozar Marović, that Justice Minister Željko Šturanović should be nominated. His Government was approved on 10 November.

On 31 January 2008 Šturanović resigned due to ill health. A week later Đukanović was nominated to resume the premiership, and was approved on 29 February. Vujanović was re-elected to the presidency on 6 April 2008, securing 52.3% of the vote—well ahead of second-placed Andrija Mandić of the Serbian List on 19.3%. He was inaugurated on 21 May.

At the 29 March 2009 Assembly elections, called by Đukanović to seek a fresh mandate for major economic reforms, the DPSCG-led Coalition for a European Montenegro increased its majority, winning 48 seats (and 52% of the vote). Formation of Đukanović's new administration took several months as leading figures within the party jostled for prominence, until a largely unchanged Government was finally announced in early June. Đukanović later intimated that he would step down in 2010, so long as Montenegro was firmly on the path towards membership of the **European Union** (EU) and **North Atlantic Treaty Organization** (NATO).

Leadership: Milo Đukanović (Chair.).

Address: Jovana Tomaševića, 81000 Podgorica.

Telephone: (20) 243952.

Fax: (20) 243347.

E-mail: office@dps.me

Internet: www.dpscg.org

Democratic Rally
Dimokratikos Synagermos (DISY)

A conservative **Greek Cypriot** party in **Cyprus**, a member of the **International Democrat Union** and **Centrist Democrat International**, and currently in opposition. DISY was founded in 1976 by Glafcos Clerides as a union of elements of the former Progressive Front and the United and Democratic National parties. Since the introduction of proportional representation in 1981, DISY has vied with the left-wing **Progressive Party for the Working People** (AKEL) for the status of largest parliamentary party.

The 1983 presidential elections resulted in Clerides winning 34% in the first round and being defeated by the **Democratic Party** (DIKO) incumbent, Spyros Kyprianou. In the 1988 contest, Clerides was again defeated, winning 48.4% of the second-round vote against the victorious AKEL-supported independent candidate. In the 1993 presidential elections, however, Clerides was the unexpected victor, with 50.3% in the second round. In further talks on the Cyprus problem, Clerides sought, unsuccessfully, to use his longstanding personal relationship with **Turkish Cypriot** leader Rauf **Denktaş** to expedite a settlement.

In the 1998 presidential elections, Clerides came second in the first round (with 40.1%), behind an independent candidate backed by AKEL and most of DIKO, but narrowly secured re-election in the second round (with 50.8%) by attracting dissident DIKO support. He then formed a national unity Government which included DISY, the **Movement of Social Democrats EDEK** and rebel DIKO members. Clerides controversially ran again in 2003, saying that he would serve for 16 months in order to achieve a Cyprus settlement and to complete accession negotiations with the **European Union** (EU). He received 38.8% of the first-round vote, well behind DIKO-AKEL-EDEK candidate Tassos Papadopoulos, and was defeated in the run-off.

In opposition, DISY took a majority decision in favour of acceptance of a UN settlement plan in a referendum in April 2004, only to see it heavily rejected by Greek Cypriot voters on the recommendation of Papadopoulos, as an anti-plan DISY faction broke away to form what became the European Party (EVROKO). In parliamentary elections in May 2006, DISY lost ground, falling from 19 to 18 seats and 30.3% of the vote, but a concurrent decline in support for AKEL meant the two parties tied as the largest in the **House of Representatives**.

In the February 2008 presidential election the DISY candidate, MEP Ioannis Kasoulidis, led on the first round with 33.5% of the vote, but was defeated in the run-off by the AKEL candidate, Dimitris **Christofias**, who (gaining support from DIKO and EDEK) beat Kasoulidis by 53.4% to 46.6%.

Leadership: Nicos Anastasiades (President).
Address: 25 Pindarou Street, PO Box 25305, 1308 Nicosia.
Telephone: (22) 883000.
Fax: (22) 753821.
E-mail: disy@disy.org.cy
Internet: www.disy.org.cy

Denktaş, Rauf

Long-term President of the **Turkish Cypriot** area of **Cyprus** (1975–2005). A British-trained barrister whose role as a political advocate for Turkish Cypriots dates back to before the ending of British rule in 1960, Rauf Denktaş presided over the Turkish Federated State of Cyprus, from 13 February 1975, after the island was partitioned *de facto* between **Greek Cypriot** and Turkish Cypriot communities following Turkish military intervention the previous year. For over 21 years commencing on 15 November 1983 Denktaş was President of the self-proclaimed **Turkish Republic of Northern Cyprus** (TRNC), which is recognized only by Turkey.

Rauf Denktaş was born in Baf (Paphos) on 27 January 1924 and was educated at the English School in **Nicosia** and then as a barrister at Lincoln's Inn, London. A teacher from 1942 to 1943, he practised law in Nicosia from 1947 to 1949, becoming a Junior Crown Counsel to the Attorney General's Office in that year, Crown Counsel in 1952 and then acting Solicitor General from 1956 to 1958.

In 1948 he had become a member of the Consultative Assembly seeking Cypriot independence from the United Kingdom and a member of the Turkish Cypriot Affairs Committee. As Chairman of the Federation of Turkish Cypriot Associations, he attended the UN General Assembly in 1958 and led the Turkish Cypriot delegation at the 1959 London conference, at which it was agreed that Cyprus should be a bicommunal partnership state; the rights of the Turkish Cypriot minority, and the independence of the country as a whole, were to be guaranteed by **Greece**, Turkey and the United Kingdom. Denktaş headed the Turkish Cypriot delegation on the Constitutional Committee drafting the Constitution under which Cyprus became independent on 16 August 1960.

As President of the Turkish Communal Chamber from 1960, Denktaş led the opposition to Greek Cypriot proposals to modify the Constitution, an issue which led to inter-communal conflict (and the interposition of a UN peacekeeping force) in 1964. Exiled from the island for four years, Denktaş became interlocutor at inter-communal talks that followed a fresh upsurge of violence in 1967, and was re-elected as President of the Turkish Communal Chamber in 1970. The nominal position of Vice-President of Cyprus, to which he was elected unopposed in February 1973, was increasingly irrelevant to the real situation, however, with talks achieving nothing and the Turkish Cypriots focusing instead on organizing their own Government within the area in which they were the majority population.

A short-lived extreme right-wing coup backed by the Greek military junta on 15 July 1974, and the Turkish response of sending troops to occupy northern Cyprus, crystallized the partition of the island. A Turkish Federated State of Cyprus was proclaimed in the Turkish-occupied north in February 1975. Denktaş was designated as its first President, and won an overwhelming victory when presidential elections were held in June 1976, with his **National Unity Party** (UBP) dominating that year's elections to a Turkish Cypriot Assembly. He retained this post until 15 November 1983, when the Federated State was replaced by the TRNC, whose 'declaration of full independence' was recognized only by Turkey.

Although indisputably the leading figure in Turkish Cypriot politics, Denktaş saw his share of the vote in successive TRNC presidential elections fall from over 70% in 1985 to only 44% in 2000. The decline in his popularity reflected concern over the deteriorating economic situation in the internationally isolated north, the perceived dangers of being left out of Cyprus's forthcoming membership of the **European Union** (EU—achieved in 2004), and the absence of any breakthrough in the protracted talks on a negotiated Cyprus settlement. Denktaş continued with these talks under UN auspices, but without contributing any real new ideas, while his core demand for recognition of the 'sovereignty' of the TRNC was a key stumbling-block, given that the Greek Cypriot side's core demand was the maintenance of Cyprus as a single sovereign state. The UBP split in 1992 when he rejected the idea of abandoning the talks and formalizing the partition. His supporters set up a breakaway **Democrat Party** (DP) which he subsequently joined. In May 1996 the DP leadership was taken by Denktaş's son Serdar, following which the DP joined the ruling coalition (until 1998) and Serdar became Deputy Prime Minister.

Denktaş maintained that the Greek Cypriots had no right to negotiate EU entry on behalf of the Turkish Cypriots. He therefore condemned the signature of the Cyprus-EU accession treaty in April 2003 and responded by opening the line of division (known as the **Green Line**) to free movement of people, enabling large numbers from each community to visit the other side.

In a defeat for the Denktaş line, Assembly elections in December 2003 resulted in the pro-EU, pro-reunification **Republican Turkish Party–United Forces** (CTP-BG) led by Mehmet Ali **Talat** becoming the largest party and forming a coalition with the DP. However, Denktaş remained chief negotiator for the Turkish Cypriot side and refused to endorse a settlement plan tabled by UN Secretary-General Kofi Annan envisaging the creation of a federal United Cyprus Republic consisting of two 'constituent states'. Nevertheless the plan was put to referendum, and supported by the Turkish Cypriots, but rejected by the Greek Cypriots. Accordingly, the accession of the Republic of Cyprus to the EU on 1 May 2004 applied only to the area under the control of the Greek Cypriot Government, with its extension to the TRNC suspended pending a settlement.

Denktaş did not stand for re-election in 2005, ending three decades in power on 25 April. The departure of his son Serdar's DP from the ruling coalition in September

2006 meant that for the first time since the creation of the breakaway Turkish Cypriot entity there was no Denktaş in office.

Rauf Denktaş is married to Aydın Münür. They have had two daughters and three sons, one of whom has died.

DeSUS *see* **Democratic Party of Slovenian Pensioners**.

Diet
Sejm

The lower house of the **National Assembly** of **Poland**.

DIKO *see* **Democratic Party (Cyprus)**.

Direction–Social Democracy
Smer–Sociálna demokracia (Smer)

A left-wing political party in **Slovakia**, affiliated to the **Socialist International**, and currently heading the Government. Smer was founded in December 1999 by Róbert **Fico** as a 'Third Way'.

Fico had been a Deputy Chair of the Party of the Democratic Left (SDĽ), the direct descendant of the Slovak Communist Party. Re-established as an autonomous formation following the collapse of communist rule in **Czechoslovakia** in late 1989, the Slovak Communist Party adopted the SDĽ title in 1990. In the June 1992 elections, the SDĽ became the second-largest party in the Slovak **National Council**, winning 29 seats on a 14.7% vote share and thereafter overcoming its initial reservations about the creation of an independent Slovakia from 1 January 1993.

After the Government of the Movement for a Democratic Slovakia (HZDS) had been reduced to minority status in March 1993, the SDĽ declined to join a coalition with the HZDS and instead became the leading party in the Common Choice (SV) centre-left opposition alliance, which also included the Social Democratic Party of Slovakia (SDSS), the Slovak Green Party and the Farmers' Movement of Slovakia. In the autumn 1994 elections, however, the SV won only 18 seats (the SDĽ itself falling back to 13), as voters preferred the incumbent HZDS as the real 'party of continuity'. In 1995–96 the SDĽ became increasingly divided over whether to accept further HZDS offers of coalition status, the election of the relatively unknown Jozef Migaš as leader in April 1996 being a compromise between the contending factions.

Standing on its own in the September 1998 National Council elections, the SDĽ advanced to 23 seats on a 14.7% vote share and opted to join a centre-left coalition headed by the centrist Slovak Democratic Coalition. Fico and his supporters broke away in late 1999 and Fico's popular appeal brought the new Smer party immediate support. It won 25 seats (13.5% of the vote) in the 2002 election, putting it in third place. It then backed Ivan **Gašparovič**'s ultimately successful candidacy for the presidency in 2004. Meanwhile in 2003 Smer had absorbed the Party of Civic Understanding, and in January 2005 it merged with the SDĽ, the SDSS and the small Social Democratic Alternative, adopting the new title Direction–Social Democracy.

At the June 2006 election, Smer won 50 seats, with 29.1% of the vote. Fico was invited to form a Government, but his controversial decision to forge a coalition with the far-right **Slovak National Party** (SNS) as well as Vladimír **Mečiar**'s **People's Party–Movement for a Democratic Slovakia** (ĽS–HZDS) was viewed with concern at home and abroad. Smer was temporarily suspended from the Party of European Socialists in the European Parliament. However, the popularity of Smer seems to have helped to keep both SNS leader Ján Slota and Mečiar in line, fearful that their parties would suffer the fallout from the electorate if the Government were brought down.

Leadership: Róbert Fico (Chair.).
Address: Súmračná 25, 82102 Bratislava.
Telephone and fax: (2) 43426297.
E-mail: generalny.manager@strana-smer.sk
Internet: www.strana-smer.sk

DISY *see* **Democratic Rally**.

Djukanović, Milo *see* **Đukanović, Milo**.

Dobruja question

A dormant territorial dispute between **Bulgaria** and **Romania** concerning the fertile plain between the River Danube and the Black Sea. Dobruja has long been an ethnically diverse region and a vital economic centre for the south-west **Balkans**. Incorporation into the Ottoman Empire in 1419 ended rival Romanian and Bulgarian claims to the region. The dispute was renewed in 1878, however, when the Ottoman Empire's loss of control in the area was formalized in the Treaty of Berlin. This treaty awarded the larger northern part of Dobruja to the newly-emerged Romanian state, and the smaller southern 'quadrilateral' to the Bulgarian principality.

After the Second Balkan War of 1913 all of Dobruja was assimilated into Romania, only to be redivided in 1940 under Nazi supervision. The modern border, similar to that of 1878, was drawn up in 1947 under the Treaty of Paris. Friendly cross-Danube relations since then have laid the dispute to rest. Bulgarian Dobruja is home to a large minority of **Bulgarian Turks**, who mostly farm tobacco there. In Romania the Dobruja has diversified its agricultural industry with heavy communist-era industrialization: the port of Constanţa is Romania's major Black Sea port.

Dodik, Milorad

Prime Minister of the **Serb Republic** (RS) in **Bosnia and Herzegovina**.

Milorad Dodik was born in 1959 in **Banja Luka**, and graduated in political science from the University of Belgrade. From 1986 he chaired the executive board of Laktasi's local assembly, before securing election in the former **Yugoslavia**'s first multi-party elections as a member of the Bosnian parliament. Opposed to the nationalist **Serbian Democratic Party** (SDS), he founded the moderate **Party of Independent Social Democrats** (SNSD), of which he is still the President. He first held office as RS Prime Minister from 1998 to 2001, and began a second tenure on 28 February 2008.

Dodik is married and has two children.

Address: Office of the Prime Minister, 78000 Banja Luka.
Telephone: (51) 331333.
Fax: (51) 331332.
E-mail: kabinet@vladars.net
Internet: www.vladars.net

Dom Naroda
(House of Peoples)

The upper house of the **Parliamentary Assembly** of **Bosnia and Herzegovina**.

Dombrovskis, Valdis

Prime Minister of **Latvia**.

A physicist and economist by training, Dombrovskis spent four years at the **Bank of Latvia** before entering politics. He joined **New Era** (JL) when it was founded in 2002 by former Bank of Latvia Governor Einars Repše, and nine months later was Latvia's Minister of Finance. In 2004 he won election to the European Parliament, but was recalled in early 2009 to become the new Latvian Prime Minister at a time of grave economic crisis.

Born on 5 August 1971 in **Rīga**, he graduated in physics from the University of Latvia in 1993 and two years later also earned a degree in economics from Rīga Technical University. He continued physics research, at Mainz University (Germany), the University of Latvia, where he gained a master's degree, and the University of Maryland (USA), where he gained a doctorate from the Department of Electrical Engineering in 1998. Returning to Latvia he joined the Bank of Latvia's Monetary Policy Board, rising to become chief economist. (He would also later gain a master's degree in customs and tax administration from Rīga Technical University in 2007.)

His political career took off rapidly in 2002. A founder member of JL in February, he was elected to the **Parliament** in October, and was Minister of Finance in Repše's Government from November until it collapsed in early 2004.

In July 2004 he left the Parliament following his election to the European Parliament, where he headed the Latvian delegation of the European People's Party–European Democrats. From December of that year he was also a member of the Council of the Nordic Investment Bank and an adviser to the Latvian Minister of Economics (holding both of these positions until 2006).

When Ivars Godmanis's Government collapsed in February 2009, amid a severe economic crisis, Dombrovskis was nominated to be the new Prime Minister, and took office on 12 March, initially also holding the portfolio for Children, Family and Integration Affairs.

He is married, and can speak English, German, Russian and a little Spanish.

Address: Office of the Prime Minister, Brivibas bulv. 36, Rīga 1520.

Telephone: 67082934.

Fax: 67280469.

E-mail: vk@mk.gov.lv

Internet: www.mk.gov.lv

DOS *see* **Democratic Opposition of Serbia**.

DP (Lithuania) *see* **Labour Party**.

DP (Turkish Republic of Northern Cyprus) *see* **Democrat Party**.

DPS *see* **Movement for Rights and Freedoms**.

DPSCG *see* **Democratic Party of Socialists of Montenegro**.

Drnovšek, Janez

A key figure in **Slovenia**'s post-independence politics as Prime Minister (1992–2000, 2000–02) and then as President (2002–07), and long-term leader of the centre-left **Liberal Democracy of Slovenia** (1991–2003). An economist by training, he was elected to the Slovenian parliament within the **Socialist Federal Republic of Yugoslavia** (SFRY) in 1986 and was President of the SFRY's collective Presidency in 1989–90. After playing a prominent role in talks on Slovenia's independence, he was the country's Prime Minister for all but six months of the next decade, and then won the presidency.

Born on 17 May 1950 in Celje, north-east of Ljubljana, he obtained a doctorate in economics from the University of Maribor in 1986. Having completed his education, he worked first with a construction company, then as Chief Executive of a branch of Ljubljanska Bank, and finally as adviser on economic affairs at **Yugoslavia**'s Embassy in Egypt. In 1989 he was elected as the Slovenian representative on the collective State Presidency of the SFRY, standing as an independent and defeating the communist candidate in the first such election to be genuinely contested. In May 1989 he took office for a year as President of the Presidency, on the principle of the rotation of this post among the SFRY's constituent republics, but with the distinction of being the first non-communist to hold this office. In October 1990, however, he withdrew from the SFRY Presidency, protesting over its manipulation by its new **Serbian** President. As Slovenia moved to obtain its independence from the disintegrating SFRY the following year, he was the principal negotiator in efforts to halt the countervailing military action by the federal Yugoslav People's Army (JNA).

Also in 1991 Drnovšek co-founded and headed the Liberal Democratic Party, precursor of the LDS, which dominated Slovenian politics in the 1990s. He headed a coalition which took office, with himself as Prime Minister, in April 1992, while the first post-independence elections in December saw the Liberal Democrats established as the largest grouping in the parliament.

Throughout Drnovšek's career as Prime Minister, Slovenia's closer integration with Western Europe was the key priority. In March 1994 Slovenia joined the **Partnership for Peace** programme of the **North Atlantic Treaty Organization** (NATO), but was left out of the first round of NATO expansion announced in mid-1997. In June 1996 Drnovšek signed an Association Agreement with the **European Union** (EU) and negotiations for membership began in November 1998. Accession to both bodies was achieved in 2004.

Drnovšek's broad left-of-centre coalition survived until April 2000, when he was ousted for a six-month period while Andrej Bajuk of the Slovene People's Party (SLS+SKD) held office in a shaky centre-right alliance. Drnovšek and the LDS were returned to office at the November 2000 elections, and two years later Drnovšek stood as the LDS candidate in the presidential election. He led the first round on 10 November with 44.4% and went on to secure 56.5% in the run-off. He was inaugurated on 22 December, and in February 2003 he stepped down as LDS leader.

The LDS lost the 2004 **National Assembly** election, and became riven with internal disputes in opposition; in January 2007 Drnovšek resigned from the party.

Drnovšek announced in early 2007 that he would not be seeking re-election that November due to ill health. He fulfilled his term in office, stepping down on 22 December, but then died in February 2008.

Državni Zbor *see* **National Assembly (Slovenia)**.

DS *see* **Democratic Party (Serbia)**.

DSS *see* **Democratic Party of Serbia**.

Dubček, Alexander

The communist party leader of **Czechoslovakia** during the 1968 '**Prague Spring**', who attempted to abandon Stalinism in favour of 'socialism with a human face'. When he replaced Antonín Novotný as leader of the Communist Party of Czechoslovakia (KSČ) in January 1968 the 47-year-old Dubček's name was not widely known, despite his role as leader of the **Slovak** communists. His appointment was regarded as a bid to placate disgruntled Slovaks in the party. The reforms introduced under Dubček's leadership won him wide popularity. When **Warsaw Pact** forces invaded in August 1968 Dubček was arrested but then released after effectively being pressured into abandoning his reform policies. By April 1969 he had been ousted as KSČ leader. After a brief spell as Ambassador to Turkey, Dubček was expelled from the KSČ in 1970. He returned to obscurity as an administrator in the Slovak Forestry Service. During the November 1989 '**velvet revolution**' Dubček was received ecstatically at mass pro-democracy rallies. Although suggested as a possible figurehead President, he stood aside in favour of Václav **Havel**, and instead became Speaker of the Federal Parliament. Dubček joined the **Public Against Violence** movement, switching to the **Movement for a Democratic Slovakia** in July 1991 but strongly opposing the dissolution of the Czechoslovak federation. In March 1992 he was elected as Chairman of the small Social Democratic Party in Slovakia. The party performed poorly in the 1992 elections and Dubček resigned as Speaker of the Federal Parliament. In September 1992 Dubček suffered grave injuries in a car crash and he died on 7 November 1992. Thousands of mourners attended his funeral.

Dubrovnik

A historic port on the southern **Dalmatian** coast, one of **Croatia**'s main cities and the focus of international outrage when it was besieged by Yugoslav forces in 1991. *Population*: 30,436 (2001 census). The south **Slav** settlement of Dubrovnik (from the Serbo-Croatian for 'grove') was incorporated by the Italian community on the nearby island of Ragusa into a city-state which for much of its history was known as Ragusa. Its connection with the Venetian trading empire ensured a distinctly west European feel to the city and enabled it to increase its influence along the Dalmatian coast.

Dubrovnik maintained its autonomy under the Ottomans but was finally subjugated by the Austro-Hungarian Empire in 1815. It was incorporated into the Croatian state within the Kingdom of Serbs, Croats and Slovenes in 1918. The city's splendid medieval architecture made it one of **Yugoslavia**'s main tourist attractions in the later 20th century. However, some of the historic buildings were severely damaged during the 1991 siege. The city has been largely rebuilt and repaired, and the tourist trade has since been regenerated. Other economic activity revolves around the city's port and the production of quality consumer goods.

Đukanović, Milo

Prime Minister, **Montenegro**.

Milo Đukanović, Chairman of the centre-left **Democratic Party of Socialists of Montenegro** (DPSCG), was initially a supporter of former Yugoslav dictator Slobodan **Milošević**, but in the late 1990s distanced the DPSCG and **Montenegro** from their ties with **Serbia** and ultimately led the republic to independence on 21 May 2006. Only 29 when first appointed on 15 February 1991 as Prime Minister of Montenegro, he became the republic's President on 15 January 1998, and returned to the post of Prime Minister after the October 2002 elections. Having secured his country's independence, he stepped down in October 2006, but returned to office a year and a half later, in February 2008, when Prime Minister Željko Šturanović resigned due to ill health.

Born into a socially prominent Montenegrin family in Nikšić on 15 February 1962, he graduated in economics from the Titograd (now **Podgorica**) University in 1986. While at university he became active in politics and joined the **League of Communists of Yugoslavia** (SKJ) in 1979. After graduating he became a member of the SKJ's Central Committee. The party was transformed into the DPSCG in 1991. As a supporter of Milošević, he was rewarded in February 1991 with the post of Prime Minister of Montenegro.

Over the course of the disintegration of the **Socialist Federal Republic of Yugoslavia** (SFRY) in the 1990s, however, he became increasingly a voice of discontent against Milošević's authoritarian regime, and in 1996 he led the anti-Milošević faction within the DPSCG against the incumbent Montenegrin President Momir Bulatović. The party was split in two and Đukanović successfully campaigned for the rump DPSCG in presidential elections in late 1997. After a slim victory in the second round he finally replaced Bulatović in January 1998.

As President, he consistently defied the republic's Serbian partner in the new **Yugoslavia**, within which Montenegro was run almost as an independent country under his leadership. The two constituent republics came close to conflict in mid-2000 as Đukanović increased his anti-Milošević rhetoric. The fall of the dictator in October 2000 did little to thaw relations with Serbia, but a very slim electoral victory for the DPSCG in April 2001 cut the party's pro-independence momentum.

In November 2001 the **European Union** (EU) helped to mediate talks between Serbia and Montenegro, and on 14 March 2002 Đukanović, along with his federal and Serbian counterparts, signed a framework agreement providing for the establishment of a State Union of Serbia and Montenegro. Under the accord, the two semi-independent republics were to maintain separate economies, but have a joint foreign and defence policy, and to elect a new, joint presidency and legislature. Montenegro was to retain the right to refer the issue of independence to a referendum after a period of three years. This agreement (which would eventually take effect on 4 February 2003) angered Đukanović's coalition partner, which withdrew its support.

Early elections were held on 20 October 2002, and the DPSCG-led Democratic List for a European Montenegro secured a majority of 39 out of 75 seats. Đukanović resigned as President on 5 November in order to be nominated as Prime Minister, and his Government was approved on 8 January 2003.

Once the prescribed three-year waiting period had elapsed, the independence referendum was held on 21 May 2006, and independence was declared on 3 June. At the 10 September 2006 elections the DPSCG-led **Coalition for a European Montenegro** retained a small majority with 41 out of 81 seats. Đukanović announced that he would not remain as Prime Minister, as he wished to develop his business interests (although he would remain leader of the DPSCG). (Đukanović had been accused of involvement with organized crime, and was under investigation by the Italian authorities, mainly in connection with large-scale illicit tobacco trade in the **Balkans**.) On 10 November Željko Šturanović was approved as Prime Minister.

On 31 January 2008 Prime Minister Šturanović resigned due to ill health. A week later Đukanović was nominated to resume the premiership, and was approved on 29 February. (His return to office gave him immunity from prosecution, though the criminal investigation continued.)

Đukanović called early elections for March 2009, claiming he needed a fresh mandate before pushing through major economic reforms, though the opposition declared he was holding the poll before the global economic crisis could bite any deeper. At the 29 March poll, the DPSCG-led Coalition for a European Montenegro increased its majority, winning 48 seats. Formation of Đukanović's new Government took several months as leading figures within the DPSCG jostled for prominence, looking ahead to becoming the successor to Đukanović. The largely unchanged Government was finally announced in early June. Đukanović later intimated that he would step down in 2010, providing Montenegro was firmly on the path towards membership of the **European Union** (EU) and the **North Atlantic Treaty Organization** (NATO).

Đukanović is married to Lidija Kuč and they have one son.

Address: Office of the Prime Minister, Karađorđeva bb, 81000 Podgorica.

Telephone: (20) 242530.

Fax: (20) 242329.

E-mail: kabinet.premijera@gov.me

Internet: www.gov.me

E

EAPC *see* **Euro-Atlantic Partnership Council**.

Eastern Europe

A term commonly applied to the European region comprising states east of **central Europe**. This region may be regarded as extending south to the **Balkan** states of **Albania**, **Bulgaria**, **Greece**, **Romania** and the former **Yugoslavia** (although these countries may also be placed in the separate category of **south-eastern Europe**), and eastwards to include the Russian Federation and the other former Soviet Republics, except those of central Asia (which lie outside Europe's geographical borders). Wider definitions can also include **Cyprus** and even Turkey. Following the post-war division of Europe along the 'iron curtain', the term eastern Europe gained a political connotation, denoting all communist (and more recently post-communist) states east of the **Oder-Neisse line**. In this usage it excluded two Balkan states, Greece and Turkey, and included, on political rather than geographical criteria, the communist states of central Europe.

Eastern Slavonia *see* **Slavonia**.

EBRD *see* **European Bank for Reconstruction and Development**.

ECCI *see* **Estonian Chamber of Commerce and Industry**.

ECE *see* **United Nations Economic Commission for Europe**.

ECHR *see* **European Court of Human Rights**.

Economic Chamber of Macedonia
Stopanska Komora na Makedonija

The principal organization in **Macedonia** for promoting business contacts, both internally and externally, in the post-communist era. Originally founded in 1962.
President: Branko Azeski.
Address: Dimitrija Čupovski 13, 1000 Skopje.
Telephone: (2) 3244000.
Fax: (2) 3244088.
E-mail: ic@ic.mchamber.org.mk
Internet: www.mchamber.org.mk

Economic Chamber of the Czech Republic
Hospodářská komora České republiky

The principal organization in **the Czech Republic** for promoting business contacts, both internally and externally, in the post-communist era. Originally founded in 1850.
Chair.: Zdeněk Somr.
Address: Freyova 27, 190 00 Prague 9.
Telephone: (2) 96696111.
Fax: (2) 96646221.
E-mail: office@komora.cz
Internet: www.komora.cz

EDEK *see* **Movement of Social Democrats EDEK**.

EKe *see* **Estonian Centre Party**.

ELTA *see* **Lithuanian News Agency**.

Enterprise Restructuring Agency
Agjensia e Ristrukturimit te Ndermarrjeve (ARN)

Government body in **Albania** charged with assisting state-owned enterprises to become privately owned. It offers enterprise sector surveys, strategic plans, consultancy services and technical assistance.
Director: Adriatik Bankja.
Address: Rruga e Durrësit 83, Tirana.
Telephone: (4) 227878.
Fax: (4) 225730.

Epirus question

An issue arising from the division of the ancient **Balkan** province of Epirus between **Albania** and **Greece** in 1913, and residual (and non-official) Greek aspirations to unite Albanian-ruled northern Epirus with the Greek province of (southern) Epirus. Northward expansion of the independent Greek state established in 1830 focused on historic **Macedonia**, the Greek claim to which encompassed not only the whole of Epirus but also much of what is now Albania. In the Balkan Wars of 1912–13 most of Macedonia was partitioned between Greece, **Serbia** and **Bulgaria**, but plans for Greece to acquire the whole of Epirus were thwarted by the declaration in November 1912 of an independent principality of Albania. Under the Treaty of Bucharest of August 1913, Albania's independence was internationally recognized within virtually its present-day borders, including northern Epirus (where ethnic **Albanians** outnumbered Greeks), while Greece acquired Greek-majority southern Epirus. Greece occupied northern Epirus soon after the outbreak of the First World War in 1914, but was eventually persuaded to accept a post-war settlement, signed in Paris in July 1926, under which northern Epirus was recognized as belonging to Albania.

Dominated by fascist Italy from 1926 and occupied by Italian forces in April 1939, Albania provided a springboard for Italy's attack on Greece in October 1940. The resounding victory of Greek forces brought them into occupation of southern Albania, where northern Epirus was declared 'liberated'. In 1941, however, German forces overran both **Yugoslavia** and Greece, whereupon **Greater Albania** was restored to Italian control. Following Italy's exit from the war in 1943, the Albanian communists gradually established control, their Government being recognized by the Allies in October 1945. The Paris peace conference in 1946 reaffirmed the independence of Albania within its 1926 borders.

With Albania under communist rule and Greece becoming a member of the **North Atlantic Treaty Organization** (NATO) in 1952, the Epirus question remained frozen during the **Cold War** era. In 1958 Albania expressed a desire to normalize relations with Greece, but rejected the Greek response that a termination of the technical state of war between the two countries should encompass negotiations on the status of northern Epirus. The establishment of diplomatic relations between Albania and Greece in 1971 was understood to imply Greek recognition of Albania's existing borders. However, not until 1987 did the Greek Government formally agree to ending the state of war with Albania, one aim being to encourage better treatment of the ethnic Greek minority in northern Epirus. The Albanian census of 1989 recorded 59,000 inhabitants as being of self-declared ethnic Greek origin, but Greek estimates continued to put the actual number at over 300,000.

The end of communist rule in Albania in 1991 and the relaxation of exit restrictions resulted in an accelerating exodus to Greece, at first mainly of ethnic Greeks but later also of ethnic Albanians in search of a better life. Anxious to reverse the tide, the Greek Government urged better treatment for ethnic Greeks within

157

Albania, while also stressing that there was no territorial issue between the two countries. Nevertheless, as violence against ethnic Greeks in southern Albania increased in 1992, some on the Greek right called for a reopening of the territorial question, while the Albanian Government accused Greece of launching a new 'cold war' against Albania. Relations worsened in mid-1994 when activists of the Democratic Union of the Greek Minority—Concord (Omonia) were prosecuted in a government crackdown on alleged subversion in southern Albania.

The release of the Omonia members facilitated an improvement in Albanian-Greek relations in 1995, assisted by Albanian moves to meet Greek demands for independent Greek-language schools in southern Albania. However, Albania's descent into virtual anarchy following the collapse of the country's **'pyramid' investment schemes** in 1997 produced particular instability in southern Albania. About 830 Greek troops returned to Albania (for the first time since 1941) as part of the multinational force sent in to restore order; with the Albanian Government's agreement they remained deployed in southern Albania after the withdrawal of the main force. With stability restored in the border area, the remaining Greek forces were almost entirely withdrawn in August 2000.

ER *see* **Estonian Reform Party**.

Erdut Agreement
(or Basic Agreement)

A peace treaty signed on 12 November 1995 by ethnic **Croat** and **Serb** forces, following the conclusion of hostilities, concerning the eastern **Slavonia** region of **Croatia**. Under the terms of the Erdut (or Basic) Agreement the region of eastern Slavonia, Baranja and western Sirmium was placed under the mandate of a United Nations transitional administration (UNTAES) for a period of 12 months. UNTAES was charged with maintaining security in the region, which was to be demilitarized, and ensuring the peaceful return of refugees of all ethnic backgrounds. In the first years following the Erdut Agreement the UN administration noted that the right-wing regime of Franjo **Tudjman** was apparently unwilling to leave the region demilitarized following the departure of UNTAES, and that little progress had been made regarding the return of refugees. None the less the 3,000-strong peacekeeping force, whose mandate had been extended for two six-month periods, finally wound up its operations in January 1998.

Eroğlu, Derviş

President of the **Turkish Republic of Northern Cyprus** (TRNC). A former doctor, he leads the right-wing **National Unity Party** (UBP), established in 1975. He was TRNC Prime Minister in 1985–93, 1996–2004 and from May 2009 until his election to the presidency in April 2010.

Derviş Eroğlu was born in Ergazi, Famagusta, on the eastern coast of **Cyprus**, in 1938. Having studied medicine at Istanbul University, Turkey, he worked as a medical doctor before resuming his medical studies in 1969, specializing as a urologist at Ankara University. He is married with four children.

Following the Turkish invasion and occupation of northern Cyprus in 1974, Eroğlu entered the Assembly of the self-proclaimed Turkish Federated State of Cyprus in 1976 and has been re-elected ever since. Between 1976 and 1977 he served as the territory's Minister of Education, Culture, Youth and Sports and, following the TRNC's declaration of independence, became a member of the Constituent Assembly in November 1983. He first became Chairman of the UBP that year, after its internal division between supporters and opponents of President Rauf **Denktaş**, and was Prime Minister of four successive Governments between 1985 and 1993.

Eroğlu went into opposition from the beginning of 1994, the TRNC Assembly elections the previous month having brought to power a coalition of the **Democrat Party** (DP—a pro-Denktaş splinter of the UBP formed in 1992) and the leftist Republican Turkish Party (CTP). In the territory's presidential elections in April 1995 Eroğlu went through to a second-round run-off against Denktaş (who on previous occasions had won outright in the first round of voting). Although Eroğlu took only 37.5% of the second-round vote, the unprecedented strength of his challenge reflected the TRNC's growing economic problems as a result of its political isolation and concerns about Denktaş's increasing personal power. When the DP-led coalition Government collapsed on 4 July 1996, Eroğlu went on to form a new coalition between the UBP and the DP six weeks later.

In elections on 6 December 1998 the UBP fell only two seats short of a majority itself and Eroğlu formed a new coalition with the leftist Communal Liberation Party (TKP). With talks with the **Greek Cypriot** Government continuing to founder into the new century, Eroğlu was able to claim 30% in the first round of presidential elections in April 2000, but withdrew from the second round against Denktaş. The UBP-TKP coalition collapsed in May 2001 after disagreeing over whether to support continuing talks with the Greek Cypriots, and Eroğlu returned to his earlier coalition formula with the DP.

The UBP lost the Assembly elections in December 2003 and went into opposition in January 2004. It continued in opposition after early Assembly elections in February 2005, and in presidential elections in April 2005 Eroğlu again came second with 22.7%, this time behind Mehmet Ali **Talat** of the ruling **Republican Turkish Party– United Forces** (CTP-BG). In February 2006 Eroğlu stepped down from the UBP leadership, succeeded by Hüseyin **Özgürgün** and then Tahsin Ertuğruloğlu. However, he returned to the post in November 2008 and led the party to outright victory at the April 2009 legislative elections, with 26 seats in the 50-member Assembly. Eroğlu returned as Prime Minister, naming a single-party Government on 5 May. He stood for the presidency again in April 2010, securing victory in the first round with 50.4% of the vote, ahead of Talat on 42.9% and five other candidates. He was inaugurated on 23 April.

Address: TRNC Presidency, Şht. Selahattin Sonat Sokak, Lefkoşa/Nicosia.
Telephone: +90-392-2283444.
Fax: +90-392-2272252.
Internet: www.kktcb.eu

ESI *see* **European Stability Initiative**.

Estonia
Eesti Vabariik

An independent **Baltic State** in north-eastern Europe, bordered to the south by **Latvia** and to the east by the Russian Federation. The Gulf of Finland lies on its northern coastline, and the Baltic Sea to the west. The country is divided administratively into 15 districts (maakonnad).

Area: 45,227 sq km; *capital*: **Tallinn**; *population*: 1.34m. (2009 estimate), comprising **Estonians** 68.6%, **Russians** 25.6%, Ukrainians 2.1%, Belarusians 1.2%, Finns 0.8%, others 1.7%; *official language*: Estonian; *religion*: majority Evangelical Lutheran, Russian and Estonian **Orthodox Christianity**; others include **Roman Catholic**, Baptist, Methodist, Pentecostal, **Muslim**, Jewish, Buddhist and Hindu.

Legislative authority is vested in the unicameral **Parliament** (Riigikogu), which has 101 members directly elected for a four-year term by a system of proportional representation. The Head of State is the President who is elected for a five-year term by a two-thirds majority of the Riigikogu (or, if the required majority is not secured after three rounds of voting, by simple majority of an electoral assembly composed of parliamentary deputies and 266 local government representatives). Executive authority is vested in the Prime Minister, who is appointed by the President and nominates the Council of Ministers.

History: The ancestors of modern Estonians are believed to be Finno-Ugric-speaking tribes from further east or south-east who began settling in the Baltic area possibly as long ago as 4000 BC, although other theories date their arrival at around 1800 BC or later. The first independent state of Estonia was conquered by the Vikings in the ninth century AD. By the 13th century the German Teutonic Knights controlled southern Estonia; in the 14th century they purchased northern Estonia from Denmark.

The country was partitioned in 1561 between Sweden (the north) and **Poland** (the south), and most of present-day Estonia had come under Swedish rule by the mid-17th century. The end of the Great Northern War between Russia and Sweden brought Estonia under tsarist Russian rule from the early 1700s until the time of the Russian Revolution in 1917. Estonia was occupied by German and then Bolshevik forces in the First World War, but in 1918 declared its independence, which was recognized by the Treaty of **Tartu** with Soviet Russia in 1920 and by the League of Nations in 1921. An authoritarian regime seized power in 1934.

In 1940, shortly after the start of the Second World War, Soviet forces occupied Estonia (as had been agreed under the terms of the 1939 **Nazi-Soviet Pact**) and the country was incorporated into the **Soviet Union** as the Estonian Soviet Socialist Republic. German forces subsequently invaded and occupied Estonia from 1941 until the Soviet Union regained control in 1944. The 'Sovietization' of Estonia followed, including agricultural collectivization and the immigration of ethnic **Russians** and other groups.

In the late 1980s the influence of the *glasnost* (openness) initiative in the Soviet Union encouraged the growth of a popular movement in Estonia to campaign for democratization and independence. Close links with popular fronts in Latvia and **Lithuania** were also established. In 1988 the Estonian Supreme Soviet declared the sovereignty of the republic and a law was subsequently passed replacing Russian with Estonian as the state language. In late 1989 the Estonian Supreme Soviet denounced the 1940 Soviet incorporation of the republic as illegal. In 1990 the communist monopoly of power was abolished, the broad-based Estonian Popular Front led by Edgar Savisaar secured a majority of seats in multi-party elections to the Estonian Supreme Soviet, and a pro-independence coalition Government was formed. A referendum held in 1991 returned a vote of 78% in favour of independence. Following the failure of the attempted August coup in the Soviet Union, Estonia declared its independence. This was recognized in September by the Soviet Union and by Western nations.

Presidential and legislative elections were held in 1992, following the approval of the new Constitution by referendum. As the presidential poll failed to produce a clear winner, the Riigikogu chose the former Foreign Minister, Lennart Meri, as the new President. The parliamentary elections returned a centre-right coalition Government led by Mart Laar, who embarked upon a radical policy of free-market reform and was widely credited with reviving Estonia's ailing post-communist economy. Laar's Government fell when it was voted out of office by the Riigikogu in 1994.

Following the March 1995 general election, Tiit Vähi, the leader of the Estonian Coalition Party (EK) and a caretaker Prime Minister in 1992, formed a centre-left coalition Government with Savisaar's **Estonian Centre Party** (Kesk) and a rural party. This coalition collapsed (over a phone-tapping scandal) six months later, and Vähi formed a new coalition with the **Estonian Reform Party** (ER). President Meri was re-elected by an electoral assembly vote in September 1996. Vähi resigned (accused of corruption) in February 1997, having formed another minority Government a month before, and was replaced by Mart Siimann, also of the EK.

In the March 1999 parliamentary elections Savisaar's Kesk became substantially the largest party, winning 28 seats on a populist platform. However, he was unable to form a coalition, and Laar returned to the premiership with a centre-right coalition between his own Pro Patria Union (IL), the ER and the Moderates. Its narrow majority of 53 of the 101 parliamentary seats led to periodic political crises, notably over the passage of a supplementary austerity budget for 1999. The Government nevertheless remained in office, buoyed by economic recovery in 2000 (*see* **Estonia, economy**). However, its privatization programme met with increasing opposition within the Riigikogu, and it faced a number of no-confidence votes through the course of 2001. Divisions within the coalition itself became clear when the former transitional President Arnold Rüütel, now of the opposition Estonian People's Union (ERL), was elected President on 21 September but only after successive rounds of voting in the Assembly. The pressure of dissent within the coalition eventually proved too much and Laar announced in December that he would resign in the new year.

Savisaar thereupon took his Kesk party into an opportunistic coalition with the ER, resulting on 19 January 2002 in a Government taking office for the remainder of the parliamentary term with ER leader and former Finance Minister Siim Kallas as Prime Minister. Controlling less than half of the seats, it relied on support from the ERL in the Riigikogu.

In the March 2003 parliamentary elections Kesk held on to the support it had achieved four years earlier, emerging as the party with the most votes, but tied for seats with the right-wing Union for the Republic—Res Publica (founded in 2001). Each obtained 28 seats, ahead of the ER with 19 seats. The ensuing coalition negotiations, however, again left Savisaar without a viable set of partners. Instead, Res Publica formed a coalition with the ER and the ERL in early April under Res Publica leader Juhan Parts.

This fragile coalition survived one potential rift in November, when the ERL voted against the Government on a key tax bill, and another the following February when ER Foreign Minister Kristiina Ojuland was dismissed over the disappearance of 91 classified documents. The final blow came with a vote of no confidence in Justice Minister Ken-Marti Vaher over a controversial anti-corruption plan. Parts resigned on 24 March, and a week later a new rainbow coalition was formed between Kesk, the ER and the ERL. New ER leader Andrus **Ansip** took office as Prime Minister on 13 April.

Protracted presidential elections in August–September 2006 eventually led to the election of former Foreign Minister Toomas Hendrik **Ilves** of the **Social Democratic Party** (SDE—formerly the People's Party Moderates).

Latest elections: In the March 2007 parliamentary elections (in which all voters were entitled to cast their votes by way of the internet) the liberal ER emerged for the first time as the largest party, winning 31 seats with 27.8% of the vote. Kesk won 29 seats (26.1% of the vote), followed by the **Union of Pro Patria and Res Publica** (IRL—a merger of Union for the Republic—Res Publica and the Pro Patria Union) with 19 seats (17.9%), the SDE with 10 seats (10.6%), and the ERL and the new Estonian Greens (EER) each with six seats (7.1%).

Recent developments: Ansip formed a centre-right Government between his ER, the IRL and the SDE, controlling 60 of the 101 seats in the Riigikogu. A key issue in the 2007 election was the controversial bronze statue of a Soviet soldier in Tallinn's central square. Erected under Soviet rule to commemorate the liberation of Estonia from the Nazis in the Second World War, for many Estonians it had become a hated symbol of the years of Soviet domination. Electoral victory for the pro-European ER led to the statue's relocation in April, which provoked riots by local Russians and a deterioration in Estonia's relations with Russia (see below).

Having entered economic recession in 2008, the Government tried to curb spending, but moves in May 2009 to reform employment laws to reduce levels of benefits produced protests from unions and from the junior coalition partner, the SDE. Ansip responded by ejecting the SDE from his coalition, forming a minority Government of just his ER and the IRL.

International relations and defence: As a newly-recognized independent state, Estonia was admitted to the UN in 1991 and also joined the **Organization for Security and Co-operation in Europe**. The republic's prime objective is to integrate into Western institutions. It was admitted to the **Council of Europe** in 1993. Further to its 1995 application for membership of the **European Union** (EU), Estonia opened formal accession negotiations with the EU in March 1998. An offer of membership was made in December 2002, as part of a major wave of EU expansion. It was supported by referendum in September 2003, and Estonia acceded on 1 May 2004. In December 2007 Estonia also joined the EU's Schengen Agreement, allowing free movement of citizens within the Schengen zone's borders. It is expecting to join the eurozone on 1 January 2011 (*see* **Estonia, economy**).

A member of the **Partnership for Peace** programme since 1994, Estonia became a full member of the **North Atlantic Treaty Organization** (NATO) in March 2004 along with six other countries. The participation of the Baltic States in both the EU and NATO meant that both these organizations now extended to Russia's main eastern border.

A central feature of Estonian foreign policy is close links with the other Baltic states within the framework of revived trilateral institutions dating from the inter-war period. The **Council of the Baltic Sea States** provides the organizational framework for political, economic and other co-operation between Baltic littoral and adjacent countries. In 1998 the Presidents of Estonia, Latvia, Lithuania and the USA signed a **US-Baltic Partnership** charter.

Post-communist relations with the Russian Federation have not been smooth. Russian troops were not removed from Estonia until 1994. Against the backdrop of the sole remaining unresolved Russia–Baltic border dispute (*see* **Jaanilinn question**), the Russian Federation opposed Estonia's attempts to join NATO and has criticized Estonian citizenship laws as being discriminatory against Estonia's Russian minority. The issue of the removal of a Soviet-era statue from Tallinn's central square in 2007 caused a serious downturn in relations. The Russian Government imposed a partial trade blockade, and Russian hackers launched a cyber-attack on Estonian websites.

Estonia's defence budget for 2008 amounted to some US $450m., equivalent to about 1.9% of GDP. The size of the armed forces in 2010 was some 5,000 personnel, including those serving under compulsory conscription of eight months (or 11 months for officers and specialists). Reservists numbered an estimated 25,000.

Estonia, economy

Now one of the most liberal economies in the world, Estonia experienced strong growth (but with unemployment remaining persistently high) until it was badly hit by the recent global economic downturn. In the preceding period it had made a rapid and comprehensive transition from communist-era state control to a free-market system, assisted by its maritime traditions and links with the Nordic region. It joined the European Union (EU) in 2004 and plans to adopt the euro on 1 January 2011.

GNP: US $19,131m. (2008); *GNP per capita*: $14,270 (2008); *GDP at PPP*: $27,700m. (2008); *GDP per capita at PPP*: $20,700 (2008); *real GDP growth*: –14.0% (2009 estimate); *exports*: $12,401m. (2008); *imports*: $16,027m. (2008); *currency*: kroon (plural: krooni; US $1 = K11.16 in mid-2009); *unemployment*: 15.5% (end 2009); *government deficit as a percentage of GDP*: 1.7%; *inflation*: 0.0% (2009).

In 2007 industry accounted for 30% of GDP, agriculture for 3% and services for 67%. Around 37% of the workforce is engaged in industry, 5% in agriculture and 58% in services.

About 22% of the land is arable, 11% permanent pasture and 31% forests and woodland. The main crops are grains, potatoes, fruit and vegetables, although the principal agricultural activity is animal husbandry and the production of dairy products. There is fishing along the lengthy coastline and a major forestry industry.

The main mineral resource is oil-shale. There are also deposits of peat and phosphorite ore. The principal industries are machine building, electronics, electrical engineering and textiles and clothing, and some shipbuilding. The exploitation of its oil-shale resources and the production of phosphates are also significant in terms of economic activity, but both these industries are under considerable pressure on environmental and pollution grounds. The main energy sources are the oil extractable from shale, and natural gas which can also be extracted from shale-based geological formations.

Estonia's main exports are machinery and transport equipment, other manufactured goods, mineral fuels, forestry products, food products and chemicals. Principal imports are machinery and transport equipment, foodstuffs, chemical products, metal products and textiles. The three biggest destinations for Estonian exports in 2008 were Finland (18%), Sweden (14%) and the Russian Federation (10%). The largest suppliers of Estonia's imports in 2008 were Finland (14%), Germany (13%) and Sweden (10%).

In the 1950s and 1960s, within the **Soviet Union**, Estonia moved away from its earlier largely agricultural base in an intense period of industrialization. When Estonia regained its independence in 1991, the country accelerated the moves towards a market economy which had already been taking place. The post-independence changes resulted in initial falls in GNP and real GDP, but successful stabilization measures yielded real GDP growth of 4% in 1995 and 1996, rising to a remarkable 10% in 1997. Inflation, which had been as high as 954% in 1992, dropped rapidly to 36% in 1993 and to around 10% in 1997. Measures introduced in the 1992–97 period to create a sound financial sector included the creation of an independent board to manage the currency and strict restraints on public expenditure. The privatization process was initially slow, but the pace later accelerated. By the end of 1996 almost all state-owned small enterprises and three-fifths of medium-sized businesses had been transferred to the private sector, largely through a version of the **voucher privatization** system. In 1997 a programme was launched for the privatization of some of the largest concerns, including the state shipping corporation and Estonia Telecoms, to which the post-1999 Government added the railways, the alcohol industry and the power grid. Conversely, only 30% of state-owned agricultural land had been privatized by the end of 1999, partly because of the entrenched position of communist-era functionaries.

The 1998 financial crisis in the Russian Federation had an adverse knock-on effect in Estonia. GDP growth dropped back to 4% in 1998, but the real impact was felt in 1999, when real GDP contracted by 1.4% and foreign trade volumes dropped sharply. However, austerity measures introduced by the new centre-right Government appointed in March 1999 had the desired effect, preparing the way for renewed GDP growth of around 5% in 2000 and reining in the budget deficit to only 1.2% of GDP. Inflation remained high by **Baltic** standards, at 5% in 2000, while unemployment continued at a stubborn 15%, many affected being long-term jobless. Nevertheless, the overall record since independence was positive, real GDP per head having risen by 40% and real wages by around 25%.

As one of the original six 'fast-track' EU entry candidates, Estonia began formal accession negotiations in November 1998, with the result that harmonization of domestic policy with EU requirements was accelerated. Estonia also joined the **World Trade Organization** in November 1999.

Meanwhile, the country became a popular location for high-technology firms to establish outsourced operations, as a result of its well-educated, multilingual workforce as well as the relatively low rates of wages and corporate taxation. After joining the EU in May 2004, Estonia was one of three new EU member states to qualify immediately for membership of the Exchange Rate Mechanism II. However, despite hopes that Estonia would be among the first of the new EU member states to accede to the **eurozone**, a subsequent increase in the rate of inflation had the effect of delaying the country's adoption of the currency. Growth began to slow in 2007, partly as a result of the weakening of the real estate market and a decline in domestic demand, and the economy entered a deep recession in 2008 as the onset of the global financial crisis exacerbated Estonia's own domestic downturn. GDP declined by 14% in 2009, but inflation also dropped sharply, from 10.4% in 2008 to nil. Government spending was slashed to keep the budget deficit down, most notably by cutting state employees' wages by 10%. This brought the economy within the convergence criteria for euro adoption, which Estonia is now planning for 1 January 2011.

Estonian Centre Party
Eesti Keskerakond (Kesk or EKe)

A populist party in **Estonia**, currently the second-largest and the main opposition party in the Riigikogu (**Parliament**). Kesk was founded in October 1991 as an offshoot of the Estonian Popular Front, which had spearheaded the post-1988 independence movement but had split into various parties after independence was achieved. As Popular Front Chairman, Edgar Savisaar had been Prime Minister from April 1990 to January 1992, having previously been Chairman of the Estonian branch of the Soviet-era Planning Committee (Gosplan). Kesk used the Popular Front designation in the September 1992 Riigikogu and presidential elections, winning 15 seats (with 12.2% of the vote) and achieving third place (with 23.7%) for its presidential candidate, Rein Taagepera. In the March 1995 parliamentary elections Kesk won 16 seats with 14.2% of the vote, following which it joined a coalition Government headed by the Estonian Coalition Party (EK), obtaining four portfolios, including that of internal affairs for Savisaar.

This Government collapsed in October 1995 over the dismissal of Savisaar for alleged involvement in a phone-tapping scandal. Kesk was not included in the succeeding coalition, even though Savisaar announced his retirement from politics and was replaced as Kesk leader by Andra Veidemann. The following year Savisaar made his political comeback. Heading an anti-Veidemann group within the party, he regained the party leadership in March, and in July he was cleared of the allegations against him. Meanwhile, Veidemann and her supporters founded a breakaway Progress Party, whose political influence proved short-lived although it initially attracted seven of the 16 Kesk deputies.

In opposition, Kesk absorbed the small Green Party in June 1998 and pursued plans for a prospective ruling alliance with the Estonian Rural People's Party (EME). In the March 1999 parliamentary elections Kesk advanced strongly to become the largest party with 28 seats (winning 23.4% of the vote), on a platform calculated to appeal to voters who were disenchanted with the free-market economy. However, the relatively poor performance of its prospective coalition party, the EME, which won only seven seats, meant that a Kesk-EME Government was not feasible. Kesk instead continued in opposition, to a centre-right coalition led by the Pro Patria Union (IL). In late 2001 Kesk forced a no-confidence vote against the IL Mayor of Tallinn, and Savisaar was elected to replace him. This was one of several issues that brought down the IL-led Government in January 2002, giving Kesk an opening to form a somewhat improbable coalition with the liberal **Estonian Reform Party** (ER), under its leader Siim Kallas.

In the March 2003 parliamentary elections Kesk won the most votes (25.4%), but tied for seats with the right-wing Union for the Republic—Res Publica, winning 28 each. Kesk was pushed back into opposition by a coalition of Res Publica, the ER and the Estonian People's Union (ERL—which had absorbed the EME).

In December 2004 Kesk signed a co-operation agreement with United Russia, the *de facto* ruling party of Russia, in an attempt to increase support for Kesk among the ethnic Russian population of Estonia; several Kesk members who supported closer co-operation and integration with the EU left the party, reducing its faction in the Riigikogu from 28 to 19 seats. However, by April 2005 the party was back in government in a rainbow coalition with the ER and ERL, under new ER leader Andrus **Ansip**. Kesk absorbed the Estonian Pensioners' Party in August 2005, and scored well in local elections in late 2005, winning majority control of the Tallinn City Council, though Savisaar did not return to the mayoralty until 2007.

In the March 2007 parliamentary elections Kesk came second (behind ER) with 29 seats and 26.1% of the vote, but it was not included in Ansip's new coalition Government.

Leadership: Edgar Savisaar (Chair.).
Address: Toom-Rüütli 3/5, Tallinn 10130.
Telephone: 6273460.
Fax: 6273461.
E-mail: keskerakond@keskerakond.ee
Internet: www.keskerakond.ee

Estonian Chamber of Commerce and Industry (ECCI)

The principal organization in **Estonia** for promoting business contacts, both internally and externally, in the post-communist era. Originally founded in 1925.

President: Toomas Luman.
Address: Toom-Kooli 17, Tallinn 10130.
Telephone: 6460244.
Fax: 6460245.
E-mail: koda@koda.ee
Internet: www.koda.ee

Estonian Investment Agency

Government agency to promote inward investment in **Estonia**.
Director: Andrus Viirg.
Address: Roosikrantsi 11, Tallinn 10119.
Telephone: 6279420.
Fax: 6279427.
E-mail: invest@eas.ee
Internet: www.investinestonia.com

Estonian Reform Party
Eesti Reformierakond (ER)

A 'liberal-rightist' pro-market formation in **Estonia**, affiliated to the **Liberal International**, currently the largest party in the Riigikogu (**Parliament**) and heading the ruling coalition. The ER was launched in 1994 by **Bank of Estonia** Governor Siim Kallas. Using the unofficial designation 'Liberals', the ER took second place in the March 1995 Riigikogu elections, winning 19 seats and 16.2% of the vote. Having thus effectively become leader of the opposition, Kallas resigned from his post at the Bank of Estonia. Six months later, in November 1995, he became Deputy Prime Minister and Foreign Minister when the ER joined a new coalition Government headed by the Estonian Coalition Party (EK). However, in late 1996 the ER left the Government, while continuing to give it qualified external support.

In the March 1999 parliamentary elections the ER slipped to 18 seats with 15.9% of the vote. It nevertheless joined a centre-right coalition headed by the Pro Patria Union (IL) (with Kallas as Finance Minister), which remained in office until January 2002. The new Government that took over for the remainder of the parliamentary term was an unlikely coalition of the ER with the populist **Estonian Centre Party** (Kesk), with Kallas as Prime Minister. Controlling less than half of the seats, it relied on support from the Estonian People's Union (ERL) in the Riigikogu.

In the March 2003 parliamentary elections the ER finished third with 19 seats, and joined a centre-right Government with the Union for the Republic—Res Publica and the ERL, led by Res Publika leader Juhan Parts. In 2004 Kallas was appointed as Estonia's member of the European Commission in Brussels, and Andrus **Ansip** was chosen as his successor as party Chairman.

The dismissal of ER Foreign Minister Kristiina Ojuland in February 2005 over the disappearance of 91 classified documents was one of several crises for the ruling coalition. It fell the following month, and Ansip was appointed as Prime Minister in April, heading a rainbow coalition between Kesk, the ER and the ERL.

The March 2007 parliamentary elections marked a breakthough for the ER as it became the largest party for the first time, winning 31 seats with 27.8% of the vote. Ansip formed a centre-right Government between his ER, the IRL and the SDE, controlling 60 of the 101 seats in the Riigikogu. When the SDE refused to back employment law reforms in May 2009, Ansip dismissed the party from the coalition and continued in office as head of a minority Government.

Leadership: Andrus Ansip (Chair.).

Address: Tonismägi 9, Tallinn 10119.

Telephone: 6808080.

Fax: 6808081.

E-mail: info@reform.ee

Internet: www.reform.ee

Estonians

An Indo-European people, the name 'Estonian' deriving from the ancient **German** word 'Aisti', first recorded by the Roman historian Tacitus.

The Estonian language belongs to the Baltic-Finnic group of **Finno-Ugric** languages, and is closely related to Finnish. It replaced Russian as the official language in **Estonia** in 1989. Written in the Latin script, it dates back to the 16th century. The proportion of ethnic Estonians decreased from 1940 following the 'Sovietization' policies, but the people retain the cultural and religious legacy of German and Scandinavian rule, adhering to the Evangelical Lutheran Church (*see* **Protestantism**).

Ethnic cleansing

A euphemism for the use of terror by one ethnic group to expel another from an ethnically-mixed community. The phrase was first widely used in war-torn **Bosnia and Herzegovina** in the summer of 1992, when Bosnian **Serbs** systematically drove many **Bosniaks** (Bosnian Muslims) from their homes. Their property was often then seized by Serb families. Serb ethnic cleansing was allegedly part of a plan to create an ethnically homogeneous **Greater Serbia** from the ruins of **Yugoslavia**. The Bosnian Serb tactics allegedly included systematic murder and rape, siege and starvation. By the spring of 1993 there were allegations that all three parties in the conflict in Bosnia and Herzegovina had perpetrated ethnic cleansing. These allegations led to the establishment by the UN Security Council in May 1993 of the **International Criminal Tribunal for the former Yugoslavia**, which began its investigations in November 1993.

EU *see* **European Union**.

EUFOR

The **EU**-led peacekeeping force stationed in **Bosnia and Herzegovina** to assist in the implementation of the 1995 **Dayton Agreement**. EUFOR is the legal successor to the **NATO**-led Stabilization Force (SFOR), which itself was the legal successor to the Implementation Force (IFOR). IFOR began overseeing the military aspects of Dayton from December 1995 with the full backing of the UN. It was the largest ever NATO operation, numbering around 60,000 personnel, and had a one-year mandate. In that year it secured the peace in the war-torn country and helped to rebuild the shattered infrastructure. At the end of its mandate and following the successful conduct of a general election in Bosnia and Herzegovina in September 1996, IFOR was replaced in December by the much smaller SFOR mission with responsibility for, literally, stabilizing the peace. SFOR's troops came from all NATO countries as well as a number of non-NATO countries, including many from **eastern Europe**.

The EU-led military operation, known officially as Operation EUFOR Althea, commenced on 2 December 2004. Its mandate is currently extended until November 2010. Troops initially numbered around 7,000 (the same size as the outgoing SFOR) and now number around 2,000, drawn from 20 EU and five non-EU countries.

Commander: Maj.-Gen. Bernhard Bair (EUFOR COM).

Address: HQ EUFOR, Public Information Office (PIO), Building 200 Camp Butmir, 71000 Sarajevo.

Telephone: (33) 495000.

Fax: (33) 495221.

E-mail: cpic_forum@eufor.eu.int

Internet: www.euforbih.org

EULEX

(European Union Rule of Law Mission)

A civilian mission of over 2,000 personnel launched by the **European Union** (EU) under the European Security and Defence Policy (ESDP) to assist the **Kosovo** authorities in the areas of police, judiciary and customs. Contributing states include most EU member states as well as Norway, Switzerland, Turkey, **Croatia**, the USA and Canada. The mission was approved in December 2007, but deployment was delayed for months by **Serbian** opposition. It finally launched in December 2008, replacing **UNMIK** personnel, after pledging to be neutral on the status of Kosovo.

Head of Mission: Yves de Kermabon.

Address: Farmed Building, Muharrem Fejza St, PO Box 268, 10000 Pristina.

Telephone: (38) 222 010 2000.

Fax: (38) 222 010 6333.

E-mail: info@eulex-kosovo.eu

Internet: www.eulex.kosovo.eu

Euro-Atlantic Partnership Council (EAPC)

A partnership of the **North Atlantic Treaty Organization** (NATO). The EAPC was inaugurated in May 1997 as a successor to the North Atlantic Co-operation Council (NACC), which had itself been established in December 1991 to provide a forum for consultation on political and security matters with the countries of **central** and **eastern Europe**, including the former Soviet republics. The EAPC meets on a regular basis to discuss political and security-related issues. As of 2010, there were 50 members: the 28 NATO member countries (including **Albania, Bulgaria, Croatia, Czech Republic, Estonia, Greece, Hungary, Latvia, Lithuania, Poland, Romania, Slovakia** and **Slovenia**) and 22 partner countries (including **Bosnia and Herzegovina, Macedonia, Montenegro** and **Serbia**). All non-NATO EAPC members are members of NATO's **Partnership for Peace** programme.

European Bank for Reconstruction and Development (EBRD)

A multilateral financial institution founded in May 1990 and inaugurated in April 1991 with the objective of providing loan capital and project support in **central** and **eastern Europe**, to contribute to the progress and the economic reconstruction of the region. Participant countries must undertake to respect and put into practice the principles of multi-party democracy, pluralism, the rule of law, respect for human rights and a market economy.

Currently **Albania, Bosnia and Herzegovina, Bulgaria, Croatia, Estonia, Hungary, Latvia, Lithuania, Macedonia, Montenegro, Poland, Romania, Serbia, Slovakia** and **Slovenia** receive investment funding. However the EBRD plans to cease investing in Estonia, Hungary, Latvia, Lithuania, Poland, Slovakia and Slovenia in the near future (having already ceased investing in the **Czech Republic** in 2007).

Members: 61 countries, including Albania, Bosnia and Herzegovina, Bulgaria, Croatia, **Cyprus**, Czech Republic, Estonia, **Greece**, Hungary, Latvia, Lithuania, Macedonia, Montenegro, Poland, Romania, Serbia, Slovakia and Slovenia.

President: Thomas Mirow.

Address: One Exchange Square, London EC2A 2JN, United Kingdom.

Telephone: (20) 73386000.

Fax: (20) 73386100.

E-mail: press@ebrd.com

Internet: www.ebrd.com

European Court of Human Rights (ECHR)

Established in 1959 in Strasbourg, France, part of the activities of the **Council of Europe**, overseeing the implementation of the Convention for the Protection of Human Rights and Fundamental Freedoms (usually known as the European Convention on Human Rights). Council member countries are required to adhere to the Convention, which should entail among other things the abolition of the death penalty.

President: Jean-Paul Costa.
Address: Avenue de l'Europe, 67075 Strasbourg-Cedex, France.
Telephone: (3) 88412018.
Fax: (3) 88412730.
Internet: www.echr.coe.int/echr

European Organization for Nuclear Research
Organisation européenne pour la recherche nucléaire (CERN)

A scientific organization founded in 1954 (initially with 12 member countries including **Greece** and **Yugoslavia**, which left in 1961) to provide for collaboration among European states in nuclear research of a pure scientific and fundamental character. The work of CERN is for peaceful purposes only and concerns sub-nuclear, high-energy and elementary particle physics. Its membership amounts to 20 European countries, including **Hungary** (joined in 1992), **Poland** (1991), **Czech Republic** and **Slovakia** (1993) and **Bulgaria** (1999). Non-member states currently involved in CERN programmes include **Croatia**, **Cyprus**, **Estonia**, **Lithuania**, **Montenegro**, **Romania**, **Serbia** and **Slovenia**. In 2010 Romania signed an agreement beginning a five-year period of candidacy for membership.

Director General: Rolf Heuer.
Address: 1211 Geneva 23, Switzerland.
Telephone: (22) 7676111.
Fax: (22) 7676555.
E-mail: cern.reception@cern.ch
Internet: www.cern.ch

European Stability Initiative (ESI)

A non-profit research and policy institute, established in 1999 to assist international efforts to promote stability and prosperity in south-eastern Europe.

Chairman: Gerald Knaus.
Address: Grossbeerenstrasse 83, 10963 Berlin, Germany.

Telephone: (30) 53214455.
Fax: (30) 53214457.
E-mail: info@esiweb.org
Internet: www.esiweb.org

European Union (EU)

The principal organization of European integration, which most of the former communist countries of **central** and **eastern Europe** have applied to join. For these countries, EU membership represents a means of cementing the process of transition to free-market economies and pluralist democracies. The EU is also a major source of funding and expertise for their economic reform and development programmes.

The EU developed from the original basis of a 1951 Treaty setting up what was then the six-member European Coal and Steel Community (ECSC), and the 1957 Treaties of Rome setting up the European Economic Community (EEC) and Euratom. Since then it has developed substantially in the economic, monetary, social and (to a lesser extent) political spheres, and also in its membership. Its largest single expansion was on 1 May 2004, from 15 to 25 member countries (**Cyprus**, the **Czech Republic**, **Estonia**, **Hungary**, **Latvia**, **Lithuania**, Malta, **Poland**, **Slovakia** and **Slovenia** joined the existing group of Austria, Belgium, Denmark, Finland, France, Germany, **Greece**, Ireland, Italy, Luxembourg, Netherlands, Portugal, Spain, Sweden and the United Kingdom) and it reached a membership of 27 with the admission of **Bulgaria** and **Romania** on 1 January 2007.

The EU has established a Stabilization and Association Process (SAP) for aspirant members in the Balkans. Stabilization and Association Agreements were signed on the following dates:

Macedonia—9 April 2001 (entered into force on 1 April 2004).

Croatia—29 October 2001 (entered into force on 1 February 2005).

Albania—12 June 2006 (entered into force on 1 April 2009).

Montenegro—15 October 2007 (not yet ratified).

Serbia—29 April 2008 (not yet ratified).

Bosnia and Herzegovina—16 June 2008 (not yet ratified).

Kosovo under UN Security Council Resolution 1244/99 has also been named as a potential candidate.

Candidate status was granted to Croatia in June 2004 and to Macedonia in December 2005. Turkey also has candidate status (since December 1999). Accession negotiations began with Croatia and Turkey in October 2005, but have not yet begun with Macedonia.

Other applications for membership (not yet granted candidate status) have been submitted by Albania (28 April 2009); Iceland (23 July 2009); Montenegro (15 December 2009); and Serbia (22 December 2009).

President of the European Council: Herman von Rompuy.
President of the European Commission: José Manuel Durão Barroso.
Address of the European Commission: rue de la Loi 200, 1049 Brussels,
    Belgium.
Telephone: (2) 2991111.
Fax: (2) 2950138.
Internet: europa.eu

European Union Rule of Law Mission *see* **EULEX**.

European Union Special Representative *see* **Office of the High Representative**.

Eurozone

The zone within which the **European Union**'s euro functions as a single currency.
Initially it covered 11 of the member states, from 1999, namely Austria, Belgium,
Finland, France, Germany, Ireland, Italy, Luxembourg, Netherlands, Portugal and
Spain. **Greece** joined in 2001, prior to the currency's full adoption in January 2002.

Under the 2003 Treaty of Accession, all new EU members are obliged to join the
eurozone once they meet the convergence criteria. They must also have been part of
the Exchange Rate Mechanism II (ERM II) for at least two years prior to euro
adoption.

The first of the new members to join the eurozone was **Slovenia** (1 January 2007),
followed by **Cyprus** and Malta (1 January 2008) and **Slovakia** (1 January 2009). The
only other firmly scheduled adoption so far is **Estonia** (1 January 2011), which has
been in the ERM II since June 2004.

Bulgaria is expected to join the Exchange Rate Mechanism II soon. It already
meets most of the convergence criteria due to its low budget deficit and its currency
being pegged to the euro. Some analysts believe, however, that euro adoption on 1
January 2013 is now unlikely, and may be delayed at least until 2015.

Lithuania joined the Exchange Rate Mechanism II in June 2004 and had planned
to join the eurozone on 1 January 2007, but it was rejected as its inflation rate was
slightly above the prescribed level. Adoption is not likely before 2014 at the earliest.

Latvia joined the Exchange Rate Mechanism II in May 2005 and had planned to
join the eurozone on 1 January 2008, but this has been repeatedly pushed back and
now adoption is not likely before 2014 at the earliest.

Hungary had hoped to join the eurozone on 1 January 2010, but it still needs to
reduce its budget deficit and public debt to meet all the convergence criteria. It is
expected to join the Exchange Rate Mechanism II soon. It had hoped to adopt the
euro by 2014, but this is likely to prove optimistic.

The **Czech Republic** is not expected to join the eurozone before 2015. It has postponed the 2010 target for entry to the Exchange Rate Mechanism II as it will not meet the convergence criteria in time, having seen a recent rise in the budget deficit due to the global downturn.

Romania is expected to join the Exchange Rate Mechanism II in 2012 and then the eurozone in 2015, if it can meet the convergence criteria.

Poland has not yet set a planned date for joining the eurozone or even the Exchange Rate Mechanism II. In 2009 the Finance Minister said that the economy might meet the convergence criteria by 2012.

EUSR (European Union Special Representative) *see* **Office of the High Representative**.

F

FBiH *see* **Muslim-Croat Federation**.

Federal Republic of Yugoslavia (FRY) *see* **Yugoslavia**.

Federation News Agency
Federalna novinska agencija (FENA)

The main news agency for the **Muslim-Croat Federation** of **Bosnia and Herzegovina**, founded in November 2000.
Director: Zehrudin Isaković.
Address: Cemalusa 1, Sarajevo 71000.
Telephone: (33) 445247.
E-mail: direktor@fena.ba
Internet: www.fena.ba

Federation of Bosnia and Herzegovina *see* **Muslim-Croat Federation**.

Federation of Young Democrats–Hungarian Civic Alliance
Fiatal Demokraták Szövetsége–Magyar Polgári Szövetség (FiDeSz–MPS)

A conservative political party in **Hungary**, affiliated to the **Centrist Democrat International** and the **International Democrat Union**. Having headed the Hungarian Government in 1998–2002, it was in opposition from 2003, but won a huge majority of seats in the April 2010 **National Assembly** election.

Originally known simply as the Federation of Young Democrats, the grouping finished only fifth in the 1990 National Assembly election, winning 22 of 378 seats on a 9% vote share. Later that year it won mayoral elections in nine of the country's largest cities, but in the May 1994 general election its national representation declined further, to 20 seats, and it remained in opposition. A 35-year-old age limit on membership was abandoned in April 1993, paving the way for the adoption of the FiDeSz–Hungarian Civic Party (FiDeSz–MPP) designation two years later.

The FiDeSz–MPP was strengthened in 1997 and early 1998 by its absorption of part of the **Christian Democratic People's Party** (KDNP), which had won 22 seats in 1994. Benefiting from public disenchantment with the ruling centre-left coalition, the FiDeSz–MPP achieved a major advance in the May 1998 National Assembly elections, winning 147 seats on a 29.5% vote share. As Chairman of the largest party, its leader Viktor **Orbán** formed a centre-right coalition with the Independent Smallholders' and Civic Party (FKgP) and the **Hungarian Democratic Forum** (MDF), in which the FiDeSz–MPP took 12 of the 17 ministerial posts. The new Government took Hungary into the **North Atlantic Treaty Organization** in March 1999 and set accession to the **European Union** as its key objective.

In January 2000 a FiDeSz congress decided to split the posts of party Chairman and premier and elected László Kövér to the party post. However, having come under criticism for his aggressive style, Kövér stood down in March 2001 and was replaced by Zoltán Pokorni, the Interior Minister.

In September 2001 FiDeSz–MPP signed an electoral co-operation agreement with the MDF, and this was joined by several FKgP deputies. In the April 2002 election the FiDeSz–MDF coalition won the most seats (188) with 48.7% of the vote. However, all remaining seats were won by the allied centre-left parties, the **Hungarian Socialist Party** (MSzP) and the Alliance of Free Democrats (SzDSz), which together pushed the FiDeSz–MDF coalition into opposition. In July Pokorni quit the party leadership following revelations that his father had been a communist informer. (János Áder was chosen to lead the party until its next congress in May 2003.) Several other members of FiDeSz–MPP (which had emphasized its anti-communist past) were also accused of having had counter-intelligence associations, which severely damaged the party's popularity. It performed badly in the subsequent October local elections.

In May 2003 the party re-formed itself as FiDeSz–Hungarian Civic Alliance (FiDeSz–MPSz), with a new charter, and Orbán was elected as the party Chairman. This fresh start did help reinvigorate the party, but at the April 2006 elections, which the party contested jointly with the KDNP, it failed to unseat the ruling MSzP–SzDSz coalition, securing only 164 seats with 42.5% of the vote (141 seats for FiDeSz–MPSz and 23 for the KDNP). The two parties agreed to form separate parliamentary blocs in opposition, but work together under a Solidarity Union.

Capitalizing on the Government's unpopularity over the country's economic situation, FiDeSz–MPSz organized repeated anti-Government demonstrations, which frequently resulted in violent clashes between extreme nationalist protesters and the security forces. It also organized a public referendum against the introduction of medical fees in March 2008, in which more than 80% of voters voted against the fees, forcing the Government to scrap this particular reform.

At the National Assembly elections on 25 April 2010, voters punished the outgoing MSzP, resulting in an overall majority for the opposition FiDeSz–MPSz–KDNP alliance, with 262 seats in the 386-seat chamber and 52.7% of the vote. Orbán was nominated as Prime Minister, to take office in late May.

Leadership: Viktor Orbán (political leader); László Kövér (Chair.).

Address: Visi Imre utca 6, 1089 Budapest.

Telephone: (1) 5552000.

Fax: (1) 2695343.

E-mail: fidesz@fidesz.hu

Internet: www.fidesz.hu

FENA *see* **Federation News Agency**.

Fico, Róbert

Prime Minister of **Slovakia**. A criminal lawyer, Fico founded the left-wing Direction (Smer) party in 1999. It won the June 2006 election, and Fico took office as Prime Minister on 4 July.

Róbert Fico was born on 15 September 1964 in Topoľčany in western Slovakia. He graduated in law from Komenský University, **Bratislava**, in 1986, took his judicial exam two years later, and was awarded a doctorate in criminal law (with a thesis on the death penalty in **Czechoslovakia**) from the Institute of State and Law of the Slovak Academy of Sciences in 1992. That year he was appointed Deputy Director of the Law Institute of the Ministry of Justice, where he had also been working since graduation; he held this post for three years.

He was elected to the Slovak Parliament in 1992, representing the Party of the Democratic Left (SDĽ), the direct descendant of the Slovak Communist Party, and became a member of the Parliamentary Constitutional Committee in the run-up to the dissolution of Czechoslovakia. In 1994 he became Leader of the SDĽ Parliamentary Group and two years later was appointed a Deputy Chairman. Meanwhile, his legal expertise was being utilized as Slovak representative to the **European Court of Human Rights** (1994–2000) and to the Parliamentary Assembly of the **Council of Europe** (1994–2005, heading the delegation in 1999–2001). Also from 1995 to 2003 he chaired the Prison Commission of the Parliamentary Constitutional Committee.

In late 1999 Fico and his supporters broke away from the SDĽ and formed the new Smer party as a 'Third Way' in Slovak politics. Fico's popular appeal brought the party immediate support: it won 25 seats (with 13.5% of the vote) in the 2002 parliamentary election, putting it in third place. Fico joined the Parliamentary Committee on Human Rights, National Minorities and Women's Rights, and became an observer at the European Parliament.

Having absorbed several social democratic parties, Smer adopted the new title **Direction–Social Democracy**, and won the 2006 election with 29.1% of the vote and 50 seats. Fico was invited to form a Government, but his controversial decision to forge a coalition with the far-right **Slovak National Party** (SNS) as well as Vladimír Mečiar's **People's Party–Movement for a Democratic Slovakia** (ĽS–HZDS) was viewed with concern at home and abroad.

Fico is married with one child. He speaks English and Russian.

Address: Office of the Government of the Slovak Republic, Nám. Slobody 1, 81370 Bratislava.

Telephone: (2) 57295111.

Fax: (2) 52497595.

E-mail: premiersr@vlada.gov.sk

Internet: www.premiersr.sk

FiDeSz–MPS *see* **Federation of Young Democrats–Hungarian Civic Alliance**.

Finno-Ugric peoples

An ethnic group, thought to have originated in the west Kazakh steppe but now inhabiting areas from **Hungary** to the River Volga. From the original Uralic group there arose four main descendant groups. Listed in order of separation from original community, these were: the **Magyars** (Hungarians) in **central Europe** and Siberia; the Permians in the centre of European Russia—Udmurts and Komi; the Volga Finns around the River Volga—Mordvin and Mari; and the Baltic Finns in the **Baltic** and Scandinavian areas—**Estonians**, Finns, Karelians and Sami.

This wide geographic spread, and the influence of the other European peoples, has emphasized the differences between the various Finno-Ugric peoples. The Volga Finns have largely embraced the **Muslim** faith, while the European Magyars converted to Catholicism (*see* **Roman Catholic Church**) in 1000. Some isolated Finno-Ugric people in the far north still practise a form of the original Uralic animist religion. There are strong linguistic connections between the Finno-Ugric languages, with varying degrees of borrowing from neighbouring tongues.

Fischer, Jan

Prime Minister of the **Czech Republic**. Head of the Czech Statistical Office, he was nominated on 6 April 2009 to head a non-partisan caretaker Government until the elections due in June 2010. He took office on 8 May.

Jan Fischer was born on 2 January 1951 in **Prague**. He graduated in statistics and econometrics from Prague's University of Economics in 1974, subsequently also earning a doctorate in 1985. He began his career at the Central Statistical Office, initially as a research worker in the early 1980s at the Research Institute of Socio-economic Information, and rising to Deputy Chairman by 1990. Then, after the split of **Czechoslovakia** in 1993, he was appointed Vice-President of the Czech Statistical Office. He was then responsible for the processing of election results, and for liaison with Eurostat, the European Statistical Office.

From 2000 he worked as Production Director for Taylor Nelson Sofres Factum. In early 2001 he worked on an International Monetary Fund project considering the establishment of a statistical service in East Timor. and two years later became the Director of Research Facilities at the University of Economics' Faculty of Informatics and Statistics. In April 2003 he was appointed President of the Czech Statistical Office.

Fischer is married, for the second time, and has three children.

Address: Office of the Prime Minister, nábř. Edvarda Beneše 4, 118 01 Prague 1.
Telephone: (2) 24002111.
Fax: (2) 57531283.
E-mail: posta@vlada.cz
Internet: www.vlada.cz

FNM *see* **National Property Fund**.

For a European Serbia—Boris Tadić
Za Evropsku Srbiju—Boris Tadić (ZES)

The pro-European coalition formed to contest the May 2008 **National Assembly** election by **Serbian** President Boris **Tadić**. Based around his **Democratic Party** (DS) and the **G17 Plus**, it also includes the Serbian Renewal Movement and some ethnic minority parties. It won 102 seats, making it the largest bloc in the 250-member Assembly.

Leadership: Dragoljub Mićunović.
Internet: www.zaevropskusrbiju.rs

For Real—New Politics
Zares—Nova Politika

A centre-left political party in **Slovenia**, and an observer member of **Liberal International**, currently part of the ruling coalition. Zares was established by a splinter group from **Liberal Democracy of Slovenia** (LDS) in October 2007. At the presidential election the following month, it joined those parties backing the ultimately successful candidacy of Danilo **Türk**, and at the September 2008 **National**

Assembly election it achieved third place, though with only nine seats (9.4% of the vote). It joined the coalition headed by Borut **Pahor** of the **Social Democrats**.

Leadership: Gregor Golobič (President).
Address: Trg Prekomorskih brigad 1, 1000 Ljubljana.
Telephone: (1) 5005750.
Fax: (1) 5005753.
E-mail: info@zares.si
Internet: www.zares.si

Foreign Investment Promotion Agency of Bosnia and Herzegovina

Government agency to encourage foreign direct investment into **Bosnia and Herzegovina**. Founded in 1999.

Director: Mirza Hajrić.
Address: Branilaca Sarajeva 21, Sarajevo 71000.
Telephone: (33) 278000.
Fax: (33) 278081.
E-mail: fipa@fipa.gov.ba
Internet: www.fipa.gov.ba

Foreign Trade Institute
Institut za Spoljnu Trgovinu

Government agency in **Serbia**.
Director: Slobodan Mrkša.
Address: Moše Pijade 8, 11000 Belgrade.
Telephone: (11) 3235391.
Fax: (11) 3235306.
E-mail: radovank@eunet.rs

Former Yugoslav Republic of Macedonia (FYROM) *see* **Macedonia**.

FRY

The Federal Republic of Yugoslavia, *see* **Yugoslavia**.

FYRM *or* FYROM

The Former Yugoslav Republic of Macedonia, *see* **Macedonia**.

G

G17 Plus

A centre-right political party in **Serbia**, currently part of the government coalition, and an observer of the **International Democratic Union**. Initially a reform-orientated think tank of 17 non-party economists set up in the late 1990s, it was transformed into a political party in December 2002 by Miroljub Labus.

At the Serbian **National Assembly** elections a year later, it stood in alliance with the Social Democratic Party (SDP) and won 34 seats (31 G17 Plus, three SDP—with a total of 11.46% of the vote), making it the fourth-largest bloc. It joined the new Serbian minority Government headed by Vojislav Koštunica's **Democratic Party of Serbia** (DSS) from March 2004, and soon also gained a ministry at the federal level. Labus resigned from his post as Deputy Prime Minister in May 2006 in protest at the failure of the authorities to apprehend indicted war criminal Gen. Ratko Mladić, and the **European Union**'s consequent suspension of Stabilization and Association Agreement talks. He then quit the party when it refused to follow suit and withdraw from the Government. He was succeeded by Mlađan Dinkić in September.

At the January 2007 Assembly election, G17 Plus dropped to 19 seats (6.8% of the vote), but remained in Koštunica's new coalition Government. It contested the May 2008 elections as part of President Boris **Tadić**'s **For a European Serbia** coalition headed by the **Democratic Party** (DS). This bloc won 102 seats in the 250-member Assembly (G17 Plus winning 22 seats itself) and headed the new coalition Government of Prime Minister Mirko **Cvetković**. Dinkić was appointed Deputy Prime Minister and Minister for Economy and Regional Development, and G17 Plus members were assigned five other ministerial portfolios. Dinkić has announced plans to merge G17 Plus with some small regional parties to form the Party of Regions.

Leadership: Mlađan Dinkić (President).
Address: Trg Republike 5/IV, 11000 Belgrade.
Telephone: (11) 3210355.
Fax: (11) 3284054.
E-mail: office@g17plus.rs
Internet: www.g17plus.rs

Gabčíkovo-Nagymaros Dam

A controversial hydroelectric dam on the River Danube in southern **Slovakia**, at the point where the Danube forms the border with **Hungary**. It was originally conceived in 1977 as a joint project between Hungary and **Czechoslovakia**. By 1989 Hungary had pulled out, on economic, ecological and domestic grounds, but Czechoslovakia (and later Slovakia) chose to complete its part of the project, which had become a symbol of national pride. The main loser in Slovakia was the Magyar (**Hungarian**) community, which had historically lived on land which was to be partially inundated by dammed water.

Both Hungary and Slovakia appealed to the **International Court of Justice** which ruled in 1997 that both sides had breached the original contract and that negotiations should proceed between the two countries until a new binding treaty was agreed. The latest step is a joint study into the dam's potential environmental consequences.

Galicia

A historic region stretching from southern **Poland** into western Ukraine. The concept of Galicia was effectively invented by the Habsburg Empire in 1772 when it was awarded the region at the first partition of Poland. It comprised a western and Polish half known as Malopolska (literally 'little Poland'), and an eastern and Ukrainian (or Ruthenian) half consisting roughly of the ancient duchy of Halychina-Wolyn, from which the name Galicia was derived. Briefly during the Revolutionary–Napoleonic period Galicia stretched to include **Warsaw** but its reduced borders were finally established when the semi-autonomous Republic of Kraków was added in 1846.

Following the dismemberment of the Habsburg Empire after the First World War, Galicia was included in the new Polish Republic. It was briefly redivided into east and west at the start of the Second World War in 1939 before it was swallowed *en masse* into the Nazi General Government district in 1941. During the Nazi occupation the large **Jewish** population of Galicia, the centre of the Hasidic branch of Orthodox Judaism, was all but wiped out. Under the Polish-Soviet Treaty of 1945 Galicia ceased to exist, with east and west becoming integral parts of Ukraine and Poland respectively. The ethnic **Polish** and Ukrainian populations were redistributed to fall within their new states, although traditionally they had been largely restricted to their respective halves in any case.

The main urban centres of the region are Kraków in Poland and Lvov in Ukraine. The area is rich in oil and gas deposits as well as other minerals, and the two halves have become important economic centres in their respective countries.

Gašparovič, Ivan

President of the Republic, **Slovakia**.

Ivan Gašparovič defeated former Prime Minister Vladimír **Mečiar** in the second round of the presidential elections in April 2004 on the eve of Slovakia's entry to the **European Union** (EU), taking office on 15 June 2004. A former colleague of Mečiar, he left the Movement for a Democratic Slovakia (HZDS, *see* **People's Party–Movement for a Democratic Slovakia**, ĽS–HZDS) in 2002 along with several other members in protest at Mečiar's autocratic leadership, despite having supported many of Mečiar's more controversial policies. Gašparovič apologized for past actions and overtook Mečiar in the second round of the election after the candidates eliminated in the first round came out in his favour. He won a second term in 2009.

Ivan Gašparovič was born on 27 March 1941 in the town of Poltár near Lučenec and Banská Bystrica in south-central Slovakia. His father had migrated to Slovakia from Rijeka, **Croatia**, at the end of the First World War, and worked as a teacher at a secondary school in **Bratislava**. Ivan was educated at Komenský University, Bratislava, where he studied law. Upon graduation in 1964, he entered the Public Prosecutor's Office in Martin. He married Silvia Gašparovičová (*née* Beníková) that year; they have one son and one daughter. Between 1966 and 1989 he served as the Vice-Chairman of the Czechoslovak Ice Hockey Federation International Commission.

By 1966 Gašparovič had become Bratislava's Municipal Public Prosecutor. Two years later he joined the Communist Party of Slovakia to support Alexander **Dubček**'s reforms, but he was deprived of his party membership after the **Warsaw Pact** invasion of **Czechoslovakia** in August 1968. That year he acquired his doctorate and returned to Komenský University as a lecturer in the Faculty of Law, where he remained until 1990.

Gašparovič was appointed Pro-Rector in 1990, the year after the '**velvet revolution**' that brought down the communist regime. He was chosen by President Václav **Havel** to become the Prosecutor General of Czechoslovakia based in **Prague** from July 1990 to March 1992, through a period of significant political upheaval. Then Gašparovič briefly became Vice-President of the Legislative Council of Czechoslovakia, before the country ceased to exist in January 1993; he was one of the authors of independent Slovakia's Constitution.

In 1992 Gašparovič became a member of the HZDS, led by the charismatic and controversial Mečiar. Prime Minister from 1992 to 1998, Mečiar was constantly criticized by his opponents and the West for corruption, autocracy and the manner in which state assets were privatized under his rule. In 2002 Gašparovič resigned from the party after an internal split—his name did not appear on the ballot for that year's general election—and several others joined him from the HZDS to set up the Movement for Democracy (HZD), of which he became the first leader. In the September election the HZD polled just 3.3% of the vote, not enough to win a seat, and Gašparovič returned to Komenský University and wrote several university textbooks as well as working papers and studies on criminal law.

Gašparovič apologized for his past support for Mečiar's controversial policies in the area of minority rights and tight controls on the media, and announced that he would stand against Mečiar in presidential elections in 2004. Mečiar won 32.7% of the first-round vote on 3 April in a surprise result that saw the Government-backed favourite, Foreign Minister Eduard Kukan, trail in third place with just 22.1% behind Gašparovič's 22.3%. Mečiar and Gašparovič went forward to the second round on 17 April. Gašparovič won the run-off with 59.9% of the vote after receiving the support of the eliminated candidates. He was inaugurated on 15 June. He stepped down as HZD leader and pledged to remain above politics while in office. In March–April 2009 he secured a second term in office, backed by two of the three ruling parties (**Direction–Social Democracy** and the **Slovak National Party**, but not by Mečiar's ĽS–HZDS), winning 46.7% in the first round, and defeating opposition candidate Iveta Radičová in the run-off by 55.5% to 44.5%.

Address: Office of the President of the Republic, Hodžovo nám. 1, POB 128,
        81000 Bratislava 1.
Telephone: (2) 57888155.
Fax: (2) 57888103.
E-mail: informacie@prezident.sk
Internet: www.prezident.sk

Gazprom

A partially state-run gas monopoly in the Russian Federation, founded in 1989 as part of the **Soviet Union**'s Gas Ministry. Gazprom is now Russia's biggest company and the largest commercial gas producer in the world, accounting for almost 20% of global gas output and 85% of the Russian Federation's output. Its activities provide a sixth of the country's GDP and up to a quarter of tax revenues. It employs over 400,000 people and boasts that 430,000 people are shareholders, the company having been part privatized in 1993. Gazprom controls all aspects of gas prospecting, mining, production, refining and supply. In 2005 it bought a 73% share in Russia's fifth-largest oil producer Sibneft, now renamed Gazprom Neft. It also has a massive commercial interest in other economic areas, most notably in the country's media industry. Plans were even announced in 2005 for the construction of Gazprom City, a business centre near the heart of St Petersburg.

The state-owned share in Gazprom was increased to just over 50% in 2005, paving the way for the lifting of foreign ownership restrictions on Gazprom shares in July 2006. That same month Gazprom was granted the exclusive right to export Russia's natural gas.

Gazprom is now the sole or majority gas supplier to many **eastern** and **central European** countries, with the **European Union** receiving about 25% of its gas supplies from Gazprom. This has given the company considerable influence in foreign affairs. The gas price wars with Ukraine, Georgia, Belarus and other former Soviet states, which have been receiving subsidized gas since the break-up of the Soviet Union, have become known as 'petropolitics'. Temporary cessations of supply to Ukraine and Belarus in the winters of 2006 and 2007 had knock-on effects in European countries that use gas from transit pipes passing through the affected countries. Gazprom has also invested in pipelines connecting to central Asia and the enormous Chinese market.

Chair of the Board of Directors: Viktor Zubkov.

Chair of the Management Committee: Alexei B. Miller.

Address: ul. Nametkina 16, 117997 Moscow, V-420, GSP-7, Russia.

Telephone: (495) 7193001.

Fax: (495) 7198333.

E-mail: gazprom@gazprom.ru

Internet: www.gazprom.com

Gdańsk

A major port on the Baltic Sea in northern **Poland**. *Population*: 505,881 (2008 estimate). Gdańsk was a prosperous northern port for much of the medieval period, declining after its separation from Poland and incorporation into **Prussia** in 1772. It re-emerged as a free city in 1919 but its **German** population made it a target for Nazi territorial demands, a contributing factor to the German invasion of Poland in 1939 which marked the beginning of the Second World War in Europe. As Danzig, the city was thoroughly destroyed in the war and reconstructed by the Polish communist regime along industrial designs. In 1980 labour unrest at the Lenin shipyards led to the formation of the **Solidarity** movement, led by locally born Lech **Wałęsa**, and the authorization of free trade unions in Poland under the so-called Gdańsk Accords of August. The city remains of significant economic value to the country.

GERB *see* **Citizens for European Development of Bulgaria**.

Germans

An ethnic group concentrated in **central Europe** but spread in small communities throughout **eastern Europe**, and sharing a common language (although regional variations can be extreme). Thought to have originated on the shores of the Baltic Sea, the Germans spread south to occupy much of the north European plain. Several mini-states flourished in this region in the medieval period, rather than one contiguous German state, with **Prussia** and Austria the most powerful of many German entities. A unified Germany, stretching as far south as Bavaria, did not emerge until the mid-19th century (with Austria even then remaining separate, bound up as it was with the Habsburg Empire).

Meanwhile, steady eastward migration created German communities whose presence in the central European states of the 20th century was to prove a source of conflict. Many Germans were despatched specifically as frontier settlers, notably the Saxons in Northern **Transylvania**. Penetration of the east by German settlers extended as far as the River Volga where they settled under the invitation of Catherine the Great of Russia from 1763. In the Soviet era a German autonomous republic was even created within the **Soviet Union**, although it was disbanded during the Second World War and the so-called Volga Germans deported *en masse* to internment camps in Siberia. The survivors were later allowed to return to the Volga region where they consider themselves to be among Russia's oppressed peoples.

The irredentist ambitions of Hitler and the Nazi regime were briefly realized in the creation of the so-called Third Reich in the 1930s. Defeat in the Second World War, however, was followed by the forcible movement of thousands of Germans across eastern Europe to the new reduced German state, devastating areas of previous German settlement. A similar, this time voluntary, movement occurred in the 1990s following the collapse of communism in the east. Thousands of ethnic Germans migrated to Germany away from the economic uncertainty of the emerging post-Soviet states.

Officially, the largest ethnic German population in eastern Europe is in Russia, where 600,000 Germans were identified in the 2002 census, mainly in the Volga region. There could be as many as 1m. Germans living in modern **Poland** where they are largely considered autochthonous, and where the pursuit of their ethnic identity has only recently been encouraged: only 150,000 people identify themselves as German. The size of this population was greatly affected by the forced post-war migrations (*see* **Yalta Agreements** and **Potsdam Agreements**). The same is true of the once large German population in the **Czech Republic** which was expelled after 1945. An original community of 750,000 Germans in Transylvania has been cut down to just 60,000 through voluntary and forced migration. Some 75,000 were deported to the Soviet Union after 1945. Representation in **Romania** is plagued by a lack of resources. Around 120,000 Germans are scattered throughout **Hungary**, where there is some German-language schooling, but where assimilation has reduced German to a 'grandmother language'. In an attempt to accommodate the many Germans stranded throughout the former Soviet Union, Germany and Ukraine agreed in 1992 to assist 400,000 to settle in the south of Ukraine, although many chose to emigrate to Germany instead.

Goražde

A town on the River Drina in eastern **Bosnia and Herzegovina**, deep into Bosnian Serb territory (*see* **Serb Republic**). The town and surrounding region was traditionally home to a **Bosniak** majority and a large **Serb** minority. It was declared a UN 'safe haven' in May 1993 during the Bosnian civil war. Unlike other safe havens, such as **Srebrenica** and Žepa, Goražde did not permanently fall to Bosnian Serb forces and was spared the atrocities of '**ethnic cleansing**'. The surrounding hills were the target of the first **NATO** air-strikes against Bosnian Serb forces in April 1994, signalling the beginning of direct international military involvement in the war.

GPW *see* **Warsaw Stock Exchange**.

Greater Albania

A historical term applied to the area extending beyond the present-day territory of **Albania** to include those adjoining areas with an ethnic **Albanian** majority population. The independent state of Albania, declared in November 1912 during the First Balkan War, encompassed the whole of the area with an ethnic Albanian majority. However, under the 1913 Treaty of Bucharest and a final demarcation agreement signed in 1926, independent Albania was recognized within borders that excluded Albanian-majority **Kosovo** as well as smaller areas of **Macedonia** and **Montenegro** with a dominant Albanian population and southern **Epirus**. Albania's aspiration to acquire these areas was a constant theme of inter-war regional politics and impelled some Albanian nationalists to see fascist Italy as the potential deliverer of a Greater Albania, on the basis of Mussolini's recognition of the 'Illyrian' Albanians as an ancient Mediterranean people.

The Italian occupation of Albania in April 1939 was followed in the autumn by a joint Italian-Albanian assault on Greece, whose forces quickly repelled the attackers and themselves invaded and occupied southern Albania. The German defeat of Greece and **Yugoslavia** in 1941 enabled a Greater Albania to be created under Italian protection, including Kosovo and other parts of Yugoslavia as well as the whole of Epirus. However, Italy's exit from the war in 1943 was followed by the gradual establishment of communist control, the communist Government being recognized by the Allies in October 1945 on the understanding that Greater Albania aims had been abandoned. At the 1946 Paris peace conference Albania's independence was reaffirmed within its 1926 borders.

The post-war communist regime disavowed any territorial ambitions, a line followed by governments of the post-communist era. In 1991 Albania joined the **Organization for Security and Co-operation in Europe**, acceding to its requirement that existing borders should be regarded as inviolable. At the time of the break-up of the old **Socialist Federal Republic of Yugoslavia** in the early 1990s, and even more acutely during the Kosovo crisis of the late 1990s, there were serious anxieties among **Serbs** about possible Albanian aspirations for territorial expansion. Kosovo's ethnic Albanian majority has, however, followed a separate path, with that country's transition to independence in 2008.

Greater Croatia

A concept involving the territorial expansion of **Croatia** into neighbouring, and largely ethnic **Croat**, regions, which retains some support among nationalists. The modern state of Croatia was formed from the former **Yugoslav** republic of the same name and covers an area that has been considered 'Croatian' for centuries. However, millions of ethnic Croats are to be found in adjoining regions of **Bosnia and Herzegovina**, particularly in the south-eastern region of **Herzegovina** itself. During the Second World War Croat irredentist ambitions were realized briefly with the creation of the enlarged Croatian puppet State by the invading Nazis, which swallowed modern-day Bosnia and Herzegovina and regions of western **Serbia**. The short-lived state's fascist Government persecuted ethnic **Serbs** and **Muslims** (**Bosniaks**) and so the concept of a Greater Croatia became entwined, in Serbian eyes in particular, with the concept of racial discrimination.

The possibility of a Greater Croatia was raised again at the time of the violent disintegration of the **Socialist Federal Republic of Yugoslavia** in the early 1990s, as nationalist Croat factions in Croatia and Bosnia called for the unification of all ethnic Croats in the region. The division of Bosnia and Herzegovina between Croatia and Serbia (*see* **Greater Serbia**) was even mooted as a viable option to end the Bosnian civil war. A particularly strong proponent of the Greater Croatia idea was Franjo **Tudjman**, the Croatian President at this time, who championed the so-called Greater Greater Croatia which involved annexing not only Herzegovina but also the entire western half of Bosnia, including the modern Bosnian Serb capital **Banja Luka**, in an uneasy reminder of the earlier Nazi State of Croatia. The creation of an intact Bosnia and Herzegovina under the 1995 **Dayton Agreement**, and the death of Tudjman, have since lessened the influence of the Greater Greater Croatia faction. However, nationalist parties continue to pursue the idea of uniting Croatia with Herzegovina (in a so-called Lesser Greater Croatia), and have lent support to Croat nationalists in Bosnia and Herzegovina (*see* **Herceg-Bosna**).

Greater Hungary

A nationalist concept of an enlarged **Hungarian** state based on that country's historical domination of the surrounding area. **Hungary** was a major regional power from early medieval times until the disintegration of the Habsburg Empire in 1918.

From a very early period, and at various stages from then on, it covered the entire Pannonian plain, which is still dominated by the modern state of Hungary, and adjoining territories in modern southern **Slovakia**, **Transylvania**, **Vojvodina** and **Croatia**. The restructuring of this inland Empire was completed at the conclusion of the First World War under the points of the 1920 Treaty of **Trianon**, which left Hungary's borders much as they are today. Consequently the idea of a Greater Hungary has been created to match nationalist and romantic resentment at the country's reduction at the hands of the Allied powers. The concept is not seriously championed by mainstream parties, although relations with the Hungarian minorities in the historic Hungarian lands are a major concern for the Government and a source of regional tension.

Greater Romania

A nationalist concept of an enlarged **Romania** covering regions inhabited by ethnic **Romanians** (and Moldovans) and lands historically connected to the Romanian state. Ethnically isolated among **Slavic** neighbours, Romanian nationalists held tight to the idea of uniting all Romanian peoples in a single state. This goal was practically achieved following the First World War when Romania was rewarded with the annexation of **Transylvania**, **Bukovina**, southern **Dobruja** and all of historic Moldavia (*see* **Bessarabia question**). However, this Greater Romania was short-lived and was greatly reduced after the Second World War, losing Dobruja, northern Bukovina, and most importantly eastern Moldavia (Moldova).

The possibility of the unification of Moldova and Romania was immediately raised following the collapse in 1991 of the **Soviet Union**, of which Moldova had been a part. However, it was soon rejected in the following years and is now only championed by nationalist Romanian parties and some fringe Moldovan parties.

Greater Serbia

A nationalist concept of an enlarged **Serbia** covering regions inhabited by ethnic **Serbs** and lands historically connected to the Serbian state. Greater Serbia was in the 1990s perhaps the strongest of such irredentist ideas in **eastern Europe**. Serbia had reached its territorial zenith under Emperor Stephen Dushan in the mid-14th century, and stretched to incorporate **Herzegovina** (modern-day south-east **Bosnia and Herzegovina**), **Montenegro**, **Macedonia**, **Albania** and much of northern Greece. This short-lived Empire has gone on to form the basis of the concept of a Greater Serbia, although it did not include the **Vojvodina**, the Bosnian **Serb Republic** or even the modern Serb capital **Belgrade**. Conquered by the Ottoman Turks, the Serbian state was buried for over 500 years until it regained autonomy in the late 19th century. By this time ethnic Serbs had been spread by their **Muslim** rulers across lands to the north and west, and many had fled into neighbouring, Christian, states (*see* **Krajina** *and* Vojvodina), laying the basis for a more northerly Greater Serbian idea. In Bosnia in particular a large Serb community was now established.

Under the **Socialist Federal Republic of Yugoslavia** Serbia came to dominate the eastern half of the country and, with its capital serving as the federal centre as well, it also dominated the bureaucracy of the Yugoslav state. As the federation began to splinter in the late 1980s, Serb nationalist movements began to equate Yugoslavism with the idea of a Greater Serbia, and the territorial integrity of the Serbian lands led to the quashing of regional autonomy in the Vojvodina and **Kosovo**. In the later war in neighbouring Bosnia and Herzegovina, Bosnian Serb nationalists looked to the Yugoslav state as their protector and openly called for a Greater Serbia. The division of Bosnia and Herzegovina between Serbia and **Croatia** (*see* **Greater Croatia**) was even mooted as a possible solution to the war there. However, as the violent excesses of the Bosnian Serb campaign became clear, and the prospect of a 'winnable' war there receded, the idea of a Greater Serbia was dropped from the political mainstream.

Greece
Elleniki Dimokratia

An independent republic in south-eastern Europe located on the southern coast of the **Balkan** peninsula, bounded to the north by Albania, the Former Yugoslav Republic of Macedonia and Bulgaria, to the east by Turkey, and to the south and west by the Ionian, Aegean and Thracian Seas. The country is divided administratively into 13 regions (periphereies), which are subdivided into 54 prefectures (nomoi).

Area: 131,957 sq km; *capital*: Athens; *population*: 11.2m. (2009 estimate), consisting of **Greeks** 98%, **Turks** 1%, others 1%; *official language*: Greek; *religion*: Eastern **Orthodox** Christian 98%, **Muslim** 1%, others 1%.

Officially called the Hellenic Republic, Greece is a parliamentary democracy with a largely ceremonial President as Head of State, elected by the 300-member unicameral Parliament (Vouli) for a five-year term, renewable once only. Executive power resides with the Prime Minister and members of the cabinet. The Parliament is elected for a four-year term by universal adult suffrage under a system of proportional representation. Parties must pass a minimum threshold of 3% of the vote to secure representation. 260 of the seats in the parliament are allocated among the qualifying parties in proportion to their percentage of the vote; the remaining 40 seats are then awarded to the party with the largest number of votes, to raise the probability of the leading party having a secure majority.

History: The Minoan civilization in Crete from c.2300–1400 BC, Europe's first advanced society, spread to Mycenae on the mainland, where from c.1900 BC Ionians, Achaeans and Aeolians entered from the north. Centred on the Peloponnese peninsula, the Mycenaean culture flourished until the 12th century BC, when a new wave of migrants from the north, notably the Dorians, led to fragmentation into many city states, although a common Greek language and religion maintained cultural cohesion. The most powerful city states were **Athens**, Sparta, Thebes, Corinth and Argos on the Greek mainland and Syracuse in Greek Sicily. Between 499 BC and 478 BC the Greeks repulsed two Persian invasions, following which the golden age of classical Greece laid the intellectual foundations of European civilization. The Peloponnesian Wars, mainly between Athens and Sparta, weakened the city states, which lost their independence to the northern Greek kingdom of Macedon in 338 BC. Alexander the Great conquered the Persian Empire, founding Alexandria in Egypt in 331 BC and spreading Hellenistic civilization to his vast empire, which was partitioned after his death in 323 BC. Conquest by Rome followed in the second century BC.

Within the Roman Empire, Greece embraced Christianity early in the fourth century AD and in 395 became part of the Eastern Roman, later Byzantine, Empire, which from its capital at Constantinople preserved versions of the Greek language and cultural heritage while assimilating many races. Doctrinal disputes between Constantinople and the Church of Rome led to the Great Schism of 1054, after which the Greek Orthodox Church regarded itself as the sole spiritual embodiment of the universal Empire. Weakened by assaults by Latin crusaders in the 13th century, the Byzantine Empire was gradually overrun by Ottoman Turks, to whom Constantinople fell in 1453, followed by mainland Greece in 1456. The larger Greek-populated islands of the Aegean held out much longer under the control of powerful Italian city states, notably Venice. However, by the late 16th century all of the Greek world was under Muslim Turkish rule.

Greek cultural revival inspired by the Orthodox Church led to the outbreak in 1821 of the Greek War of Independence, in which the Greeks received support from British and French intellectuals and also from Russia. Independence was declared at Epidauros in 1822, but not until British, French and Russian warships had destroyed the Turkish–Egyptian fleet at Navarino in 1827 were the great powers able to force Turkey to recognize an independent Greece in 1829, albeit consisting only of the Peloponnese and the western Aegean islands. Prince Otto of Bavaria was installed as King of the Hellenes in 1832, but his despotic inclinations led to his replacement by Prince George of Denmark in 1862. The cession by the United Kingdom of its Ionian Islands protectorate to Greece in 1863 was followed by the acquisition from Turkey of Thessaly in 1881 and of Macedonia (*see* **Macedonian question**), southern Epirus (*see* **Epirus question**), Crete and the eastern Aegean islands in the Balkan Wars of 1912–13. King George I was assassinated in the northern port of Thessaloniki in 1913 and succeeded by Constantine I.

The outbreak of the First World War divided Greeks between the pro-German Constantine and the Liberal Prime Minister, Eleftherios Venizelos, who in 1917 secured the King's abdication and replacement by Alexander I, following which Greece entered the war on the Entente powers' side and against Turkey. However,

Venizelos's 'Greater Greece' aspirations, as partially achieved on paper in the **Versailles** and Sèvres peace treaties of 1919 and 1920, foundered as a result of Alexander receiving a fatal monkey bite in Gibraltar in October 1920 and Constantine being restored to the throne. Without support from the United Kingdom and France, Greece sought to impose the Sèvres terms on the revived Turkey of Kemal Atatürk, who proceeded to eject the Greek army and population from Anatolia. Constantine abdicated again and was succeeded by George II in 1922. Under the 1923 Treaty of Lausanne, Greece accepted Turkey's possession of Anatolia as well as Italy's acquisition of the Dodecanese islands and British rule in **Cyprus**. A republic was declared in 1924, but George II was restored by a plebiscite in 1935. Appointed Prime Minister in 1936, Gen. Ioannis Metaxas established a quasi-fascist dictatorship called the Third Civilization.

In the Second World War, Greece bravely repelled an attempted invasion by Italy in 1940, but was overrun by German forces in 1941. Occupation by the Axis powers was resisted mainly by the Greek People's Liberation Army (ELAS), the military wing of the National Liberation Front (EAM), which was dominated by the **Communist Party of Greece** (KKE). On the liberation of Greece in late 1944, civil war broke out between ELAS-EAM and the pro-monarchy Free Democratic Greek Army (EDES). George II was again restored to the throne by a plebiscite in 1946, but he died the following year and was succeeded by his brother Paul. Under the 1947 Paris peace treaty with Italy, the Dodecanese islands were ceded to Greece. British, and later US, troops then helped royalist forces to defeat ELAS-EAM by 1949, whereupon thousands of communists went into exile. In 1952 Greece, with Turkey, joined the **North Atlantic Treaty Organization** (NATO), as the right achieved electoral ascendancy under the premierships of Alexander Papagos (1952–55) and Constantine Karamanlis (1955–63).

The 1963 elections brought to power a minority Government of the centre-left Centre Union (EK) led by George Papandreou, who won a landslide majority in further elections in 1964. In 1965, however, Papandreou resigned over a clash with the new king, Constantine II, over an alleged plot by left-wing army officers in the so-called Aspida group to install a dictatorship under his son, Andreas **Papandreou**. Popular pressure forced the calling of elections, but these were pre-empted by a military coup in April 1967, believed by the Greek left to have been instigated by the US Central Intelligence Agency (CIA). The so-called 'colonels' regime' suspended parliamentary rule, banned left-wing organizations and drove democratic leaders, including Karamanlis, into exile. An abortive counter-coup by Constantine II in December 1967 resulted in the King going into exile. The regime proclaimed a republic in June 1973, following which a further military coup in December 1973 brought more hard-line officers to power. They were brought down in July 1974 by events in Cyprus, where they backed a short-lived coup by elements favouring union with Greece, precipitating a Turkish invasion and the establishment of what later became the **Turkish Republic of Northern Cyprus** (TRNC).

Karamanlis returned from exile in Paris to lead his newly-formed **New Democracy** (ND) party to a decisive victory in parliamentary elections in November 1974. The following month the restoration of the monarchy was rejected by a two-thirds majority in a referendum. A new Constitution in 1975 declared Greece to be a democratic republic and the new Parliament elected Constantine Tsatsos as President. Returned to power in the 1977 elections, Karamanlis was elected President in 1980 and succeeded as Prime Minister by George Rallis. In January 1981 Greece joined the European Communities (EC), later the **European Union** (EU), but popular opposition to membership contributed to ND's defeat in the 1981 parliamentary elections by the **Pan-Hellenic Socialist Movement** (PASOK) led by Andreas Papandreou. Initially committed to withdrawal from the EC and the removal of US bases from Greece, the PASOK Government in 1983 switched to a pro-EC stance after securing changes in Greece's membership terms and signed a new defence agreement with the USA. PASOK declined to renominate Karamanlis for the presidency and in 1985 secured the election of its own nominee, Christos Sartzetakis (although Karamanlis was returned to this essentially ceremonial office for a second term five years later). The 1985 parliamentary elections resulted in PASOK retaining power with a reduced majority.

The PASOK Government came under intense pressure in 1988 over the Koskotas affair, involving the alleged involvement of ministers and officials in fraud and embezzlement at the Bank of Crete. Also controversial was Papandreou's extramarital affair with a much younger air hostess called Dimitra Liani, whom he later married. Elections in June 1989 resulted in PASOK losing its majority and being replaced by a coalition of ND and what later became the **Coalition of the Left of Movements and Ecology** (Synaspismos) under the premiership of Tzannis Tzannetakis. Further elections in November 1989 resulted in the formation of a temporary three-party coalition of ND, PASOK and Synaspismos under Zenophon Zolotas, without the inclusion of the three party leaders. The third general election in less than a year, in April 1990, gave ND half the seats, enabling party leader Constantine Mitsotakis to form a Government with the external support of one non-ND deputy. The following month Karamanlis was again elected President.

Beset by internal divisions, the Mitsotakis Government resigned in September 1993 and was heavily defeated in elections the following month by PASOK, which returned to power with Andreas Papandreou again Prime Minister. Growing dissatisfaction with Papandreou's leadership and the political ambitions of his new wife escalated into a succession struggle when the ageing Prime Minister fell seriously ill in November 1995.

Papandreou eventually resigned in January 1996 and was succeeded as Prime Minister by Costas Simitis. Following Papandreou's death in June 1996, Simitis became PASOK leader. He led the party to victory in parliamentary elections that September, and to a further victory, albeit a narrow one, in April 2000.

Amid feverish preparations for Athens to host the Summer Olympics in 2004, Simitis stepped down at the start of the year, calling an early general election, and also resigning the PASOK leadership, in which he was succeeded by George **Papandreou** (the son of Andreas). The elections in March resulted in ND winning 165 of the 300 seats with 45.4% of the vote, PASOK 117 (40.6%), the KKE 12 (5.9%) and the **Coalition of the Radical Left** (SYRIZA), led by Synaspismos, six (3.3%). ND leader Costas Karamanlis (the nephew of the party's founder), aged 47, became Greece's youngest Prime Minister for a century. The main parties agreed on a consensus choice of President in February 2005 when the Parliament overwhelmingly elected the veteran left-wing politician Karolos Papoulias to succeed two-term outgoing President Costas Stephanopoulos.

The boost to national morale from hosting the 2004 Olympics was somewhat dissipated by the subsequent uncovering of serious irregularities in the state finances (see **Greece, economy**) and also by the disclosure in February 2006 that the mobile telephones of the Prime Minister and some 100 officials had been tapped during and after the Games.

In August 2007 Karamanlis called elections for the following month, six months before the end of the full four-year term. His expectations of strengthening the ND's majority were confounded, however, largely because of criticism that the Government was too slow to respond to a wave of forest fires that swept across the country, killing 65 people. Nevertheless, the ND narrowly managed to retain a majority of seats, with 152 in the 300-member Parliament (and 41.8% of the vote), while PASOK won 102 seats (38.1%), the KKE won 22 seats (8.2%), SYRIZA won 14 seats (5%) and the populist **Popular Orthodox Rally** (LAOS) passed the 3% threshold for the first time, winning 10 seats (3.8%).

Proposed pension reforms provoked strikes in 2008, while a financial scandal brought down two ministers and reduced ND's majority to just one seat. The international financial crisis from late 2008 pushed unemployment and public debt upwards, along with public opposition to necessitated austerity measures. The shooting of a student by a police officer in December triggered a mass outcry against the authorities, and demonstrations became commonplace, often turning violent. The Government struggled on into 2009, but finally conceded the need for early elections.

Latest elections: The October election resulted in victory for PASOK, with 160 seats (43.9% of the vote), and ND retaining 91 seats (33.5%), while the KKE fell to 21 seats (7.5%), the LAOS increased to 15 seats (5.6%) and SYRIZA secured the remaining 13 seats (4.6%). In February 2010 incumbent President Papoulias was re-elected unopposed by the Parliament for a second term.

Recent developments: Taking office as Prime Minister on 6 October 2009, George Papandreou named a cabinet that included economic technocrats to focus on the struggling economy, and in particular public sector reform. His Government faced a major crisis over its soaring public debt, and was compelled to bring in a further succession of tough measures to cut spending and meet the conditions of a joint

European Union—**International Monetary Fund** emergency economic support package in early May 2010. As the extent and severity of the austerity measures and wage and pension cuts became known, public hostility was manifested in violent demonstrations and rioting in Athens in which several people were killed.

International relations and defence: The cornerstones of Greek foreign and defence policy are NATO and the EU, which Greece joined in 1952 and 1981 respectively. Greece is also a member of the **Council of Europe**, the **Organization for Security and Co-operation in Europe** and the **Organization of the Black Sea Economic Co-operation**, as well as of the **World Trade Organization** and the **Organisation for Economic Co-operation and Development**. Relations with neighbouring Turkey were seriously strained for decades, notably over disputed demarcation of the Aegean Sea; both sides have pursued rapprochement in recent years, but the unresolved Cyprus problem, particularly Turkey's recognition of the self-proclaimed TRNC, continues to be a source of difficulty.

The dispute over the use of the name Macedonia by Greece's northern neighbour (*see* **Macedonian question**) has flared up each time that the two countries come into contact in international affairs; it is currently a stumbling block in the former Yugoslav republic's application to join NATO and the EU.

Budgeted defence expenditure was some US $10,141m. in 2008, equivalent to 2.9% of GDP. Consisting of an army, navy, air force and coast guard, the armed forces have an active strength of 157,000, while reservists numbered an estimated 238,000. There is compulsory military conscription of 12 months.

Greece, economy

A free-market economy with a large state-owned sector in a country which, as a member of the **European Union** (EU) since 1981, has made uneven progress away from dependence on agriculture and low-value-added industries. Its high levels of public debt exposed it to harsh realities when the global economic crisis hit home in 2009, compelling the Government to adopt severe austerity measures, which were intensified in May 2010 under the terms of a rescue package from other **eurozone** member countries and the **International Monetary Fund** (IMF).

GNP: US $321,972m. (2008); *GNP per capita*: $28,650 (2008); *GDP at PPP*: $329,963m. (2008); *GDP per capita at PPP*: $29,400 (2008); *real GDP growth*: –0.8% (2009 estimate); *exports*: $23,472m. (2008); *imports*: $75,100m. (2008); *currency*: euro (US $1 = €0.7129 in mid-2009); *unemployment*: 10.6% (Nov. 2009); *government deficit as a percentage of GDP*: 12.7% (2009); *inflation*: 1.1% (2009).

In 2007 industry accounted for 20% of GDP, agriculture 4% and services 76%. Around 23% of the workforce is engaged in industry, 11% in agriculture and 66% in services.

About 30% of the land is arable (including 9% under permanent crops), 40% meadow and pasture and 20% forested. The main crops are cereals (wheat, maize and barley), sugar beet, olives, tomatoes, grapes, potatoes and tobacco; animal husbandry (sheep, goats and cattle), forestry and fishing are also important.

The main mineral resources are lignite, bauxite, magnesite, silver ore, marble and natural gas. The principal manufacturing industries are food and tobacco processing, textiles, chemicals, metal-working, ship-building and petroleum products. The services sector is dominated by shipping management (Greece having Europe's largest merchant fleet registered under its flag), financial services and tourism, the last yielding about 15% of GDP and employing 17% of the workforce.

Greece's main exports are food and beverages, textiles and clothing, manufactured goods and petroleum products, while imports are headed by machinery, transport equipment, fuels and chemicals. The principal purchasers of exports in 2008 were Italy (12%), Germany (11%) and **Bulgaria** (7%). The main sources of imports in 2008 were Germany (12%), Italy (11%) and the Russian Federation (7%).

Accession in January 1981 to what became the EU, and the subsequent receipt of substantial EU funds, accelerated the gradual transition of Greece from being one of Europe's most underdeveloped countries, with a large agricultural sector, into a modern economy with a dominant services sector. The centre-right **New Democracy** (ND) Government elected in 1990, claiming that the previous administration of the **Pan-Hellenic Socialist Movement** (PASOK) had left Greece in its worst economic crisis since 1945, introduced draconian austerity measures and initiated the privatization of hugely indebted and overmanned state-owned industries, against fierce opposition from public-sector employees.

PASOK's return to power in 1993 resulted at first in the reversal or suspension of much of the privatization programme. In 1994, however, the Government announced plans to privatize 25% of the OTE telecommunications monopoly, thereby generating strong trade union opposition. In the same year, the lifting of exchange control restrictions gave rise to a short-lived currency crisis. In 1995 the annual rate of inflation fell below 10% for the first time in two decades. Re-elected in 1996, the PASOK Government set as its principal economic goal the participation of Greece as a founder member of the EU's single currency, the euro. Austerity measures designed to bring the state finances into compliance with the criteria for **eurozone** membership, thereby provoking serious labour unrest. In March 1998 the Greek drachma entered the EU's Exchange Rate Mechanism II, the obligatory staging-post to adopting the euro, as the Government pushed ahead with its privatization programme and introduced tough wage restraint measures.

Greece was unable to join the euro at its launch for non-cash transactions in January 1999, but in June 2000 it satisfied its EU partners that it met the various criteria for membership. As a result, it became the 12th member of the eurozone in January 2001 and joined the others in making the euro its sole legal tender in January 2002. The adoption of the euro provided Greece with access to competitive loan rates and also to the low rates of the eurobond market. This led to a dramatic increase in consumer spending, which in turn boosted economic growth to about 4% in both 2002 and 2003. However, the PASOK Government's resultant more relaxed fiscal policy, combined with big overruns in the cost of staging the Olympic Games in **Athens** in 2004, meant that the ND Government elected in March 2004 faced another crisis in the public finances.

It was eventually established that the budget deficit had spiralled from 5.4% of GDP in 2003 to 6.1% in 2004, more than double the ceiling prescribed under eurozone rules and the highest rate of any participating country since the launch of the euro. In October 2004, moreover, it emerged that Greece had under-reported its deficit and public debt figures in the years preceding its admission to the eurozone and had not been qualified for membership because it had consistently breached the 3% budget deficit ceiling rule. In December 2004 the European Commission launched 'excessive deficit' legal proceedings against Greece, giving it until the end of 2006 to comply with eurozone rules. The Government responded in March 2005 by increasing excise duties on alcohol and tobacco and by raising value-added tax (VAT) from 18% to 19%. Nevertheless, the budget deficit in 2005 remained high at 5.1%, as did unemployment at around 10% of the registered workforce, despite further strong GDP growth of 4.2% in 2004 and 3.7% in 2005.

Additional austerity measures, a crackdown on tax evasion, further privatizations and GDP growth of 3.8% resulted in the anticipated 2006 budget deficit falling to 2.6% of GDP, so that Greece could claim to have come into compliance with eurozone rules. However, in October 2006 the European Commission announced that it would conduct a 'complete verification' of Greek economic data after it emerged that Greece, in a revision of its statistical methods, had begun to include the proceeds of prostitution and drug-trafficking in its calculation of GDP. In May 2007 the Commission announced that it would end budgetary supervision of Greece. In 2008 legislation was introduced to counter tax evasion, which had, hitherto, contributed to low yields from personal income tax relative to other EU countries. However, efforts to reduce expenditure, particularly with regard to proposed pension reforms, have provoked frequent bouts of civil unrest and industrial action. The international financial crisis that gathered momentum from September 2008 resulted in a shortfall in liquidity and some Greek financial institutions needed recapitalizing. The Government appropriated 28,000m. euros to this end. International credit agency Standard & Poor's downgraded the country's investment status in January 2009, following a Eurostat estimate that the budget deficit would likely exceed 3% that year; in fact by the end of the year, Greece's deficit was 12.7% of GDP, with debt above 110% of GDP and unemployment passing 10%.

In early 2010 the international dimensions of the deepening Greek economic crisis came to the fore as EU leaders debated what action they would take if Greece were unable to pay its debts. Reluctant to underwrite the costs of a bail-out but even more anxious to avoid the repercussions of a member country being forced to abandon the euro, in May 2010 they eventually agreed a support package, in tandem with the IMF, worth a total of 110,000m. euros in emergency loans and IMF credits over three years. The package was conditional on Greece's adoption of a further raft of stringent austerity measures and spending cuts, prompting more protests, violent demonstrations and strike action by Greek workers.

Greek Cypriots *see* **Greeks**.

Greeks

An ethnic group speaking the Greek language, centred on **Greece** and **Cyprus**, but found in diaspora communities worldwide. From earliest antiquity Greeks occupied land around the Aegean Sea, spreading to colonies around the entire Mediterranean. From medieval times to the early 20th century Greeks inhabited many lands of the eastern Mediterranean; after the Greco-Turkish war (1919–22) a population exchange confined ethnic Greeks almost entirely to the borders of modern Greece and Cyprus.

The majority of Greeks follow the Greek Orthodox religion (*see* **Orthodox Church**). In Greece they comprise 93% of the country's population, while Greek Cypriots make up 78% of the population in Cyprus. There are over 1m. Greeks living in the USA, around 400,000 in each of the United Kingdom, Australia, Germany and Canada, and 200,000 in **Albania**.

Green Line

The 1974 ceasefire line that became the *de facto* division between **Cyprus** proper and the self-proclaimed **Turkish Republic of Northern Cyprus**. Also known as the Attila Line, it passes east to west across the island, cutting through **Nicosia**. The UN established a buffer zone along the line, which is administered by the UNFICYP peacekeeping force.

The Turkish Cypriot Government opened the first crossing point in 2003, in Nicosia, allowing the first movement of Cypriots between the two partitioned regions for almost 30 years. Several more crossing points have opened since then, including the Ledra Street crossing in 2008.

Green Party
Strana Zelených (SZ)

A political party in the **Czech Republic**, currently part of the ruling coalition. Founded in 1990, the SZ contested several elections before securing its first legislative seat—in the Senate (upper house of **Parliament**) in 2004.

At the June 2006 lower house elections, the SZ won six seats, with 6.3% of the vote, and agreed in July to join the Government led by the **Civic Democratic Party** (ODS). Several months of political crisis ensued as the 'hung' chamber would not approve the coalition. Eventually approval was gained in January 2007, and SZ leader Martin Bursík became one of the Deputy Prime Ministers (and Minister of the Environment). The foreign affairs portfolio was assigned to Karel Schwarzenberg (an independent representing the SZ), and the SZ received two other ministerial posts.

The Government was defeated in a vote of no confidence in the Chamber of Deputies on 24 March 2009. On 6 April Jan **Fischer**, head of the Czech Statistical Office and of no political party, was nominated to be interim Prime Minister; Fischer took office on 8 May with a caretaker non-partisan cabinet, including members nominated by the SZ. The party's poor showing in the European elections in June led to Bursík's resignation as SZ Chairman, succeeded by Deputy Chairman Ondřej Liška.

Leadership: Ondřej Liška (Chair.).
Address: Stroupežnického 30, 150 00 Prague 5.
Telephone: 775587500.
E-mail: info@zeleni.cz
Internet: www.zeleni.cz

Gruevski, Nikola

Prime Minister of **Macedonia**.

Nikola Gruevski is Chairman of the right-of-centre **Internal Macedonian Revolutionary Organization–Democratic Party for Macedonian National Unity** (VMRO–DPMNE). He was appointed Prime Minister on 27 August 2006.

Born on 31 August 1970 in **Skopje**, he graduated from the Economics Faculty in Prilep in 1994. He began his career at the Balkanska Banka in 1995 as director for securities, planning and analysis, before being drafted into the cabinet as Minister without Portfolio on 30 November 1998. He was switched to the Ministry of Trade in January 1999 before arriving in the Finance Ministry in December that year. He was among a number of senior officials who discovered in early 2001 that they had been the subject of wiretapping by the secret service.

He rose to the leadership of the VMRO–DPMNE party after its defeat in the 2002 election, being appointed Chairman of the party in May 2003, and leading it to an improvement in its fortunes at the next elections in July 2006. This poll saw the

VMRO–DPMNE-led coalition reclaim its position as the largest bloc and gave Gruevski the opportunity to form a new Government. He was approved as Prime Minister on 27 August.

Address: Office of the Prime Minister, Ilindenska b.b., 91000 Skopje.
Telephone: (2) 3115389.
Fax: (2) 3112561.
Internet: www.vlada.mk

Grybauskaite, Dalia

President of **Lithuania**. A diplomat and economist, Dalia Grybauskaite spent most of the 1990s negotiating on **European Union** (EU) affairs for Lithuania. Three years as Finance Minister then saw her move to the European Commission, where she won respect for her work on the EU budget. The press call her 'Lithuania's Iron Lady' for her steely determination and outspokenness. She won the Lithuanian presidency in May 2009 by a landslide, and took office on 12 July, becoming Lithuania's first female head of state.

Dalia Grybauskaite was born on 1 March 1956 in **Vilnius**. In 1983 she graduated in economics from Zhdanov University in Leningrad (now St Petersburg), where she had also worked in a fur factory. After returning to Vilnius, she lectured in political economy and global finance at Vilnius Party High School. Continuing her studies while teaching, she gained a doctorate from Moscow Academy of Social Studies in 1988.

After the collapse of the **Soviet Union**, she went to the USA for a special programme for senior executives at the School of Foreign Service of Georgetown University, Washington, DC. Between 1991 and 1993 she was director of the European Department at Lithuania's Ministry of International Economic Relations, and then moved to the Foreign Ministry as Director of the Economic Relations Department, where she led negotiations for Lithuania's free trade agreement with the EU. In 1994 she was appointed Extraordinary Envoy and Plenipotentiary Minister at Lithuania's diplomatic mission to the EU, where she was deputy chief negotiator for Lithuania's Association Agreement with the EU, prior to its application for EU membership. Two years later, she was appointed Plenipotentiary Minister at the Lithuanian Embassy in the USA.

In 1999 she returned to Lithuania to become Deputy Minister of Finance in the centre-right Government of Andrius **Kubilius** of the Homeland Union–Lithuanian Conservatives. As part of this role, she led Lithuanian negotiations with the **World Bank** and **International Monetary Fund** (IMF). In 2000 she became Deputy Minister of Foreign Affairs, but in 2001 returned to the Finance Ministry as full Minister in the centre-left Government of Algirdas Brazauskas of the **Lithuanian Social Democratic Party**.

Three years later when Lithuania joined the EU, she was named as its European Commissioner, initially assigned responsibility for education and culture, and then transferred in November 2004 to financial programming and budget. She was chosen as Commissioner of the Year in November 2005 'for her unrelenting efforts to shift EU spending towards areas that would enhance competitiveness such as research and development'.

She announced in February 2009 that she would stand as an independent for the Lithuanian presidency, and quickly became the front runner. Her candidacy was supported by the ruling **Homeland Union–Lithuanian Christian Democrats**. At the election on 17 May she won in the first round with 68.2% of the vote, the largest ever margin.

Grybauskaite speaks English, Russian, Polish and French.

Address: Office of the President, Simono Daukanto a. 3, 01122 Vilnius.

Telephone: (5) 2664154.

Fax: (5) 2664145.

E-mail: info@president.lt

Internet: www.president.lt

Gypsies *see* **Roma**.

H

Harmony Centre
Saskaņas Centrs (SC)

A centre-left political party in **Latvia**, currently in opposition, advocating reconciliation between **Latvians** and non-Latvians with guaranteed rights for minorities. Harmony Centre was formed in 2005 as an electoral alliance between the National Harmony Party (TSP), Latvian Socialist Party (LSP), New Centre and Daugavpils City Party. The alliance won 17 seats and 14.4% of the vote at the October 2006 elections, making it the fourth-largest party in the **Parliament**. In December 2006 the alliance officially merged into a single entity, though the LSP remained just affiliated to the organization.

The TSP consisted of the residue of the Harmony for Latvia–Rebirth grouping which split in 1994. Led by Jānis Jurkāns, it won only six of the 100 seats in the autumn 1995 elections and was reduced to four seats by a further split in July 1996, although it was strengthened in September 1997 by a parliamentary alliance with the five-strong LSP group led by Alfreds Rubiks, who had been leader of the Soviet-era Latvian Communist Party.

For the October 1998 elections a pro-Russian alliance was created called For Human Rights in a United Latvia (PCTVL), which included the TSP, the LSP and two ethnic **Russian** groupings, but failed to secure registration in time to run under that label. The alliance's candidates therefore stood under the TSP banner, winning 16 seats on a 14.1% vote share. The formation thus became the largest component of the opposition to the centre-right coalition. Support for the PCTVL grew, and Jurkāns's relations with the Russian Government improved after President Vladimir Putin took office in 1999. At the October 2002 elections the PCTVL alliance secured 25 seats (with 19% of the vote), placing it second behind the populist **New Era** (JL). However, the alliance's left-wing agenda resulted in it remaining in opposition. In February 2003 Jurkāns withdrew the TSP from the alliance, distancing the party from its more radical partners to increase its future chances of joining a ruling coalition. In 2004 it gave parliamentary backing to the minority coalition of Indulis Emsis of the **Union of Greens and Farmers**, though this Government only lasted from March to October.

After a poor showing in the March 2005 **Rīga** municipal elections, when the TSP failed to pass the 5% threshold, it decided to form a Harmony Centre alliance with the New Centre, a party that had formed only a few months earlier from a breakaway faction of the TSP. Jurkāns disagreed with the alliance, and resigned as TSP leader in July. The LSP, the small Daugavpils City Party and the Social Democratic Union also subsequently joined the Harmony Centre alliance.

Leadership: Nils Ušakovs (Chair.).
Address: Rīga.
Telephone: 69218855.
Internet: www.saskanascentrs.lv

Havel, Václav

The former dissident playwright who became leader of **Czechoslovakia**'s '**velvet revolution**' in 1989 and thereafter President first of Czechoslovakia, then (from 1993 to 2003) of the **Czech Republic**.

Born on 5 October 1936 in **Prague**, he was initially denied a university place under the post-war communist regime because he had a bourgeois family background. A career in the theatre in the 1960s, and increasingly as a successful playwright with an international reputation, ensured him a high profile as an enthusiastic supporter of new ideas of liberal communism in the so-called '**Prague Spring**' of 1968. Havel chaired the Circle of Independent Writers, and was a fierce opponent of the invasion by **Warsaw Pact** forces that August. The subsequent period of repression saw his work banned in Czechoslovakia, although it circulated as *samizdat* (illegal 'self-published' manuscripts) and was published in the West. As spokesperson for a small group of dissident intellectuals, he was a founding signatory on 1 January 1977 of what became the rallying call of the human rights movement, **Charter 77**. He spent four years in prison from 1979 to 1983 on a charge of sedition, and in January 1989 was again arrested, with a group of human rights demonstrators, and sentenced to nine months' imprisonment for incitement and obstruction. This aroused a major international protest, which embarrassed the regime into releasing him in May.

The astonishingly rapid collapse of communist rule in late 1989 propelled Havel into a national leadership role. Heading the **Civic Forum** which he helped set up in November, he was at the forefront of the protest movement and the massive popular demonstrations which swept the old regime from power. On 29 December he was elected by the legislature as interim President, pending the holding of a general election the following June. The new Federal Assembly, meeting on 5 July 1990, then confirmed him in office for two years. During this period his relations with **Slovak** nationalist leader Vladimír **Mečiar** were often difficult, while it was common knowledge that he differed with Václav **Klaus**, then Finance Minister (and later

Czech Prime Minister and Havel's eventual successor as Czech President), over the speed and uncompromising radicalism of the switchover to a free-market economy.

Havel stood down as Czechoslovakia's President in July 1992, after his federalist constitutional proposals were rejected, and it was becoming increasingly unlikely that any form of Czech and Slovak Federation would survive the pull of Slovak separatism. When the separation of the two states had been formalized, the Parliament of the Czech Republic elected him unopposed to the presidency on 26 January 1993. Although the presidency is required to be non-partisan, Havel's moral stature gave him considerable weight in Czech public life and in promoting the country's interests in integration within a democratic Europe. It nevertheless took two rounds of voting among members of Parliament for him to win re-election for a further five-year term of office in January 1998—mainly because supporters of Klaus resented Havel's role in relegating him to a period in opposition after his Government collapsed in late 1997. Havel took the opportunity of his inaugural speech to rededicate himself to the development of democracy and civic society and to combating the growth of nationalism and xenophobia. On several occasions during his second term he decried prejudice and discrimination against the **Roma** minority, calling for greater tolerance and the renewal of the 'spirit of 1989'. His second term ended on 2 February 2003.

Since leaving office, Havel has focused on European affairs, human rights and environmental issues. Politically, he has voiced support for the **Green Party** (SZ), helping to revive the party's popularity. He has also returned to the theatre, writing his first play for almost two decades in 2007.

Havel's first wife Olga died in January 1996. A year later he married the acclaimed Czech actress Dagmar Veskrnova. His health has on several occasions caused serious alarm. A heavy smoker, he had surgery for lung cancer in December 1996, and he has undergone a succession of subsequent health crises and hospitalizations.

HDZ (Bosnia and Herzegovina) *see* **Croatian Democratic Union (Bosnia and Herzegovina)**.

HDZ (Croatia) *see* **Croatian Democratic Union (Croatia)**.

HELCOM *or* **Helsinki Commission** *see* **Baltic Marine Environment Protection Commission**.

Helsinki Final Act

The diplomatic agreement signed in Helsinki, Finland, on 1 August 1975 at the end of the first Conference on Security and Co-operation in Europe (*see* **Organization for Security and Co-operation in Europe**). The 35 participants, including the members of the **North Atlantic Treaty Organization** and the **Warsaw Pact** and 13 neutral and non-aligned European countries, effectively accepted the post-1945 status quo in Europe. Four 'baskets' of agreement in the Final Act (also known as the Helsinki Accord) covered: security and confidence-building; co-operation on economic, scientific and environmental issues; human rights and freedoms; and the holding of follow-up conferences.

Helsinki process

The continuing round of negotiations and follow-up conferences set in train by the 1973–75 Helsinki conference. The Helsinki process was officially known as the Conference on Security and Co-operation in Europe (CSCE). Over a period of 25 years, the CSCE and its successor the **Organization for Security and Co-operation in Europe** (OSCE) became a significant element in the architecture of European dialogue and ultimately co-operation during and after the **Cold War**. The so-called Basket One of the Helsinki Accord of 1975 set up the process which led ultimately to the conclusion of the landmark multilateral arms reduction treaty on **Conventional Forces in Europe** (CFE) in 1990. Basket Two dealt with co-operation in science, technology and environmental protection. Basket Three, in which the participant states made commitments on human rights and freedoms, had a special significance for the emergence of movements pressing for greater respect for civil liberties within communist countries. Notable among these were the Moscow Helsinki Group founded in 1976 in Russia by a group including Yuri Orlov, Yelena Bonner and Anatoly Shcharansky; **Charter 77** in **Czechoslovakia**; and the Helsinki Watch group founded in **Poland** in 1979. These initiatives were supported by 'Helsinki Watch' committees across western Europe, Canada and the USA, leading to the holding of a conference in 1982 and the creation in 1983 of the International Helsinki Federation for Human Rights (IHF).

Herceg-Bosna

The self-declared **Croat** entity in south **Bosnia and Herzegovina**, founded by Croat nationalists in July 1992 during the early phase of the Bosnian civil war and proclaimed as a separate republic on 28 August 1993. The declaration by nationalist leader Mate Boban prompted the widening of the conflict in Bosnia, drawing the **Bosniak** Muslims and the Croat populations into open hostility and encouraging the military intervention of **Croatia** in 1993. The entity was governed by the Croatian Defence Council (HVO) which successfully gained ground in the region and captured the city of **Mostar**, which became the entity's capital, in October 1992. Mostar became the centre for some of the war's most ferocious fighting between Muslims and Croats.

Herceg-Bosna was effectively absorbed into the **Muslim-Croat Federation** in March 1994 at the start of the alliance between the two groups. The region today contains a majority of Bosnia's c.750,000-strong Croat population and is the centre for their aspirations to self-rule.

Herzegovina

The south-eastern corner of **Bosnia and Herzegovina**. Historically the region stretches with indeterminate reach into **Montenegro** and south-eastern **Croatia** and is renowned as the first home of the **Serbs**. It draws its name from the *Herceg*, local leaders who resisted the encroachment of Ottoman rule in the Middle Ages. Now Herzegovina is dominated by ethnic **Croats** (*see* **Herceg-Bosna**). The main urban area is **Mostar** which serves as a regional administrative centre. The region is blocked from the Adriatic Sea by a Croatian coastal strip, apart from a small port at Neum.

HFP *see* **Croatian Privatization Fund**.

HGK *see* **Croatian Chamber of Economy**.

High Representative of the International Community *see* **Office of the High Representative**.

HINA news agency
Hrvatska Izvjes Tajna Novinska Agencija

Croatia's main news agency, founded in 1990, which also produces an electronic news service online known as Hina News Line and a news database, EVA.
Manager: Mirko Bolfek.
Address: Marulićev trg 16, 10000 Zagreb.
Telephone: (1) 4808700.
Fax: (1) 4808820.
E-mail: newsline@hina.hr
Internet: www.hina.hr

HIV—Human Immuno-deficiency Virus *see* **AIDS**.

HNB *see* **Croatian National Bank**.

HNS–LD *see* **Croatian People's Party—Liberal Democrats**.

Homeland Union–Lithuanian Christian Democrats
Tėvynės Sąjunga–Lietuvos Krikščionys Demokratai (TS–LKD)

The leading centre-right political party in **Lithuania**, currently heading the Government, and a member of the **International Democrat Union** and **Centrist Democrat International**. It took its current name in May 2008 when the Homeland Union (TS) merged with the Lithuanian Christian Democrats (LKD). At the October 2008 Seimas (**Parliament**) election, the TS–LKD won 45 seats (with 19.7% of the vote), becoming substantially the largest party in parliament.

The Homeland Union–Lithuanian Conservatives (TS–LK) was launched in May 1993 as successor to the remnants of the Lithuanian Reform Movement (**Sąjudis**), which had spearheaded the independence campaign. Under the leadership of Vytautas Landsbergis, the broadly-based Sąjudis had been the leading formation in the 1990 elections, but in the face of economic adversity had suffered a heavy defeat in the 1992 contest, winning only 20.5% of the popular vote. The new TS–LK proclaimed a centre-right orientation, while announcing that its ranks were open to former communists.

Profiting from the unpopularity of the post-1992 left-wing Government, the TS–LK swept to an overall majority of 70 seats in the autumn 1996 parliamentary elections, opting to form a centre-right coalition with the Lithuanian Christian Democratic Party (LKDP) and the Lithuanian Centre Union (LCS) under the premiership of Gediminas Vagnorius. In direct presidential elections in late 1997 and early 1998, Landsbergis came a poor third in the first round with only 15.7%, but the party then gave crucial backing to the narrow second-round victor, Valdas Adamkus (non-party).

Vagnorius was succeeded as Prime Minister in May 1999 by Rolandas Paksas, then the TS–LK Mayor of **Vilnius**, but growing divisions between the coalition partners resulted in his replacement in October 1999 by Andrius **Kubilius**. Splits within the TS–LK followed, so that in parliamentary elections in October 2000 the rump party was heavily punished, slumping to only nine seats and 8.6% of the vote. It returned to opposition.

In May 2003 Kubilius succeeded Landsbergis as party Chairman, then in November the TS–LK absorbed the Lithuanian Rightist Union, and in February 2004 merged with the Lithuanian Union of Political Prisoners and Deportees, at which point its full name became Homeland Union—Conservatives, Political Prisoners and Deportees, Christian Democrats, or more simply just Homeland Union (TS). At the October 2004 Seimas election, the TS finished in third place with 25 seats (14.6% of the vote); it remained in opposition, and absorbed the small Lithuanian National Union in March 2008, shortly before the May 2008 merger with the LKD which formed the basis of its return to power.

The LKD's own origins lay in the Lithuanian Christian Democratic Party (LKDP), launched in 1989 as the revival of a pre-Soviet party dating from 1905. It adopted a

Christian democratic programme on the western European model, favouring Lithuania's integration into Western institutions. The party's third-place vote share of 12.2% and 18 seats in the 1992 parliamentary elections was achieved in co-operation with other groups, notably the Sąjudis reform movement. It was nevertheless in opposition until the 1996 elections. Although it slipped to 16 seats and 10% of the vote in that poll, it became the second-largest party, and joined a centre-right coalition Government headed by the TS–LK. Serious strains in coalition relations from mid-1999 were accompanied by factional strife in LKDP ranks and the formation of alternative Christian democratic groupings. In the October 2000 parliamentary elections the rump LKDP slumped to only two seats and 3.1% of the vote, going into opposition. In late 2000 the LKDP initiated talks with other Christian democratic factions on reunifying the historic party. The first stage of this was achieved in April 2001 when the LKDP merged with the Christian Democratic Union to form the Lithuanian Christian Democrats (LKD). This new party won no seats at the 2004 Seimas election, but was beginning to improve its ratings, including some success in the 2007 municipal elections, prior to its merger with the TS in 2008.

Leadership: Andrius Kubilius (Chair.).
Address: L.Stuokos-Gucevičiaus g. 11, LT- 01122 Vilnius.
Telephone: (5) 2121657.
Fax: (5) 2784722.
E-mail: sekretoriatas@tsajunga.lt
Internet: www.tsajunga.lt

HOS *see* **Croatian Defence Force**.

House of Deputies
Camera Deputaţilor

The lower house of the **Parliament of Romania**.

House of Peoples
Dom Naroda

The upper house of the **Parliamentary Assembly** of **Bosnia and Herzegovina**.

House of Representatives (Bosnia and Herzegovina)
Predstavnički Dom (Bosnian); *Zastupnički Dom* (Croatian)

The lower house of the **Parliamentary Assembly** of **Bosnia and Herzegovina**.

House of Representatives (Croatia)
Zastupnički Dom

The single chamber of the **Assembly** of **Croatia**.

House of Representatives (Cyprus)
Vouli Antiprosópon (Greek); *Temsilciler Meclisi* (Turkish)

The unicameral legislature of **Cyprus**. It theoretically has 80 members elected for a five-year term by proportional representation, 56 by the Greek Cypriot community and 24 by the **Turkish Cypriots**. Since 1963, however, the Turkish Cypriot community has refused to participate in these arrangements. Three further representatives are elected by the Armenian, Maronite and Latin religious communities and have a consultative role in the House. The last elections were held on 21 May 2006.

> *Address*: House of Representatives, Dyiavaharlal Nehrou, Omerou Avenue, 1402 Nicosia.
> *Telephone*: (22) 407300.
> *Fax*: (22) 668611.
> *E-mail*: s.g@parliament.cy
> *Internet*: www.parliament.cy

Hoxha, Enver

The dictatorial head of the communist regime in **Albania** from 1944 until his death in office in 1985. A southern Albanian from Gjirokastër, Hoxha (born in 1908) joined the communist party in the 1930s while at university in France. Returning to Albania in 1936 as a French teacher after abandoning his studies in law, he joined a Marxist group in Korçë to organize against the regime of King Zog. In 1941 Hoxha was chosen as first Secretary-General of the newly-constituted Albanian Communist Party. The resistance struggle brought this small group to prominence, thanks in part to Hoxha's charismatic leadership and ruthlessness. In power from 1944, he formally relinquished in 1954 his government post as Prime Minister, but retained the first secretaryship of the renamed Party of Labour of Albania (PPS). He consolidated his personal supremacy in a series of purges beginning with the 'pro-**Yugoslav**' faction (Hoxha himself having always been associated with the rival Albanian nationalist standpoint). Hoxha oversaw the creation of a Stalinist centralized power structure and command economy, but fell out with the Soviet leadership over the Sino-Soviet split in 1960–61, whereupon Khrushchev denounced the 'bloody atrocities' of his purges. Ever more xenophobic in the cocoon of his personality cult after the break with the People's Republic of China in the late 1970s, Hoxha in 1982 denounced his long-time associate Mehmet Shehu (who had died in mysterious circumstances the previous December) for having been a US, Yugoslav and Soviet agent since the war. Further purges followed. When Hoxha died in April 1985 his personality cult remained intact. His widow Nexhmije continued to wield much influence as a hard-liner in the Party Central Committee, chairing the umbrella Democratic Front until December 1990. The violence of attacks on the statues and symbols of Hoxha all over Albania in 1991 underlined the extent to which the communist period had been defined by his omnipresence.

HSLS *see* **Croatian Social-Liberal Party**.

HSS *see* **Croatian Peasants' Party**.

Hungarian Chamber of Commerce and Industry
Magyar Kereskedelmi és Iparkamara(MKIK)

The principal organization in **Hungary** for promoting business contacts, both internally and externally, in the post-communist era. Originally founded in 1850.
  President: László Parragh.
  Secretary-General: Péter Dunai.
  Address: Kossuth Lajos tér 6–8, 1055 Budapest.
  Telephone: (1) 4745141.
  Fax: (1) 4745105.
  E-mail: mkik@mail.mkik.hu
  Internet: www.mkik.hu

Hungarian Coalition Party
Strana Maďarskej Koalície (SMK)

A political party in **Slovakia** which is the main political representative of the ethnic **Hungarian** minority population. In Hungarian its name is Magyar Koalíció Pártja (MKP). It is an observer at the **Centrist Democrat International**, and is currently in opposition.
    The SMK was launched in January 1998 as a merger of three ethnic Hungarian parties in Slovakia, namely: (i) Coexistence (ESWS), an alliance of Hungarian and other ethnic minority parties which was founded in 1990 and which won nine seats in the 1994 **National Council** elections; (ii) the Hungarian Christian Democratic Movement (MKdH/MKdM), which was founded in 1990 and which won seven seats in 1994; and (iii) the Hungarian Civic Party (MOS), which obtained one seat in 1994. In July 1998 the SMK registered as a single party, in light of new electoral rules

specifying that each component of an alliance must surmount the 5% threshold to obtain representation.

In the September 1998 parliamentary election the SMK lost ground slightly, returning 15 deputies on a vote share of 9.1%. It opted to join a centre-left coalition Government headed by Prime Minister Mikuláš Dzurinda of the centrist Slovak Democratic Coalition (SDK, *see* **Slovak Democratic and Christian Union–Democratic Party**), receiving three ministerial portfolios.

At the September 2002 election the SMK improved to 20 seats (with 11.2% of the vote), and joined Dzurinda's new coalition Government, receiving a fourth ministerial portfolio. For the 2004 presidential election it endorsed the candidacy of František Mikloško of the Christian Democratic Movement, but he finished fifth with 6.5% of the vote.

At the June 2006 election the SMK again won 20 seats (this time with 11.7% of the vote), but went into opposition to a coalition led by the left-wing **Direction–Social Democracy** but which included the far-right, nationalist **Slovak National Party** (SNS). Anti-Hungarian sentiment immediately began to surface, stirred up by contentious statements attributed to SNS leader Ján Slota on the issues of deportation and Slovakia's ethnic Hungarian population. Tensions rose between Slovakia and Hungary, and several key European leaders condemned the racial intolerance manifesting itself in Slovakia. In September the National Council voted overwhelmingly to adopted a declaration against extremism and intolerance.

In March 2007 Pál Csáky was elected SMK Chairman, replacing Béla Bugár who had led the party since its launch in 1998.

The SMK supported the candidacy of Iveta Radičová, a Vice-Chair of the SDKÚ–DS, in the 2009 presidential election, but she lost to incumbent President Ivan **Gašparovič** in the run-off.

Leadership: Pál Csáky (Chair.).
Address: Čajakova 8, 81105 Bratislava.
Telephone: (2) 52495546.
Fax: (2) 52495264.
E-mail: smk@smk.sk
Internet: www.mkp.sk

Hungarian Democratic Forum
Magyar Demokrata Fórum (MDF)

A party of populist/nationalist orientation in **Hungary**, affiliated to the **Centrist Democrat International**. The party headed Hungary's first post-communist Government. Founded in September 1987, the MDF held its first national conference in **Budapest** in March 1989, when it demanded that Hungary should again become 'an independent democratic country'. In the April 1990 **National Assembly** elections the party achieved first place with 165 of 378 elective seats. Its leader József Antall became Prime Minister, in a coalition Government also including the Independent Smallholders' and Civic Party (FKgP) and the **Christian Democratic People's Party**.

In January 1993 Antall survived a challenge to his leadership by the MDF's nationalist right, led by István Csurka. In early June Csurka and three parliamentary colleagues were expelled from the party, promptly forming the Hungarian Justice and Life Party. Antall died in December 1993 and was succeeded as MDF leader by the then Defence Minister, Lajos Für.

In the May 1994 National Assembly elections the MDF slumped to 37 seats on a vote share of only 11.7% and went into opposition. Internal divisions ensued, the confirmation of right-winger Sándor Lezsák as Chairman in early 1996 precipitating the defection of several MDF deputies.

Allied with the Federation of Young Democrats–Hungarian Civic Party (FiDeSz–MPP) in the May 1998 elections, the MDF declined further to 18 seats and 3.1% of the vote, but was nevertheless included in the new three-party centre-right Government headed by the FiDeSz–MPP. In January 1999 Lezsák was ousted as MDF leader by Ibolya Dávid, the Justice Minister, who in February 2000 launched the Right Hand of Peace 2000 alliance of assorted right-wing groups with the aim of recovering lost support for the MDF.

In September 2001 the MDF signed an electoral co-operation agreement with the FiDeSz–MPP, and this was joined by several FKgP deputies. In the April 2002 election the FiDeSz–MDF coalition won the most seats (188, 24 of which were won by the MDF) with 48.7% of the vote. However, all remaining seats were won by the allied centre-left parties, which together pushed the FiDeSz–MDF coalition into opposition.

The MDF fell out with the (renamed) **Federation of Young Democrats–Hungarian Civic Alliance** (FiDeSz–MPSz) ahead of the 2006 elections, and contested them separately, just achieving the 5% vote to pass the threshold to secure Assembly seats. It was awarded 11 seats in the new Assembly, where it remained in opposition.

The party fared even worse at the April 2010 elections, scoring only 2.7% of the vote and thus receiving no seats in the National Assembly. Dávid immediately resigned as party leader.

Leadership: vacant (Chair.).
Address: Sziágyi Erszébet fasor 73, 1026 Budapest.
Telephone: (1) 2252280.
Fax: (1) 2252290.
E-mail: velemeny@mdf.hu
Internet: www.mdf.hu

Hungarian Democratic Union of Romania

Uniunea Democrata Maghiara din România (UDMR) or *Romániai Magyar Demokrata Szövetség* (RMDSz)

The principal party of the ethnic **Hungarian** minority in **Romania**, affiliated as an observer to the **Centrist Democrat International**, and currently part of the ruling coalition. The UDMR was registered in 1990 with the aim of furthering ethnic Hungarian rights within the framework of a democratic Romania. It took 7.2% of the vote in the May 1990 **Parliament** elections, winning 29 House of Deputies seats and becoming the largest single opposition formation. Despite then being affiliated to the broad centre-right Democratic Convention of Romania (CDR), the UDMR contested the September 1992 elections separately, winning 7.5% of the vote and 27 House seats.

Following the resignation of Géza Domokos as UDMR President, the moderate Béla Markó was elected as his successor at a party congress in January 1993, after the more radical Bishop László Tökés (hero of anti-**Ceauşescu** protest actions in Timişoara, Northern **Transylvania**, in the late 1980s) had withdrawn his candidacy and accepted appointment as Honorary President. The same congress urged the Government to assist with the preservation of Hungarian language and culture, while calling for self-administration of majority Hungarian districts (rather than full autonomy, as demanded by some radicals). In mid-1995 the UDMR was rebuffed in its efforts to re-establish political co-operation with the CDR parties, whose spokesmen contended that it had become a party of extreme nationalism.

In 1996 the UDMR came under increasingly fierce attack by the extreme nationalist Greater Romania Party (PRM), which called openly for the UDMR to be banned. In the November 1996 presidential election UDMR candidate György Frunda came fourth with 6% of the first-round vote, while in the simultaneous House elections the UDMR slipped to 25 seats with 6.6% of the vote. It then opted to join a coalition Government headed by the CDR.

Despite frequent strains with CDR parties over Hungarian language rights, the UDMR's participation in government survived until the November–December 2000 elections, in which Frunda came fifth in the presidential contest with 6.2% of the vote, while in the parliamentary contest the UDMR improved slightly to 27 seats, with 6.8%. It thereafter gave qualified external support to a minority Government of the Social Democratic Pole of Romania (whose two main constituents later formed the **Social Democratic Party**—PSD) on the understanding that legislation would be enacted granting more language rights to ethnic Hungarians. However, this support caused internal divisions in the party, including the resignation of Tökés from his honorary presidency.

At the November 2004 elections, the UDMR dropped to 22 House seats and 10 Senate seats (with 6.2% of the vote). Markó stood as the UDMR candidate in the presidential election, coming fourth with 5.1% of the vote. The UDMR agreed to join a four-party governing coalition headed by Călin Popescu-Tăriceanu of the **National Liberal Party** (PNL), which took office in December, but this fell apart in April 2007. Popescu-Tăriceanu formed a new minority Government on 3 April between just his PNL and the UDMR, with external backing from the PSD.

In the November 2008 elections the UDMR again won 22 House seats but only nine Senate seats (6.2% and 6.4% of the vote). It was not part of the coalition Government that was formed subsequently between the **Democratic Liberal Party** (PD-L) and the PSD under Emil **Boc**. That Government fell in October 2009, and no new Government had been formed by the time of the November presidential election, in which UDMR candidate Hunor Kelemen came fifth with 3.8% of the vote. Incumbent President Traian Băsescu (PD-L) ultimately won a second term by a tiny margin against the PSD candidate Mircea Dan Geoană, and three days after his victory was confirmed by the Constitutional Court, he reappointed Boc as Prime Minister, who this time formed a coalition with the UDMR and five independents.

Leadership: Béla Markó (President).
Address: Str. Avram Iancu 8, PO Box 34–26, 024015 Bucharest 2.
Telephone and fax: (21) 3146849.
E-mail: elhivbuk@rmdsz.ro
Internet: www.rmdsz.ro

Hungarian National Asset Management Company
Magyar Nemzeti Vagyonkezelő Zrt. (MNV Zrt.)

State-controlled company founded in 2008 to manage **Hungary**'s state assets. Formed from the merger of the State Treasury Directorate, the Hungarian Privatization and State Holding Company (ÁPV Zrt.) and the National Land Fund.

Chief Executive Officer: Miklós Kamarás.
Address: Pozsonyi út 56, 1133 Budapest.
Telephone: (1) 2374400.
Fax: (1) 2374100.
E-mail: info@mnvzrt.hu
Internet: www.mnvzrt.hu

Hungarian News Agency
Magyar Távirati Iroda (MTI)

The national news agency of **Hungary** which was founded in 1880 and continues to provide news and analysis from around the world from a 'Hungarian perspective'. It also provides foreign news services with information and photographs relating to Hungarian news items.

President: Mátyás Vince.
Address: Naphegy tér 8, 1016 Budapest.
Telephone: (1) 4419000.
Fax: (1) 3188297.
E-mail: mtiadmin@mti.hu
Internet: www.mti.hu

Hungarian Socialist Party
Magyar Szocialista Párt (MSzP)

The successor to the former ruling (communist) Hungarian Socialist Workers' Party (MSzMP), now of social democratic orientation, and affiliated to the **Socialist International**. In government in 1994–98 and again for seven years from 2002, it supported the interim Government of Gordon **Bajnai**, who was nominated as Prime Minister by outgoing MSzP Prime Minister Ferenc Gyurcsány in 2009. It was heavily defeated in the April 2010 election.

Founded in November 1918, the original Hungarian Communist Party was outlawed under the inter-war Horthy dictatorship but in 1945 joined a Soviet-backed provisional Government with the Smallholders, Social Democrats and Agrarians. Having become the largest single party in the 1947 elections, the communists then eliminated their coalition partners as independent parties, forcing a merger with the Social Democrats in June 1948 and thereafter exercising complete power, although the façade of a political front was preserved. The drama of the abortive Hungarian Uprising in 1956, in which an attempt to throw off Moscow's yoke was brutally crushed by Soviet tanks, was followed by the reassertion of communist rule under János **Kádár**. It was at this time that the party adopted the MSzMP designation. Economic and cultural liberalization from the 1960s was followed in the 1980s by partial democratization, although within the framework of MSzMP supremacy.

Responding to the rapid collapse of **eastern European** communism, an MSzMP extraordinary congress in October 1989 renounced Marxism in favour of democratic socialism and adopted the MSzP title. This did not prevent the party's defeat in the April 1990 multi-party elections. Gyula Horn, who then became MSzP leader, rebuilt the party in opposition and led it to an overall majority in the May 1994 National Assembly elections, with a tally of 209 seats on a 32.6% first-round vote share. Mainly for purposes of international respectability, the centrist Alliance of Free Democrats (SzDSz) was brought into the resultant Horn Government as junior coalition partner.

Quickly unpopular for its economic austerity measures, the post-1994 MSzP Government was also troubled by various corruption scandals and by dissent within the party. In the May 1998 **National Assembly** elections it fell back to second place with 134 seats, although its share of the proportional vote increased to 32.9%. The party went into opposition and in September 1998 Horn was succeeded as its Chairman by former Foreign Minister László Kovács.

MSzP deputies backed the accession of Hungary to the **North Atlantic Treaty Organization** in March 1999 and also formed part of the consensus in favour of accession to the **European Union**. The MSzP fought the April 2002 election in coalition with the SzDSz; the parties won 178 and 20 seats respectively, thereby narrowly securing control of the National Assembly. On 27 May 2002 Péter Medgyessy of the MSzP took office as Prime Minister. Media allegations in June led to an investigation of Medgyessy's alleged role in the Soviet-era security service, though subsequent revelations of links between current politicians and the communist regime were far more damaging to the opposition Federation of Young Democrats–Hungarian Civic Party (FiDeSz–MPP), whose popularity plummeted.

In August 2004 Medgyessy resigned following a second dispute with the SzDSz over a cabinet reshuffle and a fall in his personal popularity. He was replaced by business tycoon Ferenc **Gyurcsány** on 24 August (in an acting capacity until 4 October). Istvan Hiller was elected as Chairman of the party at its congress that October, following Kovács's announcement in June that he would be standing down.

The June 2005 presidential election saw MSzP candidate Katalin Szili defeated, after most SzDSz Assembly members abstained from the vote. However, the two parties remained in alliance for the April 2006 legislative election, and won 54.4% of the vote and 210 seats: the first time that an incumbent government had won re-election since the fall of communism.

After several weeks of coalition talks between the MSzP and SzDSz over the legislative programme, Gyurcsány was sworn in again as Prime Minister in early June. In September the media released a clandestine recording of a post-election speech by Gyurcsány to MSzP members, in which he admitted having repeatedly lied to the electorate over the country's economic situation. Mass anti-Government riots on the streets of Budapest prompted Gyurcsány to apologize for not having addressed the economic problems sooner (but not for having misled the public). The ruling coalition performed badly in the following month's local elections. Hiller announced that he would step down as MSzP Chairman at the party congress in February 2007, but the party rallied behind Gyurcsány, who was elected as Hiller's successor.

Just over a year later, in April 2008, the SzDSz announced it was withdrawing from the Government after Gyurcsány dismissed the SzDSz Health Minister. This left the MSzP running a minority Government. The global credit crunch hit Hungary hard that year and, with the economy shrinking and the forint plummeting, unpopular Prime Minister Gyurcsány came under intense pressure to step down. He nominated his Economy Minister, independent businessman Bajnai as his successor, who named a reshuffled cabinet of technocrats and MSzP members. The party also voted to support Bajnai's programme of drastic cuts in social welfare and other austerity measures. Meanwhile, Ildikó Lendvai took over as Chair of the party on 5 April.

At the National Assembly elections a year later on 25 April 2010, voters showed their displeasure with the MSzP, resulting in an overall majority for the opposition alliance led by the **Federation of Young Democrats–Hungarian Civic Alliance** (FiDeSz–MPSz). The MSzP retained just 59 seats (19.3% of the vote), only just beating the nationalist Movement for a Better Hungary (Jobbik), who won 47 seats (16.7% of the vote). Lendvai immediately resigned as party Chairman.

Leadership: vacant (Chair.).
Address: 26 Köztársaság tér, 1081 Budapest.
Telephone: (1) 2100046.
Fax: (1) 2100081.
E-mail: info@mszp.hu
Internet: www.mszp.hu

Hungarians

Magyars

A **Finno-Ugric** people, Hungarians form the majority population in **Hungary** and sizeable minorities in neighbouring countries. Their language, quite different from the neighbouring Slavic, Romance and German tongues, has its closest modern European relatives in Finnish and Estonian. Originating in central Asia, the Magyars/Hungarians arrived in **central Europe** in the late ninth century and established a Magyar kingdom across the eastern Pannonian plain including the southern Tatras (modern-day **Slovakia**) and **Transylvania**. This kingdom quickly became a significant force in European politics and a part of Christendom after the conversion to **Roman Catholicism** under King (Saint) Stephen in 1000. Defeated by the Turks at Mohács in 1526, Hungary elected a Habsburg as its new king, and Hungarians spread out to fill the furthest reaches of the Habsburg Empire. As part of the ruling elite, Hungarians filled high positions in the imperial system. Their elevated and separate status, along with their use of the Hungarian language, made integration with the local people extremely difficult. The existence of well-established Hungarian communities, with distinct identity, created problems in several of the successor states to the Habsburg Empire after 1918, providing fuel for Hungarian nationalists eager to reassert Hungary's former territorial glory under the concept of a **Greater Hungary**.

The most significant of these communities is in Transylvania, in **Romania**, where roughly 1.5m. Hungarians live today. Another 500,000 live in Slovakia, and 300,000 in the **Vojvodina** region of northern **Serbia**. In all three cases there are moves to achieve greater autonomy for the communities, with varying success and backed in all instances by the Hungarian Government. The use of the Hungarian language in schools was eventually given support by the Slovakian and Romanian Governments in early 2001. In the Vojvodina, Hungarians were promised a return to 'territorial autonomy' in March 2001.

Hungary
Magyar Köztársaság

An independent landlocked republic in **central Europe**, bounded by Slovakia to the north, Ukraine to the north-east, Romania to the east, Serbia and Croatia to the south and Slovenia and Austria to the west. Administratively, Hungary is divided into 19 counties (megyei) and the capital city.

Area: 93,030 sq km; *capital*: **Budapest**; *population*: 10m. (2009 estimate), comprising ethnic **Hungarians** 92.3%, **Roma** 1.9%, other 5.8%; *official language*: Hungarian; *religion*: **Roman Catholic** 51.9%, **Protestant** 19.3%, other 28.8%.

The President of the Republic, elected by the unicameral **National Assembly** (Országgyűlés) for a five-year term, renewable once only, is the Head of State. The Head of Government is the Prime Minister, who is elected by the National Assembly on the recommendation of the President. Constitutionally, supreme power is vested in the legislature, which has 386 members elected by popular vote for a four-year term. The complex electoral system involves 210 proportionally-allocated seats and 176 single-member constituencies.

History: The original **Hungarians** were Magyar tribes who invaded the region in 896 and settled the territory, driving out or absorbing the existing population mix and founding a kingdom. Christianity was accepted during the reign of King Stephen I (997–1038) of the Arpad dynasty, who was canonized after his death. Hungary was devastated in 1241 by Mongol invaders, recovering to achieve its peak of medieval power during the reign of King Louis I (1342–82). A protracted struggle against the advancing Ottoman Turks began in the late 14th century. When the Turks crushed the Hungarian army at Mohács in 1526, western and northern Hungary accepted Habsburg rule to escape Ottoman occupation. Intermittent hostilities between the Habsburg and Turkish dominions continued until the close of the 17th century, when the Turks were driven out.

Oppressive Habsburg rule bred Hungarian resentment, culminating in an armed rebellion in 1848–49 led by Louis Kossuth, which was put down with the help of the Russian army. In 1867 the Hungarians concluded a compromise (Ausgleich) with the Habsburgs, whereby the dual monarchy of Austria-Hungary was set up. This disintegrated in 1918 upon the defeat of the central European powers in the First World War. The Austro-Hungarian Empire was dismembered. The Hungarian State created under the 1920 Treaty of **Trianon** was divested of two-thirds of Hungary's pre-war territory. The declaration of a republic and brief period of communist rule ended in 1920 with the reconstitution of Hungary as a kingdom and the proclamation of Admiral Nikolaus Horthy as regent. Under his authoritarian rule Hungary entered the Second World War on the side of Germany in 1941, but was itself occupied by the Nazis in 1944.

Liberation by Soviet troops led to the formation of a provisional Government which signed an armistice in early 1945. A republic was proclaimed the following year. By 1949 the communist Hungarian Workers' Party, with Soviet support, had gained a monopoly of power and Hungary was declared a people's republic under a new Constitution.

In October 1956 a popular revolt against the Stalinist system broke out in Budapest, but the uprising was crushed by Soviet military intervention the following month and a new Hungarian Socialist Workers' Party (HSWP) regime led by János **Kádár** was installed. Under Kádár's leadership (until 1988), Hungary remained within the communist camp but became the most liberal of the Soviet-bloc nations of **eastern Europe**.

The HSWP voluntarily abandoned its monopoly on power in 1989, and the Constitution was amended in October of that year to allow for a multi-party democracy. Free elections in April and May 1990 led to the formation of a centre-right coalition Government led by the **Hungarian Democratic Forum** (MDF). The following August, acting Head of State Árpád Göncz of the liberal Alliance of Free Democrats (SzDSz) was elected President by the National Assembly. The last Soviet troops left Hungary in 1991.

In legislative elections in May 1994 the MDF suffered a heavy defeat. The **Hungarian Socialist Party** (MSzP, the renamed former communist party) won an overall majority of seats in the National Assembly and formed a new coalition Government with the SzDSz under the premiership of Gyula Horn. President Göncz was re-elected President for a second term in June 1995.

After four years of Socialist-led Government, elections to the National Assembly in May 1998 resulted in the centre-right Federation of Young Democrats–Hungarian Civic Party (FiDeSz–MPP) becoming the largest party with 148 seats on a 29% vote share, 14 seats ahead of the MSzP (although the latter actually achieved a larger 33% of the vote). In July 1998 a new centre-right coalition was formed under the premiership of Viktor **Orbán** of the FiDeSz–MPP. His coalition partners were the third-placed Independent Smallholders' and Peasants' Party (later renamed the Independent Smallholders' and Civic Party—FKgP), controlling 48 seats, and the MDF which had dropped to fifth (17 seats).

Although commanding a relatively small National Assembly majority, the Orbán coalition remained securely in power in 1999–2000, the principal threat to its stability being bitter factional dissension within the FKgP. In June 2000 non-party candidate Ferenc Mádl was elected President in succession to Göncz and took the opportunity of stressing the importance of good relations with neighbouring countries containing ethnic Hungarian minorities, notably **Romania**. Domestically, legislative measures continued to be implemented to protect the cultural, civil and political rights of the various minority groups in Hungary. At the same time, increasingly overt nationalism on the right, including within the ruling coalition, focused on Hungary's territorial grievances and the perceived mistreatment of ethnic Hungarians abroad.

In September 2001 FiDeSz–MPP and the MDF signed an electoral co-operation agreement (in advance of the April 2002 polls) and several FKgP Assembly members also subsequently joined the pact. At the election, this bloc won 188 seats, but the MSzP and SzDSz won all remaining seats (MSzP 178; SzDSz 20), giving them together a small majority. On 27 May 2002 Péter Medgyessy of the MSzP took office as Prime Minister. Media allegations in June led to an investigation of Medgyessy's alleged role in the Soviet-era security service, but subsequent revelations of links between current politicians and the communist regime proved far more damaging to the opposition FiDeSz–MPP, whose popularity plummeted.

Constitutional amendments were passed in December 2002 to enable EU membership, and a fiscal austerity plan was adopted in 2004 in an attempt to keep the country heading towards adoption of the euro in the longer term. Later that year, Medgyessy resigned following a second dispute with the SzDSz over a cabinet reshuffle and a fall in his personal popularity. He was replaced by business tycoon Ferenc Gyurcsány on 24 August (in an acting capacity until 4 October).

The June 2005 presidential election was narrowly won by independent politician László Sólyom, candidate of the main opposition parties, after most SzDSz Assembly members abstained from the vote. He took office on 5 August.

In the April 2006 legislative election, the electoral alliance of the MSzP and the SzDSz won 54.4% of the vote and 210 seats. This was the first time that an incumbent government had won re-election since the fall of communism. The main opposition party (re-formed as **Federation of Young Democrats—Hungarian Civic Alliance**, FiDeSz–MPSz) in alliance with the **Christian Democratic People's Party** (KDNP) won 164 seats (with 42.5% of the vote), the MDF won 11 seats (2.9% of the vote) and the remaining seat was won by an independent candidate.

After several weeks of coalition talks between the MSzP and SzDSz over the legislative programme, Gyurcsány was sworn in again as Prime Minister in early June 2006. Stringent fiscal adjustment measures were introduced to reduce the budget deficit, in compliance with EU requirements. In September the media released a clandestine recording of a post-election speech by Gyurcsány to MSzP members, in which he admitted having repeatedly lied to the electorate over the country's economic situation. Mass anti-Government riots on the streets of Budapest prompted Gyurcsány to apologize for not having addressed the economic problems sooner (but not for having misled the public). The ruling coalition performed badly in the following month's local elections, but won a vote of confidence instigated by Gyurcsány in the National Assembly. FiDeSz–MPSz organized repeated anti-Government demonstrations, which frequently resulted in violent clashes between extreme nationalist protesters and the security forces.

Controversial health-care reforms, including the introduction of medical fees, were proposed in 2007 as part of the austerity programme to reduce the budget deficit. Despite a widespread public-sector strike, repeated protests and an initial veto from President Sólyom, the Assembly passed the reforms in February 2008. FiDeSz–MPSz organized a public referendum in March, in which more than 80% of voters voted against the fees, forcing the Government to scrap this particular reform. Gyurcsány subsequently dismissed the SzDSz Health Minister, prompting the SzDSz to withdraw from the coalition. The Prime Minister remained in office, heading a minority Government.

The global credit crunch hit Hungary hard that year (*see* **Hungary, economy**) and, with the economy shrinking and the forint plummeting, the unpopular Gyurcsány came under intense pressure to step down. He nominated Gordon **Bajnai**, an independent businessman who had been serving as Gyurcsány's Economy Minister, as his successor, charged with managing the crisis until elections due in spring 2010. Bajnai took office on 14 April 2009, appointed a reshuffled cabinet of technocrats and MSzP members, and immediately announced drastic cuts in wages, pensions and social services.

Latest elections: At the National Assembly elections on 25 April 2010, voters punished the outgoing MSzP, resulting in an overall majority for the opposition FiDeSz–MPSz–KDNP alliance, with 262 seats in the 386-seat chamber and 52.7% of the vote. The MSzP retained just 59 seats (19.3% of the vote), only just beating the nationalist Movement for a Better Hungary (Jobbik), who won 47 seats (16.7% of the vote). The only other party to secure representation was the new green Politics Can Be Different party, with 16 seats (7.5% of the vote). FiDeSz leader Viktor Orbán was nominated as Prime Minister, to take office in late May.

International relations and defence: In the post-Soviet era, as Hungary restructured itself as a market economy, the country pursued twin goals of membership of the **European Union** (EU) and of the **North Atlantic Treaty Organization** (NATO). A recipient of the EU's **PHARE programme** of economic aid after 1989, Hungary signed an association agreement with the EU in 1991. Its application for full EU membership was made in 1994, and formal negotiations beginning in March 1998. An offer of membership was made in December 2002, as part of a major wave of expansion. It was supported by referendum in April 2003, and Hungary acceded on 1 May 2004. In December 2007 Hungary also joined the EU's Schengen Agreement, allowing free movement of citizens within the zone's borders. It is unlikely to join the eurozone before 2014 (*see* **Hungary, economy**). Hungary joined NATO's **Partnership for Peace** programme in 1994 and formally joined NATO itself in March 1999 (together with the Czech Republic and Poland). Hungary's other multilateral links include membership of the United Nations, the **Organization for Security and Co-operation in Europe**, the **Council of Europe**, the **Central European Initiative**, the **Central European Free Trade Area** and the **Danube Commission**. It has also been admitted to the **Organisation for Economic Co-operation and Development** and the **World Trade Organization**.

Bilaterally, relations with Romania and **Slovakia** have been strained over issues arising from the treatment of sizeable ethnic Hungarian communities in these countries, although recent treaties include minority protection provisions. There has also been friction with Slovakia over the **Gabčíkovo-Nagymaros Dam**, a hydroelectric construction project on the River Danube, initiated jointly in the communist period by Hungary and Czechoslovakia in 1977 but suspended controversially at the end of the 1980s. The issue was the subject of a ruling by the **International Court of Justice** in 1997, which instructed Hungary and Slovakia to resume negotiations, which are still ongoing.

Hungary's defence budget for 2008 amounted to some US $1,869m., equivalent to about 1.2% of GDP. The size of the armed forces in 2010 was 29,000 personnel, while reservists numbered an estimated 44,000. The last conscripts were discharged in November 2004, and the army is now fully professional.

Hungary, economy

A free-market system that transitioned mostly successfully from state command before joining the **European Union** (EU) in 2004. Suffering high public debt and a large budget deficit, so not yet eligible for adoption of the euro, Hungary's economy was then exposed to a severe blow from the global financial crisis as exports fell and the currency plummeted, requiring the IMF to step in with a rescue package.

GNP: US $128,581m. (2008); *GNP per capita*: $12,810 (2008); *GDP at PPP*: $194,023m. (2008); *GDP per capita at PPP*: $19,300 (2008); *real GDP growth*: –6.7% (2009 estimate); *exports*: $107,466m. (2008); *imports*: $106,380m. (2008); *currency*: forint (plural: forint; US $1 = F194 in mid-2009); *unemployment*: 11.1% (end 2009); *government deficit as a percentage of GDP*: 3.9%; *inflation*: 4.5% (2009).

In 2007 industry contributed 30% of GDP, agriculture 4% and services 66%. Around 32% of the workforce is engaged in industry, 5% in agriculture and 63% in services.

Some 51% of land is arable, 2% under permanent crops, 13% permanent pasture and 19% forests and woodland. The main crops are wheat, maize, other grains, sunflower seed, sugar beet and vegetables, while there are important vineyards and there is a developed dairy industry.

The main mineral resources are bauxite, hard and brown coal (lignite), and some oil and considerable natural gas reserves. The main industries are food, beverages and tobacco, chemicals (especially pharmaceuticals), petroleum and plastics, and metallurgy and engineering. Almost 40% of Hungary's domestic energy requirements are met from nuclear power.

Hungary's main exports are machinery and transport equipment, basic manufactures, food, beverages and tobacco. The principal imports are machinery and transport equipment, other manufactures, fuels and electricity. In 2008 Germany was the largest purchaser of Hungarian exports (27%), followed by Italy (5%) and Austria (4%). Germany was also the principal supplier of Hungarian imports (25%), followed by the Russian Federation (7%) and Austria (5%).

After communist rule ended in 1989–90, successive governments pursued the creation of a free-market economic system and the dismantling of the previous

223

centralized industrial structure, assisted by the relative economic freedom permitted in non-industrial sectors under the previous regime. A four-year restructuring programme initiated in 1991 had an initial adverse effect on GDP, which contracted by nearly 20% in 1991–93, while unemployment rose to around 12% in 1994 and inflation to over 20% in 1995.

As GDP began to recover in 1994–95, a comprehensive stabilization programme introduced in March 1995, including a currency devaluation, produced modest GDP growth in 1996 and then an acceleration to annual expansion of around 5% in each of the four years of 1997 to 2000, assisted by large inflows of foreign direct investment. Over the same period, unemployment showed a marked fall, to an estimated 7% in 2000, while the inflation rate also came down, although it remained relatively high at around 10% in both 1999 and 2000.

In 1991 legislation had been approved authorizing the partial compensation of former owners of expropriated land and property, through the issue of vouchers (*see* **voucher privatization**) which could then be used to purchase state assets; this measure applied not only to property seized during the communist era but was backdated to May 1939. An accompanying privatization programme resulted in the transfer to the private sector by 1995 of some 80% of the hitherto state-owned assets, and the sale of most state farms. Privatization of the major utilities and the commercial banks followed, so that by 1999 the private sector accounted for over 80% of GDP and over two-thirds of employment. In December 2000 the Prime Minister declared that the privatization process had been completed and that the extent of private ownership in Hungary was now similar to western European levels.

As a staging post to EU membership, Hungary was in 1993 a founder member of the **Central European Free Trade Area** (CEFTA) of EU aspirant countries. It also joined the **World Trade Organization** (WTO) in 1995 and the following year became the second ex-communist state to join the **Organisation for Economic Co-operation and Development** (OECD). The EU accepted Hungary as one of the first six 'fast-track' central and eastern European candidates for entry, and formal negotiations opened in November 1998.

With GDP growing by 5.3% in 2000, the fastest since the end of communism, output and living standards that year officially exceeded 1990 levels for the first time, thus marking the completion of the transition phase. In early 2001 the worst floods for a century imposed a huge unexpected cost on the economy. Nevertheless average annual GDP growth of around 4% was maintained through 2001–06. EU membership was achieved in May 2004, and the next target became meeting the convergence criteria for joining the **eurozone**, initially set for 2010.

However, the Government failed to reduce the budget deficit (the largest among EU member nations in 2006) to a level consistent with this objective. Stringent austerity measures proposed in June 2006 precipitated mass anti-Government riots in the capital in September, and further demonstrations and strike action were staged in 2007 in protest at planned reforms, particularly in the health sector. Growth began to slow in 2007, dropping to 1.2%, while inflation doubled to nearly 8%. Towards the end of the year the Government indicated that it had abandoned its target date of 2010 for adoption of the euro, and hoped to adopt the single currency by 2014. In early 2008 the Government allowed the forint to float against the euro in order to allow the **National Bank of Hungary** to focus on reducing inflation.

Following the onset of the global financial crisis in late 2008, demand for exports declined and the over-exposed banking sector was badly hit by the credit crunch. There was a dramatic fall in the value of the forint, until the **International Monetary Fund** offered a rescue package of US $25,100m. to stabilize Hungary's economy; the **World Bank** and EU also offered support. Gordon **Bajnai** took over as Prime Minister in April 2009; he had previously headed the National Development Agency and the Ministry of National Development and the Economy, so was regarded as better equipped to proceed with structural reform than his predecessor. He cut government expenditure on pensions, welfare payments, public sector salaries and subsidies in order to maintain control of the budget deficit—a precondition of the IMF rescue package which would also help meet the euro convergence criteria. As of early 2010, Hungary was intending to join the Exchange Rate Mechanism II soon, but its 2014 target date for adoption of the euro was looking increasingly unlikely.

Husák, Gustáv

Hard-line communist party leader in **Czechoslovakia** until he was forced to resign by the '**velvet revolution**' of November–December 1989. Born in 1913, he first made his name in the Communist Party of Slovakia and helped to lead the 1944 **Slovak** uprising against the German occupation. The victim of one of the party purges of the 1950s, he was imprisoned by Czechoslovakia's hard-line Stalinist regime in 1954 as a Slovak 'bourgeois nationalist' and not released until 1960. He then rose to become part of the leadership group in the Communist Party of Czechoslovakia (KSČ) and Czechoslovak Government, and was initially associated with the 1968 '**Prague Spring**' liberalization headed by Alexander **Dubček**. When that experiment was crushed by the tanks of invading **Warsaw Pact** forces, the Soviet leadership turned to Husák to take charge of 'normalizing' Czechoslovakia and he became known principally for establishing a neo-Stalinist regime. He replaced Dubček as KSČ leader in April 1969 and held that office until his replacement by Miloš Jakeš in 1987. He was also Head of State from 1975 until he was forced to resign by mass pro-democracy rallies on 10 December 1989, a moment which marked the triumph of the 'velvet revolution'. Expelled from the KSČ in February 1990, he died on 18 November 1991.

HZDS *see* **People's Party–Movement for a Democratic Slovakia**.

I

IAEA *see* **International Atomic Energy Agency**.

IBRD

The International Bank for Reconstruction and Development, a constituent part of (and generally known as) the **World Bank**.

ICJ *see* **International Court of Justice**.

ICPDR *see* **International Commission for the Protection of the Danube River**.

ICR *see* **International Civilian Representative**.

ICTY *see* **International Criminal Tribunal for the former Yugoslavia**.

IDU *see* **International Democrat Union**.

IFOR *see* **EUFOR**.

Ilves, Toomas Hendrik

President of **Estonia**.

Toomas Hendrik Ilves was a member of the **Social Democratic Party** (SDE) prior to his election as President. Educated in the USA, he had an academic career and worked for Radio Free Europe before becoming an ambassador for the newly independent Estonia in 1993. He held ministerial office twice as Foreign Minister in 1996–98 and 1999–2002, and then became a Member of the European Parliament (MEP) from 2004 until his election as President of Estonia in September 2006.

Born in Stockholm, Sweden, on 26 December 1953, he graduated from Columbia University, USA, in 1976 and received his master's degree in psychology in 1978. His academic career began as an English teacher in 1979 and went on to include administrative roles in Canadian universities from 1981 to 1984. He joined the Munich-based Radio Free Europe as a research analyst in 1984, working there until 1993 and rising to be Director of its Estonian service. He returned to the USA in 1993 as Estonia's ambassador, with additional remit for Canada and Mexico. He was recalled to Estonia and served as Foreign Minister from 1996 to 1998. He was reappointed Foreign Minister in the coalition cabinet of Prime Minister Mart Laar in March 1999 and became deputy head of the People's Party Moderates, on the merger of the two parties. Two years later he rose to become party leader. The coalition lasted until early 2002, after which the People's Party Moderates returned to opposition. They fared badly in municipal elections, and Ilves stepped down from the party leadership. In 2004 he was elected as an MEP for the newly-renamed Social Democratic Party.

In 2006 Ilves was chosen as a consensus candidate to oppose the incumbent President Arnold Rüütel in the presidential elections. He was supported by the SDE, the **Estonian Reform Party** and the **Union of Pro Patria and Res Publica**. The protracted balloting, which began in August, had to go to an electoral college vote in September which Ilves won by 174 votes to 162. He took office on 9 October, having resigned his seat in the European Parliament and his membership of the SDE.

Toomas Hendrik Ilves had a son and a daughter by his first wife, Merry Bullock, and a daughter by his second wife, Evelyn Int-Lambot, whom he married in 2004. He speaks Estonian, English, German and Spanish.

Address: Office of the President, A. Weizenbergi 39, Tallinn 15050.

Telephone: 6316202.

Fax: 6316250.

E-mail: vpinfo@vpk.ee

Internet: www.president.ee

IMF *see* **International Monetary Fund**.

Implementation Force *see* **EUFOR**.

Internal Macedonian Revolutionary Organization–Democratic Party for Macedonian National Unity
Vnatrešno-Makedonska Revolucionerna Organizacija–Demokratska Partija za Makedonsko Nacionalno Edinstvo (VMRO–DPMNE)

A nationalist political party in **Macedonia**, currently leading the Government. It claims descent from the historic VMRO, which had fought for independence from the Turks before the First World War. In 1990 the revived VMRO merged with the DPMNE (originally founded by **Macedonian** migrant workers in Sweden) to create a party seeking to promote the revival of Macedonian **Slavic** cultural identity. The merged party became the largest single formation in the 1990 **Assembly** elections (with 38 seats) and formed the core of the resultant 'Government of experts' which asserted Macedonia's independence. However, a mid-1992 government crisis resulted in the VMRO–DPMNE going into opposition, from where it failed to gain representation in the controversial October 1994 elections. Party leader Ljubčo Georgievski was the runner-up in simultaneous presidential polling, receiving 21.6% of the vote.

The VMRO–DPMNE staged a revival while in opposition to the post-1994 Government headed by the **Social Democratic Union of Macedonia** (SDSM), forming an alliance with the new pro-business Democratic Alternative (DA) for the autumn 1998 legislative elections. The alliance emerged as substantially the largest grouping, with 59 of the 120 seats, and formed a coalition Government under Georgievski which, to the surprise of many observers, also included the (ethnic **Albanian**) Democratic Party of Albanians (DPA). The VMRO–DPMNE consolidated its authority in the late 1999 presidential elections, in which party candidate Boris Trajkovski was elected with 53% of the second-round vote.

The VMRO–DPMNE was weakened in March 2000 by the formation of a break-away VMRO led by former Finance Minister Boris Zmejkovski, while at the end of the year the withdrawal of the DA from the Government left the remaining VMRO–DPMNE/DPA coalition dependent on DA dissidents and the small Liberal-Democratic Party for a parliamentary majority. The reconstituted Government faced its greatest challenge, however, from an insurgency launched in February 2001 by ethnic Albanian rebels seeking greater rights for the Albanian community.

Under intense international pressure a Government of National Unity was established in May 2001, still headed by Georgievski but comprising parties from all sides of the Assembly, including the opposition PDP and SDSM. The alliance was volatile as the struggle for greater Albanian autonomy was largely backed by the Albanian parties and had prompted a powerful nationalist backlash among their ethnic Macedonian counterparts. Once the process of approving the various key elements of an August peace deal—providing limited autonomy and social equalization for the Albanian community—had gradually been completed, the SDSM and the Liberals withdrew from the grand coalition. The Government's majority, however, was reinforced by the participation of New Democracy (ND), which had been formed in March from a small splinter of the DA.

At the 15 September 2002 elections, the coalition of the VMRO–DPMNE and the Liberal Party of Macedonia (LPM) won only 33 seats (24.4% of the vote) and was faced with a term in opposition. The following May Nikola Gruevski was elected as the party's new Chairman.

In February 2004 President Trajkovski was killed in a plane crash. Elections were held in April to choose a successor: SDSM candidate Crvenkovski easily defeated VMRO–DPMNE candidate Saško Kedev, leading him 42.5% to 34.1% in the first round on 14 April, and then 60.6% to 39.4% in the run-off two weeks later.

At the 5 July 2006 Assembly election, the coalition of the VMRO–DPMNE, the Socialist Party of Macedonia (SPM), the LPM and 11 smaller parties emerged as the largest bloc with 45 seats (and 32.5% of the vote). Gruevski was approved as Prime Minister in August, having negotiated a coalition with the DPA and New Social Democratic Party.

Early elections were called in June 2008 in an attempt to boost support for Gruevski's reforms. The For a Better Macedonia coalition of the VMRO–DPMNE, SPM and 17 smaller parties a majority of 63 seats in the 120-member chamber (with 48.8% of the vote). Gruevski was approved as Prime Minister again on 26 July.

In the 2009 presidential elections VMRO–DPMNE candidate Gjorge **Ivanov** easily defeated SDSM candidate Ljubomir Frčkoski, leading him 35.1% to 20.5% in the first round on 22 March, and then 63.1% to 36.9% in the run-off two weeks later.

Leadership: Nikola Gruevski (Chair.).
Address: Macedonia 17A, Skopje 1000.
Telephone: (2) 3215550.
Internet: www.vmro-dpmne.org.mk

International Atomic Energy Agency (IAEA)

The UN organization founded in 1957 to promote and monitor peaceful use of atomic energy.

Members: 151 countries, including **Albania**, **Bosnia and Herzegovina**, **Bulgaria**, **Croatia**, **Cyprus**, **Czech Republic**, **Estonia**, **Greece**, **Hungary**, **Latvia**, **Lithuania**, **Macedonia**, **Montenegro**, **Poland**, **Romania**, **Serbia**, **Slovakia**, **Slovenia**.

Director General: Yukiya Amano.
Address: POB 100, Wagramerstrasse 5, 1400 Vienna, Austria.
Telephone: (1) 26000.
Fax: (1) 26007.
E-mail: official.mail@iaea.org
Internet: www.iaea.org

International Bank for Reconstruction and Development (IBRD)

Generally known as the **World Bank**.

International Civilian Representative (ICR)

The diplomat charged with overseeing the implementation of the UN's Comprehensive Proposal for the **Kosovo** Status Settlement by the Kosovan authorities. At Kosovo's declaration of independence on 17 February 2008 the appointment of an ICR was requested, as envisaged by the Proposal. Dutch diplomat Pieter Feith was chosen on 28 February; he also is the EU Special Representative for Kosovo.

Address: Blue Building, Ahmet Krasniqi PN St, 10000 Pristina, Kosovo.
Telephone: (38) 20 44 100.
Fax: (38) 20 44 210.
E-mail: office@ico-kos.org
Internet: www.ico-kos.org

International Commission for the Protection of the Danube River (ICPDR)

A body set up in 1998 to implement the Danube River Protection Convention. The Commission promotes co-operation between Danube basin countries on water management and environmental issues. In 2009 it produced a co-ordinated international River Basin Management Plan for the Danube. It is also in charge of implementing the transboundary aspects of the **European Union**'s Water Framework Directive. This also involves the participation of **Albania**, Italy, **Macedonia**, **Poland** and Switzerland.

The presidency of the Commission rotates annually on an alphabetical basis between its contracting parties; Slovenia holds the presidency for 2010 and will be succeeded by Ukraine in 2011.

Contracting Parties: Austria, **Bosnia and Herzegovina**, **Bulgaria**, **Croatia**, **Czech Republic**, Germany, **Hungary**, Moldova, **Montenegro**, **Romania**, **Serbia**, **Slovakia**, **Slovenia**, Ukraine and the **European Union**.
President: Mitja Bricelj.
Executive Secretary: Philip Weller.
Address: Vienna International Centre, Room D0412, PO Box 500, 1400 Vienna, Austria.
Telephone: (1) 260605738.
Fax: (1) 260605895.
E-mail: icpdr@unvienna.org
Internet: www.icpdr.org

International Court of Justice (ICJ)

The principal judicial organ of the United Nations, founded in 1945.
President: Hisashi Owada.
Address: Peace Palace, Carnegieplein 2, 2517 KJ The Hague, Netherlands.
Telephone: (70) 3022323.
Fax: (70) 3649928.
E-mail: information@icj-cij.org
Internet: www.icj-cij.org

International Criminal Tribunal for the former Yugoslavia (ICTY)

The UN Tribunal established in The Hague, Netherlands, by Security Council Resolution 827 on 25 May 1993, to try cases relating to war crimes committed in the former **Yugoslavia** since 1991. The ICTY covers charges relating to breaches of the Geneva Convention, violations of the laws or customs of war, genocide and crimes against humanity. It consists of 15 permanent Judges and 12 *ad litem* Judges, all of whom are elected by the UN General Assembly.

One of the ICTY's most significant rulings was made on 22 February 2001 when Zambian Judge Florence Ndepele Mwachande Mumba ruled that rape was to be considered as an 'instrument of terror' and a war crime. The sentences passed for this crime on three Bosnian **Serb** defendants ranged from 12 to 28 years in prison, and ranked second only to those for genocide in severity.

The most celebrated spectacle was the pre-trial of Slobodan **Milošević** in October 2001—the first former Head of State ever to face such proceedings. The former Yugoslav President denounced the Court's legitimacy and refused to enter a plea against charges including genocide and relating to the wars in **Croatia** and **Bosnia and Herzegovina**, and Yugoslavia's actions in **Kosovo**. The trial proper, at which

231

Milošević chose to defend himself, having refused legal counsel, began on 12 February 2002 but Milošević died before its completion on 11 March 2006.

By the beginning of 2010, proceedings had been concluded against 121 people, with 61 convictions, 11 acquittals and 49 proceedings being terminated due to death or withdrawal of charges. Only two of the 161 indictees—Ratko Mladić and Goran Hadžić—remain at large. All remaining trials should be completed by mid-2011, except for that of Radovan **Karadžić**, which is expected to last at least a year longer.

Leadership: Patrick L. Robinson (President).

Addresses: Churchillplein 1, 2517 JW The Hague, Netherlands;

POB 13888, 2501 EW The Hague, Netherlands.

Telephone: (70) 512 8752.

Fax: (70) 512 5355.

E-mail: press@icty.org

Internet: www.icty.org

International Democrat Union (IDU)

An international grouping of centre-right political parties founded in 1983, which holds conferences every six months. Its membership includes the member parties of the European Democrat Union (EDU). Most European countries have at least one political party that is a member or observer, including **Albania**, **Bosnia and Herzegovina** (observer party only), **Bulgaria**, **Croatia**, **Cyprus**, **Czech Republic**, **Estonia**, **Greece**, **Hungary**, **Lithuania**, **Macedonia** (observer party only), **Poland**, **Romania**, **Serbia** and **Slovenia**.

Chairman: John Howard.

Executive Secretary: Eirik Moen.

Address: POB 1536 Vika, 0117 Oslo, Norway.

Telephone: (2) 2829000.

Fax: (2) 2829080.

E-mail: secretariat@idu.org

Internet: www.idu.org

International Monetary Fund (IMF)

The principal organization of the international monetary system, founded in December 1945 to promote international monetary co-operation, the balanced growth of trade and exchange rate stability. A critical role of the IMF has been to provide credit resources to members, on condition that specified (and sometimes domestically highly controversial) conditions are met for management of the economy and attainment of monetary targets.

The IMF's 186 member countries now include all the countries of central and eastern Europe. **Czechoslovakia** and **Poland** were both early members but withdrew in the 1950s. **Yugoslavia** was a founder member and remained one throughout the communist era. The years in which each country joined were:

1945 **Greece**.

1961 **Cyprus**.

1972 **Romania**.

1982 **Hungary**.

1986 Poland (rejoined).

1990 **Bulgaria**; **Czech Republic/Slovakia** (replacing the former membership of Czechoslovakia).

1991 **Albania**.

1992 **Bosnia and Herzegovina**; **Croatia**; **Estonia**; **Latvia**; **Lithuania**; **Macedonia**; **Slovenia**.

2000 Yugoslavia (readmitted in December as the FRY, the membership of the former SFRY (dating originally from 1945) having been suspended since December 1992. **Serbia** has since inherited this membership.

2007 **Montenegro**.

2009 **Kosovo**.

Managing Director: Dominique Strauss-Kahn.

Address: 700 19th St, NW, Washington, DC, 20431, USA.

Telephone: (202) 6237300.

Fax: (202) 6234661.

E-mail: publicaffairs@imf.org

Internet: www.imf.org

International Organization for Migration (IOM)

Founded as the International Committee for Migration (ICM) in 1951, the organization changed its name in 1989.

> *Members*: 127 countries, including **Albania**, **Bosnia and Herzegovina**, **Bulgaria**, **Croatia**, **Cyprus**, **Czech Republic**, **Estonia**, **Greece**, **Hungary**, **Latvia**, **Lithuania**, **Montenegro**, **Poland**, **Romania**, **Serbia**, **Slovakia** and **Slovenia**. **Macedonia** is one of 17 observer states.

Director General: William Lacy Swing.

Address: route des Morillons 17, 1211 Geneva 19, Switzerland.

Telephone: (22) 7179111.

Fax: (22) 7986150.

E-mail: info@iom.int

Internet: www.iom.int

Investment and Export Promotion Agency of the Republic of Serbia
Agencija za strana ulaganja i promociju izvoza Republike Srbije (SIEPA)
Government agency in **Serbia** to promote trade. Founded in 2001.
Director: Jasna Matić.
Address: Vlajkovićeva 3, 11000 Belgrade.
Telephone: (11) 3398550.
Fax: (11) 3398814.
E-mail: office@siepa.sr.gov.rs
Internet: www.siepa.sr.gov.rs

Investment Promotion Agency of Kosovo (IPAK)

Established as an Executive Agency under the Ministry of Trade and Industry to attract foreign investors through aggressive and pro-active marketing.
Acting Chief Executive Officer: Mustafë Hasani.
Address: Perandori Justinian No.3–5, Qyteza Pejton, Pristina.
Telephone: (38) 20036044.
Fax: (38) 20036041.
E-mail: info@invest-ks.org
Internet: www.invest-ks.org

Inzko, Valentin

UN High Representative and EU Special Representative to **Bosnia and Herzegovina**.
Valentin Inzko is an Austrian diplomat who has been involved in south-east Europe for three decades. He worked in Belgrade and Sandzak before becoming Austria's first resident ambassador in Bosnia in the late 1990s. He was ambassador to Slovenia from 2005 until taking up his appointment as High Representative on 26 March 2009 (*see* **Office of the High Representative**).
Born on 22 May 1949, he was educated bilingually in Slovene and German, and then specialized in Russian and Serbo-Croat at Graz University. He is married to the mezzo-soprano Bernarda Fink and they have two children.
Address: Emerika Bluma 1, 71000 Sarajevo.
Telephone: (33) 283500.
Fax: (33) 283501.
Internet: www.ohr.int

IOM *see* **International Organization for Migration**.

IPAK *see* **Investment Promotion Agency of Kosovo**.

IRL *see* **Union of Pro Patria and Res Publica**.

Islam *see* **Muslim peoples**.

Islamic fundamentalism

An extreme interpretation of Islam which promotes *jihad* (holy war) against non-Muslims, and aims to implement strict *sharia* (Islamic) law. Since the terrorist attacks in the USA on 11 September 2001 by the fundamentalist al-Qaida group, Islamic fundamentalism has taken on a renewed political importance in **eastern Europe**. Although the small size of **Muslim** communities in the region and their largely peaceful coexistence with Christian neighbours has somewhat negated its threat, the rapid growth of Islamic fundamentalism, fuelled by Arab nationalism and the success of such Islamic states as Iran, has seen it take on an almost evangelic-revolutionary tinge. It is often linked to nationalist causes in separatist regions to further polarize the antagonists. In particular Islamic fundamentalism has influenced separatist struggles in Chechnya and Dagestan, but it was also somewhat invoked during the civil war in **Bosnia and Herzegovina** in the 1990s, to draw Islamic mercenaries to fight alongside fellow Muslim **Bosniaks**. However, in all cases the major motivation for conflict has been ethno-political, rather than religious.

Istria

A small peninsula at the northern end of the Adriatic Sea, divided politically between **Slovenia** and **Croatia**, but with the area around its principal city, **Trieste**, under the administration of adjacent Italy. While the north and interior of the peninsula are hilly and dry, the coasts provide fertile land for agricultural production. Along with cultivation and grazing, Istria also produces anthracite coal and bauxite.

The region has had a long history of conquest and domination by the various regional powers. After a reasonably prolonged period of peace under Austrian control, Istria was ceded to Italy in 1919. However, the peninsula was overrun by Allied and Yugoslav forces at the end of the Second World War, and was absorbed, bar the region around Trieste, into the re-formed **Yugoslavia** in 1947. Tensions over sovereignty of the area, particularly the municipality of Trieste, continued for years, but did not flare up as some predicted when both Slovenia and Croatia proclaimed independence in 1991. Italians form minorities in the Istrian regions of both countries.

Ivanov, Gjorge

President of the Republic, **Macedonia**.

Ivanov, Gjorge

Gjorge Ivanov trained as a lawyer and then became a renowned professor in political science. He was nominated for the presidency by the **Internal Macedonian Revolutionary Organization–Democratic Party for Macedonian National Unity** (VMRO–DPMNE) in early 2009, easily winning the election, and took office on 12 May.

Born on 2 May 1960 in Valandovo, he graduated in law from the University of Saints Cyril and Methodius in **Skopje** in 1982. He joined national broadcaster Macedonian Radio in 1988, rising to become an editor. Involved with liberal organizations since his days at university, he campaigned for political reform in the early 1990s.

In 1994 he returned to his university for a master's degree in political science, then joined its law department and gained a doctorate in 1998 for a thesis on *Democracy in Divided Societies*. He was appointed assistant professor in Skopje, teaching political theory and political philosophy. In 1999 he was a visiting professor at Athens University in Greece, and he has since also been involved with courses on democracy and human rights at the universities in **Sarajevo (Bosnia and Herzegovina)** and Bologna (Italy).

Ivanov was appointed Director of Political Studies at Skopje University in 2001, associate professor the following year, Vice-Dean of the law faculty in 2004, and a full professor in 2008. He has also co-founded Macedonia's first political science journal *Political Opinion*, the Institute for Democracy think tank, and the Macedonian Political Science Association, of which he is Honorary President.

He has also been active in higher education reforms, participating in the European Union's TEMPUS programme, and becoming Chair of Macedonia's Higher Education Accreditation Council in 2008.

He is not a member of the VMRO-DPMNE, but has advised the party on reform policies, and was its nominee for the presidency in 2009. He easily defeated Social Democratic Union of Macedonia candidate Ljubomir Frčkoski, leading him 35.1% to 20.5% in the first round on 22 March, and then 63.1% to 36.9% in the run-off two weeks later.

Ivanov is married to Maja Ivanova, and they have one child.

Address: Office of the President, 11 Oktomvri b.b., 91000 Skopje.
Telephone: (2) 3113318.
Fax: (2) 3112643.
E-mail: office@president.gov.mk
Internet: www.president.gov.mk

J

Jaanilinn question

A border dispute between **Estonia** and the Russian Federation over the division of the historic town of Narva. The town itself is divided by the River Narva which, from 1945, came to serve as the border between Estonia and Russia (then one of the Soviet republics). The incorporation of Estonia into the **Soviet Union** made this distinction somewhat arbitrary, and the two halves of the town continued to interact as one, although its eastern district, known as Jaanilinn—in Russian, Ivangorod—was administered as part of the Leningrad (St Petersburg) oblast. Factories in Narva employed almost half of the residents of Jaanilinn, which thus acted to draw Russian migrants into eastern Estonia, in line with Soviet efforts to reduce the ethnic homogeneity of its constituent republics.

With the collapse of the Soviet Union in 1991 and the independence of Estonia that summer, the question of the sovereignty of Jaanilinn was raised. However, the fact of its by now overwhelming ethnic **Russian** majority population negated Estonian claims. The dispute has been muted since initial attempts to redraw the border were resolved in 1995 with grudging recognition of the Soviet-era division.

Russia and Estonia signed a border treaty in May 2005, following Estonia's accession to the **North Atlantic Treaty Organization** and the **European Union**. However, when during the ratification process Estonia's **Parliament** amended the preamble to retain its claim to Jaanilinn with a reference to the 1920 Treaty of **Tartu** Russia withdrew from the new treaty. Russia offered to reopen talks in 2006, but the offer was rejected by Estonia.

Jaruzelski, Gen. Wojciech

The last leader of communist-era **Poland**. Jaruzelski was head of both government and party from the time of the regime's crisis in dealing with the **Solidarity** movement in 1981, until the partially free elections of mid-1989. He was born in 1923 in a minor aristocratic family, in part of eastern Poland which was annexed by the **Soviet Union** in 1939. After fighting the Nazis with the Polish Army in the Soviet

Union in 1943–45, he combined his post-war military career with party and government posts, becoming Defence Minister in 1968 and gaining a place two years later on the Politburo of the ruling Polish United Workers' Party (PZPR). Named Prime Minister in February 1981, he also took over as PZPR First Secretary in October. His decision to introduce martial law in December 1981, for which his opponents would never forgive him, was an act he always insisted was justified as the only way of averting a Soviet invasion to crush the Solidarity movement. In November 1985 he took the post of President, while remaining party First Secretary. When he took the party into round-table negotiations in 1989, to work out **eastern Europe**'s first pluralist system, the gamble did not succeed for the PZPR, which was comprehensively rejected by the electorate at the June 1989 partially free parliamentary elections. He himself, however, stood for the restyled post of President and was narrowly elected by the parliament, thanks to key Solidarity votes cast in his favour for the sake of stability. As President, Jaruzelski briefly enjoyed high approval ratings, peaking at 74% in September 1989, as measured by opinion polls. Accepting ultimately that he would always symbolize the old regime, and taking note of the revolutionary changes across eastern Europe, Jaruzelski was persuaded within little over a year to step down and make way for the direct election of his successor, Lech **Wałęsa**. Efforts to have him brought to trial for his actions while in office are still continuing, though he has avoided most court appearances citing ill health.

Jehovah's Witnesses

A religion based on Christianity with some 600,000 adherents in **eastern Europe**. Founded in the USA in the late 19th century, it has been spread across the world by 'publishers', who are encouraged to canvass their neighbours door-to-door. The largest communities in eastern Europe are found in the Russian Federation (150,000), Ukraine (140,000) and **Poland** (128,000). Jehovah's Witnesses believe in a strict interpretation of the Bible and the essential humanity of Jesus Christ, and they reject the symbol of the cross. Their religion, which isolates its followers from other religious groups, is often vilified by mainstream Christian denominations as a cult. One of its greatest areas of conflict with modern states is its prohibition on members fulfilling military service. In countries where there is no civilian alternative to the draft, Jehovah's Witnesses often end up being prosecuted.

Jews

A religious group once found in large communities in many parts of **eastern Europe**, including especially Belarus, **Poland** and regions of European Russia, but now greatly reduced in numbers as a result of the Second World War, the Holocaust and large-scale emigration. Eastern Europe was home to the greatest proportion of the world's

Jews for many centuries. Sidelined by mainstream society for their religion, Jews often took up industries deemed unfit for Christians, such as moneylending, and promoted their own educational institutions through close-knit communities. Their successes bred resentment and they were the targets of various attacks, early instances of which occurred during the Crusades which began in the 11th century. Anti-Semitism is now officially condemned but low-level discrimination continues across the region, with Jews particularly targeted by far-right nationalist groups.

Most of the Jews from eastern Europe are known as Ashkenazi. The Yiddish language, widely spoken among Ashkenazi Jews, is a hybrid of Hebrew and German. Jewish communities in **Bulgaria**, however, tend to be Sephardic, i.e. Hispanic, in origin. All of **Albania's** 300 Sephardic Jews migrated on the invitation of the Israeli Government in 1990–91. The liberalization of the **Soviet Union** from the 1980s opened up a new mass migration of Jews to Israel. Between 1989 and 1998 over 768,000 Jews made *aliyah* (migration to Israel) from the former Soviet Union, with 375,000 departing in 1990–91 alone. Today the largest populations of Jews in eastern Europe are found in the Russian Federation (around 228,000, mainly in urban centres), among the ethnic **Russian** communities in Ukraine (80,000, down from 486,000 in 1989) and **Hungary** (estimated at 80,000–100,000, though only 13,000 declared Jewish religion on the 2001 census).

JL *see* **New Era**.

John Paul II, Pope

The first Polish pope in history, in office from 1978 until his death in 2005 (*see* **Roman Catholic Church**). Born Karol Jozef Wojtyła on 18 May 1920 in Wadowice, the son of an army officer, he was reputedly active in Christian underground wartime activities, and was ordained to the priesthood on 1 November 1946. Gaining a reputation as a theologian with conservative views on marriage, he rose to become Archbishop of Kraków in 1964 and a cardinal in June 1967. He was elected as Pope on 16 October 1978. He was treated by many in his native **Poland** as a symbol of freedom against the power of the communist state, and his visits to Poland in the ensuing years accordingly took on a special significance. He became better known worldwide than any of his predecessors, making over 100 foreign trips and clearly revelling in the acclamation he received. Retaining his conservative orientation on Catholic moral doctrine, he sought to stem the growing acceptance of more liberal ideas on such issues as birth control, abortion, homosexuality and the ordination of women. A convinced anti-communist, he nevertheless also developed a critique of global capitalism and the operation of the free market, concerned that it fails to guarantee the global good and the exercise of economic and social rights.

Josipović, Ivo

President of the Republic, **Croatia**.

Ivo Josipović was born on 28 August 1957 in **Zagreb**. He studied law at the city's university, graduating in 1980, passing the bar examination and also earning a master's degree and a doctorate. He has represented Croatia at the **International Court of Justice** and the **International Criminal Tribunal for the former Yugoslavia**, and has worked as a **Council of Europe** expert advising on prison conditions in various countries including Ukraine, Mongolia and Azerbaijan. He is also an accomplished classical musician; he studied composition at the Zagreb Academy of Music, has had about 50 of his works performed professionally and won a European Broadcasting Award in 1999.

A member of the Communists' Union of Croatia in the 1980s, he helped draft the first statute of the **Social Democratic Party** (SDP) in the early 1990s but then quit politics in 1994 to focus on his legal and music careers. He returned to politics in 2003, becoming an independent member of the **Assembly** but backing the SDP; during two terms, he worked on various parliamentary committees on legislation, judiciary, parliamentary rules of procedure, political system and constitutional affairs. In 2005 he also sat in the Zagreb assembly. In 2008 he formally rejoined the SDP, and in 2009 was chosen as the SDP presidential candidate. He led the first round on 27 December with 32.4%. His nearest rival on 14.8% was independent Milan Bandić, who had been expelled from the SDP the previous month for announcing his own rival candidacy. Josipović went on to win the run-off on 10 January by 60.3% to 39.7% and took office on 18 February.

Ivo Josipović is married to Tatjana and they have one daughter. He speaks English and some German.

Address: Office of the President, Pantovčak 241, 10000 Zagreb.

Telephone: (1) 4565191.

Fax: (1) 4565299.

E-mail: office@president.hr

Internet: www.predsjednik.hr

Jubmes Banka *see* **Yugoslav Bank for International Economic Co-operation**.

K

Kaczyński, Lech

Former President of **Poland** (2005–10). A lawyer with a strong involvement in the Solidarity trade union movement of the 1980s, Lech Kaczyński formed the centre-right **Law and Justice** (PiS) party (along with his twin brother Jarosław) in 2001, following an immensely popular stint as Justice Minister, spearheading an anti-corruption drive. Elected President in October 2005, he took office in December, overseeing a PiS administration. From July 2006 his brother held the premiership, making Poland the first country to have twins in the two key executive roles. Early elections in October 2007 sent the PiS into opposition, however, and Kaczyński's presidency continued in a cohabitation with a Government formed by **Civic Platform** (PO). On 10 April 2010 Kaczyński was killed in a plane crash over Russian territory en route to a memorial service for those who died in the 1940 **Katyń massacre**.

Lech Kaczyński was born in **Warsaw** in 1949. He studied law at Warsaw University and then at the University of Gdańsk, receiving a doctorate in labour law in 1980 and a post-doctoral degree a decade later. Meanwhile he had been involved in trade union activities, initially at the Interventions Office of the Worker Defence Committee, then with the Independent Trade Unions and the Gdańsk Inter-plant Strike Committee, and was a delegate to the first congress of the **Solidarity** trade union movement. He was interned during the period of martial law in the early 1980s, but resumed trade union activities on his release, assisting the underground Solidarity movement. As Solidarity emerged as a major force in the late 1980s, Kaczyński became a member of the Civic Committee with Lech **Wałęsa**, and took part in the round-table negotiations with the Government. In 1989 he was elected to the Senat (upper house of the **National Assembly**) and in 1990 became a deputy of Solidarity.

In 1991, following the fall of communism, he became a Sejm (lower house) deputy for the Centre Civic Alliance, and was appointed to head the National Security Office at the Office of the President. From 1992 to 1995 he was President of the Supreme Chamber of Control.

In mid-2000 Prime Minister Jerzy Buzek of Solidarity Electoral Action (AWS) appointed Kaczyński as Minister of Justice. He launched a hugely popular anti-crime drive, and was regularly cited as the second-most popular politician in Poland after President Aleksander Kwaśniewski. However, his crusade against organized crime and corruption ran into conflict with the State Prosecutor's Office, prompting tensions with Buzek. Kaczyński was finally dismissed from the cabinet in July 2001 and immediately set about transforming the faction that he had led within AWS into a separate, fully-fledged political party—the PiS—with the help of his brother Jarosław, former leader of the right-wing minority Centre Agreement. Lech Kaczyński was the first Chairman of the party, elected as a PiS deputy in September, and winning election as Mayor of Warsaw a year later (after which the PiS leadership passed to his brother Jarosław in 2003). During his mayoral term he continued to pursue anti-corruption and anti-crime policies.

In the October 2005 presidential election he was second in the first round with 33% of the vote behind Donald **Tusk** of Civic Platform with 36%. He defeated Tusk in the run-off, however, in which he secured 54%, and he was sworn into office on 23 December.

On 10 April 2010 Kaczyński, his wife Maria and around 90 other Polish dignitaries were en route to a memorial service for the 70th anniversary of the Katyń massacre when their plane crashed near Smolensk, Russia, killing everyone on board.

Kádár, János

Leading figure in communist-era **Hungary**, First Secretary of the party for over three decades (1956–88) and the dominant figure of what became known as the 'Kádár era'. Born in 1912, he was active in clandestine communist youth movements and as a wartime resistance leader, and emerged after the liberation as Party Secretary in **Budapest**. In 1948–50 he was Minister of the Interior. In the party's factional disputes he turned against his close friend László Rajk, who was executed in 1949, but was himself purged in turn in 1950, and then imprisoned from 1951 to 1954. Rehabilitated in 1954, he was soon identified with Imre **Nagy** and the reformism of 1956, but swiftly changed horses when Soviet troops moved to crush the Hungarian uprising. The Soviet authorities left Kádár in charge—as Prime Minister (1956–58) as well as party leader—of pursuing the repressive process of 'normalization'. In the 1960s Kádár launched a new experiment: 'whoever is not against us is with us' on the ideological front, and the 'new economic mechanism' (introduced in 1968) which encouraged a 'regulated market' to deliver material benefits which would win public support. It was only in the 1980s, when Hungary's economic situation deteriorated, that Kádár came seriously under challenge, and he became entrenched in a sterile defensiveness against calls for 'reform of the reform'. The May 1988 party conference provided the occasion for the reformers to oust him, designating him as President of the party but without a Politburo seat. Seriously ill, he died in hospital on 6 July 1989.

Kaliningrad

A city and exclave of the Russian Federation adjoining the south-western corner of the Baltic Sea. *Population*: 937,360 (2009 estimate). The Kaliningrad oblast (region), roughly rectangular in shape, extends 140 km inland from the city of the same name. It was formed from the northern half of the **German** territory of East **Prussia**, which had been occupied by advancing Soviet troops at the end of the Second World War (1945). Bordering **Poland** to the south, it is separated from the rest of the Russian Federation by territory belonging to **Lithuania** (which borders Kaliningrad to the north and east) and by the entire width of Belarus.

Germanized since the era of the medieval Teutonic Order, the region around the city of Königsberg (literally 'king's mountain'), the administrative capital of East Prussia, was the centre for the reawakening of German nationalism during the Napoleonic Wars. It was incorporated into the Prussian-dominated unified Germany in 1871. It experienced 20 years as a German exclave from 1919 to 1939, cut off from the rest of Germany by Polish territory under the territorial settlement imposed on defeated Germany at the end of the First World War. Rejoined to Germany by the Nazi military advance eastwards in the Second World War, East Prussia was then split in two by the **Potsdam Agreements** in 1945. The northern half was annexed to Russia and the southern half ceded to the reorganized state of Poland, while the German population left to seek new homes in the rump Germany. For the next 46 years Kaliningrad was merely the edge of the vast **Soviet Union**, abutting only Soviet-dominated **eastern Europe** and repopulated with Russian colonists.

The collapse of the Soviet Union and the emergence of independent **Baltic States** in 1991 turned administrative isolation into a real political distance. With the admission of Poland and Lithuania into the **North Atlantic Treaty Organization** and the **European Union** (EU), Kaliningrad's position has become of even greater diplomatic significance. Civil authorities in the oblast have toyed with and ultimately rejected independence from Russia, but have been forced to take a decidedly more Western view than their masters in Moscow, calling for EU investment to help solve their dire socio-economic problems. Kaliningrad was made a free economic zone soon after the fall of the Soviet Union, with the intention of creating a 'Baltic Hong Kong'. However, prosperity proved elusive in the 1990s, as the region's economy fared even worse than that of Russia as a whole; unemployment, violence, poverty and environmental degradation set in. In early 2001 rumours of the Russian Federation's intention of using the oblast as a base for nuclear missiles caused uproar among its neighbours. There has also been friction over the freedom of movement from Kaliningrad to Russia proper. The introduction of border checks and visa requirements by Lithuania and Poland seriously strained regional relations, but a system of transit documents is now in place.

Economic growth has returned since the Russian financial crisis of the late 1990s, with the region consistently outperforming the Russian economy. Foreign investment is now growing along with EU co-operation, and the Special Economic Zone has been redefined and extended, though Russian accession to the **World Trade Organization** could affect its terms.

The city of Kaliningrad is home to almost half of the oblast's population—422.300 (2009 estimate). Built on the ruined north-western suburbs of Königsberg, Kaliningrad underwent heavy industrialization under Soviet rule and economic activity now centres on engineering and metalworking, although the traditional amber industry is still active. For their size, the city and oblast provide an above average proportion of the Russian Federation's industrial output—and draw a similar proportion of aid. Georgy Boos has headed the Kaliningrad administration since September 2005.

Karadžić, Radovan

Former **Serb** leader during the 1992–95 war in **Bosnia and Herzegovina**, now facing war crimes charges at the **International Criminal Tribunal for the former Yugoslavia** (ICTY).

Radovan Karadžić was born on 19 June 1945 in the village of Petnjica in **Montenegro**. His father fought with the **Chetniks** against the wartime Nazi occupation and against **Tito**'s Partisans, the rival communist resistance movement, and later served a prison sentence under the Tito regime for these activities. When Radovan Karadžić was 15, the family moved to **Sarajevo**, where he was a university student in the 1960s, studying medicine and psychiatry, writing poetry, and doing a one-year placement at Columbia University, New York. After qualifying as a psychiatrist he worked in various Sarajevo hospitals, but spent several months in prison in the mid-1980s on charges related to alleged involvement in corruption rackets such as selling prescriptions and false medical certificates and misusing government materials and funds.

In 1990, as the **Socialist Federal Republic of Yugoslavia** (SFRY) moved towards multi-party elections along increasingly nationalistic lines, Karadžić entered politics, co-founding the radical Serb nationalist **Serbian Democratic Party** (SDS) of which he was elected President. The SDS won 72 seats in November–December 1990 in a reorganized 240-seat Assembly in Bosnia and Herzegovina, when the ruling communists were heavily defeated.

With the SFRY fast fragmenting, Karadžić opposed the creation of an independent Bosnia and Herzegovina, in which ethnic Serbs would be outnumbered. Allying himself closely at this stage with **Serbia**'s President Slobodan **Milošević**, he successfully urged Bosnian Serb voters to boycott the referendum on independence, held in February–March 1992, and warned **Bosniaks** (Bosnian Muslims) the following month that a declaration of Bosnian sovereignty could result in their annihilation. With the outbreak of war he moved the Bosnian Serb administration to

Pale and in December 1992 was elected President of the self-proclaimed **Serb Republic** of Bosnia and Herzegovina, or Republika Srpska.

The Bosnian Serb army held the upper hand until the latter stages of the 1992–95 war, conducting a brutal campaign and committing atrocities which led to Karadžić and others being charged with war crimes. Although he attended a series of abortive peace negotiations in London, Geneva and New York, pretending a willingness to negotiate, he was never prepared to deliver any settlement in practice, until the **Croatian** offensive of mid-1995 turned the military tide decisively against the Serbs. Remaining obdurate under growing international pressure even when Milošević had begun to want a settlement, Karadžić was strongly critical of the late-1995 **Dayton Agreement**. Unable to attend the Dayton talks himself because of the war crimes indictment issued against him in July 1995, he eventually had no choice but to accept the accord under pressure from Milošević.

The indictment against Karadžić related to the crime of genocide, crimes against humanity, and crimes against the civilian population and places of worship throughout Bosnia and Herzegovina between April 1992 and July 1995. In particular they relate to the unlawful detention, murder, rape, sexual assault, torture, beating, robbery and inhumane treatment of thousands of Bosniak and Bosnian Croat civilians, as part of a programme of **'ethnic cleansing'**, the killing of civilians in sniper attacks during the siege of Sarajevo and other towns, and the taking as hostages of UN peacekeepers in mid-1995. In November 1995 he was further indicted over the mass killings of Bosniaks after Bosnian Serb forces overran the so-called 'safe area' of **Srebrenica** in July that year.

In July 1996, as stipulated by the Dayton Agreement, Karadžić was obliged formally to resign as Bosnian Serb leader and was replaced by his deputy and former ally, Biljana Plavšić. He also resigned as President of the SDS, although he continued to play an influential role behind the scenes, and to be regarded as a symbol of resistance by many Bosnian Serbs resentful of the Dayton settlement. An international warrant for his arrest was issued in July 1996, but despite the offer of a large bounty for his capture, he remained at large for well over a decade.

On 21 July 2008 the Serbian authorities unexpectedly announced that Karadžić had been arrested in **Belgrade**, where it turned out he had been a long-term resident, gaining some renown under the assumed identity of an alternative medicine practitioner. His arrest was enthusiastically welcomed by the international community, which urged that Gen. Ratko Mladić also be taken into custody. He was extradited to the ICTY on 30 July and on 28 August refused to enter pleas to the 11 charges against him, on the grounds that the Tribunal had no jurisdiction to try him. In February 2009, following a prosecution request that the number of counts against Karadžić be reduced in order to avoid an excessively prolonged trial, the ICTY approved an amended indictment of 11 charges. This involved fewer alleged crime areas, but included two rather than one counts of genocide, of which one related to war crimes in 1992 and one to the massacre of Srebrenica. In early March, after

Karadžić again failed to plead to the charges against him, a plea of not guilty was entered on his behalf. The trial began on 26 October, but Karadžić refused to appear for several days. It was then adjourned to 1 March 2010 to give time to prepare the defence, and then adjourned again until June.

Katyń massacre

The mass murder of some 22,000 **Poles** (mostly army officers) by the Soviet secret police (NKVD) in April–May 1940 during **Soviet** occupation of **Poland** in the Second World War. The victims were buried in mass graves in the Katyń Forest (which were discovered by the Nazis in 1943) and two other similar sites. For decades the official Soviet accounts blamed Nazi troops for carrying out the Katyń killings after they invaded the area in 1941, but in April 1990 the Soviet Union officially admitted reponsibility. An inquiry by the Russian Prosecutor General's office confirmed this in March 2005, but enumerated fewer than 2,000 Polish victims and declined to describe the massacre as either a war crime or an act of genocide.

A notably more sympathetic Russian attitude to the affair emerged when over 90 other Polish dignitaries, including President Lech **Kaczyński**, flying to a 70th anniversary commemoration were killed in a plane crash on 10 April 2010.

KDNP *see* **Christian Democratic People's Party**.

KDU–ČSL *see* **Christian Democratic Union–Czechoslovak People's Party**.

KECG *see* **Coalition for a European Montenegro**.

Kesk *see* **Estonian Centre Party**.

KFOR
(Kosovo Force)

A UN-mandated multinational peacekeeping force, led by the **North Atlantic Treaty Organization** (NATO), which maintains security in **Kosovo**. KFOR entered the Yugoslav province of Kosovo on 12 June 1999 following the conclusion of NATO's bombing campaign against **Yugoslavia** under the terms of UN Resolution 1244. Dividing the province into five sectors controlled by Italian, French, British, US and, later, non-NATO **Russian** troops, KFOR oversees the military aspects of the enforced peace in Kosovo and protects the UN administration there (**UNMIK**). The initial strength of KFOR totalled 50,000 personnel drawn from over 30 countries including obviously many non-NATO countries; in 2010 it numbered around 10,700 personnel.

Although sectors are effectively run by the five original forces, all troops obey a single command structure, headed since 8 September 2009 by German Lt-Gen. Markus Bentler.

Following Kosovo's independence declaration on 17 February 2008, NATO reaffirmed that KFOR should remain in place, unless the UN Security Council were to decide otherwise. KFOR was also tasked with supporting the development of professional, democratic and multi-ethnic security structures, and with assisting the European Union's planned policing mission (**EULEX**).

Address: Pristina, Kosovo.
Telephone: +389-22682849.
Fax: +389-22682070.
E-mail: pao@hq.kfor.nato.int
Internet: www.nato.int/kfor

KIG *see* **Polish Chamber of Commerce**.

KISOS–EDEK *see* **Movement of Social Democrats EDEK**.

KKE *see* **Communist Party of Greece**.

KKTC *see* **Turkish Republic of Northern Cyprus**.

Klaipeda

A port in the centre of **Lithuania**'s **Baltic** coast, formerly the East Prussian city of Memel. *Population*: 192,954 (2001 census). The original **Lithuanian** settlement was occupied by the Germanic Teutonic Knights in 1252 and became the base for their colonization of the Baltic region. Developed as a vitally important ice-free port, the city of Memel was inherited by the **Prussian** state and ultimately the newly-formed German state in 1871. After Germany's defeat in the First World War the region was made a ward of the League of Nations before being handed to the new state of Lithuania and renamed Klaipeda in 1923. The city's German history made it a prime target for the irredentism of the Nazi regime and between 1939 and 1945 it was returned to German rule. Since the end of the Second World War it has been an integral part of Lithuania (under **Soviet** control until 1991). The redrawing of the European map after 1945, and the mass expulsion of **Germans** from **eastern Europe**, ensured that German claims to the city have been reduced to the fanciful dreams of the extreme right.

The port has major shipbuilding yards and is the base for a large deep-sea fishing fleet. The city also has light industries, such as papermaking and electrical equipment. It is fairly well connected to the Lithuanian interior and **Latvia** to the north.

Klaus, Václav

President of the **Czech Republic**.

Former Finance Minister in post-communist **Czechoslovakia** and then first Prime Minister (1993–97) of the independent Czech Republic, Klaus was a leading advocate of a rapid and comprehensive transition to a free-market economy. He was elected as the country's second President in February 2003, and won a second term in 2008.

Born in **Prague** on 19 June 1941, he graduated in foreign trade economics from the Prague University of Economics in 1963. He identified with the 1968 reformists as a young economist, but took a low profile under the subsequent repressive regime, working in the state bank. He joined **Civic Forum** in December 1989 and was Czechoslovak Finance Minister from December 1989 until June 1992. Describing himself as a 'Thatcherite', he earned a reputation for ruthless efficiency, with achievements including, in particular, masterminding the mass privatization scheme. Klaus's views on economic policy hastened the split in Civic Forum, of which he became Chairman in October 1990. He co-founded the right-wing liberal **Civic Democratic Party** (ODS) in February 1991 and became its leader.

The ODS scored a striking success in the Czech Republic in the 1992 elections. Klaus became Czech Prime Minister in July 1992 and, grasping that the Czechoslovak federation was doomed, he resolved to end it on terms as favourable as possible to the Czechs. On this and other issues, his relations with President Václav **Havel** thereafter became sensitive.

The new Czech Constitution passed in autumn 1992 gave the presidency a limited, mainly ceremonial role, making the Prime Minister the dominant political figure in what became from 1 January 1993 the independent Czech Republic. As Prime Minister, Klaus continued to concentrate on transforming the economy. Elections in mid-1996 left his ODS-led coalition short of an absolute majority, but he remained as Prime Minister, with 'external' support from the **Czech Social Democratic Party** (ČSSD), until the defection of two minor coalition parties brought down his Government in November 1997.

The ODS lost further ground at the June 1998 elections, overtaken by the ČSSD. The party agreed to give qualified external support to a ČSSD-led minority Government and Klaus was appointed Chairman of the Chamber of Deputies (lower house of **Parliament**).

Support for the ODS declined further at the June 2002 election, and Klaus stood down as ODS Chairman in December. However, just two months later, he was elected President of the Czech Republic. He went on to win a second term five years later. During his terms in office, he has spoken out controversially against many issues such as Kosovan independence and action to limit global warming. He also held out as long as he could against signing the **European Union**'s Lisbon Treaty, despite its ratification by the Czech Parliament.

He is married to Livia Klausova, with two sons.

Address: Office of the President of the Republic, Pražský hrad, 119 08 Prague 1.
Telephone: (2) 24371111.
Fax: (2) 24373300.
E-mail: president@hrad.cz
Internet: www.hrad.cz

Komorowski, Bronisław

Marshal (Speaker) of the Sejm (lower house of the **National Assembly** of **Poland**), in which capacity he became acting President of Poland on the death of President Lech **Kaczyński** in a plane crash on 10 April 2010.

Bronisław Komorowski was born in Oborniki Śląskie on 6 April 1952. He studied history at Warsaw University and then taught at a seminary. A supporter of Poland's underground opposition movement in the 1970s and 1980s, he published dissident leaflets and newsletters. Arrested several times for taking part in anti-communist rallies, he was sent to an internment camp in the early 1980s while Poland was under martial law.

After the fall of communism in 1989, Komorowski joined the Cabinet Office and then was elected as a member of the Sejm from 1991 onwards. He served as Defence Minister from June 2000 to October 2001. In October 2005 he became Deputy Marshal of the Sejm and in November 2007 he secured election as its Marshal.

In early 2010 Komorowski was nominated as the **Civic Platform** (PO) presidential candidate for the presidential election due by October, just ahead of the conclusion of Kaczyński's five-year term. In light of the latter's death in April, however, an early election was scheduled for 20 June 2010.

Bronisław Komorowski is married to Anna Dembowska and they have two sons and three daughters.

Address: Office of the President, ul. Wiejska 10, 00-902 Warsaw.
Telephone: (22) 6952900.
Fax: (22) 6952237.
E-mail: listy@prezydent.pl
Internet: www.prezydent.pl

Komšić, Željko

Member of the Presidency (**Croat**), **Bosnia and Herzegovina**.

Željko Komšić was born on 20 January 1964 in **Sarajevo**. He graduated in law from the University of Sarajevo and also studied at the School of Foreign Service at the University of Georgetown, USA. He joined the Bosnian army when conflict broke out, receiving the Golden Lily for conduct and courage.

Working as a lawyer, he entered politics supporting the **Social Democratic Party of Bosnia and Herzegovina** (SDPBiH) and eventually rising to become one of the party's Vice-Presidents. From 2000 to 2001 he headed the Municipality of New Sarajevo, and then was appointed Bosnia's first ambassador to the rump **Yugoslav** state of Serbia and Montenegro. However, he resigned in 2002 when the SDPBiH left government. At the local elections in 2004 he was returned to his former post in New Sarajevo. He stood as SDPBiH candidate for the union Presidency in the October 2006 election, and won the Croat seat with 41% of the vote. The tripartite Presidency was inaugurated on 6 November 2006, and Komšić held the Chair of the Presidency, from July 2007 to March 2008 and, secondly, from July 2009 to March 2010.

Željko Komšić is married to Sabina Komšić and they have one daughter.

Address: Office of the Presidency, Titova 16, 71000 Sarajevo.
Telephone: (33) 663863.
Fax: (33) 555620.
E-mail: press@predsjednistvobih.ba
Internet: www.predsjednistvobih.ba

Kosor, Jadranka

Prime Minister of **Croatia**. A member of the **Assembly** since 1995, representing the **Croatian Democratic Union** (HDZ), Jadranka Kosor was a Deputy Prime Minister and Minister of the Family, Veterans' Affairs and Intergenerational Solidarity prior to her appointment as Croatia's first female Prime Minister on 3 July 2009.

Born on 1 July 1953 in Pakrac, she graduated in law from the University of Zagreb, and began a career in journalism. As a correspondent for Radio Zagreb, she became noted for her radio shows for refugees and veterans during the early 1990s conflict.

In 1995 she was elected to the House of Representatives for the HDZ, and was chosen as Vice-President of the House for the 1995–2000 term. Within the party, she was a Vice-President, and from 1998 was President of the HDZ Women's Association. From 2002 she rose to be HDZ Deputy President, and when the HDZ won elections in November 2003 she joined the new Government as a Deputy Prime Minister and Minister of the Family, Veterans' Affairs and Intergenerational Solidarity.

In January 2005 she stood in the presidential election as the HDZ candidate, going through to the second round but only securing 34.1% against incumbent Stipe Mesić's 65.9% in the run-off.

When Prime Minister Ivo Sanader announced on 1 July 2009 that he was quitting politics, he recommended Kosor as his successor. She was nominated on 3 July, secured the presidency of the HDZ the following day, and took office on 6 July.

Kosor speaks English and some German.

Address: Office of the Prime Minister, Trg sv. Marka 2, 10000 Zagreb.
Telephone: (1) 4569222.
Fax: (1) 6303023.
E-mail: predsjednik@vlada.hr
Internet: www.vlada.hr

Kosovo
Kosova, Kosovë

A newly independent (but not universally recognized) landlocked republic located in south-eastern Europe in the **Balkan** peninsula, bounded by Serbia to the north and east, Macedonia to the south-east, Albania to the south-west and Montenegro to the west. Administratively, Kosovo is divided into seven districts (rrethe).

Area: 10,887 sq km; *capital*: **Pristina**; *population*: 2.1m. (2009 estimate), comprising **Albanians** 88%, **Serbs** 7%, others 5%; *official languages*: Albanian and Serbian; *religion*: **Muslim** 92%, **Orthodox Christian** 4%, **Roman Catholic** 4%.

Under Kosovo's post-independence 2008 Constitution, the head of state is a President elected by the legislature for a five-year term. The unicameral legislature, the **Assembly of Kosova** (Kuvendi i Kosovës or Skupština Kosova), has a total of 120 members. Directly elected members hold 100 seats, 10 seats are reserved for Serbs, and 10 more for other minorities. All members are elected for a term of four years.

History: Kosovo was historically an integral part of Serbia, until the loss of the province to the invading Ottoman Turks at the Battle of Kosovo in 1389. This defining event forms a cornerstone of **Serb** nationalism. Its consequences also laid the foundations for centuries of ethnic tension. Ethnic Albanians began to arrive in the region following its incorporation into the **Muslim** Ottoman Empire but did not become the dominant population until the mid-20th century, by which time it was part of the **Socialist Federal Republic of Yugoslavia** (SFRY).

Kosovo, known as Kosovo and Metohija, acquired a degree of autonomy within the Serbian republic under the SFRY framework, but calls for greater rights for the ethnic Albanian community created a backlash among Serb nationalists, who felt their position increasingly beleaguered within what they regarded as the heartland of their national identity. The aspiring Serbian leader Slobodan **Milošević** exploited these feelings in building a nationalist platform for himself, and in 1989 the autonomous status of both Kosovo and **Vojvodina** was withdrawn. The Kosovo Assembly responded by demanding that Kosovo become a full republic within the SFRY, at which point Serbia dissolved the Assembly. Autonomous status was restored, but the ethnic Albanian Kosovans were not satisfied and declared independence on 19 October 1991 (recognized only by Albania). An alternative Government was set up under 'President' Ibrahim Rugova and 'Prime Minister' Bujar Bukoshi.

Repression and discrimination against Kosovo's Albanian-speaking community gathered pace under Milošević's rule later in the decade. Full-scale fighting between Serbian paramilitary police and the **Kosovo Liberation Army** (UÇK) nationalist militia broke out in 1998. The Yugoslav police, soon backed by the regular Yugoslav army, implemented a brutal policy of '**ethnic cleansing**', prompting worldwide condemnation and the threat of international intervention. Hundreds of thousands of Kosovar Albanians were forced from their homes and found shelter in neighbouring countries. US-led military intervention to force a halt to the 'ethnic cleansing' campaign took the form of sustained aerial bombing, under the aegis of the **North Atlantic Treaty Organization** (NATO). Although this began in March 1999, Serbian forces were not finally withdrawn until June.

The province was then divided into sectors to be patrolled by British, US, French, German, Italian and later Russian troops as part of an international **KFOR** peacekeeping force. Ethnic Albanian refugees began returning to their homes, and plans were laid for a multi-ethnic police force, and later a full domestic administration. In the interim, Kosovo was placed under the UN Interim Administration Mission in Kosovo (**UNMIK**), which was established as the supreme legal and executive authority, overseeing civilian administration and reconstruction as an autonomous province. On 1 February 2000 the authority of UNMIK was recognized both by Rugova's 'alternative' Government and by a rival provisional Government formed by the UÇK in March 1999.

Tensions between the ethnic Albanian and remaining minority Serb communities remained high, particularly in the heavily divided town of Mitrovica where a number of clashes took place (*see also* **Preševo valley**). Ethnic Serbs frequently condemned the alleged bias of the UN administration in favour of Albanians and repeatedly withdrew their support for the UN administration. On the other hand ethnic Albanians continued to press for the province's full independence. When elections for a UN-sponsored Assembly were held in November 2001, the moderate **Democratic League of Kosovo** (LDK), headed by Rugova, became the largest party (47 seats, 45.7% of the vote), ahead of the more radical **Democratic Party of Kosovo** (PDK—26 seats, 25.7%). A Serb coalition, Return, won 12 seats (11.3%) and the Alliance for the Future of Kosovo (AAK) won eight seats (7.8%). Repeated attempts in the Assembly to elect Rugova as President failed as the other parties boycotted the proceedings. Eventually inter-party negotiations enabled his election on 4 March 2002, while a power-sharing Government took office with Bajram Rexhepi of the PDK as Prime Minister. Return joined this Government in April.

In early 2003 when the Federal Republic of Yugoslavis was dissolved and a looser Union of Serbia and Montenegro was created, ethnic Albanians in Kosovo objected to the province's inclusion in the Union as part of Serbia. Calls for independence continued.

At the 23 October 2004 Assembly election, the LDK retained its 47 seats (with 45.4% of the vote), the PDK rose to 30 seats (28.9% of the vote) and the AAK won nine seats (8.4%). A new coalition was formed on 3 December, with AAK leader Ramush Haradinaj as Prime Minister. Haradinaj, once a key figure in the KLA, was under investigation for war crimes by the ICTY: his appointment was criticized by Serb parties. He resigned on 8 March 2005 (succeeded by fellow AAK member Bajram Kosumi), after the ICTY had indicted him on 37 charges—he surrendered to the Tribunal, and was subsequently cleared three years later.

The Assembly had re-elected Rugova as President in December 2004, but on 21 January 2006 he died of lung cancer. The LDK nominated Fatmir **Sejdiu** to succeed him, and the Assembly elected him unopposed on 10 February. Rugova's death caused a shift in the dynamics both within the LDK, and between it and its coalition partners. One outcome was the resignation of Prime Minister Kosumi on 10 March. Kosumi was succeeded by former UÇK commander Agim Çeku—a choice regarded as particularly inflammatory by the Serb community.

Meanwhile, in February 2006 the UN had held the first round of negotiations on the final status of Kosovo. These were followed in July (a month after **Montenegro** achieved independence) by the first talks to involve the Presidents and Prime Ministers of Serbia and Kosovo since 1999. Both sides had already stated their positions—the Serbs refusing to accept independence for Kosovo, and the Kosovans refusing to accept anything else—and remained intransigent through months of negotiations. The new Serbian Constitution promulgated later that year explicitly referred to Kosovo as an integral part of the Republic of Serbia.

In March 2007 UN Special Envoy Martti Ahtisaari submitted to the UN Security Council his finalized Comprehensive Proposal for the Kosovo Status Settlement. He recommended independence for the province, to be supervised for an initial period by an international military and civilian presence. Under the Proposal, an **International Civilian Representative** would be appointed to supervise the implementation of the settlement, and would be empowered to veto legislation and dismiss local officials. On 3 April, at the beginning of a debate in the UN Security Council, Serbia rejected the Proposal; two days later, the Kosovo Assembly approved it by 100 of the 101 votes cast. International negotiators continued their attempts to bring the two sides together and reach a resolution, but reported in December that neither side would compromise. Meanwhile, at the UN Security Council, Russia refused to approve the Proposal until it was acceptable to Serbia.

Latest elections: At the 17 November 2007 Assembly election, the PDK overtook the LDK, winning 37 seats (with 34.3% of the vote) against the LDK's 25 seats (22.6% of the vote). The pro-business New Kosovo Alliance (AKR) won 13 seats (12.3%), while 11 went to the alliance of the Democratic League of Dardania (a splinter from the LDK) and the Albanian Christian Democratic Party of Kosovo, with 10% of the vote. The AAK won 10 seats (9.6%) and the remaining 24 seats (including 10 reserved for Serbs and 10 for other minorities) went to 13 smaller parties. On 9 January 2008 the Assembly approved a PDK-LDK coalition with PDK leader Hashim

Thaçi as Prime Minister, and re-elected the LDK's leader Fatmir Sejdiu as President, for a term now extended to five years.

Recent developments: With both governing parties in favour of independence, Kosovo unilaterally declared independence on 17 February 2008, with a request for implementation of the terms of the UN's unapproved Proposal. The draft of a new Constitution was completed, approved by the Assembly on 9 April, and came into effect on 15 June. However, Serbia continued to regard Kosovo as a Serbian province: balloting for Serbia's legislative elections in May 2008 took place in the Serb-dominated regions of Kosovo, and the following month Kosovo's Serbs set up a 45-member autonomous Assembly.

International relations and defence: International recognition is the key issue for Kosovo: on declaring independence on 17 February 2008 it was immediately recognized by the USA, the United Kingdom, France and Albania, and by a total of 22 countries by the end of the month. By the first anniversary of independence the total had risen to 55 countries (including neighbours **Macedonia** and Montenegro). Significantly, however, Russia and the People's Republic of China backed Serbia in not recognizing Kosovan independence: both hold vetoes on the UN Security Council, which has prevented UN recognition. Also, within the **European Union** (EU), five of the 27 members have withheld recognition (namely Spain, Romania, Cyprus, Slovakia and Greece); however, this has not prevented the EU from deploying its **EULEX** mission to assist the Kosovan authorities with policing, judiciary and customs issues, taking over many duties from UNMIK. In October 2008, the UN agreed to a Serbian proposal for the **International Court of Justice** (ICJ) to rule on whether Kosovo's unilateral secession was 'in accordance with international law'. The ICJ opened its consideration of the matter on 1 December 2009, with a verdict not expected for several months; its ruling will only be an advisory opinion, and supporters of Kosovan independence viewed Serbia's requesting it as a delaying tactic.

Meanwhile, with the UN's 1999 resolution setting up UNMIK still in force, many international organizations are required to view UNMIK as the territory's executive authority. This has prevented Kosovo's admission to many international organizations. However, enough countries voted to allow Kosovan membership of the **International Monetary Fund** and the **World Bank** in mid-2009. Kosovo plans eventually to apply for membership of the **Council of Europe**, the EU, the **Organization for Security and Co-operation in Europe** (OSCE) and NATO.

At independence, KFOR was in charge of defence, with emergency services assistance from the civilian **Kosovo Protection Corps** (TMK), formed in 1999 from the demilitarized UÇK. The first Defence Minister was appointed in August 2008, and a new professional, multi-ethnic Kosovan Security Force was created to replace the TMK in January 2009. By September, when it began operational duties, it had 300 troops; this was expected to rise to an eventual 2,500 personnel.

Kosovo, economy

One of the poorest economies in Europe, whose transition from communist-era central control has been badly damaged by the conflicts of the 1990s, the effects of UN sanctions and embargoes, the entry of **NATO** forces into Kosovo and the region's struggle to obtain its independence from **Serbia**. It has one of Europe's highest rates of unemployment and an enormous imbalance of trade, leaving it very dependent still on support from the international community.

GNP: US $3,030m. (2008); *GNP per capita*: $1,800 (2008); *GDP at PPP*: US $5,300m. (2008); *GDP per capita at PPP*: $2,452 (2007); *real GDP growth*: 3.5% (2007); *exports*: $272m. (2008); *imports*: $2,700m. (2008); *currency*: euro (US $1 = €0.7129 in mid-2009), the Serbian dinar is used in Serb-dominated areas; *unemployment*: 45% (2008); *government deficit as a percentage of GDP*: 2.4% (2009); *inflation*: 9.3% (2008).

In 2007 industry contributed 20% of GDP, agriculture 20% and services 60%. Around 21% of the workforce is engaged in industry, 15% in agriculture and 64% in services.

Some 53% of land is arable and 41% forests and woodland. The main crops are wheat, potatoes, maize, peppers and grapes (for wine).

Mineral resources include brown coal (lignite), halloysite (a clay mineral used in the production of porcelain and bone china), lead, zinc, chromium and bauxite. Industries include machine-building, metallurgy, and mining.

The main exports are base metals, metal goods, mineral products, machinery and mechanical products, leather and leather goods, and prepared foodstuffs, beverages, alcohol and tobacco. There is some potential for Kosovo as an energy exporter, utilizing what are the world's fifth-largest reserves of brown coal, but it has so far lacked the ability to exploit these deposits (which are also prospectively a highly polluting form of energy). The principal imports are mineral products, prepared foodstuffs, beverages and tobacco, machinery and mechanical products, base metals and metal good and chemical products. The main destinations of exports in 2006 were Serbia (19%), **Bulgaria**, Italy and **Albania**, while the principal sources of imports were **Macedonia** (20%), Serbia, Germany and Turkey.

When **UNMIK** took over the administration of Kosovo in 1999 it introduced the Deutsche Mark as the region's currency (subsequently replaced with the euro), established a Banking and Payments Authority of Kosovo to fulfil the traditional roles of a central bank (now the **Central Banking Authority of Kosovo**), and formed a separate tax collection structure, mainly focused on border taxes. Serbia objected to these moves, and although UNMIK still recognized Serbia's ultimate sovereignty over the region it could not function administratively without these measures. Also uncertainty over the province's political future made strategic policy-making difficult.

Nevertheless, modest annual GDP growth of around 3% was achieved through 2003–05 and accelerated to 4.1% in 2006 and over 5% in 2007–08. Inflation remained well under control, partly due to Kosovo's use of the euro, until global food price rises pushed it to 12% in 2008. However, wages are low in all sectors, and a third of the population lives below the poverty line, with 15% living in extreme poverty. Unemployment, rising since 2004, has reached heights that could only be remedied by rapid and sustained economic growth over many years. Around 80% of farmland is privately owned, but farming is inefficient and usually near subsistence, and industrial production is also weak. Imports significantly exceed exports resulting in a trade deficit of up to half of GDP each year. This is funded by remittances from Kosovans abroad (mainly from Germany and Switzerland, and accounting for about a seventh of GDP) and by foreign aid.

In mid-2003, a privatization programme for the 500 state-owned enterprises (SOEs) was launched. These SOEs operated throughout Kosovo in all sectors of the economy and represented both small and large-scale enterprises, active in agro-industrial ventures, textiles, wine-making, distribution, hotels, building materials, mining and metal-processing. By 2008, more than 350 had been privatized, generating revenue of over US \$500m, but the **European Union** (EU) has criticized the slow pace of privatization for large-scale public companies.

UNMIK (on behalf of Kosovo) joined the **Central European Free Trade Area** (CEFTA) in 2006, but two of its member countries, Serbia and **Bosnia and Herzegovina**, have refused to recognize Kosovo's customs stamp or extend it any privileges under CEFTA. In July 2008 a donors' conference pledged US \$1,900m. to fund a socio-economic reform programme. In mid-2009 Kosovo joined the **World Bank** and **International Monetary Fund**, and subsequently began servicing its share of the former **Yugoslavia**'s debt with those institutions. While Kosovo is likely to strengthen its economic links with **Albania** over the next few years, its unresolved rift with Serbia remains a barrier to development. Meanwhile, it remains heavily reliant on donor aid. The (distant) prospect of membership of the EU will form and focus government policies for many years to come.

Kosovo Chamber of Commerce
Oda Ekonomike ë Kosovës (OEK)

An independent organization in **Kosovo** supporting members' interests and promoting the development of trade and industry. Established in 1962.

President: Besim Beqaj.
Address: Nënë Tereza 20, 10000 Pristina.
Telephone: (381) 38224741.
Fax: (381) 38224299.
E-mail: oek@oek-kcc.org
Internet: www.odaekonomike.org

Kosovo Force *see* **KFOR.**

Kosovo Liberation Army
Ushtria Çlirimtare e Kosovës (UÇK)

The principal armed movement of ethnic **Albanians** in **Kosovo** seeking the province's independence from **Serbia/Yugoslavia** in the late 1990s. The UÇK came to prominence in 1998 as the focus of ethnic Albanian resistance to a ruthless assertion of Serbian authority by government forces, mounting a well-armed and well-financed military campaign which established effective control over substantial areas of Kosovo. UÇK representatives participated in the Rambouillet talks on Kosovo in early 1999 but failed to secure Western support for independence, whereupon the UÇK announced that its political leader, Hashim **Thaçi**, had become 'Prime Minister' of a provisional Kosovo Government.

The withdrawal of Serbian forces from Kosovo in June 1999 accentuated divisions between UÇK 'moderates', prepared to co-operate with the succeeding UN administration, and hard-liners advocating continued struggle for independence and eventual union with **Albania** (*see* **Greater Albania**). The UÇK was officially disbanded in June 1999. Little real progress was made at this stage on disarming its rank-and-file militants, some of whom joined new groups which in early 2001 became involved in an insurgency in ethnic Albanian areas of neighbouring **Macedonia**. Politically the UÇK was succeeded by the **Democratic Party of Kosovo** under Thaçi's leadership. It was also provided that former UÇK members, once demilitarized, could enter the **Kosovo Protection Corps** (TMK), a civilian emergency services organization headed by former UÇK Commander Agim Çeku and charged with assisting the **NATO**-led **KFOR**. After Kosovo's independence in 2008, the TMK was progressively replaced by a professional force and it was formally disbanded in June 2009.

Kosovo Press
Kosova Press

Independent media source in **Kosovo**, publishing news in Albanian and English. Established in 1999.

Manager: Skender Krasniqi.
Address: Nënë Tereza 20, 10000 Pristina.
Telephone and fax: (38) 248721.
E-mail: info@kosovapress.com
Internet: www.kosovapress.com

Kosovo Protection Corps
Trupat e Mbrojtjes së Kosovës (TMK)

A civilian emergency services organization in **Kosovo** created in mid-1999 to define a new role for the former members of the **Kosovo Liberation Army** and to assist the **NATO**-led **KFOR**. Following Kosovo's declaration of independence in February 2008, it was announced that the TMK would be replaced with a military defence force. On 20 January 2009 the TMK ceased operational activities, and the following day the Kosovo Security Force came into existence. The TMK was officially disbanded in June.

Koštunica, Vojislav

Former President of the Federal Republic of **Yugoslavia** (2000–03) and Prime Minister of **Serbia** (2004–08). Vojislav Koštunica heads the small nationalist **Democratic Party of Serbia** (DSS). A consistent and vocal opponent of Yugoslav governments since the 1970s, he was chosen in 2000 to stand against Slobodan **Milošević** as presidential candidate for the **Democratic Opposition of Serbia** (DOS), largely because he was free from connections with the disgraced Milošević regime. He held the presidency until the restructuring of the Federal Republic of Yugoslavia into the looser Union of Serbia and Montenegro. He then secured two terms heading the Serbian Government in various coalitions, ultimately falling out with President Boris **Tadić** over the issues of Kosovo and **European Union** (EU) integration, and losing power after his party's poor showing in the 2008 legislative elections.

Born in **Belgrade** on 24 April 1944, he graduated from the University of Belgrade's Faculty of Law, achieving a master's degree in 1970 and a doctorate in 1974. His firm nationalist politics jarred with the communist regime and his support of prominent critics of Marshal **Tito**'s 1974 federal Constitution, which ensured autonomy within Serbia for **Kosovo** and **Vojvodina**, led to his dismissal from the faculty. When offered a professorship at the same faculty in 1989 he famously refused. From 1974 he worked at the Institute for Social Sciences in Belgrade and was briefly its Director in the mid-1980s. During this period he also edited several well-respected political and legal journals and had his own writings on law and politics published. He mixed **Serbian** nationalism with advocacy of human rights and was prominent on the Board for the Protection of the Freedom of Thought and Expression. In 1989 he co-founded the **Democratic Party** (DS). In elections in 1990 he won a seat in the lower house which he held through consecutive elections (and the break-up of Yugoslavia) until 1997.

Koštunica left the DS in 1992 because he considered its stance during the Yugoslav civil war to be insufficiently nationalistic. Instead he created the DSS, of which he has been President ever since. By 1993 the DSS was on the very fringe of Serbian politics, becoming known derisively as the 'van party' on the basis that all of its supporters could fit in one van. He earned the dubious honour of being lumped among the 'war party' in the Federal Assembly for his continual attacks on the various Western-proposed peace plans, and his support for the extreme nationalist Radovan **Karadžić** and the rebellious Serbs in **Bosnia and Herzegovina**—although he condemned the excessive violence of the various paramilitary groups. His belligerent policies kept him out of popular politics until the Kosovo conflict in 1999 when hostility to Milošević grew in strength. The disparate opposition parties turned to him in July 2000 as a unifying candidate, who was utterly free from the taint of the corrupt regime, to represent the DOS in the presidential election. After the electoral commission admitted to having been ordered to falsify the results of the 24 September elections, a wave of mass demonstrations on 5 October forced Milošević to resign. Koštunica took office as federal President two days later. The October revolution brought offers for Yugoslavia to rejoin the international community and Koštunica was universally hailed as a champion of democracy. However, he proved to be as consistent as ever and continued to condemn outside interference while warning of a future conflict with ethnic Albanian guerrillas in Kosovo. In January 2001 he sent shock waves through the DOS when he met with Milošević to discuss the issues of the day, and he openly condemned the **International Criminal Tribunal for the former Yugoslavia** (ICTY) as a 'monstrous institution'. When Milošević was arrested in April on charges of misappropriation of state funds and abuse of his official position, Koštunica insisted that the ex-President and other indicted war criminals would be tried in Yugoslavia rather than by the ICTY. However, the Serbian Government subsequently extradited Milošević to The Hague in June. This was just one among several issues that undermined the DOS, pitting Koštunica against the Serbian Prime Minister Zoran Đinđić, leader of the **Democratic Party** (DS) component of the DOS. In August Koštunica accused the Serbian Government of failing to tackle widespread crime, and withdrew his DSS.

Meanwhile, following protracted negotiations on the issue of Montenegro's independence, Koštunica and both of the republican Presidents signed a framework agreement on 14 March 2002, providing for the establishment of a State Union of Serbia and Montenegro. It took effect on 4 February 2003, and a new Union President was elected. This federal-level restructuring appeared to have left Koštunica out in the cold—but he was not interested in the less-powerful Union presidency and had his eyes set on the Serbian presidency. He had led the first-round vote held the preceding September, but the run-off vote held in October was invalidated due to a below-50% turnout. A fresh election in December (in which Koštunica polled over 50% in the first round) again failed to muster the required turnout.

In November 2003 the DOS coalition finally collapsed and early elections were called. At the December poll, Koštunica's DSS-led coalition finished in second place behind the the ultra-nationalist **Serbian Radical Party** (SRS). After lengthy inter-party talks, the radicals were kept from power by a minority coalition headed by Koštunica as Prime Minister, which took office on 3 March 2004.

Following the independence of Montenegro in June 2006, fresh **National Assembly** elections were held in January 2007. Again the SRS secured the most seats, but this time the DS (now led by President Tadić) came second and Koštunica's DSS alliance third. Lengthy coalition talks again ensued, resulting in May with Koštunica remaining as Prime Minister, heading a new coalition Government that this time also included the DS.

Tensions grew between Tadić (whose key priority was Serbia's accession to the EU) and Koštunica (whose key priority was to retain the UN-administered province of Kosovo as part of Serbia). On 8 March, shortly after Kosovo's secession, the coalition collapsed and Koštunica resigned. In the ensuing early elections the DSS alliance finished a distant third, and was not included in the new DS-led Government.

Vojislav Koštunica is married to Zorica Radović, who is also a lawyer. He famously eschewed the trappings of power, living in a modest Belgrade apartment, and was seen driving through the streets of the capital in his battered old Yugo car.

Krajina

The border territories, literally 'border lands', of **Croatia**. These regions, forming a broad bulge along the central and southern Croatia–**Bosnia and Herzegovina** border and the far eastern edge of **Slavonia**, were populated by **Orthodox Christian Serbs** fleeing the occupation of Bosnia by the Ottomans in 1463. Relations between them and the (**Roman Catholic**) **Croats** were characterized by repeated acts of brutality. During the Second World War the fascist Croat Government persecuted the Serb population with mass killings. In the early 1990s, as **Yugoslavia** collapsed and Croats asserted their nationalist identity, the ethnic Serbs, fuelled by the territorial ambitions of the proponents of **Greater Serbia**, voted in a referendum on 12 May 1991 to secede from Croatia and remain part of Yugoslavia. Exactly a week later the rest of Croatia voted for independence. The contrasting decisions led within two months to open conflict between ethnic Serbs, backed by the regular Yugoslav army, and Croat forces—effectively heralding the beginning of war.

The Republic of Serbian Krajina (RSK) was declared during a hiatus in the conflict on 4 April 1992 and was led by self-styled President Milan Babić. A call for the RSK to be amalgamated with the **Serb Republic** in neighbouring Bosnia and other Serb lands (Greater Serbia) in June 1993 led to a continuing low-level offensive against the Krajina by Croat troops. Ethnic Serbs became themselves the victims of a concerted policy of '**ethnic cleansing**' wherever settlements in the Krajina came under Croat military domination. The RSK was eventually destroyed in the decisive Operation Storm mounted by Croat forces in August 1995, although the border region of eastern Slavonia remained under Serb control. Eastern Slavonia was eventually returned to Croatia under the terms of the **Dayton Agreement** of November 1995, averting further bloodshed.

Hundreds of thousands of Serbs fled the advancing Croat forces during Operation Storm, arriving for the most part in the Serb-controlled areas of Bosnia and Herzegovina and in Yugoslavia itself. This demographic shift in the Krajina helped to settle relations between Croatia and Yugoslavia after the war. Following the collapse of the overtly nationalist regimes in Croatia and Yugoslavia, after the death of **Tudjman** and the downfall of **Milošević** respectively, the Krajina is no longer a focus of cross-border tension.

Krišto, Borjana

President of the **Muslim-Croat Federation** of **Bosnia and Herzegovina**—the first woman to hold the post.

Borjana Krišto was born on 13 August 1961 in Livno and graduated in law in Banja Luka, working in various businesses' legal departments before becoming a cantonal Minister of Justice and Administration in 1999, cantonal Secretary in 2000 and Federation Minister of Justice from 2002 to 2006. A Vice-President of the **Croatian Democratic Union** (HDZ), she was elected Federation President on 22 February 2007.

Address: Office of the President, Alipašina 41, 71000 Sarajevo.

KSČM *see* Communist Party of Bohemia and Moravia.

Kubilius, Andrius

Prime Minister of **Lithuania**. Chairman of the conservative **Homeland Union– Lithuanian Christian Democrats** (TS–LKD), Kubilius first served as Prime Minister from November 1999 until October 2000. His second appointment followed the October 2008 election. His political career has been described as a 'textbook' example of a Lithuanian politician, from independence activist to mainstream party member.

Andrius Kubilius was born on 8 December 1956 in the Soviet Socialist Republic of Lithuania, to two literature critics. He graduated from Vilnius University in 1979 with a degree in physics. Through the course of the 1980s he found employment at the same university as a laboratory assistant, engineer and a scientific research assistant. His political carer began in 1988 when he joined the emerging Lithuanian independence movement, **Sąjudis**. He quickly worked his way up the movement's hierarchy and was soon appointed as executive secretary.

In 1991 Lithuania achieved full independence from the **Soviet Union** and Kubilius was appointed to the newly-created unicameral **Parliament** (Seimas) the following year. In May 1993 Sąjudis was transformed into the Homeland Union–Lithuanian

Conservatives (TS–LK) and Kubilius was a founding member. In the general election held in November 1996 the TS–LK swept into power with around 30% of the vote and Kubilius was appointed as First Deputy Speaker of Parliament. It was in this role that he earned himself a reputation as a forthright manager with an easy sense of humour who was able to control parliamentary debates effectively. He also served as Chairman of the European Affairs Committee and speaks fluent English as well as Russian.

In 1999 the TS–LK-led Government came under severe crisis when first in April Prime Minister Gediminas Vagnorius resigned over tensions between himself and the President, and then in October his replacement Rolandas Paksas also stepped down, this time over the controversial decision to semi-privatize the state-owned Mazeikiai Oil company. Kubilius was appointed to take over in November and, despite his political gravitas, his Government faced immediate public opposition over the oil sale and the rise in unemployment along with the harsh austerity measures deployed in an attempt to resuscitate the economy. In March 2000 the TS–LK suffered a crushing defeat in local elections, foretelling the disaster of the general election held later in the year, when it only won nine seats.

In May 2003 Kubilius succeeded Landsbergis as party Chairman. He became Leader of the Opposition following the October 2004 election, at which the TS (having dropped the LK from its name) recovered some ground to finish in third place with 25 seats, behind the **Labour Party** (DP) and the alliance of the **Lithuanian Social Democratic Party** (LSDP) and the New Union (Social Liberals) (NS), which formed the new Government. When the DP withdrew from the coalition in mid-2006, the resulting minority Government relied on external support from the TS. Kubilius was rewarded by being reappointed to his former position as Deputy Speaker and as Chairman of the Parliamentary Committee on European Affairs in October 2006.

Ahead of the October 2008 election the TS merged with the Lithuanian Christian Democrats (LKD) to form the TS–LKD, with Kubilius remaining as Chairman. It won 45 seats (with 19.7% of the vote), well ahead of the second-placed LSDP; Kubilius was nominated as Prime Minister in late November and took office in December. As in his first term, he was immediately faced with a struggling economy, requiring harsh austerity measures, which provoked mass demonstrations on the streets of Vilnius in early 2009.

Andrius Kubilius is married to Rasa, a violinist with the National Symphony Orchestra, and they have two sons.

Address: Office of the Prime Minister, Gedimino pr. 11, 01103 Vilnius.

Telephone: (5) 2663711.

Fax: (5) 2663895.

E-mail: kanceliarija@lrvk.lt

Internet: www.lrvk.lt

Kuvendi i Kosovës *see* **Assembly of Kosova**.

Kuvendi Popullor *see* **People's Assembly (Albania)**.

Kuzmanović, Rajko

President of the **Serb Republic** (RS) in **Bosnia and Herzegovina**.

Rajko Kuzmanović was born on 1 December 1931 in Čelinac. He attended university in **Zagreb, Croatia**, graduating first in law and then from the Faculty of Philosophy. He worked at the University of Banja Luka, rising to professor, head of constitutional science and Chancellor of the University (1988–92). He was also involved in local government and education management. He was a member of the Bosnian Assembly in the early 1960s and has frequently given expert advice on constitutional issues. In 1994 he became a judge and from 1998 to 2002 he was President of the Constitutional Court of the RS. Following the unexpected death of RS President Milan Jelić in September 2007, Kuzmanović stood as candidate of the **Alliance of Independent Social Democrats** (SNSD) and was elected on 9 December with 42% of the vote. He was sworn in on 28 December 2007.

Address: Office of the President, Bana Milosavljevića 4, 78000 Banja Luka.
Telephone: (51) 248100.
Fax: (51) 248161.
E-mail: info@predsjednikrs.net
Internet: www.predsjednikrs.net

KZB *see* **Coalition for Bulgaria**.

L

Labour Party
Darbo Partija (DP)

A centrist political party in **Lithuania**, member of the **Alliance of Democrats** and founded by Russian-born businessman Viktor Uspaskich in 2003. It performed well in the May 2004 European elections, winning five of Lithuania's 13 mandates, and it went on to win the October **Parliament** election, with 39 seats (28.4% of the vote).

The existing parties feared that if Uspaskich took power he might allow the Russian Federation to reassert its influence over Lithuania, so they attempted to form a coalition without the DP. However, no agreement could be reached, and the new Government that eventually took office in December did include the DP, though it was still led by incumbent Prime Minister Algirdas Brazauskas of the **Lithuanian Social Democratic Party** (LSDP). Uspaskich became Minister of the Economy, but he resigned the following June after the Chief Commission on Ethics declared he had a conflict of interests between his government position and his business empire. Mounting allegations of corruption were levelled against him and the DP, and internal divisions in the party deepened. In May 2006 seven deputies defected to the Civil Democracy Party, then Uspaskich stepped down from the party leadership, and at the end of the month the party withdrew from the Government, forcing the resignation of Prime Minister Brazauskas. Uspaskich, under investigation for financial irregularities, went to Russia for his brother's funeral and did not return. Now in opposition, the DP elected Kęstutis Dauksys as its new Chairman in August 2006.

Uspaskich eventually returned to Lithuania in September 2007 and was immediately placed under house arrest. Despite this, he was re-elected as DP Chairman in November. At the October 2008 Parliament election, the Coalition Labour Party + Youth finished in sixth place with 10 seats (with a 9% share of the vote). It remained in opposition to the new centre-right Government.

Leadership: Viktor Uspaskich (Chair.).
Address: Ankštoji 3, 01109 Vilnius.
Telephone: (5) 2107152.
Fax: (5) 2107153.
E-mail: info@darbopartija.lt
Website: www.darbopartija.lt

LAOS *see* **Popular Orthodox Rally**.

Latvia
Latvijas Republika

An independent **Baltic State** located in north-eastern Europe bounded to the north by Estonia, to the south by Lithuania and Belarus, to the east by the Russian Federation and to the west by the Baltic Sea. Administratively, the country is divided into 26 counties (rajoni) and seven municipalities.

Area: 64,589 sq km; *capital*: **Rīga**; *population*: 2.3m. (2009 estimate), comprising **Latvians** 59%, **Russians** 28.3%, Belarusians 3.7%, Ukrainians 2.5%, **Poles** 2.4%, **Lithuanians** 1.4%, others 2.7%; *official language*: Latvian (Lettish); *religion*: Lutheran, **Roman Catholic**, **Russian Orthodox**.

Legislative authority is vested in a unicameral **Parliament** (Saeima), which has 100 deputies directly elected for a four-year term by a system of proportional representation, subject to a threshold of 5% for each party. The Head of State is the President, who is elected for a four-year term (once renewable) by the Parliament. Executive authority is vested in the Prime Minister, who is responsible to Parliament. The Cabinet of Ministers is appointed by the Prime Minister.

History: Settled by the Balts in ancient times, Latvia was conquered by the **German** Teutonic Knights during the 13th century and became part of the state of **Livonia** for the next 200 years. During the religious wars of the 16th century Livonia was partitioned and Latvia came successively under Polish and Lithuanian, and then Swedish, rule. The 1721 Treaty of Nystad between Russia and Sweden, concluding the Great Northern War, brought much of Livonia, with **Estonia**, under Russian rule. Latvia was fully integrated by the late 18th century and remained part of the Russian Empire until the 1917 revolution. By this time nationalist groups had developed into a political force and Latvia declared its independence in 1918, although this was only fully achieved once Bolshevik forces had been expelled and the 1920 **Rīga Treaty** had been signed with the **Soviet Union**. A coup in 1934 replaced the democratic Government with a right-wing authoritarian regime.

In 1940, after the start of the Second World War, Soviet forces occupied Latvia, along with neighbouring Estonia and **Lithuania**, and all three countries were incorporated into the Soviet Union as Soviet Socialist Republics. This Soviet expansion was carried out with prior German agreement under the 1939 **Nazi-Soviet Pact**, but when Germany turned against the Soviet Union in 1941 German forces invaded, occupying Latvia from 1941 until 1944. The Soviet Union then regained control and resumed the process of 'Sovietization'. Neither the USA, the United Kingdom nor other Western powers ever formally recognized the Soviet absorption of Latvia and the other two Baltic republics.

In the late 1980s, influenced by the **Solidarity** movement in **Poland** and the *glasnost* (openness) initiative in the Soviet Union, the growing opposition movements in Latvia united in a political force—the Latvian Popular Front (LPF)—to campaign for sovereignty and democracy. At the same time, close links were established with popular fronts in Estonia and Lithuania. Official status was given to the Latvian language, and the 1989 elections to the Latvian Supreme Soviet returned the LPF with a majority of seats, so bringing to an end the communist monopoly of power.

The initial declaration of Latvian independence in May 1990 (subject to a transitional period for negotiation) caused violent clashes between independence supporters and communists. President Gorbachev of the Soviet Union annulled the declaration and in early 1991 Soviet forces briefly went into Rīga. Latvia boycotted an all-Union referendum on the future of the Soviet Union and instead held a referendum in March 1991 on outright Latvian independence, which received a 73% vote in favour. Following the failure of the attempted August coup against Gorbachev, Latvia declared itself an independent republic, gaining recognition from the Soviet Government the following month.

Latvia has had unstable, often minority, ruling coalitions since leaving the Soviet Union, averaging less than two years in office. In the first post-independence legislative and presidential elections, held in 1993, the LPF suffered a huge loss of popular support and was replaced as the governing party by a centre-right coalition led by Valdis Birkavs, of the newly-formed Latvian Way (LC), and the Latvian Farmers' Union (LZS). Guntis Ulmanis, leader of the LZS, was elected as the first President. Maris Gailis (the Deputy Prime Minister) replaced Birkavs in a new coalition formed following the withdrawal of LZS support in 1994.

After the 1995 general election had produced a hung Parliament, President Ulmanis opposed the creation of a coalition government by two of the largest parties—the Democratic Party Saimnieks (the Master) and the radical right-wing Popular Movement for Latvia–Zigerists (TKL–ZP). The result was that a broad centre-right coalition was formed instead, headed by a non-party Prime Minister, Andris Škele. Ulmanis was re-elected to the presidency in 1996. When Škele resigned as Prime Minister in July 1997 (because of opposition to his authoritarian style and conflicts of interest over ministerial appointments), Guntars Krasts of the right-wing For Fatherland and Freedom Union/Latvian National Independence Movement (TB/LNNK) formed a new coalition administration in August.

In the October 1998 legislative elections, the newly-established **People's Party** (TP) led by former Prime Minister Škele was returned as the largest single party with 24 seats and 21.2% of the vote, but it was Vilis Krištopans, of the second-placed LC (with 21 seats and 18.1% of the vote), who in November formed a minority coalition with the TB/LNNK and the New Party (JP). In February 1999 a co-operation agreement with the Latvian Social Democratic Union (LSDA) gave the Government qualified external support. The LSDA subsequently became the Latvian Social Democratic Workers' Party (LSDSP).

At the same time as the legislative polling in October 1998, a referendum was held on amending Latvia's controversial citizenship laws. As introduced in 1991, these required residents who were not citizens of the pre-1940 republic (or their descendants) to apply for naturalization, and made this subject to qualifications which included 16 years' residence and knowledge of the Latvian language. In the closely contested referendum, just over 50% of voters approved the amendments, which ended naturalization quotas, granted citizenship to those children born in Latvia after independence if their parents requested it, and provided for simpler language tests for older residents. The amendments would therefore make it easier for (mainly Russian) non-citizens currently resident in Latvia to obtain Latvian citizenship, and for that reason were welcomed by the **Organization for Security and Co-operation in Europe** (OSCE) and the **European Union** (EU). In a further adaptation to European norms, the Parliament in April 1999 overcame its earlier reluctance to abolish the death penalty in Latvia.

In presidential elections in the Parliament in June 1999 the politically neutral Vaira Vike-Freiberga was elected Latvia's first female President after seven rounds of voting. (She was re-elected unopposed in 2003 for a second four-year term.)

Plagued by its lack of a stable parliamentary majority, the Krištopans Government collapsed in July 1999. Škele of the TP then formed a majority centre-right coalition including the LC and the TB/LNNK, but this Government in turn collapsed after just nine months, damaged by political infighting and the implication of Škele and other senior officials in a paedophilia scandal (from which they were later cleared). The outcome in May 2000 was the formation of a four-party coalition headed by Andris Berzinš of the LC and including the TP, the TB/LNNK and the JP (renamed as the New Christian Party (JKP) in 2001).

In the October 2002 legislative elections six parties passed the 5% threshold required for seats in the Parliament, but these did not include the ruling LC. The right-wing **New Era** (JL) party (founded by former Bank of Latvia Governor Einars Repše in late 2001) won 26 seats and 23.9% of the vote, ahead of the leftist, pro-Russian For Human Rights in a United Latvia (PCTVL) alliance with 25 seats and the TP with 20 seats.

Repše formed a centre-right coalition of his JL with the **Union of Greens and Farmers** (ZZS), the Latvian First Party (LPP—founded in May 2002) and the TB/LNNK. Their alliance did not prove an easy one; within a year Repše's coalition partners were jointly accusing him of authoritarianism. When the LPP backed calls for an inquiry into Repše's property dealings he dismissed the LPP Deputy Prime Minister in January 2004, whereupon the LPP withdrew from the ruling coalition, forcing Repše to resign.

On 20 February 2004 Indulis Emsis was nominated as Latvia's (and the world's) first Green Prime Minister, and on 9 March he formed a centre-right coalition between the ZZS, the LPP and the TP, which was also supported in the Parliament by the National Harmony Party (TSP—which had contested the 2002 elections as part of the PCTVL alliance). This coalition oversaw NATO and EU accession, but only lasted seven and a half months, collapsing in late October when the Parliament rejected Emsis's budget proposals.

On 2 December 2004 Aigars Kalvītis of the TP became Prime Minister at the head of a majority centre-right coalition of his TP, the JL, the ZZS and the LPP. Over the next 17 months various ministers were plagued by corruption allegations, and in April 2006 the JL withdrew after Kalvītis refused to eject the LPP, leaving once again a minority coalition of the TP, ZZS and LPP.

Latest elections: In the October 2006 legislative elections the TP regained pole position in the Parliament with 23 seats and 19.6% of the vote. The ZZS and JL tied for second place with 18 seats (and 16.7% and 16.4% of the vote respectively), just ahead of the **Harmony Centre** (SC) with 17 seats and 14.4% of the vote (the SC's constituent parties, including the TSP, were formerly part of the previous PCTVL grouping). An alliance of the LPP and LC won 10 seats (8.6% of the vote), the TB/LNNK won eight seats (6.9%) and the PCTVL won six seats (6%).

Recent developments: Kalvītis's incumbent coalition, now commanding 51 seats in the 100-member Parliament, was the first since independence in 1991 to retain power at an election. His new Government, which took office in November 2006, was strengthened by the addition of the TB/LNNK. The four parties backed the candidacy of Valdis **Zatlers**, a non-political doctor, in the May 2007 presidential election; he was inaugurated on 8 July. By the end of the year Kalvītis was under fire for alleged abuse of power—in particular his dismissal of Latvia's anti-corruption chief. He resigned in December and was replaced by LPP/LC co-leader Ivars Godmanis, who had previously held the post of Prime Minister from 1990 to 1993 overseeing Latvia's transition to independence.

Economic crisis bit deeply in 2008–09 (*see* **Latvia, economy**), with unemployment and inflation rising and standards of living falling; tax rises prompted riots on the streets of Rīga in January 2009. Under pressure from the TP and ZZS, Godmanis resigned on 20 February. Valdis **Dombrovskis** of JL was approved as the new Prime Minister on 12 March, heading a Government of the TP, ZZS, JL, TB/LNNK and Civic Union (formed in 2008 from splinter groups from the JL and TB/LNNK).

International relations and defence: Upon its recognition as an independent state, Latvia was admitted to the United Nations in 1991 and became a member of the OSCE; it also joined the **World Trade Organization** (in 1999). Pursuing closer links with Western institutions, Latvia was admitted to the **Council of Europe** in 1993. In December 1999 it was accorded official candidate status by the **European Union** (EU), formal negotiations beginning in February 2000. An offer of membership was made in December 2002, in a major wave of expansion. It was supported by referendum in September 2003, and Latvia acceded on 1 May 2004. In December 2007 Latvia also joined the EU's Schengen Agreement, allowing free movement of citizens within the Schengen zone's borders. It is unlikely to join the eurozone before 2012 (*see* **Latvia, economy**).

A member of the **Partnership for Peace** programme since 1994, Latvia became a full member of the **North Atlantic Treaty Organization** (NATO) in March 2004, despite opposition from the Russian Federation, as part of a NATO expansion including six other new member countries. The participation of the Baltic States in both the EU and NATO meant that both these organizations now extended to Russia's main eastern border.

A treaty delimiting the Latvian–Russian border (based on the 1920 Treaty of Rīga—*see* **Abrene question**) was formulated in 1997, but was not signed until 2007, amid continuing unhappiness in Russia over the effect of Latvian citizenship laws on Latvia's ethnic Russian minority.

Latvia maintains close co-operation with its Baltic and Nordic neighbours, and is a member of the **Council of Baltic Sea States**. In January 1998 the Presidents of Latvia, Estonia and Lithuania and the USA signed a **US-Baltic Partnership** charter.

Latvia's defence budget for 2008 amounted to some US $542m., equivalent to about 1.6% of GDP. The size of the armed forces in 2010 was some 6,000 personnel, while reservists numbered an estimated 11,000. Conscription ended in 2007.

Latvia, economy

Latvia has made the transition over the last two decades from a state-controlled economy to a free-market system, assisted by links with the countries of the Nordic region. However, after recording the highest economic growth in the **European Union** (EU) for the years immediately following its accession in 2004, it was one of the countries worst hit by the global economic crisis, with a GDP contraction estimated at 18% in 2009.

GNP: US $26,883m. (2008); *GNP per capita*: $11,860 (2008); *GDP at PPP*: $38,750m. (2008); *GDP per capita at PPP*: $17,100 (2008); *real GDP growth*: −18.0% (2009 estimate); *exports*: $9,210m. (2008); *imports*: $15,645m. (2008); *currency*: lats (plural: lats; US $1 = L0.502 in mid-2009); *unemployment*: 22.9% (end 2009); *government deficit as a percentage of GDP*: 6.8% (2009); *inflation*: 3.1% (2009).

In 2008 industry accounted for 23% of GDP, agriculture for 3% and services for 74%. Around 28% of the workforce is engaged in industry, 10% in agriculture and 62% in services.

Some 27% of the land is arable, 13% permanent pasture and 46% forests and woodland. The main crops are grain, sugar beet and vegetables. Dairy farming and pig breeding are a more important element of agriculture than arable farming. Latvia has a developed fishing fleet, and forest resources are exploited.

Mineral resources include small reserves of amber, peat, limestone, gypsum and dolomite. Some petroleum reserves have, however, been identified and exploration has begun with foreign partners. The main industries are food products, textiles and clothing, wood products and transport equipment. Latvia is heavily dependent on imports to meet its energy requirements, notably electrical energy from **Estonia** and **Lithuania** and petroleum products from the Russian Federation and Lithuania.

Latvia's main exports are timber and timber products, metals and metalwork, and machinery and electrical equipment. Principal imports are machinery and electrical equipment, vehicles and transport equipment, and mineral products. The principal purchasers of Latvian exports in 2008 were Lithuania (17%), Estonia (14%) and the Russian Federation (10%). The main suppliers of Latvia's imports in 2008 were Lithuania (17%), Germany (13%) and the Russian Federation (11%).

After regaining independence in 1991, Latvia experienced considerable difficulties in realigning its trading patterns with the other former Soviet republics, being notably dependent in respect of fuels and other raw materials. Agricultural output dropped sharply, many manufacturing sectors suffered extreme difficulties in securing supplies, manufacturing output fell drastically and inflation rose to around 1,000% in 1992. However, as economic reform measures introduced in 1992 began to take effect, buttressed by the introduction of the lats as the currency in 1993, gradual improvements were experienced from 1994.

Land reform and the process of land privatization, which had already begun before independence, was accelerated in 1992 with the division of collectivized land into individual plots, although some of the resultant private farms were uneconomically small. The privatization of state-owned enterprises was launched in 1994, but encountered strong political and trade union opposition especially over the sell-off of the larger entities.

Real GDP growth of 3.3% in 1996 was followed by rapid expansion of 8.6% in 1997, during which the inflation rate was brought down to single figures and unemployment to 7% of the labour force. By 1997 almost all price controls had been removed, along with most subsidies, and a new competition law had been enacted.

The Russian financial crisis of mid-1998 caused serious repercussions, aggravated by disputes over the rights of ethnic **Russians** in Latvia. GDP growth fell back to under 4% in 1998 and to only 0.1% in 1999, while unemployment rose to nearly 10% by the end of 1999. Strong recovery began in 2000, with real GDP growth of 6.6% and a reduction in unemployment to under 8%. The Government reported in

December 2000 that tax collection and social insurance payment rates had risen to over 70% of sums due and that the size of the 'black' economy was declining, although its share of economic activity remained worrying high at over 40%. By 2001 the privatization of the small and medium-sized state-owned businesses had been largely completed. However, moves to privatize certain large shipping, energy and other enterprises continued to be dogged by problems of domestic opposition and failure to find suitable buyers.

Latvia became a full member of the **World Trade Organization** in February 1999 and formal negotiations on EU membership opened in February 2000. The key determinant of domestic economic policy therefore became the perceived need to adapt Latvian laws and procedures to EU requirements and to ensure that Latvian economic indicators were brought within the EU's Maastricht criteria. Meanwhile, trade was reorientated eastwards, to capitalize on rapid growth in the Russian economy. Strong GDP growth reduced unemployment significantly, but also led to price and wage inflation and a large current-account deficit.

Following accession to the EU in May 2004, the lats was pegged to the euro, and in May 2005 Latvia joined the Exchange Rate Mechanism II. It initially planned to join the **eurozone** on 1 January 2008, but adoption has been repeatedly pushed back, and is now unlikely before 2014 at the earliest.

Growth steadily increased from 6.5% in 2002 to 12% in 2006 (the highest rate in the EU), with tourism, financial services and construction the key sectors of expansion. Living standards were among the highest of ex-Soviet states. However, the Government failed to act on advice from the **International Monetary Fund** (IMF) to address its growing budget deficit and cut spending, and in 2007 the economy began to slow. The following year the international financial crisis had an immediate negative impact, leading to a GDP contraction of 4.6%, while inflation soared to 15%. In November the Government had to bail out the country's largest privately-owned financial institution, Parex Banka. In December, after the legislature had adopted extensive austerity measures, the IMF approved an economic stabilization programme for Latvia, which was to be funded by a loan amounting to US $7,500m.

Public discontent with the Government's perceived economic mismanagement precipitated substantial protests in January 2009, while disputes within the governing coalition resulted in a new administration in March. In April the IMF suspended disbursements to Latvia until the Government demonstrated progress in implementing the stipulated austerity measures, emphasizing the necessity of achieving sustained reductions in the budget deficit in order to meet the criteria for Latvia's long-term objective of adopting the euro. Unemployment more than doubled that year, while the economy contracted by an estimated 18% of GDP, with a further contraction of at least 4% predicted for 2010.

Latvian Chamber of Commerce and Industry
Latvijas Tirdzniecības un Rūpniecības Kamera (LTRK)

The principal organization in **Latvia** for promoting business contacts, both internally and externally, in the post-communist era. Originally founded in 1934, and re-established in 1990.

President: Andris Larmanis.
Address: K. Valdemāra iela 35, Rīga.
Telephone: 67225595.
Fax: 67820092.
E-mail: info@chamber.lv
Internet: www.chamber.lv

Latvian Farmers' Union
Latvijas Zemnieku savienība (LZS)

A centre agrarian political party in **Latvia**, part of the **Union of Greens and Farmers** (ZZS) alliance, which is a member of the ruling coalition. Founded in 1917 the LZS was a key party until it was banned after the 1934 coup. Refounded in 1990, it has been part of the ZZS alliance since 2002.

Leadership: Augusts Brigmanis (Chair.).
Address: Republikas laukumā 2, Rīga 1010.
Telephone: 67323628.
Fax: 67027467.
E-mail: lzs@latnet.lv
Internet: www.lzs.lv

Latvian Green Party
Latvijas Zaļā partija (LZP)

A green political party in **Latvia**, part of the **Union of Greens and Farmers** (ZZS) alliance, which is a member of the ruling coalition. Founded in 1990, it has been part of the ZZS alliance since 2002.

Leadership: Viesturs Silenieks and Raimonds Vējonis (Co-Chairs).
Address: Kalnciema ielā 30, Rīga 1046.
Telephone and fax: 67614272.
E-mail: birojs@zp.lv
Internet: www.zp.lv

Latvian Investment and Development Agency
Latvijas Investīciju un Attības Ağentūra (LIAA)

Promotes foreign investment and exports in **Latvia**. Founded in 1993.
Director General: Andris Ozols.
Address: Pērses iela 2, Rīga 1442.
Telephone: 67039400.
Fax: 67039401.
E-mail: invest@liaa.gov.lv
Internet: www.liaa.gov.lv

Latvian News Agency *see* **LETA**.

Latvian Privatization Agency
Latvijas Privatizācijas Agentūra (LPA)

The agency in **Latvia** established in April 1994, which was charged with the privatization of all state assets by the Andris Škele Government in 1996. Although more than 300 entities were privatized by 1997, the process was inhibited by political differences which caused several Economy Ministers to resign. In 2004 it became a state joint-stock company.
Director General: Arturs Grants.
Address: K. Valdemāra iela 31, Rīga 1887.
Telephone: 67021358.
Fax: 67830363.
E-mail: lpa@mail.bkc.lv
Internet: www.lpa.bkc.lv

Latvians

An Indo-European people. The name 'Latviji' is thought to have derived from a river 'Latve' and was modified to 'Latvis' by **Finno-Ugric** settlers. German rulers changed the name to Lette and renamed the state **Livonia**. Closely related to Lithuanian, the Latvian language belongs to the Baltic group, a highly inflective language written in the Latin script. It replaced Russian as the official language in **Latvia** in 1988. The earliest written forms are from 16th-century catechisms. The proportion of ethnic Latvians fell significantly following the policy of 'Sovietization' and a substantial number moved abroad, notably to the USA. Western Latvia retains the cultural and religious ties of German and Scandinavian rule, while eastern Latvia (Latgale) retains more Polish and Russian influences.

Law and Justice
Prawo i Sprawiedliwość (PiS)

A conservative anti-crime political party in **Poland**. Its candidate Lech **Kaczyński** held the presidency from 2005 until his death in April 2010, but since 2007 the PiS has been in opposition to the centre-right coalition Government.

The PiS was originally a faction within the Solidarity Electoral Action (AWS) party led by Lech Kaczyński. His hugely popular anti-crime drive while Minister of Justice in 2000–01 made him the second-most popular politician in Poland after President Aleksander Kwaśniewski. Following his dismissal in July 2001 he immediately set about transforming the PiS group into a fully-fledged political party with the help of his twin brother Jarosław Kaczyński, the former leader of the right-wing minority Centre Alliance.

The PiS was among a trio of rightist parties to achieve an unexpected degree of success in the September 2001 elections, when it won 9.5% of the vote and 44 seats in the Sejm (lower house of the **National Assembly**). In 2002 Lech Kaczyński was elected Mayor of Warsaw and the following year Jarosław took over as Chairman of the party.

At the 2005 election the PiS won 27% of the vote, 155 seats in the Sejm and 49 in the Senat, as the centre-right parties benefited from public discontent with the left-wing **Democratic Left Alliance** (SLD). However, the PiS and second-placed Civic Platform (PO) failed to reach a coalition agreement, despite the apparently conciliatory PiS move of nominating Kazimierz Marcinkiewicz as Prime Minister rather than its own leader Jarosław Kaczyński. Their negotiations were overshadowed by a run-off between their respective candidates in the presidential election, which was eventually won by Lech Kaczyński with 55% of the vote.

On 31 October 2005 Marcinkiewicz was sworn in to head a minority Government of the PiS and independents. In spring 2006 the agrarian Self-Defence of the Republic of Poland (SRP) and nationalist League of Polish Families (LPR) joined this Government, giving it a parliamentary majority. In July Marcinkiewicz resigned after a rift with the Kaczyńskis, and Jarosław Kaczyński took over the premiership, Poland thus becoming the first country ever to be ruled by twins.

Within two months the PiS-led coalition was in trouble, however, with the dismissal of SRP leader Andrzej Lepper from the post of Deputy Prime Minister, leading to the withdrawal of all SRP ministers. Surprisingly in October the same coalition was reformed.

In July 2007 Lepper was dismissed again, but this time the SRP did not immediately quit the Government. After four weeks of uncertainty, President Kaczyński fired the SRP members in a move to precipitate the dissolution of the Assembly and the calling of early elections.

At the October 2007 elections the PiS increased its position in the Sejm (32% of the vote and 166 seats) but was overtaken by the PO (with 42% of the vote and 209 seats). In December Jarosław Kaczyński won a vote of confidence in his leadership, but several members of the party have defected.

Lech Kaczyński was intending to run for re-election in autumn 2010, but he was killed in a plane crash on 10 April of that year. Instead the PiS put forward his brother Jarosław, for the early election scheduled for 20 June.

Leadership: Jarosław Kaczyński (Chair.).
Address: ul. Nowogrodzka 84–86, 02-018 Warsaw.
Telephone: (22) 6215035.
Fax: (22) 6216767.
E-mail: biuro@pis.org.pl
Internet: www.pis.org.pl

LCY *see* **League of Communists of Yugoslavia**.

LDK *see* **Democratic League of Kosovo**.

LDS *see* **Liberal Democracy of Slovenia**.

League of Communists of Yugoslavia (LCY)
Savez Komunista Jugoslavije (SKJ)

The single ruling party of the **Socialist Federal Republic of Yugoslavia** (SFRY) until 1990. Founded in 1919 as the Communist Party of Yugoslavia (KPJ), the party supported the communist partisan resistance during the Second World War and came to power in 1945. The KPJ stuck closely to the format of the **Communist Party of the Soviet Union** (KPSS) until 1952, when at the KPJ's sixth party congress it broke its ties to the KPSS and renamed itself the SKJ. The various republican branches of the party were named in turn as the Serbian League of Communists and so on.

Under the leadership of **Tito**, the SKJ was the centre of political power in the SFRY and membership was seen as the main route to influence and power. However, from 1952 to Tito's death in 1980 the party underwent moves to reduce its grip on the state, particularly on the economy. Despite attempts by Tito to reassert its position every now and then, by the 1980s its membership and influence had decreased considerably. Under the reformist 1974 Constitution other political parties were tolerated as appendages of the SKJ, leading to the erosion of its central power.

The defining moment in the party's demise came at the 14th party congress, in 1990. The single-party state was abandoned and multi-party elections were agreed in principle. However, attempts to formalize the process of decentralization and reverse the growing influence of the Serbian League were floated and blocked, prompting the

Slovenian delegation to stage a walk out from the conference which effectively engendered the collapse of the SFRY. The republican divisions of the SKJ reorganized themselves as new parties, ranging from left-of-centre to nationalist.

Lefkoşa *see* **Nicosia**.

Left and Democrats
Prawo i Sprawiedliwość (LiD)

A centre-left political alliance in **Poland** formed in September 2006 between the left-wing **Democratic Left Alliance** (SLD), its splinter **Polish Social Democracy** (SDPL), the small left-wing Labour Union (UP) and the centrist **Democratic Party** (PD). In the September 2007 election the LiD alliance finished in third place, well behind the two main centre-right parties, with 13% of the vote and 53 seats in the Sejm (lower house of the **National Assembly**). It won no seats in the Senat (upper house). Its campaign had been led by former President Aleksander **Kwaśniewski** of the SLD. Of the 53 seats gained, 37 were won by the SLD, 10 by the SDPL, one by the PD, none by the UP and five went to non-party candidates (three of whom were affiliated with the SLD and two with the PD).

The uneasy position of the centrist PD within the alliance, and the discomfort of the juxtaposition of the SLD and its splinter SDPL, caused the alliance to collapse in March–April 2008. The 40 SLD-affiliated Sejm members and two of the SDPL Sejm members remained in alliance as The Left.

LETA
(Latvian News Agency)

The main news agency in **Latvia** which was founded as the state service in 1919 by the provisional Latvian Government under the name Latopress. It was transformed into the Latvian Telegraph Agency (LETA) in 1920. Under **Soviet** rule it was 'subordinated' to the Telegraph Agency of the Soviet Union (TASS—later ITAR-TASS), and renamed Latinform in 1971. On independence LETA was reformed as the state news agency. It was privatized in 1997 but remains the country's 'national' news agency.

Chair.: Mārtiņš Barkāns.
Address: Palasta iela 10, Rīga 1502.
Telephone: 67222509.
Fax: 67223850.
E-mail: leta.marketing@leta.lv
Internet: www.leta.lv

LIAA *see* **Latvian Investment Development Agency**.

Liberal and Centre Union
Liberalų ir Centro Sąjunga (LiCS)

A centrist political party in **Lithuania**, affiliated to the **Liberal International**, and currently part of the ruling coalition. It was formed in May 2003 by the merger of the Lithuanian Liberal Union (LLS), the Lithuanian Centre Union (LCS) and the Modern Christian-Democratic Union (MKDS).

The LLS was founded in November 1990 by pro-independence activists of Vilnius University and elsewhere. It failed to gain representation in the 1992 elections and won only one seat in 1996, but it polled strongly in the March 1997 local elections. In December 1999 it was greatly strengthened by the adhesion of a breakaway faction of the Homeland Union–Lithuanian Conservatives (TS–LK, *see* **Homeland Union–Lithuanian Christian Democrats**) led by former Prime Minister Rolandas Paksas, who became LLS Chairman.

In the October 2000 **Parliament** elections the LLS achieved a major advance, to 34 seats on a 17.3% vote share. Paksas was therefore able to form a centrist majority coalition. However, divisions between the parties over the Government's privatization programme led to its collapse in June 2001. Unable to form a new coalition, the LLS went into opposition, and in September Paksas was forced to resign as LLS Chairman. At the October party congress, Eugenijus Gentvilas was elected as the new Chairman with Paksas as Deputy Chairman. In December Paksas and 10 other deputies left the LLS parliamentary faction, and were duly expelled from the party the following month. Gentvilas stood in the first round of the December 2002 presidential election, finishing a disappointing eighth with 3.1% of the vote (the run-off was in fact won by Paksas, beating the incumbent Valdas Adamkus, though just over a year after taking office Paksas was impeached).

The LCS, founded in 1992, won two seats in that year's parliamentary elections and advanced strongly to 13 seats in 1996, becoming a junior partner in a centre-right coalition headed by the TS–LK. It paid the penalty for the Government's unpopularity in the October 2000 elections, falling back to two seats and 2.9% of the vote, but nevertheless became part of the post-election centre-right coalition Government headed by the LLS. Divisions over the pace of the privatization programme led to this Government's collapse in June 2001, however, and the LCS was left out of a new centre-left coalition headed by the **Lithuanian Social Democratic Party** (LSDP).

The MKDS formed from a splinter of the Lithuanian Christian Democratic Party (LKDP) in April 2000. It won one seat in the October 2000 Parliament election.

The three parties merged as the LiCS in May 2003. Artūras Zuokas, recently elected as Mayor of Vilnius, was chosen as LiCS Chairman. One faction of the LiCS that did not support the merger broke away and founded the National Centre Party.

At the October 2004 election the LiCS finished in fourth place with 18 seats (9.1% of the vote). Initially the LiCS remained in opposition, but following the collapse of the LSDP-led Government on the withdrawal of the **Labour Party** in May 2005, a new centre-left coalition was negotiated by July, still led by the LSDP but this time including the LiCS. Meanwhile, Zuokas was under investigation for alleged corruption; his refusal to resign led to a group of deputies leaving the party in early 2006 and forming the **Liberal Movement of the Republic of Lithuania** (LRLS).

This split in the party showed its effect at the October 2008 election, when the LiCS won just eight seats (with 5.3% of the vote). Nevertheless, the LiCS negotiated to remain in government this time in a centre-right coalition led by the TS–LKD. In June 2009 Gintautas Babravičius was elected as the new party Chairman in succession to Zuokas.

Leadership: Gintautas Babravičius (Chair.).
Address: Vilniaus g. 22/1, 01119 Vilnius 2001.
Telephone: (5) 2313264.
Fax: (5) 2619363.
E-mail: info@lics.lt
Internet: www.lics.lt

Liberal Democracy of Slovenia
Liberalna Demokracija Slovenije (LDS)

A centre-left party which dominated political life in **Slovenia** in the 1990s, but then declined in influence and was weakened by factional defections; it is now a junior partner in the ruling coalition. It is a secular party affiliated to the **Liberal International**.

The present LDS was founded in 1994 as a merger of the then ruling Liberal Democratic Party, itself derived from the communist-era Federation of Socialist Youth of Slovenia (ZSMS), and three small formations, including the Slovenian Greens. The Liberal Democrats had come to power in April 1992 at the head of a centre-left coalition under Janez **Drnovšek** (a former member of the collective Presidency of the **Socialist Federal Republic of Yugoslavia**) and had become the largest party in the first post-independence elections in December 1992, winning 22 seats on a 21.4% vote share. A third of the deputies in the **National Assembly** joined the new LDS, which advocated the decentralization of power and rapid transition to a market economy.

Despite losing two of its coalition partners in the interim, the LDS retained power until the November 1996 Assembly elections, in which it remained the largest single party but with only 25 seats on a 27% vote share. The following month Drnovšek narrowly secured re-election as Prime Minister on the basis of a disparate coalition which included the left-wing United List of Social Democrats (ZLSD), the far-right

Slovenian National Party (SNS) and the **Democratic Party of Slovenian Pensioners** (DeSUS). In February 1997, however, he succeeded in forming a more stable coalition which included the **Slovenian People's Party** (SLS) and the DeSUS.

In presidential elections in November 1997 the LDS candidate, Bogomir Kovač, came a distant seventh with only 2.7% of the vote. Thereafter, increasing strains in the coalition culminated in the withdrawal of the SLS in April 2000 and Drnovšek's resignation after he had lost a confidence vote, whereupon an SLS-led coalition took office in June.

Drnovšek obtained revenge in parliamentary elections in October 2000, when the LDS advanced to 34 of the 90 seats on a vote share of 36.3%. He proceeded to form a broad-based centre-left coalition which included what had become the SLS+SKD, the ZLSD and the DeSUS.

Drnovšek stood as the LDS candidate in the 2002 presidential election. He led the first round on 10 November with 44.4% and went on to secure 56.5% in the run-off. LDS Minister of Finance Anton Rop was nominated to replace Drnovšek as Prime Minister; his new Government, which maintained the same coalition, was approved on 19 December and Drnovšek was inaugurated as President three days later. Rop took over as LDS President in February 2003.

At the October 2004 Assembly elections the LDS dropped to 23 seats (with 22.8% of the vote), and went into opposition to a coalition led by the **Slovenian Democratic Party** (SDS). In 2005 Jelko Kacin replaced Rop as LDS President, but he was unable to unite the divided party.

In January 2007 Drnovšek resigned from the party, and in March a group, including Rop, defected to the **Social Democrats** (SD, the renamed ZLSD). Another faction broke off in October to form **For Real—New Politics** (Zares). Meanwhile, Katarina Kresal had been elected LDS President in June, tasked with reviving the party, which by the end of the year controlled only 11 Assembly seats.

With Drnovšek not seeking re-election in November 2007 due to ill health, the LDS backed independent candidate Mitja Gaspari, who finished a close third in the first round but was therefore eliminated. Drnovšek died in February 2008.

At the September 2008 Assembly elections the LDS only managed to hold five seats (with 5.2% of the vote). Nevertheless, it managed to return to government as a junior partner in an SD-led coalition.

Leadership: Katarina Kresal (Chair.).
Address: Slovenska cesta 29, 1000 Ljubljana.
Telephone: (1) 2000310.
Fax: (1) 2000311.
E-mail: lds@lds.si
Internet: www.lds.si

Liberal International

The world union of 67 liberal parties (with a further 27 observer parties) in 66 countries or territories, founded in 1947. These include parties from **Bosnia and Herzegovina** (observer only), **Bulgaria, Croatia, Estonia, Hungary, Kosovo, Latvia, Lithuania, Macedonia, Romania, Serbia** and **Slovenia**.

President: Hans van Baalen.
Address: 1 Whitehall Place, London, SW1A 2HD, United Kingdom.
Telephone: (20) 78395905.
Fax: (20) 79252685.
E-mail: all@liberal-international.org
Internet: www.liberal-international.org

Liberal Movement of the Republic of Lithuania
Lietuvos Respublikos Liberalų Sąjūdis (LRLS)

A centre-right political party in **Lithuania**, currently part of the ruling coalition. The LRLS was founded in early 2006 by a group of defectors from the **Liberal and Centre Union** (LiCS). The initial party leader Petras Auštrevičius was succeeded in February 2008 by his former deputy Eligijus Masiulis. The party won 11 seats (with 5.7% of the vote) at the October 2008 **Parliament** election, and subsequently joined the new centre-right Government.

Leadership: Eligijus Masiulis (Chair.).
Address: Sėlių g. 48, 08125 Vilnius.
Telephone and fax: (5) 2496959.
E-mail: info@liberalai.lt
Website: www.liberalai.lt

LiCS *see* **Liberal and Centre Union**.

LiD *see* **Left and Democrats**.

Lithuania
Lietuvos Respublika

An independent **Baltic State** in north-eastern Europe, bounded to the north by Latvia, to the east and south-east by Belarus, to the south-west by Poland and by the **Kaliningrad** exclave of the Russian Federation, and to the west by the Baltic Sea. Administratively, the country is divided into 10 counties.

Area: 65,300 sq km; *capital*: **Vilnius**; *population*: 3.3m. (2009 estimate), comprising **Lithuanians** 84.5%, **Russians** 6.4%, **Poles** 6.8%, Belarusians 1.2%, others 1.1%; *official language*: Lithuanian; *religion*: **Roman Catholic** 79%, with **Russian Orthodox** 4.1% and **Protestant** 1.9%, other or none 15%.

Legislative authority is vested in the unicameral **Parliament** (Seimas). It has 141 deputies elected for a four-year term, of whom 71 are returned from single-member constituencies by majority voting and 70 by proportional representation subject to a 5% threshold. The Head of State is the President, who is elected for a five-year term (renewable once) by universal suffrage. Executive power is held by the Prime Minister, who is appointed by the President with the approval of the Seimas.

History: The kingdom of Lithuania emerged in the mid-13th century, as the Lithuanian tribes united to resist the repeated invasions of the **German** Teutonic Knights. A dynastic union with **Poland** in 1386 enabled Vytautas the Great to win a decisive victory over the Knights at Tannenberg in 1410, following which the dual monarchy became Europe's largest state, stretching from the Baltic to the Black Sea. Under the 1569 Union of Lublin Lithuania became a principality of the unified Polish kingdom, as part of which it was annexed by the Russian Empire in the partitions of Poland in 1772–95.

Occupied by Germany at the outbreak of the First World War, Lithuania declared its independence in 1918, although this was only fully achieved once German and Soviet troops were expelled and a peace treaty was signed with the **Soviet Union** in Moscow in 1920. The fact that Vilnius, the historic Lithuanian capital, was taken by revived independent Poland fuelled inter-war nationalist sentiment in Lithuania, where an authoritarian regime seized power in 1926. Following the outbreak of the Second World War in 1939 and the German–Soviet partition of Poland, Soviet forces handed Vilnius back to Lithuania in October 1939 but within nine months the whole country was forcibly incorporated into the Soviet Union, in June 1940, as the Lithuanian Soviet Socialist Republic. Germany invaded and then occupied Lithuania from 1941 (many thousands of Lithuanian **Jews** being murdered), but Soviet forces regained control in 1944. The 'Sovietization' of Lithuania followed, including agricultural collectivization and mass deportations, despite Lithuanian guerrilla resistance. Neither the USA, the United Kingdom nor other Western powers ever formally recognized the Soviet absorption of Lithuania and the other two Baltic republics.

In the late 1980s, encouraged by the Polish **Solidarity** movement and the *glasnost* (openness) initiative in the Soviet Union, dissident movements of Roman Catholics (*see* **Roman Catholic Church**) and anti-communist intellectuals united to form the **Sąjudis** popular front to campaign for Lithuanian independence. Links with popular fronts in **Estonia** and **Latvia** were also established. The 1990 elections to the Lithuanian Supreme Soviet returned pro-independence Sąjudis candidates with a majority of seats, so abolishing the communist monopoly of power, while the majority wing of the Lithuanian Communist Party severed its Soviet ties and became the Lithuanian Democratic Labour Party (LDDP). The new legislature declared the independent Republic of Lithuania and elected Vytautas Landsbergis, the Sąjudis Chairman, as Head of State. In retaliation, the Soviet Union imposed an economic blockade. This was lifted when the legislature agreed to suspend the independence declaration, but in early 1991, after Soviet troops had fired on civilians in Vilnius, Lithuanian voters gave overwhelming support in a national referendum (90%) for outright independence. Following the failure of the attempted coup to remove Soviet President Mikhail Gorbachev in August 1991, Lithuania achieved its independence the following month.

Legislative and presidential elections were held in 1992 and 1993 respectively, following the approval of a new Constitution by referendum. The parliamentary elections resulted in a heavy defeat for the increasingly right-wing Sąjudis and the unexpected return to power of the LDDP on a platform of gradual transition to a free-market economy. In the presidential contest in early 1993, LDDP candidate Algirdas Brazauskas (former First Secretary of the Lithuanian Communist Party) was directly elected with 60% of the vote.

Appointed as Prime Minister in 1993, Adolfas Šleževičius (LDDP) had nearly completed a full term when disclosures of alleged corruption forced him to resign in February 1996. In a general election in October–November of that year the Sąjudis successor party, the Homeland Union–Lithuanian Conservatives (TS–LK), won a large majority (70 seats) but opted to form a centre-right coalition with the Lithuanian Christian Democratic Party (LKDP) and the Lithuanian Centre Union (LCS) under the premiership of Gediminas Vagnorius. In presidential elections in late 1996 and early 1997, TS–LK-backed independent candidate Valdas Adamkus narrowly-defeated former prosecutor Arturas Paulauskas, who was supported by the left, by 50.3% to 49.7% in the second round. Adamkus had emigrated to the USA in 1944, after fighting against Nazi and Soviet occupation during the Second World War, and had obtained US citizenship, which he relinquished in order to contest the election.

In one of a series of adaptations to European norms, the Seimas in December 1998 approved the abolition of the death penalty in Lithuania.

An escalating conflict between Adamkus and Vagnorius, highlighting differences of government style, forced the latter out of office in April 1999, whereupon the premiership was entrusted to Rolandas Paksas, the conservative Mayor of Vilnius. Growing divisions between the coalition parties compelled Paksas to resign in October 1999, the new Prime Minister being Andrius **Kubilius** (TS–LK). Paksas and his supporters promptly defected to the opposition Lithuanian Liberal Union (LLS), of which Paksas became Chairman.

Parliamentary elections held in October 2000 resulted in the left-wing A. Brazauskas Social Democratic Coalition, including the LDDP and the **Lithuanian Social Democratic Party** (LSDP), winning 51 of the 141 seats with 31.1% of the vote. In second place came the reinvigorated LLS with 34 seats (17.3%), followed by Paulauskas's New Union (Social Liberals) (NS) with 29 (19.6%), the TS–LK with nine (8.6%), the Lithuanian Farmers' Party (LVP) with four (4.1%), the LKDP with two (3.1%), the LCS with two (3.1%) and the Lithuanian Poles' Electoral Action (AWPL) with two (1.9%). Five other parties won one seat each and three independents were elected.

Despite having become substantially the largest parliamentary group in the October 2000 elections, the Social Democratic Coalition was outmanoeuvred in subsequent inter-party negotiations on a new Government by the ascendant centrist parties. The outcome was a three-party majority coalition headed by Paksas of the LLS and including the NS and the LCS, committed to accelerated liberalization of the economy and to achieving speedy accession to the **European Union** (EU) and the **North Atlantic Treaty Organization** (NATO).

However, divisions within the coalition over the pace of Paksas's privatization drive led to the departure of the NS on 18 June 2001 and Paksas's resignation two days later. In the meantime, the LDDP and the LSDP had responded to their continued opposition status by formally merging in January 2001 under the historic LSDP party name and under the leadership of former President Brazauskas. Now the largest single party in the Seimas, the LSDP could not be ignored and, in an informal coalition with the NS, it formed a new Government with Brazauskas as Prime Minister in early July.

Paksas, now in opposition, fell out with the LLS in late 2001. He and 10 other deputies were expelled, and in March 2002 founded the Liberal Democratic Party under the leadership of Paksas, who then went on to launch a successful bid for the presidency. Although he trailed behind the incumbent Adamkus in the first round in December 2002 (Adamkus winning 35.3% to Paksas's 19.7%), their positions were reversed in the run-off in January 2003, when Paksas clinched the vote with 54.7% to Adamkus's 45.3%.

Paksas was inaugurated as President on 26 February, and reappointed Brazauskas as Prime Minister in early March. However, by the end of the year Paksas was under investigation for leaking classified material and giving citizenship to a Russian businessman, with alleged links to organized crime, in return for financial support. Following the conclusion of an investigative commission, the Seimas voted to impeach Paksas on 6 April 2004. Paulauskas as Speaker became acting President, pending a fresh election. This was won by Adamkus, who led with 30.7% of the vote in the first round against 21.4% for Kazimiera Prunskienė, leader of the Farmers and New Democracy Party Union (VNDPS—an alliance of the LVP and New Democracy Party), and then secured 52.6% in the run-off.

Meanwhile the new **Labour Party** (DP) led by Russian-born businessman Viktor Uspaskich was emerging as a new force in Lithuanian politics. Having performed well in the May European elections, winning five of Lithuania's 13 mandates, it went on to a notable victory in the October 2004 Seimas election, taking 39 seats (28.4% of the vote), with the coalition of Brazauskas's LSDP and Paulauskas's NS finishing in second place (those parties winning 20 and 11 seats respectively, on a combined vote share of 20.7%). The TS (having dropped the LK from its name) came third with 25 seats (14.6% of the vote), followed by the **Liberal and Centre Union** (LiCS—a merger of the LCS and the LLS) with 18 seats (9.1%), Paksas's For Order and Justice coalition of the LDP and the Lithuanian People's Union with 11 seats (11.4%), the VNDPS with 10 seats (6.6%) and the AWPL with two seats (3.8%). Five seats were won by independents.

Brazauskas, despite his party no longer being the largest, nevertheless retained the post of Prime Minister in a new coalition Government formed by the DP, LSDP, NS and VNDPS in November 2004 and approved by the Seimas in December.

Corruption allegations plagued several parties during 2005 and 2006, gradually eroding the position of the Government. The removal of Paulauskas as Speaker in April 2006 led to the withdrawal of the NS from the coalition, and the following month seven DP deputies defected to an opposition Civil Democracy Party (PDP), leaving the Government in control of only 62 seats in the 141-member Parliament. The DP's withdrawal from the coalition at the end of May effectively forced Brazauskas's resignation.

Negotiations between the parties (while Minister of Finance Zigmantas Balčytis held office as acting Prime Minister) led to the formation in July 2006 of a new coalition. In its initial form it comprised the LSDP, with LSDP Vice-Chairman Gediminas Kirkilas as Prime Minister, plus the Lithuanian National Farmers' Union (LVLS, as the VNDPS had renamed itself), the PDP and the LiCS. This was insufficient for a parliamentary majority, leaving the Government reliant on external support from the TS until January 2008, when the TS withdrew its support but the NS joined the coalition.

Ahead of the 2008 election the TS merged with the Lithuanian Christian Democrats (LKD) to form the **Homeland Union–Lithuanian Christian Democrats** (TS–LKD).

Latest elections: At the October Seimas 2008 election, the TS–LKD won 45 seats (with 19.7% of the vote), well ahead of the LSDP with 25 seats and 11.7%. In third place was the new centre-right **National Resurrection Party** (TPP) with 16 seats (15.1%), followed by **Order and Justice** (TT—formerly the LDP) with 15 seats (12.7%), the **Liberal Movement of the Republic of Lithuania** (LRLS—a splinter from the LiCS) with 11 seats (5.7%), the Coalition Labour Party + Youth with 10 seats (9%), the LiCS with eight seats (5.3%), the AWPL and the LVLS with three seats each and the NS with one seat. The remaining four seats were won by independents.

Recent developments: The eclipse of the centre-left in the October 2008 elections ushered in a period of right-of-centre government, based on a coalition of the resurgent TS–LKD and the TPP plus the LRLS, the LiCS and one independent. The new Government headed by TS–LKD leader Andrius Kubilius took office in December. Austerity measures attempting to address the problems with the struggling economy provoked mass demonstrations on the streets of Vilnius in early 2009.

The May 2009 presidential election was won outright in the first round by independent candidate Dalia **Grybauskaite**, Lithuania's EU Commissioner for Financial Programming and the Budget, with 69.1% of the vote. She took office on 12 July, becoming Lithuania's first female head of state. Kubilius was renominated as Prime Minister a few days later.

International relations and defence: Lithuania was admitted to the United Nations in 1991 and also joined the **Organization for Security and Co-operation in Europe**. In 1993 it became a full member of the **Council of Europe**. Following the completion in 1993 of the Russian military withdrawal from its territory, Lithuania joined NATO's **Partnership for Peace** programme in 1994. A Treaty of Friendship and Co-operation with Poland, stressing the two countries' strong historical ties, was signed in 1994, guaranteeing the rights of ethnic minorities and recognizing the existing borders. In 1997 Lithuania signed a treaty with the Russian Federation delimiting the common border and guaranteeing Russian access to its Kaliningrad enclave. Despite the Russian Federation's continuing anxieties about Lithuania joining NATO, Lithuania went on to accede to full NATO membership in March 2004.

Meanwhile, in May 2001 Lithuania's membership of the **World Trade Organization** (WTO) was formally approved, and in December 2002 negotiations with the EU reached the point where full membership was offered, in a major wave of expansion. A nationwide referendum in May 2003 endorsed joining the EU, and Lithuania acceded on 1 May 2004. In December 2007 Lithuania also joined the EU's Schengen Agreement, allowing free movement of citizens within the zone's borders. As of 2010, however, Lithuania had not fulfilled its declared intention of taking the further integrationist step of joining the eurozone (*see* **Lithuania, economy**).

Independent Lithuania has pursued close co-operation with the other two Baltic states, while membership of the **Council of Baltic Sea States** provides an organizational basis for political, economic and other co-operation between Lithuania and other littoral and adjacent countries.

Lithuania's defence budget for 2008 amounted to some US $547m., equivalent to about 1.2% of GDP. The size of the armed forces in 2010 was some 9,000 personnel, including those serving under compulsory conscription of 12 months, while first-line reservists numbered an estimated 7,000.

Lithuania, economy

The economy has achieved a transition from state control to a free-market system over the last two decades. It was assisted by its regional links with other Nordic countries. Accession to the **European Union** (EU) in 2004 was followed by several boom years, but the global credit crunch burst the housing bubble in 2008 and a GDP contraction estimated at 18.5% followed in 2009.

GNP: US $39,866m. (2008); *GNP per capita*: $11,870 (2008); *GDP at PPP*: $63,217m. (2008); *GDP per capita at PPP*: $18,800 (2008); *real GDP growth*: –18.5% (2009 estimate); *exports*: $23,755m. (2008); *imports*: $31,120m. (2008); *currency*: litas (plural: litai; US $1 = L2.46 in mid-2009); *unemployment*: 14.9% (Sept. 2009); *government deficit as a percentage of GDP*: 8.9% (2009); *inflation*: 3.5% (2009).

In 2007 industry accounted for 34% of GDP, agriculture for 5% and services for 61%. Around 31% of the workforce is engaged in industry, 10% in agriculture and 59% in services.

The main crops are grain, vegetables and sugar beet; animal husbandry declined sharply after independence in 1991, with the dismantling of the large collective and state farms which had supplied the **Soviet Union**.

Lithuania has hardly any mineral resources, although there are reserves of peat and various construction materials; small-scale oil production began in 1990. The main industries include peat and construction material extraction, the refining of imported oil, food products and textiles. Nuclear generation used to provide over 70% of electricity production until the closure of the Ignalina nuclear plant in 2010. Now Lithuania is reliant on electricity imports, but it is planning to construct a new nuclear plant to come online within a decade.

Lithuania's main exports are machinery and electrical equipment, vehicles and transportation equipment, chemical products, plastics and rubber, and textiles. Principal imports include machinery and electrical equipment, mineral products, vehicles and transportation equipment, chemical products, base metals, and plastics and rubber. The principal purchasers of Lithuanian exports in 2008 were the Russian Federation (16%), **Latvia** (12%) and Germany (7%). The main suppliers of Lithuania's imports in 2008 were the Russian Federation (30%), Germany (12%) and **Poland** (10%).

During the Soviet era the Lithuanian economy was shifted by central planners away from agriculture and into industry. Over 90% of Lithuania's trade was with Russia and other Soviet republics by the 1980s. Following the regaining of independence in 1991, Soviet-era trading patterns continued to be important, but the ending of the direct link and difficulties in adjusting to the global marketplace resulted in a sharp contraction in real GDP, by over 20% in 1992 alone, while inflation spiralled to over 1,000% in 1992.

Legislation adopted in 1991 provided for the restitution of land to former owners or their heirs, and for the privatization of state-owned farms and the reorganization of collective farms. The privatization of industry also began, initially through the **voucher** system. Although the process was complicated by the sharp post-independence economic downturn, over 80% of state assets had been privatized by the end of 1995.

Despite the setback of a financial crisis affecting two major banks in late 1995, GDP growth gathered pace in 1996, and the 7.3% GDP expansion in 1997 was one of the highest rates in the region. Over the same period, new currency board arrangements and fiscal stringency brought the inflation rate down to 2.4% in 1998. The share of GDP generated by the private sector had risen to 70% by 1998, and that year substantial stakes were sold to foreign companies in the main oil refining, telecommunications and dockyards enterprises, with much of the proceeds to be devoted to recompensing those who had lost savings in the 1992 hyperinflation and the 1995–96 banking crisis.

The Russian financial crisis in mid-1998 impacted adversely on Lithuania, where GDP growth slowed and then contracted by 4% in 1999; also that year the budget deficit rose to 8.6% of GDP. The Government therefore launched a new **International Monetary Fund**-approved stabilization and restructuring programme, geared in particular to preparing Lithuania for membership of the **European Union** (EU), on which formal negotiations began in February 2000. The restructuring included privatization of the remaining two large state-owned banks, the natural gas company and the power distribution network. The result was renewed growth of around 3% in 2000 and a partial recovery in external trade, while the budget deficit was reduced to 3.3% of GDP. An adverse consequence of the programme was sharply rising unemployment, reaching 13% in 2001. In December 2000 Lithuania joined the **World Trade Organization** (WTO).

In February 2002 the litas was switched from being pegged to the US dollar to being pegged to the euro. Following accession to the EU in May 2004, Lithuania joined the Exchange Rate Mechanism II in June. It applied in March 2006 to join the **eurozone** on 1 January 2007, but was rejected as its inflation rate was slightly above the prescribed level. Unable to bring inflation down sufficiently, the Government now says that adoption is not likely before 2014 at the earliest.

Annual growth of 7%–8% characterized 2001–07, with peaks of 10% in 2003 in the run-up to EU accession and of 9% in 2007. However, in 2008 the international financial crisis caused the inflated housing market to crash, while the credit crunch on over-extended borrowers prompted a fall in domestic consumption, which had been a principal driver of economic growth. Meanwhile, inflation was pushed to 12.5% due to high global fuel prices. In early 2009, as the economy began to contract and protesters took to the streets demanding action, the Government introduced a number of austerity measures, which included a 15% reduction in public sector salaries, pension reforms and an increase in value-added tax, and then an economic stimulus plan to support the ailing construction sector and to improve the provision of credit to businesses affected by the financial crisis. Nevertheless a sharp contraction in the economy saw GDP fall by 18.5% in 2009, with a further fall of 4% expected in 2010, while rising unemployment is predicted to reach 18%. The closure of the Ignalina nuclear power plant has already increased energy import bills, a significant factor in slowing any recovery.

Lithuanian News Agency (ELTA)
Lietuvos Naujienų Agentūra

The main news agency in **Lithuania**. Founded on 1 April 1920, ELTA was a source of regional information for major foreign news agencies until the **Soviet** invasion in 1940. Thereafter it was subordinated to the Telegraph Agency of the Soviet Union (TASS—later ITAR-TASS) until 1990. In 1996 the agency was divorced from its direct links to the Lithuanian state and has become a joint stock company; it has also rebuilt its links with other international agencies.

Director: Raimondas Kurliansksis.
Address: Gedimino pr. 21/2, Vilnius 01103.
Telephone: (5) 2628864.
Fax: (5) 2619507.
E-mail: zinios@elta.lt
Internet: www.elta.lt

Lithuanian Reform Movement
Sajudis

The pro-democracy movement which led Lithuania's campaign for independence from the **Soviet Union**. Founded on 3 June 1988 by around 500 activists, Sajudis went on to organize anti-communist demonstrations, gaining rapid support. In free elections held in 1990 the Movement won a clear majority in the Lithuanian **Parliament** and declared the country's independence on 11 March 1990. However, the arrival of independence exposed the internal divisions within the Movement and it was ousted from power in elections held in October–November 1992. Following this defeat Sajudis transformed itself in May 1993 into the right-wing Homeland Union–Lithuanian Conservatives (TS–LK, *see* **Homeland Union–Lithuanian Christian Democrats**).

Lithuanian Social Democratic Party
Lietuvos Socialdemokratų Partija (LSDP)

A centre-left political party in **Lithuania**, currently in opposition. A member of the **Socialist International**, it is directly descended from the original LSDP founded in 1896.

Prominent in the inter-war period of independence and maintained in exile under Soviet communist rule, the LSDP was revived in Lithuania in 1989 and formed part of the broad pro-independence movement under the umbrella of **Sajudis**. The party contested the 1992 parliamentary elections independently, winning 5.9% of the vote and eight seats. It subsequently formed part of the parliamentary opposition to a

Government of the Lithuanian Democratic Labour Party (LDDP, the relaunched pro-reform successor to the Communist Party of Lithuania), led by Algirdas Brazauskas.

In the October 1996 parliamentary elections, which represented a serious reverse for the LDDP, the LSDP by contrast advanced to 12 seats and 7% of the vote. The LSDP candidate, Vytenis Andriukaitis, came a disappointing fourth, with 5.7% of the vote, in the presidential elections of late 1997 and early 1998. However, the LSDP and the LDDP mounted increasingly effective joint opposition to the post-1996 centre-right Government headed by the Homeland Union–Lithuanian Conservatives (TS–LK).

The October 2000 parliamentary elections were contested jointly by the LSDP and the LDDP within the A. Brazauskas Social Democratic Coalition, which also included the small New Democratic Party (NDP) and the Lithuanian Russians' Union (LRS). The Coalition became substantially the largest group, winning 51 of the 141 seats with 31.1% of the vote. However, its leaders were outmanoeuvred in the subsequent party negotiations, which resulted in the formation of a centrist coalition Government headed by the Lithuanian Liberal Union (LLS).

Continuing in opposition, the LSDP and the LDDP formally merged at a **Vilnius** congress in January 2001. Brazauskas was elected Chairman of the unified party, which adopted the historic LSDP name to signify the reunification of the Lithuanian left after 80 years of division. In June when the coalition Government collapsed amid divisions over its own privatization programme, the reinvigorated LSDP could not be overlooked. It formed a coalition with the New Union (Social Liberals) (NS), and Brazauskas was appointed Prime Minister on 3 July.

Overtaken at the October 2004 Seimas election by the newly emergent **Labour Party** (DP), the coalition of the LSDP and the NS finished second (its constituent parties winning 20 and 11 seats respectively, on a combined vote share of 20.7%), but Brazauskas continued as Prime Minister heading a coalition of the DP, LSDP, NS and the Farmers and New Democracy Party Union (VNDPS).

This Government collapsed in May 2006, however, following first the withdrawal of the NS, then the defection of seven DP deputies and the withdrawal of the DP. In July a new coalition was formed comprising the LSDP, the Lithuanian National Farmers' Union (LVLS, as the VNDPS had renamed itself), the Civil Democracy Party (PDP) and the **Liberal and Centre Union** (LiCS), with LSDP Vice-Chairman Gediminas Kirkilas as Prime Minister; this minority Government relied on external support from the Homeland Union (TS).

At the May 2007 party congress, Kirkilas was elected as LSDP Chairman in succession to Brazauskas. In January 2008, following the withdrawal of TS support for the Government, the NS joined the coalition, giving it a slim majority of seats in the Seimas.

The LSDP won 25 seats and 11.7% of the vote in the October Seimas 2008 election, putting it in second place, but some distance behind the newly-merged **Homeland Union–Lithuanian Christian Democrats** (TS–LKD). The LSDP went into opposition to a centre-right coalition. At the March 2009 party congress Algirdas Butkevičius was elected as the new LSDP Chairman.

Leadership: Algirdas Butkevičius (Chair.).
Address: B. Radvilaites 1, Vilnius 01124.
Telephone: (5) 2613907.
Fax: (5) 2615420.
E-mail: info@lsdp.lt
Internet: www.lsdp.lt

Lithuanians

A **Baltic** people dominant in modern **Lithuania**. The Baltic tribes have long been associated with the territory on the eastern bank of the Baltic Sea (from where their collective name is derived). The Lithuanian language is most closely related to Latvian and is similarly transcribed using the Latin script. The distinct history of the Lithuanians has set them culturally apart from their northern neighbours. Long connected since the later medieval period with the **Poles**, the Lithuanians adopted **Roman Catholicism**. They successfully managed to avoid russification after the incorporation of Lithuania into the **Soviet Union** in 1940.

Livonia

A historic term for an area in the hinterland of the Baltic coast comprising territory now in modern **Estonia, Latvia** and the Russian Federation. After the conquest of the region by the German Teutonic Knights in the early 13th century it was given the name Livland (Livonia in Latin) after the Livs, a **Finno-Ugric** tribe native to the area but later replaced by **Latvians** and **Estonians**. After centuries of rule the area was divided and redivided by conquest and war until the 18th century when Livonia was occupied by Russia and split into the administrative districts of Estonia (to the north), Livonia (in the centre: modern-day southern Estonia and northern Latvia) and Courland (modern-day southern Latvia). The concept of Livonia was effectively lost in 1917 when Estonia and Latvia claimed their independence, dividing historic Livonia once again. These territorial boundaries were passed down to the present day.

LjSE *see* **Ljubljana Stock Exchange**.

Ljubljana

The capital of **Slovenia** situated in the centre of the country's mountainous terrain. *Population*: 244,000 (2007 estimate). After centuries of destruction and reconstruction, the city became an important regional centre under Austrian suzerainty in the 15th century (known in German as Laibach). Its role as a base for Slovene and south **Slavic** autonomy began when it was designated as the capital of Napoleon I's Illyrian Provinces. Agitation for an autonomous south Slav union was also based in Ljubljana in the late 19th century. On Slovenia's inclusion in the Kingdom of Serbs, Croats and Slovenes in 1918 the city maintained its role as the Slovene capital and developed its transport links with the rest of the **Balkans**. Economic activity is varied including metalwork, textiles and general consumer goods.

Ljubljana Stock Exchange
Ljubljanska borza vrednostnih papirjev (LjSE)

The stock exchange in **Slovenia**, established in December 1989. Trading began in March 1990. Market capitalization as at December 2009 totalled 19,668m. euros. At March 2010 there were 27 members trading on the LjSE.

President and Chief Executive: Marko Simoneti.
Address: Slovenska 56, 1000 Ljubljana.
Telephone: (1) 4710211.
Fax: (1) 4710213.
E-mail: info@ljse.si
Internet: www.ljse.si

LPA *see* **Latvian Privatization Agency**.

LRLS *see* **Liberal Movement of the Republic of Lithuania**.

L'S–HZDS *see* **People's Party–Movement for a Democratic Slovakia**.

LSDP *see* **Lithuanian Social Democratic Party**.

LTRK *see* **Latvian Chamber of Commerce and Industry**.

Lustration laws

Post-communist **Czechoslovakia**'s controversial process of identifying and purging those found to have collaborated in the past with the **StB** (secret police) under the communist regime. Lustration (or 'purification') was regarded by some as a key part of the decommunization process. The first significant act of lustration took place in March 1991, when several parliamentary deputies were publicly denounced as former collaborators by a parliamentary commission on the basis of evidence in the StB archive. In June 1991 a screening law was passed, allowing the dismissal of state employees found to have collaborated with the StB. Critics of lustration argued that the StB archive was unreliable and incomplete; that although many had been forced to collaborate under duress, there was no formal legal means of refuting allegations; and that the process would be manipulated by unscrupulous politicians keen to discredit their rivals.

LZP *see* **Latvian Green Party**.

LZS *see* **Latvian Farmers' Union**.

M

Macedonia
(Former Yugoslav Republic of Macedonia, FYROM)
Republika Makedonija

A landlocked republic located in south-eastern Europe in the **Balkan** peninsula, part of the former Yugoslavia until independence in 1991, and bounded by Albania to the west, Kosovo and Serbia to the north, Bulgaria to the east and Greece to the south. Administratively, the country is divided into 85 municipalities.

Area: 25,713 sq km; *capital*: **Skopje**; *population*: 2m. (2009 estimate), comprising ethnic **Macedonians** 64.2%, **Albanians** 25.2%, **Turks** 3.9%, **Roma** 2.7%, **Serbs** 1.8%, others 2.2%; *official languages*: Macedonian and Albanian; *religion*: Eastern **Orthodox** 64.7%, **Muslim** 33.3%, other 2%.

Under the 1991 Constitution, legislative power rests with a unicameral **Assembly** (Sobranie), which has 120 members elected by universal suffrage for a four-year term, 85 in single-member constituencies and 35 by proportional representation. The President is directly elected for a five-year term. Executive authority rests with the Prime Minister, who is appointed by the President.

History: The present-day republic occupies the western part of the ancient kingdom of Macedon, dating from the sixth century BC and from 338 BC the ruler of the Greek Hellenistic world. A Roman province from 148 BC, Macedon came under the authority of the Byzantine Emperor after the Roman Empire was divided in AD 395. In the sixth century **Slavic peoples** settled the region, which subsequently fell under intermittent **Bulgarian** and Byzantine influence until it became a part of the Ottoman Empire in the 14th century. Ottoman Turkish rule lasted for the next 500 years, up to the Balkan Wars of 1912–13, when the geographical area of Macedonia was divided between **Serbia** (which took the territory of the present-day republic), **Bulgaria** and **Greece**. After the First World War Serbian Macedonia became part of the Kingdom of Serbs, Croats and Slovenes (renamed **Yugoslavia** in 1929). During the Second World War it was occupied by Bulgaria (which was allied with Nazi Germany), before becoming at the end of the war a separate republic within a reconstituted (and communist-ruled) Yugoslav federal state under **Tito**.

Following President Tito's death in 1980, Yugoslavia's federal structure became increasingly unable to contain ethnic and nationalist rivalries between the constituent republics. Macedonia's aspirations towards independence were complicated by the presence of a large Albanian minority in the territory and by Greek objections to the name 'Macedonia' (also a province in northern Greece) being used in the official title of another state. Following the collapse of communist rule, multi-party elections to the Assembly were held in late 1990, although with inconclusive results. No single party won an overall majority, the largest number of seats being won by the nationalist **Internal Macedonian Revolutionary Organization–Democratic Party for Macedonian National Unity** (VMRO–DPMNE), which formed the core of the resultant 'Government of experts'.

In a referendum in September 1991, some 95% of the two-thirds of eligible voters who participated—ethnic Albanians having boycotted the poll—backed an independent and sovereign Macedonia. A new Constitution was promulgated in November 1991 and Macedonia achieved its secession from the Yugoslav federation without violence, although inter-ethnic tensions and an increase in unrest necessitated the deployment of a United Nations peacekeeping contingent in the country from late 1992 until early 1999 (see below). The international controversy over the country's official name was partially resolved in September 1995 when Greece agreed to the formula 'Former Yugoslav Republic of Macedonia' (FYROM) and the two countries signed an agreement to establish diplomatic relations.

Presidential elections in late 1994 were won by the incumbent, Kiro **Gligorov** (in office since January 1991), standing as the candidate of the Union of Macedonia (SM), comprising the (ex-communist) **Social Democratic Union of Macedonia** (SDSM), the Liberal Party of Macedonia (LPM) and the Socialist Party of Macedonia (SPM). In simultaneous legislative elections the VMRO-DPMNE failed to win any seats at all, while pro-Gligorov coalition parties won 95 of the 120 seats (the SDSM taking 58 of these, the LPM 29 and the SPM eight), and went on to form a coalition Government which also included the (Albanian) Party for Democratic Prosperity (PDP). In February 1996, following discord within the coalition, Prime Minister Branko Crvenkovski formed a new Government without the Liberals.

The legislative elections of October–November 1998 took place against a regional backdrop of escalating conflict between Serbian security forces and the majority Albanian population in the neighbouring Yugoslav province of **Kosovo**. The parties of the outgoing Government suffered a setback as a resurgent VMRO–DPMNE, in coalition with the recently-formed Democratic Alternative (DA), won 59 of the 120 seats with 38.8% of the proportional vote. The SDSM saw its share of seats halved to 29 (with 25.1% of the vote), and an alliance of the SPM and the Roma Union of Macedonia won two and one respectively (4.7%), while the Liberal-Democratic Party (LDP—a merger of the LPM and the Democratic Party of Macedonia) won four seats (7.0%). The remaining 25 seats were split between the Albanian parties, the PDP and the Democratic Party of Albanians (DPA), with 19.3% of the vote between them. A coalition Government of the VMRO–DPMNE, the DA and the DPA was formed in December 1998, with VMRO–DPMNE leader Ljubčo Georgievski as Prime Minister.

Presidential elections were held in October–November 1999, with a partial re-run of the second round being required in December because of irregularities in the main polling. The outcome was that Boris **Trajkovski** of the VMRO–DPMNE won in the second round with 52.9% of the vote against 45.9% for Tito Petkovski of the SDSM.

Increasing strains between the VMRO–DPMNE and the DA resulted in the latter's withdrawal from the Government in November 2000, whereupon Georgievski formed a new coalition between the VMRO–DPMNE and the DPA, dependent for a parliamentary majority on Liberal and dissident DA deputies. The reconstituted Government faced its greatest challenge, however, from an insurgency launched in February 2001 by ethnic Albanian rebels seeking greater rights for the Albanian community. The so-called National Liberation Army (UÇK) fought government troops for six months, prompting fears in the international community of a recurrence of the bloody conflicts which had engulfed other former Yugoslav states in the 1990s. Under intense international pressure a Government of National Unity was established in May comprising parties from all sides of the Assembly, including the opposition PDP and SDSM. The coalition was volatile as the struggle for greater Albanian autonomy was largely backed by the Albanian parties and had prompted a powerful nationalist backlash among their ethnic Macedonian counterparts. However, peace initiatives gradually gained ground in July and a final agreement was signed between the Government and the UÇK at Ohrid on 13 August 2001. A **North Atlantic Treaty Organization** (NATO) peace mission, dubbed Operation Essential Harvest, moved in to disarm the rebels and oversee the implementation of the accord. By September 3,875 weapons had been collected, and the UÇK disbanded itself.

The process of approving the various key elements of the peace deal—providing limited autonomy and social equalization for the Albanian community—was complex and frequently delayed. At its conclusion in November, the SDSM and the Liberals withdrew from the grand coalition. New Democracy (ND), which had been formed in March from a small splinter of the DA, was drafted in to take their place. In May 2002 the Assembly approved making Albanian an official language, alongside Macedonian. Then in July it dissolved itself and called early elections, according to the terms of the peace deal.

At the 15 September 2002 elections, the Together for Macedonia (ZMZ) coalition, of the SDSM, LDP and eight smaller parties, won exactly half of the seats in the 120-member Assembly (with 40.5% of the vote). The coalition of the VMRO–DPMNE and the re-emerged LPM won 33 seats (24.4% of the vote), the new Democratic Union for Integration (DUI—comprising many former members of the UÇK) won 16 seats (11.9%), the DPA won seven seats (5.2%), the PDP won two seats (2.3%), and the National Democratic Party (NDP) and the SPM each won one seat and 2.1% of the vote. The DUI joined with the ZMZ to give it a majority to form a Government, and Crvenkovski was approved by the Assembly as Prime Minister on 1 November.

On 26 February 2004 President Trajkovski was killed in a plane crash. Elections were held in April to choose a successor. Standing as the SDSM candidate, Crvenkovski easily defeated VMRO–DPMNE candidate Saško Kedev, leading him 42.5% to 34.1% in the first round on 14 April, and then 60.6% to 39.4% in the run-off two weeks later. Crvenkovski was inaugurated on 12 May, and on 2 June Hari Kostov was approved by the Assembly as the new Prime Minister.

In July, after pressure from the international community, the Government reached agreement on re-demarcation of administrative districts, reducing the total number from 123 to 85 with 26 becoming predominantly ethnic Albanian. Opposition nationalist parties forced a referendum on the issue, held on 7 November but invalidated due to low turnout after the Government recommended a boycott.

In mid-November Kostov resigned, claiming that the DUI was obstructing economic reforms and that a DUI minister was involved in corrupt practices. Vlado Bučkovski, hitherto the Minister of Defence, was appointed SDSM Chairman and nominated as Prime Minister; his new Government, still including the DUI, was approved by the Assembly on 17 December.

At the 5 July 2006 Assembly election, the coalition of the VMRO–DPMNE, SPM, LPM and 11 smaller parties emerged as the largest bloc with 45 seats (and 32.5% of the vote). The ZMZ coalition of the SDSM, LDP and seven smaller parties, dropped to 32 seats (23.3% of the vote). An alliance of the DUI and PDP won 17 seats (12.1%), the DPA won 11 seats (7.5%), the New Social Democratic Party (NSDP) won seven seats (6%), the splinter VMRO–People's Party won six seats (6.1%), and one seat each went to the Democratic Renewal of Macedonia and the Party for European Future (1.9% and 1.2% of the vote respectively). Nikola **Gruevski**, VMRO–DPMNE Chairman since May 2003, was approved as Prime Minister in August, having negotiated a coalition with the DPA and NSDP. The DUI and PDP boycotted the Assembly from January 2007, protesting over their exclusion from the governing coalition. Both parties ended their boycotts in May, although only the PDP was invited to join the Government; the DUI recommenced its boycott in September. In March 2008 the DPA left the Government over Macedonia's reluctance to recognize Kosovo's declaration of independence, but it was persuaded to retract later in the month.

In early April Greece vetoed Macedonian membership of NATO over the unresolved name dispute. A few days later, the Assembly voted to dissolve itself and call early elections, in an attempt to give the Government a clearer mandate to push through necessary reforms.

Latest elections: At the 1 June 2008 Assembly election, polling in ethnic Albanian-dominated areas was affected by clashes between DUI and DPA supporters. After re-runs were held at several stations, the final results gave the For a Better Macedonia coalition of the VMRO–DPMNE, SPM and 17 smaller parties a majority, with 63 seats in the 120-member chamber (with 48.8% of the vote). The Sun—Coalition for Europe of the SDSM, NSDP, LDP, LPM and four smaller parties won just 27 seats

(23.7% of the vote). The DUI won 18 seats (12.8%), the DPA won 11 seats (8.5%) and the Party for European Future won one seat (1.5%). Gruevski was approved as Prime Minister again on 26 July.

In the 2009 presidential elections VMRO–DPMNE candidate Gjorge **Ivanov** easily defeated SDSM candidate Ljubomir Frčkoski, leading him 35.1% to 20.5% in the first round on 22 March, and then 63.1% to 36.9% in the run-off two weeks later.

International relations and defence: Following independence and the adoption of the interim FYROM designation as its official title, the new state of Macedonia was admitted to the United Nations in April 1993. After Greece had accepted the FYROM formula in September 1995 subject to further negotiations on a definitive name, Macedonia was admitted to the **Council of Europe**, to the **Organization for Security and Co-operation in Europe** and to NATO's **Partnership for Peace** programme. In April 1996 Macedonia and the Federal Republic of Yugoslavia (comprising Serbia and **Montenegro**) established full diplomatic relations, recognizing each other's sovereignty, independence and territorial integrity. A friendship and co-operation agreement was signed with the Russian Federation in February 1998.

In a controversial move in January 1999, the Macedonian Government established full diplomatic relations with Taiwan, joining the Vatican as the only European states to recognize the Taipei regime as the 'Republic of China'. The People's Republic of China responded in February by using its veto in the UN Security Council to block the renewal of the mandate of the UN Preventive Deployment Force (UNPREDEP) in Macedonia, which therefore wound up its operations in March. Taiwan subsequently denied that it had promised Macedonia US $1,000m. in aid in return for recognition. Some Taiwanese aid did arrive, but during the ethnic conflict in 2001 (see above) Macedonia, feeling the need for Chinese support for international intervention, formally revoked its recognition of Taiwan on 18 June.

In February 1999 Bulgaria and Macedonia signed a declaration settling a longstanding language dispute involving Bulgaria's refusal to recognize Macedonian as a language separate from Bulgarian. The agreement also resolved potential territorial disputes and provided for the finalization of 20 bilateral accords that had remained unsigned since Macedonia's independence.

Macedonia's limited resources were stretched severely by the refugee and humanitarian crisis in neighbouring Kosovo, arising from the repression of Kosovar Albanians by the Serbian authorities there, which provoked punitive military action against Serbia by NATO in the first half of 1999. Macedonia was therefore allocated substantial **European Union** (EU) and other Western reconstruction aid within the framework of the South-East European Co-operation Process (SEECP).

NATO forces were called directly into Macedonia itself in August 2001 following the signing of a peace accord between the Government and ethnic Albanian rebels. They remained there until 14 Dec 2002, succeeded by a series of EU or EU-led missions to assist Macedonia's police and armed forces over the next three years.

Macedonia had hoped for an invitation to join NATO at the organization's April 2008 summit—but instead Greece blocked accession over the unresolved issue of the country's name. Macedonia responded by suing Greece at the **International Court of Justice** (ICJ) for breaching the 1995 agreement not to object to future Macedonian integration into the EU and NATO under the FYROM designation. Until a ruling is delivered, the dispute is unlikely to get any nearer to a resolution.

A Stabilization and Association Agreement (SAA) was signed with the EU in April 2001 and came into force three years later. Just ahead of that, in March 2004, Macedonia had submitted a membership application. It was granted candidate status in December 2005, and sufficient progress had been made with reforms for it to be invited to begin membership talks in late 2009. However, the name dispute with Greece is likely to stall the process.

Macedonia was initially reluctant to recognize the independence of Albanian-dominated Kosovo from Serbia in March 2008, despite pressure from the junior coalition partner, the DPA. Recognition was approved six months later, but it took a further year for the two countries to resolve a border dispute and therefore establish full diplomatic relations.

Macedonia's defence budget for 2008 amounted to some US \$192m., equivalent to about 2.1% of GDP. The size of the armed forces in 2010 was some 8,000 personnel, including those serving under compulsory conscription of six months, while reservists numbered an estimated 5,000.

Macedonia, economy

Attempts to build up the economic base after communist-era neglect, and to secure a transition to a market economy, have been hampered by regional conflict and internal ethnic divisions. Despite modest growth from 2003, living standards have not yet returned to pre-independence levels and unemployment is high.

GNP: US \$8,432m. (2008); *GNP per capita*: \$4,140 (2008); *GDP at PPP*: \$20,460m. (2008); *GDP per capita at PPP*: \$10,000 (2008); *real GDP growth*: –2.5% (2009 estimate); *exports*: \$3,920m. (2008); *imports*: \$6,844m. (2008); *currency*: denar (plural: denars; US \$1 = D43.6 in mid-2009); *unemployment*: 32% (Sept. 2009); *government deficit as a percentage of GDP*: 2.8% (2009); *inflation*: –0.5% (2009).

In 2007 industry accounted for 31% of GDP, agriculture for 11% and services for 58%. Around 31% of the workforce is engaged in industry, 18% in agriculture and 51% in services.

Some 24% of the land is arable, 2% under permanent crops, 25% permanent pastures and 39% forests and woodland. The main crops are rice, grain, sugar beet, vegetables, grapes (for wine) and tobacco, and there is an important dairy industry.

The main mineral resources are brown coal (lignite) and iron ore; other mineral deposits remain largely unexploited. The main industries are metallurgy, chemicals, textiles and the production of tobacco. The main energy sources are coal-fired plants and hydroelectric power, while natural gas is now imported from the Russian Federation via **Bulgaria**.

Macedonia's main exports by value are basic manufactures, miscellaneous manufactured articles, food and live animals, beverages, tobacco, iron, steel and other metals. Principal imports include basic manufactures, machinery and transport equipment, petroleum and petroleum products and chemical products. **Serbia** was the main purchaser of Macedonia's exports in 2008 (21%), followed by Germany (16%) and **Greece** (13%). Imports in that year came mainly from Germany and Greece (13% each) and **Bulgaria** (10%). Over half of Macedonia's trade is with EU members.

Having been the poorest of the republics within the former **Socialist Federal Republic of Yugoslavia**, Macedonia immediately encountered external threats to its economy when it declared full independence in November 1991. Not only was it heavily dependent on its relations with the rest of the former Yugoslavia (especially **Serbia**), it also suffered from the international sanctions placed on that country to 1995. Moreover, in 1994–95 Greece acted on its objections to the new state being called Macedonia by imposing an economic blockade which cut off much of its oil and other essential imports. However, GDP stabilized in 1996, having fallen by an average of 5.5% a year in the period 1990–95, and increased modestly in 1997 by 1.5% and by 3% in 1998. Severe post-independence inflation, rising to nearly 2,000% in 1992, was brought down to around nil by the end of 1996 and remained at a low level thereafter.

A privatization programme introduced in 1992 made little headway during the initial post-independence years of external pressure. At this stage it consisted mainly of management buy-outs ('**nomenklatura** privatization'). After the lifting of the sanctions on Yugoslavia and of the Greek blockade, however, the programme made real progress, special attention being paid to the privatization of the banking sector. The situation was complicated by the collapse in early 1997 of a fraudulent **'pyramid' investment scheme** which led to an overall lack of economic confidence. Nevertheless, by mid-1998 around 95% of industrial, commercial and mining enterprises had been privatized, as had about half of state-owned farms. A landmark privatization in 1999 was that of the OKTA oil refinery, whose sale to a Greek company resulted in a Macedonian-Greek agreement to build a US $90m. pipeline from **Skopje** to Thessaloniki. The sale of Macedonia's largest bank to Greek and other interests followed in April 2000, in which month further legislation was approved providing for the return to former owners or their heirs of property and land confiscated since 1945.

The economic situation in Macedonia was thrown into some disarray in the spring of 1999, when the unrest in **Kosovo** (the Serbian province of **Yugoslavia** to the north of Macedonia) erupted into warfare, causing the massive exodus to Macedonia of ethnic **Albanian** refugees and **NATO** air-strikes against Serbia. However, **International Monetary Fund** (IMF) credits and other aid from Western Governments enabled Macedonia to cope with the crisis sufficiently well that modest GDP growth of 2.5% was recorded in 1999, rising to 3% in 2000. A range of economic restructuring and liberalization measures began to take effect, but unemployment remained very high at around 35% officially in the late 1990s and in reality even higher (partly masked by the existence of a huge 'black' economy).

Ethnic hostilities in the north in early 2001 caused the economy to contract, but considerable aid pledges to support reconstruction followed in 2002. A new stand-by credit agreement with the IMF was also signed in 2003.

In 2001 Macedonia signed a Stabilization and Association Agreement with the **European Union** (EU). It joined the **World Trade Organization** (WTO) in 2003 and the **Central European Free Trade Agreement** (CEFTA) in 2006.

GDP grew by 0.9% in 2002 and 2.8% in 2003. In 2004 the Government eased business restrictions to encourage foreign investment, and in mid-2005 the IMF approved a further three-year stand-by arrangement. Moderate growth of around 4% a year was achieved in 2004–06, while the Government struggled to combat corruption, strengthen the judiciary, improve contract enforcement and tax collection, and fund high domestic finance costs. In 2007 it launched an expensive marketing campaign promoting the country to foreign investors, and GDP growth rose to 6%. The following year the Government reduced corporation tax from 15% to 10%, increased pensions (despite the pension system being in deficit) and raised public sector wages by 10%.

Critical areas of concern remained the need to diversify exports, the high rate of unemployment and the widening current account deficit. Inflation rose sharply in 2008 as a result of higher international prices for food and oil, and the global economic downturn towards the end of the year led to declines in remittances from workers abroad, foreign investment and exports. The trade deficit rose to 25% of GDP. In 2009 the country moved into recession, with GDP contracting by 2.5%, and also experienced a brief period of deflation. To stimulate the economy the governing coalition announced a seven-year programme to invest 8,000m. euros in the country's infrastructure. Growth of 2% is predicted for 2010.

Macedonian question

A territorial and diplomatic dispute based on the division of historical Macedonia and the emergence of a separate state of **Macedonia**. A powerful country in ancient times, Macedonia was absorbed by the **Turkic** Ottoman Empire in the 14th century. When that Empire's last remaining **Balkan** possessions were finally partitioned in the Balkan Wars of 1912–13, the Macedonian elements were carved up under the Treaty of London in 1913 between the three Balkan allies, **Bulgaria**, **Serbia** and **Greece**.

Although Bulgaria was allocated one of the larger shares, the **Bulgarian royal family** of the time aspired to sovereignty over all of Macedonia—based on the ethnic similarity between **Macedonians** and **Bulgarians**, and on the state's brief annexation of Macedonia under the 1878 Treaty of San Stefano. Late in 1913 Bulgaria turned on its erstwhile allies and attempted to seize historic Macedonia for itself. It was easily defeated. Under the resultant Treaty of Bucharest, Macedonia was finally divided along the modern borders it has today. The territory known as Vardar Macedonia, after the river of the same name, was awarded to Serbia (and forms the basis of the modern Macedonian state). A small chunk to the east, known as Pirin Macedonia, was left in Bulgarian hands and the final southern belt (Aegean Macedonia) became a part of Greece. Tensions persist between Macedonia (the heir to the Serbian cession) and its eastern and southern neighbours. Bulgarian, and even some Macedonian, nationalists still call for greater ties if not full reunification with Bulgaria.

Meanwhile, Greece has shown great reluctance since 1991 to accept that a new 'Macedonian' state can lay title to that name. This is more than mere semantics. Greeks take pride in the Macedonian element of their own ancient heritage, dating back to the era of Philip of Macedon and his son Alexander the Great. They are also anxious not to encourage any possible Macedonian irredentism affecting northern Greece—where the largest of Greece's 10 traditional regions has long been known as Macedonia too. The international controversy over the new state's official name was partially resolved in September 1995 when Greece agreed to the formula 'Former Yugoslav Republic of Macedonia' (FYROM) and the two countries signed an agreement to establish diplomatic relations. In 2008, however, Greece blocked FYROM's accession to the North Atlantic Treaty Organization (NATO) over the unresolved issue of the country's name. Macedonia responded by suing Greece at the **International Court of Justice** (ICJ) for breaching the 1995 agreement. Until a ruling is delivered, the dispute is also likely to stall FYROM's accession negotiations with the **European Union** (EU).

Macedonian Stock Exchange
Makedonska Berza (MSE)

The first organized stock exchange in **Macedonia**. The MSE was founded in September 1995 and trading began in March 1996. Market capitalization in March 2010 totalled US $842m. and there were 24 members.

Chair.: Zvonko Stankovski.
Address: ul. Mito Hadživasilev br. 20, 1000 Skopje.
Telephone: (2) 3122055.
Fax: (2) 3122069.
E-mail: mse@mse.org.mk
Internet: www.mse.org.mk

Macedonians

A south **Slavic people** who had established themselves in north and central (geographical) Macedonia (*see* **Macedonian question**) by the eighth century. They now constitute around 67% of the population of modern (political) **Macedonia**. The conquest of the area by the **Bulgarians** to the east in the ninth century resulted in the merging of the two peoples. Consequently there is dispute as to whether Macedonian is even a separate language or merely a dialect of Bulgarian, which it closely resembles. The issue is a cause for tension between Macedonia and **Bulgaria**.

The separate identity of the Macedonians was denied by the royal **Yugoslav** authorities in the inter-war years but was resurrected by the communist regime which founded Yugoslavia's Socialist Republic of Macedonia in 1943. In the following years Macedonian grammar was established as part of an effort to reduce Bulgarian influence in the region.

The Macedonians converted to **Orthodox Christianity** while under Bulgarian and Serbian rule in the early second millennium. A separate Macedonian Orthodox Church was established by the communist authorities in 1967. Although it is not officially recognized by other Orthodox Patriarchates it receives much support within Macedonia. However, some Macedonians converted to Islam under Ottoman rule; their descendants are known as **Pomaks**.

Communities of ethnic Macedonians live in neighbouring countries. Over 10,000 live in south-western Bulgaria although their identity and number are contested by both Macedonian and Bulgarian authorities. Around 50,000 live in **Serbia**. Upwards of 4,500 live in the east of **Albania**. Most Macedonians living in Aegean Macedonia in **Greece** emigrated north after the First World War. A small community remains and are known as Slavomacedonians, although many have assimilated with the Greek population.

Magyar Koalíció Pártja (MKP) *see* **Hungarian Coalition Party**.

Magyars *see* **Hungarians**.

Makarios III

First President of the Republic of Cyprus (1960–74 and 1974–77).

Born Mihail Christodoulou Mouskos on 13 August 1913 in Panayia, he entered the Kykkos Monastery at the age of 13 and graduated in theology and law from the University of Athens during the Second World War. In 1948 he was elected Bishop of Kitium, and two years later was elected Archbishop of Cyprus, making him head of the autocephalous Cypriot **Orthodox Church** and Ethnarch or national leader of the **Greek Cypriot** community. He used this position to campaign for colonial ruler, the

United Kingdom, to quit Cyprus, in favour of the island's union (*enosis*) with **Greece**. Accused of links with the insurgent National Organization of Cypriot Fighters (EOKA), Makarios was forced to leave Cyprus by the British in 1956, initially sent to exile in the Seychelles and then permitted to go to **Athens**, from where he continued to campaign vehemently for *enosis*. However, both the Greek and British Governments now favoured independence for the island as the preferred outcome, and Makarios was eventually persuaded to back down and accept this solution.

When the British at last allowed him to return to Cyprus, Makarios arrived on 1 March 1959 to an enormous welcome. He won the presidential election in December, and took office as the new republic's first independent head of state on 16 August 1960. The next decade, however, saw rising tensions between the Cypriot communities, with many Greek Cypriots still campaigning for *enosis* with Greece while Turkish Cypriots claimed they were being subjugated by the Greek Cypriot majority. Makarios's own position grew increasingly difficult as the Greek Cypriot agitation for *enosis*, and consequent opposition to his independent state, was supported (and funded) by the military junta which had seized power in Greece in 1967. This culminated on 15 July 1974 in a coup in **Nicosia** that forced Makarios to flee the island. Five days later Turkey, one of the three signatories of Cyprus's Treaty of Guarantee, invaded the north of the island—ostensibly to restore peace, but in fact leading to *de facto* partition. To this day its troops remain stationed in the self-proclaimed **Turkish Republic of Northern Cyprus**. With the Greek junta itself now on the brink of collapse, the Cypriot coup leaders were forced to resign after just eight days in power. The Speaker of the **House of Representatives** Glafcos Clerides took over as acting President until Makarios's return on 7 December. Restored to the presidency, he campaigned unsuccessfully for the removal of the Turkish troops and re-unification of the island. He died from a heart attack on 3 August 1977 and was buried on Throni Mountain near the Kykkos Monastery.

Makfax

The main private news agency in **Macedonia**. Founded in 1992, Makfax began services the following year and promotes itself as a major regional source of independent and objective reporting.

Executive Director: Risto Popovski.
Address: Goce Delčev 66, POB 738, 1000 Skopje.
Telephone: (2) 3110125.
Fax: (2) 3110184.
E-mail: makfax@ makfax.com.mk
Internet: www.makfax.com.mk

MDF *see* **Hungarian Democratic Forum.**

Mečiar, Vladimír

Former Prime Minister of **Slovakia**, its leader through the **'velvet divorce'** from the **Czech Republic** at the end of 1992, and subsequently a prominent but controversial figure on the right wing of Slovak politics.

Born in Zvolen, north-east of **Bratislava**, on 26 July 1942, Vladimír Mečiar held a post in local government after completing secondary school, then did military service, and began rising rapidly within the communist youth movement. In 1969, however, at the all-Slovakia conference of the Youth Union, Mečiar expounded progressive and reformist ideas that resulted in his expulsion from the communist party. During the period of 'normalization' following the 1968 **'Prague Spring'**, Mečiar was offered high rank in the Slovak Central Committee of the Youth Union on the condition that he retract his statements but he refused to do so. Initially unable to find employment because of his political views, he eventually began work six months later as an assistant smelter at the heavy engineering works, Dubnica nad Váhom. During this time he enrolled for an external course at the Comenius University of Bratislava, graduating with a law degree in 1974. From 1974 until 1990 he worked at the Skloobal concern in Nemšová, quickly rising to the position of company lawyer.

In 1989 Mečiar joined the **Public Against Violence** (VPN) movement which, together with its Czech counterpart **Civic Forum**, was instrumental in bringing down the communist regime in December 1989. In the non-communist Government which was then formed on an interim basis, he held the post of Slovak Minister of the Interior and the Environment. In the June 1990 legislative elections to the federal and Slovak legislatures, Mečiar was elected to the Federal Assembly and was appointed Prime Minister of a Slovak coalition Government dominated by the VPN.

Increasingly overt in his advocacy of full autonomy for Slovakia, and accused of abusing his access to secret information, he was obliged to resign in March 1991. He left the VPN to form the nationalist Movement for a Democratic Slovakia (HZDS) and was elected as its Chairman later the same year. In the federal and republican elections, which were held in June 1992, the HZDS became the strongest Slovak party in both the Federal Assembly and the Slovak **National Council**. Mečiar was accordingly again appointed Slovak Prime Minister and proceeded to negotiate the dissolution of **Czechoslovakia** with the then Czech Premier, Václav **Klaus**.

The ensuing period was marked by growing tensions between Mečiar and Michal Kováč, elected President of the newly independent Slovakia in February 1993. A series of government resignations and the formation of a breakaway party eventually led to the fall of Mečiar's Government in March 1994 after he lost a parliamentary vote of confidence. However, after the September–October 1994 general election Mečiar was again able to form a Government in December, this time comprising his HZDS, the **Slovak National Party** (SNS) and the Association of Workers of Slovakia. Upon his return to power Mečiar used his party's majority in the National Council to repeal privatization legislation approved under Jozef Moravčík, while the animosity between Mečiar and Kováč continued to paralyse the process of government. Differences culminated in May 1997 over the holding of a referendum on Slovakia's proposed membership of the **North Atlantic Treaty Organization** (NATO) and the nature of the Slovak presidency, with both sides accusing the other of acting undemocratically. In the event the referendum was boycotted by 90% of the electorate in protest at the Government's decision to omit the question on presidential elections and was thus declared invalid. Elections in 1998 saw Mečiar ousted and a new Government formed by the former opposition grouping, the Slovak Democratic Coalition (*see* **Slovak Democratic and Christian Union–Democratic Party**).

Following the adoption of a constitutional amendment by the new legislature in January 1999 providing for direct presidential elections, Mečiar emerged from post-election seclusion to become the HZDS presidential candidate. However, in the elections in May 1999 he was defeated in the second round by the centre-left nominee on a 57% to 43% split. In March 2000 Mečiar was re-elected HZDS Chairman by a party congress which also approved the conversion of the HZDS into a formal political party with the suffix People's Party, signifying a shift to a less nationalistic stance, while the party declared its full support for membership of the **European Union** (EU) and NATO.

In April 2000 Mečiar suffered the indignity of being arrested and fined for refusing to testify on the murky affair of the kidnapping of President Kováč's son in 1995 at the height of Mečiar's confrontation with the President.

After the HZDS had won a plurality at the September 2002 parliamentary election, Mečiar was invited to form a government, but again found himself unable to form a coalition, so remained in opposition. In the first round of the April 2004 presidential election Mečiar led with 32.7% of the vote, with Ivan **Gašparovič** (a former ally of Mečiar, who had defected from the HZDS in 2002 to form the rival Movement for Democracy) edging out the ruling coalition's candidate by 22.3% to 22.1%. However, Gašparovič then went on to win the run-off by 59.9% to 40.1%.

The June 2006 election was the worst ever showing for Mečiar's party, now renamed as the **People's Party–Movement for a Democratic Slovakia** (ĽS–HZDS), but it was invited, along with the SNS, to join the new Government headed by **Direction–Social Democracy** (Smer) leader Róbert **Fico**. The junior coalition partners received only two and three ministerial portfolios respectively, and neither party's controversial leader was invited to fill any of the positions.

Memel *see* **Klaipeda**.

Milošević, Slobodan

President of **Yugoslavia** in 1997–2000, and before that the President of **Serbia** from 1989. His ruthless pursuit of a **Serb** nationalist agenda contributed significantly to inflaming the violent conflicts which accompanied the disintegration of the **Socialist Federal Republic of Yugoslavia** (SFRY). He became the first ex-head of state ever to face charges for war crimes in an international court.

Slobodan Milošević was born in Požaravec, near **Belgrade**, on 20 August 1941. His father was an **Orthodox Christian** priest of Montenegrin descent, who left home soon after Slobodan's birth, and later committed suicide, as did his mother in 1973. Milošević met his future wife Mirjana Marković, who came from a leading Serb communist family, while at secondary school in Požaravec. She subsequently became a university professor and a significant political figure in her own right as head of the nationalist Yugoslav United Left. They have one son, Marko Milošević, and one daughter, Marija.

Milošević joined the ruling **League of Communists of Yugoslavia** (SKJ) when he was 18, graduated in law from the University of Belgrade in 1964, and worked at the national gas extraction company, Tehnogas, rising to become its Director General in 1973. Meanwhile he held several party posts in Belgrade, became a member of the Presidium of the SKJ Central Committee in 1984 and two years later took over the leadership of the party in Serbia. In April 1987 he famously told **Kosovo**'s Serbs (who had been in a violent confrontation with police while demonstrating against greater autonomy for the province's ethnic **Albanians**): 'No one has the right to beat you. No one will ever beat you again.' His words struck a chord and he returned to Belgrade as the hero of the Serb nationalists, using this to strengthen his position in the party hierarchy and, in May 1989, to win election by the republican parliament as President of Serbia. Within months the autonomous status of Kosovo and **Vojvodina** within Serbia had been revoked.

Dominating Serbia's first multi-party presidential elections in December 1990, Milošević won 65% of the vote, as the candidate of the **Socialist Party of Serbia** (SPS), the renamed communist party. He was re-elected two years later, by which time Serbia was no longer one of six republics under the old Yugoslav structure, but the larger of two (with **Montenegro**) in a 'rump' state, formed in April 1992 as the Federal Republic of Yugoslavia (FRY).

During the bloody break-up of Yugoslavia, Milošević initially gave full backing to the idea of a **'Greater Serbia'**, but he has consistently denied conniving at providing military support from the regular Yugoslav army for Bosnian Serb militias (who attempted to advance the Greater Serbia cause by **'ethnic cleansing'** of non-Serbs in **Bosnia and Herzegovina**). In the later stages of the Bosnian war it became expedient for the international community to deal directly with Milošević, rather than with Bosnian Serbs, in negotiating what became the **Dayton Agreement** to end the conflict. This initially boosted his regime in Serbia, but mass demonstrations over the manipulation of municipal elections in 1996 highlighted growing domestic dissatisfaction with his Government, at least in Belgrade. Seeking to maintain his position of power beyond the end of his second and final term as Serbian President, he switched to the federal presidency in July 1997 and worked to transform what was effectively a figurehead position into a powerful executive position, without ever altering the constitutional role. Opposition within the FRY was severely repressed, in a climate of fear carefully managed by Milošević's powerful state machine.

The 1999 **NATO** bombing campaign, prompted by the actions of Serb security forces against ethnic Albanians in Kosovo, laid the seeds for Milošević's eventual downfall. Despite public outrage at the NATO 'aggression', the humiliation of having to retreat from Kosovo, the cradle of Serb nationalism, made him politically vulnerable. This was compounded by his indictment for war crimes by the **International Criminal Tribunal for the former Yugoslavia** (ICTY), and by the imposition of crippling economic sanctions which would only be rescinded on his own removal. Rival forces came together in the **Democratic Opposition of Serbia** (DOS) coalition in time for simultaneous presidential and legislative elections called for 24 September 2000, Milošević having gambled by changing the Constitution to allow him to seek a fresh term as federal President by introducing direct elections to that post. It was not obvious at the time if he considered his support to be sufficiently strong, or the resolve of the opposition sufficiently weak in the face of his own ability and willingness to control results. Either way, it was a miscalculation. The DOS claimed victory, and a massive public outcry greeted his initial attempts to have the first round of the presidential contest declared inconclusive. When it was made known that he himself had ordered the results doctored in his favour, the protestors took over the streets on 5 October, demanding his resignation. Milošević conceded defeat and DOS candidate Vojislav **Koštunica** was inaugurated in his place two days later.

Koštunica himself regarded Milošević as having a legitimate political role, and strongly maintained that he should never be extradited to the ICTY in The Hague. Many still saw him as a defender of Serb national pride against Western aggression. However, the new Serbian Prime Minister elected in December 2000, Zoran Đinđić, was keenly aware that Yugoslavia's international rehabilitation, and particularly the return of international aid, depended on bringing Milošević to justice. On 1 April 2001 Milošević was arrested after a dramatic police siege of his Belgrade home; and on 28 June, contrary to initial promises that he would only be tried in Yugoslavia, he was extradited to the ICTY. At the pre-trial in October 2001 he took a typically combative stance, denying the legitimacy of the Tribunal and refusing either to appoint legal representation or to enter pleas. In November he was charged, in addition, with genocide. At the start of his trial on 12 February 2002, he refused to recognize the court's authority. He died while the trial was still in progress on 11 March 2006.

MKIK *see* **Hungarian Chamber of Commerce and Industry**.

MKP (Magyar Koalíció Pártja) *see* **Hungarian Coalition Party**.

MNB *see* **National Bank of Hungary**.

MNV Zrt. *see* **Hungarian National Asset Management Company**.

Molotov-Ribbentrop Pact *see* **Nazi-Soviet Pact**.

Montenegrins

A south **Slavic people** dominant in modern **Montenegro** and forming a significant minority in neighbouring **Serbia**. Like **Serbians**, most Montenegrins are **Orthodox Christians**. The Montenegrin language is almost identical to Serbian, although it is more commonly written in the Latin alphabet rather than the **Cyrillic alphabet**.

Montenegro
Crna Gora

A landlocked republic located in south-eastern Europe on the western coast of the **Balkan** peninsula, independent since June 2006, and bounded by Albania to the south, Kosovo to the east, Serbia to the north-east, Bosnia and Herzegovina to the north-west, Croatia to the west and the Adriatic Sea to the south-west. Administratively, Montenegro is divided into 21 municipalities.

Area: 13,812 sq km; *capital*: **Podgorica**; *population*: 624,200 (2009 estimate), comprising **Montenegrins** 43%, **Serbs** 32%, **Bosniaks** 8%, **Albanians** 5%, others 12%; *official language* Montenegrin; *religion*: **Orthodox** Christian 74.2%, **Muslim** 17.7%, **Roman Catholic** 3.5%, other 4.6%.

Under the 2007 Constitution, the Head of State is a directly-elected President, with a five-year term of office. The unicameral legislature, the **Assembly of the Republic of Montenegro** (Skupština Republike Crne Gore) has 81 members, elected for a four-year term, five of whom are elected from the ethnic Albanian community. Executive authority lies with the Prime Minister, who appoints the cabinet.

History: The Montenegrin people, ethnically similar to the neighbouring **Serbs** and **Croats**, arrived in the area during the south **Slav** migration into the region in the seventh century. Montenegro held on tenaciously to its independence in the impenetrable Black Mountain region (from which the country derives its name) against the encroaching power of the Ottoman Turks. Although most of its current territory was nominally part of the Ottoman Empire from 1498, Turkish control was never secure. Montenegro was internationally recognized as an independent state in the 1878 Treaty of Berlin, with its territory enlarged to include border areas in **Albania** and the plains around **Podgorica**, and to give it access to the Adriatic. After the First World War Montenegro was absorbed into the new Kingdom of the Serbs, Croats and Slovenes (**Yugoslavia**) in 1918 but reappeared as a separate state during the Second World War. Once more it disappeared into the Yugoslav state in 1945.

During the collapse of the post-communist Yugoslavia in the early 1990s, Montenegro's pro-Serbian Government sided with the Belgrade authorities and joined **Serbia** in the 'third Yugoslavia': the Federal Republic of Yugoslavia. However, criticism of Serbian strategies ultimately led to the removal of Montenegrin forces from the Yugoslav army. A split in the ruling **Democratic Party of Socialists of Montenegro** (DPSCG) in 1997 led to the election of Milo Đukanović as Montenegrin President. His rival, Momir Bulatović, the former Montenegrin President and DPSCG leader, subsequently left the DPSCG and formed the pro-federation **Socialist People's Party of Montenegro** (SNPCG); in mid-May 1998 he was appointed federal Prime Minister. Montenegrin Assembly elections later that month were won outright by Đukanović's For a Better Life coalition of his DPSCG, the People's Party (NS) and the Social Democratic Party of Montenegro, securing 42 seats in the 78-member chamber and 49% of the vote. The SNPCG were second with 29 seats and 36% of the vote; the Liberal Alliance of Montenegro (LSCG) won five seats (6.2%), and the Democratic Alliance of Montenegro (DSCG) and the Democratic Union of Albanians (DUA) won one seat each (1.6% and 1% of the vote respectively).

Tensions with the central and Serbian authorities increased dramatically. Đukanović steadily argued the case for greater autonomy, and even independence, for Montenegro despite strong opposition from Serbia, the international community and within Montenegro among the 'White Montenegrins' (those in favour of closer connection with Serbia).

During 1999, which saw Serbian forces attack ethnic Albanian communities in **Kosovo** and the ensuing **NATO** bombardment and sanctions, Montenegro cut almost all ties with the central federal regime. The DPSCG ordered a boycott of federal elections in 2000, protesting at alterations in the Yugoslav Constitution which downgraded Montenegro's position in the federation. The effect of this boycott was to allow the SNPCG and the Serbian People's Party (SNS—a pro-federation splinter from the NS) to secure the republic's seats in the federal-level legislature. Across Yugoslavia as a whole, however, the election was highly controversial and was followed within days by the ousting of President Milošević. The new regime's President, Vojislav Koštunica, stated that he intended to preserve the federation of Serbia and Montenegro, a position supported by the West.

Đukanović now pressed more strongly for independence for Montenegro, and pledged to hold a referendum. Opposing this course, the NS withdrew from his ruling coalition, which resulted in early elections being called. Held in April 2001, these proved to be a much tighter contest than had been expected. The pro-independence

Victory is Montenegro's coalition of Đukanović's DPSCG and the Social Democrats won 42% of the vote (36 seats) against 40.6% (33 seats) for the pro-federation Together for Yugoslavia coalition of the SNPCG, the SNS and the NS. The LSCG won 7.8% (six seats), the DUA 1.3% (two seats) and the DSCG 1.1% (one seat). The DPSCG, after attempting but failing to negotiate a coalition with the pro-independence nationalist LSCG, instead formed a minority Government with that party's backing in the Assembly.

The narrowness of the election result took away some of the momentum for the promised independence referendum, but the DPSCG suggested that it could be held in 2002. In November 2001 the **European Union** (EU) helped to mediate talks between Serbia and Montenegro, and on 14 March 2002 the federal and both republican Presidents signed a framework agreement providing for the establishment of a State Union of Serbia and Montenegro. Under this accord, the two semi-independent republics were to maintain separate economies, but have a joint foreign and defence policy, and elect a new, joint presidency and legislature. Montenegro was to retain the right to refer the issue of independence to a referendum after a period of three years. The agreement was approved by both republican Assemblies in April, and by the Federal Assembly in May, and a Constitutional Charter was drawn up over the next few months. This was approved at republican level in late-January 2003, and took effect when the Federal Assembly approved it on 4 February 2003. Later that month, a 126-member Assembly of Serbia and Montenegro was elected from the existing federal and republican legislatures, with 91 members from Serbia and 35 from Montenegro, split party-wise in the same proportions as the republican Assemblies. On 7 March this new Assembly elected Svetozar Marović unopposed as President of Serbia and Montenegro, and on 18 March a five-member Council of Ministers was approved, chaired by Marović.

Meanwhile the LSCG, which was hostile to this new Union even as a temporary arrangement, had withdrawn its support from the Đukanović Government, precipitating early elections in which, on 20 October 2002, the DPSCG-led Democratic List for a European Montenegro secured a majority of 39 out of 75 seats (with 47.3% of the vote). The rebranded Together for Change coalition of the SNPCG, the SNS and the NS won 30 seats (37.9% of the vote), the LSCG-led Montenegro Can Do It dropped to four seats (5.8%), and the DUA and DSCG allied as the Democratic Coalition—Alliance Together retained their two seats (with 2.4% of the vote). Đukanović resigned as President on 5 November in order to be nominated as Prime Minister, in which capacity he formed a Government which was approved on 8 January 2003. Two attempts to hold a presidential election, in December 2002 and February 2003, were invalidated by low turnout after the SNPCG and LSCG boycotted the poll. The Assembly then voted to remove the turnout condition for future elections, and on 11 May former Prime Minister Filip Vujanović of the DPSCG secured the presidency with 64% of the vote (he had polled 84% and

82% in the previous two polling attempts, but this time the LSCG did participate, its candidate receiving 31% of the vote); turnout was still just under 50%.

In preparation for the eventuality of independence, a new flag, anthem and national day (13 July) were chosen by the Assembly in July 2003. Once the prescribed three-year waiting period had elapsed, the independence referendum was set for 21 May 2006. The EU, which was supervising the poll, stipulated that a minimum 55% 'yes' vote, on a turnout of at least 50%, was necessary to approve independence: the result just passed this threshold, with 55.5% in favour (on a healthy 86% turnout). Independence was duly declared on 3 June 2006. Two days later the Serbian **National Assembly** proclaimed that the Republic of Serbia was the successor state to the Union of Serbia and Montenegro, and the Union bodies were dissolved. The Serbian Government officially recognized Montenegro's independence 10 days later.

At the 10 September 2006 elections the DPSCG-led **Coalition for a European Montenegro** retained a small majority with 41 out of 81 seats (and 48.6% of the vote). The Serbian List, led by the SNS, finished second with 12 seats (14.7% of the vote), just ahead of the coalition of the SNPCG, NS and Democratic Serb Party, with 11 seats (14.1%), and the Movement for Changes, with 11 seats (13.1%). The Liberal Party of Montenegro (LPCG—a splinter from the LSCG, now itself defunct) in alliance with the Bosniak Party won three seats (3.8%), and one seat each went to the DSCG, DUA and Albanian Alternative. Đukanović announced that he would not remain as Prime Minister, as he wished to develop his business interests (although he would remain leader of the DPSCG). (Đukanović had been accused of involvement with organized crime, and was under investigation by the Italian authorities, mainly in connection with large-scale illicit tobacco trade in the Balkans.) On 10 November Željko Šturanović was approved as Prime Minister.

On 2 April 2007 the Assembly approved a new draft Constitution, although debate continued for several months thereafter over the alternative options for state symbols, official languages and religious communities. The new Constitution, finally approved on 19 October and promulgated three days later, was denounced by Serbian parties as discriminating against Serbs. (In particular, Montenegrin replaced Serbian as the main official language.)

On 31 January 2008 Prime Minister Šturanović resigned due to ill health. A week later Đukanović was nominated to resume the premiership, and was approved on 29 February. (His return to office gave him immunity from prosecution, although the criminal investigation continued.)

Vujanović was re-elected to the presidency on 6 April 2008, securing 52.3% of the vote—well ahead of second-placed Andrija Mandić of the Serbian List on 19.3%. Vujanović was inaugurated on 21 May.

Latest elections: Đukanović called early elections for 29 March 2009. He claimed that he needed a fresh mandate before pushing through major economic reforms, whereas the opposition accused him of holding the poll before the global economic crisis could bite any deeper. The result was that the DPSCG-led Coalition for a

European Montenegro increased its majority, winning 48 seats (and 52% of the vote). The SNPCG reclaimed its position as the largest opposition party with 16 seats (16.8% of the vote), while Mandić's New Serb Democracy won eight seats (9.2%), the Movement for Changes won five seats (6%) and four Albanian minority seats went to the DUA, the new FORCA party, the Albanian List coalition and the Albanian Coalition—Perspective.

Recent developments: Formation of Đukanović's new Government took several months, as leading figures within the DPSCG jostled for prominence, looking ahead to becoming the successor to Đukanović. A largely unchanged Government was finally announced in early June. Đukanović later intimated that he would step down in 2010, so long as Montenegro was firmly on the path towards membership of the EU and NATO.

International relations and defence: Montenegro's gradual and negotiated progression to independence had the benefit that, within two weeks of the formal declaration on 3 June 2006, recognition of the new state had been extended by Serbia, its other Balkan neighbours, the EU and all the permanent members of the UN Security Council. Montenegro was admitted to the **Organization for Security and Co-operation in Europe** on 22 June and to the UN as the 192nd member on 28 June. On 14 December, Montenegro was one of the new entrants to NATO's **Partnership for Peace** programme, the first step towards its ambition for full NATO membership. Two years later it joined the **Adriatic Charter** to help advance its case for accession. In 2007 it also joined the **World Bank, International Monetary Fund** and **Council of Europe**.

A Stabilization and Association Agreement was initialled with the EU on 15 March 2007, and signed in October once the country's new Constitution had been adopted. Montenegro officially submitted a full EU membership application on 15 December 2008.

Montenegro did not immediately recognize Kosovo when it declared independence from Serbia on 17 February 2008, fearing this might endanger national security. Recognition was finally extended in October. A dispute over the maritime border between Montenegro and Croatia has been referred to the **International Court of Justice** at The Hague for resolution.

Following independence, a Ministry of Defence was created with responsibility for the former Union's military units within Montenegrin territory. Montenegro's defence budget for 2008 amounted to some US $71m., equivalent to about 2.3% of GDP. The size of the armed forces in 2010 was some 3,000 personnel. Conscription was abolished in 2006.

Montenegro, economy

The transition from communist-era central control was badly damaged by the regional conflicts of the 1990s and UN sanctions and embargoes. Tourism and foreign investment subsequently spurred several years of growth, but the 'grey' economy remains large and organized crime is widespread.

GNP: US $4,008m. (2008); *GNP per capita*: $6,440 (2008); *GDP at PPP*: US $8,682m. (2008); *GDP per capita at PPP*: $14,000 (2008); *real GDP growth*: –4.0% (2009 estimate); *exports*: $827m. (2007); *imports*: $3,206m. (2007); *currency*: euro (US $1 = €0.7129 in mid-2009); *unemployment*: 11% (2009); *government deficit as a percentage of GDP*: 3% (2009); *inflation*: 3.4% (2009).

In 2007 industry accounted for 18% of GDP, agriculture for 8% and services for 74%. Around 27% of the workforce is engaged in industry, 2% in agriculture and 71% in services.

The main crops are maize, wheat, vegetables and fruit.

Mineral resources include brown coal (lignite), red bauxite and sea salt. Industries include machine-building, metallurgy, mining, chemical goods and consumer goods.

The principal exports are manufactured goods, while the main imports are machinery and transport equipment, and fuels and lubricants. The principal purchasers of Montenegro's exports in 2008 were Italy (24%), **Serbia** (23%) and **Greece** (22%). The main suppliers of Montenegro's imports in 2008 were Serbia (32%), Italy (8%) and **Slovenia** (7%).

While Montenegro was still part of the Federal Republic of Yugoslavia (FRY), its Government began distancing the economy from the Serbian regime under Slobodan **Milošević**. It adopted the Deutsche Mark as the official currency in November 1999, in place of the Yugoslav dinar, which had recently plummeted in value; this was replaced in turn by the euro in January 2002. It forged ahead with a mass privatization programme, and 50% of the sector had been privatized by 2003. The dissolution of the FRY that year in favour of a looser union of the two republics officially gave Montenegro control over most of its economic affairs.

Following independence in June 2006, Montenegro joined the **International Monetary Fund** (IMF) and **World Bank** in January 2007. The following September it joined the **Central European Free Trade Agreement** (CEFTA), and in October signed a Stabilization and Association Agreement with the **European Union** (EU); the country submitted its application for EU membership in December 2008. Key EU requirements are the restructuring of the remaining public enterprises prior to privatization, improvement of state administration, and implementation of measures to combat endemic corruption, the 'black' market and organized crime.

High GDP growth of 8.6% was achieved in 2006, rising again to 10.7% in 2007, based largely on capital growth and massive inflows of foreign direct investment, particularly in the tourism, banking and construction sectors. Unemployment was nearly halved during these boom years, from 20% in 2005 to 11% in 2008. Global economic slowdown affected tourism and foreign investment from 2008, however, and GDP contracted by around 4% in 2009, while unemployment started to rise again. High wage increases were also affecting the country's competitiveness, although businesses are attracted by the region's lowest corporate tax rate (9%).

Montenegro Stock Exchange
Montenegroberza

The stock exchange in **Montenegro**, established in June 1993 with a licence for trading from the Federal Ministry of Finance. As of March 2010, it had 25 members.
Director General: Dejana Šuškavčević.
Address: Moskovska 77, 81000 Podgorica.
Telephone: (20) 228502.
Fax: (20) 228502.
E-mail: mberza@t-com.me
Internet: www.montenegroberza.com

Moravia

One of the two ancient states which in combination form the modern **Czech Republic**, the other being **Bohemia**. Moravia, now the south-eastern third of the republic, was an important early medieval **central European** kingdom. At its maximum expansion, the Great Moravian kingdom occupied all of neighbouring Bohemia, southern **Poland** and the western Pannonian plain of modern **Hungary**, as well as the **Slovak** lands in between. King Rostislav greatly influenced the future of the region when he invited the renowned Byzantine missionaries, Saints Cyril and Methodius, to convert his people to Christianity in 864. The resulting Slavic liturgy won the enthusiastic approval of the Pope in Rome, encouraging the Moravians to adopt **Roman Catholicism** and to introduce the Latin script to transcribe their language—somewhat ironically, since it was the other great achievement of the mission to create the modified Greek script known as **Cyrillic**, which was adopted by the south **Slavs** along with Byzantine **Orthodox Christianity**.

Moravia was absorbed into the kingdom of Bohemia from 1029 and has remained tied to its western neighbour ever since, though it retained a distinct relationship with the Habsburg Austrian overlords who dominated the region from 1526 onwards. It ceased to exist as a separate administrative region in 1949 under the communist regime. On the disintegration of **Czechoslovakia** in 1993 Moravia was included in the Czech Republic without question.

Mostar

A historic town in south-eastern **Bosnia and Herzegovina**, traditionally the capital of **Herzegovina** and now in the **Croat**-dominated canton of **Herceg-Bosna**. *Population*: 111,198 (2007 estimate). The town's single-span stone bridge, after which it was named (from the Serbo-Croat word *most* meaning bridge), was constructed over the River Neretva in 1566 by Ottoman engineers, and was one of the former **Yugoslavia**'s most celebrated historic monuments. The bridge was destroyed during heavy bombardment by Croat forces during the Bosnian war in November 1993. Its destruction, after months of brutal fighting between local Muslims and Croats in a town formerly famed for its multiculturalism, was a heavy symbolic blow to the ideal of inter-ethnic harmony. The city became the base of a briefly revived separate Croat state during 2001. The bridge has now been rebuilt.

Movement for Rights and Freedoms
Dvizhenie za Prava i Svobodi (DPS)

The main political formation representing the **Muslim** ethnic **Bulgarian Turks** in **Bulgaria**, and a member of the **Liberal International**. It was part of successive coalition governments in 2001–09 but is currently in opposition.

The policies of compulsory assimilation practised in the 1980s by the communist regime, resulting in the flight of many ethnic Turks to Turkey and elsewhere, formed the background to the DPS's aims on its creation in January 1990. These aims included full political, cultural and religious rights, but excluded any fundamentalist or separatist objectives. In the June 1990 **National Assembly** elections the DPS won 23 of the 400 seats at issue with 6% of the national vote. From December 1990 it participated in a national unity coalition under a non-party Prime Minister, together with the dominant **Bulgarian Socialist Party** (BSP) and the Union of Democratic Forces (SDS). In further elections in October 1991 the DPS improved its position, winning 24 of 240 seats with 7.6% of the vote.

From November 1991 the DPS gave crucial parliamentary backing to a minority SDS administration, being rewarded with the lifting of a ban on optional Turkish-language instruction in secondary schools. But the SDS Government's subsequent pro-market policies were described as 'blue fascism' by the DPS, which withdrew its support in September 1992, thereby precipitating the Government's fall in October. After the BSP had failed to fill the political vacuum, the DPS successfully nominated a non-party Prime Minister (Lyuben Berov) to head a 'Government of experts' which included semi-official DPS representation. In 1993 the DPS backed the Berov Government but was weakened by internal dissension and by continuing emigration of ethnic Turks. Since this time the party has attempted to broaden its support base among Bulgaria's other non-**Slavic** minority groups, principally the Muslim **Pomaks**.

In March 1994, after Berov had suffered a heart attack, DPS Deputy Premier Evgeni Matinchev (an ethnic **Bulgarian**) briefly became acting Prime Minister.

Weakened by the launching of the breakaway Party of Democratic Change (PDP) in 1994, the DPS slipped to 5.4% of the vote and 15 seats out of 240 in the December elections, therefore reverting to opposition status. It recovered to 8.2% of the vote nationally in municipal elections in October 1995, thereafter backing the successful candidacy of Petar Stoyanov of the SDS in the autumn 1996 presidential elections. Prior to the April 1997 legislative elections, the DPS's decision not to join the SDS-led United Democratic Forces (ODS) caused a pro-SDS faction to form the breakaway National Movement for Rights and Freedoms. For the elections the rump DPS headed the Union for National Salvation (ONS), including the Green Party and the New Choice Union, which won 19 seats on a 7.6% vote share. In opposition, the DPS in July 1998 participated in the launching of the four-party Liberal Democratic Alliance, while in January 2000 the PDP rejoined the DPS.

At the head of an alliance with the Liberal Union and Euroroma, the DPS retained a 7.5% share of the vote in legislative elections in June 2001, and was again allocated 19 seats in the Assembly. When the ODS refused to take part in a coalition with the overwhelming victors of the poll, the newly-formed National Movement Simeon II, the Prime Minister-designate Simeon Saxecoburggotski turned to the DPS to provide the overall majority his movement needed in the Assembly. For the first time in its history the DPS was directly part of the Government, gaining two seats in the cabinet.

In the June 2005 election the DPS improved its position to 34 seats (14.1%), becoming the third-largest bloc. BSP leader Sergey Stanishev was nominated as Prime Minister in mid-July, but later that month his proposed KzB–DPS cabinet was rejected by the Assembly. Saxecoburggotski, as head of the second-placed party, was given the next mandate, though he struggled to form a coalition. With pressure mounting for a government to take office in order to carry though the reforms needed to achieve EU membership, a cabinet headed by Stanishev and comprising members of the BSP, NDS II, DPS and an independent took office in mid-August.

In the July 2009 elections the DPS won 38 seats, including five of the new constituency seats (with 14.5% of the vote). Again this made it the third-largest bloc behind the new centre-right **Citizens for European Development of Bulgaria** (GERB) and the BSP-led **Coalition for Bulgaria**. (A February 2010 ruling from the Constitutional Court on electoral violations adjusted the results, reducing the DPS to 37 seats.) GERB leader Boiko **Borisov** formed a minority Government with backing from the small right-wing parties, and the DPS returned to opposition.

Leadership: Ahmed Dogan (Pres.).

Address: Bul. Al. Stamboliyski 45A, 1301 Sofia.

Telephone: (2) 8114466.

Fax: (2) 8114460.

E-mail: info@dps.bg

Internet: www.dps.bg

Movement of Social Democrats EDEK
Kinima Socialdimokraton–Eniaia Dimokratiki Enosi Kyprou
(KISOS–EDEK)

A left-of-centre **Greek Cypriot** party in **Cyprus**, a member of the **Socialist International**, and currently in opposition, having left the ruling coalition in February 2010. The party was founded by Vassos Lyssarides in 1969 as the United Democratic Union of Cyprus (EDEK) and opted to retain the familiar EDEK suffix in its title after it became the broader Movement of Social Democrats in 2000.

Having supported the return to power of President **Makarios** in late 1974, EDEK participated in the 1976 elections in a pro-Makarios alliance with the centre-right **Democratic Party** (DIKO) and the left-wing **Progressive Party for the Working People** (AKEL), winning four seats. In subsequent parliamentary elections, its best result was seven seats in 1991, while Lyssarides's highest vote in three attempts at the presidency was 10.6% in 1998.

In the second round of the 1988 presidential elections, EDEK supported the successful AKEL-backed independent candidate, George Vassiliou. Thereafter, however, EDEK quickly came to oppose President Vassiliou's more accommodating line in inter-communal talks, making common cause with DIKO against AKEL and the conservative **Democratic Rally** (DISY). In the 1993 presidential elections, EDEK and DIKO presented a joint candidate, Paschalis Paschalides, who obtained only 18.6% in the first round. In the second round, EDEK backed Glafcos Clerides of DISY, who was narrowly victorious over Vassiliou. Clerides' re-election in 1998 was followed by the appointment of a national unity Government in which EDEK was given two portfolios. However, EDEK withdrew from this Government in January 1999 in protest against the President's decision to abandon a plan to deploy Russian-made surface-to-air missiles in Cyprus.

In the 2001 parliamentary elections, EDEK slipped to four seats, whereupon Lyssarides resigned as party leader and was succeeded by Yiannakis Omirou. In February 2003 EDEK joined with AKEL in backing the successful presidential candidacy of Tassos Papadopoulos of DIKO, becoming part of the subsequent three-party coalition Government. EDEK strongly opposed the UN settlement plan decisively rejected by Greek Cypriot voters in April 2004. In the May 2006 parliamentary elections, EDEK advanced to five seats out of 56 with 8.9% of the vote.

EDEK initially supported Papadopoulos in his bid for re-election as President in February 2008, but his elimination in the first round left AKEL General Secretary Dimitris **Christofias** as the party's preferred candidate in the run-off against the DISY front-runner Ioannis Kasoulidis. Following the victory of Christofias, EDEK was included in his new Government. However, it opposed Christofias's pro-unification negotiations and some of his other policies, and eventually decided to withdraw from the Government in February 2010.

Leadership: Yiannakis Omirou (President).
Address: 4th Floor, 40 Byron Avenue, PO Box 21064, 1096 Nicosia.
Telephone: (22) 670121.
Fax: (22) 678894.
E-mail: socialdimokrates@cytanet.com.cy
Internet: www.edek.org.cy

Mrkonjič Grad

A town in the western half of what is now the **Serb Republic**, in west-central **Bosnia and Herzegovina**, the site of mass killings of ethnic **Serbs** at the hands of **Croat** forces during the Bosnian civil war. The town is an important administrative centre in the region of **Banja Luka** and is of such strategic value that it was 'liberated' 39 times as fighting flowed back and forth during the Second World War.

The town fell to Croatian forces on 10 October 1995 during the successful Operation Storm. Although most of the Serb population fled, around 220 people were killed by Croat forces and buried in a mass grave.

MSE *see* **Macedonian Stock Exchange**.

MSzP *see* **Hungarian Socialist Party**.

MTI *see* **Hungarian News Agency**.

Mujezinović, Mustafa

Prime Minister of the **Muslim-Croat Federation** in **Bosnia and Herzegovina**.

Mustafa Mujezinović was born on 27 December 1954 in **Sarajevo**. He graduated in electrical engineering from the University of Sarajevo in 1978, and then joined Energoinvest Sarajevo, rising from being a constructor up to Sales Manager and Member of the Board by the early 1990s. In 1995 he became Mayor of the Municipality of Stari Grad Sarajevo, the following year was appointed the first Prime Minister of the Sarajevo Canton, and from 1998 to 2000 was the canton's Governor. In 2000 he was appointed Bosnia's ambassador to the **Organization for Security and Co-operation in Europe**, then directed the Prevent Invest Privatization Fund in 2002–04. After that he spent four years as ambassador to Malaysia, before returning to Bosnia as Adviser to the Management of the Development Bank of the Federation. He was nominated as Federation Prime Minister on 11 June, and his appointment was approved two weeks later.

Address: Office of the Prime Minister, Alipašina 41, 71000 Sarajevo.
Telephone: (33) 650457.
Fax: (33) 664816.
E-mail: info@fbihvlada.gov.ba
Internet: www.fbihvlada.gov.ba

Muslim-Croat Federation
Federacija Bosne i Hercegovine (FBiH)

The autonomous **Bosniak** and Bosnian **Croat** entity within **Bosnia and Herzegovina**.
It is formally, if confusingly, known simply as the Federation of Bosnia and
Herzegovina. Bordered to the north and east by Bosnia's **Serb Republic** and to the
south along the **Dalmatian** coast by **Croatia**, it forms a rough triangle of land with its
north-eastern point near the town of **Brčko**. The Federation was established during
the Bosnian conflict of 1992–95, by the Washington Accords agreed on 18 March
1994, sealing an alliance between Bosniak and Croat forces. Under the **Dayton
Agreement** of December 1995 the Federation was formalized alongside the Serb
Republic in the current loose confederal arrangement. The Federation is a loose
framework of eight cantons—four Bosniak, two Croat (**Herzegovina**) and two multi-
ethnic—with its capital at **Sarajevo**. The strength of the Federation was tested in
2001 when Bosnian Croats in Herzegovina briefly established a separate state.

Muslim peoples

People who have embraced Islam, including over 20 ethnic groups in **eastern
Europe**. Islam is the second-largest religion in the world with over 1,500m.
adherents. It is divided into two main denominations, the majority Sunni and the
smaller Shi'a sect. The biggest populations of Muslims in Europe can be found in the
Balkans, in southern European Russia and the Caucasus. Islam was brought to these
regions by the invading Turkic peoples in the 14th century and, although their
political power was shattered by the early 20th century, their religious legacy has
been the source of ethnic tensions into the 21st century, and a significant element in
conflicts in **Bosnia and Herzegovina**, Chechnya, Dagestan and **Macedonia**. The
wide variety of languages, and intermingling of Muslim with non-Muslim peoples,
dilutes pan-Islamic sentiment among European Muslims, but such sentiment is
nevertheless significant, notably in the Caucasus, where it has heightened since the
start of the war in Afghanistan in 2001 and the 2003 US-led invasion of Iraq.

The only majority Muslim independent states in Europe (not including Turkey
which lies mostly in Asia) are Azerbaijan (94% Muslim), **Kosovo** (92%) and **Albania**
(70%). Ethnic groups in eastern Europe with a majority of Muslim followers include
Albanians, Bosniaks, Bulgarian Turks and **Pomaks**.

N

NACC

The North Atlantic Co-operation Council, replaced in 1997 by the **Euro-Atlantic Partnership Council**.

Nagy, Imre

Hungarian reformist premier during the 1956 revolution. Born in 1896, Nagy was in Russia as a prisoner of war at the time of the 1917 revolution there. He fought in the Russian civil war as a communist party member, returning to Hungary in the 1920s but then going back to the **Soviet Union**, and working there until the Red Army liberated his native country in 1944. He was briefly Agriculture Minister, then Interior Minister (until February 1946), but became a critic of the agricultural collectivization programme, and was expelled from the Politburo in 1949. Nagy escaped further punishment in the purges, however; he returned to government in 1951, and was made Prime Minister in July 1953 at the urging of the Soviet leadership, charged with improving living standards in an attempt to mitigate the unpopularity of the regime of Mátyás Rákosi. Ousted in April 1955, he retired to write and then advocate a 'revisionist' alternative to the Stalinism of Rákosi. In the dramatic conditions of October 1956 he was recalled to office by a hard-line leadership hoping to harness his popularity. His declaration of Hungarian neutrality hastened the Soviet invasion which crushed the attempted Hungarian uprising. Nagy's arrest, secret trial and June 1958 execution made him a potent martyr figure. His ceremonial reburial in June 1989 was attended by some 200,000 mourners.

Národná Rada *see* **National Council of the Republic of Slovakia**.

Narodna Skupština *see* **National Assembly of the Republic of Serbia**.

Narodna Sabranie *see* **National Assembly (Bulgaria)**.

Narva

A town in the far north-east of **Estonia** on the border with the **Russian Federation**. *Population*: 66,712 (2007 estimate). As with much of the industrialized north-east of Estonia, Narva is home to a large ethnic Russian population. The town is of major importance to the regional economy, providing access to the Gulf of Finland for the Russian hinterland. As such, it has been dominated through the centuries by the Swedish and Russian Empires, and was secured for the latter by Peter the Great in 1704. Since the mid-19th century the town has been a major centre for cotton textiles. The River Narva came to form the border between the Russian Federation and Estonia in the 20th century, placing most of the town in the Estonian republic, but leaving the **Jaanilinn** district in the Leningrad (St Petersburg) oblast. On Estonia's independence in 1991 the majority Russian inhabitants of Narva voted for regional autonomy in a ballot deemed illegal by the Estonian authorities.

NASDAQ OMX Rīga

The stock exchange in **Latvia**, now owned by NASDAQ OMX. The Rīga Stock Exchange was founded originally in 1816, and reopened after the communist period in December 1993. Trading began in July 1995. It has been intimately involved in the privatization process and most of the companies listed have emerged from this process. On 1 January 2009 the Rīga Stock Exchange renamed itself NASDAQ OMX Rīga. It had 31 members in 2009. NASDAQ OMX Baltic comprises the stock exchanges and central depositories of **Estonia**, Latvia and **Lithuania**.

Chair. of the Management Board: Daiga Auziņa-Melalksne.
Address: Vaļņu iela 1, Rīga 1050.
Telephone: (6) 7212431.
Fax: (6) 7229411.
E-mail: riga@nasdaqomx.com
Internet: www.nasdaqomxbaltic.com

NASDAQ OMX Tallinn

The stock exchange in **Estonia**, now owned by NASDAQ OMX. The Tallinn Stock Exchange was originally founded in 1920 during Estonia's brief inter-war period of independence. It was relaunched in 1995 after the collapse of the **Soviet Union**, and trading began in May 1996. In 2009 it was renamed NASDAQ OMX Tallinn. It had 33 members in 2009. NASDAQ OMX Baltic comprises the stock exchanges and central depositories of Estonia, **Latvia** and **Lithuania**.

Chair. of the Management Board: Andrus Alber.
Address: Tartu mnt. 2, Tallinn 10145.

321

Telephone: 6408800.
Fax: 6408801.
E-mail: tallinn@nasdaqomx.com
Internet: www.nasdaqomxbaltic.com

NASDAQ OMX Vilnius

The stock exchange in **Lithuania**, now owned by NASDAQ OMX. The Vilnius Stock Exchange was founded in September 1993. In 2009 it renamed itself NASDAQ OMX Vilnius. It had 35 members in 2009. NASDAQ OMX Baltic comprises the stock exchanges and central depositories of **Estonia**, **Latvia** and Lithuania.

Chair. of the Management Board: Arminta Saladžienė.
Address: Konstitucijos pr. 7, 15A, Europa Business Centre, Vilnius 08501.
Telephone: (5) 2723871.
Fax: (5) 2724894.
E-mail: vilnius@nasdaqomx.com
Internet: www.nasdaqomxbaltic.com

National Agency for Privatization
Agjencia Kombetare e Privatizimit (AKP)

The agency in **Albania** established in 1992 under the Council of Ministers, charged with proposing and preparing the legal framework for the privatization of state-owned assets (*see* **Albania, economy**).

Gen. Director: Kozeta Fino.
Address: Bul. Dëshmorët e Kombit, Tirana.
Telephone: (4) 257457.
Fax: (4) 227933.

National Assembly (Bulgaria)
Narodno Sabranie

The unicameral legislature of **Bulgaria**. It has 240 members, directly elected for a four-year term. The last elections were held 5 July 2009.

Address: Narodno Sabranie Square 2, 1169 Sofia.
Telephone: (2) 93939.
Fax: (2) 981313.
E-mail: infocenter@parliament.bg
Internet: www.parliament.bg

National Assembly (Hungary)
Országgyűlés

The unicameral legislature of **Hungary**. It has 386 members, directly elected for a four-year term. The complex electoral system involves 210 proportionally-allocated seats and 176 single-member constituencies. The last elections were held on 11 and 25 April 2010.

Address: Országgyűlés, Kossuth tér 1–3, 1055 Budapest.
Telephone: (1) 4414000.
Fax: (1) 4415972.
E-mail: ktk@parlament.hu
Internet: www.mkogy.hu

National Assembly (Poland)
Zgromadzenie Narodowe

The bicameral legislature of **Poland**, comprising the Diet (Sejm) and the Senate (Senat). The lower Diet has 460 members, directly elected for a four-year term by a complex system of proportional representation subject to a 5% threshold. The upper Senate has 100 members, directly elected for a four-year term by a majority vote on a provincial basis. The last elections were held on 21 October 2007.

Address of lower house: Sejm, ul. Wiejska 4/6/8, 00902 Warsaw.
Telephone: (22) 6942500.
Fax: (22) 6941863.
E-mail: zjablon@sejm.gov.pl
Internet: www.sejm.gov.pl

Address of upper house: Senat, ul. Wiejska 4/6/8, 00902 Warsaw.
Telephone: (22) 6942410.
Fax: (22) 6942224.
E-mail: senat@nw.senat.gov.pl
Internet: www.senat.gov.pl

National Assembly (Slovenia)
Državni Zbor

The unicameral legislature of **Slovenia**. It has 90 members, directly elected for a four-year term. The last election was held on 21 September 2008. A National Council (Državni Svet), with 40 indirectly-elected members, has an advisory role and its nature and status are under discussion. The last election was held on 21–22 November 2007.

National Assembly of the Republic of Serbia

Address: Državni Zbor, Šubičeva 4, 1000 Ljubljana.
Telephone: (1) 4789400.
Fax: (1) 4789845.
E-mail: info@dz-rs.si
Internet: www.dz-rs.si

National Assembly of the Republic of Serbia
Narodna Skupština Republike Srbije

The unicameral legislature of **Serbia**. It has 250 members, directly elected for a four-year term. The last elections were held on 11 May 2008.
Address: Narodna Skupština, Kralja Milana 14, 11000 Belgrade.
Telephone: 113222001.
Internet: www.parlament.sr.gov.rs

National Bank of Hungary
Magyar Nemzeti Bank (MNB)

The central bank of **Hungary**. The first Hungarian central bank was formed in 1848–49 during a brief period of revolutionary autonomy from the Habsburg Empire. It was resurrected at the end of the First World War after the collapse of the Empire, and the Royal Hungarian State Bank was transformed into the National Bank of Hungary in June 1924. The national currency, the forint, was introduced by the MNB in August 1946. Under communist rule the country's banking system was effectively nationalized, but a two-tier system was reintroduced in January 1987, with commercial banks being separated from the MNB. The political independence of the Bank was reasserted in October 1991. The MNB's role as a supervisor of the banking sector was restricted by new legislation in 1997, leaving it mainly in control of monetary policy. As of December 2007, the Bank had reserves of 81,364m. forint.
President: András Simor.
Address: Szabadság tér 8–9, 1850 Budapest.
Telephone: (1) 4282600.
Fax: (1) 4282500.
E-mail: info@mnb.hu
Internet: www.mnb.hu

National Bank of Macedonia
Narodna Banka na Republika Makedonija (NBRM)

Established as a central bank in April 1992, following **Macedonia**'s secession from the **Socialist Federal Republic of Yugoslavia**. The Bank is charged with maintaining the stability of the domestic currency (the denar), ensuring liquidity in the economy and supervising the functioning of the banking system. Although the National Bank is independent of the Government, it is the latter that sets the nation's major economic objectives, such as inflation and growth targets. However, the Bank is free to undertake monetary measures and determine the monetary instruments necessary to achieve these goals. As of December 2007, the Bank had reserves of 7,971.0m. new Macedonian denars.

Governor: Petar Goshev.
Address: POB 401, Kompleks banki b.b., 1000 Skopje.
Telephone: (2) 3108203.
Fax (2) 3124054.
E-mail: governorsoffice@nbrm.gov.mk
Internet: www.nbrm.gov.mk

National Bank of Poland
Narodowy Bank Polski (NBP)

The central bank of **Poland**. A centralized bank for Poland first came into being under Russian rule in 1828 in that part of the country which **Russia** had incorporated in recent partitions. This Bank of Poland began issuing złotys in 1830. Between 1885 and the First World War the Bank was subsumed into the Russian State Bank but it was reborn in the independent Poland of the inter-war period. The eventual National Bank of Poland was constituted in January 1945 from the various institutions created by the puppet governments of the Second World War, and złotys were reintroduced that year. From the beginning the Bank was subordinate to the Government and from 1948 it oversaw the country's transition to a planned economy. A two-tier, market-economy banking system did not reappear until the late 1980s. A revalued new złoty was introduced in 1995. The role of the Bank was last revised in the Act on the NBP adopted in August 1997. In its new role it governs monetary policy and regulates the banking industry. As of December 2006, the Bank held reserves of 943m. new złotys.

President: vacant.
Address: ul. Świętokrzyska 11/21, POB 1011, 00919 Warsaw.
Telephone: (22) 6531000.
Fax: (22) 6208518.
E-mail: nbp@nbp.pl
Internet: www.nbp.pl

National Bank of Romania
Banca Naţională a României (BNR)

The central bank of **Romania**. The BNR predates Romanian independence and was first established in 1880. On its creation it took over the running of the national currency, the leu, whose regulation remains a primary function for the Bank. After 1945 the Bank operated within a single-tier system but was released and charged with steering the country to a market economy in 1990. The BNR enjoys a large amount of autonomy but works closely with the **Parliament of Romania**. As of December 2007, the Bank held reserves of 670.8m. lei.

Governor: Mugur Constantin Isărescu.
Address: Str. Lipscani 25, 030031 Bucharest.
Telephone: (21) 3130410.
Fax: (21) 3123831.
E-mail: info@bnro.ro
Internet: www.bnro.ro

National Bank of Serbia
Narodna Banka Srbije (NBS)

The central bank of **Serbia**. A central bank for the newly independent Kingdom of Serbia was first founded in **Belgrade** in 1884. It was transformed in to a central financial institution for the Kingdom of Serbs, Croats and Slovenes in 1920. Freeing itself from reliance on foreign printers the Bank began printing dinars in 1927. During the Second World War the Bank operated in exile in London, but returned to Belgrade in 1944. It became the National Bank of Yugoslavia (NBJ) in 1945 and it was nationalized the following year with the creation of the **Socialist Federal Republic of Yugoslavia**. Reconstituted as an independent central bank in 1992, it controlled monetary policy and regulated the banking sector, but the Federal Assembly appointed the Governor and set the exchange rate of the dinar. In 2003, following the reconstitution of the Federal Republic of Yugoslavia as the State Union of Serbia and Montenegro, the NBJ became Serbia's central bank, and was renamed the National Bank of Serbia. As of December 2007, the Bank held reserves of 7,692m. dinars.

Governor: Radovan Jelašić.
Address: Kralja Petra 12, POB 1010, 11000 Belgrade.
Telephone: (11) 3027100.
Fax: (11) 3027113.
E-mail: kabinet@nbs.rs
Internet: www.nbs.rs

National Bank of Slovakia
Národná Banka Slovenska (NBS)

The central bank of **Slovakia**. The NBS was founded on 1 January 1993 following the dissolution of **Czechoslovakia** and the emergence of a separate Slovakian state. Its main functions are to supervise monetary policy and regulate the country's banking industry. It is independent of the Government although the Bank's Governor is appointed by the President. The koruna was introduced in August 1993. As of December 2007, the Bank had reserves of –91,270m. koruny.

Governor: Jozef Makúch.
Address: Imricha Karvaša 1, 813 25 Bratislava.
Telephone: (2) 57871111.
Fax: (2) 57871100.
E-mail: webmaster@nbs.sk
Internet: www.nbs.sk

National Council of the Republic of Slovakia
Národná Rada Slovenskej Republiky

The unicameral legislature of **Slovakia**. It has 150 members, directly elected for a four-year term. The last elections were held on 17 June 2006.

Address: Národná Rada, Nám. Alexander Dubčeka 1, 812 80 Bratislava.
Telephone: (2) 59341111.
Fax: (2) 54415324.
E-mail: info@nrsr.sk
Internet: www.nrsr.sk

National Liberal Party
Partidul Naţional Liberal (PNL)

A centre-right political formation in **Romania**, currently in opposition, affiliated to the **Liberal International**. Dating originally from 1848 and founded as a party in 1875, it has its roots in 19th-century liberalism, and favours the restoration of the **Romanian royal family** deposed in 1947. The PNL ceased to function in 1947 following the communist takeover and was revived in January 1990 after the fall of the **Ceauşescu** regime. The party came third in the May 1990 **Parliament** elections, winning 29 House of Deputies seats on a 6.4% vote share, and in 1992 was briefly a member of the broad centre-right Democratic Convention of Romania (CDR) before most of the PNL withdrew because of policy differences. In the same year the exiled King Michael declined nomination as the PNL presidential candidate.

In 1993–94 the party went through a lengthy leadership struggle from which Mircea Ionescu-Quintus emerged as Chairman, following which some dissident PNL elements rejoined the party. The PNL re-entered the CDR for the November 1996 elections, backing the successful presidential candidacy of Emil Constantinescu (CDR) and winning 25 House seats under the CDR banner. The party became a component of the resultant CDR-led coalition Government, although frequent strains with other CDR components were accompanied by internal divisions and defections, notably over the choice of a presidential candidate for 2000.

In the event, the PNL contested the November–December 2000 elections outside the CDR and therefore escaped the obliteration of the latter by an electorate experiencing economic and social deterioration. The party's presidential candidate, Theodor Stolojan, came third in the first round with 11.8% of the vote, while in the parliamentary contest the PNL advanced to 30 House seats on a vote share of 6.9%. It thereafter gave qualified external support, although without great enthusiasm within the party, to a minority Government of the Social Democratic Pole of Romania (whose two main constituent parties later formed the **Social Democratic Party**— PSD). In February 2001 a PNL congress elected former Justice Minister Valeriu Stoica as party Chairman in succession to Ionescu-Quintus, but in August 2002 he in turn was succeeded by Stolojan. The next couple of years saw the PNL absorb the Alliance for Romania, the Union of Rightist Forces and the remaining dissident Liberal factions that had split off in the late 1990s. Stolojan resigned in October 2004 due to health reasons, and Călin Popescu-Tăriceanu took over as PNL Chairman.

The PNL contested the November 2004 elections in the Justice and Truth Alliance (ADA) with the Democratic Party (PD). It finished in second place with 112 seats (64 PNL, 48 PD) and 31.5% of the vote. In the simultaneous Senate elections it also became the second-largest bloc, with 49 seats (31.8% of the vote). In the presidential election it supported PD leader Traian **Băsescu**, standing as the candidate of the ADA, who overtook PSD Prime Minister Adrian Năstase in the second round to secure election. In late December Popescu-Tăriceanu negotiated a coalition of his PNL, PD, **Hungarian Democratic Union of Romania** (UDMR) and Humanist Party of Romania (PUR), even though the PUR had contested the election as part of the PSD-led alliance. His Government, commanding just one seat more than the minimum required in Parliament to secure approval, took office on 28 December. Its main programme was to continue to push through reforms required by the EU as prerequisites to Romanian membership. The Constitutional Court blocked a judicial reform package in July 2005, prompting Popescu-Tăriceanu to offer his Government's resignation; however, Parliament rapidly passed an amended package to resolve the impasse.

In December 2006 the PUR, now renamed as the **Conservative Party** (PC), withdrew from the ruling coalition, reducing it to a minority Government. In the early months of 2007 tensions rose between Băsescu and Popescu-Tăriceanu, reaching a head at the start of April when Băsescu's PD was ejected from the ruling coalition. Popescu-Tăriceanu formed a new minority Government on 3 April between his PNL and the UDMR, with external backing from the PSD. On 19 April Parliament backed a motion to suspend Băsescu on grounds of unconstitutional conduct. However, in a national referendum on 19 May Băsescu's removal from office was opposed by three-quarters of voters. He was reinstated four days later.

At the November 2008 election the PNL (in alliance with the Christian Democratic National Peasants' Party—PNȚCD) dropped to third place, with 65 seats (18.6% of the vote) in the House of Deputies and 28 seats (18.7%) in the Senate. It did not join the new coalition Government headed by the **Democratic Liberal Party** (PD-L), a 2007 merger of the PD with the Liberal Democratic Party.

In March 2009 Crin Antonescu was chosen as PNL Chairman. He stood in the November presidential election, but won only 20% of the vote (in third place).

Leadership: Crin Antonescu (Chair.).
Address: blvd Aviatorilor 86, 011866 Bucharest.
Telephone: (21) 2310795.
Fax: (21) 2310796.
E-mail: dre@pnl.ro
Internet: www.pnl.ro

National Property Fund
Fond Národného Majetku (FNM)

Supervises the privatization process in **Slovakia**. Founded in 1993.
President: Peter Imko.
Address: Drieňová 27, 821 01 Bratislava.
Telephone: (2) 48271448.
Fax: (2) 48271484.
E-mail: fnm@natfund.gov.sk
Internet: www.natfund.gov.sk

National Regional Development Agency (NRDA)
Nacionaliné Regionų Plétros Agentūra

A public non-profit company owned by the Lithuanian Association of Chambers of Commerce, and partly state-funded. Established in 1999, it has grown to become one of the biggest consulting and technical assistance companies in the area of regional development in **Lithuania**.

Director: Vaidas Kazakevičius.
Address: Lukiskių g. 5/502, Vilnius 01108.
Telephone: (5) 2334151.
Fax: (5) 2334151.
E-mail: nrda@nrda.lt
Internet: www.nrda.lt

National Resurrection Party
Tautos Prisikėlimo Partija (TPP)

A new force which emerged in centre-right politics in **Lithuania** in 2008. Founded in May of that year by television show host Arūnas Valinskas, it won 16 seats in the October 2008 elections (with 15.1% of the vote), making it the third-largest party. It joined Andrius **Kubilius**'s coalition Government, and Valinskas was elected Speaker of **Parliament**, but he was dismissed from this post in September 2009 over allegations of links with organized crime.

Leadership: Arūnas Valinskas (Chair.).
Address: Pranciškonų g. 4A–10, Vilnius.
Telephone: (6) 7882816.
Fax: (5) 2400493.
E-mail: bustine@prisikelimopartija.lt
Website: www.prisikelimopartija.lt

National Unity Party
Ulusal Bırlık Partisi (UBP)

A conservative party in the self-proclaimed **Turkish Republic of Northern Cyprus** (TRNC), currently in government and holding the presidency, and generally seen as resisting most proposals for the reunification of the island.

The UBP was founded in 1976 by Rauf **Denktaş**, then leader of the **Turkish Cypriot** community, espousing the political principles of Kemal Atatürk, the founder of the modern Turkish state. It was consistently the largest Assembly party until 2003 and headed successive coalition governments during that time except for a period of opposition in 1994–96. Having been formally elected to the Turkish Cypriot presidency in 1976, Denktaş was re-elected in 1981 as the UBP candidate with 51.8% of the vote. Following the declaration of the TRNC in 1983, Denktaş was re-elected to the presidency in 1985 as the UBP candidate with 70.5% of the vote.

Standing as an independent, Denktaş was in 1990 re-elected TRNC President with 66.7% of the vote. Strains then intensified between Denktaş and UBP Prime Minister Derviş **Eroğlu**, who advocated the formal partition of Cyprus on the basis of the existing territorial division, whereas the President favoured further UN-sponsored talks. This divergence resulted in 1992 in the formation of the breakaway **Democrat Party** (DP), which included 10 former UBP deputies. The rump UBP remained the largest party in early elections in December 1993, but with only 17 seats out of 50 gave way to a coalition of the DP and the Republican Turkish Party (CTP, later renamed as **Republican Turkish Party–United Forces**, CTP-BG).

Eroğlu came in second place in the first round of TRNC presidential elections in 1995 (winning 24.2% of the vote), but was easily defeated in the second by Denktaş. In 1996 Eroğlu returned to the premiership, heading a coalition of the UBP and the

DP until the DP was replaced by the Communal Liberation Party (TKP) in 1999. In the April 2000 presidential elections Eroğlu again came second with 30.1% of the first-round vote. In November 2000 the UBP strongly backed Denktaş's decision to withdraw from UN-sponsored 'proximity' talks. Increasing strains with the pro-settlement TKP impelled the UBP to terminate the coalition in May 2001 and to form a new coalition with the DP. In April 2003 the UBP-DP Government took the decision to open the line of division (known as the **Green Line**) to freedom of movement.

Assembly elections in December 2003 reduced the UBP to second place, with 18 seats, whereupon it went into opposition to a coalition headed by the CTP-BG. It continued in opposition after early Assembly elections in February 2005, in which it advanced to 19 seats with 31.7% of the vote. In presidential elections in April 2005 Eroğlu again came second with 22.7%, behind Mehmet Ali **Talat** of the CTP-BG. In February 2006 Eroğlu stepped down from the UBP leadership, succeeded by Hüseyin **Özgürgün** and then Tahsin Ertuğruloğlu; however, he returned to the post in November 2008.

In the April 2009 legislative elections, the UBP secured 44.1% of the vote and a slim majority of 26 seats in the 50-member Assembly. Eroğlu returned as Prime Minister, naming a single-party Government on 5 May.

Eroğlu stood for the presidency again in April 2010, securing victory in the first round with 50.4% of the vote, ahead of Talat on 42.9% and five other candidates. He was inaugurated on 23 April. Özgürgün took over as acting Prime Minister.

Leadership: Derviş Eroğlu (Chair.).

Address: 9 Atatürk Meydani, Lefkoşa/Nicosia.

Telephone: +90-392-2283669.

Fax: +90-392-2288732.

E-mail: ubpbasin@ulusalbirlikpartisi.com

Internet: www.ulusalbirlikpartisi.com

NATO *see* **North Atlantic Treaty Organization**.

Nazi-Soviet Pact

A non-aggression pact signed between Nazi Germany and the **Soviet Union** on 23 August 1939 which enabled Germany to invade **Poland** unopposed on 1 September, effectively beginning the Second World War. Red Army troops crossed the Polish border on 17 September, dividing the briefly independent state between the two aggressors. The pact also included the division of the **Baltic States** into German and Soviet zones of influence, with the Soviet Union gaining access to Finland, **Estonia** and **Latvia** and leaving Germany with proposed control of **Lithuania**. Also known as the Molotov-Ribbentrop Pact, after the Foreign Ministers of the Soviet Union and Germany respectively, it came as a severe shock to the international community which had hitherto witnessed the two countries engaging in a vicious war of rhetoric against one another. Collaboration with Germany ended abruptly in June 1941 when Adolf Hitler tore up the non-aggression pact and launched Operation Barbarossa—the Nazi invasion of the Soviet Union.

NBP *see* **National Bank of Poland**.

NBRM *see* **National Bank of Macedonia**.

NBS (Serbia) *see* **National Bank of Serbia**.

NBS (Slovakia) *see* **National Bank of Slovakia**.

ND *see* **New Democracy**.

Neman question

A question of the border between southern **Lithuania** and the Russian enclave of **Kaliningrad** along the River Neman (Nemunas in Lithuanian). At the end of the Second World War the borders of the **Baltic States** were redrawn by the Soviet authorities to create ethnic republics and guarantee direct Russian access to an ice-free port on the Baltic Sea at Kaliningrad. Following the disintegration of the **Soviet Union** in 1991 and the resurrection of an independent Lithuania the issue of this somewhat arbitrary border was raised. Elements on the far right of Lithuanian politics called for the total annexation of the Kaliningrad enclave (home to a mixed **Russian-German** population) in light of its geographic separation from the rest of the Russian Federation by around 750 km. However, Lithuania and Russia signed a border treaty in 1997, ratified by Lithuania two years later and by Russia in 2003. It came into force in August 2003, making Lithuania the first ex-Soviet state to secure a border agreement with Russia.

Neuilly, Treaty of

A treaty signed on 27 November 1919 at the Paris Peace Conference, convened following the conclusion of the First World War, concerning the territorial restructuring of **Bulgaria** which had allied itself during the war with the defeated Central Powers. The treaty fixed Bulgaria's borders, significantly ceding the coastal region of Western Thrace to Greece, and the agriculturally important region of southern **Dobruja** to **Romania**. *See also* Treaties of **Trianon** and **Versailles**.

New Democracy
Nea Demokratia (ND)

A moderate conservative party in **Greece**, a member party of the **International Democrat Union** and the **Christian Democrat International**, and the party of government in 2004–09, but currently in opposition. ND was founded in 1974 by Constantine Karamanlis, who had been Prime Minister in 1956–63 as leader of the National Radical Union (ERE) and had opposed the 'colonels' regime' of 1967–74 from exile in Paris. The new party won an absolute majority in the November 1974 elections, securing 220 of the 300 **Parliament** seats. It was confirmed in power in 1977, although it slipped to 172 seats, with Karamanlis continuing as Prime Minister until being elected President in May 1980, when he was succeeded by George Rallis. In January 1981 a key ND policy aim was achieved when Greece became a member of the European Community (later the **European Union**, EU).

In the 1981 elections ND was heavily defeated by the **Pan-Hellenic Socialist Movement** (PASOK), retaining only 115 seats. Rallis was then replaced as leader by right-winger Evangelos Averoff-Tossizza, but the latter resigned in 1984 following the ND's poor showing in European Parliament elections. He was succeeded by the moderate Constantine Mitsotakis, who led ND to another election defeat in 1985, although it improved to 126 seats. In the June 1989 elections ND won a relative majority of 145 seats, after which it formed a temporary coalition with what became the **Coalition of the Left of Movements and Ecology** (Synaspismos). Further polling in November 1989 produced another stalemate, with ND representation edging up to 148 seats, so that a temporary three-party coalition of ND, PASOK and Synaspismos representatives plus non-party technocrats was formed. Yet more elections in April 1990 gave ND half the seats (150), so that Mitsotakis was able to form a Government with the external support of one non-ND deputy.

The Mitsotakis Government experienced growing internal rifts in 1992–93, culminating in the formation of the breakaway Political Spring (PA) in June 1993. Deprived of a parliamentary majority, Mitsotakis resigned in September 1993, precipitating early elections in October, in which ND was heavily defeated by PASOK, falling to 111 seats. Mitsotakis immediately resigned as ND leader and was succeeded by Miltiades Evert. In January 1995 Parliament voted to drop phone-tapping and various corruption charges against Mitsotakis arising from his term as Prime Minister. In the 1996 elections the ND failed to oust the PASOK Government, winning only 108 seats. In March 1997 Evert was replaced as ND leader by Costas Karamanlis, nephew of the ND founder.

In the 2000 elections, the party narrowly failed to oust PASOK from power, advancing to 42.7% of the vote and 125 seats. It returned to government at the March 2004 elections, winning 165 seats with a 45.4% vote share, with Karamanlis becoming, at 47, Greece's youngest Prime Minister for a century. In a major reshuffle in February 2006, Dora Bakoyannis, the daughter of Mitsotakis and hitherto Mayor of Athens, became Foreign Minister.

In August 2007 Karamanlis called elections for September. His calculation, in going to the electorate six months before the end of his full term, was widely expected to strengthen ND's position. In the month before the poll, however, a wave of forest fires swept across the country, killing 65 people, and the Government came under public criticism for failing to respond more speedily. Nevertheless, the ND narrowly managed to retain a majority of seats, with 152 in the 300-member Parliament (and 41.8% of the vote).

Proposed pension reforms provoked strikes in 2008, while a financial scandal brought down two ministers and reduced ND's majority to just one seat. The international financial crisis from late 2008 pushed unemployment and public debt upwards, along with public opposition to austerity measures. The shooting of a student by a police officer in December triggered a mass outcry against the authorities, and demonstrations became commonplace, often turning violent.

The Government struggled on into 2009, but finally conceded the need for early elections, held in October. These resulted in defeat for the ND, leaving the party with only 91 seats (33.5% of the vote). Karamanlis resigned the presidency of the party, and Antonis Samaras was elected as his successor in November.

Leadership: Antonis Samaras (President).
Address: Odos Rigillis 18, 10674 Athens.
Telephone: (210) 7418221.
Fax: (210) 7418275.
E-mail: koinonia@nd.gr
Internet: www.nd.gr

New Era
Jaunais Laiks (JL)

A liberal right-wing political party in **Latvia**, founded in 2002 and currently heading the Government.

Einars Repše stepped down as **Bank of Latvia** Governor in December 2001 to found this populist, anti-corruption party, which was launched in February 2002. Repše's trusted image and popularity enabled JL to win the parliamentary elections in October of that year, with 23.9% of the vote and 26 seats in the **Parliament**. Repše became Prime Minister on 7 November, heading a centre-right coalition with the **Union of Greens and Farmers** (ZZS), Latvian First Party (LPP) and For Fatherland and Freedom Union/Latvian National Independence Movement (TB/LNNK).

In September 2003 the JL's three coalition partners jointly accused Repše of authoritarianism. This disagreement was patched up, but in January 2004 Repše dismissed the LPP Deputy Prime Minister, after that party had backed calls for an inquiry into Repše's property dealings. The LPP withdrew from the ruling coalition, forcing Repše to resign. The JL then went into opposition to the short-lived Government of Indulis Emsis of the ZZS, but returned to power in December 2004 in the coalition formed by Aigars Kalvītis of the **People's Party** (TP). Repše became Minister of Defence.

In December 2005 a criminal investigation was launched into Repše's property dealings, at which point he resigned as Minister of Defense and temporarily stepped down from the JL leadership. By April 2006 further friction over corruption allegations (involving accusations of electoral malpractice by the LPP leader, and an LPP-provoked inquiry into financial misconduct by a JL minister) led to the JL demanding that Kalvītis eject the LPP from the coalition. When he refused to do so, the JL left his Government.

At the October 2006 election the JL was less successful, its vote share reduced to a third-placed 16.4%, with 18 seats in the new Parliament. It became the largest party in opposition. In March 2007 a joint leadership structure was established for the party, occupied by Repše and Arturs Krišjānis Kariņš. In early 2008 several high-profile JL members left the party; Repše and Kariņš resigned from the leadership and were replaced by Solvita Āboltiņa and Artis Kampars.

When economic crisis brought down the Government of Ivars Godmanis in February 2009, economist and MEP Valdis **Dombrovskis**, of the JL, was nominated to form the new Government, which was approved on 12 March.

Leadership: Solvita Āboltiņa (Chair.); Artis Kampars (Parliamentary Chair.).

Address: Jēkaba kazarmās, Torņa ielā 4–IIIв, 202, Rīga 1050.

Telephone: 67205472.

Fax: 67205473.

E-mail: sekretare@jaunaislaiks.lv

Internet: www.jaunaislaiks.lv

News Agency of the Serb Republic
Srpska Novinska Agentsija (SRNA)

The main news agency for the **Serb Republic** of **Bosnia and Herzegovina**. Founded in 1992.

Director: Dragan Davidović.

Address: Sofke Nikolić 66, Bijeljina 75320.

Telephone: (55) 201819.

Fax: (55) 201810.

E-mail: redakcija@srna.rs

Internet: www.srna.rs

News Agency of the Slovak Republic
Tlačová agentúra Slovenskej republiky (TASR)

The partially state-funded news agency in **Slovakia**. Established in 1992, TASR collects and compiles news from Slovakia under the guidance of the 1996 statute demanding objectivity. The General Director is responsible to the Government.

Director: Peter Nedavska.
Address: Pribinova 23, 819 28 Bratislava.
Telephone: (2) 59210152.
Fax: (2) 52962468.
E-mail: market@tasr.sk
Internet: www.tasr.sk

Nicosia
(Lefkoşa)

The capital of **Cyprus**, situated in the centre of the island on the River Pedieos. It is the seat of government for both parts of the divided island (being itself divided), and the main centre for business. *Population*: 270,000, plus 84,893 in the Turkish northern sector (2004 estimates). Nicosia has been settled since the Bronze Age, and became the capital of Cyprus in the 11th century, when a palace and many churches were built. City walls built by the Venetians in the 16th century enclose the heart of the city. Nicosia was divided in the 1960s between the **Greek** and **Turkish Cypriot** communities, but after the Turkish invasion in 1974 the northern part of the city became the capital of the **Turkish Republic of Northern Cyprus** (TRNC) (recognized only by Turkey). The **Green Line** dividing the city was opened in April 2008 to allow free passage as part of efforts to reunify the island. Nicosia is an important trade and manufacturing centre for textiles, leather, pottery and plastic.

Nomenklatura

(Russian, 'list of names and offices'.) The system of appointments in the **Soviet Union**, co-ordinated by the security police (the KGB or its precursor the NKVD) and the Cadres Department of the Central Committee of the Communist Party of the Soviet Union, which together assigned 'suitable' candidates to a range of state offices. The nomenklatura system ensured discipline and deference to the party. Those rewarded by the nomenklatura came to be regarded as an elite and were treated preferentially in the distribution of resources such as apartments, cars and holidays. In the early post-communist period, well-placed officials were sometimes able to reinvent themselves as business leaders and secure the choicest assets when state industries were sold—a process described derisively as 'nomenklatura privatization'.

North Atlantic Co-operation Council (NACC)

Replaced in 1997 by the **Euro-Atlantic Partnership Council**.

North Atlantic Treaty Organization (NATO)

The key institution of the Atlantic Alliance, which after the end of the **Cold War** underwent a reappraisal of its identity and purpose, seeking ways of co-operating with, instead of confronting, the countries of **eastern Europe** that had hitherto been members of the **Warsaw Pact**. The original 1949 North Atlantic Treaty was a defensive and political military alliance of a group of European states (then numbering 10) and the USA and Canada. Its objectives were (and remain) to provide common security for its members through co-operation and consultation in political, military and economic fields, as well as scientific, environmental and other non-military aspects. Since January 1994, NATO's **Partnership for Peace** programme has provided a loose framework for wider co-operation.

A Founding Act on Mutual Relations, Co-operation and Security was signed between the Russian Federation and NATO in May 1997. This addressed some Russian concerns about the implications of an eastward expansion of NATO itself, for which a number of countries were pressing. The **Czech Republic**, **Hungary** and **Poland** were the first three such countries to join NATO, on 12 March 1999. A further expansion in March 2004 brought in **Bulgaria**, **Estonia**, **Latvia**, **Lithuania**, **Romania**, **Slovakia** and **Slovenia**. A further two countries, **Albania** and **Croatia**, joined the Alliance on 1 April 2009, while **Macedonia** will be invited to start accession talks once the issue of its name has been resolved. **Montenegro** was invited to join the Membership Action Plan (MAP—the stage prior to accession talks) in December 2009, but **Bosnia and Herzegovina** still needs to achieve necessary progress in its reform process before it will be invited to join MAP.

> *Members*: Albania, Belgium, Bulgaria, Canada, Croatia, Czech Republic, Denmark, Estonia, France, Germany, **Greece**, Hungary, Iceland, Italy, Latvia, Lithuania, Luxembourg, Netherlands, Norway, Poland, Portugal, Romania, Slovakia, Slovenia, Spain, Turkey, United Kingdom, USA.
>
> *Secretary-General*: Anders Fogh Rasmussen.
> *Address*: blvd Léopold III, 1110 Brussels, Belgium.
> *Telephone*: (2) 7074111.
> *Fax*: (2) 7074579.
> *E-mail*: nato-doc@hq.nato.int
> *Internet*: www.nato.int

Northern Bukovina *see* **Bukovina question**.

337

Northern Dobruja *see* **Dobruja question**.

Northern Epirus *see* **Epirus question**.

Northern Transylvania *see* **Transylvania**.

NRDA *see* **National Regional Development Agency**.

NSG *see* **Nuclear Suppliers' Group**.

NSZZ *see* **Solidarity**.

Nuclear Suppliers' Group (NSG)

A group formed in the 1970s, at US instigation and spurred by India's nuclear test in 1974, to create common guidelines among the countries supplying nuclear material and technology so as to prevent their being used by non-nuclear-weapon states for weapons development. The NSG included France, which was then not party to the 1968 Nuclear Non-Proliferation Treaty (NPT), and had 15 member countries by early 1978 when its guidelines and control list were published.

The NSG did not meet throughout the 1980s, but resumed annual meetings beginning in The Hague in March 1991. Its membership has expanded to 45 (including **Bulgaria**, **Croatia**, **Cyprus**, **Czech Republic**, **Estonia**, **Greece**, **Hungary**, **Latvia**, **Lithuania**, **Poland**, **Romania**, **Slovakia** and **Slovenia**). It also holds two consultations annually on its arrangement to control nuclear-related 'dual-use' exports, of material and technology which could be used both for nuclear weapons and fuel-cycle activities and for other, non-nuclear purposes.

O

Oder-Neisse line

The border between eastern Germany and **Poland** formed from the Oder-Neisse river system and extending from the Baltic Sea to the **Czech Republic**. In the closing stages of the Second World War, as the Allied Powers debated the future make-up of a post-Nazi Europe, the reconstruction of Poland, and therefore also of Germany, became of central importance. Poland was liberated by Soviet forces that went on to occupy Berlin in 1945, putting the **Soviet Union** in a commanding position in negotiations over Poland's future. Since the country was losing substantial eastern territories to the Soviet Union itself, the new communist authorities in Poland pressed for territory in the west at the expense of defeated Germany. The Soviet leadership consequently proposed the course of the lower Oder (Odra in Polish) river, and its tributary the Neisse (Nysa), as a natural frontier, pushing the new Poland far into historically German lands. Initially the idea was opposed by the Western allies, seeking to limit the consequent population movements and national upheaval for Germany. However, the presence of Soviet troops on the ground, and the desire of the Western leaders to be accommodating towards Stalin on this issue, led the Allies to agree to the Oder-Neisse proposal in the **Yalta** and **Potsdam Agreements**. Millions of **Germans** were forcibly deported from the annexed territory.

The post-1945 borders were recognized by the newly-established East German state in 1950. West Germany, however, continued to regard them as no more than a temporary administrative border until 1971, when a change in stance on policy towards the East was marked by recognition of the enduring status of the Oder-Neisse line. At the time of German reunification in 1990, the Federal Republic of Germany moved quickly to attest the legitimacy of the Oder-Neisse line as Poland's inviolable western border. This was confirmed in the German-Polish Treaty signed in **Warsaw** on 14 November 1990.

ODS *see* **Civic Democratic Party**.

OECD *see* **Organisation for Economic Co-operation and Development**.

OEK *see* **Kosovo Chamber of Commerce**.

OF *see* **Civic Forum**.

Office of the High Representative (OHR)

The body created, under the terms of the 1995 **Dayton Agreement** at the end of the Bosnian civil war, as highest civilian authority in **Bosnia and Herzegovina**, to oversee all civilian aspects of the peace treaty. The High Representative is nominated by the international Peace Implementation Council (PIC) and then endorsed by the UN. He or she does not have authority over the military aspects of the peace accord. The High Representative (Valentin **Inzko** since March 2009) is also concurrently the Special Representative of the **European Union** (EUSR). The PIC is preparing to close the OHR, though it does not yet consider Bosnia and Herzegovina capable of taking full responsibility for its own affairs so the date of cessation has been repeatedly postponed. The proposed closure will not affect the role of EUSR.

Address: Emerika Bluma 1, 71000 Sarajevo.
Telephone: (33) 283500.
Fax: (33) 283501.
Internet: www.ohr.int

OIC *see* **Organisation of the Islamic Conference**.

Open Society Institute *see* **Soros Foundations network**.

Orbán, Viktor

Prime Minister-designate of **Hungary**. A leading light of the radical liberal Young Democrats from the dying days of the communist regime, Orbán served as Prime Minister from 1998 to 2002, and then led the **Federation of Young Democrats— Hungarian Civic Alliance** (FiDeSz–MPSz) in opposition from 2003 until its landslide election victory in April 2010.

Born in May 1963, Orbán gained a reputation as an activist and outspoken critic of the communist system during his time as a law student in **Budapest** in the mid-1980s. He continued in this vein with the Federation of Young Democrats (FiDeSz), launched formally in March 1988, and attracted wide attention in July 1989, in a speech at the state reburial of Hungarian national hero Imre **Nagy**, calling for multi-party elections and the full withdrawal of Russian troops. In September of that year he won a scholarship to Pembroke College in Oxford, United Kingdom, to study the philosophy of English liberal politics, but returned to Hungary after the announcement that multi-party elections were to be held in 1990.

In April 1990, in the first free elections to be held since 1947, Orbán was elected to the **National Assembly** and led FiDeSz's small parliamentary group. The party's profile was raised in the international arena in 1992 when it joined the **Liberal International** (LI) and Orbán was elected to be Vice-President of that organization. The following year he became a member of the LI's Executive and was also elected as FiDeSz's first Chairman.

Once he was officially leader of the movement, Orbán began the transformation of FiDeSz in 1993, away from its radical image as a youth movement to make it a more widely acceptable, and electable, political force. He was unable to turn around its fortunes in time for the elections held in May 1994, when its proportion of seats in the Assembly actually fell. In 1995 the party added the suffix Hungarian Civic Party (MPP) to its name, stressing the traditionally conservative civic qualities of respect and fairness. In legislative elections held in May 1998, FiDeSz–MPP increased its share of seats in the National Assembly from just 20 to 148 out of 386, and the following month Orbán was nominated to form a new Government. In July his three-party coalition was sworn in.

As part of Hungary's drive to be accepted into the **European Union**, and in an effort to elevate its international image as a serious and independent political contender, Orbán made a point of breaking with tradition to make France, and not Germany, his first foreign visit as Prime Minister. He also oversaw the country's popular accession to membership of the **North Atlantic Treaty Organization** (NATO) in March 1999. The immediate afterglow of this diplomatic coup was quickly eroded when NATO launched military action in neighbouring **Serbia** by the end of the same month. Genuine fears of physical retaliation from **Yugoslavia** forced Orbán to agree to Hungary's involvement being limited to allowing its larger NATO allies the use of Hungarian military bases and airspace during their airstrikes. Following an internal FiDeSz–MPP vote in December 1999 it was agreed that party and governmental roles should be clearly separated and Orbán duly stepped down as Chairman in January 2000.

At the April 2002 polls the FiDeSz-led alliance won 188 seats, but the Socialist-led opposition won all the remaining 198 seats, pushing FiDeSz–MPP into opposition. A year later, Orbán was re-elected as party Chairman, at the same time as the party took its current name.

FiDeSz–MPSz performed well at the 2004 European elections, but failed to unseat the Socialists at the 2006 Assembly election. However, by 2010 the electorate had had enough of the Socialists and voted the FiDeSz-led alliance into power with a sizeable majority. Orbán was nominated as Prime Minister, to take office in late May.

Order and Justice
Tvarka ir Teisingumas (TT)

A centre-right political party in **Lithuania**, formerly known as the Liberal Democratic Party (LDP), and currently in opposition.

The LDP was formed in March 2002 by Rolandas Paksas and 10 other defectors from the Lithuanian Liberal Union (*see* **Liberal and Centre Union**). After Paksas won the Lithuanian presidency in January 2003, Valentinas Mazuronis took over as LDP Chairman. However, Paksas lost the presidency when he was impeached in April 2004, and he resumed the leadership of the party the following December. Meanwhile, in the October 2004 **Parliament** election, the For Order and Justice coalition of the LDP and the Lithuanian People's Union had won 11 seats (with 11.4% of the vote). In May 2006 the LDP renamed itself as Order and Justice, and at the October 2008 election it again won 11 seats, this time with a vote share of 12.7%.

Leadership: Rolandas Paksas (Chair.).
Address: Gedimino pr.10/ Totorių g.1, 01103 Vilnius.
Telephone and fax: (5) 2691618.
E-mail: tt@tvarka.lt
Website: www.tvarka.lt

Organisation for Economic Co-operation and Development
(OECD)

An influential grouping within which the governments of industrialized countries discuss, develop and attempt to co-ordinate their economic and social policies. Founded in 1961, it replaced the Organisation for European Economic Co-operation (OEEC), which had been established in 1948 in connection with the Marshall Plan for post-war reconstruction. The OECD's officially-stated aims are to promote policies designed to achieve the highest level of sustainable economic growth, employment and increase in the standard of living while maintaining financial stability, and to contribute to economic expansion in member and non-member states and to the expansion of world trade.

Members: 30 countries, including the **Czech Republic**, **Greece**, **Hungary**, **Poland** and **Slovakia**.
Secretary-General: Angel Gurría.
Address: 2 rue André-Pascal, 75775 Paris Cédex 16, France.
Telephone: (1) 45248200.
Fax: (1) 45248500.
E-mail: webmaster@oecd.org
Internet: www.oecd.org

Organisation of the Islamic Conference (OIC)

An organization that groups 57 countries and territories, principally in the Middle East, Africa and Asia, to promote Islamic solidarity and co-operation. Azerbaijan and **Albania**, its only European members, both joined in 1992. Observers include **Bosnia and Herzegovina**, Russia and the **Turkish Republic of Northern Cyprus**. The observer status of **Kosovo** was blocked at Egypt's instigation in 2008.

The organization had formally been established in May 1971, when its Secretariat became operational. The impetus for the creation of the organization had come from the summit meeting of **Muslim** Heads of State at Rabat, Morocco, in September 1969, followed up by conferences at foreign ministerial level in Jeddah, Saudi Arabia, and Karachi, Pakistan, during 1970.

Secretary-General: Ekmeleddin İhsanoğlu.
Address: Kilo 6, Mecca Road, POB 178, Jeddah 21411, Saudi Arabia.
Telephone: (2) 6515222.
Fax: (2) 6512288.
E-mail: cabinet@oic-oci.org
Internet: www.oic-oci.org

Organization for Security and Co-operation in Europe (OSCE)

The Organization for Security and Co-operation in Europe was established in 1972 as the Conference on Security and Co-operation in Europe (CSCE), providing a multilateral forum for dialogue and negotiation. The areas of competence of the CSCE were expanded by the Charter of Paris for a New Europe (1990)—which transformed the CSCE from an ad hoc forum to an organization with permanent institutions—and the Helsinki Document 1992. CSCE membership had reached 52 by 1994, as it sought to encompass all recognized states in Europe and the former **Soviet Union**, together with Canada and the USA.

The CSCE's role included securing the observance of human rights, and providing a forum for settling disputes among member countries. Some member countries, notably the Russian Federation, advocated its development as the principal organization for managing the responses of European countries on a range of continent-wide concerns. Its initial impact, however, was principally in promoting East-West détente, bringing together 35 countries including the rival **North Atlantic Treaty Organization** and **Warsaw Pact** alliances for the Helsinki CSCE conference which began in July 1973 and culminated in the 1975 **Helsinki Final Act**.

In December 1994 the summit conference adopted the new name of OSCE, in order to reflect the organization's changing political role and strengthened Secretariat. The OSCE's main decision-making body, the Permanent Council, convenes weekly in Vienna to discuss and make decisions on current developments in the OSCE area. Also meeting weekly in Vienna is the Forum for Security Co-operation, which is concerned with military aspects of security in the OSCE area, in particular confidence- and security-building measures. The OSCE's Economic and Environmental Forum annually holds a preparatory meeting and a conference to focus on economic and environmental issues.

The OSCE also has: a Parliamentary Assembly; an Office for Democratic Institutions and Human Rights (ODIHR), based in **Warsaw** and originally created (in 1990) as the Office for Free Elections, concerned to promote human rights and democracy; a High Commissioner on National Minorities and a Representative on Freedom of the Media; and a Court of Conciliation and Arbitration overseeing its disputes settlement procedures. The position of Chairperson-in-Office is held by the Minister of Foreign Affairs of the member state that is holding the one-year chairmanship of the OSCE; it is held for 2010 by Kanat Saudabayev of Kazakhstan.

Members: 56 participating states, comprising all the recognized countries of Europe and the former Soviet republics, Canada and the USA.

Secretary-General: Marc Perrin de Brichambaut.

Address: Wallnerstrasse 6, 1010 Vienna, Austria.

Telephone: (1) 514366000.

Fax: (1) 514366996.

E-mail: info@osce.org

Internet: www.osce.org

Organization of the Black Sea Economic Co-operation (BSEC)

An organization derived from the Black Sea Economic Co-operation (BSEC) grouping formed in 1992 to strengthen regional co-operation, particularly on economic development. In June 1998, at a summit meeting held in Yalta, Ukraine, participating countries signed the BSEC Charter, thereby officially elevating the BSEC to regional organization status. The Charter entered into force on 1 May 1999, at which time the BSEC formally became the Organization of the Black Sea Economic Co-operation, retaining the same acronym. The chairmanship of the BSEC rotates alphabetically between its member states every seven months. It passed to Bulgaria on 1 November 2009, and will pass on to Georgia on 1 June 2010.

Members: **Albania**, Armenia, Azerbaijan, **Bulgaria**, Georgia, **Greece**, Moldova, **Romania**, Russian Federation, **Serbia**, Turkey and Ukraine.

Secretary-General: Leonidas Chrysanthopoulos.

Address: Sakıp Sabancı Caddesi, Müşir Fuad Paşa Yalısı, Eski Tersane 34460, Istanbul, Turkey.

Telephone: (212) 2296330.

Fax: (212) 2296336.

E-mail: info@bsec-organization.org

Internet: www.bsec-organization.org

Országgyűlés *see* **National Assembly (Hungary)**.

Orthodox Christianity

The form of Christianity most widespread in south-eastern and **eastern Europe**. Its formal separation from western Christianity (**Roman Catholicism**) was completed by the Great Schism in 1054. The eastern Orthodox Catholic Church was championed by the Eastern Roman (Byzantine) Empire centred on Constantinople, and was spread to the pagan tribes north and east of that city. This geographical spread, and conversely the success of Catholicism elsewhere in Europe, has given Orthodox Christianity a distinctly 'eastern' feel. Its practices are dominated by the belief that the form of worship has not changed since the days of Jesus Christ. The tradition of iconic art is strong. The symbol of the Orthodox Church is the three-barred cross (representing the crucifix upon which Jesus Christ was executed, and including the nameplate above his head and the footplate). Orthodox missionaries also provided **Slav** converts with the **Cyrillic alphabet** and the original Slavonic liturgy.

Unlike the Roman Catholic Church with its Pope, the Orthodox Church does not have a single head, but rather is divided into separate *autocephalous* (independent) Churches or Patriarchates, most of which are part of the Eastern Orthodox Communion. The Churches are headed by a local Patriarch or Metropolitan. The original branch, the Greek-speaking Autocephalous Church of Constantinople (Istanbul), is deemed the 'first among equals' and the Patriarch of Constantinople is considered 'ecumenical', but theoretically does not have any actual powers over the other Churches. Ecumenical Patriarch Bartholomew I ascended the throne of the Constantinople See on 2 November 1991. The Russian Orthodox Church also carries great weight within the religion, having by far the largest single congregation.

Estimates of the number of Orthodox Christians worldwide range from 200m. to 300m. The biggest congregations are in the Russian Federation (up to 125m.) and **Romania** (c.20m.). Orthodox Christians were persecuted by the communist authorities; 98% of churches in the **Soviet Union** were closed and many priests executed. However, a general revival in religious activity since the late 1980s has seen a resurgence in the size of congregations and the social influence of the Church hierarchy.

Eastern European countries with autocephalous Churches are: **Albania**, **Bulgaria**, **Cyprus**, **Czech** lands and **Slovakia**, Georgia, **Greece**, **Poland**, **Romania**, Russian Federation and **Serbia**. The autonomous Churches of **Latvia**, Moldova and Ukraine are subordinated to the Russian Church, while there are two autonomous Churches of **Estonia**, one subordinated to the Russian Church and the other to the Ecumenical Patriarchate of Constantinople. Small congregations in other countries are subordinate to various neighbouring Churches. The **Macedonian** and **Montenegrin** Orthodox Churches are not formally recognized as part of the Eastern Orthodox Communion.

OSCE *see* **Organization for Security and Co-operation in Europe**.

Özgürgün, Hüseyin

Deputy Prime Minister and Minister of Foreign Affairs of the **Turkish Republic of Northern Cyprus** (TRNC) from 5 May 2009, and acting Prime Minister from 23 April 2010.

Hüseyin Özgürgün was born in Lefkoşa in 1965. He graduated in political science from Ankara University in Turkey and then studied language and administrative science in the United Kingdom. A member of the **National Unity Party** (UBP), he was first elected to the TRNC Assembly in 1998. He was briefly leader of the UBP for 10 months in 2006. He was also a national athlete and football player and has two children.

After the UBP won the April 2009 legislative elections, Özgürgün was appointed Deputy Prime Minister and Minister of Foreign Affairs. Then when Prime Minister Derviş **Eroğlu** won the presidency in April 2010, Özgürgün was appointed as acting Prime Minister.

Address: Prime Ministry, Selçuklu Caddesi, Lefkoşa/Nicosia.

Telephone: +90-392-2283141.

Fax: +90-392-2287280.

E-mail: info@kktcbasbakanlik.org

Internet: www.kktcbasbakanlik.org

P

Pahor, Borut

Prime Minister of **Slovenia** and leader of the Social Democrats. Pahor served three terms in the **National Assembly** and one term in the European Parliament prior to his appointment as Prime Minister in November 2008.

Borut Pahor was born on 2 November 1963 in Postojna, south-west Slovenia. He studied international relations at the Faculty of Sociology, Political Sciences and Journalism of the University of Ljubljana, graduating in 1987. Three years later he was elected to the Slovenian Assembly and chaired its youth and international affairs committees. After Slovenia gained its independence, he was elected to the new National Assembly, representing the United List of Social Democrats (ZLSD), of which he became Vice-President in 1993 and President in March 1997. He served three terms in the Assembly, and was variously involved in its committees for EU Affairs, Intelligence and Security Services, Defence, International Relations, Constitutional Affairs. He was also Chairman of the Slovenian Delegation to the Parliamentary Assembly of the **Council of Europe** and a member of the Executive Committee of the Inter-Parliamentary Union. In 2000–04 he was Speaker of the National Assembly. In June 2004 he was elected to the European Parliament, where he joined the Committees on Budgetary Control and Constitutional Affairs, and was Vice-Chairman of the Delegation to the EU-Croatia Joint Parliamentary Committee.

The ZLSD changed its name to **Social Democrats** (SD) in April 2005 on Pahor's initiative, and went on to win the September 2008 Assembly election. Pahor resigned his seat in the European Parliament in mid-October, was nominated as Prime Minister on 3 November and took office on 21 November.

Pahor speaks English, Italian and a little French. He is married and has a son.
Address: Prime Minister's Office, Gregorčičeva 20, 25, 1000 Ljubljana.
Telephone: (1) 4781000.
Fax: (1) 4781721.
E-mail: gp.kpv@gov.si
Internet: www.kpv.gov.si

347

PalilZ *or* **PAIZ** *see* **Polish Information and Foreign Investment Agency**.

Pan-Hellenic Socialist Movement
Panellinio Sosialistiko Kínima (PASOK)

A social democratic party in **Greece**, a leading force in its modern politics and currently the party in power, and a member of the **Socialist International**. PASOK was founded in 1974, being derived from the Pan-Hellenic Liberation Movement (PAK) created by Andreas **Papandreou** in 1968 to oppose the military dictatorship which held power in Greece in 1967–74. The party was originally committed to the socialization of key economic sectors and also to withdrawal from the **North Atlantic Treaty Organization** (NATO) and what became the **European Union** (EU), but revised such policies when it came into government.

Having become the strongest opposition party in 1977, PASOK in 1981 won an absolute majority with 170 seats in the 300-seat **Parliament** (with 48.1% of the vote) and formed a Government under Papandreou's premiership. Four years later PASOK was returned for a second term, although with its representation down to 161 seats on a 45.8% vote share. In office, PASOK experienced internal divisions over foreign and economic policies, including a new five-year agreement signed in 1983 allowing US bases to remain in Greece, the dropping of opposition to EU and NATO membership, and the introduction of an economic austerity programme in 1985.

In the June 1989 election PASOK was damaged by the Koskotas affair, involving financial malpractice in the Bank of Crete, and by Papandreou's extramarital affair with a young air hostess called Dimitra Liani, with whom he later contracted his third marriage. The party's representation slumped to 125 seats (on a 39.2% vote share) and it went into opposition to a temporary coalition between **New Democracy** (ND) and what became the **Coalition of the Left of Movements and Ecology** (Synaspismos). Further elections in November 1989 produced another stalemate, with PASOK improving slightly to 128 seats and 40.7% of the vote, well behind ND, although the latter's lack of an overall majority necessitated the formation of another temporary coalition, this time of the three main parties, but not including their leaders. Greece's third general election in less than a year, held in April 1990, broke the deadlock, with PASOK slipping to 123 seats and 38.6% and going into opposition to an ND Government.

In the 1993 elections PASOK jettisoned much of its left-wing theses of the 1980s and instead professed a 'social democratic' identity. It won an overall majority of 170 seats (on a 46.9% vote share) and returned to government with Papandreou once again Prime Minister. However, growing unrest within PASOK over the ageing Papandreou's continued leadership and the political ambitions of his wife Dimitra developed into a succession struggle when the Prime Minister fell seriously ill in November 1995. Papandreou eventually resigned in January 1996 and was succeeded as Prime Minister by Costas Simitis, who had resigned from the Government in September 1995 in protest against alleged sabotage of his reform plans by the PASOK hierarchy. Following the death of Papandreou in June 1996, Simitis was elected PASOK leader despite strong internal opposition.

Simitis consolidated his position in the September 1996 general election, which PASOK won with 162 seats on a 41.5% vote share. His Government's economic austerity measures to prepare Greece for the single European currency were resisted by the PASOK 'old guard'. PASOK narrowly retained power in the April 2000 election, winning 158 seats with 43.8% of the vote. Simitis continued in office until January 2004, when he called early elections. George **Papandreou**, Andreas's son, took over the PASOK leadership in February, ahead of to the March poll, at which the party was removed from power, winning only 117 seats on 40.6% vote share. In the August 2007 elections it fell further back, winning only 102 seats (38.1% of the vote). However, ND also declined, barely retaining a two-seat majority. Its Government struggled through the first half of its term, against economic crisis, public discontent and corruption scandals, but eventually called early elections for October 2009. These resulted in victory for PASOK, with 160 seats (43.9% of the vote) and George Papandreou took office as Prime Minister on 6 October.

Leadership: George Papandreou (President).
Address: Odos Hippocrates 22, 10680 Athens.
Telephone: (210) 3665000.
Fax: (210) 3606958.
E-mail: pasok@pasok.gr
Internet: www.pasok.gr

Pan-Slavism

The idea that promotes the closer integration and possible unification of all **Slavic peoples** based on their shared ethnic and linguistic background. In practice, the creation of **Yugoslavia** was the main, partial and ultimately unsuccessful implementation of this idea. The agitation of **Croat** and **Slovene** pan-Slavists for a union of south Slavs, or Yugoslavs, was the basis for the creation in 1918 of the Kingdom of Serbs, Croats and Slovenes, but the deep religious divides and historical animosities among south Slavs violently undid the Yugoslav experiment in the 1990s. More recently, the close ethnic similarities of the east Slavs were the foundation for initiatives towards a Belarus-Russia Union and for closer links between these two countries and Ukraine.

PAP *see* **Polish Press Agency**.

Papandreou, Andreas

Prime Minister of **Greece** (1981–89 and 1993–96) and founder of the **Pan-Hellenic Socialist Movement** (PASOK), and father of the current Prime Minister and party leader George **Papandreou**. His first election victory, in 1981, ended almost 50 years of conservative political dominance. An articulate US-educated economist, Andreas Papandreou made waves with left-wing rhetoric, particularly the unfulfilled threat of pulling Greece out of both the **North Atlantic Treaty Organization** (NATO) and the European Communities (EC), later the **European Union** (EU). Towards the end of the 1980s, however, his authority was eroded by illness, corruption scandals and by the spotlight turned on his affair with an airline hostess who became his third wife. An unexpectedly vigorous election campaign in 1993 gave him a further term in office, but his ensuing government drifted without clear direction until his eventual retirement and death in 1996.

Andreas George Papandreou was born on the island of Chios on 5 February 1919. His father George Papandreou was a lawyer and a leading political figure, who was Prime Minister briefly in 1944, and again in 1963 and 1964–65.

Initially following his father's example, Andreas studied law at Athens University. He was arrested in 1939, under the nationalist dictatorship of Metaxas, but was then permitted to go to the USA to continue his studies. Having switched from law to economics, he completed a doctorate at Harvard University in 1943, became a US citizen in 1944, held a series of professorships at American universities, and served in the US Navy. While in the USA he married Christina Rasia in 1941, but divorced her a decade later to marry Margaret Chant, with whom he had three sons and a daughter; they were divorced in 1989.

Papandreou returned to Greece and resumed his Greek citizenship in 1959. In 1961 he was appointed Director of the Centre of Economic Research in **Athens** (a post he held until 1964) and adviser to the **Bank of Greece** (until 1962). His father George Papandreou came to power following the 1963 general election and then strengthened his position further in the 1964 election, when Andreas Papandreou secured a seat in **Parliament** as a deputy for Achaia. Papandreou senior appointed his son to the cabinet as Minister to the Prime Minister and then Deputy Minister in charge of Co-ordination, in preference to more senior members of his own republican Centre Union party. The Government fell in July 1965, both Papandreous going into opposition.

When Georgios Papadopoulos seized power in April 1967, initiating the seven years of repressive military government known as the 'colonels' regime', Andreas Papandreou was at first arrested and imprisoned, but was then allowed to go into exile in Sweden and then Canada, where he resumed work as an economics professor. In exile he became a prominent campaigner against the colonels, founding and leading the Pan-Hellenic Liberation Movement in 1968. When the regime did eventually collapse in July 1974, Papandreou returned to Greece and founded PASOK that September.

Between the general elections of 1974 and 1977, Papandreou gradually built up PASOK's popular support, increasing its share of the vote so that it became the main opposition party. PASOK's eventual general election victory in 1981, when it secured 48% of the vote and 172 seats, allowed Papandreou to form a Government, in which he was not only Prime Minister but also Minister of National Defence. He had pledged to withdraw from the EC (which the country had just joined in January 1981) and from NATO, but did neither when in office, although he did inaugurate lavish spending policies at home, subsidized by large-scale EC subsidies.

In the 1985 general election Papandreou successfully secured a second term of office, but his position was undermined by his own poor health (he had several spells in hospital including two months in the United Kingdom in 1988). The opposition also sought to discredit him by linking him to embezzlement scandals concerning the Bank of Crete and the Greek-American businessman Georgios Koskotas. Meanwhile Papandreou announced that he was seeking a divorce so that he could marry Dimitra Liani, a former air hostess half his age, whom he eventually married in 1989 and who held increasing influence over him until his death.

Two sets of elections in 1989 provided no clear winner and two short-lived Governments followed, although renewed elections in April 1990 gave **New Democracy** (ND) a clearer majority over the discredited PASOK. Reinvigorated by a spell in opposition, however, and acquitted of involvement in the diversion of funds from the Bank of Crete to PASOK, Papandreou was able to make a strong comeback. In the October 1993 election he projected his party as a model of 1990s social democracy and playing down its previous radical socialist image.

Papandreou's 1993 victory (PASOK won 47% of the vote) was based partly on his own charisma, but was helped by the unpopularity of the austerity measures of the outgoing Government, and by divisions within ND itself. Papandreou went on to form a Government, in which his young wife headed the Prime Minister's private office, and his son George Papandreou was initially Deputy Minister for Foreign Affairs and from July 1994 Minister of Education and Religion (a post he had also held in 1987–89). Andreas proceeded to renationalize the Athens bus network, but a year later also announced plans for the partial privatization of the national telecommunications concern OTE. His position was, however, increasingly undermined by his deteriorating health. He was taken into hospital in late 1995 with pneumonia and kidney failure, and placed in intensive care. He was eventually persuaded to resign as Prime Minister on 15 January 1996, although he clung on to the leadership of PASOK until his death on 23 June 1996.

Papandreou, George

Prime Minister of **Greece**. The third member of his family to be Greece's socialist leader and Prime Minister in successive generations, George is noted for a more reserved temperament than his father Andreas **Papandreou** and grandfather George. Born in the USA and educated mainly abroad, he subsequently rose through the hierarchy of the **Pan-Hellenic Socialist Movement** (PASOK). He has been a member of **Parliament** since 1981 and held ministerial posts in education, culture and foreign affairs, notably co-ordinating Athens' bids to host the 1996 and 2004 Olympic Games (successful on the second attempt), and improving diplomatic relations with Greece's neighbours. He has led PASOK since February 2004, losing two elections before winning a large majority at the October 2009 poll. He took office as Prime Minister the following day, pledging to rebuild the economy and clean up government.

George Papandreou was born on 16 June 1952 in St Paul, Minnesota, USA. His father Andreas, exiled from Greece in 1939, had come to the USA to study; he married for the first time in 1941, but was divorced a decade later and married Margaret Chant, with whom he had all four of his children. George attended schools in Greece, the USA, Sweden and Canada. He was 11 when his grandfather George became Prime Minister of Greece (for the second time), this tenure lasting only a couple of months; a third appointment in 1964 lasted just over a year, but led to a series of crises that climaxed with the 1967 coup, which ushered in the repressive 'colonels' regime'. By the time Greece returned to civilian rule in 1974, the young George was enjoying his undergraduate years, spent mostly at Amherst College, Massachusetts, but also at Stockholm University, Sweden. He graduated in sociology a year later, and then gained a master's degree in sociology and development from the London School of Economics in the United Kingdom.

Returning now to Greece, George joined the party that his father Andreas had founded in 1974. He served on various party committees, and won a seat in Parliament in 1981, at the election that resulted in a PASOK majority and his father becoming Prime Minister. George chaired the Parliamentary Committee on Education until 1985, and then joined the Ministry of Culture, responsible for diaspora affairs and adult education. After a brief stint as Vice-Chair of the Parliamentary Committee for Free Radio in 1987, he was appointed Minister of Education and Religious Affairs, and co-ordinated Athens' unsuccessful bid to host the 1996 Olympic Games. PASOK lost power from 1989 (the same year that his parents divorced) and, in opposition, Papandreou became Chair of the Parliamentary Committee for Culture and Education. In 1992 he secured a fellowship post at Harvard University's Center for International Affairs in the USA.

Back in Greece the following year he joined the new PASOK Government as Deputy Minister for Foreign Affairs, responsible for relations with the USA and, during Greece's presidency of the **European Union** (EU), was part of the negotiating team on the accession of Sweden, Finland, Austria and Norway. In 1994 he was reappointed Minister for Education and Culture. The following year his elderly father suffered kidney failure, and in January 1996 stepped down as Prime Minister; he died the following June.

Elected as one of Athens' parliamentarians in 1996, George was put in charge of the city's second, and this time successful, bid to host the Olympics, for 2004. He was also appointed Alternate Minister of Foreign Affairs, rising to full Minister in 1999. In 2000 the East-West Institute awarded Papandreou and his Turkish counterpart Ismail Cem their Statesman of the Year award for their efforts to improve Greco-Turkish relations. He also improved ties with neighbouring **Albania** and **Bulgaria**, and was involved in efforts to reunite **Cyprus** ahead of its EU accession in 2004.

PASOK's ratings were low ahead of the 2004 election, and the popular Papandreou was handed the party's reins in an attempt to attract back voters disillusioned by corruption scandals, the state of the economy and the behind-schedule preparations for the Olympics coming up that summer. PASOK still lost to **New Democracy** and, finding himself in opposition, Papandreou pledged to clean up and rebuild the party. Lacking the flamboyant leadership skills of his forebears, however, he managed to please neither the reformists nor the left-wing faction of the party. PASOK performed even worse at the September 2007 poll, but Papandreou fought off a challenge for the party leadership later in the year.

At the 2009 election the party capitalized on the poor state of the economy and corruption scandals embroiling ND politicians to secure a comfortable majority. Papandreou took office as Prime Minister on 6 October.

George Papandreou is married to Ada, with a son and a daughter. In addition to Greek he speaks fluent English and Swedish.

Address: Office of the Prime Minister, Maximos' Mansion, Irodou Attikou 19, 10671 Athens.
Telephone: (210) 6717732.
Fax: (210) 6715799.
E-mail: mail@primeminister.gr
Internet: www.primeminister.gr

Papoulias, Karolos

President of **Greece**. A lawyer by training, Papoulias spent many years in exile before returning to Greece and helping to found the **Pan-Hellenic Socialist Movement** (PASOK). He was first elected to **Parliament** in 1977 and served for 27 years before he was elected President in February 2005 by a huge majority in Parliament, and sworn in on 12 March.

Karolos Papoulias was born on 4 June 1929 in the city of Ionnina, **Epirus**, in north-west Greece. He studied law in the University of Athens, followed by the University of Munich in Germany, and has a doctorate from the University of Cologne—he went into exile in Germany for the seven-year 'colonels' regime' from 1967 and became a member of PASOK's Central Committee when the party was founded in 1974.

Papoulias was elected to Parliament for his home city of Ionnina in 1977, and re-elected eight times, serving a total of 27 consecutive years. He was appointed Deputy Minister for Foreign Affairs in October 1981, then Alternate Minister in February 1984 and full Minister from July 1985. He held this post until just after the 1989 election, when he became Alternate Minister for National Defence. PASOK lost power between 1990 and 1993, after which Papoulias returned to the post of Minister for Foreign Affairs. Then from January 1996 he led Greece's parliamentary representation to the **Organization for Security and Co-operation in Europe**.

During the course of his career, Papoulias had also been a pole-vault champion, an official of the national volleyball team and President of the National Athletics Association. In June 2000, he was appointed as a member of the Board of Directors and Executive Committee of the International Olympic Truce Foundation.

In February 2005 both main parties backed his candidacy as President and he was elected by an unprecedented 279 votes in the 300-seat Parliament. He secured a second term, unopposed, on 3 February 2010.

Papoulias is married to May Panou, and they have three daughters. He speaks German, French and Italian.

Address: Presidential Mansion, Vassileos Georgiou B2, 10028 Athens.

Telephone: (210) 7283111.

Fax: (210) 7248938.

Internet: www.presidency.gr

Parlamentarna Skupština *see* **Parliamentary Assembly**.

Parlamentul României *see* **Parliament of Romania**.

Parliament (Czech Republic)
Parlament

The bicameral legislature of the **Czech Republic**, comprising the Chamber of Deputies (Poslanecká Sněmovna) and the Senate (Senát). The lower Chamber of Deputies has 200 members, directly elected for a four-year term. The upper Senate has 81 directly-elected members; one-third of the seats come up for re-election every two years, and Senators then serve six-year terms. The last elections were held on 2–3 June 2006 (Chamber of Deputies) and 17–18 and 24–25 October 2008 (Senate).

Address of lower house: Poslanecká Sněmovna, Sněmovní 4, 11826 Prague 1.

Telephone: (2) 57175111.

Fax: (2) 57534469.

E-mail: posta@psp.cz

Internet: www.psp.cz

Address of upper house: Senát, Valdštejnské náměstí 17/4, 11801 Prague 1.
Telephone: (2) 57071111.
Fax: (2) 57075700.
E-mail: info@senat.cz
Internet: www.senat.cz

Parliament (Estonia)
Riigikogu

The unicameral legislature of **Estonia**. It has 101 members, directly elected for a four-year term. The last elections were held on 4 March 2007.
Address: Riigikogu, Lossi plats 1A, 15165 Tallinn.
Telephone: 6316331.
Fax: 6316334.
E-mail: riigikogu@riigikogu.ee
Internet: www.riigikogu.ee

Parliament (Greece)
Vouli

The unicameral legislature of **Greece**. It has 300 members, directly elected for a five-year term under a system of proportional representation. Parties must pass a minimum threshold of 3% of the vote to secure representation. Two hundred and sixty of the seats in the Parliament are allocated among the qualifying parties in proportion to their percentage of the vote; the remaining 40 seats are then awarded to the party with the largest number of votes, to raise the probability of the leading party having a secure majority. The last elections were held on 4 October 2009.
Address: Parliament, Palaia Anactora, Vas. Sophias 2, 10021 Athens.
Telephone: (210) 3707000.
Fax: (210) 3692170.
E-mail: info@parliament.gr
Internet: www.parliament.gr

Parliament (Latvia)
Saeima

The unicameral legislature of **Latvia**. It has 100 members, directly elected for a four-year term by a system of proportional representation, subject to a threshold of 5% for each party. The last elections were held on 7 October 2006.

Parliament (Lithuania)

Address: Saeima, Jekaba iela 11, Rīga 1811.
Telephone: 67087321.
Fax: 67830333.
E-mail: saeima@saeima.lv
Internet: www.saeima.lv

Parliament (Lithuania)
Seimas

The unicameral legislature of **Lithuania**. It has 141 members, directly elected for a four-year term. The last elections were held on 12 and 26 October 2008.

Address: Seimas, Gedimino pr. 53, 01109 Vilnius.
Telephone: (523) 96060.
Fax: (523) 96339.
E-mail: priim@lrs.lt
Internet: www.lrs.lt

Parliament of Romania
Parlamentul României

The bicameral legislature of **Romania**, comprising the Chamber of Deputies (Camera Deputaților) and the Senate (Senatul). The lower Chamber of Deputies has 345 members (with 18 seats reserved for minorities), directly elected for a four-year term. The upper Senate has 137 members, directly elected for a four-year term. The last elections were held on 30 November 2008.

Address of lower house: Camera Deputaților, Palatul Parlamentului, St Izvor 2–4, Sector 5, 70647 Bucharest.
Telephone: (1) 3160300.
Fax: (1) 3126600.
E-mail: infocdep@cdep.ro
Internet: www.cdep.ro

Address of upper house: Senatul, Calea 13 Septembrie 1–3, Sector 5, 050711 Bucharest.
Telephone: (1) 4021111.
Fax: (1) 3121184.
E-mail: gsterea@unix1.senat.ro
Internet: www.senat.ro

Parliamentary Assembly
Parlamentarna Skupština

The bicameral legislature of **Bosnia and Herzegovina**, comprising the House of Representatives (Predstavnički Dom/Zastupnički Dom) and the House of Peoples (Dom Naroda). The lower House of Representatives has 42 members who are directly elected to the two constituent chambers: the Chamber of Deputies of the **Muslim-Croat Federation** (known as the Federation), with 28 members, and the Chamber of Deputies of the **Serb Republic** (Republika Srpska), with 14 members. The upper House of Peoples has 15 members elected indirectly by the legislatures of the two entities, 10 of them from the Federation and five from the Serb Republic. Both Houses have four-year terms.

The Federation also has a bicameral Assembly (Skupština), comprising a House of Representatives (Predstavnički/Zastupnički Dom Federacije) with 98 directly elected members, and a 58-member House of Peoples (Dom Naroda Federacije), which has one-half Bosniak and one-half Croat representation. Both houses have a four-year term. The Serb Republic has two legislative bodies, comprising a People's Assembly (Narodna Skupština) with 83 members directly elected, and a Council of Peoples (Vijeće Naroda), whose members (eight Bosniaks, eight Croats, eight Serbs and four others) are chosen by the People's Assembly. Both houses have a four-year term.

The last elections were held on 1 October 2006 for the House of Representatives, and the Federation and Serb Republic legislatures.

Address: Parlamentarna Skupština, Trg BiH 1, 71000 Sarajevo.
Telephone: (33) 284401.
Fax: (33) 211028.
E-mail: branka.todorovic@parlament.ba
Internet: www.parlament.ba

Partnership for Peace (PfP)

A mechanism to promote a rapprochement between the **North Atlantic Treaty Organization** (NATO) and the countries of **central** and **eastern Europe** after the end of the **Cold War**. The Partnership for Peace programme was established in January 1994 within the framework of the North Atlantic Co-operation Council (NACC—*see* **Euro-Atlantic Partnership Council**). The PfP incorporated practical military and defence-related co-operation activities that had originally been part of the NACC Work Plan. Participation in the PfP required an initial signature of a framework agreement, establishing the common principles and objectives of the partnership, the submission of a presentation document, indicating the political and military aspects of the partnership and the nature of the future co-operation activities, and finally the development of individual partnership programmes establishing country-specific objectives. Many initial PfP participants have since become full members of NATO.

Participating states: 22 countries. Armenia, Austria, Azerbaijan, Belarus, **Bosnia and Herzegovina**, Finland, Georgia, Ireland, Kazakhstan, Kyrgyzstan, **Macedonia**, Malta, Moldova, **Montenegro**, Russian Federation, **Serbia**, Sweden, Switzerland, Tajikistan, Turkmenistan, Ukraine and Uzbekistan.
Internet: www.nato.int/pfp/pfp.htm

Party for Bosnia and Herzegovina
Stranka za Bosne i Hercegovine (SBiH)

A moderate non-sectarian formation in **Bosnia and Herzegovina** which has sought to challenge the dominance of the ethnic nationalist parties. The SBiH was founded in April 1996 by Haris **Silajdžić**, who had resigned as Prime Minister of the Bosnian Government in January in opposition to apparent Islamic fundamentalist tendencies in the dominant **Party of Democratic Action** (SDA). In the first post-**Dayton** elections in September 1996, Silajdžić came second in the contest for the **Muslim** member of the collective Presidency, winning 13.5% of the Muslim vote, while the SBiH took two seats in the union lower house and 11 in the **Muslim-Croat Federation** lower house. In December 1996 Silajdžić was appointed as one of the two union Co-Prime Ministers, continuing in the post until the move to a single Prime Minister in June 2000.

The SBiH contested the September 1998 elections within the SDA-led Coalition for a Single and Democratic Bosnia and Herzegovina (KCD). Standing alone in the November 2000 elections, the SBiH won five union lower house seats with 11.4% of the vote, 21 in the Federation lower house and four in the People's Assembly of the **Serb Republic** (RS).

The party joined the Alliance for Change grouping of moderate parties in early 2001, and Beriz **Belkić** of the SBiH was appointed as the Bosniak member of the union Presidency, replacing Halid Genjac of the SDA.

At the October 2002 elections, Silajdžić narrowly lost the race for the Muslim seat on the union Presidency, securing 34.8% while SDA candidate Sulejman Tihić gained 37.3%. In the all-Bosnia lower house the SBiH improved to second with six seats (12% of the vote), retained its four seats in the RS Assembly, but dropped to 15 seats in the Federation lower house (which had been downsized from 140 members to 98 members). Adnan Terzić of the SDA formed a cross-party union Government which included representatives of the SBiH.

Four years later Silajdžić regained the Bosniak seat on the union Presidency with a convincing 62.8% of the vote. The SBiH, meanwhile, performed well in all the legislative polls, winning eight seats (with 15.5% of the vote) in the all-Bosnia lower house, 24 seats in the Federation lower house (only four behind the largest bloc, the SDA) and again four in the RS Assembly.

Leadership: Haris Silajdžić (President).
Address: 7A Maršala Tita, Sarajevo.
Telephone and fax: (33) 214417.
Internet: www.zabih.ba

Party of Democratic Action
Stranka Demokratske Akcije (SDA)

The dominant political formation of the majority **Muslim** population in **Bosnia and Herzegovina**. Founded in May 1990, the SDA became the largest Assembly party in elections in late 1990 and also won three seats on the then seven-member collegial Presidency, with SDA leader Alija Izetbegović becoming its Chairman. Under Izetbegović's presidency, Bosnia and Herzegovina moved to full independence in March 1992; but the intention that the new state's Government should be a coalition of the SDA, the **Serbian Democratic Party** (SDS) and the **Croatian Democratic Union** (HDZ) proved unattainable, as deepening hostilities between the communities resulted in the effective breakdown of inter-party co-operation by late 1992. In the mid-1990s the SDA was weakened by splits, resulting in the creation of the breakaway Democratic People's Union and the **Party for Bosnia and Herzegovina** (SBiH). Nevertheless, in the first post-**Dayton** elections in September 1996 the SDA maintained its hold on the Muslim vote. Izetbegović was elected as the Muslim representative on the new three-member collective Presidency, with over 80% of the Muslim vote, while the SDA won 19 of the 42 seats in the lower house of the union legislature and 78 of 140 seats in the **Muslim-Croat Federation** lower house. In the September 1998 elections, Izetbegović was candidate of the SDA-led Coalition for a Single and Democratic Bosnia and Herzegovina (KCD), which included the non-sectarian SBiH, and was re-elected with 86.8% of the Muslim vote (and about 32% nationally). However, the KCD won only 17 seats in the union lower house and 68 in the Federation lower house.

Having succeeded to the rotating Presidency of the Muslim-Croat Federation from the beginning of 2000, Ejup Ganić of the SDA was expelled from the party in May for refusing to resign over the SDA's poor showing in local elections the previous month. Standing on its own in the November 2000 legislative elections, the SDA won only eight of the union lower house seats and only 38 in the Federation lower house, being challenged in both legislatures by the multi-ethnic **Social Democratic Party of Bosnia and Herzegovina**. Prior to the elections, Izetbegović had finally retired as a member of the union collective Presidency (being succeeded by Halid Genjac of the SDA), although he continued as SDA Chairman until October 2001, when Sulejman Tihić was appointed to replace him.

Tihić won the Muslim seat on the union Presidency in October 2002 with 37.3% of the vote, and in the simultaneous legislative elections the SDA became the largest party in both the all-Bosnia lower house (with 10 seats and 23.7% of the national vote) and in the Federation lower house (with 32 seats in a downsized chamber of 98 members) and retaining its position as the main Muslim party in the People's Assembly of the **Serb Republic** (RS) with six seats. Adnan Terzić of the SDA was nominated as union Prime Minister in January 2003, while Ahmet Hadžipašić became Federation Prime Minister the following month.

In February 2006 the SDA joined a new coalition Government in the RS, under Milorad **Dodik** of the **Alliance of Independent Social Democrats** (SNSD).

The moderate parties fought back at the October 2006 elections, with Tihić losing his seat on the union Presidency to Haris **Silajdžić**, who scored a convincing 62.8% of the vote compared to Tihić's 28%. The SDA dropped one seat in the all-Bosnia lower house for a total of nine (with 16.9% of the vote nationally) but remained the largest party. However, Nikola Špirić of the SNSD was nominated as union Prime Minister, though he included the SDA in his coalition.

In the RS Assembly the SDA fell to three seats, while in the Federation lower house, the SDA dropped to 28 seats but again remained the largest bloc. A new Federation Government led by Nedžad Branković of the SDA was approved on 22 March, but it was immediately suspended by the UN **High Representative** as his office had not yet approved all the proposed ministers. On 30 March the Government, with a replacement Interior Minister, was again approved by the Federation parliament. Branković resigned on 27 May 2009, after being charged with misappropriation of funds while he was CEO of Energoinvest; Mustafa **Mujezinović** replaced him the following month.

Leadership: Sulejman Tihić (Chair.).

Address: 14 Mehmeda Spahe, Sarajevo.

Telephone: (33) 216906.

Fax: (33) 650429.

E-mail: sda@bih.net.ba

Internet: www.sda.ba

Party of Democratic Progress
Partija Demokratskog Progresa (PDP)

A centrist **Serb** political formation in the **Serb Republic** (RS), a member of the **International Democrat Union**. The PDP was launched in September 1999 by Mladen Ivanić, a well-known economist who had come second in the Serb section of the elections for the union collective Presidency in September 1996 as a moderate non-party candidate, with 30% of the vote. In the November 2000 elections the PDP won 11 of the 83 seats in the RS Assembly. Ivanić become RS Prime Minister in January 2001. In March 2002, after the union Presidency had rotated, Dragan Mikerević of the PDP was appointed as all-Bosnia Prime Minister.

In the October 2002 elections to the all-Bosnia lower house, the PDP retained its two seats (taking 4.7% of the vote) and was included in the new union Government led by the **(Muslim) Party of Democratic Action** (SDA). In the RS Assembly it dropped to nine seats but Mikerević (who had come third in the union presidential race for the Serb seat on the collective Presidency) was appointed as RS Prime Minister. However, he resigned in December 2004, though the PDP remained in the successor coalition led by Pero Bukejlović of the **Serbian Democratic Party** (SDS). It withdrew its support for Bukejlović the following November and when his Government collapsed in January 2006 it joined the new SNSD-led coalition of Milorad **Dodik**. At the October 2006 elections it won only one seat in the all-Bosnia lower house and eight in the RS Assembly, but it remained in Dodik's RS coalition.

Leadership: Mladen Ivanić (Chair.).
Address: First Krajina Corps 130, 78000 Banja Luka.
Telephone: (51) 346210.
Fax: (51) 300956.
E-mail: pdp@blic.net
Internet: www.pdpinfo.net *or* www.pdp.rs.ba

PASOK *see* **Pan-Hellenic Socialist Movement**.

PC *see* **Conservative Party**.

PCA *see* **Permanent Court of Arbitration**.

PD *see* **Democratic Party (Poland)**.

PD-L *see* **Democratic Liberal Party**.

PDK *see* **Democratic Party of Kosovo**.

PDP *see* **Party of Democratic Progress**.

PDSh *see* **Democratic Party of Albania**.

People's Assembly
Kuvendi Popullor

The unicameral legislature of **Albania**. It has at least 140 members under the 1998 Constitution, directly elected for a maximum of four years, 100 in single-member consituencies and at least 40 by proportional representation. The last elections were held on 28 June 2009.

Address: Kuvendi Popullor, Bulevardi Dëshmorët e Kombit 4, Tirana.
Telephone: (4) 237418.
Fax: (4) 227949.
E-mail: marlind@parlament.al
Internet: www.parlament.al

People's Party
Tautas Partija (TP)

The largest centre-right political party in the **Parliament** of **Latvia**, advocating family values and national regeneration, and part of the ruling coalition. The TP was officially launched in May 1998 by Andris Škele, a former businessman who had been non-party Prime Minister in 1995–97 attempting to lead a series of fractious centre-right coalitions. In the October 1998 parliamentary elections the TP emerged as narrowly the largest party, winning 24 of the 100 seats on a 21.2% vote share. It nevertheless went into opposition to a coalition headed by Latvian Way (LC) until July 1999, when Škele returned to the premiership at the head of a majority centre-right coalition. Škele was forced to resign in April 2000 over a paedophilia scandal (later being cleared of allegations against him personally), whereupon the TP again became a junior partner in a coalition headed by the LC.

At the October 2002 parliamentary election the TP finished in third place with 20 seats and 16.6% of the vote. It was not included as part of the new centre-right coalition, and the following month Škele was replaced by Atis Slakteris as party Chairman.

In March 2004 the TP re-entered government in a four-party minority coalition headed by Indulis Emsis of the **Union of Greens and Farmers** (ZZS). Despite being part of the Government, the TP in October opposed Emsis's 2005 budget proposals. When Emsis resigned, Aigars Kalvītis of the TP was invited to form the new Government, which was a majority centre-right coalition of the TP, **New Era** (JL), ZZS and Latvian First Party (LPP). Over the next 17 months various ministers were plagued by corruption allegations, and in April 2006 the JL withdrew after Kalvītis refused to eject the LPP, leaving once again a minority coalition of the TP, ZZS and LPP.

Kalvītis took over from Slakteris as TP leader later that year, and in the October 2006 legislative elections the TP regained pole position in the Parliament with 23 seats and 19.6% of the vote. Kalvītis's incumbent coalition, now commanding 51 seats in the 100-member Parliament, was the first since independence in 1991 to retain power at an election. His new Government, which took office in November 2006, was strengthened by the addition of the TB/LNNK. By the end of the year Kalvītis was under fire for alleged abuse of power—in particular his dismissal of Latvia's anti-corruption chief. He resigned in December though the TP remained in the ruling coalition, now headed by LPP/LC co-leader Ivars Godmanis. Economic crisis in 2008–09 brought down this Government, but again the TP was part of the new coalition Government under Valdis **Dombrovskis** of JL from 12 March 2009. Meanwhile, Mareks Segliņš had replaced Kalvītis as TP leader in October 2008.

Leadership: Mareks Segliņš (Chair.).
Address: Jēkaba ielā 16, Rīga 1811.
Telephone: 7087207.
Fax: 7087289.
E-mail: tautpart@saeima.lv
Internet: www.tautaspartija.lv

People's Party–Movement for a Democratic Slovakia
Ľudová strana–Hnutie za Demokratické Slovensko (ĽS–HZDS)

A populist centre-right party in **Slovakia**, currently a junior partner in the ruling coalition, and a member of the **Alliance of Democrats**.

The HZDS was launched in May 1991 a month after Vladimír **Mečiar** (a former communist) had been ousted from the premiership of Slovakia (then still part of **Czechoslovakia**) after coming into conflict with the mainstream leadership of the pro-democracy **Public Against Violence** (VPN). The HZDS quickly confirmed that it was Slovakia's leading political formation, winning 74 of the 150 Slovak Council seats in the June 1992 elections. Restored to the premiership, Mečiar led Slovakia to sovereignty from the beginning of 1993 and formed a governing coalition with the radical right-wing **Slovak National Party** (SNS).

The Mečiar Government quickly came under criticism for its authoritarian tendencies and the entrenched position of former communists in the state bureaucracy. Policy and personal clashes precipitated a series of defections from the HZDS in 1993–94, while the appointment of a former communist as Defence Minister in March 1993 caused the SNS to leave the Government, which was thus reduced to minority status. Having failed to persuade the (ex-communist) Party of the Democratic Left (SDĽ) to join the Government, Mečiar restored the coalition with the SNS in October 1993. However, chronic divisions within the HZDS led to the Prime Minister's defeat in a no-confidence motion and reluctant resignation in March 1994. The HZDS went into opposition to a centrist coalition, but remained the country's strongest formation with its combination of economic conservatism and strident nationalism.

Allied in the autumn 1994 elections with the small Agrarian Party of Slovakia, the HZDS won a decisive plurality of 61 seats in the **National Council** (on a 34.9% vote share) and became the lead partner in a 'red-brown' coalition with the SNS and the left-wing Association of Workers of Slovakia. Public commitments notwithstanding, the return of the HZDS to power meant a slowdown in the pace of transition to a market economy. It also revived earlier political conflict between Mečiar and President Michal Kováč, who had been elected by the legislature in February 1993 as candidate of the HZDS but who had subsequently distanced himself from the movement. The tension flared up in March 1995 when the President refused at first to sign a bill transferring overall control of the security services from the Head of State to the Government. Although he signed the measure the following month when the National Council had readopted it, the HZDS executive called for his resignation and expulsion from the party.

The confrontation between Mečiar and President Kováč rumbled on in 1996–97, with the HZDS Government blocking opposition moves for a referendum on a proposal that the President should be directly elected. As Kováč's five-year term came to an end, the legislature failed to produce the required three-fifths majority for a successor, so that in March 1998 Mečiar, as Prime Minister, assumed key presidential functions. HZDS deputies thereafter blocked further attempts to elect a President, with damaging effects on the party's public standing. In National Council elections in September 1998 the HZDS narrowly remained the largest party, but slumped to 43 seats on a 27% vote share and went into opposition to a centre-left coalition.

Following the adoption of a constitutional amendment by the new legislature in January 1999 providing for direct presidential elections, Mečiar emerged from post-election seclusion to become the HZDS presidential candidate. However, in the elections in May 1999 he was defeated in the second round by the centre-left nominee on a 57% to 43% split. In March 2000 Mečiar was re-elected HZDS Chairman by a party congress which also approved the conversion of the HZDS into a formal political party with the suffix People's Party, signifying a shift to a less nationalistic stance, while the party declared its full support for membership of the **European Union** (EU) and the **North Atlantic Treaty Organization** (NATO).

In April 2000 Mečiar suffered the indignity of being arrested and fined for refusing to testify on the murky affair of the kidnapping of President Kováč's son in 1995 at the height of Mečiar's confrontation with the President. The HZDS then succeeded in collecting sufficient signatures to force a referendum on its proposal that early parliamentary elections should be held. However, only 20% of the electorate voted when the consultation was held in November 2000, so that the result had no validity.

At the September 2002 parliamentary election the HZDS remained the largest party, though now with only 36 seats and 19.5% of the vote. Mečiar was invited to form a government, but again found himself unable to form a coalition, so remained in opposition.

Just before the election, Ivan **Gašparovič** and some fellow HZDS members who had not been selected as candidates for the poll broke away and established the Movement for Democracy (HZD). In May 2003 another group broke off the HZDS and formed the People's Union (ĽU). The HZDS responded in June by changing its name to the People's Party–Movement for a Democratic Slovakia (ĽS–HZDS). In the first round of the April 2004 presidential election Mečiar led with 32.7% of the vote, with Gašparovič edging out the ruling coalition's candidate by 22.3% to 22.1%. However, Gašparovič then went on to win the run-off by 59.9% to 40.1%.

At the June 2006 election, the ĽS–HZDS fell to fifth place on 15 seats (8.8% of the vote). The poll was won by **Direction–Social Democracy** (Smer), whose leader Róbert **Fico** formed a coalition with the ĽS–HZDS and the SNS. The junior coalition partners received only two and three ministerial portfolios respectively, and neither party's controversial leader was invited to fill any of the positions.

Leadership: Vladimír Mečiar (Chair.).

Address: Tomášikova 32/A, POB 49, 83000 Bratislava 3.

Telephone: (2) 48220309.

Fax: (2) 48220329.

E-mail: predseda@hzds.sk

Internet: www.hzds.sk

Permanent Court of Arbitration (PCA)
(also known as *Cour permanente d'arbitrage*, CPA)

An international court based in The Hague, Netherlands, designed to provide a peaceful forum for the solution of international disputes. The PCA was established by the Convention on Pacific Settlement of International Disputes, which was signed in 1899 during the first Hague Peace Conference—convened by Russian Tsar Nicholas II as an attempt to prevent future international conflict and to de-escalate the arms race of the time.

The Convention was revised at the second Conference in 1907 and 110 countries have signed up to either one or both of the Conventions, giving them access to the PCA. These included **Bulgaria**, **Croatia**, **Cyprus**, **Czech Republic**, **Estonia**, **Greece**, **Hungary**, **Latvia**, **Lithuania**, **Macedonia**, **Montenegro**, **Poland**, **Romania**, **Serbia**, **Slovakia** and **Slovenia**. The court also now hears cases of international commercial arbitration in a specially-convened Council. The court uses two official languages, English and French.

Secretary-General: Tjaco van den Hout.

Address: Peace Palace, Camegieplein 2, 2517 KJ, The Hague, Netherlands.

Telephone: (70) 3024165.

Fax: (70) 3024167.

E-mail: bureau@pca-cpa.org

Internet: pca-cpa.org

Petseri question

A dormant territorial dispute between **Estonia** and the Russian Federation over the Petseri county area (known in Russian as Pechory), which lies south-east of Narva. The county was ceded to Estonia under the first Treaty of **Tartu** in 1920 along with other **Russian**-dominated areas, but the Soviet authorities reannexed Petseri in 1944. The collapse of the **Soviet Union** in 1991 and the creation of an independent Estonia raised calls for a return to the borders agreed in 1920. However, Petseri has a predominantly Russian community, a fact which did not leave the Estonian claim with much weight, and in November 1995 Estonia agreed to drop its claims to the county.

Russia and Estonia signed a border treaty, which confirmed the Petseri area as part of Russia, in May 2005, following Estonia's accession to the **North Atlantic Treaty Organization** and the **European Union**. However, when during the ratification process Estonia's Parliament amended the preamble with a reference to the 1920 Treaty of Tartu, Russia withdrew from the new treaty.

PfP *see* **Partnership for Peace**.

PHARE programme

The programme in the early 1990s for **European Union** aid initially to **Poland** and **Hungary**, and thereafter extended to the rest of **central** and **eastern Europe**. The name Phare, meaning 'lighthouse' in French, comes from the French acronym for 'Poland and Hungary: economic reconstruction assistance'.

Pirin Macedonia *see* **Macedonian question**.

PiS *see* **Law and Justice**.

PNL *see* **National Liberal Party**.

PO *see* **Civic Platform**.

Podgorica

The capital, and main urban centre, of **Montenegro**. *Population*: 174,000 (2007 estimate). Founded by the ancient Illyrians and adopted by the Romans, the city of Podgorica lies at the confluence of the Morača and Ribnica rivers. It was given its modern name in 1326, having previously been known as Ribnica while it served, briefly, as the capital of **Serbia**. Through most of the long Ottoman rule in the region the city lay outside the domain of the fiercely independent Montenegrin rulers. It became the Montenegrin capital for the first time when *de facto* independence was finally recognized by the international community in 1878. It remained in this capacity when the republic was absorbed in 1918 into the Kingdom of Serbs, Croats and Slovenes (which would later become **Yugoslavia**), and indeed the Great People's Council at which Montenegro was voluntarily united with Serbia, was held in Podgorica on 26 November 1918. Much of the old city was destroyed during the Second World War and socialist reconstruction has left a thoroughly 'modern' city in its place. From 1946 until the collapse of the **Socialist Federal Republic of Yugoslavia** in 1992, Podgorica was known as Titograd in honour of the Yugoslav leader Marshal **Tito**.

As the capital of the now independent Montenegro, Podgorica is the centre of the country's economy and home to a wide variety of light industries. It is a key transport hub and contains the country's main airport, which is still known internationally by the ex-Titograd code TGD.

Poland

Rzeczpospolita Polska

An independent republic situated in northern central Europe, bordered to the west by Germany, to the south-west by the Czech Republic, to the south by Slovakia, to the east by Ukraine and Belarus, to the north-east by Lithuania, and to the north by the **Kaliningrad** territory of the Russian Federation and the Baltic Sea. Administratively, the country is divided into 16 provinces (voivodships) and 308 districts (powiats).

Area: 312,685 sq km; *capital*: **Warsaw**; *population*: 38.1m (2009 estimate), comprising **Poles** 96.7%, **Germans** 0.4%, Ukrainians 0.1%, Belarusians 0.1%, other 2.7; *language*: Polish; *religion*: **Roman Catholic** 88%, **Orthodox** 1.3%, other 10.7%.

Under the Constitution approved by referendum in 1997, legislative authority is vested in the bicameral **National Assembly** (Zgromadzenie Narodowe), which consists of a 460-member Diet (Sejm) and a 100-member Senate (Senat). Sejm members are elected for a four-year term by a complex system of proportional representation subject to a 5% threshold; the Senat is directly elected for a four-year term by a majority vote on a provincial basis. Executive authority is vested in the President (Head of State) and Prime Minister. The President is directly elected for a five-year term (renewable once). The Prime Minister is appointed by the Diet on the basis of a motion by the President. The Council of Ministers is also appointed by the Diet.

History: Slavic tribes united under Prince Mieszko I of the Piast dynasty in the late 10th century to form the first Polish state. After subsequent feudal fragmentation, Poland was reunited and royal authority restored in the 14th century. Existing close dynastic links with **Lithuania** led in 1569 to the formation of a powerful confederation under the Union of Lublin. However, after 200 years of elective monarchy marked by wars and territorial losses, **Russia**, **Prussia** and Austria partitioned Poland in three stages between 1772 and 1795. At the Congress of Vienna in 1815, Poland remained partitioned and the Napoleonic Duchy of Warsaw (created by the Treaty of Tilsit in 1807) became the puppet Kingdom of Poland under tsarist Russian domination.

Polish nationalists led by Marshal Jozef Piłsudski declared Poland's independence in 1918 following the collapse of Germany and tsarist Russia during the First World War. Independence was guaranteed by the 1919 **Versailles** settlements, but was only fully achieved after Soviet troops had been expelled and the 1921 Treaty of **Rīga** signed with the new **Soviet Union**. After a period of crisis-ridden democratic politics, Marshal Piłsudski became virtual dictator of Poland in 1926. In September 1939, despite Anglo-French guarantees, Germany and the Soviet Union invaded and divided Poland (as had been secretly agreed under the 1939 **Nazi-Soviet Pact**). In April–May 1940 the Soviet secret police perpetrated (but for many year's denied) the **Katyń massacre** of some 22,000 Poles. Following the German attack on the Soviet Union in 1941, all of Poland was occupied by German forces.

In 1944 the Soviet-backed 'Lublin Committee' declared itself the provisional Polish Government, as the Red Army drove out German forces. At the Allies' **Potsdam** conference in 1945 Poland's borders were redrawn westwards to include former German territory up to the **Oder-Neisse line**, in partial compensation for the cession of a larger area of eastern Poland to the Soviet Union. Having ruthlessly suppressed its opponents, the communist Polish Workers' Party engineered a victory for itself and allied parties in the 1947 elections, following which it declared a people's republic and renamed itself the Polish United Workers' Party (PUWP). In 1952 Poland adopted a Soviet-style Constitution and in 1955 joined the **Warsaw Pact** military alliance.

In 1980, following a visit by the Polish Pope **John Paul II** the previous year, workers' strikes in **Gdańsk** led to the birth of **Solidarity**, a free trade union led by Lech **Wałęsa**. Martial law was imposed in 1981 and Solidarity was outlawed, but by the late 1980s the influence of the *glasnost* ('openness') initiative in the Soviet Union had rekindled public unrest. Unable to contain the political challenge, the PUWP regime agreed to a measure of power-sharing and representation for the opposition. In elections in 1989 Solidarity candidates won all the unreserved seats in the Sejm (around two-thirds being reserved for approved organizations, particularly the PUWP) and all but one seat in the Senat. Tadeusz Mazowiecki, a Solidarity activist, was appointed Prime Minister, leading a coalition Government with a non-communist majority. The PUWP voted to disband, re-forming as Social Democracy of the Polish Republic in early 1990 and later becoming the dominant component of the **Democratic Left Alliance** (SLD). In December 1990 Wałęsa was overwhelmingly elected as Poland's first post-communist President, his first Prime Minister being pro-marketeer Jan Bielecki.

Political instability followed the first fully democratic parliamentary elections in October 1991, which gave 29 parties representation in the Sejm. A fragile centre-right coalition Government led by Jan Olszewski, then a centrist, resigned after seven months and was succeeded in July 1992 by a seven-party coalition headed by Hanna Suchocka of the Democratic Union. In May 1993 the President dissolved the Sejm and new electoral rules were enacted to exclude parties which won less than 5% of the vote. The September 1993 elections returned the SLD as the largest party with 171 lower house seats, followed by the **Polish People's Party** (PSL) with 132. The SLD and PSL formed a left-wing coalition Government under PSL leader Waldemar Pawlak, but he was replaced by Józef Oleksy of the SLD in early 1995 following serious tensions between the Government and the President. Wałęsa narrowly failed to secure a second term in the November–December 1995 presidential elections, being defeated in the second round by Aleksander **Kwaśniewski** of the SLD. In early 1996 he appointed Włodzimierz **Cimoszewicz** (the SLD Deputy Prime Minister) to replace Oleksy, who had resigned over spying allegations. Thereafter, amid economic and social difficulties associated with transition to a market economy, the SLD-PSL coalition became increasingly unpopular.

Parliamentary elections in September 1997 were won by the centre-right **Solidarity Electoral Action** (AWS), a multi-party Christian-orientated alliance which took 201 seats in the Sejm. The SLD was pushed into opposition as Jerzy Buzek of the AWS was appointed Prime Minister and formed a centre-right coalition Government with the liberal Freedom Union (UW). The new Government went on to secure the ratification in January 1998 of a concordat with the Vatican, signed in 1993 but shelved by the SLD-PSL Government, providing *inter alia* for the legalization of church marriages. It also ensured the abolition of capital punishment under a new penal code introduced in September 1998. However, increasing strains in the ruling coalition culminated in the withdrawal of the UW in June 2000, leaving Buzek as head of a minority AWS Government with diminishing parliamentary and popular support.

Presidential elections in October 2000 were won in the first round by SLD incumbent Kwaśniewski, who took 53.9% of the vote, while AWS nominee Marian Krzaklewski, leader of the Solidarity trade union wing, came a poor third with only 15.6%. The popularity of the Government slipped even further as the Solidarity movement withdrew its support for AWS altogether in May 2001 and the party became mired in corruption scandals. Buzek became the first Prime Minister to complete a term in office in post-communist Poland but had the indignity of seeing the AWS wiped out of the Assembly entirely in elections in September. The poll saw a great success for more radical right-wing parties on the political fringe. The SLD, in alliance with the Labour Union (UP), secured 216 seats in the Sejm and 75 seats in the Senat. Leszek **Miller** of the SLD formed a coalition Government with the UP and the PSL (who had secured 42 seats in the Sejm and four seats in the Senat).

In March 2003 Miller ejected the PSL from his coalition Government after it refused to support his tax plans. Thereafter his Government could not command a majority in the Sejm, despite gaining the support of the small Peasant Democratic Party (until January 2004). His position became untenable when 27 SLD politicians defected in March 2004 to form **Polish Social Democracy** (SDPL), and he announced that he would resign on 2 May, the day after Poland's accession to the **European Union** (EU).

Former Finance Minister Marek Belka, an independent, was nominated to succeed Miller, heading a Government of SLD/UP members and independents, with support from the SDPL. Although the Sejm rejected Belka's nomination on 14 May, raising the possibility that early elections would be needed, it endorsed him at a second vote on 24 June. Belka remained in office until the September 2005 elections, despite the difficulties of minority rule: he offered his resignation to President Kwaśniewski in May 2005, but it was refused.

In the 2005 elections the two main centre-right parties were victorious. Law and Justice (PiS), led by the Kaczyński twins, won 27% of the vote, 155 seats in the Sejm and 49 in the Senat, while Civic Platform (PO), led by Donald **Tusk**, won 24% of the vote, 133 Sejm seats and 34 Senat seats. The SLD lost ground heavily, retaining only 55 Sejm seats and no representatives in the Senat. With coalition talks ongoing between the PiS and PO in October, Tusk and Lech **Kaczyński** faced off in the presidential ballot, which was won by Kaczyński (with 54% of the vote to Tusk's 46%). His twin brother Jarosław had been expected to become Prime Minister, but in an effort to improve relations with the PO economist, Kazimierz Marcinkiewicz was nominated for the post. However, the coalition talks still collapsed. Marcinkiewicz then formed a minority Government of the PiS and independents, which took office on 31 October.

In spring 2006 the agrarian Self-Defence of the Republic of Poland (SRP) and nationalist League of Polish Families (LPR) joined the Government, giving it a parliamentary majority. In July Marcinkiewicz resigned after a rift with the Kaczyńskis, and Jarosław Kaczyński took over the premiership, Poland thus becoming the first country ever to be ruled by twins. Within two months the coalition was in trouble, however, with the dismissal of SRP leader Andrzej Lepper from the post of Deputy Prime Minister, leading to the withdrawal of all SRP ministers. Surprisingly in October the same coalition was reformed. In July 2007 Lepper was dismissed again, but this time the SRP did not immediately quit the Government. After four weeks of uncertainty, President Kaczyński fired the SRP members in a move to precipitate the dissolution of the Assembly and the calling of early elections.

Latest elections: In the early polls, held in October 2007, an enormous swing of support behind Tusk's PO enabled it to win 209 Sejm seats and 41.5% of the vote. The PiS was second—on an increased vote share of 32% and 166 Sejm seats. The left-wing alliance, the **Left and Democrats** (LiD—including the SLD) won 13% of the vote and 53 seats, while the centrist PSL was the only other party to pass the 5%

vote threshold to secure representation, with 9% of the vote and 31 seats; the German Minority (not required to reach the threshold) were awarded one seat. In the Senat, the PO won 60 seats, the PiS won 39 and the final seat went to an independent. On 9 November Tusk was formally nominated as Prime Minister heading a majority Government of his PO and the PSL.

Recent developments: On 10 April 2010 President Lech Kaczyński, his wife and around 90 other Polish dignitaries were en route to a memorial service for the 70th anniversary of the Katyń massacre when their plane crashed near Smolensk, Russia, killing everyone on board. Bronisław **Komorowski**, Marshal (Speaker) of the Sejm, became acting President, and an early election was scheduled for 20 June.

International relations and defence: Post-communist Poland signed a Treaty of Friendship and Co-operation with reunified Germany in 1991, giving legal recognition to the Oder-Neisse border and the rights of the German minority in Poland. A similarly-named treaty was signed with the Russian Federation in 1992. In the early 1990s Poland joined the **Organization for Security and Co-operation in Europe**, the **Council of Europe**, the **Central European Initiative** and the **Central European Free Trade Area**, later becoming a member of the **Organisation for Economic Co-operation and Development** and the **World Trade Organization**. Having acceded to **NATO**'s **Partnership for Peace** programme in 1994, Poland formally joined the NATO Alliance (together with the **Czech Republic** and **Hungary**) in March 1999. Following its 1994 application for membership of the EU, Poland opened formal accession negotiations in March 1998 and was offered membership in December 2002, as the organization undertook a major expansion. The Polish people supported membership in a referendum in June 2003, and Poland acceded on 1 May 2004. In a further stage of integration, in December 2007 Poland also joined the EU's Schengen Agreement, allowing free movement of citizens within the borders of the Schengen zone. It is unlikely to join the eurozone before 2012 (*see* **Poland, economy**).

Poland's defence budget for 2008 amounted to some US $10,176m., equivalent to about 1.9% of GDP. The size of the armed forces in 2010 was some 100,000. Conscription was phased out by August 2009, so the armed forces are now entirely professional. Around 200 Polish soldiers participated in the 2003 invasion of Iraq— making Poland one of only four countries to take part in the major combat operations. In 2008 Poland signed an agreement with the USA to host 10 interceptor missiles for the US missile defence shield, in return for assistance with air defence and modernization of its armed forces. Russia has voiced strong disapproval of this arrangement. In October 2009 US President Obama modified the US missile defence plan: now Poland is only expected to host a small US base equipped with short-range missiles.

Poland, economy

One of the largest economies in central-eastern Europe. Having made the transition to a free-market economy from communist-era central control, and joined the **European Union** (EU) in 2004, Poland was the only EU member to continue posting positive growth throughout the recent global economic recession.

GNP: US $453,034m. (2008); *GNP per capita*: $11,880 (2008); *GDP at PPP*: $671,927m. (2008); *GDP per capita at PPP*: $17,600 (2008); *real GDP growth*: 1.0% (2009 estimate); *exports*: $168,725m. (2008); *imports*: $204,951m. (2008); *currency*: złoty (plural: złotys; US $1 = Z3.18 in mid-2009); *unemployment*: 8.9% (end 2009); *government deficit as a percentage of GDP*: 7.2% (2009); *inflation*: 3.4% (2009).

In 2007 industry accounted for 31% of GDP, agriculture for 4% and services for 65%. Around 31% of the workforce is engaged in industry, 15% in agriculture and 54% in services.

Some 47% of the land is arable, 1% under permanent crops, 13% permanent pasture and 29% forests and woodland. The main crops are vegetables, grain and sugar beet; there is a significant animal husbandry sector, including dairy farming.

The main mineral resources are hard and brown coal (lignite), some oil and natural gas, and various non-ferrous metal ores, including copper, zinc, lead and silver, together with sulphur reserves. The principal industries are machine-building, iron and steel, chemicals, shipbuilding, food processing, textiles and beverages. Coal is by far the greatest energy source, although petroleum is imported to supplement the indigenous coal; there are no plans for nuclear-sourced electricity.

Poland's main exports are machinery and transport equipment, manufactured goods, food and live animals, and chemicals and related products. Principal imports are machinery and transport equipment, manufactured goods, chemical products, mineral fuels and lubricants, and food and live animals. In 2008 Germany was by far the greatest purchaser of Polish exports (26%), followed by Italy (7%) and France (6%). Germany is also the biggest provider of Polish imports (24% in 2008), followed by the Russian Federation (9%) and the People's Republic of China (7%). Over 80% of trade is with other EU member states.

Poland avoided the protracted slump in output experienced by most other post-communist countries in the early 1990s, becoming in 1994 the first to improve on its 1989 GDP and achieving average annual GDP growth of 5% in the period 1993–98. Within this framework, the share of the industrial sector dropped sharply as the old, centralized economy with a concentration on heavy industry was replaced by a more modern service-orientated market economy. The relative importance of the agricultural sector also declined as Poland became more integrated into the wider European market. Annual inflation dropped from around 30% in 1994 to 13.2% in 1997 and to 8.6% at the end of 1998, while unemployment fell from 14% in 1996 to 10% in 1998.

The role of the state was always less dominant in Poland than in other communist states, especially in that the agricultural sector was mostly under private ownership, so the privatization process in the 1990s was less disruptive, although nevertheless controversial. After initial concentration on eliminating subsidies and liquidating uneconomic concerns, legislation was enacted in 1990 providing for the privatization of over 7,500 enterprises, the first sales taking place later that year. The first mass privatization programme was initiated from 1993. Later stages, which were finally implemented after procedural delays, involved also the 'commercialization' rather than necessarily the full privatization of enterprises, with the state retaining the main ownership stake, and other privatizations in which vouchers were issues to citizens to enable them to acquire shares (*see* **voucher privatization**). The new Constitution which entered into force in October 1997 committed Poland to a social market economy based on freedom of economic activity and private ownership.

Poland was a founder member of the **Central European Free Trade Area** (CEFTA) in 1993 and the third post-communist state to join the **Organisation for Economic Co-operation and Development** (in 1996), having also become a founder member of the **World Trade Organization** in 1995.

Economic policy from the late 1990s onwards was wholly geared to the aim of joining the EU, Poland being one of the five original 'fast-track' entry candidates among the former communist states. Accession negotiations opened in 1998. The złoty was floated from April 2000 and became freely convertible against the euro.

GDP growth slowed to around 4% in 1998–2000, as Poland was adversely affected by the mid-1998 financial crisis in the Russian Federation—still an important trading partner—by rising world oil prices and by the slowdown in EU countries. In late 1998 and early 1999 there were a number of strikes and other expressions of industrial unrest as some workers resisted certain of the Government's reform measures. Inflation rose to 10%, and unemployment to 12% in 1999 and 15% in 2000.

By mid-2000 the number of state-owned concerns had been reduced by half to less than 2,800, but these included over 400 larger enterprises in highly-unionized sectors such as mining and heavy industry in which union opposition to privatization was strong.

GDP grew by only just over 1% a year in 2001–02, but economic recovery was evident by 2003, and was further sustained by Poland's accession to the EU in 2004, with GDP growth exceeding 5% that year. Unemployment declined as increasing numbers of Poles moved abroad to find work, notably to the United Kingdom and Ireland. By the end of 2006 an estimated 1.95m. Poles had emigrated, equating to over 10% of the workforce. GDP growth dipped to 3.6% in 2005, but rose to 6.2% in 2006 and further to 6.8% in 2007.

The new Government of Prime Minister Donald **Tusk** that took office in late 2007 favoured a strategy of liberalizing the labour market in order to improve productivity, privatizing state enterprises and reducing bureaucracy. The need to reduce the budget deficit to below 3% of GDP remained the most challenging element of the EU's financial criteria for joining the **eurozone**. In September 2008, with unemployemnt down to 6.5% and inflation under control, the Government outlined a series of moves aimed at adoption of the euro by 2012. The decision came in the wake of the global financial crisis, which led to a significant weakening of the złoty. Furthermore, by early 2009 the Government announced its application for $20,500m. of credit from the **International Monetary Fund** (IMF), which would support the economy in the event of further financial turmoil. The złoty strengthened on the news, reaching a three-month high against the euro by April 2009. GDP growth was a respectable 4.9% in 2008, and remained positive, at 1%, in 2009—the only EU-member economy to avoid recession in the global economic downturn.

However, unemployment is on the rise again, and the Government is attempting to get the budget deficit back under control by cutting spending and accelerating the privatization of the remaining large, state-owned enterprises, particularly in the transport, mining, chemical, energy, finance and defence sectors.

In 2009 the Finance Minister said that the economy was unlikely to meet the convergence criteria until 2012, an admission which extended indefinitely the Government's schedule for joining the eurozone.

Poles

A west **Slavic people** overwhelmingly dominant in modern **Poland** with sizeable minority populations in Belarus, Germany and **Lithuania**. The Polish language is very similar to Czech and Slovak. The ancestors of the Poles were dominant in the east of the north European plain by the 10th century when the northern Polanie united with the southern Wislanie to create a single Polish state. Despite their proximity to their east Slavic relations the Poles followed a westward-leaning path through history after accepting **Roman Catholicism** and the Latin script from the **Czechs** of **Bohemia** in 966. In the modern period the decline of Polish power was mirrored by the growing importance of **Prussia** (originally based on Königsberg, now called **Kaliningrad**), as a focal point of German unification, and by the westward extension of Russian power. The Poles' ethnic homogeneity was greatly challenged as their territory was swallowed up by the neighbouring powers, the Polish state disappearing entirely in the late 18th century. The influx of non-Polish people was accompanied by attempts to germanize and russify the population, with most Poles reduced to little better than the status of serfs. However, the preservation throughout this period of a sense of Polish identity, enhanced by the brief existence of the Napoleonic Duchy of **Warsaw**, provided a basis for nationalism in the independent state established in 1918. The devastation of the country under Nazi domination after 1939, the obliteration of its minority population of **Jews**, the mass deportations and then the displacement of ethnic **Germans** (and redrawing of boundaries) in 1945, left modern Poland with an almost entirely ethnic Polish population.

Polish Chamber of Commerce
Krajowa Izba Gospodarcza (KIG)

The principal organization in **Poland** for promoting business contacts, both internally and externally, in the post-communist era. Founded in 1990.
President: Andrzej Arendarski.
Address: ul. Trębacka 4, POB 361, 00074 Warsaw.
Telephone: (22) 6309600.
Fax: (22) 8279478.
E-mail: aarendarski@kig.pl
Internet: www.kig.pl

Polish Information and Foreign Investment Agency
Polska Agencja Informacji i Inwestycji Zagranicznych (PAIZ or PAIiIZ)

Government agency supervising the search for and administration of inward investment in **Poland**'s privatization and economic development programmes. Founded in 2003.
President: Andrzej Kanthak.
Address: ul. Bagatela 12, 00585 Warsaw.
Telephone: (22) 3349800.
Fax: (22) 3349999.
E-mail: post@paiz.gov.pl
Internet: www.paiz.gov.pl

Polish People's Party
Polskie Stronnictwo Ludowe (PSL)

A traditional political formation of **Poland**'s large agricultural population, currently part of the ruling coalition. The PSL is descended from the historic Peasant Party founded in **Galicia** in 1895, and more precisely from the group led by Stanisław Mikolajczyk, which in 1945 rejected the party leadership's decision to enter into close co-operation with the communists. In November 1949, after Mikolajczyk had been ousted by leftist PSL members, the two groups merged as the United Peasant Party (ZSL), which became part of the communist-dominated 'unity front'. The ZSL was thus committed to the goal of transforming Poland into a socialist society, although private peasant ownership of land was guaranteed from 1956.

As communist rule collapsed, the PSL was revived in August 1989 and reconstituted in May 1990 at a congress which unified various strands of the peasant movement. The then PSL leader, Roman Bartoszcze, received only 7.2% of the vote in the first round of presidential elections in November 1990 and was replaced in June

1991 by Waldemar Pawlak. Pawlak restored unity to the party and led it to a respectable 8.7% of the vote and 48 seats in the October 1991 **National Assembly** elections. Although it broadly supported the subsequent centre-right Olszewski Government, the PSL opposed its proposal to release secret police files to expose informers of the communist era. This issue brought down the Government in June 1992, whereupon Pawlak was endorsed by the Sejm (lower house) as the new Prime Minister, but was unable to form a Government.

Benefiting from rural disenchantment with economic 'shock therapy', the PSL polled strongly in the September 1993 parliamentary elections, becoming the second-largest party with 132 seats on an overall vote share of 15.4% (and a historically high 46% of the peasant vote). It then opted to join a coalition Government with the **Democratic Left Alliance** (SLD), the largest formation. In the light of lingering doubts about the SLD's pro-communist ancestry, the SLD agreed that Pawlak should become Prime Minister. The new coalition quickly displayed internal tensions, while the PSL also came into conflict with President **Wałęsa** because of its objections to what it regarded as precipitate moves to a free-market economy. The outcome was Pawlak's resignation in February 1995 and the appointment of an SLD Prime Minister, although the coalition was maintained.

The PSL's stint in government came to an end at the September 1997 parliamentary elections, in which its vote share slumped to 7.3% and its Sejm representation to 27 seats. The following month Pawlak gave way as party Chairman to former Agriculture Minister Jarosław Kalinowski, a representative of the PSL's conservative Christian-democratic wing that favoured tariff protection for Polish agriculture. In February 1998 the PSL was weakened by the formation of the breakaway Peasant Democratic Party (PLD) by former Deputy Prime Minister Roman Jagieliński, while in January 2000 radical farmers' groups launched the National Peasant Bloc. In the September 2001 legislative elections the PSL improved to 9% of the vote, gaining 42 seats in the Sejm and four in the Senat (upper house). It re-entered government in a SLD-led coalition (together with the Labour Union) which was headed by Leszek Miller. In March 2003 Miller ejected the PSL after it refused to support his Government's tax plans. In the September 2005 elections the PSL dropped back to 7% of the vote and only secured 25 seats in the Sejm and two in the Senat. It was one of several small parties to give parliamentary support to the minority **Law and Justice** Goverment, but never joined its coalition. In the early elections held in October 2007 the party won 9% of the vote and 31 Sejm seats. It joined the new Government formed by Donald **Tusk** of **Civic Platform** (PO) in November.

Leadership: Waldemar Pawlak (Chair.).
Address: ul. Grzybowska 4, 00-131 Warsaw.
Telephone: (22) 6206020.
Fax: (22) 6543583.
E-mail: biuronkw@psl.org.pl
Internet: www.psl.pl

Polish Press Agency
Polska Agencja Prasowa (PAP)

The state news agency in **Poland**. Established by the **Soviet** authorities in 1944 to replace the pre-war Polish Telegraph Agency, the PAP is now the major news provider in Poland with branches in 28 Polish towns and 22 foreign capitals. Made a joint stock company in 1998, it was partly privatized in 2001.

President: Piotr Skwiecinski.
Address: ul. Bracka 6/8, 00502 Warsaw.
Telephone: (22) 6280001.
Fax: (22) 6286407.
E-mail: webmaster@pap.com.pl
Internet: www.pap.com.pl

Polish Social Democracy
Socjaldemokracja Polska (SDPL)

A centre-left political party in Poland, currently in opposition and formed in March 2004 when more than 20 parliamentary deputies from the **Democratic Left Alliance** (SLD), led by Marek Borowski, announced their defection to form a new party.

At the September 2005 election it only won 3.9% of the vote, failing to pass the 5% threshold to secure seats in the Sejm (lower house of the **National Assembly**). A year later it formed a centre-left alliance **Left and Democrats** (LiD) with its 'parent' SLD, the small Labour Union (UP) and the centrist **Democratic Party** (PD), initially just to contest local elections. In early 2007 a common policy programme was devised, and the SDPL candidates in the early legislative elections held in October 2007 stood under the LiD banner. The alliance achieved 13% of the vote, and 53 Sejm seats (10 of which were SDPL candidates). The uneasy collaboration between the SLD and its splinter was one factor in the dissolution of the alliance in March–April 2008; eight of the 10 SDPL deputies broke away to form their own parliamentary grouping, though two remained in alliance with the SLD deputies as The Left.

Leadership: Marek Borowski (Chair.).
Address: ul. Mokotowska 29A, 00560 Warsaw.
Telephone: (22) 6213640.
Fax: (22) 6215342.
E-mail: sdpl@sdpl.pl
Internet: www.sdpl.pl

Pomaks

A widely-used name for Muslim **Slavs** living in the southern **Balkans**. Around 132,000 Pomaks live in **Bulgaria** and around 50,000 in **Macedonia**. Ethnically identical to their Slavic neighbours, the Pomaks embraced **Islam** during the 500 years of Ottoman rule.

The Pomaks in Bulgaria came under severe pressure to abandon their faith and culture under the repressive communist regime. They suffered from policies to Bulgarianize the population and the use of Muslim and Arabic names was forbidden. Aligning themselves with the similarly-treated **Bulgarian Turks**, some Pomaks were forcibly dispersed across the country. Unlike the Turks, the Pomaks were denied the option of emigrating to Turkey. The Pomak population is in a crisis of self-identity, often claiming either Bulgarian or Turkish ethnicity. Pomaks do not have official political representation, as ethnically-based political parties are banned in Bulgaria, but the **Movement for Rights and Freedoms** has increasingly wooed the Pomak vote as its own traditional support base among the Bulgarian Turks has dwindled.

Some Pomak communities living in Macedonia complain of deliberate campaigns to assimilate them into the **Albanian** community, with whom they are mistakenly lumped together because of their common Muslim identity. However, the existence of the substantial Albanian minority in Macedonia has meant greater cultural and religious freedom in that country, from which the Pomaks also benefit.

Popular Orthodox Rally
Laikos Orthodoxos Synagermos (LAOS)

A small populist party in **Greece**, opposed to globalization and rejecting traditional left/right definitions. LAOS was founded in 2000 by journalist George Karatzaferis after he was expelled from **New Democracy**. It won only 2.2% of the vote in the March 2004 parliamentary elections, not enough to pass the threshold to gain representation. In the June 2004 European Parliament elections, however, it obtained 4.1% of the vote and one of Greece's 24 seats. It entered the Greek **Parliament** in August 2007, securing 10 seats and 3.8% of the vote. Then in the early elections in October 2009 it increased to 15 seats (5.6% of the vote), overtaking the **Coalition of the Radical Left**.

Leadership: Georgios Karatzaferis (President).
Address: Leoforos Kallirrois 52, 11745 Athens.
Telephone: (210) 7522700.
Fax: (210) 7522704.
E-mail: pr@laos.gr
Internet: www.laos.gr

Posavina Corridor *see* **Brčko**.

Poslanecká Sněmovna

(Chamber of Deputies)

The lower house of **Parliament** of the **Czech Republic**.

Potsdam Agreements

The conclusion of the Potsdam Conference on 17 July 1945 between the Heads of Government of the United Kingdom, the USA and the **Soviet Union**, held at Potsdam in Germany following the conclusion of the war in Europe. The Potsdam meeting essentially endorsed the conclusions of the previous summit held in **Yalta**, placing **eastern Europe** effectively within the Soviet sphere of influence. It also established the principle of an international tribunal for war criminals (which became the basis for the Nuremburg trials, and more recently the **International Criminal Tribunal for the former Yugoslavia**), and agreed a framework for the mass repatriation of ethnic **Germans** from all over eastern Europe.

Prague

The capital city of the **Czech Republic**, situated in the centre of **Bohemia**. *Population*: 1.2m. (2008 estimate). The city has been the administrative centre of Bohemia since it was a kingdom in the Holy Roman Empire (Prague was the imperial capital under Charles IV in the 14th century), through its incorporation into the Habsburg Empire. Its long history has left an array of intriguing architecture, making the city the republic's major tourist attraction and sparing it some of the worst excesses of communist planning. It was also spared the damage experienced elsewhere during Europe's many wars. Even the city's **Jewish** quarter was saved from the devastation wreaked elsewhere, although only as Hitler intended to preserve it as a monument to the Jewish people. As capital of the **Czechoslovak** state from 1919 to 1993, Prague was the centre of the country's cultural and political life and as such played a significant role in the major events of the last 50 years. In 1968 it saw the brief blossoming of liberal culture during the **Prague Spring**, and in 1989 it was the centre stage for the dramatic '**velvet revolution**'.

Prague Spring

Communist **Czechoslovakia**'s brief experiment in 1968 with socialism with a human face. An 'action programme' in April set out plans to extend democracy and civil rights, and the newly-freed press radicalized the political climate, although communist party leader Alexander **Dubček** never questioned the leading role of the communist party while in office. The **Prague Spring** was crushed by an invasion by **Warsaw Pact** tanks and troops in September 1968.

The brief rise of **Croatian** reform communism and moderate nationalism in 1969–71, under the **Tito** regime in communist **Yugoslavia**, was sometimes referred to, by analogy, as the Croatian Spring.

Prague Stock Exchange (PSE)
Burza cenných papírů Praha

The stock exchange in the **Czech Republic** originally founded in 1871, which reopened after the communist period in November 1992. In May 2004 the Exchange became a full member of the Federation of the European Securities Exchanges (FESE) in connection with accession of the Czech Republic into the European Union. As of 1 June 2007, it had 22 members.

General Secretary: Petr Koblic.
Address: Rybná 14, 11005 Prague 1.
Telephone: (2) 21832411.
Fax: (2) 21833040.
E-mail: info@pse.cz
Internet: www.pse.cz

Predstavnički Dom
(House of Representatives)

The lower house of the **Parliamentary Assembly** of **Bosnia and Herzegovina**.

Preševo valley

The disputed border region between eastern **Kosovo** and south-western **Serbia**. Although never a part of mainly **Albanian**-populated Kosovo, the Preševo valley is home to a significant ethnic Albanian community, particularly in the towns of Bujanovac, Medvedja and Preševo. Militant Albanians there were prompted to take up arms during the conflict over control of Kosovo in 2000, with the Liberation Army of Preševo, Medvedja and Bujanovac (known by its Albanian initials UCPMB) attacking **Serb** police. Benefiting from the protection of the UN buffer zone established to keep Serb security forces out of Kosovo, they subsequently sought to have the Preševo valley included in the UN administration of Kosovo. However, neither the post-**Milošević** Serbian authorities, nor the international community were sympathetic to this. In May 2001 Serb paramilitary police were given permission to re-enter the buffer zone and by the end of the month the UCPMB had agreed to disarm. The Albanian coalition from Preševo valley, which won one seat in the Serbian parliament in 2007, controls the Bujanovac local authority. Protracted talks between the coalition and local Serb leaders aim to forge a multi-ethnic authority, but Albanian demands for greater influence in Serbia's state institutions are not heeded by the Government.

Prevlaka peninsula

A strategic spit of land forming the southernmost extreme of **Croatia** and jutting out into the Bay of Kotor, effectively controlling access to the south-western **Montenegrin** ports. The area was overrun by Yugoslav forces, particularly Montenegrins, in 1991–92 but control was handed back to Croatia at the end of the war under the **Dayton Agreement** of November 1995 despite initial attempts by **Yugoslavia** to demand control of the area. It became a demilitarized zone, monitored by a UN observer mission. Sovereignty over the region remains in dispute between the two countries, although relatively good regional relations in the early 21st century took some of the heat out of the argument. In 2002 a temporary agreement returned the region to Croatian control (the UN ending its mission on 15 December), pending a ruling on sovereignty by the **International Court of Justice** (ICJ) in The Hague. Following Montenegro's independence, the Montenegrin and Croatian Governments confirmed that they would abide by any ICJ ruling.

Pristina
Prishtinë or *Prishtina* (Albanian); *Priština* (Serbian)

The capital of **Kosovo**, situated in the north-east of the country near the Silver Mountains and straddling major European trade routes. *Population*: 500,000 (2009 est.). The majority of the population is **Albanian** with smaller communities of **Turks**, **Serbs**, **Bosniaks** and **Roma**.

Pristina served as the capital city of King Milutin (1282–1321) and later Serbian rulers until the Ottoman invasion following the Battle of Kosovo in 1389. Under Ottoman rule, many of the inhabitants, both Albanian and **Slav**, converted to Islam (*see* **Muslim peoples**). In 1946 Pristina became the capital of the autonomous region of Kosovo within Serbia, itself a constituent part of **Yugoslavia**. Particularly after the dissolution of Yugoslavia in the 1990s, Albanian Kosovars suffered under Serbian oppression, and the University of Pristina became a centre for Albanian nationalism. At the outbreak of the Kosovo conflict in 1999 Pristina was placed under a state of emergency, several districts were shelled by Serb and Yugoslav forces, and many ethnic Albanians were expelled. Since then the ethnic balance of the city has changed dramatically, with large numbers of Albanians returning and few Serbs remaining.

Privatization Agency

Organizes the privatization in **Bulgaria** of state-owned enterprises whose assets exceed 70m. leva. Founded in 1992.

Executive Director: Todor Nikolov.
Address: Aksakov St 29, Sofia 1000.
Telephone: (2) 8977579.
Fax: (2) 9816201.
E-mail: rstaneva@priv.government.bg
Internet: www.priv.government.bg

Privatization Agency of the Federation of Bosnia and Herzegovina

Government agency in the **Muslim-Croat Federation**.

Director: Adnad Mujagić.
Address: Alipašina 41, Sarajevo 71000.
Telephone: (33) 212884.
Fax: (33) 212883.
E-mail: apfbih@bih.net.ba
Internet: www.apf.com.ba

Progressive Party for the Working People
Anorthotiko Komma Ergazomenou Laou (AKEL)

A left-wing **Greek Cypriot** party in **Cyprus**, currently holding the presidency and heading the ruling coalition. AKEL is directly descended from the Communist Party of Cyprus (CPC) founded in 1925.

The CPC was declared illegal by the British authorities in 1931 and reconstituted as AKEL in 1941, emerging after the Second World War as an orthodox pro-Soviet Marxist-Leninist formation and again being banned in 1955. Legalized in 1959, it consolidated its dominant position in the trade union movement after independence in 1960.

In the 1976 parliamentary elections AKEL was part of a victorious alliance with the centre-right **Democratic Party** (DIKO) and what became the **Movement of Social Democrats EDEK**. Following the death of President **Makarios** in 1977, AKEL gave general backing to the new Government of President Spyros Kyprianou (DIKO) and headed the poll in the 1981 parliamentary elections, winning 12 of the 35 available seats. The alliance with DIKO was terminated by AKEL in 1984 on the grounds that the President was showing insufficient flexibility in inter-communal talks with the **Turkish Cypriots**. In the 1985 parliamentary elections AKEL slipped to third place, winning 15 seats out of 56.

In the 1988 presidential elections, AKEL backed an independent candidate, George Vassiliou, who was elected in the second round by a narrow margin over Glafcos Clerides of the conservative **Democratic Rally** (DISY). The collapse of communism in **eastern Europe** in 1989 and the demise of the **Soviet Union** in 1991, although regretted by AKEL hard-liners, set the party on a democratic socialist path. In the 1991 parliamentary elections, AKEL increased its representation to 18 seats. AKEL again endorsed Vassiliou in the 1993 presidential elections, but the opposition of DIKO and EDEK to his handling of the national question resulted in their supporters swinging behind Clerides (DISY) and giving him a narrow victory in the second round.

AKEL gained ground in the 1996 parliamentary elections, winning 19 seats but failing to supplant DISY as the largest party. In the 1998 presidential elections, AKEL joined with DIKO to back the independent candidacy of George Iacovou, who led in the first round but was narrowly defeated by incumbent Clerides in the second. AKEL continued in opposition and was rewarded in the 2001 parliamentary elections by overtaking DISY as the largest party with 20 seats and 34.7% of the vote. An immediate benefit was the election of AKEL General Secretary Dimitris **Christofias** as President of the **House of Representatives** (the second highest state post).

In the February 2003 presidential elections, AKEL joined with EDEK in backing the successful candidacy of Tassos Papadopoulos of DIKO and became part a coalition Government with DIKO and EDEK. It backed Papadopoulos' rejection of a UN settlement plan that was heavily rejected by Greek Cypriot voters in a referendum in April 2004 and supported Cyprus's accession to the **European Union** (EU) the following month, although its past antipathy to the EU resurfaced in its call in 2006 for Cyprus to delay entry into the euro single currency until social welfare provision had been strengthened. In the May 2006 parliamentary elections, AKEL fell back to 18 seats and 31.2% of the vote, resulting in a tie with DISY to be the largest party in the House of Representatives.

In July 2007 AKEL withdrew from the ruling coalition in order for Christofias to stand as a separate candidate in the February 2008 presidential election. He stood in second place after the first round, but gained the support of DIKO and EDEK to defeat the front-running DISY candidate Ioannis Kasoulidis in the run-off by 53.4% to 46.6%. He was inaugurated on 28 February, becoming the first communist head of state of an EU member country, and appointed an AKEL-DIKO-EDEK Council of Ministers the following day.

Christofias promised to push forward with reunification negotiations with the **Turkish Republic of Northern Cyprus** (TRNC), and held his first meeting with TRNC President Mehmet Ali **Talat** just three weeks later. He stepped down as AKEL General Secretary in December 2008, and Andros Kyprianou was elected as his successor.

Leadership: Andros Kyprianou (General Secretary).
Address: 4 E. Papaioannou St, PO Box 21827, 1513 Nicosia.

Telephone: (22) 761121.
Fax: (22) 761574.
E-mail: k.e.akel@cytanet.com.cy
Internet: www.akel.org.cy

Protestantism

Any Christian denomination founded on the principles of the 16th-century reformers who rejected the hierarchy and supremacy of the **Roman Catholic Church**. Started in Germany by Martin Luther, the Reformation, the adherents of which 'protested' against the authority of the Pope and the decay of the Church, spread across western and northern Europe. Protestantism represented a two-pronged attack on medieval society, on the one hand affirming the political independence of European states from Rome, and on the other attempting to democratize and personalize Christianity for the laity. It served as both a revolutionary movement for greater democracy and at the same time as a means to increase the power of local rulers. The establishment of Protestant states in northern Europe and the rationalist development of the enlightenment stripped mainstream Protestantism of its antagonistic vein and pushed it firmly into the religious mainstream. It is now represented by many different denominations, the major ones of which in **eastern Europe** are Lutheranism and Calvinism. Eastern European countries with significant Protestant populations are **Estonia** (56% Lutheran), **Latvia** (55% Lutheran) and **Hungary** (19%, mainly Calvinist). Elsewhere in the region Protestantism is greatly overshadowed by Roman Catholicism and **Orthodox Christianity**.

Prussia

Historically, the ethnically **German** state whose original centre was around Königsberg (now **Kaliningrad**) and the southern Baltic coast. The Kingdom of Prussia was a key player in European and **pan-German** politics from the 17th century and a key driving force in shaping the German unification process, culminating in 1870–71. Prussia's growth during this period saw it stretch across the economically important regions of Pomerania (along the Baltic coast) and Silesia, both of which are now integral parts of modern **Poland**. Prussia was effectively reintroduced into the European story in 1919 with the territorial changes imposed on Germany under the Treaty of **Versailles**. Parts of Pomerania were ceded to Poland, leaving the isolated German exclave of East Prussia as a focus for German nationalism and regional tensions. Following the mass resettlement of populations after the Second World War, most of what was Prussia is now indisputably Polish, with the remainder forming the **Russian** enclave of Kaliningrad.

PSD *see* **Social Democratic Party (Romania)**.

PSE *see* **Prague Stock Exchange**.

PSL *see* **Polish People's Party**.

PSSh *see* **Socialist Party of Albania**.

Public Against Violence
Verejnosť proti násiliu (VPN)

Slovakia's sister party to the Czech **Civic Forum**, founded in November 1989 during the '**velvet revolution**'. Public Against Violence was a popular front drawing together various disparate political forces in opposition to the communist regime, to demand free elections. It fragmented after elections in 1990.

Purvanov, Georgi

President of **Bulgaria**. The unexpected winner of presidential elections in November 2001 as candidate of the former communist **Bulgarian Socialist Party** (BSP), Purvanov secured re-election in October 2006, and began his second five-year term on 22 January 2007.

Georgi Sedefchov Purvanov was born in Sirishtnik in western Bulgaria on 28 June 1957. He served two years in the army from 1975 before studying history at Sofia University. After graduating in 1981 he joined the Bulgarian Communist Party (BKP) and worked as a researcher in the party's Institute of History, specializing in the emergence of the modern Bulgarian state at the turn of the 20th century. He was elected to the recently-renamed BSP's Supreme Council in 1991 and championed the realignment of the party towards a more centrist approach in the newly democratic Bulgaria. The BSP was returned to power in elections in 1994, but faced increasing political and economic problems. Although his faction within the party gained the ascendancy and he was elected party Chairman in December 1996, Purvanov realized how untenable the Government's position had become, and he and the new Prime Minister, Nikolai Dobrev, refused a further mandate, instead leading the BSP into opposition. From here he worked to transform the party in line with other social democratic parties elsewhere in Europe. Although he led the party's opposition to **NATO** bombing in **Yugoslavia** in 1999, the following year he pledged its support for Bulgaria's campaigns to join both NATO and the **European Union** (EU).

The personal prestige of the incumbent President Petar Stoyanov, who also had the full backing of the hugely popular and newly-elected Prime Minister Simeon Saxecoburggotski, made Purvanov's electoral victory in presidential elections in

November 2001 all the more surprising. He was inaugurated as President on 22 January 2002, vowing to pursue his predecessor's policies of promoting Bulgaria's ties to the West as well as deepening relations with former allies to the east. During this five-year term, Bulgaria acceded to NATO and received a formal invitation for EU membership from 2007. He comfortably secured re-election in October 2006, with only the low turnout denying him an outright victory in the first round.

Address: Office of the President, 2 Dondukov blvd, Sofia 1123.

Telephone: (2) 9239333.

E-mail: press@president.bg

Internet: www.president.bg

'Pyramid' investment schemes

Essentially fraudulent savings schemes offering very high interest rates, whose spread and then dramatic collapse in **Albania** threw the country into deep turmoil in 1997. A feature of several post-communist countries, the 'pyramid' schemes became especially popular in Albania as a means of supplementing meagre salaries and pensions and as an alternative to the suspect banking system. They also provided a channel for money laundering. The schemes offered substantially higher interest rates (25% in some cases) than were obtainable elsewhere, but interest payments were in reality financed from new deposits rather than from any real return on investment.

The inevitable collapse of the Albanian schemes from late 1996, with losses totalling an estimated US \$1,500m., impelled the **People's Assembly** in January 1997 to freeze their assets and to ban new schemes. However, faced with the loss of their life savings, tens of thousands of people took to the streets, fuelling an open insurrection and bringing about the effective demise of central government authority by March, particularly in the south. A central complaint of the protesters was that the Government of the **Democratic Party of Albania** (PDS) under President Sali **Berisha** had connived with the 'pyramid' scheme operators, notably Vefa Holdings, which had become Albania's largest private company.

Although the Berisha regime responded with a plan under which investors were supposed to recover 50%–60% of their savings over time, the crisis led to the installation of a new Government headed by the **Socialist Party of Albania** (PSS) and to the resignation of Berisha in July 1997. In November 1997 a new PSS-dominated Assembly adopted constitutional amendments allowing the Government to audit and administer private companies whose activities were deemed to threaten the 'the economic interests of citizens'. In December 1999 the official liquidator of the schemes said that only about 6% of savings would be recovered by about 150,000 investors, whereas hundreds of thousands would recover nothing at all.

Pytalovo *see* **Abrene question**.

R

Radmanović, Nebojša

Member of the Presidency (**Serb**), **Bosnia and Herzegovina**.

Nebojša Radmanović was born on 1 October 1949 in Gračanica. After schooling in Banja Luka, he graduated in philosophy from the University of Belgrade. During a varied career he has been Director of the Bosanska Krajina Archives and the Archives of the Republic of Srpska; Director of the National Theatre in Banja Luka; Director and the editor-in-chief of GLAS; and President of the Executive Board of the Town of Banja Luka. He was elected to the **Serb Republic**'s National Assembly and was appointed Minister of Administration and Local Self-Management. He stood as union presidential candidate for the **Alliance of Independent Social Democrats** (SNSD) in the October 2002 election, finishing second with 19.9% behind Mirko Šarović's 35.5%. However, he fared better in the 2006 election, winning the Serb seat with 53% of the vote. The tripartite Presidency was inaugurated on 6 November 2006, and Radmanović was first in rotation to hold the Chair of the Presidency, from November 2006 to July 2007 and, secondly, from November 2008 to July 2009.

Address: Office of the Presidency, Titova 16, 71000 Sarajevo.

Telephone: (33) 663863.

Fax: (33) 555620.

E-mail: press@predsjednistvobih.ba

Internet: www.predsjednistvobih.ba

Regional Co-operation Council (RCC)

The Regional Co-operation Council was officially launched on 27 February 2008, as the successor to the **Stability Pact for South-Eastern Europe**. It promotes mutual co-operation and the European and Euro-Atlantic integration of **south-eastern Europe** in order to reinvigorate economic and social development in the region. Its members include representatives from the **Balkan** countries, as well as neighbouring states, the **European Union** (EU), non-EU members of the Group of Eight industrialized countries and international financial institutions

Members: 45   members,   including   **Albania**,   **Bosnia   and   Herzegovina**, **Bulgaria**, **Croatia**, **Czech Republic**, **Greece**, **Hungary**, **UNMIK** (on behalf of **Kosovo**), **Latvia**, **Macedonia**, **Montenegro**, **Poland**, **Romania**, **Serbia**, **Slovakia** and **Slovenia**.
Secretary-General: Hido Biščević.
Address: RCC Secretariat, Trg Bosne i Hercegovine 1/V, 71000 Sarajevo.
Telephone: (33) 561700.
Fax: (33) 561701.
E-mail: rcc@rcc.int
Internet: www.rcc.int

Republican Turkish Party–United Forces
Cumhuriyetçi Türk Partisi–Birleşik Güçler (CTP-BG)

A centre-left party in the self-proclaimed **Turkish Republic of Northern Cyprus** (TRNC), currently in opposition.

The CTP was founded in 1970 as a Marxist-Leninist party espousing anti-imperialism and non-alignment, but by the 1990s had evolved into a democratic socialist formation in favour of the reunification of Cyprus and entry into the **European Union** (EU). Having usually trailed in Assembly and presidential elections in the 1970s and 1980s, the CTP advanced in the 1993 Assembly elections, winning 13 of 50 seats and entering a coalition Government led by the recently-formed **Democrat Party** (DP) associated with then **Turkish Cypriot** leader Rauf **Denktaş**. CTP leader Özker Özgür took third place in the 1995 presidential elections (with 18.9% of the vote), after which the CTP joined a coalition Government with the DP.

In January 1996 Özgür was ousted as CTP leader by Mehmet Ali **Talat**, who in July 1996 took the party into opposition. The party fell back to six seats in the 1998 Assembly elections, remaining in opposition. In the April 2000 presidential elections Talat came fourth in the first round with only 10% of the vote. Adding the suffix United Forces to its electoral title to broaden its appeal, the CTP-BG achieved a breakthrough in the December 2003 Assembly elections, becoming the largest party with 19 seats and 35.2% of the vote on a platform supporting the entry of a reunified Cyprus into the EU. Talat formed a coalition with the DP, which obtained the endorsement of a UN settlement plan by 64.9% of Turkish Cypriot voters in a referendum in April 2004, although **Greek Cypriot** voters' rejection of the plan meant that the Turkish Cypriot area was effectively excluded when Cyprus joined the EU in May 2004. The CTP-BG strengthened its position in early Assembly elections in February 2005, winning 24 seats on a 44.5% vote share and forming a new coalition with the DP. In April 2005 Talat was elected TRNC President in succession to Denktaş with 55.6% of the vote, following which Ferdi Sabit Soyer replaced him as Prime Minister and CTP-BG leader. In September 2006 the DP was ejected from the coalition and replaced by the newly-formed Freedom and Reform Party (ÖRP).

Meanwhile, Talat and Greek Cypriot President Tassos Papadopoulos had agreed in July 2006 to resume talks, which were reinvigorated by the presidential victory of Greek Cypriot communist leader Dimitris **Christofias** in February 2008. The April 2009 TRNC Assembly elections represented a setback for the CTP-BG, however; it dropped to 15 seats (29.2%), while the hard-line **National Unity Party** (UBP) won 26 out of the 50 seats and went on to form a Government. Talat sought re-election for a second presidential term in April 2010, but UBP Prime Minister Derviş **Eroğlu** secured 50.4% of the vote in the first round, ahead of Talat on 42.9% and five other candidates.

Leadership: Ferdi Sabit Soyer (Chair.).
Address: 99 Salahi Sevket Street, Lefkoşa/Nicosia.
Telephone: +90-392-2273300.
Fax: +90-392-2281914.
E-mail: info@ctp-bg.com
Internet: www.ctp-bg.com

Republika Srpska *see* **Serb Republic**.

Republika Srpska Directorate for Privatization

Government agency in the **Serb Republic** that oversees the privatization process. Established in 1998.

Director: Borislav Obradović.
Address: Mladena Stoganovića 4, Banja Luka 78000.
Telepone: (51) 308311.
Fax: (51) 311245.
E-mail: dip@inecco.net
Internet: www.rsprivatizacija.com

Rīga

Capital city of **Latvia** and a major Baltic port situated near the mouth of the River Daugava on the northern coast. *Population*: 717,371 (2008 estimate).

An ancient Liv settlement, Rīga was founded by the Bishop of **Livonia** in 1201 and was converted to Christianity. The privileges of the bishopric granted some freedom to the city, which joined the Hanseatic League in 1282. In the 1520s the country converted to Lutheranism (*see* **Protestantism**). Under Polish rule from 1581, and Swedish rule from 1621, Rīga was granted self-government until ceded to **Russia** by the Treaty of Nystad in 1721. Rīga was the capital city of independent Latvia from 1918 until its Soviet occupation in 1940. Under German occupation from 1941, much of the old town centre was destroyed before it was reoccupied by the **Soviet Union** as the capital of the Latvian Soviet Socialist Republic from 1944 until independence was regained in 1991.

Rīga Stock Exchange *see* **NASDAQ OMX Rīga.**

Rīga, Treaties of

Two peace treaties signed by the **Soviet Union** with neighbouring countries. The first, signed with **Latvia** on 11 August 1920 at the conclusion of the brief war between the two countries, included the recognition of Latvian independence by the Soviet Government (later revoked) and the cession of the **Abrene** region to Latvia. The second was signed with **Poland** on 18 March 1921 after the defeat of a Polish invasion of Russia. It fixed the two countries' border mid-way between the medieval Polish border far to the east and its modern edge to the west. The second treaty was revoked with the division of Poland between Soviet and Nazi forces in 1939 (*see* **Nazi-Soviet Pact**). *See also* Treaties of **Tartu.**

Riigikogu *see* **Parliament (Estonia).**

RMDSz *see* **Hungarian Democratic Union of Romania.**

Roma

A nomadic people of traditionally-mixed ethnicity who arrived in Europe from the Indian sub-continent in waves of migration beginning in the ninth century. They are also known in English as the Gypsies, a name generally considered to be derogatory and which is derived from the misconception that they originated in Egypt. As a nomadic people, they spread across the European continent and have been subject to serious discrimination and outright abuse ever since. As a language, Romani is most closely related to Punjabi (Hindi) and three main dialects exist in Europe: Romani in the west, Lomarven in **central Europe** and Domari in the east. There is no official written form. The language is in decline, as a large proportion of Roma have adopted the language of fellow minorities in their home countries. The Roma are divided into four main tribes or 'nations'—the Kalderash, Machavaya, Lovari and Churari—and various sub-tribes. Romani culture has been generally eroded owing to assimilation into the fringe of other European cultures. Loyalty to the extended family remains its cornerstone.

Throughout history the Roma have been subject to violent discrimination. They were often enslaved in feudal societies. Following the end of Romani slavery in the mid-19th century, great numbers joined other disfavoured groups of European society in emigrating to the New World. One of the most systematic persecutions of Roma was in the Nazi Holocaust when an estimated half a million were liquidated in death camps across occupied territories.

Persecution continued after the Second World War on a local level, with many regional authorities reflecting popular prejudice in open discrimination. Often Roma have been forced to take on a settled lifestyle so as to participate in the industrialization of the European economies. To this day the Roma are seriously maligned as a minority across **eastern Europe**, with poor access to education and employment, and are targeted in violent attacks by the extreme right. Attempts to organize better collective representation resulted in a resolution to press for greater rights at the Fifth World Romani Congress (2001—the first to be conducted in the Romani language), while the Sixth Congress (2004) pledged to step up the fight against racism. However, the division of Romani society into sub-tribes has greatly hindered collective action. The most recent Congress, the seventh, was held in 2008.

Of the roughly 10m.–15m. Roma living worldwide, just over a third (around 4m.) reside in eastern Europe, although their exact number is hard to pin down, owing to fear of persecution and wholesale integration with other minorities. Of these populations the most significant are the up to 2.5m. Roma resident in **Romania**, where they are officially known as Rroma to distinguish from **Romanians** (official census information put the figure at only 535,140 in 2002). Well over half of adult Rroma are unemployed, only three out of 10 have access to running water, and many children fail to attend the first years of schooling. Rroma are also subject to frequent and poorly-investigated violence.

Other major populations are in **Hungary** (official number: 205,720; highest estimate: 1m.), **Bulgaria** (370,908; 800,000) **Slovakia** (92,500; 550,000) and **Serbia** (108,193; 450,000). In all cases official discrimination stopped after the fall of communism in 1989 but continues in entrenched public and local government attitudes.

Roman Catholic Church

The predominant Christian denomination centred on the Vatican City in Rome. Roman Catholicism (often just called Catholicism, taking its name from catholic, meaning 'universal') is the largest single religious denomination in the world and is prevalent over much of Europe, particularly in western and **central Europe**. It chiefly differs from other Christian Churches in its belief in the primacy of the Bishop of Rome (Pope) as the 'Vicar of Christ'. It was divided from **Orthodox Christianity** in the Great Schism of 1054 (a split which, more than 900 years later, formed the basis of one of the principal divisions in **Yugoslavia**), and from **Protestantism** during the 16th-century Reformation. The cult of the saints and particularly the Virgin Mary are very strong. The role of priests is central to the religion. Unlike in most other Christian denominations, Roman Catholic priests (only men) take a vow of celibacy. The election of the Polish Cardinal Karol Wojtyła as Pope John Paul II in 1978 (the first Polish Pope ever, and the first non-Italian pontiff for over 400 years) brought Catholicism closer to the communist-dominated east and helped link it to pro-democracy movements such as **Poland**'s **Solidarity**. Pope John Paul II also attempted to breach the divide between Catholicism and Orthodoxy, making historic visits to Greece and Ukraine in 2001. Pope John Paul II died in April 2005 and was succeeded by Pope Benedict XVI.

The connection between spiritual and temporal power and the Church's inherent conservatism have led to the formation of Catholic-orientated right-of-centre political parties in many central European countries, often called Christian Democrats or People's parties. Catholic political activity and influence often attracted repression under communist rule, although the Church's popularity in some countries led to efforts to integrate it into the political mainstream.

Despite the close association of much of **eastern Europe** with Orthodoxy, there are some 70m. Catholics in the region with the largest congregations in Poland (37m.—96% of the population), **Hungary** (7.4m.—77%) and the **Czech Republic** (4m.—43%). Countries with majority Catholic populations are **Croatia**, Hungary, **Lithuania**, Poland, **Slovakia** and **Slovenia**. All Roman Catholic Churches are subordinate to the papacy, as is the **Uniate Church**.

Romania
România

An independent republic located in south-eastern Europe on the eastern coast of the **Balkan** peninsula, bounded by Ukraine to the north and east, Moldova to the north-east, the Black Sea to the south-east, Bulgaria to the south, Serbia to the south-west, and Hungary to the north-west. Administratively, the country is divided into 40 counties and one municipality.

Area: 238,391 sq km; *capital*: **Bucharest**; *population*: 21.3m (2009 estimate), comprising **Romanians** 89.5%, **Hungarians** 6.6, **Roma** 2.5%, other 1.5% (although the Roma probably comprise a significantly larger percentage of the population—possibly even as high as 8%—as their numbers are frequently underestimated in censuses owing to the method of designation and the high proportion of this group which does not register); *official language*: Romanian; *religion*: Romanian **Orthodox** 86.7%, **Roman Catholic** 4.7%, **Protestant** 3.7%, other 4.9%.

Legislative authority is currently vested in a bicameral **Parliament of Romania** (Parlamentul României), but a referendum in November 2009 approved a change to a unicameral Parliament with a maximum of 300 seats. The existing legislature consists of the upper 137-member Senate (Senatul) and the lower 334-member House of Deputies (Camera Deputaţilor), which includes 18 seats reserved for minorities. Both houses are directly elected for a four-year term by a system of proportional representation, but parties win no seats if their vote is below the 5% minimum threshold. Members of Parliament are barred from holding ministerial office, following the principle of executive–legislative separation. Executive power is vested in the President, who is directly elected for a five-year term (renewable once) and who appoints the Prime Minister, who in turn appoints the cabinet.

History: Once part of the Roman province of Dacia, and then subjected to successive waves of invasions and foreign domination, present-day Romania evolved from the union of the two Danubian principalities of **Wallachia** and Moldavia in the 1850s. These principalities had emerged in the 14th century and subsequently came under nominal Ottoman rule from the 1500s. Romania was recognized as an independent state in 1878 (by the Treaty of Berlin) and became a kingdom under the Hohenzollern dynasty in 1881. After Romania had fought with the Western powers in the First World War, it was rewarded under the post-war settlement by the creation of a **Greater Romania** which included **Bessarabia** (formerly under Russian rule) and **Bukovina** and **Transylvania** (from the dismembered Austro-Hungarian Empire). In 1938 King Carol II established a royal dictatorship, abolishing the democratic Constitution of 1923.

Having been forced in 1940, under the second of the so-called **Vienna Awards** (and as agreed in the 1939 **Nazi-Soviet Pact**), to cede Bessarabia and northern Bukovina to the **Soviet Union** and northern Transylvania to **Hungary**, Romania then sided with Nazi Germany during the Second World War until 1944, when the fascist regime of Ion Antonescu was ousted prior to Soviet occupation. Under the post-war treaties Romania recovered northern Transylvania (so that ethnic **Hungarians** in Romania formed post-war Europe's largest single minority group), but lost Bessarabia and northern Bukovina to the Soviet Union and southern **Dobruja** to **Bulgaria**. A communist-led Government won elections in 1946 and the Romanian People's Republic was declared in 1947, following the abdication of King Michael. Having adopted a Soviet-style Constitution, Romania joined the **Warsaw Pact** in 1955. Nicolae **Ceauşescu** became First Secretary of the Romanian Communist Party (PCR) in 1965 (replacing Gheorghe Gheorghiu-Dej) and was made President of the Republic in 1974. Under Ceauşescu, Romania adopted an independent foreign policy (refusing, for example, to participate in the Warsaw Pact invasion of **Czechoslovakia** in 1968), while maintaining a repressive and rigid orthodox line at home.

In 1989 internal opposition to economic austerity and human rights abuses led to the violent overthrow and execution of Ceauşescu (along with his wife) in December. A National Salvation Front (FSN) formed a provisional Government, which abolished the communist monopoly of power and dissolved the feared Securitate secret police, proceeding to win about two-thirds of the vote in free elections in May 1990. Its leader, Ion Iliescu (a former communist official), was elected President with over 85% of the vote and Petre Roman was appointed Prime Minister. Roman resigned the premiership in September 1991 following serious civil unrest, and a national referendum the following December endorsed a new Constitution providing for political pluralism, guaranteed human rights and a commitment to a market economy.

In 1992 the FSN split, with the pro-Iliescu wing of the party (opposed to the rapid economic change) forming the Democratic National Salvation Front, which quickly became the Social Democracy Party of Romania (PDSR). Iliescu was re-elected to the presidency in September 1992, and concurrent parliamentary elections returned a PDSR-led minority Government under Nicolae Vacaroiu. In 1994 the ultra-nationalist Romanian National Unity Party (PUNR) was brought into the ruling coalition, with support from the extreme right-wing Greater Romania Party (PRM) and the neo-communist Socialist Party of Labour (PSM). However, serious differences between the parties developed, resulting in the collapse of the coalition arrangement by September 1996.

A dramatic change in the political landscape took place in November 1996 as the opposition Democratic Convention of Romania (CDR), a centre-right alliance headed by the Christian Democratic National Peasants' Party (PNȚCD), successfully contested concurrent presidential and parliamentary elections. The CDR leader, Emil Constantinescu, won a clear second-round victory over President Iliescu, and the alliance secured nearly 30% of the vote in the legislative polling. A new administration was formed, led by Victor Ciorbea of the PNȚCD and including representatives of the **National Liberal Party** (PNL), the **Hungarian Democratic Union of Romania** (UDMR) and the Social Democratic Union (USD), consisting of the Democratic Party (PD) and the Romanian Social Democratic Party (PSDR).

A radical economic reform programme and anti-corruption drive were introduced in 1997, but in February 1998 the USD withdrew from the coalition, precipitating the resignation of Ciorbea the following month and his replacement as Prime Minister by Radu Vasile of the PNȚCD. The reconstituted centre-right coalition, despite persistent internal divisions, subsequently survived political challenges from left-wing and nationalist parties but became deeply unpopular against a background of deteriorating economic and social conditions and extreme industrial unrest. Vasile resigned in December 1999 and was succeeded by Mugu Constantin Isărescu (non-party), hitherto Governor of the **National Bank of Romania**.

The political pendulum again swung sharply in the November–December 2000 presidential and parliamentary elections, as the centre-right was heavily defeated by the new Social Democratic Pole of Romania, an alliance of the PDSR, the PSDR and the small Humanist Party of Romania (PUR). Iliescu regained the presidency for the PDSR, having faced Corneliu Vadim Tudor of the far-right PRM in the second round. Tudor had taken second place in the first round, benefiting from a strong vein of popular disenchantment with both the left and the centre-right. In the parliamentary contest, the Pole alliance became substantially the largest formation, winning a total of 155 seats with 36.6% of the vote, while the second-placed PRM took 84 (19.5%). In the simultaneous Senate elections, the Pole parties won 65 seats, ahead of the PRM with 37.

In December 2000 the Pole alliance formed a minority Government under the premiership of Adrian Năstase, who secured qualified pledges of external support from the PD, the PNL and the UDMR, with the particular aim of excluding the ascendant PRM from any policy-making role. The new administration undertook to continue the pro-market economic reforms of its predecessor, with an admixture of greater concern for their social consequences, and to pursue Romania's aspiration to join the **European Union** (EU). It introduced new legislation to strengthen the language rights of ethnic Hungarians and other minorities, thereby triggering a national campaign of opposition by the PRM, while strains quickly appeared in the Government's fragile understanding with the PD and the PNL. In June 2001 the PDSR and the PSDR merged to form the **Social Democratic Party** (PSD), with Năstase at its head. In the same month the Government, despite the potential for public controversy, moved to bring Romania in line with western Europe in lifting the longstanding ban on homosexuality (Article 200 of the penal code).

A referendum held on 18–19 October 2003 overwhelmingly approved 79 proposed amendments to the Constitution, which aimed to bring it into conformity with EU requirements (by, *inter alia*, guaranteeing the right to private property, strengthening legal rights for ethnic minorities and limiting the powers of the executive branch of government). The revised Constitution entered into force on 29 October.

In the run-up to the November 2004 elections, electoral alliances were announced between the PSD and PUR, to be known as the National Alliance (UN), and between the PNL and the PD, to be known as the Justice and Truth Alliance (ADA). The election was won by the former, with 132 seats in the 332-member House of Deputies (113 seats for the PSD and 19 for the PUR) and 36.8% of the vote. The rival ADA alliance won 112 seats (64 PNL, 48 PD) and 31.5% of the vote. The PRM took 48 seats (13%), the UDMR 22 (6.2%) and ethnic minorities 18. In the simultaneous Senate elections the UN won 57 seats (with 37.2% of the vote), the ADA 49 (31.8%), the PRM 21 (13.6%) and the UDMR 10 (6.2%). In the presidential election, however, Traian **Băsescu**, candidate of the ADA, overtook Năstase, candidate of the UN, in the second round to secure election.

Despite the UN's leading position in the legislature, it was Călin Popescu-Tăriceanu of the PNL who in late December negotiated a coalition of the PNL, PD, UDMR and PUR (the last-named having contested the election as part of the UN alliance). It commanded just one seat more than the required minimum in Parliament to secure approval. It took office on 28 December. This Government continued moves to push through reforms required by the EU as prerequisites to Romanian membership. The Constitutional Court blocked a judicial reform package in July 2005, prompting Popescu-Tăriceanu to offer his Government's resignation; however, Parliament rapidly passed an amended package to resolve the impasse.

Far-reaching corruption allegations brought down key figures in several parties during 2006, most notably Năstase. In December 2006 the PUR, now renamed as the **Conservative Party** (PC), withdrew from the ruling coalition, reducing it to a minority Government.

In the early months of 2007 tensions rose between President Băsescu and Prime Minister Popescu-Tăriceanu, reaching a head at the start of April when Băsescu's PD was ejected from the ruling coalition. Popescu-Tăriceanu formed a new minority Government on 3 April between his PNL and the UDMR, with external backing from the PSD. On 19 April Parliament backed a motion to suspend Băsescu on grounds of unconstitutional conduct. Senate Chair Vacaroiu became interim President. However, in a national referendum on 19 May Băsescu's removal from office was opposed by three-quarters of voters. He was reinstated four days later.

Latest elections: Băsescu's fraught relationship with the Parliament was strengthened by the outcome of legislative elections in November 2008, in which the **Democratic Liberal Party** (PD-L, formed by a merger of the PD and the Liberal Democratic Party in December 2007) won 115 seats in the House of Deputies (with 32.4% of the vote), just one more seat than the PSD–PC Alliance (whose constituent parties won 110 seats and four seats respectively), which actually had won a slightly larger 33.1% of the vote. The PNL won 65 seats (with 18.6% of the vote), the UDMR won 22 seats (6.2%) and representatives of ethnic minorities secured 18 seats (3.6%). In the simultaneous Senate election the PD-L won 51 of the 137 seats (with 33.6% of the vote), the PSD–PC Alliance won 49 seats (34.2%), with 48 seats and one seat to the respective parties, the PNL won 28 seats (18.7%) and the UDMR won nine seats (6.4%). The PRM lost all its seats in both houses.

Recent developments: On 10 December 2008 Theodor Stolojan of the PD-L was nominated as Prime Minister, but he resigned the mandate within days, and PD-L leader Emil **Boc** was nominated in his place. On 18 December Parliament approved a coalition Government between the PD-L and the PSD, which took office four days later.

The PSD ministers resigned on 1 October 2009 in protest over the dismissal three days earlier of the Minister of the Interior, and Boc's Government was defeated in a vote of no confidence 12 days later. Lucian Croitoru, a politically independent economist, and Liviu Negoita of the PD-L were each in turn nominated to form a cabinet but both were unsuccessful. Meanwhile, the first round of the presidential election in November saw incumbent Băsescu lead with 32.4%, ahead of PSD leader Mircea Dan Geoană with 31.2%. A concurrent referendum on changing to a unicameral Parliament was approved by 78% of voters, and just received the required 50%-plus-one turnout to validate it. The presidential run-off on 6 December proved to be ever so close, with official results giving Băsescu 50.33% of the vote—a margin of just over 70,000 votes. With over 138,000 votes having been deemed as invalid, the PSD called for the result to be annulled. Instead the Constitutional Court decided that the invalid votes should be recounted; only around 2,000 votes were validated, and so the result was upheld. A few days later, on 17 December, Băsescu again nominated Boc as Prime Minister. His new Government was a coalition of the PD-L and the UDMR, with five independents also included, and was approved by Parliament on 23 December.

International relations and defence: Romania is a member of the United Nations, the **Organization for Security and Co-operation in Europe**, the **Council of Europe**, the **Danube Commission** and the **Stability Pact for South-Eastern Europe**, also becoming a founder member of the **Organization of the Black Sea Economic Co-operation** in 1992 and joining the **Central European Initiative** in 1996 and the **Central European Free Trade Area** in 1997. Successive governments have sought closer integration with the West. Romania joined the **North Atlantic Treaty Organization** on 29 March 2004 (having participated in the **Partnership for Peace** programme since 1994). Having applied for EU membership in 1995, Romania was accepted as an official candidate in December 1999 and formal negotiations opened in February 2000. Although Romania remained the most economically backward of the ex-communist applicants, an offer of membership was made in April 2005, and Romania acceded on 1 January 2007. Romania plans to implement the EU's Schengen Agreement, allowing free movement of citizens within the zone's borders, in 2011. It is unlikely to join the eurozone before 2014 (*see* **Romania, economy**). In 1996 Romania signed a treaty of reconciliation with Hungary, under which the latter formally renounced any claim to parts of Transylvania, while Romania guaranteed rights to its ethnic Hungarian population. Economic and military co-operation accords were reached with Ukraine in 1997 and a treaty was signed agreeing to try to settle differences over territorial issues and minority rights. A lingering territorial dispute with Ukraine over the maritime border around **Serpent's Island** in the Black Sea, with potentially rich offshore oil deposits at stake, was resolved by the **International Court of Justice** in 2009, granting Romania a large part of the territorial waters it was claiming. Attempts to sign a new Romanian-Russian treaty have made little progress since the end of communist rule in Moscow. A basic treaty initialled with neighbouring Moldova in 2000 remains unratified, in part because of its ambiguity about the goal espoused by some Romanian parties of reunification with the ethnic **Romanian** majority of Moldova. Negotiations began afresh, and in January 2009 the Romanian and Moldovan Foreign Ministers agreed that treaties on friendship, co-operation and borders could be signed later that year. However, in April the Moldovan President Vladimir Voronin accused the Romanian Government of inciting an outbreak of civil unrest in the Moldovan capital Chişinau, causing relations to fall to a low ebb. Voronin's departure from office and the election of a new pro-EU Moldovan Government later that year revived hopes for a friendship treaty.

Romania's defence budget for 2008 amounted to some US \$3,005m., equivalent to about 2% of GDP. The armed forces in 2010 numbered about 73,000 personnel, while reservists totalled an estimated 45,000. Compulsory military service ended in 2006.

Romania, economy

Romania's formerly centrally-planned economy has made a slow and difficult transition to a free-market system. It joined the **European Union** (EU) in 2007.

GNP: US $170,560m. (2008); *GNP per capita*: $7,930 (2008); *GDP at PPP*: $302,566m. (2008); *GDP per capita at PPP*: $14,100 (2008); *real GDP growth*: −8.5% (2009 estimate); *exports*: $49,398m. (2008); *imports*: $82,450m. (2008); *currency*: new leu (plural: new lei; US $1 = L3.00 in mid-2009); *unemployment*: 72% (Sept. 2009); *government deficit as a percentage of GDP*: 7.2% (2009); *inflation*: 5.5% (2009).

In 2006 industry accounted for 36% of GDP, agriculture for 9% and services for 55%. Around 31% of the workforce is engaged in industry, 30% in agriculture and 39% in services.

About 41% of the land is arable, 3% under permanent crops, 21% permanent pasture and 29% forests and woodland. The main crops are grain, grapes (for wine), sugar beet, fruit and vegetables, and there is important animal husbandry and also timber extraction.

The main mineral resources are petroleum, natural gas, hard coal and brown coal (lignite), iron ore and bauxite. Onshore oil production increased in the 1990s, but has since declined, though Romania remains the largest producer in central and eastern Europe, with proven reserves of 500m. barrels at the end of 2007; offshore exploitation now accounts for 10% of production. Among the main industries are mining, petroleum production and refining, metal-working, timber extraction, machine-building and chemical processing. The main energy sources have been petroleum, natural gas and coal, and hydroelectricity. Romania's first nuclear power station unit opened in December 1996, with the second coming onstream in 2008, and two more expected in 2016; each of them supplies approximately 10% of the country's electricity production.

Romania's main exports by value are machinery and equipment, textiles and footwear, metals and metal products, mineral fuels and chemical products. Principal imports include machinery and transport equipment, manufactured goods, mineral fuels and lubricants and chemicals. Germany took about 17% of Romania's exports in 2008, followed by Italy (16%) and France (7%). Germany was the supplier of 16% of Romania's imports in 2000, with Italy providing 11% and **Hungary** 7%.

With the overthrow of **Ceauşescu**, at the end of 1989, the inefficiencies and corruption of the former regime meant that the new administration was faced with severe problems in seeking to restore order, while external support was difficult to secure. The change of Government accelerated the decline of the heavy industrial sector, which the Ceauşescu regime had promoted, largely at the expense of traditional agriculture, in its abortive effort to make Romania a key industrial nation. Simmering social problems and deteriorating living standards sparked off massive strike actions, particularly by coal miners fearful of the contraction of their inefficient industry and consequential job losses. The post-communist Governments introduced successive programmes to reform the economy, but for the first six years these were relatively cautious and not fully implemented. Some initiatives were announced on privatization of state-owned enterprises, but little actual progress was made. Among the factors inhibiting industrial disposals were continuing bureaucratic lethargy and government reluctance to antagonize key elements of the workforce.

GDP fell sharply in the early 1990s but incomes were allowed to rise, so that inflation in the 1991–93 period was at or above 200% per year. Government measures brought the inflation rate down to 28% in 1995, when substantial real GDP growth of 7% was achieved. The economy continued to grow, albeit more slowly, in 1996, but inflation in that year doubled again, to 57%, and the situation deteriorated under the centre-right Government elected in late 1996. GDP actually fell for three successive years—by 6.1% in 1997, 5.4% in 1998 and 3.2% in 1999—while inflation reached as high as 150% in 1997, and was only partially curbed to a rate of 55% in 1999. Officially-recorded unemployment also rose, from 6.5% at the end of 1996 to 11.5% at the end of 1999. New efforts towards 'realistic' privatization and industrial restructuring were announced in 1998 but again were subject to change and delay in the face of overall economic deterioration.

The appointment of the central bank Governor as Prime Minister in December 1999 resulted in some improvement in 2000, in which GDP growth of about 2% was achieved and exports increased by 25% in dollar terms, although inflation remained high at 41% and about a third of the population were living below the poverty line.

At this stage in Romania's transition process, although the private sector already accounted for 60% of GDP, this was largely due to the privatization of small and medium-sized enterprises, some 4,000 of which were in private hands by 2000. By contrast the heavy industrial sector, textiles, utilities and communications was still largely under state ownership. In February 2001, therefore, the incoming left-wing Government announced an extensive new privatization programme under which over 60 larger concerns would be sold off as quickly as possible, although in such a way as not to damage 'social equilibrium'. That month a controversial restitution law was also promulgated under which properties nationalized between 1945 and 1989 could be recovered by their former owners. This followed on from a 1995 restitution law under which only about 1% of an estimated 300,000 eligible properties had been recovered by former owners. The new programme also proved to be complex and not very effective.

Also in February 2001 the **International Monetary Fund** (IMF) suspended the 1999 stand-by facility, demanding real progress on the economic reform programme.

Romania had joined the **Central European Free Trade Area** (CEFTA) in 1997 and EU accession negotiations opened in 2000, but Romania was deemed the least advanced of the ex-communist applicants towards meeting EU accession requirements. In October 2003 the EU nevertheless stated that Romania could be considered to have achieved the status of a functioning market economy, provided it continued to consolidate the progress that it had made. Uncomfortable reforms remained to be implemented in preparation for EU membership and in conformity with a two-year IMF stand-by agreement (finalized in July 2004); the Government committed to making some 7,000 redundancies in the mining sector in 2005, as part of a national restructuring plan that also encompassed the iron, steel and railway industries. The Romanian currency was redenominated in July, but was subject to strong appreciation pressures thereafter. Romania's largest commercial bank was privatized in 2006, though the privatization of the remaining state-owned bank was postponed indefinitely. Similarly, some progress was made with privatization of the energy sector, but the remainder was put on hold.

In the years prior to EU accession on 1 January 2007, the Romanian economy demonstrated considerable growth (generally 4%–6% with peaks of 8% in 2004 and 2006). Inflation was finally brought down into single figures by 2004. However, public-sector wage increases were criticized as unsustainable, the rate of tax collection was one of the lowest in Europe and high-level corruption remained endemic, despite the establishment of a national agency to monitor the activities of civil servants.

With the onset of the global economic crisis, international credit rating agency Standard & Poor's downgraded the country's sovereign debt rating in October 2008, as a consequence of which the new leu decreased in value by 2%. Sharp contractions followed in foreign direct investment and demand for Romanian exports, particularly for the automobiles and car-parts sector. In March 2009 multilateral 'pre-emptive' financial assistance amounting to 20,000m. euros was approved for Romania to support an IMF-supervised programme of reforms, which were to include large reductions in government spending and the strengthening of supervisory powers over the financial sector. The economy was expected to register minimal positive growth in 2010, after a 2009 contraction of 8.5%. The Government set a target of limiting the budget deficit to 3% of GDP by 2011. If it could also meet the other convergence criteria, Romania planned to join the Exchange Rate Mechanism II in 2012 and then the **eurozone** in 2015.

Romanian Agency for Foreign Investment
Agentia Romana pentru Investitii Straine (ARIS)

Promotes foreign investment in **Romania**. Founded in 2002.
  President: Ana-Maria Cristina.
  Address: bd Primaverii 22, Bucharest 1.
  Telephone: (21) 2339103.
  Fax: (21) 2339104.
  E-mail: aris@arisinvest.ro
  Internet: www.arisinvest.ro

Romanian National News Agency *see* **Rompres**.

Romanian royal family—Hohenzollern-Sigmaringen dynasty

The family which gave rise to the hereditary monarchs of **Romania** from 1881 to 1947. The current claimant to the Romanian throne is Mihai (Michael) Hohenzollern-Sigmaringen, who has spent most of his life as a businessman based in the United Kingdom and Switzerland. The dynasty was founded by the German Prince Karl of Hohenzollern-Sigmaringen who was proclaimed King Carol in 1881. The last reigning monarch was Michael himself. Having been proclaimed King as a small child in 1927, he was deposed by his own father in 1930, but became King for the second time at the age of 19 when his father (Carol II) abdicated in 1940. In 1944 Michael headed the coup which overthrew the pro-Nazi regime of Gen. Ion Antonescu. The communist regime established in the post-war period forced him to abdicate in December 1947 and he fled to the West, initially to the United Kingdom. Following the overthrow of the **Ceauşescu** Government, he attempted to return to the post-communist Romania, but was initially deported and faced hostility from the leftist regime of President Ion **Iliescu**. However, he returned in 1992, had his citizenship and passport restored in 1997, and was granted the same rights as other former heads of state in mid-2001. In recent years he has lobbied for the return of royal property confiscated by the state. His heir apparent is his eldest daughter Princess Margareta; her husband, Prince Radu, has considered running for the Romanian presidency.

Romanians

An Indo-European people indigenous to the fertile banks of the eastern end of the Danube and now comprising around 90% of people in the modern state of Romania. Romanians are ethnically and linguistically identical to the neighbouring Moldovans, differing only in that they use the Latin alphabet rather than the **Cyrillic alphabet**. Both are descended from ancient **Vlach** communities. At the 2004 Moldovan census, there were 75,000 Romanians in Moldova, but a further 2m. Moldovans (out of a total population of 4.2m.) identified Romanian as their main language. A growing number of Romanians live outside Romania and Moldova, with around 35,000 in **Serbia**, 25,000 in **Greece** and 15,000 in **Hungary**.

The Romanian language is derived ultimately from Latin and has strong similarities with modern Italian. The region converted to Christianity at the time of the Roman Empire. A majority of modern Romanians practise **Orthodox Christianity**. Despite their shared creed the Romanians foster a sense of cultural distinctiveness amid the predominantly Slavic countries around them (*see* **Slavic peoples**).

Rompres
(Romanian National News Agency)

The official state news agency of **Romania**. Rompres was created in 1990 but traces its lineage back to the Romanian Telegraph Agency (Ruomagence) which was founded as a government mouthpiece in 1889. Rompres was reorganized under state control after the emergence of democracy in Romania but prides itself on its constitutional independence.

General Manager: Constantin Badea.
Address: Piaţa Presei Libere 1, 013701 Bucharest.
Telephone: (21) 2228340.
Fax: (21) 2220089.
E-mail: webmaster@rompres.ro
Internet: www.rompres.ro

RS *see* **Serb Republic**.

Russians

An east **Slavic people** dominant throughout the constituent republics of the Russian Federation and with sizeable minorities in most of the former **Soviet** states. Russian migrations to the former Soviet states fall into two distinct phases: pre-20th century (historic) migrations and the larger Soviet-era movement of workers.

In **Estonia** and **Latvia**, where Russians came to number almost a third of the population, the question of language dominated relations with Russia in the post-Soviet period. Policies such as denying Russian its former status as an official language, and requiring competence in the local language as a qualification for citizenship, encouraged a large exodus of Russians and created significant bilateral tension.

S

Sabor *see* **Assembly (Croatia)**.

Saeima *see* **Parliament (Latvia)**.

Sąjudis *see* **Lithuanian Reform Movement**.

Sandžak

A region straddling the border between **Serbia** and **Montenegro** with a sizeable Muslim population. The area was the site of bitter inter-ethnic conflict during the Second World War. A considerable number of the Sandžak's Muslims fled the area during the conflicts which followed the collapse of the **Socialist Federal Republic of Yugoslavia**, reducing the chance of conflict in the region itself in the 1990s. The major urban centre in the Sandžak is the town of Novi Pazar.

Sarajevo

The capital of **Bosnia and Herzegovina**, situated in the heart of the country and the seat of the federal institutions. It has long been home to a **Bosniak** majority and has developed a distinctly **Muslim** identity. *Population*: 304,136 (2006 estimate). The ancient city was established as the capital of the Ottoman province of Bosnia and Herzegovina in 1850 and retained that role after the region was ceded to the Habsburg Empire in 1878. It was perhaps most famous for the assassination of Austrian Archduke Ferdinand in 1914, which sparked the First World War. A more positive claim to fame came 70 years later when the city, by then the capital of the Bosnian republic within communist **Yugoslavia**, hosted the 1984 Winter Olympics in an unusual display of international harmony between east and west.

The city became internationally renowned for negative reasons once more during the Bosnian war; designation as a UN 'safe haven' in May 1993 failed to protect it and the surrounding area from heavy Bosnian **Serb** bombardment, leaving its inhabitants facing sniper fire and incessant shelling. In the final phase of the war Sarajevo was linked to the rest of the Muslim-Croat territory. With peace restored the work to rebuild the shattered city began.

Sarajevo Stock Exchange (SASE)
Sarajevska Berza-Burza

The main stock exchange in **Bosnia and Herzegovina**. Founded in 2002. In March 2010 it had 18 members.
Director General: Zlatan Dedić.
Address: Đoke Mazalića 4, Sarajevo 71000.
Telephone: (33) 251460.
Fax: (33) 559460.
E-mail: contact@sase.ba
Internet: www.sase.ba

SARIO *see* **Slovak Investment and Trade Development Agency**.

SASE *see* **Sarajevo Stock Exchange**.

SBiH *see* **Party for Bosnia and Herzegovina**.

SC *see* **Harmony Centre**.

SCCI *see* **Slovak Chamber of Commerce and Industry**.

SD *see* **Social Democrats**.

SDA *see* **Party of Democratic Action**.

SDE *see* **Social Democratic Party (Estonia)**.

SDKÚ–DS *see* **Slovak Democratic and Christian Union–Democratic Party**.

SDP *see* **Social Democratic Party of Croatia**.

SDPBiH *see* **Social Democratic Party of Bosnia and Herzegovina**.

SDPL *see* **Polish Social Democracy**.

SDS (Bosnia and Herzegovina) *see* **Serbian Democratic Party**.

SDS (Slovenia) *see* **Slovenian Democratic Party**.

SDSM *see* **Social Democratic Union of Macedonia**.

Seimas *see* **Parliament (Lithuania)**.

Sejdiu, Fatmir

President of **Kosovo**.

Fatmir Sejdiu is a law professor and was a founding member of Kosovo's first ethnic **Albanian** party, the **Democratic League of Kosovo** (LDK). A member of Kosovo's **Assembly** since 1992, he was elected by the Assembly as the republic's President in February 2006, and re-elected for a five-year term in January 2008, making him the country's first President upon its declaration of independence the following month.

Born on 23 October 1951 in Pakashtica, in the Municipality of Podujeva, he graduated in law from the University of Pristina in 1974, then staying on to complete a doctorate. Specializing in juridical-historical and juridical-constitutional fields, he was appointed a professor at the university, but has also studied at foreign universities, including in Paris, France, and Arizona, USA.

Sejdiu was a founder member of the LDK in 1989, joined its presidency three years later, and was elected Secretary-General in 1994. He was also a member of the Kosovan legislature from 1992, serving on Judicial, Legislative and Constitutional Affairs Committees and latterly on the Committee for International Co-operation and Integration with the **European Union**.

When on 21 January 2006 President Ibrahim Rugova died of lung cancer, the LDK nominated Sejdiu to succeed him, and the Assembly elected him unopposed on 10 February. Rugova's death caused a shift in the dynamics within the LDK. After Assembly Speaker Nexhat Daci and Deputy Prime Minister Adem Salihaj were removed from office in February and replaced by Sejdiu's supporters, a rift opened within the party between the two factions, and the vacant party leadership remained unfilled until December. Sejdiu won the eventual leadership contest (and in January 2007 Daci and his supporters left the LDK to form the Democratic League of Dardania).

Sejdiu is married with three children. He speaks French and English.

Address: Ndërtesa e Kuvendit, Rruga Nëna Tereze p.n., 10000 Pristina.
Telephone: (38) 213222.
Fax: (38) 211651.
E-mail: xh_beqiri@president-ksgov.net
Internet: www.president-ksgov.net

Sejm
(Diet)

The lower house of the **National Assembly** of **Poland**.

Senate (Czech Republic)
Senát

The upper house of **Parliament** of the **Czech Republic**.

Senate (Poland)
Senat

The upper house of the **National Assembly** of **Poland**.

Senate (Romania)
Senatul

The upper house of the **Parliament of Romania**.

Serb Republic
Republika Srpska (RS)

The autonomous Bosnian **Serb** entity which constitutes around 49% of **Bosnia and Herzegovina**. The republic is divided into a northern half, running along the northern border with **Croatia** (which contains the capital, **Banja Luka**), and an eastern half, bordering **Serbia** and **Montenegro**. The two halves are linked by a tight land corridor which passes through the disputed town of **Brčko**. It was established as the Serb Republic of Bosnia and Herzegovina on 9 January 1992 initially in an attempt to maintain links with **Yugoslavia** in the face of calls for Bosnian independence. The original multi-ethnic population of the republic was transformed into Serb dominance through a determined policy of '**ethnic cleansing**' led by the ultra-nationalist Tigers militia.

The assistance of the regular Yugoslav army ensured the Bosnian Serbs significant successes in their campaigns during the Bosnian civil war until the formation of a Muslim-Croat alliance shifted the balance in 1994. The **Dayton Agreement** of November 1995 formalized the existence of the republic, and of the **Muslim-Croat Federation**, in a loose confederal arrangement within the Bosnian state.

Serbia
Republika Srbija

An independent landlocked republic, formerly a core element of Yugoslavia, located in south-eastern Europe in the **Balkan** peninsula, and bounded by Hungary to the north, Romania and the Danube to the north-east, Bulgaria to the east, Macedonia and Kosovo to the south, Montenegro to the south-west, and Bosnia and Herzegovina and Croatia to the west. Administratively, Serbia is divided into 17 regions, seven of which comprise the northern province of **Vojvodina**.

Area: 77,474 sq km; *capital*: **Belgrade**; *population*: 7.6m. (2009 estimate), comprising **Serbs** 82.9%, **Hungarians** 3.9%, **Bosniaks** 1.8%, **Roma** 1.4%, others 10%; *official language*: Serbian; *religion*: Serbian **Orthodox** 85%, **Roman Catholic** 5.5%, **Muslim** 3.2%, other 6.3%.

Under the 2006 Constitution, the Head of State is a directly elected President. The President's term of office is five years, renewable once only. The legislature is unicameral. The sole chamber, the **National Assembly of the Republic of Serbia** (Narodna Skupština Republike Srbije), has 250 members, directly elected for a four-year term. Executive authority lies with the Prime Minister, who is appointed by the President.

History: The extent and centre of gravity of Serbian territory has shifted considerably. Historically, it included **Herzegovina**, now in the modern state of **Bosnia and Herzegovina**, but did not extend to the **Hungarian**-dominated region of Vojvodina, which it does now include. **Serbia** also used to include, as an autonomous province, the (now **Albanian**-dominated) area of Kosovo, which became fully independent as a separate state only in 2008.

Slavic tribes, including Serbs, settled in the **Balkan** peninsula from around the sixth century. Serbia was under Roman and then Byzantine rule but became increasingly independent, under the Serbian princes from 1180 onwards. The brief Serbian Empire, carved out by Stephen Dushan (1331–55), set the tone for later territorial ambitions. A major landmark in Serbian national history was their defeat in 1389 at the hands of the Ottoman Turks at the Battle of Kosovo—a defining moment also for other independent countries of the **Balkans**. Following popular uprisings against Ottoman rule, Serbia secured autonomy in the early 19th century. An independent Serbia reappeared at the Congress of Berlin in 1878 and was extended to include **Macedonia** in 1913 at the expense of Turkey and **Bulgaria** (*see* **Macedonian question**). Serbia remained embittered over Austria-Hungary's 1908 annexation of Bosnia and Herzegovina with its substantial Serb population. This hostility culminated in the assassination in **Sarajevo** in 1914 of the heir to the Austro-Hungarian throne by a Serb nationalist, precipitating the outbreak of the First World War, in which the Serbs fought (against both the Austro-Hungarian Empire and the Turks) on what proved to be the winning side.

In 1918, Serbia, Montenegro and other south Slav territories acceded to an uneasy union as the Kingdom of Serbs, Croats and Slovenes, which was renamed **Yugoslavia** in 1929. The dominant position of Serbia within the union was sealed in 1919 when the initial monarchy was handed to the Serbian royal house. The authoritarian rule instigated from **Belgrade** between 1929 and 1939 laid foundations for resentment among the other elements within Yugoslavia.

For most of the Second World War Yugoslavia was under occupation by Nazi Germany and its Axis allies. Resistance was led by Serb-based **Chetniks** and by communist Partisans. The post-war communist Yugoslav regime of Marshal **Tito** sought to achieve a better balance among the nationalities, although the Constitution he introduced in 1974 devolved greater power to the individual republics, thereby contributing to a resurgence of rival nationalisms in the next decade.

The collapse of authority of the ruling **League of Communists of Yugoslavia** (SKJ) in 1990 was followed in 1991 by the failure of efforts to negotiate a new political structure for the country, heralding declarations of independence by most of the republics and subsequent military hostilities between several of them. Having by then abolished the autonomous status of Kosovo and Hungarian-populated Vojvodina, Serbia was firmly under the control of Slobodan **Milošević**. He had become leader of the republican SKJ in 1986 and Serbian President in 1989, before converting the SKJ into the **Socialist Party of Serbia** (SPS) in 1990.

In April 1992 the rump Yugoslav state, consisting of Serbia and Montenegro, adopted a new Constitution, proclaiming a new Federal Republic of Yugoslavia and effectively acknowledging the secession of the other republics. Serbia, however, continued to support violent nationalist resistance by Serb minorities in Croatia and Bosnia and Herzegovina. International pressure and mediation brought these conflicts to a negotiated if brittle conclusion by the end of 1995, but with a continuing legacy of political instability and inter-ethnic distrust (*see* **Dayton Agreement**).

Despite considerable internal opposition to Milošević's regime, the SPS emerged as the largest party in the legislative elections in November 1996, in alliance with the Yugoslav United Left (JUL), led by Milošević's wife Mirjana Marković, and New Democracy (ND). Milošević was constitutionally barred from a third term as Serbian President, but switched the institutional basis of his authority to the federal presidency instead, securing election by the Federal Assembly in July 1997 as President of Yugoslavia under the then prevailing system of indirect election. Serbian **National Assembly** elections later that year resulted in a further SPS-led Government, although with reduced support, while in protracted Serbian presidential elections SPS candidate Milan **Milutinović** was eventually returned in balloting described as 'fundamentally flawed' by international observers.

From early 1998 Serbia's attempts to maintain control over the province of Kosovo in the face of growing insurrection by the separatist **Kosovo Liberation Army** (UCK) had severe political and military repercussions. International efforts to deal with a serious escalation of violence between ethnic Albanians and Serbian security forces led eventually to military intervention from March 1999 by forces under the command of the **North Atlantic Treaty Organization** (NATO). Following an intensive NATO bombing campaign against the Belgrade regime, Serbian security forces withdrew from Kosovo in June 1999 and were replaced by UN-endorsed NATO and **Russian** peacekeeping contingents. The province was placed under UN administration (although remaining part of Yugoslavia) and efforts were initiated to reconcile the hostile ethnic communities.

Having been indicted for alleged war crimes by the **International Criminal Tribunal for the former Yugoslavia** at The Hague, President Milošević faced growing political opposition in Serbia in 2000, while in Montenegro pressure mounted for greater autonomy leading to outright independence. An assortment of 19 anti-Milošević parties and movements came together in the **Democratic Opposition of Serbia** (DOS) to demand early elections. These were called only after the enactment in July 2000 of federal constitutional amendments providing for direct presidential elections and thus enabling Milošević to stand for a further term.

Despite widespread intimidation and vote-rigging by Milošević supporters, elections for the federal presidency in September 2000 were widely believed to have produced an outright first-round victory for DOS candidate Vojislav **Koštunica**, leader of the nationalist **Democratic Party of Serbia** (DSS). Attempts by the regime first to insist that a second round of voting was necessary and then to annul the elections provoked a massive popular uprising, which forced Milošević to surrender the presidency to Koštunica in early October. Simultaneous federal parliamentary elections were deemed to have been equally flawed. The official results showed that the DOS alliance had won 58 of the 138 seats in the Chamber of Citizens, and the SPS/JUL 44. The **Socialist People's Party of Montenegro** (SNPCG) were third with 28. Montenegro's ruling **Democratic Party of Socialists of Montenegro** (DPSCG) boycotted both federal elections. The inauguration of Koštunica on 7 October was followed in November 2000 by the formation of a transitional Federal Government pending new elections, headed by Zoran Žižić of the Montenegrin SNPCG but consisting mainly of DOS representatives.

Following the ousting of Milošević, fresh elections to the Serbian National Assembly were held in December 2000, resulting in a landslide victory for the DOS alliance, which won 176 of the 250 seats with a 64.1% vote share, against 37 for the SPS/JUL (13.8%). A new Serbian Government appointed in January 2001 was headed by Zoran Đinđić, leader of the **Democratic Party** (DS) component of the DOS, whose prospects of being able to cohabit politically with incumbent Serbian Republic President Milutinović (also an indicted war crimes suspect) were improved by the latter's resignation from the SPS leadership.

Uncertainty about the future of Milošević was partially resolved at the beginning of April 2001 when he was arrested in Belgrade on charges of misappropriation of state funds and abuse of his official position. President Koštunica insisted that the ex-President and other indicted war criminals would be tried in Yugoslavia rather than by the international tribunal at The Hague. However, the Serbian Government subsequently extradited Milošević to The Hague in June to face charges of war crimes there, the compliance of the Yugoslav Government with this course of action being secured (but a major political crisis over the extradition not being averted) by the promise of a very substantial Western aid package. In consequence Žižić resigned from his post as federal Prime Minister, taking the SNPCG with him. However, he was replaced by SNPCG moderate Dragiša Pesić in July. The controversy over the fate of Milošević had serious repercussions for the DOS coalition, exposing its inherent fragility and particularly the deep fault lines between Đinđić's Government and Koštunica. In August Koštunica accused the Serbian Government of failing to tackle widespread crime, and withdrew his DSS. Disputes between DOS factions continued, not helped by ongoing pressure from the USA for greater co-operation with the ICTY. In June 2002 the DSS boycotted the Serbian National Assembly after 21 of its deputies were expelled. It was soon also expelled from the DOS coalition.

(Milošević was charged, in addition, with genocide in November 2001, and his trial began on 12 February 2002: he refused to recognize the court's authority. He died while the trial was still in progress on 11 March 2006.)

Meanwhile, following protracted negotiations on the issue of Montenegro's independence (which were mediated by the **European Union** (EU) from November 2001), the Federal and both republican Presidents had signed a framework agreement on 14 March 2002, providing for the establishment of a State Union of Serbia and Montenegro. Under this accord, the two semi-independent republics were to maintain separate economies, but have a joint foreign and defence policy, and elect a new, joint presidency and legislature. Montenegro was to retain the right to refer the issue of independence to a referendum after a period of three years. The agreement was approved by both republican Assemblies in April, and by the Federal Assembly in May, and a Constitutional Charter was drawn up over the next few months. This was approved at republican level in late-January 2003, and took effect when the Federal Assembly approved it on 4 February 2003. Later that month, a 126-member Assembly of Serbia and Montenegro was elected from the existing Federal and republican Assemblies, with 91 members from Serbia and 35 from Montenegro, split party-wise in the same proportions as the republican Assemblies. On 7 March this new Assembly elected Svetozar Marović unopposed as President of Serbia and Montenegro, and on 18 March a five-member Council of Ministers was approved, chaired by Marović.

This federal-level restructuring appeared to have left former federal President Koštunica without a role, since he had not sought the less powerful Union presidency, and also failed in his bid to succeed Milutinović in the Serbian republican presidency. Milutinović's term ended at the end of December 2002 (and the following month he was voluntarily transferred to the ICTY to face trial for war crimes). He was succeeded in an acting capacity by Serbian National Assembly Speaker Nataša Mićić, since two attempts to elect a successor had failed to muster the required 50% turnout (Koštunica having led the field on both occasions).

On 12 March 2003 Đinđić was assassinated: 1,200 people were arrested, and 45 were subsequently charged with involvement. Fellow DS-member Zoran Živković was appointed as the new Serbian Prime Minister on 18 March.

In November two small parties withdrew from the DOS coalition, causing it to lose its majority in the Serbian National Assembly. The coalition subsequently broke up and early elections were called.

At this poll, in December 2003, the ultra-nationalist **Serbian Radical Party** (SRS) won 82 seats (with 27.6% of the vote), while Koštunica's DSS-led coalition won 53 seats (17.7%) and Boris **Tadić**'s DS-led coalition won 37 seats (12.6%). A newly emerged reformist grouping known as **G17 Plus** in alliance with the **Social Democratic Party** won 34 seats (11.5%), and the **Serbian Renewal Movement—New Serbia** (SPO–NS) and the SPS (still led in name by Milošević) each won 22 seats (7.7% and 7.1% of the vote respectively). After lengthy inter-party talks, the SRS was kept from power by a minority coalition formed between the DSS, G17 Plus and SPO–NS, with external support—surprisingly—from the SPS. Koštunica became Prime Minister at the head of the new Government on 3 March 2004. The following month, a Union-level ministerial reshuffle brought in members of the new ruling parties.

Serbia was at this time still without an elected President. The latest polling attempt in November 2003 had been led by SRS acting leader Tomislav Nikolić but again was invalidated due to only 38% turnout. In February 2004 the turnout requirement was removed, and in June a new election was held. Nikolić led Tadić in the first round, but Tadić won the run-off and was inaugurated on 17 July.

In 2005 the USA and the EU pressed Serbia for more co-operation with the ICTY, in particular for the detention and extradition of four prominent figures who had been indicted for war crimes, most notably Gen. Ratko Mladić, the former military leader of the Bosnian Serbs. Talks with the EU on a Stabilization and Association Agreement (SAA), which began in October 2005, were suspended the following April as Mladić had still not been detained.

On 21 May 2006 Montenegro held its long-awaited referendum on independence. The 'yes' campaign secured 55.5% of the vote—just above the EU's prescribed minimum of 55% for it to accept the decision. Independence was declared on 3 June, and two days later the Serbian National Assembly proclaimed that the Republic of Serbia was the successor state to the Union of Serbia and Montenegro, and the Union bodies were dissolved. The Serbian Government officially recognized Montenegro's independence 10 days later.

Serbia now needed a new Constitution: a draft was adopted by the Assembly on 30 September, approved by referendum on 29 October, and promulgated on 8 November.

At the January 2007 Assembly elections, the SRS won 81 seats (with 28.6% of the vote), Tadić's DS won 64 seats (22.7%), Koštunica's DSS in alliance with NS won 47 seats (16.6%), G17 Plus dropped to 19 seats (6.8%), the SPS (with a new leader following the death of Milošević) won 16 seats (5.6%) and a new reformist alliance led by the Liberal Democratic Party (LDS), a splinter from the DS, won 15 seats (5.3%). The remaining eight seats were won by parties representing ethnic minorities. Lengthy coalition talks again ensued, motivated by the general desire to keep the radicals out of power, and resulted on 11 May with agreement between the DS, DSS–NS and G17 Plus. Koštunica was sworn in again as Prime Minister, heading a new Government, four days later.

On 20 January 2008 the first round of the presidential election was held, with SRS leader Nikolić again heading the list with 40% ahead of incumbent President Tadić on 35.4%. However, in the run-off on 3 February Tadić emerged with 50.3% of the vote to Nikolić's 49.7%, and he was inaugurated on 15 February.

Tensions quickly heightened between Tadić (whose key priority was Serbia's accession to the EU) and Koštunica (whose key priority was to retain the UN-administered province of Kosovo as part of Serbia). Talks with the EU on an SAA had resumed in mid-June 2007, and an agreement had been initialled on 7 November, though its signing remained dependent on the arrest of Mladić. As no advance had been made by early 2008, the EU offered an Interim Agreement, but this was rejected by Koštunica, who disagreed with the EU move to set up a police and justice mission for Kosovo. Then on 17 February Kosovo issued a declaration of independence, which the Serbian Government refused to accept. On 8 March Koštunica resigned and early elections were called. Just ahead of the polls, on 29 April, Tadić and Deputy Prime Minister Božidar Đelić went to Luxembourg and the SAA was signed, despite Mladić being unapprehended. The change of heart by the EU was viewed as an attempt to boost support for the pro-European parties in the forthcoming poll.

Latest elections: At Serbia's May 2008 Assembly elections **For a European Serbia—Boris Tadić** (ZES—a coalition led by Tadić's DS and G17 Plus) won 102 seats (with 38.4% of the vote), reflecting popular backing for moves towards EU integration. The SRS came second, with 78 seats and 29.5% of the vote. Well behind in third place was the DSS–NS alliance with 30 seats (11.6%), then the SPS in alliance with the Party of United Pensioners of Serbia (PUPS) with 20 seats (7.6%). The LDS—Čedomir Jovanović received 13 seats (5.2%), while Hungarian (Vojvodina), Bosniak (**Sandžak**) and Albanian (**Preševo valley**) parties won four, two and one seats respectively.

Recent developments: On 28 June 2008 President Tadić nominated as Prime Minister Mirko **Cvetković** of the DS (who had been Finance Minister in the outgoing Council of Ministers). His new Council of Ministers, a coalition of the ZES, SPS, PUPS and some minority parties, was approved by the Assembly on 7 July. Later that month, former Bosnian Serb President Radovan **Karadžić** was arrested in Belgrade and extradited to The Hague. In September, the Assembly ratified the SAA signed with the EU back in April.

International relations and defence. Following the break-up of the former Socialist Federal Republic of Yugoslavia in the early 1990s the rump federation of Serbia and Montenegro was recognized by most countries as the successor state, one important exception being the USA, which took the view that none of the successor republics represented a continuation of the former Yugoslavia. The rump federation succeeded none the less to Yugoslavia's membership of the United Nations, the **Organization for Security and Co-operation in Europe** (OSCE) and other international organizations. Its support for ethnic Serb military action in other former Yugoslav republics, however, resulted in its suspension from most international bodies and the imposition of comprehensive UN sanctions in May 1992. These were lifted in November 1995 under the Dayton peace agreement on Bosnia and Herzegovina, following which there was some progress towards normalization of Yugoslavia's regional and international relations. The onset of the 1998–99 Kosovo crisis returned Yugoslavia to international pariah status, which continued after the withdrawal of Yugoslav forces from Kosovo in June 1999 because Milošević remained in power. Not until Milošević ceased to be President in October 2000 was Yugoslavia restored to formal UN and OSCE membership, following which the new Koštunica administration applied for membership of the **Council of Europe** and declared its aim of joining the EU 'as soon as possible'.

On the demise of the Union of Serbia and Montenegro in June 2006, Serbia was recognized as the successor state, inheriting the former Yugoslavia's memberships. Later that year Serbia was formally invited to join NATO's **Partnership for Peace** programme, which came into effect on 14 December. An EU SAA was initialled in November 2007, and signed the following April, despite the fact that the Serbian Government had still not co-operated fully with the ICTY in the matter of the extradition of Gen. Ratko Mladić.

The secession of Kosovo in February 2008 complicated Serbia's international relations. Russia staunchly supported its position of non-recognition, thereby preventing UN recognition of the new state due to the potential of a Russian veto at the UN Security Council. However, many European countries, including several neighbours, did recognize Kosovo, which strained their relations with Serbia. A Serbian application for EU candidate status is still expected soon, but the process is likely to be delayed over the unresolved issues of Kosovo and co-operation with the ICTY, as well as potentially by existing disputes with neighbours who are either already EU members, candidates 'ahead in the queue' or applicants for candidacy.

Serbia's defence budget for 2008 amounted to some US $1,034m., equivalent to about 2.1% of its GDP. The size of the armed forces in 2010 was some 29,000 personnel, including those serving under compulsory conscription of six months, while reservists numbered an estimated 50,000.

Serbia, economy

Serbia's economy is going through a difficult and uneven transition. Some initial steps away from socialist-influenced central control began before the break-up of the **Socialist Federal Republic of Yugoslavia** (SFRY) in 1991. The transition process in Serbia, as the main element in the rump state of **Yugoslavia**, was then distorted by regional and international conflict, the application of UN sanctions and embargoes, and more especially the conflict over **Kosovo** and the 1999 **NATO** air-strikes on Serbia. The damage was compounded by suspension from the **International Monetary Fund** (IMF) and other international financial and development organs. Against this background, it was extremely difficult to determine realistic data on economic performance in the 1990s, especially in view of secrecy over economic indicators on the part of the Yugoslav and Serbian Governments themselves. Not until the fall of the **Milošević** regime in late 2000 and the readmittance of Yugoslavia to the IMF and other international bodies did normal transparency begin to apply. The 2006 secession of Montenegro, which had already been functioning independently in economic terms for several years, had little impact on the Serbian economy, although it left the country landlocked. Serbia's inefficient industry and bloated public sector were badly hit by the global economic downturn from 2008, requiring IMF support.

GNP: US $41,929m. (2008); *GNP per capita*: $5,700 (2008); *GDP at PPP*: US $84,207m. (2008); *GDP per capita at PPP*: $11,500 (2008); *real GDP growth*: –4.0% (2009 estimate); *exports*: $8,817m. (2007); *imports*: $18,400m. (2007); *currency*: dinar in Serbia (plural: dinars; US $1 = YD66.7 in mid-2009); *unemployment*: 15.6% (2009); *government deficit as a percentage of GDP*: 2.9% (2009); *inflation*: 9.9% (2009).

In 2007 industry accounted for 29% of GDP, agriculture for 10% and services for 61%. Around 29% of the workforce is engaged in industry, 21% in agriculture and 50% in services.

The main crops are maize, wheat, sugar beet, and vegetables and fruit; livestock and dairy farming are also important. Mineral resources include coal, brown coal (lignite), copper ore and bauxite, together with iron ore, petroleum, natural gas and lead and zinc ore. Industries include machine-building, metallurgy, mining, chemical goods, textiles and consumer goods.

The principal exports are manufactured goods, food and live animals, and chemicals, while the main imports are machinery and transport equipment, fuels and lubricants, manufactured goods and chemicals. The main destinations of exports in 2008 were **Bosnia and Herzegovina** and **Montenegro** (12% each) and Germany (10%), while the principal sources of imports were the Russian Federation (15%), Germany (12%) and Italy (10%).

Economic development in the SFRY had fostered the growth of a series of industrial centres down Serbia's north–south axis, from Novi Sad to Niš, along the fertile Morava valley. The dissolution of the SFRY in 1991 and the attendant regional hostilities resulted in output falling by 50% in the rump Yugoslavia in 1992–93 and inflation rising to very high levels in 1993. The introduction of a new currency (the new dinar) and other economic reforms in early 1994 produced a sharp reduction in inflation, but output did not recover until after the signature of the **Dayton Agreement** brought regional conflict to a halt in 1995. Thereafter, GDP expanded by 8% in 1996 and by 10% in 1997. However, underlying weaknesses were highlighted by large fiscal and trade deficits and by a 45% devaluation of the new dinar in April 1998, as evidence accumulated that the Milošević regime was more interested in retaining power than in reforming an increasingly inefficient economy still essentially under state control. An aggravating factor was the large proportion of government expenditure devoted to the defence and security sectors.

The economic framework was further disrupted by the increasing effect of renewed UN sanctions and embargoes imposed in 1998, and by the massive destruction of Serbia's infrastructure in March–June 1999 in the air bombardment carried out by NATO because of the Government's conduct in Kosovo. Although economic growth of 2% was recorded in 1998, GDP was estimated to have contracted by 20% in 1999, so that Yugoslavia emerged from the Kosovo crisis with output at about 40% of its 1989 level and unemployment of 50%, while inflation rose to 50%.

From a very low base, GDP growth of around 10% was officially recorded in 2000, but inflation rose to nearly 100% year-on-year. Not until the defeat of Milošević in the September 2000 elections and the resultant lifting of UN sanctions were conditions created for rebuilding the Yugoslav economic infrastructure after a decade of decline and containment.

The new Government quickly gained admittance to the **European Bank for Reconstruction and Development** and the IMF and was granted the equivalent of US $150m. by the IMF in emergency post-conflict assistance in support of a programme to stabilize the economy and to rebuild administrative capacities. At the same time, the National Bank of Yugoslavia (*see* **National Bank of Serbia**) announced in December 2000 that the fixed exchange rate for the dinar would be replaced by a managed float of the currency.

The new Government also declared its intention to launch a comprehensive privatization programme, the Milošević era having ended with around 80% of all companies, most of the large agricultural sector and over 90% of all assets still under state or social ownership. Although privatization measures had been announced in 1994 and again in 1997, the limited resultant disposals of state-owned enterprises had mostly benefited members of the ruling elite, often with connections in the criminal underworld. Some 1,500 companies were privatized in 2001–05.

In early 2002 four of Yugoslavia's biggest banks were liquidated. The '**shock therapy**' seemed to work, and during that year the banking sector substantially increased its level of activity. By 2009 there were 34 banks in Serbia, 21 of which were in majority foreign ownership, 10 in majority domestic private ownership and three still in majority state ownership.

An IMF stand-by agreement secured in 2002 promised to provide a much-needed injection of foreign capital over three years. However, the collapse of the Government in late 2003, and the subsequent elections and hiatus over the formation of the new coalition, caused the IMF to suspend disbursements. The new Government quickly impressed, with good fiscal management focusing on reducing inflation, stabilizing debt-servicing and cutting the balance-of-payments deficit, and the IMF resumed lending in late 2004. The arrangement was completed by February 2006, at which point over 60% of Serbia's foreign debt was cancelled with the 'Paris Club' of international creditors, as had been agreed in 2001.

Between 2000 and 2003 industrial production decreased slightly in absolute terms. Agricultural output declined in 2002–03, and again between 2005 and 2007. However, annual growth in real wages averaged 16% during 2001–06, rising to 20% in 2007, and overall annual GDP growth averaged over 5% in 2001–08. Despite this, national income in Serbia in 2008 was equivalent to only 69% of the 1989 level. The rise in imports during 2001–08 had kept pace with the rise in exports, so the annual trade deficit continued to cause a problem.

The formation of the **State Union of Serbia and Montenegro** in 2003 had given each republic responsibility for its own economic affairs, so when Montenegro seceded from the Union in June 2006 it did not take long for the two sides to reach agreement on the division of their financial rights and obligations. Serbia inherited the existing memberships of international organizations such as the IMF and **World Bank**.

In September 2006 the Government launched a National Investment Plan (NIP), to be financed by the proceeds of the sale of Serbia's second mobile telephone licence. Plan priorities included education, the health service, public administration, environmental protection, roads, energy, agriculture, culture and sport. Originally planned to run until 2011, it was suspended briefly in 2007 and again in 2008, and had its funding reduced by more than a third in 2009.

An EU Stabilization and Association Agreement (SAA) was initialled in November 2007, and signed the following April, but its implementation remains suspended until all EU members agree that Serbia is co-operating fully with the **International Criminal Tribunal of the Former Yugoslavia** (ICTY). In January 2009 the Serbian Government unilaterally implemented the interim trade agreement that had been signed as part of the SAA, which provided for a substantial reduction in customs duties on industrial and agricultural products imported from the EU. Serbia is also applying for membership in the **World Trade Organization**.

Since 2006, the privatization agenda has been dominated by the sale of a number of large, and politically sensitive, companies, notably the petroleum concern Naftna Industrija Srbije (NIS), a 51% stake of which was sold to the Russian state-controlled energy producer **Gazprom** in February 2009. Fiat agreed to buy the state-owned car manufacturer in 2008, though the transaction has been postponed due to the global crisis. However, a quarter of the workforce is still employed in the public sector and, despite success in trade liberalization and macroeconomic stabilization, the underlying inefficiencies of both public and private sectors have not been addressed. As a result, the global recession has made many Serbian companies loss-making, with a real danger of mass bankruptcies.

In late 2008 the Government asked for a precautionary stand-by arrangement with the IMF. In January 2009 the announcement that promised public sector wage rises would be scrapped provoked strike action. In March an enhanced arrangement was agreed, under which the IMF would lend Serbia $4,000m. over a period of 27 months, to April 2011. The first instalment, disbursed in May, was used to strengthen currency reserves and fund a stimulus package, that included lower rates for business loans in order to prevent insolvencies.

Serbia and Montenegro

The name used between 2003 and 2006 for the successor state to the Federal Republic of **Yugoslavia**. Officially known as the State Union of Serbia and Montenegro, it was formed on 4 February 2003. Its two semi-independent republics of **Serbia** (including **Kosovo** and **Vojvodina**) and **Montenegro** maintained separate economies, but had a joint foreign and defence policy, and elected a joint presidency and legislature. Montenegro retained the right to refer the issue of independence to a referendum after a period of three years. This it did on 21 May 2006, and following a 'yes' vote it declared independence on 3 June, thereby dissolving the State Union of Serbia and Montenegro. Serbia officially declared itself the successor state to the State Union, thereby inheriting its membership of international organizations.

Serbian Democratic Party
Srpska Demokratska Stranka (SDS)

The once-dominant **Serb** nationalist political formation in **Bosnia and Herzegovina**, formerly led by Radovan **Karadžić**. Launched in July 1990, the SDS secured most of the ethnic Serb vote in the November–December 1990 elections, winning the two guaranteed Serb seats on the then seven-member collegial Presidency with about 25% of the popular vote. It joined a post-election coalition with the (**Muslim**) **Party of Democratic Action** (SDA) and the **Croatian Democratic Union** (HDZ), arguing that Bosnia and Herzegovina should remain within a federal **Yugoslavia**. When the Government opted for independence, the SDS withdrew from the Assembly in **Sarajevo** and in March 1992 led the proclamation of the **Serb Republic** (RS) of Bosnia and Herzegovina in Serb-controlled territory, with its own Assembly at Pale. Thereafter the SDS was closely identified with the Bosnian Serbs' military struggle and was technically banned by the central Government in June 1992.

417

Karadžić and the SDS secured the Bosnian Serbs' rejection of successive international peace plans, on the grounds that they did not guarantee sovereignty for a Bosnian Serb entity. The party therefore came into political conflict with the leadership of rump Yugoslavia, which came to favour a settlement with the aim of securing the lifting of UN sanctions. The SDS also condemned the US-inspired creation of the **Muslim-Croat Federation** in March 1994. Increasing Yugoslav and international pressure on the Bosnian Serbs in 1995 caused divisions in the SDS, especially after Karadžić was named as a suspected war criminal by the **International Criminal Tribunal for the Former Yugoslavia**. Under the US-brokered peace agreement concluded at **Dayton**, Ohio, in November 1995, indicted war criminals were specifically excluded from standing for office in post-settlement political structures. Bowing to international pressure, Karadžić relinquished the RS presidency to the more moderate Biljana Plavšić in mid-1996, but remained very much in control behind the scenes.

The SDS maintained its hold on the Serb vote in the first post-Dayton elections in September 1996. Hard-liner Momčilo Krajišnik was elected as the Serb member of the new collective Presidency of Bosnia and Herzegovina, with 67% of the Serb vote, while Plavšić was returned as RS President with 64% support. In the simultaneous legislative elections, the SDS won an overall majority of 45 seats in the RS People's Assembly as well as nine in the union lower house. Plavšić quickly came into conflict with Karadžić and the hard-liners and was expelled by the SDS in July 1997, subsequently forming what became the Serbian People's Union–Biljana Plavšić (SNS–BP). In further RS elections in November 1997, the SDS was reduced to 24 seats, with the result that Gojko Klicković (SDS) was succeeded as RS Prime Minister by Western-backed moderate Milorad **Dodik** of the Party of Independent Social Democrats (SNSD, *see* **Alliance of Independent Social Democrats**).

In June 1998 hard-liner Dragan Kalinić, having been ousted as RS People's Assembly President, replaced Aleksa Buha as SDS President. In the September 1998 elections for the RS presidency the SDS backed Nikola Poplasen of the ultra-nationalist Serbian Radical Party (SRS), ensuring his easy victory over Plavšić. However, the SDS declined further in the RS People's Assembly to only 19 seats (and to four in the union lower house), while Krajišnik failed to secure re-election as the Serb member of the union collective Presidency, winning only 44.9% of the Serb vote. The SDS staged a recovery in the November 2000 elections, securing the election of hard-line RS Vice-President Mirko **Šarović** of the SRS as RS President with 50.1% of the vote and advancing to 31 seats in the RS People's Assembly with 36.1% (and to six seats in the union lower house). From its restored dominance, the SDS agreed in January 2001 to support a new RS Government headed by Mladen Ivanić of the **Party of Democratic Progress**, who appointed one SDS Minister to his 'non-partisan' administration despite Western opposition to SDS participation.

The SDS performed well again at the October 2002 elections, with Šarović winning the Serb seat on the union Presidency with 35.5% of the vote, SDS candidate

Dragan Čavić winning the RS presidency, and the party securing 26 seats in the RS Assembly and five (with 15.2% of the vote in the all-Bosnia lower house. It was included in the new SDA-led union Government, but went into opposition to an SNSD-led Government in the RS, despite being the largest party in the Assembly.

On 2 April 2003 Šarović resigned from the union Presidency, which he had been chairing, after being implicated in two scandals involving illicit exports to Iraq and alleged espionage activities by the RS military. Borislav Paravać, also SDS, was nominated to replace him eight days later.

The RS Prime Minister on 17 December 2004, and Pero Bukejlović (SDS) replaced him on 17 February 2005. However, in January 2006 he was ousted by a vote of no confidence and the SDS returned to opposition.

In March 2005 Čavić had been elected as SDS Chair. At the October 2006 elections, the SDS faired badly, losing the RS and union presidencies, and being overtaken resoundingly in the RS Assembly, where it trailed with 17 seats behind the SNSD on 41 seats. It also retained only three seats in the all-Bosnia lower house. Čavić resigned as SDS Chair (a post he had held since March 2005, in succession to Dragan Kalinić), and Mladen Bosić was elected as the new party leader in December.

Leadership: Mladen Bosić (Chair.).

Address: Nikola Tesla 16, Banja Luka.

Telephone: (51) 211947.

Fax: (51) 217848.

E-mail: info@sdsrs.com

Internet: www.sdsrs.com

Serbian Radical Party
Srpska Radikalna Stranka (SRS)

An ultra-nationalist party in opposition in **Serbia** and a leading political advocate of a **Greater Serbia** stretching from the Adriatic to the Aegean. Founded in 1991, the SRS won 34 Federal Assembly lower house seats in December 1992 and subsequently co-operated with the dominant **Socialist Party of Serbia** (SPS) until September 1993. Its representation in the Serbian **National Assembly** was almost halved to 39 seats in December 1993, following which the party disbanded its paramilitary wing (named after the Second World War resistance **Chetniks**), which had been accused of atrocities in **Serb** separatist campaigns elsewhere in former **Yugoslavia**. In the November 1996 federal elections the party's lower house representation fell to 16 seats on a 17.9% vote share. In the September 1997 Serbian National Assembly elections, however, the SRS advanced strongly to 82 seats and 29.3% of the vote and in March 1998 was included in a Serbian coalition Government headed by the SPS. Meanwhile, SRS leader Vojislav Šešelj had stood in the protracted Serbian presidential elections in late 1997, his victory in the first contest being annulled because of a low turnout, following which his losing vote share against the SPS candidate in the second was 40%.

The SRS strongly backed President **Milošević**'s intransigence in the 1998–99 **Kosovo** crisis, and was correspondingly critical of the withdrawal of Serbian forces in June 1999, although it remained part of the ruling coalition. The party opted to run a candidate, Tomislav Nikolić, in the September 2000 federal presidential elections, but he was believed to have obtained only 6% of the first-round vote. In the post-election crisis surrounding Milošević's reluctance to accept his defeat by Vojislav **Koštunica** of the **Democratic Opposition of Serbia** (DOS), a crucial factor in his belated concession was Šešelj's declaration of support for Koštunica. Having won only five lower house seats in the simultaneous federal parliamentary elections, the SRS slumped to 23 seats (and 8.5% of the vote) in Serbian National Assembly elections in December 2000.

In February 2003 Šešelj surrendered to the **International Criminal Tribunal for the former Yugoslavia** to face charges of war crimes in the early 1990s conflicts.

The collapse of the DOS ahead of early elections in December 2003 revived the hopes of the SRS, which became the largest party in the Serbian National Assembly with 82 seats (and 27.6% of the vote). Unable to find a coalition partner, however, it fell victim to the determination of the other parties to keep it out of government. This pattern was repeated after the 2007 elections, at which it won 81 seats and 28.6% of the vote. Similarly, Nikolić, its candidate in successive presidential elections in 2003 (invalidated due to low turnout), 2004 and 2008, led in the first rounds of presidential elections but each time was overtaken in the second round by Boris Tadić—in the 2008 poll by just 50.3% to 49.7%. At the 2008 Assembly election, Tadić's **For a European Serbia** coalition pushed the SRS into second place, with 78 seats (29.5% of the vote). After the election the party fractured, with Nikolić forming a breakaway Serbian Progressive Party.

Leadership: Vojislav Šešelj (President).

Address: Magistratski trg 3, 11080 Belgrade.

Telephone: (11) 3164621.

E-mail: info@srpskaradikalnastranka.rs

Internet: www.srpskaradikalnastranka.org.rs

Serbs

A south **Slavic people** dominant in modern **Serbia** and forming significant minorities in neighbouring **Bosnia and Herzegovina, Croatia, Montenegro** and **Kosovo**. Their ancestors, who settled in the eastern **Herzegovina** area in the seventh century, converted to **Orthodox Christianity** under Byzantine suzerainty in the early Middle Ages, distinguishing them from the western **Croats** who adopted **Roman Catholicism**. The Serbian tribes were spread throughout the western **Balkans** during this period and reached their zenith under the Serbian Empire of Stephen Dushan (1331–55). The occupation of Serbian lands by the Ottomans from the 15th century led to the migration of many Serbs, perhaps as many as 25% in total, into neighbouring lands (which came under the sway of the Habsburgs), notably modern-day **Vojvodina** and Croatia.

Very much in the political ascendancy in the royalist **Yugoslav** state in the period before the Second World War, the Serbs were not overtly privileged in the same way under the subsequent communist regime set up by Marshal **Tito**, although Serbia was the largest of its constituent republics and the federal army in particular was heavily Serb-dominated. The disintegration of the **Socialist Federal Republic of Yugoslavia** in the 1990s gave free rein once again to a revived Serbian nationalism. However, the flight of many Croatia-based Serbs during the wars of the early 1990s, and the eventual Bosnian settlement giving local Serbs an autonomous status within the **Serb Republic**, moved the nationalist idea of **Greater Serbia** further down the political agenda. The failure of nationalist politics in Serbia itself in 2000 further dampened nationalist ardour.

The Serbian language is almost identical to Croatian and Bosnian but can be distinguished by its use of the **Cyrillic alphabet**.

Serpents' Island

A small island (or cliff) opposite the delta of the Danube river in the Black Sea, which is the subject of a territorial dispute between **Romania** and Ukraine. The island was ceded to Romania in 1878 but control was handed to the authorities of the **Soviet Union** in 1948 in a clandestine agreement. It remains unclear who has the legal claim to the island. The matter is of significance, not only because of the question of the movement and stationing of the post-Soviet Black Sea Fleet, but also because of the sea's deposits of oil and natural gas. In 2004 Romania submitted its claim to the **International Court of Justice**; the hearings took place in September 2008, and the ruling in 2009 confirmed that the island belongs to Ukraine, but ceded to Romania about four-fifths of the territorial waters that it was claiming.

SFOR *see* **EUFOR**.

SFRY *see* **Socialist Federal Republic of Yugoslavia**.

Shock therapy

A policy of rapid transition from a command economy to a market-based economy, which in the short term imposes economic and social hardship in pursuit of medium-to long-term gains. **Poland**'s Balcerowicz plan was the most notable example of shock therapy. Introduced by the country's first post-communist Finance Minister, Leszek Balcerowicz, in January 1990, it was the first and most radical market-orientated economic reform package in any post-communist state. It abolished price controls and state subsidies but, in an attempt to reduce inflation, it retained wage controls. State spending was to be held down and state-owned enterprises to be privatized. The Balcerowicz plan succeeded in reducing the inflation rate and brought goods into shops, ending the queues of the communist era. However, industrial production declined rapidly and unemployment grew, and the plan proved politically unpopular.

SIEPA *see* **Investment and Export Promotion Agency of the Republic of Serbia**.

Silajdžić, Haris

Chair of the Presidency (**Bosniak** member), **Bosnia and Herzegovina**.

Haris Silajdžić was born on 1 October 1945 in **Sarajevo**. He attended Benghazi University in Libya, gaining a degree and doctorate in international relations and eastern studies. He then taught engineering until 1990 at Pristina University in **Kosovo**, the region then within Serbia inhabited mainly by ethnic Albanians, and rose to be a professor there, publishing over 100 papers specializing in thermal and fluid engineering. He also edited three scientific journals and has in addition written widely on international relations, especially concerning relations between the USA and **Albania**.

Appointed Minister of Foreign Affairs for the Republic of Bosnia and Herzegovina in 1990, Silajdžić helped secure international recognition for its independence in 1992, and later appealed from a besieged Sarajevo to the UN Security Council for the establishment of secure zones to protect the civilian population from the civil war and 'ethnic cleansing'. A firm believer in a multi-ethnic nation, his nomination on 25 October 1993 as Prime Minister nevertheless effectively signalled the abandonment of the 'rotation' of posts in the Bosnian leadership among the different ethnic groups. On 30 May 1994 he was also appointed Prime Minister of the newly-created **Muslim-Croat Federation**. In the latter stages of the conflict in Bosnia, tensions grew between Silajdžić and Bosnian President Alija Izetbegović, whom he criticized for steering his **Party of Democratic Action** (SDA) increasingly towards Bosniak Muslim nationalism. When the peace accord eventually came, Silajdžić resigned all his posts on 21 January 1996, believing that the December 1995 **Dayton Agreement** had allowed the central Government to be weakened too much. He left the ruling SDA, and in April founded the **Party for Bosnia and Herzegovina**, a party intended to appeal to all ethnic groups.

In the September 1996 elections this party won 11 seats in the all-Bosnia parliament and Silajdžić himself won 14% of the vote as a Bosniak presidential candidate, finishing second behind Izetbegović who secured over 80%. In December, Silajdžić was nominated, along with Boro Bosić, as union Co-Prime Minister; he held office from 3 January 1997 for just over three years.

Silajdžić stood again for the union Presidency in October 2002, this time in a close race against Sulejman Tihić, who ultimately won with 37.3% of the vote to Silajdžić's 34.8%. However, when Tihić stood for a second term in 2006, Silajdžić trounced him by 62% to 28%. The tripartite Presidency was inaugurated on 6 November 2006, and Silajdžić held the Chair of the Presidency in March–November 2008 and from 6 March 2010.

Address: Office of the Presidency, Titova 16, 71000 Sarajevo.
Telephone: (33) 663863.
Fax: (33) 555620.
E-mail: press@predsjednistvobih.ba
Internet: www.predsjednistvobih.ba

SKJ *see* **League of Communists of Yugoslavia**.

Skopje

The capital of **Macedonia** situated on the River Vardar in the mountainous northern part of the country. *Population*: 515,419 (2004 estimate). Skopje has had a long history as a regional centre and has undergone several different incarnations after natural disasters, purposeful destruction and political changes.

Founded in ancient times as an Illyrian settlement, the city became a regional administrative centre under the Romans. After near total destruction in an earthquake in 518 the city recovered towards the end of the first millennium. It first fell into **Slavic** hands when it was conquered by **Serbian** princes in 1189. However, a long period of Turkish domination followed conquest of the region by the Ottomans in 1392. Skopje (Usküb) became the capital of the province of Macedonia but Austrian forces razed it to the ground in 1689 to combat a cholera epidemic. The region was revitalized in the late 19th century with the construction of the Belgrade–Thessaloniki railway line. With the collapse of the Ottoman Empire in Europe, Skopje and Macedonia came once more under Serbian rule in 1913, beginning an 80-year political connection with **Belgrade**. Named as the capital of the Macedonian republic within **Yugoslavia** in 1945, Skopje has since been the republic's political and cultural centre. A massive earthquake in 1963 ruined 80% of the city and international assistance in reconstruction efforts earned it the name of 'City of International Solidarity'. The post-quake city has been designed to resist future geological upheavals. It also retains a Roman aqueduct and a handful of medieval buildings.

In its latest incarnation as capital of an independent Macedonia, Skopje is home to governmental institutions (on the left bank of the Vardar) and has become a centre for light industry (on the river's right bank).

Skupština Kosova *see* **Assembly of Kosova**.

Skupština Republike Crne Gore *see* **Assembly of the Republic of Montenegro**.

Slavic peoples

The largest single ethnic family in Europe. The Slavs are an Indo-European ethnic group whose area of settlement spreads from the far-eastern shores of Asiatic Russia to the heart of **central Europe** and across the **Balkans**. Slavs are divided into three main branches: the east Slavs (Belarusians, **Russians** and Ukrainians), west Slavs (**Czechs**, **Poles**, **Slovaks** and the minority Sorbs, or Wends, in eastern Germany) and south Slavs (**Bosniaks**, **Croatians**, **Montenegrins**, **Serbs** and **Slovenes**). The **Bulgarians** and **Macedonians** are also considered south Slavs and they speak a Slavic language, although their origin is generally accepted to have been from a mixing of Slavs and Tatars.

Arising from Asian origins in the third or second millennium BC, the Slavs historically settled north of the Carpathian mountains. The divide into the three major groups occurred from the fifth century AD as **German** tribes migrated westward into central Europe. The resultant geographic division encouraged separate linguistic and cultural differences.

The most potent of these differences is the split between **Roman Catholicism** (west Slavs, Croats, Slovenes, and some Belarusians and Ukrainians) and **Orthodox Christianity** (remaining east Slavs, Bulgarians, Macedonians, Montenegrins and Serbs). Along this fault line can also be found the use of the Latin and **Cyrillic alphabets** respectively (although all Belarusians and Ukrainians use Cyrillic). **Pan-Slavic** movements, usually inspired by Russian imperialism, have generally failed owing to this religious/cultural difference, among others. The most recent experiment, uniting the majority of south Slavs in **Yugoslavia**, proved a notable disaster—the differences between rival Christian traditions there being further complicated by the existence of two groups of south Slavs which follow the Islamic faith, the Bosniaks (who use the Latin script) and the **Pomaks** in Macedonia (who use Cyrillic).

Slavic languages are similar enough for rudimentary understanding between all Slavic peoples. In some cases, particularly within the former Yugoslav states, the differences between languages are small and distinctions are inspired more by nationalism than by linguistics.

The development of the various Slavic countries today has been largely due to the political divisions of the 20th century. The west and the south Slavs now generally aspire to greater integration with western Europe whereas the east Slavs, the most homogeneous group, tentatively seek closer regional integration between themselves, based around the economic dominance of the Russian Federation.

Slavonia

The north-eastern portion of **Croatia**, geographically incorporating the south-western corner of the Pannonian plain. Historically the centre of **Croatian** settlement, literally 'land of the **Slavs**', the region was dominated by the Catholic **Hungarian** kingdom until the establishment of the Kingdom of the Serbs, Croats and Slovenes in 1918. The region contained a large proportion of Croatia's **Serbian** population in the **Krajina** areas in its south and far east. These communities were devastated by the intense fighting in the area in the mid-1990s, and the flight of hundreds of thousands of Serb refugees in the face of a successful Croat military offensive launched in August 1995.

SLD *see* **Democratic Left Alliance**.

Slovak Chamber of Commerce and Industry (SCCI)
Slovenská obchodná a priemyselná komora

The principal organization in **Slovakia** for promoting business contacts, both internally and externally, in the post-communist era.
President: Peter Mihók.
Address: Gorkého 9, 81603 Bratislava.
Telephone: (2) 54433291.
Fax: (2) 54131159.
E-mail: sopkurad@scci.sk
Internet: www.scci.sk

Slovak Democratic and Christian Union–Democratic Party
Slovenská demokratická a kresťanská únia–Demokratická strana
(SDKÚ–DS)

A centrist political party in **Slovakia**, a member of the **Centrist Democrat International**, and currently in opposition. It was registered in February 2000 by

Prime Minister Mikuláš Dzurinda as a replacement for the ruling Slovak Democratic Coalition (SDK), a wide-ranging alliance of parties that was proving unwieldy.

The SDK had been launched in April 1998 as an electoral alliance of five parties then in opposition, namely (i) the Christian Democratic Movement (KDH), which had been founded in February 1990 under the leadership of communist-era Catholic dissident Ján Carnogurský and which had won 17 seats in the 1994 **National Council** elections; (ii) the Democratic Union of Slovakia (DÚS), which had been founded in 1994 as a merger of two centrist parties and which had won 15 seats in that year's elections; (iii) the Social Democratic Party of Slovakia (SDSS), which had won two seats in 1994 in alliance with the Party of the Democratic Left (SDĽ); (iv) the Slovak Green Party (SZS), which had also won two seats in 1994 in alliance with the SDĽ; and (v) the unrepresented Democratic Party (DS).

Under the leadership of Dzurinda, a former KDH minister, the SDK in July 1998 registered as a single party, in light of new electoral rules specifying that each component of an alliance must surmount the 5% threshold to obtain representation. In the September 1998 elections, the SDK narrowly failed to overtake the then ruling Movement for a Democratic Slovakia (HZDS), winning 42 of the 150 seats with 26.3% of the vote. Nevertheless, on the basis of a pre-election agreement, Dzurinda was able to form a majority coalition Government which included the SDĽ, the Party of Civic Understanding (SOP) and the **Hungarian Coalition Party** (SMK), on a programme of accelerated pro-market reform and accession to the **European Union** and the **North Atlantic Treaty Organization**.

The reluctance of some SDK components to abandon their individual party identities became increasingly apparent, so in January 2000 Dzurinda announced the creation of the Slovak Democratic and Christian Union (SDKÚ) as the effective successor to the SDK, being elected SDKÚ Chairman at its founding conference in November. So as not to provoke open defections by SDK components, however, activation of the SDKÚ was deferred until the 2002 parliamentary elections, with Dzurinda continuing as SDK Chairman in the meantime.

Nevertheless, in December 2000 deputies associated with the KDH and the DS withdrew from the SDK parliamentary group, while the SDSS entered into 'parallel' talks for a possible merger with either the SDĽ or the SOP. Although all the SDK components said that they would continue to support the Government, Prime Minister Dzurinda expressed disappointment at the reaction to his SDKÚ concept. In the event the DÚS was the only one of the five parties to dissolve itself in favor of the SDKÚ, but the new party did gather supporters from across the SKD alliance.

The SDKÚ finished second in the September 2002 election with 28 seats (15.1% of the vote), behind Vladimír **Mečiar**'s Movement for a Democratic Slovakia (HZDS, *see* **People's Party–Movement for a Democratic Slovakia**). However, Mečiar was not able to form a coalition, so Dzurinda returned as Prime Minister heading a coalition of the SDKÚ, SMK, KDH and New Citizens' Alliance (ANO) that controlled 78 seats in the 150-member National Council.

In late 2003 several deputies left the SDKÚ to join the new Free Forum, leaving the ruling coalition in control of just 68 seats. The next setback was the third-place finish of SDKÚ candidate Eduard Kukan in the first round of the 2004 presidential election. Then in September 2005, after several weeks of dispute over the attempted dismissal of the ANO leader Pavel Rusko from his cabinet post, the ANO was expelled from the ruling coalition (though the ANO's anti-Rusko faction split off and remained in the Government). However, opposition parties began a boycott of the National Council and it was nine days before the Government won back enough support to open a parliamentary session. The minority Government struggled on for a few more months, but the withdrawal of the KDH in February 2006 reduced it to an untenable 53 seats: early elections were called, set for 17 June, instead of the end-of-term schedule of September.

In January 2006 the SDKÚ had merged with the DS, adopting its current name. It finished second in the June 2006 election with 31 seats (18.4% of the vote), this time behind the left-wing **Direction–Social Democracy**. It went into opposition to a coalition that controversially included the far-right **Slovak National Party**.

In the 2009 presidential election Iveta Radičová, a Vice-Chairperson of the SDKÚ–DS, polled 38.1% in the first round, behind incumbent President Ivan **Gašparovič** with 46.7%. Gašparovič went on to win the run-off with 55.5% to Radičová's 44.5%.

Leadership: Mikuláš Dzurinda (Chair.).
Address: Ružinovská 28, 82735 Bratislava.
Telephone: (2) 43414102.
Fax: (2) 43414106.
E-mail: sdku@sdkuonline.sk
Internet: www.sdku-ds.sk

Slovak Investment and Trade Development Agency
Slovenská Agentúra pre Rozvoj Investícií a Obchodu (SARIO)

Government agency in **Slovakia**. Founded in 1991.
General Director: Milan Juráška.
Address: Martinčekova 17, 82101 Bratislava.
Telephone: (2) 43421851.
Fax: (2) 43421853.
E-mail: sario@sario.sk
Internet: www.sario.sk

Slovak National Party
Slovenská Národná Strana (SNS)

A far-right, nationalistic political party in **Slovakia**, which has given overt political expression to hostility within Slovakia to the **Hungarian** minority and to **Roma** (Gypsies). It is currently part of the ruling coalition.

The SNS was launched in December 1989 after the collapse of communism in **Czechoslovakia**, on a platform calling for the revival of Slovak national pride, the establishment of Slovak-language schools in every district (including those with ethnic Hungarian majorities) and exclusive use of Slovak at all official levels. It obtained 13.9% of the vote in the 1990 Slovak **National Council** elections, but only 7.9% (and nine seats) in the June 1992 contest, after which it joined a coalition with the dominant Movement for a Democratic Slovakia (HZDS). It continued to support the Government after the resignation of its sole minister in March 1993, and in October resumed formal coalition status, obtaining several key ministries.

In February 1994 the SNS was weakened by a split involving the defection of the party's 'moderate' wing led by its then Chairman Ľudovit Černák. The following month, on the fall of the HZDS Government, the rump SNS went into opposition, whereupon the SNS Central Council decided in May that only ethnic **Slovaks** were eligible to be members of the party. In the autumn 1994 elections the SNS took only 5.4% of the vote (and nine seats), being nevertheless awarded two portfolios in a new HZDS-led coalition. Thereafter the party resolutely opposed the granting of any form of autonomy to ethnic Hungarian areas of Slovakia under the March 1995 Slovak-Hungarian friendship treaty and also continued to oppose Slovakian membership of **NATO**, even though the goal of accession was official government policy.

In the September 1998 parliamentary elections, the SNS advanced to 14 seats with 9.1% of the vote but went into opposition to a centre-left coalition headed by the Slovak Democratic Coalition (SDK, *see* **Slovak Democratic and Christian Union–Democratic Party**). In the May 1999 presidential elections, then SNS leader Ján Slota came a very poor fifth with only 2.5% of the first-round vote, having attracted much criticism for his anti-Hungarian tirades during the campaigning. In September 1999 Slota was ousted as SNS Chair by a party congress and succeeded the following month by Anna Malíková, hitherto Deputy Chair.

In October 2000 Malíková reaffirmed her party's opposition to NATO membership on grounds of cost and its support for an independent European security system. In January 2001 the SNS elaborated on its controversial plan for 'reservations' in which 'unadaptable' Roma would be educated to become good citizens. Later that year Slota and his supporters were expelled from the SNS, and formed the Real SNS. This division split the nationalist vote at the September 2002 election, so neither party reached the 5% threshold for securing representation in the National Council. The two parties eventually reunited in April 2005, with Slota returning to the leadership, and the SNS went on to secure 20 seats (with 11.7% of the vote) in the June 2006 election.

Direction–Social Democracy (Smer) leader Róbert **Fico** was invited to form a Government, and on 4 July a coalition of Smer, the SNS and the **People's Party–Movement for a Democratic Slovakia** (ĽS–HZDS) took office. The junior coalition partners received only three and two ministerial portfolios respectively, and neither party's controversial leader was invited to fill any of the positions. The international community was nevertheless concerned by the inclusion of the SNS in government. Assurances from Fico that the foreign and domestic policies of the previous Government would be continued, and that extremism would not be tolerated, were undermined by contentious statements attributed to Slota on the issues of deportation and Slovakia's ethnic Hungarian population. Tensions rose between Slovakia and Hungary, and several key European leaders condemned the racial intolerance manifesting itself in Slovakia. In September the National Council voted overwhelmingly to adopted a declaration against extremism and intolerance.

The SNS supported the re-election of Ivan **Gašparovič** in the 2009 presidential election.

Leadership: Ján Slota (Chair.).
Address: Šafárikovo nám. 3, 81499 Bratislava.
Telephone: (2) 52634014.
Fax: (2) 52966188.
E-mail: sns@sns.sk
Internet: www.sns.sk

Slovakia
Slovenská Republika

An independent landlocked republic in **central Europe**, bounded to the north-west by the Czech Republic, to the north by Poland, to the east by Ukraine, to the south by Hungary and to the west by Austria. Administratively, the country is divided into eight higher territorial units (VÚCs).

Area: 49,033 sq km; *capital*: **Bratislava**; *population*: 5.4m. (2009 estimate), comprising **Slovaks** 85.8%, **Hungarians** 9.7%, **Roma** 1.7%, **Czechs** 0.9%, Ruthenians and Ukrainians 0.7%, **Germans** 0.1%, others 1.1%; *official language*: Slovak; *religion*: **Roman Catholic** 69%, atheist 13%, **Protestant** 6.9%, **Orthodox** 0.9%, other 10.2%.

Supreme legislative authority is vested in the unicameral **National Council of the Slovak Republic** (Národná Rada Slovenskej Republiky) composed of 150 deputies, who are elected for a four-year term by a system of proportional representation, subject to a 5% threshold for individual parties whether or not they run in alliances. The Head of State is the President, who is directly elected for a five-year term (renewable once only) and who appoints the Prime Minister and the cabinet (the latter on the Prime Minister's recommendation).

History: The region was settled by **Slavic** tribes from the fifth century and, in the ninth century, the Great Moravian Empire (Slovakia, **Bohemia** and **Moravia**) was established. Slovakia was then conquered by the Magyars (Hungarians), however, and consolidated into the Hungarian kingdom in the 11th century. In 1526 the Austrian Habsburg dynasty inherited the Hungarian throne, retaining most of the Slovakian lands. The establishment of the Austro-Hungarian dual monarchy in 1867 restored Slovakia to separate Hungarian rule, under which a policy of 'Magyarization' was introduced and nascent Slovak nationalism suppressed. Following the collapse of the Hapsburg Empire in the First World War, Slovakia declared independence in 1918. Under the 1919 Treaty of **Versailles**, however, it became part of the new Republic of **Czechoslovakia**, together with Bohemia, Moravia and Ruthenia (*see* **Transcarpathia**).

During the first republic the Slovaks increasingly resented the political dominance of the Czechs and their unwillingness to allow internal self-government for Slovakia. Following the 1938 Munich Agreement, under which Czechoslovakia was forced to accept the annexation by Germany of its German-populated **Sudetenland** border territories, the main Slovak national party declared autonomy (and **Hungary** annexed Hungarian-speaking areas in south Slovakia). In 1939 Nazi Germany invaded Czechoslovakia and established Slovakia as a self-governing, albeit 'puppet', state under fascist leadership, while Bohemia and Moravia became a German protectorate.

Soviet forces liberated the country from German occupation in 1945, and Slovakia, with limited autonomy, was returned to the pre-war Czechoslovak state. The Hungarian-speaking south was also restored, although Ruthenia was ceded to the **Soviet Union**. In legislative elections in 1946, the Communist Party of Czechoslovakia won 38% of the vote and became the dominant political party. Two years later the communists gained full control and declared a 'People's Democracy' in the Soviet style of government. In 1968, following the repression of the post-war years, Communist Party leader Alexander **Dubček** (a Slovak) introduced a programme of political and economic liberalization known as the '**Prague Spring**'. This was perceived by the Soviet Union as a threat to its control of **eastern Europe**, with the result that **Warsaw Pact** forces invaded the country to restore orthodox communist rule. One of Dubček's reforms survived, however: in 1969, under a new federal system, Slovakia became the Slovak Socialist Republic, although with largely powerless institutions.

In 1989, encouraged by democratization movements elsewhere in eastern Europe, anti-Government demonstrations in Czechoslovakia forced the communists, in the so-called '**velvet revolution**', to relinquish their monopoly of power. By the end of that year, a new Government with a non-communist majority had been formed and Václav **Havel**, a prominent writer and former dissident, had replaced Gustáv **Husák** as state President. At the same time, a strong Slovak nationalist movement emerged. Led by Vladimír **Mečiar**, who assumed the premiership in Slovakia in 1990, the Movement for a Democratic Slovakia (HZDS) became the political platform for outright independence in the 1992 parliamentary elections. The creation of separate Slovak and Czech entities was agreed and took effect in January 1993 with the dissolution of the Czechoslovak federation (the so-called '**velvet divorce**'). Michal Kováč was subsequently elected President of the new Slovak Republic.

Having lost parliamentary support owing to defections, Mečiar's coalition Government was defeated on a vote of no confidence in March 1994 and obliged to resign. In the September–October 1994 general election, however, the HZDS was returned as substantially the largest party with 61 seats, so that Mečiar formed a new coalition in alliance with the **Slovak National Party** (SNS) and the Association of Workers of Slovakia.

Over the next four years the authoritarian nature of Mečiar's regime slowed down Slovakia's transition to a free-market economy, generating political conflict and international concern about the observance of civil and constitutional rights. Tension between Mečiar and President Kováč led to a parliamentary vote of no confidence in Kováč in 1995, although without the three-fifths majority required to oust the President, so that a lengthy political confrontation ensued. When President Kováč's term expired in March 1998, the National Council was repeatedly unable to elect a successor because no candidate could win the necessary three-fifths majority. In the political vacuum, Mečiar assumed the presidential role but his seemingly undemocratic actions served to unite the political opposition.

In the September 1998 parliamentary elections, the HZDS narrowly retained the largest number of seats, winning 43 on a vote share of 27.0%. The new centrist Slovak Democratic Coalition (SDK) came a close second with 42 seats (and 26.3% of the vote), followed by the Party of the Democratic Left (SDĽ) with 23 (14.7%), the **Hungarian Coalition Party** (SMK) with 15 (9.1%), the SNS with 14 (9.1%) and the Party of Civic Understanding (SOP) with 13 (8.0%). The outcome was the formation of a majority centre-left coalition under the premiership of Mikuláš Dzurinda (SDK) and also including the SDĽ, the SMK and the SOP.

The new Government speedily secured the enactment of constitutional amendments providing for direct elections for the presidency, the first such balloting taking place in May 1999. Nominated as the candidate of all four ruling parties, Rudolf Schuster of the SOP easily defeated Mečiar and four other candidates, winning 47.4% in the first round and 57.2% in the run-off against the HZDS leader.

Commanding a majority of 93 of the 150 National Council seats, the Dzurinda Government remained politically secure in 2000–01, as it injected greater urgency into pro-market reform after years of slow progress under the HZDS (*see* **Slovakia, economy**) and steered Slovakia more enthusiastically towards membership of the **European Union** (EU) and the **North Atlantic Treaty Organization** (NATO) (see below). In opposition, the HZDS attempted to reassert its previous dominance by forcing a referendum on its proposal that early parliamentary elections should be held, but the exercise failed dismally in November 2000 when the voter turnout was less than half of the 50% required for the result to be valid.

431

On the other hand, Dzurinda encountered difficulties in his attempt to weld the SDK into a unitary party, with the result that in January 2000 he announced the creation of a new party called the Slovak Democratic and Christian Union (SDKÚ). However, because of the reluctance of some SDK components to join a new party, it was agreed that the SDKÚ would not be activated until the start of campaigning for the September 2002 parliamentary election.

At that election the HZDS remained the largest party, though with only 36 seats and 19.5% of the vote. The SDKÚ finished second with 28 seats (15.1% of the vote), just ahead of the new Direction (Smer) party with 25 seats (13.5%). The SMK improved to 20 seats (11.2%), the Christian Democratic Movement (KDH, formerly part of the SDK) and the New Citizens' Alliance (ANO) each won 15 seats (8.3% and 8.0% of the vote respectively) and the Communist Party of Slovakia (KSS) won 11 seats (6.3%). Five parties, including the SNS and SDĽ, failed to pass the 5% threshold. Mečiar proved unable to form a coalition, so in mid-October a coalition of the SDKÚ, SMK, KDH and ANO was approved, with Dzurinda continuing as Prime Minister.

Just before the election, Ivan **Gašparovič** and some fellow HZDS members who had not been selected as candidates for the poll broke away and established the Movement for Democracy (HZD); however, the new party only secured 3.3% of the vote, thus failing to secure any seats. In May 2003 another group broke off the HZDS and formed the People's Union (ĽU). The HZDS responded in June by changing its name to the **People's Party–Movement for a Democratic Slovakia** (ĽS–HZDS).

Gašparovič's candidacy in the April 2004 presidential election was backed by the HZD, ĽU, SNS and Smer. Mečiar led the first round with 32.7% of the vote, but Gašparovič edged out the SDKÚ candidate Eduard Kukan to win second place by 22.3% to 22.1%. Gašparovič then went on to win the run-off by 59.9% to 40.1%. He was inaugurated on 15 June.

Meanwhile, in late 2003 several deputies had left the SDKÚ to join the new Free Forum, leaving the ruling coalition in control of just 68 seats in the 150-member National Council. In September 2005, after several weeks of dispute over the attempted dismissal of the ANO leader Pavel Rusko from his cabinet post, the ANO was expelled from the ruling coalition (though the ANO's anti-Rusko faction split off and remained in the Government). However, opposition parties began a boycott of the National Council and it was nine days before the Government won back enough support to open a Council session. The minority Government struggled on for a few more months, but the withdrawal of the KDH in February 2006 reduced it to an untenable 53 seats. Early elections were called, set for 17 June, instead of the end-of-term schedule of September.

Latest elections: At the June 2006 election, **Direction–Social Democracy** (a merger of Smer, the SOP and various social democratic parties including the SDĽ) won 50 seats, with 29.1% of the vote. The **Slovak Democratic and Christian Union–Democratic Party** (SDKÚ–DS, a 2006 merger of the SDKÚ and the

Democratic Party, a former component of the SDK) were second with 31 seats (18.4% of the vote), while the SNS and SMK each won 20 seats (with 11.7% of the vote each). The ĽS–HZDS won 15 seats (8.8%) and the KDH won 14 seats (8.3%). The KSS, HZD and ANO were among the parties that failed to win representation.

Recent developments: Smer leader Róbert **Fico** was invited to form a Government, and on 4 July a coalition of Smer, the SNS and the ĽS–HZDS took office. The international community was concerned by the inclusion of the far-right SNS in government. Smer's membership of the Party of European Socialists in the European Parliament was temporarily suspended because of its controversial choice of coalition partner. Contentious statements attributed to SNS leader Ján Slota, on the issues of deportation and Slovakia's ethnic Hungarian population, undermined Prime Minister Fico's assurances that the foreign and domestic policies of the previous Government would be continued and that extremism would not be tolerated. Tensions rose between Slovakia and Hungary, and several prominent European leaders condemned the racial intolerance manifesting itself in Slovakia. In September the National Council voted overwhelmingly to adopted a declaration against extremism and intolerance.

In March–April 2009 Gašparovič secured re-election as President, winning 46.7% in the first round, and defeating SDKÚ–DS candidate Iveta Radičová in the run-off by 55.5% to 44.5%.

International relations and defence: In 1993 Slovakia, as a newly sovereign state, became a member of the United Nations, the **Council of Europe**, the **Organization for Security and Co-operation in Europe**, the **Central European Initiative**, the **Central European Free Trade Area** (until 2004) and the **Danube Commission**. In 1994 Slovakia acceded to NATO's **Partnership for Peace** programme, but it did not achieve NATO membership until 1 April 2009, five years after the Czech Republic.

Having applied for EU membership in 1995, Slovakia was accepted as an official candidate in December 1999 and formal negotiations opened in February 2000. An offer of membership was made in December 2002, in a major wave of EU expansion. The idea was supported by referendum in May 2003, and Slovakia acceded on 1 May 2004. In December 2007 Slovakia also joined the EU's Schengen Agreement, allowing free movement of citizens within the zone's borders. It joined the **eurozone** on 1 January 2009 (*see* **Slovakia, economy**).

In 1995 Slovakia and Hungary signed a Treaty of Friendship and Co-operation, which guaranteed the rights of ethnic minorities in each country and confirmed existing borders. However, bilateral tensions continued over a controversial Slovak language law of 1995 which restricted the official use of any language other than Slovak and also over an ongoing dispute about the joint hydroelectric **Gabčíkovo-Nagymaros Dam** project on the Danube river. The centre-left Government elected in September 1998 enacted a new language law in 1999 which authorized the official use of Hungarian and other languages in towns with an ethnic minority population of over 20%. However, the law was criticized as inadequate in Hungary and by ethnic

Hungarian groups in Slovakia. The entry of the far-right SNS into government in July 2006, and the subsequent rise in anti-Hungarian sentiment, put a severe strain on Slovak–Hungarian relations.

Slovakia's defence budget for 2008 amounted to some US $1,477m., equivalent to about 1.6% of GDP. The size of the armed forces in 2010 was some 17,000 personnel, including those serving under compulsory conscription of six months.

Slovakia, economy

Slovakia's transition to a market system involved less economic turbulence than that of other post-communist states in the 1990s. It grew strongly in the run-up to joining the **European Union** (EU) in 2004, and continued to perform well thereafter, completing its process of joining the **eurozone**, until the global economic crisis induced a sharp downturn in 2009.

GNP: US $78,607m. (2008); *GNP per capita*: $14,540 (2008); *GDP at PPP*: $119,369m. (2008); *GDP per capita at PPP*: $22,100 (2008); *real GDP growth*: –4.7% (2009 estimate); *exports*: $70,982m. (2008); *imports*: $74,034m. (2008); *currency*: euro (US $1 = €0.7129 in mid-2009); *unemployment*: 13.7% (end 2009); *government deficit as a percentage of GDP*: 6.7% (2009); *inflation*: 1.5% (2009).

In 2008 industry accounted for 37% of GDP, agriculture for 3% and services for 60%. Around 39% of the workforce is engaged in industry, 4% in agriculture and 57% in services. Some 31% of the land is arable, 3% under permanent crops, 17% permanent pasture and 41% forests and woodland. The main crops are grain, vegetables and sugar beet, while there is significant animal husbandry.

The main mineral resources are brown coal (lignite) and some iron, copper, zinc and manganese ore; the country also has some largely-unexploited reserves of petroleum, natural gas and mercury. The principal industries are light manufacturing, iron and steel, chemicals, food and beverages, and transport equipment. In 2005 57% of domestic energy generation came from nuclear power stations, 20% from coal-based thermal stations (which are being increasingly withdrawn because of the pollution which they cause) and some 15% from hydroelectricity. Slovakia is also a net importer of electricity, mainly from the **Czech Republic**.

Slovakia's main exports by value are machinery and transport equipment (particularly road vehicles, telecommunications and sound recording equipment, and electrical machinery, apparatus and appliances) and basic manufactures (notably iron and steel). Principal imports are machinery and transport equipment, basic manufactures, mineral fuels and lubricants, other manufactured goods, and chemicals and related products. Germany took 20% of Slovakia's exports in 2008, the Czech Republic took 13% and France 7%. Germany was also the main supplier of Slovakia's imports in 2008 (20%), with the Czech Republic and the Russian Federation providing 11% each.

The division of **Czechoslovakia** into the Czech Republic and Slovakia from the beginning of 1993 presented economic problems to each of the new countries in view of the separation of their respective economic bases. Under communism, Slovakia had concentrated on various energy-intensive heavy industries, mostly run on inefficient bureaucratic lines and with relatively low productivity. Within the **Council for Mutual Economic Assistance** (Comecon), it had specialized in armaments production for the **Warsaw Pact**, the end of which left much of this sector redundant. Following the division of Czechoslovakia, uncompetitive aspects of the industrial sector became more exposed.

Despite these problems, Slovakia experienced a much lower immediate drop in output than other ex-communist countries, with GNP and GDP each falling by only about 1% per year on average during the period 1990–94. There followed three years of strong GDP growth of over 6% annually, underpinned by high foreign investment, as inflation was curbed from 23% in 1993 to 6% in 1997.

Privatization of state-owned enterprises was initiated in the early 1990s within the Czechoslovakia framework and was largely undertaken through the **voucher privatization** system. Following the 1993 separation, political differences in Slovakia delayed further disposals of state assets, despite the introduction in 1995 of direct sales through the **National Property Fund**. By early 1997 the private sector accounted for about three-quarters of Slovakia's GDP, industrial output and employment. However, the Government, led by the populist Movement for a Democratic Slovakia (HZDS, *see* **People's Party–Movement for a Democratic Slovakia**), earmarked some 30 major enterprises for retention within the public sector, with the state also retaining a holding in a further batch of large concerns.

The absence of real structural reform under the HZDS-led Government, combined with poor public and private economic governance, served to reveal underlying weaknesses from 1997, associated in particular with ill-advised or corrupt lending by unreformed state-owned banks. The budget deficit jumped to over 5% of GDP in 1997–98 and current-account deficits of over 10% were recorded, as GDP growth fell back to 4% in 1998 and unemployment increased to 14%. A speculative attack on the koruna in the wake of the mid-1998 Russian financial crisis forced the **National Bank of Slovakia** to float the currency in October 1998, immediately devaluing it by 6%.

The centre-left Government elected in September 1998 moved quickly to stabilize the economy and to initiate new structural reform measures intended to accelerate transition to a market economy. It undertook to expedite the privatization process, with priority being given to disposal of the state-owned banking sector, telecommunications and the gas and electricity utilities, although in the case of the utilities the state would retain majority stakes. The budget deficit was reduced to 3.6% of GDP in 1999 and the current-account deficit to 6% of GDP, although GDP expansion declined further to 1.9% and inflation rose to 11%. Signs of renewed progress were apparent in 2000, during which GDP growth of 2.2% was recorded, although unemployment rose to 20%. That year, after seven years of negotiation, agreement was finally reached with the Czech Republic dividing the state assets of former Czechoslovakia between the two successor countries.

EU accession negotiations opened in February 2000, while in August Slovakia was formally invited to join the **Organisation for Economic Co-operation and Development**. It became a full member of the EU on 1 May 2004.

In January 2004 a 19% uniform rate of income tax, corporate tax and value-added tax was introduced, the relatively low rate of corporate taxation subsequently leading to increased foreign direct investment, which spurred economic growth. In 2004 and 2005 the World Bank described the country as an outstanding performer, while in late 2005 the country's long-term credit rating was raised, putting it ahead of the Czech Republic. However, the new Government of Róbert **Fico**, which assumed power in July 2006, halted plans to privatize many state-run enterprises.

Slovakia was admitted to the EU's exchange rate mechanism (ERM II) in November 2005, and in May 2008 the European Commission agreed that Slovakia had fulfilled the Maastricht criteria for membership of the eurozone. Slovakia duly adopted the euro on 1 January 2009.

Real GDP growth slowed to 6.4% in 2008, from a high of 10.4% in 2007, as a consequence of the global financial crisis and consequent fall in demand for Slovakian exports. In November 2008 the Government adopted measures aimed at reducing the impact of the international downturn on Slovakia, which included improvements in the use of EU funds, reductions in public expenditure, investment in infrastructure projects, and new loan schemes for small and medium-sized enterprises. A 332m. euros plan to support employment and boost domestic demand was also announced in January 2009. Nevertheless, the unemployment rate, which had declined to 8% in late 2008 (although significant regional disparities remained), increased steadily through 2009 to over 13%, and GDP contracted by 4.7%. Recovery is expected in 2010, with growth predicted of 4%, though much will depend on the strength of the recovery elsewhere in Europe, particularly in key trading partner Germany.

Slovaks

A west **Slavic people** dominant in modern **Slovakia** who arrived in the region during the seventh century. Ethnically they are almost identical to the neighbouring **Czechs**, with whom they shared the state of **Czechoslovakia** for much of the 20th century. Slovak as a language is very similar to the other west Slavic languages (Czech and Polish) and is transcribed using the Latin script. Most Slovaks practise **Roman Catholicism**, although a sizeable minority follow Protestant faiths, and around 10% consider themselves atheists. The connection with the Czech people was broken when the empire of **Moravia** was splintered in the 10th century and Slovakia was absorbed into the **Hungarian** monarchy for the next 800 years. This long separation engendered a distinct Slovak identity. In the 20th century, ideas of separate Slovak nationhood remained muted within the Czechoslovakia of the inter-war period, although after 1939 the Nazis sought to exploit them with the creation of a puppet Slovak state. After the fall of communism, nationalist politicians placed more emphasis on the divergence of Slovak interests from those of the Czech Lands, leading to the separation of the two in the so-called '**velvet divorce**'. Sizeable Slovak minorities exist in the **Czech Republic** and **Hungary**.

Slovene Press Agency
Slovenska Tiskovna Agencija (STA)

The main news agency in **Slovenia**. Established in June 1991, STA is the first Slovenian news agency. Its creation was mooted by pro-democracy activists in the 1980s and realized during the collapse of the **Socialist Federal Republic of Yugoslavia** in 1991. From its beginnings as a mouthpiece for the emerging Slovene democracy, STA has now developed to provide news items to the international as well as the domestic press.

Director General: Igor Vezovnik.
Editor-in-Chief: Tadeja Šergan.
Address: Cankarjeva 5, p.p. 145, 1100 Ljubljana.
Telephone: (1) 2410100.
Fax: (1) 4266050.
E-mail: desk@sta.si
Internet: www.sta.si

Slovenes

A south **Slavic people** dominant in modern **Slovenia**. Early Slovene settlement south of the eastern Alps first took place in the sixth century. The 'Alpine Slavs' came into close contact with the various local powerbrokers, from the Avars to the Austrians. Although ethnically and linguistically the Slovenes are closely related to the neighbouring **Bosniaks**, **Croats** and **Serbs**, a long historical connection with western European politics and culture, particularly that of Austria, has developed a more **central European** identity. Like the Croats, Slovenes largely practise **Roman Catholicism**, and use the Latin script to transcribe their version of south Slavic (which contains many German and Italian loanwords). They were subjugated as a rural peasantry under Austrian rule and those finding themselves in modern German- or Italian-speaking states have been under pressure to assimilate into those communities. Around 100,000 Slovenes live in the **Trieste** region of north-eastern Italy, with a further 24,000 in **Croatia** and about 15,000 in southern Austria.

Slovenia
Republika Slovenija

An independent republic located in south-eastern Europe on the western coast of the **Balkan** peninsula, whose successful bid for independence in 1989–91 marked the first stage in the break-up of the **Socialist Federal Republic of Yugoslavia** (SFRY). It is bounded by Italy to the west, Austria to the north, Hungary to the north-east, Croatia to the east and south, and by a short coastal strip on the Adriatic Sea to the south-west. Administratively, the country is divided into 193 municipalities.

Area: 20,273 sq km; *capital*: **Ljubljana**; *population*: 2m. (2009 estimate), comprising ethnic **Slovenes** 83.1%, **Serbs** 2%, **Croats** 1.8%, **Muslims** 0.1%, **Bosniaks** 1.1%, others 11.9%; *official language*: Slovenian; *religion*: **Roman Catholic** 57.8%, Muslim 2.4%, **Orthodox** 2.3%, none 10.1%, other 27.4%.

Under the 1991 Constitution, executive authority is exercised by the Prime Minister and Cabinet of Ministers. The President, who is directly elected for a maximum of two five-year terms, has largely ceremonial powers. Legislative power is vested in a unicameral **National Assembly** (Državni Zbor), with 90 members elected for a four-year term, 40 directly by constituencies and 50 by a system of proportional representation subject to a 4% threshold (with one seat each reserved for the **Hungarian** and Italian ethnic minorities). There is also an advisory 40-member National Council (Državni Svet), whose members serve five-year terms, 18 being indirectly elected by socio-economic interest groups and 22 elected by communities to represent local interests.

History: Once part of the Roman province of Illyria, Slovenia was settled by **Slavic** tribes from the sixth century and came under feudal Bavarian and Frankish domination in the eighth century. By the late 10th century much of present-day Slovenia was within the Holy Roman Empire and eventually passed under Habsburg rule in the 14th century. France briefly ruled western Slovenia during the Napoleonic era, but Habsburg rule was restored in 1815 at the Congress of Vienna. In 1867 most of Slovenia was incorporated into the Austrian half of the Austro-Hungarian Empire. The collapse of this imperial structure followed defeat in the First World War. Slovenia in 1918 joined other south Slav territories within the newly-formed Kingdom of Serbs, Croats and Slovenes (renamed **Yugoslavia** in 1929).

During the Second World War Slovenia was under Italian and German occupation from 1941 until 1945. Resistance was led by the Slovene Liberation Front in alliance with the communist-led Yugoslav Partisans under **Tito**. At the end of the war, Slovenia came under communist rule as one of the six constituent republics of the Socialist Federal Republic of Yugoslavia (together with **Serbia, Croatia, Bosnia and Herzegovina, Macedonia** and **Montenegro**).

Tito's death in 1980 ushered in a period of instability as Yugoslavia's political structure began to break down because of increasing nationalism and rivalry among the constituent republics and their populations. In 1989 the Slovenian Assembly declared the sovereignty of the republic and its right to secede from Yugoslavia. Multi-party elections were held for the first time in April 1990. The parliamentary contest resulted in the defeat of the successor to the erstwhile ruling communist party (although the former communist leader Milan Kučan won election as President with 59% of the second-round vote). A nationalist Government led by the Democratic Opposition of Slovenia (DEMOS) was installed under the premiership of Lojze Peterle of the Slovenian Christian Democrats (SKD), the largest DEMOS component.

Following an overwhelming referendum vote in favour of independence, Slovenia seceded from the Yugoslav federation in June 1991, provoking military conflict with the Serb-dominated Yugoslav army. After a brief period of hostilities, the **European Union** (EU) brokered a ceasefire in July under which Yugoslav forces withdrew and Slovenia's independence was accepted by default. A new Constitution providing for a multi-party democratic system was adopted in December 1991, as the DEMOS coalition was dissolved.

Slovenia held its first post-independence parliamentary and presidential elections in December 1992. The Assembly elections returned a new centre-left coalition, mainly comprising what became **Liberal Democracy of Slovenia** (LDS), the SKD and the United List of Social Democrats (ZLSD), under the premiership of Janez **Drnovšek** of the LDS. In the presidential elections Kučan was re-elected in the first round with 64% of the vote.

Strains in the ruling coalition were underlined by the withdrawal of the ZLSD in January 1996 after Drnovšek had announced the dismissal of one of its ministers. In the November 1996 Assembly elections, the LDS secured only 25 of the 90 seats, while a centre-right Slovenian Spring (SP) opposition alliance of the SKD, the **Slovenian People's Party** (SLS) and the Social Democratic Party of Slovenia (SDS) won an aggregate of 45. Following protracted negotiations, Drnovšek narrowly secured re-election as Prime Minister on the basis of an unlikely coalition which included the ZLSD on the left, the **Slovenian National Party** (SNS) on the far right, as well as the **Democratic Party of Slovenian Pensioners** (DeSUS) and the two national minority deputies. By February 1997, however, Drnovšek had succeeded in detaching the SLS from the SP alliance, and so was able to form a more stable coalition Government with the SLS and the DeSUS. In November 1997 President Kučan was re-elected for a second term, winning outright in the first round with 55.6% of the vote, and a new National Council was elected for a five-year term.

Growing strains in the ruling coalition culminated in the withdrawal of the SLS in April 2000 and the consequential fall of the Drnovšek Government. A lengthy crisis ensued, resulting in June in the appointment, pending elections in October, of an administration headed by what had become the SLS+SKD (by a merger between the two erstwhile SP allies), with Andrej Bajuk of the SLS+SKD as Prime Minister. Bajuk quickly broke with the SLS+SKD over the issue of whether proportional representation should be abandoned and all Assembly seats filled in individual constituency contests. In August 2000 he launched the New Slovenia–Christian

People's Party (NSi), which attracted several prominent centrists, especially members of the former SKD.

The October 2000 Assembly elections resulted in a major advance for the LDS, which won 34 of the 90 seats with a vote share of 36.3%. Second place was taken by the SDS with 14 seats (15.8% of the vote), followed by the ZLSD with 11 (12.1%), the SLS+SKD with nine (9.6%), the NSi with only eight (8.6%), the DeSUS with four (5.2%), the SNS with four (4.4%) and the Slovenian Youth Party (SMS—now called the **Youth Party–European Greens**, SMS-Zeleni) with four (4.3%), just surpassing the minimum percentage threshold which had recently been raised to 4%. The Hungarian and Italian minorities again returned one Assembly member each for their reserved seats.

The election outcome resulted in the return of Drnovšek to the premiership in November 2000, at the head of a majority centre-left coalition of his LDS together with the ZLSD, the SLS+SKD and the DeSUS. Drnovšek said that the Government would avoid '**shock therapy**' but would concentrate on revision of legislation to prepare Slovenia for EU membership.

Drnovšek stood as the LDS candidate in the 2002 presidential election. In the first round on 10 November he led with 44.4%, while in second place, with 30.8%, was Barbara Brezigar whose candidacy was backed by the SDS and NSi. In the run-off on 1 December Drnovšek beat Brezigar by 56.5% to 43.5%. LDS Minister of Finance Anton Rop was nominated to replace Drnovšek as Prime Minister; his new Government, which maintained the same coalition, was approved on 19 December and Drnovšek was inaugurated as President three days later.

In early 2004 legislation was passed by the Assembly to restore Slovenian citizenship to 18,000 nationals of former Yugoslav republics, who (resident in Slovenia at the time of its independence) had been removed from population records and lost their residency rights. However, several right-wing parties opposed to the legislation forced a referendum on the issue, which was held in April and resoundingly rejected the legislation. The SLS, which had supported the holding of the referendum, subsequently withdrew from the Government.

At the October 2004 Assembly elections the SDS (which in 2003 had renamed itself the **Slovenian Democratic Party**, retaining the same acronym) became the largest party with 29 seats (with 29.1% of the vote), overtaking the LDS with 23 seats (22.8%). The ZLSD won 10 seats (10.2%), the NSi won nine seats (9.1%), the SLS won seven seats (6.8%), the SNS won six seats (6.3%) and the DeSUS won four seats (4%). The remaining two seats were reserved for the minority representatives. On 9 November SDS leader Janez Janša was nominated as Prime Minister, and his Government was approved on 3 December, comprising the SDS, the SLS, the NSi and the DeSUS.

Due to ill health, Drnovšek did not seek re-election as President in 2007. In the 21 October first round, Peterle (now an independent candidate, backed by the SDS, NSi and SLS) led with 28.7%, followed by Danilo **Türk** (independent, backed by the

Social Democrats (SD—the renamed ZLSD), DeSUS, **For Real—New Politics** (Zares) and Active Slovenia) with 24.5%, just ahead of LDS-backed independent Mitja Gaspari on 24.1%. SNS candidate Zmago Jelinčič Plemeniti also secured 19.2%. In the run-off on 11 November Türk resoundingly defeated Peterle, winning by 68% to 32%. He took office on 22 December.

Latest elections: The September 2008 Assembly elections confirmed the rise of the SD which won 29 seats (with 30.5% of the vote), pushing the SDS into second with 28 seats (29.3% of the vote). Zares won nine seats (9.4% of the vote), DeSUS won seven seats (7.5%) and five seats each went to the SNS (5.4% of the vote), the alliance of the SLS and SMS (5.2%) and the LDS (5.2%). NSi and nine other parties did not pass the 4% threshold to secure representation in the Assembly.

Recent developments: SD leader Borut **Pahor** was nominated as Prime Minister on 3 November 2008. He formed a coalition with Zares, the DeSUS and the LDS, and his Government was approved on 21 November, including several independent technocrats. Pahor said his priority would be to combat the effects of the global economic crisis.

International relations and defence: Slovenia was recognized as an independent state by the EU in January 1992, by the **Russian Federation** in February, and by the USA in April, and was admitted to the United Nations in May. It became a member of the **Council of Europe**, the **Organization for Security and Co-operation in Europe** and the **Central European Initiative**. In 1994 it joined **NATO**'s **Partnership for Peace** programme. It was unsuccessful in a bid to be included in the first round of NATO enlargement (along with the **Czech Republic, Hungary** and **Poland**), but did join in the second wave of expansion in March 2004.

In the same year (2004) Slovenia acceded on 1 May to membership of the EU, having been one of six 'fast-track' candidates in negotiations since 1998; the offer of membership was made formally in December 2002 and supported by a Slovenian referendum in March 2003. **Eurozone** membership followed relatively rapidly, on 1 January 2007 (*see* **Slovenia, economy**), and in December of that year Slovenia also joined the EU's Schengen Agreement, allowing free movement of citizens within the Schengen zone's borders.

Bilaterally, Slovenia's relations with Croatia had been clouded by various unresolved issues, including demarcation of land and maritime borders and control of the jointly-owned nuclear power station at Krško (in Slovenia). Despite an accord signed in 2001, relations have remained fractious, particularly over the still undemarcated maritime border; Slovenia has stalled the final stages of Croatia's EU accession talks because of the tensions.

One area of agreement between Slovenia and Croatia was their joint opposition to any Italian irredentism in respect of territory lost in the Second World War, and to Italian demands for the return of confiscated Italian properties in Istria. The latter issue had caused Italy to block the signing of an EU association agreement with Slovenia, until an agreement was concluded in February 1998 under which Slovenia undertook to meet more than half of the financial compensation which former Yugoslavia had agreed to pay in respect of appropriated Italian properties.

Slovenia and Yugoslavia recognized one another in 1995, but relations remained cool as Slovenia condemned Serbia's repression in **Kosovo** and supported NATO military action in 1999.

Slovenia's defence budget for 2008 amounted to some US $834m., equivalent to about 1.5% of GDP. The size of the armed forces in 2010 was some 7,000 personnel, while reservists numbered an estimated 4,000. Compulsory military service was phased out in 2003 and replaced by a voluntary option.

Slovenia, economy

Formerly the most prosperous economy among the republics of the **Socialist Federal Republic of Yugoslavia**, Slovenia has successfully adopted a market system since becoming independent, joining both the **European Union** (EU) and the **eurozone**.

GNP: US $48,973m. (2008); *GNP per capita*: $24,010 (2008); *GDP at PPP*: $56,297m. (2008); *GDP per capita at PPP*: $27,600 (2008); *real GDP growth*: –4.7% (2009 estimate); *exports*: $29,233m. (2008); *imports*: $33,937m. (2008); *currency*: euro (US $1 = €0.7129 in mid-2009); *unemployment*: 6.8% (end 2009); *government deficit as a percentage of GDP*: 6.5% (2009); *inflation*: 0.5% (2009).

In 2007 industry contributed 35% of GDP, agriculture 2% and services 63%. Around 37% of the workforce is engaged in industry, 5% in agriculture and 58% in services.

Some 12% of the land is arable, 3% under permanent crops, 28% permanent pastures and 51% forests and woodland. The main crops are grain, vegetables, fruit (including grapes for wine) and sugar beet; there is also an animal husbandry sector and forestry is important.

The main mineral resource is brown coal (lignite). The principal industries include electrical equipment, chemicals, food processing, textiles, metal manufacture and the exploitation of timber. Tourism is an important part of the economy, with most tourists coming from Italy, Germany and Austria. Nearly 40% of energy requirements are met from a nuclear power station (whose ownership and output is shared between Slovenia and **Croatia**), while hydroelectricity contributes 23%.

Slovenia's main exports are machinery and transport equipment (particularly road vehicles and parts, and electrical machinery), basic manufactures (notably metal manufactures), chemicals, and miscellaneous manufactured articles. Principal imports are machinery and transport equipment (notably road vehicles), basic manufactures, chemical products, miscellaneous manufactured articles, mineral fuels and crude materials. The main destinations for Slovenian exports in 2008 were Germany (19%), Italy (12%) and Croatia (9%). Germany was also the principal supplier of Slovenia's imports in 2008 (19%), followed by Italy (18%) and Austria (12%).

Immediately prior to the dissolution of former **Yugoslavia** in 1991, Slovenia had less than 10% of the total federal population but produced around 20% of its social product, although it had shared in the general Yugoslav economic deterioration of the 1980s. Slovenia experienced only a brief period of pre-independence hostilities in 1991, so that the economy was able to develop without the devastation suffered in Croatia and in **Bosnia and Herzegovina**. Nevertheless, the general disruption of trade in the area resulted in a 17% fall in GDP in 1990–92 and a further contraction of 3% in 1993. Inflation, which was running at a massive 500% in 1990, fell back to 32% in 1993. A new currency, the tolar, was introduced in 1991 and economic reform programmes were announced; but little real structural change was achieved in the early years of independence.

A new comprehensive reform programme launched in early 1993 with support from the international financial institutions yielded GDP growth of 5.3% in 1994 followed by expansion rates of around 4% a year in the period 1995–99. Inflation was brought down further, to 9% at the end of 1997 and to 6.5% at the end of 1998, before rising to 8% in 1999 because of the introduction of value-added tax (VAT). This progress was achieved despite a 1996 agreement under which Slovenia assumed 18% of the debts of the former Yugoslavia (a far greater proportion than relative population size).

Privatization was launched in 1992 under complex procedures for the disposal of equity in state-owned enterprises, but did not get properly under way until 1994, with the allocation of **vouchers** to employees of such businesses. Most of these privatizations were in effect management/employee buy-outs of co-operatives, and generally there was little inward investment from abroad. Whereas privatization was originally due to have been completed by 1995, in early 1998 the state sector still accounted for over half of Slovenian enterprises in terms of value added and employment. Accordingly, a new privatization programme was initiated in 1999 covering state-owned banks, telecommunications and public utilities, while plans were announced for the dismantling of the remaining restrictions on foreign investment. Progress was slow, however, and deadlines for privatizations were frequently postponed.

Assisted from February 1999 by the activation of its association agreement with the EU (following the opening of formal accession negotiations in November 1998) and by the freeing of capital movement later that year, Slovenia recorded further GDP growth of 4% in 2000, during which time inflation was curbed to 4% and the budget deficit remained low at around 1% of GDP. Although unemployment remained at over 7% in the period from 1995 to 2000, Slovenia continued to have the highest per head GDP among ex-communist countries in transition, and by 2003 this had reached about 70% of the EU average.

Slovenia formally acceded to the EU on 1 May 2004 and, following the successful adoption of measures to reduce inflation, achieved entry into the Exchange Rate Mechanism II in June. The continued reduction of inflation in order to meet EU levels was central to government policy. Slovenia joined the eurozone on 1 January 2007, the first of the new EU members to do so.

In November 2005 the Government announced extensive economic reforms, including measures to increase competitiveness, reform the labour market and the pension and health systems, and resume the privatization of state-owned enterprises. The removal of a number of barriers to foreign direct investment (FDI) in 2002 had encouraged more foreign buyers into the market, but a significant portion of the economy remains state-owned and FDI per capita is among the lowest in the EU.

Slovenia's export-driven economy was quickly affected by the global economic slowdown in late 2008, though the subsequent reduction in domestic consumption and investment helped to contain inflation, which had reached almost 7% in July 2008— the highest level in the eurozone. GDP growth of 3.5% was still achieved in 2008, though the economy contracted the following year, and the fall in exports coupled with increased government spending to stimulate the economy pushed the budget deficit for 2009 above the 3% threshold prescribed for eurozone members.

Slovenia is well placed to bounce back from the downturn, with a well-educated and productive workforce, good high-tech infrastructure, and the best credit rating among the transition economies. FDI will rise as the privatization programme continues, and businesses are good at orientating production to fit market demand.

Slovenian Democratic Party
Slovenska demokratska stranka (SDS)

A centre-right political party in **Slovenia**, currently in opposition, and a member of the **International Democratic Union** and **Centrist Democrat International**.

Founded in February 1989 as the Social Democratic Alliance of Slovenia (SDZS), but later renamed the Social Democratic Party of Slovenia (SDS), it was a component of the victorious Democratic Opposition of Slovenia (DEMOS) alliance in the 1990 elections. In December 1992 its presidential candidate took only 0.6% of the first-round vote, but the party won 3.1% and four seats in the simultaneous legislative elections, subsequently participating in the centre-left coalition Government headed by **Liberal Democracy of Slovenia** (LDS). In 1993 the SDS Defence Minister and party Chairman, Janez Janša, became enmeshed in an arms-trading scandal, which led indirectly to his dismissal from the cabinet in March 1994, whereupon the SDS joined the parliamentary opposition.

The SDS contested the November 1996 parliamentary elections as part of the Slovenian Spring (SP) alliance with the **Slovenian People's Party** (SLS) and the Slovenian Christian Democrats (SKD), making a breakthrough by winning 16 seats on a 16.1% vote share. It continued in opposition, making little impact in the November 1997 presidential elections but contributing crucially to the fall of the LDS-led coalition in April 2000 and becoming part of the SLS-led coalition formed in

June 2000. In the October 2000 parliamentary elections the SDS slipped to 14 seats and 15.8% of the vote and reverted to opposition status. In the 2002 presidential election it backed Barbara Brezigar, who lost in the run-off to LDS Prime Minister Janez **Drnovšek** by 56.5% to 43.5%.

In September 2003 the SDS renamed itself to its current title (retaining the same SDS acronym) to reflect its transition to the centre right of politics. At the October 2004 Assembly elections it became the largest party with 29 seats (with 29.1% of the vote), and on 9 November SDS leader Janez Janša was nominated as Prime Minister. His Government was approved on 3 December, comprising the SDS, the SLS, the New Slovenia–Christian People's Party (NSi) and the **Democratic Party of Slovenian Pensioners** (DeSUS).

In the first round of the 2007 presidential election, Lojze Peterle (independent, backed by the SDS, NSi and SLS) led with 28.7%, but he was beaten resoundingly in the run-off by Danilo **Türk**. Then at the September 2008 Assembly elections the SDS dropped one seat to finish on 28 seats (29.3% of the vote), just behind the **Social Democrats**, who went on to form the new Government, while the SDS returned to opposition.

Leadership: Janez Janša (President).
Address: Trstenjakova 8, 1000 Ljubljana.
Telephone: (1) 4345450.
Fax: (1) 4345452.
E-mail: tajnistvo@sds.si
Internet: www.sds.si

Slovenian National Party
Slovenska Nacionalna Stranka (SNS)

An extreme nationalist formation in **Slovenia** with some electoral support but little political influence. Founded in 1991, the SNS advocates a militarily strong Slovenia, revival of the **Slovenes'** cultural heritage and protection of the family as the basic unit of society. It is also strongly opposed to Italian and **Croatian** irredentist claims on Slovenian territory or property. The party won 9.9% of the vote and 12 **National Assembly** seats in December 1992 but experienced internal dissension in 1993 after party leader Zmago Jelinčič Plemeniti was named as a federal **Yugoslav** agent, while other leaders were reported to be listed in security service files as having been informers in the communist era.

As a result of these and other difficulties, over half of the SNS deputies left the party, which slumped to only four seats and 3.2% of the vote in the November 1996 parliamentary elections. The SNS was then briefly co-opted into a disparate coalition headed by **Liberal Democracy of Slovenia** (LDS), but reverted to opposition status when the LDS found a larger partner in February 1997. In the October 2000 parliamentary elections the SNS improved slightly to 4.4% of the vote but again won only four seats.

In early 2004 legislation was passed by the Assembly to restore Slovenian citizenship to 18,000 nationals of former Yugoslav republics, who (resident in Slovenia at the time of its independence) had been removed from population records and lost their residency rights. However, several right-wing parties including the SNS opposed the legislation and forced a referendum on the issue, which was held in April and resoundingly rejected the legislation. At the October 2004 Assembly elections the SNS won six seats (6.3% of the vote).

Having come third, with 8.5% of the vote, in the 2002 presidential election, Jelinčič stood again in 2007. Although this time he won 18.2% of the first round vote, this was only enough for fourth position. In March 2008 SNS Vice-President Sašo Peče and his supporters broke away and founded a new party, Lipa. At the September 2008 Assembly election the SNS dropped to five seats (5.4% of the vote).

Leadership: Zmago Jelinčič Plemeniti (President).
Address: Tivolska 13, 1000 Ljubljana.
Telephone: (1) 2529020.
Fax: (1) 2529022.
E-mail: info@sns.si
Internet: www.sns.si

Slovenian People's Party
Slovenska Ljudska Stranka (SLS)

A conservative peasant-based formation in **Slovenia**, affiliated to both the **Christian Democrat International** and the **International Democrat Union**, and currently in opposition. In mid-2000 it merged with the Slovenian Christian Democrats (SKD), after which it adopted the acronym SLS+SKD, though this was dropped again in 2002.

Descended from a pre-Second World War **Roman Catholic** party of the same name, the SLS was founded in 1988 as the Slovene Peasant League (SKZ), which registered as a party in January 1990 and won 11 **National Assembly** seats in 1990 as a member of the victorious Democratic Opposition of Slovenia (DEMOS) alliance. Having adopted the SLS label in 1991, it retained 11 seats in the December 1992 elections with 9% of the vote.

The SKD also claimed descent from a pre-war party and was re-established in March 1990 by a group of 'non-clerical Catholic intellectuals' advocating full sovereignty for Slovenia, gradual transition to a market economy and integration into European institutions, especially the **European Union**. In the 1990 elections it was the largest component of the DEMOS alliance, winning 11 Assembly seats in its own right, so that SKD leader Lojze Peterle became Prime Minister and led Slovenia to independence in 1991. He remained Prime Minister despite the break-up of DEMOS at the end of 1991 but was forced to resign in April 1992 by a successful no-confidence motion criticizing the slow pace of economic reform. In the December 1992 Assembly elections the SKD advanced to 15 seats (on a 13.9% vote share), thereafter joining a new coalition headed by **Liberal Democracy of Slovenia** (LDS), whereas the SLS was in opposition.

Strains in the SKD's relations with the LDS intensified in 1994, leading to Peterle's resignation as Deputy Prime Minister and Foreign Minister in September in protest against the induction of an LDS President of the National Assembly, although the SKD remained a government party.

The SLS and the SKD contested the November 1996 parliamentary elections within the Slovenian Spring (SP) alliance, the former party advancing to 19 seats on 19.4% vote share, whereas the latter fell back to 10 seats and 9.6%. The SLS then deserted the SP and joined a coalition Government headed by the LDS, whereas the SKD went into opposition. In the November 1997 presidential elections, neither the SLS candidate nor the joint nominee of the SKD and the Social Democratic Party of Slovenia (SDS) made much impact against the incumbent, Milan Kučan (non-party), who won outright in the first round.

Strains in the SLS's relations with the LDS culminated in April 2000 in the party's withdrawal from the Government, causing its collapse. Now the SLS formally merged with the SKD, with SLS Parliamentary Leader Franc Zagožen as President and Lojze Peterle of the SKD as a Vice-President. The new party now controlled 28 seats in the Assembly, so itself headed the new Government coalition appointed in June under the premiership of Andrej Bajuk. The new Prime Minister promptly left the SLS+SKD to launch New Slovenia–Christian People's Party. In the October 2000 elections the SLS+SKD obtained a disappointing nine seats with 9.6% of the vote, but was included in the new government coalition headed by the LDS. The following year Zagožen was replaced as President by Franc But, who was in turn replaced in 2003 by Janez Podobnik.

In early 2004 legislation was passed by the Assembly to restore Slovenian citizenship to 18,000 nationals of former Yugoslav republics, who (resident in Slovenia at the time of its independence) had been removed from population records and lost their residency rights. However, several right-wing parties opposed to the legislation forced a referendum on the issue, which was held in April and resoundingly rejected the legislation. The SLS, which had supported the holding of the referendum, subsequently withdrew from the Government.

At the October 2004 Assembly elections the SLS dropped again to seven seats (6.8% of the vote). It joined a coalition headed by the **Slovenian Democratic Party**, as the SDS was now known. It joined the SDS in backing the independent candidacy of Peterle in the 2007 presidential contest, but he lost to Danilo **Türk** in the run-off. The SLS fought the September 2008 Assembly election in alliance with the Slovenian Youth Party (SMS, now known as the **Youth Party–European Greens**, SMS-

Zeleni), but the alliance only won five seats (with 5.2% of the vote). Both parties went into opposition to a **Social Democrats**-led coalition. In May 2009 Radovan Žerjav took over as SLS President from Bojan Šrot, who had held the post since November 2007.

Leadership: Radovan Žerjav (President).
Address: Beethovnova 4, 1000 Ljubljana.
Telephone: (1) 2418820.
Fax: (1) 2511741.
E-mail: tajnistvo@sls.si
Internet: www.sls.si

SLS *see* **Slovenian People's Party**.

Smer *see* **Direction–Social Democracy**.

SMK (Slovakia) *see* **Hungarian Coalition Party**.

SMS *see* **Youth Party–European Greens**.

SNPCG *see* **Socialist People's Party of Montenegro**.

SNS (Slovakia) *see* **Slovak National Party**.

SNS (Slovenia) *see* **Slovenian National Party**.

SNSD *see* **Alliance of Independent Social Democrats**.

Sobranie *see* **Assembly (Macedonia)**.

Social Democratic Party (Estonia)
Sotsiaaldemokraatlik Erakond (SDE)

A social democratic political party in **Estonia**, affiliated to the **Socialist International** and currently in opposition. The name Social Democratic Party was adopted only in February 2004, the party having formerly been known as the People's Party Moderates since its formation by a merger of the People's Party and the Moderates in 1999.

The Moderates originated as a 1990 electoral alliance of the Estonian Rural Centre Party (EMK) and the Estonian Social Democratic Party (ESDP), the latter descended from the historic ESDP founded in 1905 when Estonia was part of the **Russian** Empire. The alliance won 12 seats in the 1992 **Parliament** elections and was a member of the resultant Government. In the 1995 elections, however, the Moderates slumped to six seats, despite receiving endorsement from the then Prime Minister, Andres Tarand.

The People's Party was formed in 1998 as a merger of the Estonian Farmers' Party and the right-wing Republican and Conservative People's Party.

In the March 1999 parliamentary elections a joint People's Party Moderates list advanced strongly to 17 seats on a 15.2% vote share, becoming the progressive end of a new centre-right coalition Government. The two parties formally merged later that year. Tarand, who had been Chairman of their co-ordinating council, stepped down from the party leadership in 2001 to contest (unsuccessfully) the presidential election.

The People's Party Moderates returned to opposition when the ruling coalition broke down in January 2002, and its poor performance in that year's municipal elections provoked the resignation of Chairman Toomas Hendrik **Ilves**, who was replaced by Ivari Padar. After only winning six seats and 7% of the vote in the March 2003 parliamentary election, the party decided to revert to its historic Social Democratic Party name in February 2004 in an effort to revive its popularity.

In the 2006 presidential election, Ilves was chosen as the consensus candidate to stand against the incumbent of the **Estonian People's Union** (ERL), former communist Arnold Rüütel. Ilves eventually won the protracted ballot with the support of the ER and the **Union of Pro Patria and Res Publica** (IRL).

In the March 2007 parliamentary elections the SDE won 10 seats and 10.6% of the vote. It became part of a new ER-led coalition Government, with its Chairman, Ivari Padar, as Finance Minister. However, it refused to back employment law reforms in May 2009, whereupon it was dismissed from the coalition Government (Prime Minister Andrus Ansip remaining in office at the head of a minority Government).

Leadership: Ivari Padar (Chair.).
Address: Ahtri 10A, Tallinn 10151.
Telephone: 6116040.
Fax: 6116050.
E-mail: kantselei@sotsdem.ee
Internet: www.sotsdem.ee

Social Democratic Party (Romania)
Partidul Social Democrat (PSD)

A centre-left political party in **Romania**, currently in opposition. It was formed by the merger in June 2001 of the Social Democracy Party of Romania (PDSR) and the Romanian Social Democratic Party (PSDR).

The PDSR, which defined itself as a social democratic, popular and national party supportive of transition to a market economy on the basis of social responsibility, had been launched in 1993 as a merger of the Democratic National Salvation Front

(FSND), the Romanian Socialist Democratic Party and the Republican Party, essentially to provide a party political base for President Ion Iliescu, a former senior communist apparatchik. The FSND had come into being in March 1992, when a group of pro-Iliescu deputies of the National Salvation Front (FSN) opposed to rapid economic reform withdrew from the parent party. The FSND had won a relative majority of seats in both houses of **Parliament** in the September 1992 elections and had backed Iliescu's successful re-election bid in the concurrent presidential contest. Having formed a minority Government after the 1992 elections, the PDSR in August 1994 formed a coalition with the right-wing Romanian National Unity Party (PUNR), with external support from the even more right-wing Greater Romania Party (PRM) and from the neo-communist Socialist Party of Labour (PSM). By mid-1995, however, serious differences had developed between the government parties, with the result that the PRM and the PSM withdrew their support in late 1995, while the PUNR was finally ejected from the Government in September 1996.

The other component of the new PSD, the PSDR, was descended from the historic party founded in 1893, which had been forced to merge with the Communist Party in 1948 and had thereafter been maintained in exile. Revived in Romania after the overthrow of the **Ceauşescu** regime, the party won only one seat in the House of Deputies (lower house) in the May 1990 elections, improving to 10 in 1992 as a component of the mainly centre-right Democratic Convention of Romania (CDR). In January 1996 it left the CDR, instead joining an alliance with the Democratic Party (PD), itself the anti-Iliescu rump of the original FSN.

In the November 1996 elections Iliescu failed to secure re-election as President, being defeated in the second round by 54.4% to 45.9% by CDR candidate Emil Constantinescu, while in the parliamentary contest the PDSR won only 91 House seats with 21.5% of the vote. It therefore went into opposition to a CDR-led coalition which included the PSDR, whose House representation had remained at 10 seats. The rapprochement between the two future PSD partner parties began in September 2000 when the PSDR withdrew from the CDR-led coalition Government, abandoning its alliance with the PD, to form the Social Democratic Pole with the PDSR and the Humanist Party of Romania (PUR). This new grouping triumphed in the November–December 2000 elections. Iliescu regained the presidency as the Pole candidate, winning 66.8% of the second-round vote against a serious challenge by the PRM leader, while in the parliamentary contest the Pole parties won 155 of the 346 House seats (and 36.6% of the vote), of which the PDSR obtained 142, the PSDR a disappointing seven and the PUR four. The Pole parties therefore formed a minority Government under the premiership of Adrian Năstase, which obtained qualified pledges of support from the PD, the **National Liberal Party** (PNL) and the **Hungarian Democratic Union of Romania** (UDMR).

In January 2001 Năstase was elected Chairman of the PDSR in succession to Iliescu (who was disqualified from party affiliation during his presidential term). The party then embarked upon negotiations for a formal merger with the PSDR, one consequence of which would be that the unified party would inherit the PSDR's membership of the **Socialist International** (which had declined to admit the PDSR because of doubts about its democratic credentials). The merger was completed, forming the PSD, on 16 June 2001.

The PSD contested the November 2004 elections as part of the National Alliance (UN) with the PUR. The UN won a plurality of parliamentary seats: 132 in the 332-member House of Deputies (113 seats for the PSD and 19 for the PUR) based on 36.8% of the vote, and 57 seats in the Senate (with 37.2% of the vote). Năstase won the first round of the presidential election with 40.9% of the vote, but he was overtaken in the second round by PD leader Traian **Băsescu**, with 51.2% to Năstase's 48.8%. Băsescu subsequently nominated PNL leader Călin Popescu-Tăriceanu as Prime Minister, heading a coalition of the PNL, PD, UDMR and PUR (even though the latter had contested the election as part of the UN alliance), so the PSD was pushed into opposition.

In April 2005 Năstase stepped down as PSD Chairman, as Iliescu stood again for the post. However, he was unexpectedly defeated by former Foreign Minister Mircea Dan Geoană.

Although the PSD gave external support to a minority Government formed by the PNL and the UDMR from April 2007, the PSD again allied itself with the PUR (now renamed as the **Conservative Party**, PC) for the November 2008 elections. This alliance achieved the largest vote shares with 33.1% in the House of Deputies election and 34.2% in the Senate election, but secured the second-largest number of seats in each chamber: 114 in the House (110 PSD, four PC) and 29 in the Senate (48 PSD, one PC). The **Democratic Liberal Party** (PD-L, successor to the PD) was the largest party, and its leader Emil **Boc** negotiated a coalition Government with the PSD which was approved by Parliament on 18 December, and took office four days later.

The PSD ministers resigned on 1 October 2009 in protest over the dismissal three days earlier of the Minister of the Interior, and Boc's Government was defeated in a vote of no confidence 12 days later. While attempts to form a new Government went on, the PSD's Geoană mounted a strong challenge to the incumbent Băsescu in the presidential election. The first round in November saw Băsescu lead by 32.4% to 31.2%, and in the run-off on 6 December official results gave Băsescu 50.33% of the vote—a margin of just over 70,000 votes. With over 138,000 votes having been deemed as invalid, the PSD called for the result to be annulled. Instead the Constitutional Court decided that the invalid votes should be recounted; only around 2,000 votes were validated, and so the result was upheld. The PSD was not included in the new PD-L-led coalition that took office a few days later.

Following his electoral defeat, Geoană lost the PSD presidency at the February 2010 party congress to Victor Ponta.

Leadership: Victor Ponta (President).
Address: Şos. Kiseleff 10, 011346 Bucharest 1.
Telephone: (21) 2222953.
Fax: (21) 2223272.
E-mail: psd@psd.ro
Internet: www.psd.ro

Social Democratic Party of Bosnia and Herzegovina
Socijaldemokratska Partija Bosne i Hercegovine (SDPBiH)

A moderate centre-left formation in **Bosnia and Herzegovina** which aims to be a social democratic party on the western European model and disavows any specific ethnic/national identification. The SDPBiH was created in February 1999 by a merger of the Social Democrats of Bosnia and Herzegovina (SDBiH) and the Democratic Party of Socialists (DSS), each descended from Bosnian sections of communist-era formations. Affiliated to the **Socialist International** (which had pressed for the merger), the SDPBiH favours a regulated market economy.

Social democratic forces had been marginalized during the Bosnian civil war, but the SDBiH won two seats in the union lower house and six in the **Muslim-Croat Federation** lower house in the September 1998 elections, while the DSS took four and 19 seats respectively, as well as securing second place (with 31.9% of the Croat vote) for its candidate in the **Croat** section of the elections for the Bosnian collective Presidency.

New impetus was provided by the creation of the SDPBiH, which polled strongly in local elections in April 2000 and then took first place in the November 2000 elections to the union lower house, winning nine of the 42 seats, and second place in the Federation lower house, with 37 of the 140 seats. The party also won four seats in the People's Assembly of the **Serb Republic** (RS), thus demonstrating its cross-community appeal. As the leading component of a new Alliance for Change of moderate parties, the SDPBiH then led a challenge to the union Prime Minister, a member of the nationalist **Croatian Democratic Union** (HDZ). The outcome in February 2001 was the appointment of Bozidar Matić (a Croat member of the SDPBiH) as union Prime Minister, heading the first all-Bosnia Government not dominated by nationalists.

Following the dismissal of the Croat member of the union Presidency in March, Jozo **Križanović** (SDPBiH) was appointed from the moderate Alliance for Change. He assumed the rotating chairmanship of the Presidency in June, at which point Matić had to resign (since the two posts could not be held simultaneously by the same ethnic group). Matić was replaced the following month by party leader and Foreign Minister Zlatko **Lagumdžija**.

The SDPBiH lost ground to the nationalist parties at the October 2002 elections, losing its seat on the union Presidency and only winning five seats in the union lower house (with 11.8% of the vote) and 15 in the Federation lower house (now reduced from a total of 140 members to 98 members). Some SDPBiH members broke away from the party in order to join the nationalist-led coalition that was forming the union Government.

The SDPBiH fought back at the October 2006 elections, with Željko **Komšić** winning the Croat seat on the union Presidency with 39.6% of the vote. In the simultaneous all-Bosnia lower house election the SDPBiH won five seats (with 10.2% of the vote), while in the Federation lower house it finished third with 17 seats, and it also won one seat in the RS Assembly.

Leadership: Zlatko Lagumdžija (Chair.).
Address: Alipašina 41, 71000 Sarajevo.
Telephone: (33) 563910.
Fax: (33) 563913.
E-mail: predsjednik@sdp-bih.org.ba
Internet: www.sdpbih.ba

Social Democratic Party of Croatia
Socijaldemokratska Partija Hrvatske (SDP)

A left-of-centre party derived from the former ruling **League of Communists of Yugoslavia** (SKJ). It was the principal party in the coalition Government of **Croatia** from January 2000 to late 2003. Since that time it has been in opposition, but in 2010 its candidate won the presidential election. It is a member of the **Socialist International**.

The party is descended from Croatian elements which had been prominent in attempts to liberalize and reform the SKJ regime from within. In the post-1989 move to independence and multi-partyism, the Croatian branch of the SKJ was sidelined by the nationalist **Croatian Democratic Union** (HDZ). It failed to stem the outflow of support by changing its name to Party of Democratic Reform (SDP) and committing itself to democratic socialism and a market economy. In the 1990 pre-independence elections, the SDP trailed a poor second to the HDZ. The party's current title was adopted in 1991 (although the SDP acronym was retained) and the party deferred to pro-independence sentiment by acknowledging Croatia as the 'national state of the Croatian people'.

Advocating economic modernization combined with preservation of the welfare state, the SDP was reduced to 11 seats in the August 1992 elections to the lower house of the **Assembly** and failed to secure representation in its own right in the February 1993 upper house balloting. It performed better in the October 1995 lower house elections, winning nearly 9% of the vote and 10 seats, while in the June 1997 presidential elections SDP candidate Zdravko Tomać took second place with 21%.

Following the death of President Franjo **Tudjman** of the HDZ in December 1999, the SDP contested the January 2000 Assembly elections in tandem with the **Croatian Social-Liberal Party** (HSLS) and two small regional formations. It became the dominant bloc with 71 of the 151 seats (44 on its own account) and 38.7% of the vote, and formed a six-party centre-left coalition Government headed by SDP Chairman Ivica Račan. In immediately succeeding presidential elections, the SDP backed the HSLS candidate in both rounds of voting, but welcomed the eventual victory of Stipe Mesić of the **Croatian People's Party**, which was a member of the new ruling coalition.

Controversy over the SDP Government's co-operation with the **International Criminal Tribunal for the former Yugoslavia** damaged the party's popularity, and it also attracted blame for rising unemployment. For the November 2003 parliamentary elections it formed an electoral alliance with the **Istrian Democratic Assembly** (IDS), Party of Liberal Democrats (Libra–SLD) and Liberal Party (LS), but finished in second place, behind the HDZ, having won 22.6% of the vote and 43 seats (34 in its own right). Back in opposition, the SDP supported a second term for incumbent President Mesić in 2005.

Suffering from cancer, Račan announced in January 2007 that he was resigning the party leadership, and he died in April. Zoran Milanović was elected as the SDP's new leader in June. At the November 2007 elections the SDP increased its share considerably to 56 seats (31.2% of the vote), but remained in second place behind the HDZ, which formed a new coalition with smaller parties.

Prior to the 2009–10 presidential election Milan Bandić was expelled from the party after he announced that he would stand against the SDP's official candidate Ivo **Josipović**. In the first round on 27 December Josipović led with 32.4% and Bandić took second with 14.8%. Josipović went on to win the run-off on 10 January by 60.3% to 39.7% and took office on 18 February.

Leadership: Zoran Milanović (Chair.).

Address: Trg Drage Iblera 9, 10000 Zagreb.

Telephone: (1) 4552055.

Fax: (1) 4557509.

E-mail: sdp@sdp.hr

Internet: www.sdp.hr

Social Democratic Union of Macedonia
Socijaldemokratski Sojuz na Makedonije (SDSM)

A centre-left political party in **Macedonia**, currently in opposition. The SDSM is directly descended from the **League of Communists of Yugoslavia**, but is now a pro-market party affiliated to the **Socialist International**. As the League of Communists of Macedonia–Party of Democratic Change (SKM–PDP), the party came second in Macedonia's 1990 republican **Assembly** elections, with 31 seats. In January 1991 its nominee, Kiro **Gligorov**, was elected Head of State by the Assembly, following which the party adopted its present SDSM name. In mid-1992 it became the leading component of a coalition Government. Heading the Union of Macedonia (SM) centre-left alliance, it was confirmed in power in 1994 in both presidential and Assembly elections (winning 58 seats), and SDSM leader Branko Crvenkovski was reappointed Prime Minister at the head of a coalition of the SM parties and an ethnic **Albanian** formation.

The SDSM lost power in the parliamentary elections of late 1998, retaining only 29 seats on a 25.1% vote share and going into opposition to a Government headed by the **Internal Macedonian Revolutionary Organization–Democratic Party for Macedonian National Unity** (VMRO–DPMNE). In the late 1999 presidential elections, moreover, SDSM candidate Tito Petkovski lost to the VMRO–DPMNE nominee in the second round. In May 2000 the SDSM formed an opposition alliance with the small Liberal-Democratic Party and other centrist elements.

An insurgency launched in February 2001 by ethnic Albanian rebels seeking greater rights for the Albanian community led to the establishment of a Government of National Unity in May comprising parties from all sides of the Assembly, including the SDSM, but still headed by the VMRO–DPMNE. However, following a peace deal, signed in August 2001 and put in place by November, the SDSM and the Liberals withdrew from the grand coalition.

The party improved its fortunes at the September 2002 elections. Its candidates stood as the principal element in the Together for Macedonia (ZMZ) coalition, with the Liberal-Democratic Party and eight smaller parties, and the ZMZ won exactly half of the seats in the 120-member Assembly (with 40.5% of the vote). The ethnic Albanian Democratic Union for Integration (DUI) then joined with the ZMZ to enable it to form a Government, and Crvenkovski was approved by the Assembly as Prime Minister on 1 November.

On 26 February 2004 President Trajkovski was killed in a plane crash. When elections were held in April to choose a successor, Crvenkovski achieved a convincing victory, leading the VMRO–DPMNE candidate Saško Kedev 42.5% to 34.1% in the first round and 60.6% to 39.4% in the run-off. Crvenkovski was inaugurated on 12 May, and on 2 June Hari Kostov (also of the SDSM) was approved by the Assembly as the new Prime Minister.

In mid-November Kostov resigned, claiming that the DUI was obstructing economic reforms and that a DUI minister was involved in corrupt practices. Vlado Bučkovski, hitherto the Minister of Defence, was appointed SDSM Chairman and nominated as Prime Minister; his new Government, still including the DUI, was approved by the Assembly on 17 December.

The 5 July 2006 Assembly election brought defeat for the SDSM-led ZMZ coalition. With only 32 seats (23.3% of the vote), the party was left facing a spell in opposition. This was confirmed by its renewed failure when legislative elections were held again less than two years later. The June 2008 poll saw the Sun—Coalition for Europe of the SDSM, New Social Democratic Party, LDP, Liberal Party of Macedonia and four smaller parties win just 27 seats (23.7% of the vote), although it remained the second-largest bloc.

With Crvenkovski's term as President due to end in May 2009, the SDSM chose Ljubomir Frčkoski as its candidate for the presidential election. In the first round on March 22 he trailed the VMRO–DPMNE candidate Gjorge **Ivanov** by 20.5% to 35.1%, and the run-off two weeks later confirmed his defeat by 36.9% to 63.1%. Crvenkovski resumed the leadership of the party in late May soon after stepping down from the presidency.

Leadership: Branko Crvenkovski (Chair.).
Address: Bihačka 8, Skopje 1000.
Telephone: (2) 3293100.
Fax: (2) 3293109.
E-mail: contact@sdsm.org.mk
Internet: www.sdsm.org.mk

Social Democrats
Socialni Demokrati (SD)

The party in **Slovenia** which is directly descended from the former ruling **League of Communists of Yugoslavia** and its front organization. Now of social-democratic orientation, it is a member of the **Socialist International** (SI) and currently heads the ruling coalition.

The United List of Social Democrats (ZLSD), as the party was known until 2005, was established in 1992 as an alliance of formations deriving from the ruling structures of the Yugoslav era, which had backed the successful candidacy of former communist leader Milan Kučan in the pre-independence presidential elections in 1990. In post-independence elections in December 1992, the ZLSD gained third place in the new **National Assembly**, with 14 seats and 12.1% of the vote, while in the simultaneous presidential contest Kučan (now without party affiliation) was re-elected with 64% of the vote. The ZLSD opted to join a centre-left coalition Government headed by Janez **Drnovšek** of the **Liberal Democracy of Slovenia** (LDS) and remained a coalition partner until January 1996, when Drnovšek's move to dismiss one of its four ministers caused the party to withdraw from the Government. Later in 1996 the ZLSD was admitted to SI membership, replacing the conservative-leaning Social Democratic Party of Slovenia (later renamed the **Slovenian Democratic Party**, SDS).

In the November 1996 parliamentary elections, the ZLSD declined to nine seats and 9% of the vote and continued in opposition. The following year Borut **Pahor** replaced Janez Kocijančič as party leader. In the October 2000 elections it improved to 11 seats and 12.1%, opting thereafter to join a coalition Government headed again by Drnovšek and the LDS.

The ZLSD fielded its own candidate, Lev Kreft, in the 2002 presidential election, but he only won 2.2% of the vote in the first round, finishing sixth. The poll was eventually won by Drnovšek, and Anton Rop took over as Prime Minister, maintaining the same coalition.

In the 2004 Assembly election the ZLSD fell slightly to 10 seats, though with an increased 10.2% of the vote and in fact becoming the third-largest party behind the SDS and LDS. It went into opposition to a centre-right SDS-led Government. In April 2005 Pahor proposed shortening the party's name to just Social Democrats.

The SD's decision to back the independent candidate Danilo **Türk** in the 2007 presidential election proved to be an astute one, crowned by his unexpected runaway success in defeating the Government-backed candidate in the second round by 68% to 32%. The following year's Assembly elections in September 2008 marked a victory for the SD itself. The party won 29 seats (with 30.5% of the vote), narrowly beating the SDS, which won 28 seats, into second place. **Pahor** was nominated as Prime Minister on 3 November. He formed a coalition with **For Real—New Politics**, the **Democratic Party of Slovenian Pensioners** (DeSUS) and the LDS, and his Government was approved on 21 November, including several independent technocrats. Pahor said his priority would be to combat the effects of the global economic crisis.

Leadership: Borut Pahor (President).
Address: Levstikova 15, 1000 Ljubljana.
Telephone: (1) 2444100.
Fax: (1) 2444111.
E-mail: info@socialnidemokrati.si
Internet: www.socialnidemokrati.si

Socialist Federal Republic of Yugoslavia (SFRY)

The formal name, from 1963, for the socialist state created after the Second World War on the territory of what had been the Kingdom of **Yugoslavia**. This state, which included the modern republics of **Bosnia and Herzegovina**, **Croatia**, **Kosovo**, **Macedonia**, **Montenegro**, **Serbia** and **Slovenia**, collapsed in the early 1990s.

It was the victory in 1945 of the wartime resistance Partisans, against both the Nazi invaders and the **Serb** nationalist **Chetniks**, which put the Yugoslav communists led by **Tito** in a position of control in the formation of the new Yugoslav entity. A Federal People's Republic of Yugoslavia was declared on 29 November 1945 (the

SFRY name coming into existence with the 1963 Constitution). The state that Tito masterminded was a relatively loose federation, with regional autonomy also extending to the nominally Serbian provinces of **Kosovo** and **Vojvodina**. It pursued a non-aligned foreign policy, Tito having broken as early as 1948 with the concept of a monolithic Soviet-led communist bloc. It was politically dominated by the **League of Communists of Yugoslavia**, with no multi-party elections until 1990.

Nationalist tensions between the major ethnic groups were contained until after Tito's death in 1980, but thereafter came increasingly to destabilize the SFRY, which was also badly weakened by economic problems. Autonomy for Serbia's provinces was revoked in 1989 and discontent at the increasing centralization of control in **Belgrade,** under the then Serbian President Slobodan **Milošević**, prompted the leaders of first Slovenia and then Croatia to declare their secession from the SFRY in June 1991. The declarations prompted armed invasions by the Yugoslav National Army (JNA) and the beginning of the violent wars in the former Yugoslavia which raged until 1995. Macedonia seceded after holding a referendum in September 1991 and Bosnia and Herzegovina declared its own independence shortly afterwards. The SFRY having been declared non-existent by its federal President Stipe Mesić in December 1991, the two remaining republics (Serbia and Montenegro) formed the rump Federal Republic of Yugoslavia (FRY) on 27 April 1992.

Socialist International

The world's oldest and largest association of political parties, founded in 1864 and grouping democratic socialist, labour and social democratic parties from 86 countries, including all of the recognized countries of **central** and **eastern Europe**. The Socialist International provides a forum for political action, policy discussion and the exchange of ideas.

Members: 115 full member parties, 27 consultative parties, 15 observer parties and 13 organizations.

President: George Papandreou.

Secretary-General: Luis Ayala.

Address: Maritime House, Old Town, Clapham, London, SW4 0JW, United Kingdom.

Telephone: (20) 76274449.

Fax: (20) 77204448.

E-mail: secretariat@socialistinternational.org

Internet: www.socialistinternational.org

Socialist Party of Albania
Partia Socialiste e Shqipërisë (PSSh)

The main centre-left political party in **Albania**, currently in opposition, and a member of the **Socialist International**. It is descended from the former ruling Party of Labour of Albania (PPSh), itself created in 1948 as successor to the Albanian Communist Party (founded 1941).Having won multi-party elections in March–April 1991, the PPSh switched to the PSSh designation in June 1991 to signify its renunciation of Marxism-Leninism and espousal of democratic socialism and the market economy. Former Prime Minister Fatos Nano became PSSh Chairman in succession to President Ramiz Alia, while Ylli Bufi of the PSSh was appointed to head a 'non-partisan' coalition Government. Continuing social unrest forced the PSSh to vacate the premiership in December 1991, and in the March 1992 **People's Assembly** elections the party was heavily defeated by the **Democratic Party of Albania** (PDSh).

In 1993 the opposition PSSh was weakened by the conviction of Alia, Nano and other leaders on charges of corruption and abuse of power during the communist period. Nano remained titular PSSh Chairman despite being imprisoned, with Deputy Chairman Servet Pellumbi leading the party in his absence. In November 1995 the PSSh led abortive opposition to a law requiring senior public officials to be investigated for their activities during the communist era. Many PSSh candidates were barred from the May–June 1996 elections, the second round of which was boycotted by the party in protest against malpractice in the first. With only 10 Assembly seats, the PSSh nevertheless led popular opposition to the subsequent PDSh-led Government. In March 1997 the PSSh joined a 'Government of Reconciliation' headed by Bashkim Fino and was boosted by the release of Nano on a presidential pardon. In further People's Assembly elections in June–July 1997 the PSSh returned to power with 101 of the 155 seats and 52.8% of the vote. In July 1997 Rexhep Meidani of the PSSh replaced Sali **Berisha** (PDSh) as President, whereupon Nano was appointed to head a five-party coalition Government.

Further instability resulted in Nano being replaced as Prime Minister in September 1998, his successor being PSSh Secretary-General Pandeli Majko, who at 31 became Europe's youngest Head of Government. Internal party strains caused Nano to announce in January 1999 that he would resign as PSSh Chairman in order to launch 'an emancipating movement' to restore hope among the people. At a PSSh congress in October 1999, however, Nano was re-elected Chairman by a narrow majority over Majko, who therefore resigned as Prime Minister. He was replaced by Deputy Premier Ilir Meta, who was also on the PSSh's reformist or 'Euro-socialist' wing rather than Nano's conservative faction. In October 2000 the PSSh registered substantial local election advances, winning over 50% of the popular vote and taking control of **Tirana**, hitherto a PDSh stronghold.

The success continued into 2001 when the PSSh garnered 42% of the national vote in legislative elections in June, gaining an absolute majority of 73 seats in the 140-

seat Assembly. The PDSh contested the results and boycotted the new parliamentary session for several months. However, despite this lack of parliamentary opposition, the party's internal divisions provided all the turbulence the new Government needed. Nano again clashed with Meta who had been easily re-elected Prime Minister by the party in August. Nano accused Meta and his cabinet of corruption and pressed for a reshuffle, prompting the resignation of four cabinet members in December. On 29 January 2002 Meta resigned, and Majko was nominated on 7 February to head a Government that included supporters from each of the two PSSh factions. This took office on 22 February, and the following month the opposition ended its parliamentary boycott.

Nano had his eyes set on the presidency, but the PDSh refused to accept his candidacy. Instead Gen. (retd) Alfred Moisiu was nominated as a compromise candidate; he was elected by the People's Assembly on 24 June with 97 votes out of 140, and took office a month later on 24 July. The following day Majko resigned as Prime Minister, and Nano was appointed in his place, again heading a Government containing both his supporters and Meta's. This Government lasted for a year, but in July 2003 Meta and one of his close allies resigned. Meta then obstructed the appointment of replacements, and by November the number of unfilled ministerial vacancies had risen to four. Moisiu insisted on Nano filling the posts, so he negotiated a Coalition for Integration with five smaller parties, and a new Government was approved on 29 December.

Meta left the PSSh in September 2004, and formed the Socialist Movement for Integration (LSI). Several PSSh members defected to the new party, causing the PSSh to lose its majority in the People's Assembly.

At the 3 July 2005 People's Assembly election the PSSh won 42 seats and its allies won 18, forcing the parties into opposition. Nano resigned as Chair of the PSSh, and was succeeded by Mayor of Tirana Edi Rama in October.

The PSSh boycotted the 2007 presidential election in the People's Assembly: repeated ballots left PDSh candidate Bamir **Topi** just short of the three-fifths of the vote required to secure election. Only at the fourth attempt (of a constitutionally possible five before the People's Assembly would have had to be dissolved) did five PSSh and two other deputies break the boycott to end the stalemate.

At the 28 June 2009 People's Assembly election, the PSSh-led Unification for Changes won 66 seats and 45.3% of the vote (PSSh 65; the Human Rights Union Party (PBDNj) one; three others none), meaning it remained in opposition to a new PDSh-led Government.

Leadership: Edi Rama (Chair.).
Address: Bul. Dëshmorët e Kombit, Tirana.
Telephone: (4) 227409.
Fax: (4) 227417.
E-mail: info@ps.al
Internet: www.ps.al

Socialist Party of Serbia
Socijalistička Partija Srbije (SPS)

A left-wing, nationalist political party in **Serbia**. Currently a junior partner in the ruling coalition, the SPS had been the principal ruling party in Serbia and **Yugoslavia** until the defeat of Slobodan **Milošević** in the 2000 federal presidential elections. Created in 1990 by the merging of the **Serbian** wings of the former ruling **League of Communists of Yugoslavia** (SKJ) and the associated Socialist Alliance of the Working People, the SPS acknowledged its origins in the communist-era ruling structure while officially subscribing to democratic socialism, favouring a continuing state economic role and preservation of the social security system. In fact, with Milošević (who had become leader of the Serbian SKJ in 1986 and Serbian President in 1989) as its Chairman, the SPS became the political vehicle for his hard-line pro-Serb policies in the regional conflicts of the 1990s and his increasingly repressive response to domestic opposition.

Having won an overwhelming majority in the Serbian **National Assembly** in December 1990 (when Milošević was re-elected Serbian President with 65% of the vote), the SPS obtained a narrow lower house majority in the May 1992 Federal Assembly elections. The imposition of UN sanctions from mid-1992 resulted in reduced popular support for the SPS, which lost its overall majorities in the federal lower house and the Serbian National Assembly in December 1992, although it remained the largest single party in both and Milošević was re-elected President of Serbia with 56% of the vote. In further Serbian elections in December 1993, the SPS increased its lower house representation from 101 to 123 seats out of 250, subsequently forming a Government with the New Democracy (ND) party.

Milošević's reluctant acceptance of the November 1995 **Dayton Agreement** for **Bosnia and Herzegovina** brought him into conflict with ultra-hard-liners within the SPS, several of whom defected or were expelled. In federal elections in November 1996 a Joint List alliance of the SPS, the Yugoslav United Left (JUL) led by Milošević's wife, and the ND won 64 of the 138 lower house seats, so that the SPS continued to dominate the Federal Government. In simultaneous local elections, however, opposition parties captured **Belgrade** and most other Serbian cities—results which the Government-controlled courts tried to annul but which Milošević eventually accepted in the face of mass popular protests and strikes.

Being constitutionally barred from a third term as Serbian President, Milošević was in July 1997 elected as Federal President by the Federal Assembly, under the then prevailing system of indirect election. Serbian National Assembly elections in September 1997 resulted in the SPS/JUL/ND alliance winning 110 seats, the eventual outcome being a coalition Government of the SPS, the JUL and the ultra-nationalist **Serbian Radical Party** (SRS) under the continued premiership of Mirko Marjanović. In protracted Serbian presidential elections in late 1997, SPS candidate Milan

Milutinović was eventually returned with 59% of the vote, in balloting described as 'fundamentally flawed' by international observers.

The **Kosovo** crisis of 1998–99 and the eventual air bombardment of Serbia by the **North Atlantic Treaty Organization** initially appeared to strengthen Milošević and the SPS politically. However, following the withdrawal of Serbian forces from Kosovo in June 1999 and the indictment of Milošević for alleged war crimes, demands for a change of Government intensified from what became the **Democratic Opposition of Serbia** (DOS). Milošević and his coterie resisted the pressure, the President being re-elected as SPS Chairman unopposed in February 2000 and telling a party congress that the Kosovo conflict had been 'a struggle for freedom and independence'. In July 2000, moreover, Milošević secured the enactment of constitutional amendments providing for direct elections for the federal presidency and lifting the previous ban on second federal presidential terms.

Federal elections were then called, in September 2000, in what proved to be a crucial political miscalculation by Milošević. Intimidation and vote-rigging by Milošević supporters in the presidential ballot failed to prevent what was widely seen as an outright first-round victory for the DOS candidate, Vojislav **Koštunica**. Last-ditch attempts by the regime to sidestep the outcome provoked a massive popular uprising, and Milošević eventually surrendered the federal presidency in early October. In simultaneous federal parliamentary elections, themselves marred by irregularities, the SPS/JUL alliance declined to 44 lower house seats. Three months later, the Serbian National Assembly elections in December 2000 revealed the true state of opinion by reducing the SPS/JUL to only 37 seats and 13.8% of the vote.

Milošević remained defiant after losing office, pledging that he would lead a revitalized SPS back to power in the near future. At the beginning of April, however, he was arrested at his home in Belgrade and charged with misappropriation of funds and other abuses as President. Despite the new Government's initial insistence that he should be tried in Yugoslavia, he was subsequently extradited to face the **International Criminal Tribunal for the former Yugoslavia** at The Hague. Milošević was charged, in addition, with genocide in November 2001, and his trial began on 12 February 2002: he refused to recognize the court's authority. He died while the trial was still in progress on 11 March 2006. Throughout this period he officially remained leader of the SPS. In December 2006 Ivica Dačić was elected as the party's new President.

Meanwhile, the 2003 elections had been won by the ultra-nationalist **Serbian Radical Party** (SRS); the SPS finished joint fifth with just 22 seats and 7.1% of the vote. To keep the SRS from power, the SPS agreed to give external backing to a minority coalition led by the **Democratic Party of Serbia** (DSS) under Koštunica— the man who had beaten Milošević in the 2000 presidential elections.

At the 2004 Serbian presidential poll Dačić, the SPS candidate, finished in fifth place with 4% of the vote. The party's representation in the Assembly fell further at the 2007 election, achieving just 16 seats with 5.6% of the vote. Its support was no longer needed by Koštunica's new coalition with the **Democratic Party** (DS) and others. It performed slightly better at the 2008 polls: its presidential candidate finished fourth, with 6% of the vote, and, in alliance with the Party of United Pensioners of Serbia (PUPS), it secured 20 seats and 7.6% of the vote. With the DS and DSS leaders at loggerheads, the DS invited the SPS (and PUPS) into government, with Dačić among the Deputy Prime Ministers, and four other ministerial portfolios for the party.

Leadership: Ivica Dačić (President).
Address: Studentski trg 15, 11000 Belgrade.
Telephone: (11) 2627282.
Fax: (11) 2627170.
E-mail: info.centar@sps.org.rs
Internet: www.sps.org.rs

Socialist People's Party of Montenegro
Socijalistička Narodna Partija Crne Gore (SNPCG)

A centre-left opposition party in **Montenegro**, which prior to independence was the main element in republican politics favouring continuing federation with **Serbia**. The SNPCG was first launched early in 1998 by a breakaway faction of the **Democratic Party of Socialists of Montenegro** (DPSCG) led by Momir Bulatović, following his narrow and much-resented defeat by the anti-federation DPSCG candidate Milo Đukanović in Montenegrin presidential elections of October 1997. In the May 1998 Montenegrin **Assembly** elections the SNPCG took second place (behind the DPSCG); shortly beforehand Bulatović had been appointed federal Prime Minister, charged with maintaining the Yugoslav federation at a time of national crisis over **Kosovo**.

The SNPCG maintained its pro-federation line in the September 2000 federal elections in which President Slobodan **Milošević** and his **Socialist Party of Serbia** (SPS) were defeated by the **Democratic Opposition of Serbia** (DOS). The dubious official results gave the SNPCG 28 of Montenegro's 30-seat quota in the lower house, and 19 out of Montenegro's 20-seat quota in the upper house (the DPSCG had boycotted the poll). Following Milošević's removal from power, Bulatović resigned as federal Prime Minister. Newly-elected federal President Vojislav **Koštunica** replaced him with SNPCG Deputy Chairman Zoran Žižić (under the federal Yugoslav Constitution, the President and Prime Minister had to come from different republics).

Bulatović was succeeded as party Chairman in February 2001 by Predrag Bulatović (no relation), who was aligned with the new Government in **Belgrade**. He established the Together for Yugoslavia pro-federation alliance of the SNPCG, the Serbian People's Party (SNS) and the People's Party (NS) for the April 2001 Montenegrin Assembly elections. The alliance lost very narrowly (40.6% of the vote and 33 seats, compared with the DPSCG-led coalition's 42% and 36 seats) and therefore contended that the resultant minority DPSCG-led Government had no mandate for independence.

Žizić's opposition to the arrest and subsequent extradition of Milošević in June 2001 prompted him to resign, taking most of the SNPCG cabinet members with him. Eventually Koštunica secured the co-operation of the relative moderate SNPCG candidate Dragiša Pešić as the new federal Prime Minister, after party Chairman Predrag Bulatović had rejected being nominated. Pešić held the post until it was abolished under the new, looser Union of Serbia and Montenegro that came into effect in March 2003.

Meanwhile the collapse of the minority DPSCG-led Montenegrin Government had precipitated early Assembly elections in October 2002. The rebranded Together for Change coalition dropped slightly to 30 seats (37.9% of the vote). The SNPCG boycotted the subsequent presidential election in protest at the agreement to loosen the federal structure; repeated polls failed due to insufficient turnout until this condition for the validity of the contest was removed.

Once the prescribed three-year waiting period had elapsed, the independence referendum was set for 21 May 2006. The SNPCG campaigned for a 'no' vote, but was narrowly defeated. After independence, the party's support base dwindled as it sought to redefine its ethos. At the September 2006 elections the coalition of the SNPCG, NS and Democratic Serb Party finished third with 11 seats (14.1% of the vote). Predrag Bulatović stepped down as party Chairman the following month, and Srđan Milić was chosen as his successor in November. In the 2008 presidential election, Milić stood as the SNPCG candidate but finished only fourth, with 11.9% of the vote. However, at early Assembly elections in March 2009, the SNPCG reclaimed its position as the largest opposition party with 16 seats (16.8% of the vote).

Leadership: Srđan Milić (Chair.).

Address: Vaka Đurovicá 5, 81000 Podgorica.

Telephone: (20) 272421.

Fax: (20) 272420.

E-mail: snp@t-com.me

Internet: www.snp.co.me

Sofia

The capital city of **Bulgaria**, situated in the west of the country in the southern foothills of the Balkan Mountains. *Population*: around 1.2m. (2007 estimate). Originally named Serdica, after the Thracian Serdi community which founded the settlement, the city came into Greek hands around 29 BC. It flourished as an important Byzantine centre from the fourth century AD, and began its connection with the **Bulgarians** as early as the ninth century when it was absorbed into the First Bulgarian Empire. It gained the title Sofia, meaning wisdom and taken from the still surviving

Church of St Sofia, under Byzantine administration in the 14th century. From 1382 to 1879 the city developed a distinctly eastern feel under the domination of the Ottoman Empire, but lost its regional significance until the rise of Bulgarian nationalism in the late 19th century. In 1879 Sofia became the national capital of a newly-proclaimed, small autonomous Bulgarian principality. Full independence from Ottoman control in 1908 brought a vigorous building campaign, with city authorities keen to establish a modern European city. Sofia suffered severe damage in the Second World War, however, when it was firebombed by the Allies in 1944 before falling to the Red Army. Industrial development under the subsequent communist regime also left its mark on the city's architectural heritage. As the capital of present-day Bulgaria, Sofia is an important location for light industry, including engineering and metallurgy, as well as the country's cultural and political centre.

Solidarity
Solidarność

The free trade union movememnt in **Poland** which was responsible in the 1980s for a challenge to the communist regime which ultimately helped instigatie the collapse of communism in Europe. Its full official name is now the Independent Self-Governing Trade Union Solidarity (Niezależny Samorzadny Zwiazek Zawodowy Solidarność). Its influence has declined in recent years.

Launched in 1980 to challenge the official trade union structure, Solidarity resulted from a strike at the **Gdańsk** shipyard which inspired massive countrywide stoppages and protests against economic conditions. Lech **Wałęsa** quickly emerged as the most prominent leader of Solidarity, which functioned both as an independent union and as a vehicle for national, religious and political aspirations, posing an increasing threat to the communist regime. Although Solidarity was initially granted official recognition, the possibility of a Soviet invasion impelled the Government to declare martial law in December 1981 and to ban Solidarity. At its height, Solidarity had 9.5m. members, while the Rural Solidarity peasants' counterpart had a further 2.4m.

From 1982 a new official trade union structure was created, culminating in the establishment in November 1984 of the All-Poland Alliance of Trade Unions (OPZZ). However, Solidarity remained active underground and in the late 1980s re-emerged as a major force. In April 1989, amid mounting political and economic crisis, the regime was forced to agree to the relegalization of Solidarity and also to partially free elections. Four months later the first Solidarity-backed Government was formed, setting the pattern of Solidarity's often conflicting twin identities as a political movement and a trade union.

After the collapse of communism and Wałęsa's election as Polish President in December 1990, Solidarity suffered from its identification with the new Government's austerity policies. Four consecutive years of falling real wages boosted support for the OPZZ, to which some dissident Solidarity elements defected, while others formed the breakaway Solidarity 80 movement. Roles were reversed when the (ex-communist) **Democratic Left Alliance** came to power in September 1993, following which Solidarity returned to opposition. The new Government continued the general approach of previous post-communist administrations, so that Solidarity obtained a new lease of life as it campaigned against the consequences of economic restructuring, including job losses and wage cuts.

After Wałęsa had narrowly failed to be re-elected President in December 1995, a Solidarity congress in June 1996 launched Solidarity Electoral Action (AWS) as an organizationally distinct political movement. Campaigning on a pro-market and pro-European platform in the September 1997 legislative elections, the AWS came to power in coalition with the centre-right Freedom Union, under the premiership of Jerzy Buzek, an early Solidarity leader. Solidarity trade union leader Marian Krzaklewski, who had been elected as an AWS member of the **National Assembly**, became Chairman of the AWS party caucus. The Solidarity trade union wing therefore again experienced the tensions caused by dual identity, as it frequently opposed the Buzek Government on economic and labour issues while distancing itself from the 'destabilizing' activities of the OPZZ and peasant groups. In October 2000 Krzaklewski was the AWS candidate in presidential elections but managed only third place with 15.6% of the vote. He subsequently faced renewed demands within Solidarity that he should choose between leading the union and his political ambitions. On 15 May 2001 the union members took the initiative and voted to withdraw Solidarity from the ruling coalition and to take the union out of active politics altogether. Under the new regulations union members can no longer head political parties, or work for their electoral committees. As a union movement, Solidarity has lost members steadily in the post-communist era, as state industries have been privatized and the succeeding businesses have largely eschewed union organization.

President: Janusz Śniadek.
Address: ul. Wały Piastowskie 24, Gdańsk 80855.
Telephone: (58) 3084476.
Fax: (58) 3084482.
E-mail: zagr@solidarnosc.org.pl
Internet: www.solidarnosc.org.pl

Sólyom, László

President of the Republic, **Hungary**. László Sólyom is a law professor, specializing in constitutional rights. He was prominent in Hungary's transition to democracy, attending the round-table negotiations. Aa a political independent, he was elected President on 7 June 2005.

Born on 3 January 1942 in Pécs, Sólyom graduated from the Faculty of Political and Legal Sciences of the University of Pécs in 1965. He spent the next four years in Germany, working as an assistant lecturer at the Institute of Civil Law of the Friedrich Schiller University of Jena, obtaining a doctorate in 1969 and then was appointed as a fellow of the Institute of Political and Legal Sciences of the Hungarian Academy of Sciences. He had also qualified as a librarian in the National Széchényi Library, and worked as a librarian at the Library of Parliament until 1975. From 1978 he worked at the Department of Civil Law of the Eötvös Loránd University Budapest, first as associate professor and from 1983 as university professor. During this time he became a doctor of political and legal sciences of the Hungarian Academy of Sciences.

Sólyom worked in the field of the right of personality and privacy, and introduced the right of data protection in Hungary, thus shifting the focus of his activity to constitutional rights and later to theoretical questions of constitutional jurisdiction. He has published many books on this area, and on environmental law. He has advised several civil and environmental movements, and was member of various civil organizations which played a significant role in the transition to democracy in the late 1980s. He was a founding member of the **Hungarian Democratic Forum** (MDF) and a member of its presidency between March 1989 and November 1990. He attended the sessions of the opposition round-table on behalf of MDF and participated in the national round-table negotiations in 1990. He was also elected as a judge to the new Constitutional Court in 1989, and over the next decade was three times elected as its President. In 1993 he joined the International Commission of Jurists, serving on it for eight years, and has also been a member of the European Commission for Democracy through Law. In 1995 he was appointed university professor at the Faculty of Law of the Pázmány Péter Catholic University Budapest. He held this post until his election as President in June 2005.

Sólyom and his wife have two children.

Address: Office of the President, Sándor Palace, Szent György tér 1, 1014
            Budapest.
Telephone: (1) 2245000.
Fax: (1) 2245013.
E-mail: ugyfelkapu@keh.hu
Internet: www.keh.hu

Soros Foundations network

A group of autonomous foundations across the world, but mostly in **eastern Europe**, founded by George Soros, a **Hungarian**-born billionaire fund manager and philanthropist, to promote the development of civil society and pluralist democracy. Its foundations include the New York-based Open Society Institute, established in 1993, which has been actively involved in making grants in central and eastern

Europe. Latterly this has involved the creation of a Trust for Civil Society in Central and Eastern Europe, to support the long-term sustainable development of non-governmental organizations in the region. Another Soros Foundations initiative was the creation (initially in **Prague** and **Budapest** but increasingly concentrated in the latter city) of the Central European University (CEU), which established itself during the 1990s as an internationally-recognized institution of postgraduate education in social sciences and humanities.

Chairman: George Soros.

Address: Open Society Institute, Oktober 6 ut. 12, 1051 Budapest.

Telephone: (1) 8823100.

Fax: (1) 8823101.

E-mail: info@osi.hu

Internet: www.soros.org

South-Eastern Europe

A term commonly applied to the European region comprising the **Balkan** states of **Albania**, **Bulgaria**, **Greece**, **Romania** and the former **Yugoslavia** (though Slovenia and Croatia could also be termed part of **central Europe**). It also can be defined to include **Cyprus** and Turkey.

Southern Bukovina *see* **Bukovina question**.

Southern Dobruja *see* **Dobruja question**.

Soviet Union
(Union of Soviet Socialist Republics, USSR)

The historic communist state of 1922–91, which at its height was one of two global superpowers, and stretched from the Pacific coast of Siberia in the east to the borders of **eastern Europe** in the west, and from the Arctic Circle in the north to the edges of the Middle East in the south. The Soviet Union (known in Russian by its **Cyrillic** acronym *CCCP* [SSSR]) was the largest country in the world, and adhered closely to the borders of the old Russian Empire (the **Baltic States** and modern Moldova being added to the Union through military conquest in the Second World War). Its disintegration in 1991 left 15 independent successor states: Armenia, Azerbaijan, Belarus, **Estonia**, Georgia, Kazakhstan, Kyrgyzstan, **Latvia**, **Lithuania**, Moldova, the Russian Federation, Tajikistan, Turkmenistan, Ukraine and Uzbekistan. All but the three Baltic States then joined together to form the loose Commonwealth of Independent States (CIS).

Špirić, Nikola

Prime Minister of **Bosnia and Herzegovina**. Špirić is a moderate Serb and member of the **Alliance of Independent Social Democrats** (SNSD).

Nikola Špirić was born on 4 September 1956 in Drvar in west Bosnia. He earned a degree, master's and doctrate in economics from the University of Sarajevo, and from 1992 lectured in monetary and public finance at the University of Banja Luka. He has been a member of the House of Representatives of the all-Bosnia **Parliamentary Assembly** from 1990 onwards, briefly also appointed Deputy Minister for Human Rights and Refugees in 2000 before a five-year period as Speaker or Deputy Speaker of the House. He was nominated as union Prime Minister on 3 January 2007 and confirmed eight days later, heading a seven-party coalition. On 1 November he resigned in protest at political reforms being proposed by the UN **High Representative**. However, at the end of November the Serb leaders ended resistance to the legislation, and the following month Špirić was renominated as union Prime Minister. This was approved by the Assembly on 28 December.

Špirić is married and has two children.

Address: Office of the Prime Minister, TRG BiH 1, 71000 Sarajevo.

Telephone: (33) 219923.

Fax: (33) 205347.

E-mail: mmicevska@vijeceministara.gov.ba

Internet: www.vijeceministara.gov.ba

SPS *see* **Socialist Party of Serbia**.

Srebrenica

A town deep in what is now the **Serb Republic** in north-eastern **Bosnia and Herzegovina**, the site of the mass execution of Muslim **Bosniaks** at the hands of Bosnian **Serb** forces in July 1995. Srebrenica, along with **Goražde** and **Sarajevo**, was an area with a clear Bosniak majority before the Bosnian war. It was declared a UN 'safe haven' on 6 May 1993. Dutch UN peacekeepers could do nothing to prevent the enclave falling to Bosnian Serb forces two years later on 11 July 1995, and were subsequently heavily criticized for their failure to take any effective action to protect its inhabitants. A total of 8,000 of the region's estimated 40,000 Bosniaks were executed in a deliberate campaign of '**ethnic cleansing**' in the town, the worst single atrocity of the entire war. International outrage over the massacre contributed to growing condemnation of Serb territorial aggression, and to a shift of opinion in favour of a less passive stance by international forces. Like many other previously cosmopolitan areas, Srebrenica now has a clear Serb majority.

SRNA *see* **News Agency of the Serb Republic**.

SRS *see* **Serbian Radical Party**.

STA *see* **Slovene Press Agency**.

Stability Pact for South-Eastern Europe

A forum created in June 1999 in Cologne, Germany, under the initiative of the **European Union**, to promote co-operation and peaceful relations in the **Balkans**. It was succeeded by the **Regional Co-operation Council** on 27 February 2008.

Stabilization Force *see* **EUFOR**.

State Property Fund
Valstybės Turto Fondas (VTF)

Created in 1997 and inaugurated in March 1998, incorporating the Lithuanian State Privatization Agency established in 1995. The Fund's principal tasks are to represent state interests in holding and disposing of **Lithuania**'s state-owned property.

    Chair.: Gediminas Rainys.
    Address: Vilnius g. 16, Vilnius 01507.
    Telephone: (5) 2684999.
    Fax: (5) 2684997.
    E-mail: info@vtf.lt
    Internet: www.vtf.lt

State Union of Serbia and Montenegro *see* **Serbia and Montenegro**.

StB
Státní bezpečnost

The communist-era State Security Force (secret police) of the former **Czechoslovakia**. The StB was used to suppress dissent, sometimes violently, and to provide the authorities with information on security issues within the country. It was notably put to use in undermining the pro-democracy '**Prague Spring**' of 1968. Following its dissolution in February 1990 after the collapse of the communist Government, controversy over 'collaboration' with the Force prompted the drafting of so-called **lustration laws**.

Sudetenland question

A flashpoint in the history of Europe in the 1930s, when Nazi Germany demanded the right to incorporate into the Third Reich the territory inhabited by a large **German** community within what was then **Czechoslovakia**. They were concentrated in the Sudetenland, the mountainous western border region which derives its name from the Sudeten mountains between **Bohemia** and Silesia (modern south-western **Poland**). Under the Habsburg Empire, Austrian rule over Bohemia had enabled the Sudeten Germans to flourish, and representatives of the 3m.-strong German community protested strongly, but fruitlessly, when the whole of Bohemia was incorporated into the new Czechoslovak state under the 1919 Treaty of St Germain. Their stronger cultural connection with neighbouring Germany stimulated German nationalism in the area and encouraged Hitler's ambition to include the Sudeten Germans within his Third Reich. These aims were achieved at the Munich Conference in 1938, when the territorial integrity of Czechoslovakia was sacrificed to the Western desire to appease Hitler's demands. The entire Sudetenland area was ceded to the Nazi state, and this was followed by the expulsion of the region's **Czech** minority population.

At the end of the 1939–45 war, the restored Czechoslovak authorities not only reincorporated the territory of Sudetenland, but insisted that almost all its German inhabitants be forcibly 'repatriated' to Germany. The relatively small remaining minority community of some 165,000 had dwindled to just 50,000 by 1991 through voluntary emigration. Calls for compensation or the return of property taken from the fleeing Germans have largely been sidelined by good relations between Germany and the **Czech Republic**.

SYN *or* **Synaspismos** *see* **Coalition of the Left of Movements and Ecology**.

SYRIZA *see* **Coalition of the Radical Left**.

SZ *see* **Green Party**.

Szeklers

A **Finno-Ugric people** who arrived in **central Europe** some time in the late 10th century and ultimately settled in northern **Transylvania** under the encouragement of the medieval **Hungarian** kingdom. The language of the Szeklers, known by the same name, is considered by Hungarian nationalists as the most pure form of their own language, and the Szeklers themselves are romanticized as embodying essential Hungarian traits. The modern Szeklers largely class themselves as Hungarian, making any estimate of their numbers very difficult.

T

Tadić, Boris

President of **Serbia**. Boris Tadić is a psychologist who campaigned against communism in the 1980s, and against the nationalist regime of Slobodan **Milošević** in the 1990s. Leader of the **Democratic Party** (DS) since February 2004, he has held the presidency of Serbia since July 2004, and has used his position to improve Serbia's political and economic integration with the international community.

Born on 15 January 1958 in **Sarajevo**, he graduated from the University of Belgrade with a degree in social psychology. He worked as a psychology teacher and military clinical psychologist. He joined the anti-communist dissident movement in the 1980s, and was arrested several times.

In the 1990s he became a lecturer in political advertising at the Drama Faculty of the University of Belgrade. In 1997 he founded the Centre for the Development of Democracy and Political Skills, holding the post of Director until 2002.

After Slobodan Milošević was overthrown in 2000, Tadić was appointed Minister of Telecommunications in the new Government. He was also deputy leader of the DS. In March 2003 DS leader and Prime Minister Zoran Đinđić was assassinated; Tadić became Defence Minister in the reshuffled Government, tasked with reforming the military to meet NATO standards for a modern rapid, reaction force, and the following February he was also elected as the new DS leader.

On 27 June 2004 he was elected President of Serbia, taking office on 17 July, and he secured a second term in office on 3 February 2008, taking office 12 days later. His key priority has been the international integration of Serbia, in particular with the **North Atlantic Treaty Organization** and the **European Union** (EU), though this caused friction with Prime Minister Vojislav **Koštunica**, who disapproved of international moves to support independence for Kosovo. After Kosovo declared its independence on 17 February 2008 Koštunica resigned, and elections were called for May. On 29 April 2008 Tadić went to Luxembourg and signed the long-stalled Stabilization and Association Agreement with the EU, the achievement of which gave a boost to his **For a European Serbia** coalition just ahead of the poll.

Tadić is married and has two daughters.

Address: Office of the President, Andričev venac 1, 11000 Belgrade.
Telephone: (11) 3632121.
Fax: (11) 3228408.
E-mail: izivanovic@predsednik.rs
Internet: www.predsednik.rs

Talat, Mehmet Ali

Former President of the **Turkish Republic of Northern Cyprus** (TRNC) from April 2005 to April 2010. Previously Prime Minister and leader of the left-of-centre **Republican Turkish Party–United Forces** (CTP-BG), Mehmet Ali Talat worked hard towards a solution to the **Cyprus** problem.

Mehmet Ali Talat was born in Girne (Kyrenia) in northern Cyprus on 6 July 1952, to a farming family. He first became involved in politics while studying for a degree in electrical engineering at the Middle East Technical University (METU) in Ankara, Turkey, from where he graduated in 1977. On his return to Cyprus he supported himself by repairing refrigerators and air conditioners. He is married with a son and a daughter.

Talat became Minister of Education and Culture in 1993 in the coalition Government formed by the **Democrat Party** (DP) and the CTP following the general election, and continued in the same post in the second DP–CTP coalition Government. Elected as leader of the CTP in January 1996, he first became an Assembly member in 1998 for the constituency of Lefkoşa (**Nicosia**), and was re-elected in 2003. Talat formed a coalition Government with the DP in January 2004 at the request of then-President Rauf **Denktaş** when Prime Minister Derviş **Eroğlu** found himself unable to do so. Talat was credited with leading the successful campaign to persuade **Turkish Cypriots** to accept a UN-backed proposal to reunite the island, though the plan was scuppered when **Greek Cypriots** voted 'no'. Following the victory of the ruling parties in Assembly elections in February 2005, Talat continued as Prime Minister, until his election as President on 17 April 2005. He was inaugurated on 24 April and stepped down as CTP-BG leader in May.

The presidential victory of Greek Cypriot communist leader Dimitris **Christofias** in February 2008 reinvigorated the push for a resolution to the Cyprus issue. Talat and Christofias have held over 60 sessions of talks, and though a deal has yet to be made, both leaders profess to remain fully committed to finding a lasting settlement to the island's problems. After the April 2009 Assembly elections, Talat had to cohabit with a hard-line **National Unity Party** Government under Eroğlu, but despite that party's opposition to reunification he sought to maintain the momentum of the inter-communal talks. Talat stood for a second term in April 2010, but this time was defeated by Eroğlu, who secured 50.4% of the vote in the first round, ahead of Talat on 42.9% and five other candidates.

Tallinn

Capital city of **Estonia** and a major Baltic port, situated on the northern Bay of Tallinn, on the Gulf of Finland. *Population*: 398,594 (2009 estimate).

In 1219 King Waldemar of Denmark conquered Toompea (Dome Hill), the hill fortress at what is now the centre of Tallinn. Sold to the Teutonic Knights of Germany in 1347, Tallinn prospered as a member of the Hanseatic League as the building of what is now the old town was completed. After two centuries of Swedish rule, Estonia was annexed in 1710 by Russia, which established Tallinn as a naval base for its Baltic fleet. It became a major industrial centre, a railway link to St Petersburg was established, and by 1917 the Tallinn population had increased to 160,000, largely due to the influx of Russian labourers.

Tallinn was the capital of independent Estonia from 1919 until its occupation by the **Soviet Union** in 1940. During German occupation from 1941 much of the old town architecture was destroyed. Tallinn was the Soviet capital of the Estonian Soviet Socialist Republic from 1944 until the country regained independence in 1991. Edgar Savisaar, Mayor of Tallinn in 2001–04, was re-elected in 2007.

Tallinn Stock Exchange *see* **NASDAQ OMX Tallinn**.

Tanjug
Novinska Agencija Tanjug (Tanjug News Agency)

The main state news agency in **Serbia**. Tanjug is a contraction of *Telegrafska agencija Nove Jugoslavije* (Telegraphic News Agency of New Yugoslavia). It was founded in 1943 at the height of the Second World War as a means of spreading information about the Yugoslav resistance to Nazi occupation. Under the **Socialist Federal Republic of Yugoslavia** Tanjug was one of the major international news agencies of its day, providing an alternative communist perspective against the might of the Soviet Novosti information machine, and particularly strong in international coverage of the Non-Aligned Movement. In the 1990s Tanjug was harnessed as a vital tool of Slobodan **Milošević**'s propaganda efforts. Following his downfall in 2000 it has been overhauled and purged of his supporters and its connections with the state. Tanjug is in the process of divorcing itself from government control altogether.

Director and Editor-in-Chief: Dušan Đorđević.
Address: Obilićev Venac 2, POB 439, 11001 Belgrade.
Telephone: (11) 3281608.
Fax: (11) 633550.
E-mail: agency@tanjug.co.rs
Internet: www.tanjug.co.rs

Tartu, Treaties of

Treaties signed in 1920 by **Soviet** Russia securing peaceful relations and common borders with **Estonia** (2 February) and Finland (14 October). The first treaty guaranteed Russia's recognition of Estonia's independence (later revoked), while the second significantly included the cession of the Petsamo district to Finland.

See also Treaties of **Rīga**.

TASR *see* **News Agency of the Slovak Republic**.

Temsilciler Meclisi *see* **House of Representatives (Cyprus)**.

Tetovo

The town in **Macedonia** that lies in the heart of the country's ethnic **Albanian**-dominated north-western region, and has been at the centre of support for greater autonomy. *Population* 86,580 (2004 estimate). In 1995 the community established an illegal Albanian-language university in the city. The institution was finally recognized by the Macedonian authorities in July 2000 and formally opened later the following year, following the ending of months of armed conflict between Macedonian troops and the Albanian National Liberation Army (known by its Albanian initials UCK— *see* **Kosovo Liberation Army**), a conflict in which Tetovo was very much on the front line.

Thaçi, Hashim

Prime Minister of **Kosovo**.

Hashim Thaçi was a founding member and political leader within the ethnic Albanian **Kosovo Liberation Army** (UÇK) nationalist militia in the 1990s. Party to the international talks at Rambouillet, France, that opened the way for **NATO** intervention in 1999, he then disbanded the UÇK and formed the **Democratic Party of Kosovo** (PDK) as a more radical alternative to Ibrahim Rugova's **Democratic League of Kosovo** (LDK). The PDK won elections in November 2007, and Thaçi was appointed as Prime Minister on 9 January 2008. Kosovo unilaterally declared independence six weeks later.

Born on 24 April 1968 in Burojë village, Skënderaj municipality, he was studying history at the University of Pristina in 1989 when he joined the People's Movement of the Republic of Kosova (LPRK). He led the student movement from 1990, was elected student deputy-rector of the University in 1991 and was a key figure in the founding of the Kosovo Liberation Army (UÇK) in 1992. He graduated in 1993, but found himself wanted by the police for his involvement with the UÇK; he fled abroad but frequently came back to Kosovo secretly, to support UÇK units. During his travels he studied south-eastern European history and political sciences at the University of Zurich, Switzerland (1996–98). In 1997 a Serbian court tried *in absentia* a group of UÇK members, including Thaçi, and sentenced them to prison.

As repression and discrimination against Kosovo's Albanian community gathered pace, full-scale fighting between Serbian paramilitary police and the UÇK nationalist militia broke out in 1998. Government forces ruthlessly asserted Serbian authority, implementing a brutal policy of '**ethnic cleansing**' that prompted worldwide condemnation. Thaçi, as the UÇK's political leader, led a delegation to the Rambouillet talks on Kosovo in February 1999 but failed to secure Western support for independence, whereupon the UÇK announced the establishment of an alternative provisional Kosovo Government with Thaçi as 'Prime Minister'. However, the main outcome of the Rambouillet talks was NATO military intervention in Kosovo from March.

The withdrawal of Serbian forces from Kosovo in June 1999 accentuated divisions between Thaçi, one of the UÇK 'moderates' prepared to co-operate with the succeeding UN administration, and hard-liners advocating continued struggle for independence and eventual union with **Albania** (*see* **Greater Albania**). Thaçi oversaw the official disbanding of the UÇK in June, and formed a political party, initially called the Party of Democratic Progress in Kosovo until May 2000 when it was renamed the PDK at its first congress. In February 2000 the provisional Government was disbanded, Thaçi instead recognizing the authority of the UN Interim Administration Mission in Kosovo (**UNMIK**), and becoming a member of the Interim Administrative Council pending **Assembly** elections.

In Kosovan Assembly elections in 2001 and 2004, the PDK finished second to the LDK, with Thaçi occupying the position of leader of the opposition during the Assembly's terms.

In 2005–07 Thaçi was party to the status negotiation process led by UN Special Envoy Martti Ahtisaari. At the November 2007 election, the PDK overtook the LDK, and the two parties formed an expected, if uncomfortable, grand coalition in January 2008, with Thaçi as Prime Minister. He announced the unilateral independence of Kosovo from Serbia the following month.

He is married to Lumnije, and has one son. He speaks English and German.

Address: Ndërtesa e Qeverisë, Rruga Nëna Tereze p.n., 10000 Pristina.

Telephone: (38) 540564.

Fax: (38) 213113.

Internet: www.ks-gov.net/pm

Tirana

Capital city of **Albania**, situated in the middle of the country, of which it is the political, economic and cultural centre. *Population*: 406,000 (2007 estimate). The city is reputed to have been founded in 1614 by the Turkish feudal lord of the region, Sulejman Pasha Mulleti, who built a mosque and other facilities. It developed as an economic centre in the 18th century and was declared the capital of independent Albania in 1920.

Tirana Stock Exchange

Albania's only stock exchange. Officially opened on 2 May 1996, it is the first of its kind in Albania. It is run as an appendage of the **Bank of Albania** and currently only trades in government bonds and treasury bills. There are plans to 'spin off' the exchange and allow greater trading.

General Director: Anila Fureraj.
Address: Rruga Dora D'Istria, Kutia Postare 274/1, Tirana.
Telephone: (4) 271849.
Fax: (4) 271850.
E-mail: tseinfo@abcom-al.com
Internet: www.tse.com.al

Tito

Communist **Yugoslavia**'s leader for 35 years until his death in 1980, and President from 1953 onwards.

Born Josip Broz in 1892, he was taken prisoner in the First World War when fighting as a soldier in the army of the Austro-Hungarian Empire, and was thus in **Russia** at the time of the 1917 revolution. He fought on the communist side in the Russian civil war. Returning to Yugoslavia, he established himself there as communist party leader and achieved heroic status under the adopted name of Tito as a leader of Partisan resistance to Nazi occupation from 1941.

A **Croat** himself, Tito achieved the remarkable feat of winning popularity with all Yugoslav nations, holding the tensions of the multi-ethnic state to some extent in abeyance throughout his period in power. Initially an orthodox Stalinist, he turned to his own brand of Marxism-Leninism as leader of post-1945 Yugoslavia, causing an irreparable rift with the Soviet authorities by the late 1940s. Titoism included Yugoslav neutrality, workers' self-management, economic decentralization and the concept of social ownership.

Tito showed great flexibility in adapting Yugoslav institutions in an attempt to solve the many structural problems that confronted the state. Under his stewardship,

Yugoslavia did develop rapidly, as measured by both economic and educational indexes. His death in 1980 was immediately followed by predictions of the break-up of the **Socialist Federal Republic of Yugoslavia**, although almost a decade passed before this process entered its critical phase.

Titograd *see* **Podgorica**.

TMK *see* **Kosovo Protection Corps**.

Topi, Bamir

President of the Republic, **Albania**.

Bamir Topi is a professor of veterinary medicine and specialist in toxicology and pharmacology. He has represented the centre-right **Democratic Party of Albania** (PDSh) in the People's Assembly since 1996, and was inaugurated as President of Albania on 24 July 2007.

Born on 24 April 1957 in **Tirana**, he graduated in veterinary medicine from the Agricultural University. From 1984 to 1995 he worked as a Scientific Researcher at the Institute of Veterinary Scientific Researches. During this period he also studied for a doctorate in Molecular Biology in Italy, and in the early 1990s was Director of the Food Safety and Veterinary Institute. The success of his research and papers led to appointment as professor in 1995.

Involved in politics from the early 1990s, Topi was first elected to the People's Assembly in 1996, representing the PDSh, and was appointed Minister of Agriculture and Food until the PDSh went into opposition after losing the 1997 election. Topi has served two further terms as an Assembly member, and has also been Deputy Chairman of the PDSh.

In 2007 the PDSh nominated Topi to be the next President, without consulting the opposition. The **Socialist Party of Albania** boycotted the repeated ballots, leaving Topi just short of the three-fifths of the vote which was at that time required for the election of the President. Only at the fourth attempt (of a constitutionally possible five before the People's Assembly would have had to be dissolved) did seven opposition deputies break the boycott to end the stalemate. Topi was sworn in four days later, on 24 July.

Bamir Topi is married with two daughters.

Address: Office of the President, Bulevardi Dëshmorët e Kombit, Tirana.

Telephone: (4) 228313.

Fax: (4) 233761.

E-mail: presec@presec.tirana.al

Internet: www.president.al

TP *see* **People's Party**.

TPP *see* **National Resurrection Party**.

TRACECA
(Transport Corridor Europe–Caucasus–Asia)

A project assisted by the **European Union** to promote, co-ordinate and plan alternative transport links between **eastern Europe** and central Asia, via the Caucasus. Established in May 1993 as an extension of the existing transport corridor, TRACECA aims to increase regional trade and political ties. A Permanent Secretariat of the Inter-governmental Commission TRACECA is based in Baku, Azerbaijan.

> *Members*: Armenia, Azerbaijan, **Bulgaria**, Georgia, Kazakhstan, Kyrgyzstan, Moldova, **Romania**, Tajikistan, Turkey, Turkmenistan, Ukraine and Uzbekistan.
> *Secretary-General*: Rustan Jenalinov.
> *Address*: Gen. Aliyarbekov St 8/2, 1005 Baku.
> *Telephone*: (12) 5982718.
> *Fax*: (12) 4986426.
> *E-mail*: r.jenalinov@ps.traceca-org.org
> *Internet*: www.traceca-org.org

Trade and Investment Promotion Agency
Agencija za Promicanje Izvoza i Ulaganja (APIU)

A government agency whose main tasks are to promote international investment in **Croatia** and provide full service to investors.

> *Managing Director*: Slobodan Mikac.
> *Address*: Hebrangova 34, 10000 Zagreb.
> *Telephone*: (1) 4866000.
> *Fax*: (1) 4866008.
> *E-mail*: slobodan.mikac@croinvest.org
> *Internet*: www.apiu.hr

Transport Corridor Europe–Caucasus–Asia *see* **TRACECA**.

Transylvania

A mountainous plateau situated in the corner of the eastern and southern Carpathians. It was settled by **Hungarian** invaders (**Szeklers**) in the 10th century and by ethnic **Romanians** possibly from as early as the time of the Roman conquest of the area in the second century. Under Hungarian rule the region also saw the arrival of ethnic **Germans**. It later became the subject of a prolonged territorial dispute between **Romania**, which was awarded sovereignty over the region after the First World War, and **Hungary** which regarded that award as an injustice and a humiliation.

Dominated by the Hungarians for centuries following its consquest by Hungarian leader King (Saint) Stephen in the early 11th century, Transylvania became an important part of Hungarian national aspirations under the Austro-Hungarian Empire, and was the centre of an anti-Austrian uprising in the mid-19th century. Following the break-up of the Empire at the end of the First World War, Transylvania was ceded to Romania under the 1920 Treaty of **Trianon**, on the basis that the majority of the population were ethnically Romanian. Tensions between the large Hungarian minority in Transylvania and the Romanian state were reinforced by the temporary annexation of northern Transylvania during the Second World War by a Nazi-supervised Hungarian Government. The dispute was stifled during the **Cold War** era through the wholesale repression of Hungarian culture.

At the time of the collapse of communism in the late 1980s and early 1990s Transylvania played a key role. The overthrow of the hated **Ceauşescu** regime began with protests in the western Transylvanian city of Timişoara. Tensions between the ethnic communities have since then remained subdued, and relations between the Romanian and Hungarian Governments have been strengthened. Political representation for the Transylvanian Hungarians (who include the Szeklers) is dominated by the sizeable **Hungarian Democratic Union of Romania**, but it is now challenged by a more radical Hungarian Civic Party; both parties' support at state level is offset by the racist nationalism espoused by the extreme right. In 2003 the Szeklers established a National Council, calling for autonomy.

Trianon, Treaty of

A treaty signed on 4 June 1920 at the Paris Peace Conference, convened following the conclusion of the First World War. The Treaty of Trianon was concerned specifically with the territorial restructuring of the newly independent **Hungary**, and it established what are still that country's modern borders. It remains a source of resentment for Hungarian nationalists as it ceded much of historic Hungary to neighbouring countries, including south and eastern **Slovakia**, **Transylvania** and the **Vojvodina**. These areas are still home to significant ethnic **Hungarian** populations who retain very close links with Hungary and whose treatment is a source of regional tensions. *See also* Treaties of **Neuilly** and **Versailles**.

Trieste

An Italian city situated in the north-western corner of **Istria**. Developed as a major port by the Romans, Trieste flourished once again under Austrian control from 1891. The large Italian majority in the city prompted the Allies to grant it, along with the Istrian peninsula as a whole, to Italy after the First World War. As a frontier, it has provided strong support for Italian nationalists ever since, while disputes over the adjoining territory continued.

Briefly held by **Yugoslav** communist forces from 1945 to 1947, Trieste was created a UN Free Territory with Allied and Yugoslav forces sharing control. Official claims to sovereignty over the city were not settled until a treaty in 1954 gave the eastern and northern hinterlands to Yugoslavia (shared between **Croatia** and **Slovenia**), and the city itself to Italy. The Italian Government did not drop its claims to the whole area until 1975.

TRNC *see* **Turkish Republic of Northern Cyprus**.

TS–LKD *see* **Homeland Union–Lithuanian Christian Democrats**.

TT *see* **Order and Justice**.

Tudjman, Franjo

Nationalist leader in **Croatia** and President from 1990 until his death in December 1999. Tudjman was born on 14 May 1922 in the village of Veliko Trgovišće. His father founded the wartime anti-fascist movement in his native region, but was nevertheless killed by the secret police after the war under the **Tito** regime. Franjo Tudjman himself also fought as a Partisan in north-west Croatia (as did his brother, killed in 1943). A military career after 1945 (he reached the rank of general in the Yugoslav National Army by 1960) gave way eventually to his interest in national history and political science. He resigned his commission in 1961 to pursue this research, and was expelled from the communist party in 1967 as his writing became increasingly controversial and his support for a specifically **Croat** identity more overt. His controversial *Wastelands of Historical Reality* claimed that the crimes of the wartime Ustaša regime (against which he had fought as a Partisan) were being grossly exaggerated by communist propagandists, and that the Ustaša should even be commended for achieving statehood for Croatia. He was imprisoned in 1972 and again between 1981 and 1984. Later that decade Tudjman travelled in North America and Europe, raising support among Croatian émigrés for the 1989 launch of his **Croatian Democratic Union** (HDZ).

In Croatia's first multi-party elections, in April–May 1990, the HDZ won a large majority and on 30 May the new Assembly elected Tudjman as President. Croatia declared itself independent in 1991, and bitter fighting followed as the **Serb**-dominated federal army moved in to support Croatian Serbs in resisting this secession, but by January 1992 the new state had won international recognition, albeit with a quarter of its former territory in Serb hands. As the hero of independence, Tudjman was returned to power with nearly 60% of the vote in presidential elections that August. Re-elected for another five-year term in June 1997, he was the dominant Croat nationalist figure throughout the period of conflict which followed the collapse of the **Socialist Federal Republic of Yugoslavia**. He was criticized internationally, however, both for his authoritarianism (in particular in restricting the press and broadcasting media) and for pursuing the temptation of a '**Greater Croatia**' by supporting ethnic Croat forces in the war which ravaged neighbouring **Bosnia and Herzegovina** between 1992 and 1995. Ultimately Tudjman became a firm supporter of alliance between Bosnian Croats and **Muslims**, and took the opportunity of recovering Serb-held areas of Croatia in a series of offensives in August and September 1995. Many thousands of Serb refugees were sent streaming eastwards, such '**ethnic cleansing**' having already become appallingly familiar in the region's four years of conflict. Tudjman was a signatory of the **Dayton Agreement** at the end of 1995, and also signed an accord with the rump **Yugoslavia** the following August. His narrowly nationalistic outlook, however, and lack of respect for democratic values, contributed to a loss of impetus in Croatia's bid for greater integration within a democratic and liberal free-market Europe. His death in December 1999 became the catalyst for a period of change and a more internationalist outlook in Croatian politics.

Türk, Danilo

President of **Slovenia**. A respected lawyer, specializing in human rights, Türk spent most of Slovenia's post-independence period as Ambassador to the UN. He was elected President in October–November 2007, taking office on 22 December.

Danilo Türk was born on 19 February 1952 in Maribor. He received his degree from the Faculty of Law of the University of Ljubljana in 1975, followed by a master's degree from Belgrade, and then a doctorate back in **Ljubljana** in 1982. During this period he also chaired the Commission for Minorities and Migrants of the Socialist Alliance of the Working People of Slovenia (SZDL). He then became head of the university's Institute of International Law and International Relations, rising to a full professor by 1995. Already involved with Amnesty International, he also joined the UN Sub-Commission on Prevention of Discrimination and Protection of Minorities, became noted as an adviser in cases of human rights violations in the former **Yugoslavia**, and helped found Slovenia's Human Rights Council.

As the country gained its independence, Türk became involved in diplomatic affairs, first (unofficially) representing the still unrecognized country at the UN and **Council of Europe**, then at the Conference on Yugoslavia, and in 1992–2005 serving as Ambassador to the UN in New York. In 1998–99 Slovenia held one of the non-permanent seats on the UN Security Council, and after this Türk was appointed Assistant Secretary-General for Political Affairs.

Returning to Slovenia in 2005, he resumed teaching at the University of Ljubljana, becoming Vice-Dean of the Faculty of Law the following year.

Türk stood as an independent candidate in the 2007 presidential election, gaining the backing of the **Social Democrats**, the **Democratic Party of Slovenian Pensioners, For Real—New Politics** and Active Slovenia. In the first round on 21 October, he won 24.5%, trailing Lojze Peterle with 28.7%. However, in the run-off on 11 November Türk resoundingly defeated Peterle, winning by 68% to 32%. He took office on 22 December. Türk is married and has one daughter.

Address: Office of the President, Erjavčeva 17, 1000 Ljubljana.

Telephone: (1) 4781222.

Fax: (1) 4781357.

E-mail: gp.uprs@up-rs.si

Internet: www.up-rs.si

Turkic peoples

A large ethnic group encompassing nationalities spread across **eastern Europe** and central Asia. Historically the Turks are thought to have originated among the nomadic T'u-chüeh of western Mongolia. Through their sixth-century empire the Turks spread across the Russian steppe and established the first of their European colonies.

Turkic nationality groups in Europe include **Bulgarian Turks**, **Turkish Cypriots** and many minorities in the Russian Federation. They have mixed with local peoples over the centuries, often retaining only their language—which is of the Altaic group—by which they can be identified as Turkic, although they share similarities in culture and, apart from the Chavash and Kryashens, all embrace Islam.

Turkish Cypriots

The **Turkic** community of **Cyprus**. The term usually refers not only to the indigenous Turkish-speaking Cypriots whose ancestors first arrived on the island after the Ottoman conquest in 1570, but also to Turks who migrated after the 1974 Turkish invasion (and their descendants). Most of the Turkish Cypriot community now live in the self-proclaimed **Turkish Republic of Northern Cyprus** (TRNC). The largest community of Turkish Cypriots outside Cyprus is in the United Kingdom, numbering around 50,000.

483

Turkish Republic of Northern Cyprus (TRNC)
Kuzey Kibris Türk Cumhuriyeti (KKTC)

A self-proclaimed republic in the **Turkish Cypriot** area of northern **Cyprus**, recognized only by Turkey. The TRNC was established in November 1983 as the successor to the Turkish Federated State of Cyprus (TFSC), which had been created in 1975 following the 1974 Turkish invasion and occupation of the northern 37% of Cyprus (3,355 sq km), where some 40,000 Turkish troops continue to be deployed. The area had previously come under the Turkish Cypriot Autonomous Administration dating from 1968.

Under its 1985 Constitution, the TRNC has an executive President directly elected for a five-year term and a 50-member Assembly of the Republic (Cumhuriyet Meclisi). About 20% of TRNC government expenditure is funded by subventions from Turkey and the TRNC uses the Turkish lira as its currency. A census in April 2006 showed that the TRNC had 264,172 inhabitants, a 32% increase since the previous count in 1996 and appearing to confirm that post-1974 settlers from Turkey and elsewhere outnumbered indigenous Turkish Cypriots. Although the Turkish Cypriot area contains the greater part of the island's resources and productive agricultural land, its economy suffered from its international isolation in the decades after 1974, falling increasingly behind that of the **Greek Cypriot** part of the island. GDP per capita at PPP in 2004 was estimated at US $7,135 in the TRNC, about a third of the Greek Cypriot level. Annual GDP growth of 8% in 2003–08, fuelled by a boom in the construction of holiday homes, did appear to be closing the gap, despite the severe blow of the Turkish Cypriot area being blocked from accession to the **European Union** (EU) in 2004.

The Turkish Cypriot leader since the late 1960s, Rauf **Denktaş** who became President of the TRNC in 1983 and was re-elected in 1985, 1990, 1995 and 2000, had maintained his core demand for recognition of the 'sovereignty' of the TRNC through seemingly interminable UN-brokered negotiations in quest of a Cyprus settlement. Denktaş's line on this was a key stumbling-block, given that the Greek Cypriot side's core demand was the maintenance of Cyprus as a single sovereign state. Denktaş had also maintained that the Greek Cypriots had no right to negotiate EU entry on behalf of the Turkish Cypriots. He therefore condemned the signature of the Cyprus-EU accession treaty in April 2003 and responded by opening the line of division (known as the **Green Line**) to free movement of people, enabling large numbers from each community to visit the other side.

In a defeat for the Denktaş line, Assembly elections in December 2003 resulted in the pro-EU, pro-reunification **Republican Turkish Party–United Forces** (CTP-BG) led by Mehmet Ali **Talat** becoming the largest party and forming a coalition with the **Democrat Party** (DP). However, Denktaş remained chief negotiator for the Turkish Cypriot side and refused to endorse a settlement plan tabled by UN Secretary-General Kofi Annan envisaging the creation of a federal United Cyprus Republic consisting of two 'constituent states'. The plan was also rejected by Greek Cypriot President Tassos Papadopoulos, on the grounds that it would solidify the island's division to the disadvantage of the Greek Cypriots. Annan therefore presented the UN plan directly to the Cypriot people in simultaneous referendums in April 2004. The Turkish Cypriots delivered a 64.9% vote in favour, but 75.8% of Greek Cypriots voted against. Accordingly, the accession of the Republic of Cyprus to the EU on 1 May 2004 applied only to the area under the control of the Greek Cypriot government.

Early TRNC Assembly elections in February 2005 resulted in the CTP-BG winning 24 seats, the hard-line anti-unification **National Unity Party** (UBP) 19, the DP six and the Peace and Democracy Movement (BDH) one. Presidential elections in April 2005, in which Denktaş did not stand, were won by Talat with 55.6% of the vote. Talat appointed Ferdi Sabit Soyer (CTP-BG) as Prime Minister, at first heading another coalition with the DP, which in September 2006 was replaced by the new Freedom and Reform Party (ÖRP).

Meanwhile, Talat and Papadopoulos had agreed in July 2006 to resume talks between Greek Cypriots and Turkish Cypriots. Although at first this process remained at a preparatory technical level, the presidential victory of Greek Cypriot communist leader Dimitris **Christofias** in February 2008 reinvigorated the push for a resolution of the island's division. Talat's first meeting with Christofias took place within three weeks, and direct, UN-backed negotiations began in early September. The Turkish Cypriot electorate's apparent ambivalence, however, was reflected in the April 2009 TRNC Assembly election results, with the UBP winning 26 seats (with 44.1% of the vote), while Talat's CTP-BG dropped to 15 seats (29.2%). The DP won five seats (10.7%) and the left-wing Communal Democracy Party and ÖRP won two seats each (with 6.9% and 6.2% of the vote respectively). UBP leader Derviş **Eroğlu** named a new Government on 5 May 2009.

Talat stood for a second term as president in April 2010, again facing Eroğlu as his main opponent, and with their differing positions on reunification as the key issue. Eroğlu secured victory in the first round with 50.4% of the vote, ahead of Talat on 42.9% and five other candidates. He was inaugurated on 23 April. Hüseyin **Özgürgün** took over as acting Prime Minister.

Tusk, Donald

Prime Minister of **Poland** since November 2007. Involved in the student movement of **Solidarity** while at university, Tusk has sat in both houses of the **National Assembly**, and held office as Deputy Speaker in each, prior to the electoral success of his centre-right **Civic Platform** (PO) in October 2007.

Donald Tusk was born in **Gdańsk** on 22 April 1957, and studied history at the University of Gdańsk, where he co-founded the Students' Committee of Solidarity. He worked in the Swietlik co-operative and as a journalist for the Solidarity weekly

Samorządność (Selfgovernance), while at the Maritime Publishing House he headed the Solidarity movement. He was a co-founder of the Liberal and Democratic Congress (KLD) and a member of the first Sejm (lower house of the National Assembly) following the collapse of communism. In 1994 he became a deputy Chairman of the Freedom Union (UW), a merger of the KLD and the Democratic Union, and three years later was elected to the Senat (upper house of the National Assembly), where he served as Deputy Speaker.

In 2001 he left the UW to co-found Civic Platform (PO), and since the September 2001 election he has served as a PO deputy in the Sejm, appointed as Deputy Speaker for 2001–05. In the October 2005 presidential election he led on the first round with 36% of the vote, but was beaten in the run-off with 46% to Lech **Kaczyński**'s 54%.

When early elections were held in October 2007, the PO surged ahead of the rival centre-right **Law and Justice** (PiS), and on 9 November Tusk was appointed as Prime Minister, heading a majority Government with the **Polish People's Party**.

Tusk is married with a son and a daughter.

Address: Office of the Prime Minister, Al. Ujazdowskie 1–3, 00-583 Warsaw.
Telephone: (22) 8413832.
Fax: (22) 6284821.
E-mail: cirinfo@kprm.gov.pl
Internet: www.kprm.gov.pl

U

UBP *see* **National Unity Party**.

UÇK *see* **Kosovo Liberation Army**.

UDMR *see* **Hungarian Democratic Union of Romania**.

UN Interim Administration Mission in Kosovo *see* UNMIK.

UN War Crimes Tribunal for the former Yugoslavia *see* **International Criminal Tribunal for the former Yugoslavia**.

UNECE *see* **United Nations Economic Commission for Europe**.

Union of Chambers of Commerce and Industry of Albania

The principal organization in **Albania** for promoting business contacts, both internally and externally, in the post-communist era. Originally founded in 1958.
President: Anton Leka.
Address: Rruga Kavajes 6, Tirana.
Telephone and fax: (4) 222934.

Union of Greens and Farmers
Zaļo un Zemnieku savienība (ZZS)

A green-agrarian political alliance of the Latvian Green Party (LZP) and the Latvian Farmers' Union (LZS), and part of the ruling coalition. The 2002 parliamentary election was the first fought by the two parties in alliance, and the ZZS finished fourth with 12 seats and 9.4% of the vote. The ZZS joined the **New Era**-led Government, and when this collapsed in February 2004 LZP Co-Chair Indulis Emsis was invited to form the new Government, becoming the world's first Green Prime Minister. A defeat of budget proposals in October led to Emsis's resignation, but the ZZS joined the new coalition headed by the **People's Party** (TP). In the 2006 legislative elections the ZZS again secured the second-largest share of the vote (16.7%), this time behind the TP with 19.6%. It gained 18 seats in the **Parliament**, and remained part of the ruling coalitions headed by first the TP, then the Latvian First Party/Latvian Way and currently by New Era. The leaders of the ZZS's constituent parties co-chair the alliance.

Union of Pro Patria and Res Publica
Isamaa ja Res Publica Liit (IRL)

A centre-right party in **Estonia**, formed by a merger of two existing groups in July 2006, affiliated to the **International Democrat Union** and **Centrist Democrat International**, and currently part of the ruling coalition.

The constituent elements of the IRL were the Pro Patria Union (IL) and the Union for the Republic—Res Publica.

The IL had been created in December 1995 by the merger of the Fatherland (or Pro Patria) National Coalition (RKI), an alliance of Christian Democratic and other centre-right groups whose leader had been Prime Minister in 1992–94, and the Estonian National Independence Party (ERSP), a centrist grouping from the pre-independence period which at the time of its foundation in August 1988 was the only organized non-communist party in the **Soviet Union**. Under Laar's leadership the IL had performed strongly at the March 1999 parliamentary elections, emerging as the second-largest party. The governing centre-right coalition he then formed with the Moderates and the **Estonian Reform Party** (ER) proved problematic, however, and Laar resigned as Prime Minister in January 2002, taking the IL into opposition. Laar stood down as party leader later that year. The March 2003 parliamentary elections saw the IL relegated to fifth place, with just seven seats and 7% of the vote.

The Union for the Republic—Res Publica party, by contrast, had performed strongly in the March 2003 parliamentary elections, tying for first place with 28 seats. Founded only two years earlier, it was based on the political organization Res Publica which had existed since 1989 as a club for young conservatives, most of whom were also associated with the IL. The party's leader Juhan Parts became Prime Minister at the head of a coalition Government formed in early April 2003 with the ER and the **Estonian People's Union** (ERL). The coalition proved to be a fragile one, however. In November the ERL voted against the Government on a key tax bill, and in February 2005 the ER almost withdrew when its Foreign Minister was dismissed over the disappearance of classified documents. The final blow, a vote of no confidence in the Justice Minister over a controversial anti-corruption plan, precipitated the resignation of Parts on 24 March 2005, whereupon Res Publica went into opposition under the leadership of Taavi Veskimägi.

The merger of the IL and Res Publica to form the IRL was approved in 2006, though each party retained its own leadership structure initially. In the March 2007 parliamentary elections the IRL finished third with 19 seats and 17.9% of the vote, and it entered the Government as part of an ER-led coalition under incumbent Prime Minister Andrus **Ansip**. In May 2007 the party unified its leadership, with Mart Laar as Chairman.

Leadership: Mart Laar (Chair.).
Address: Wismari 11, Tallinn 10136.
Telephone: 6691070.
Fax: 6691071.
E-mail: info@irl.ee
Internet: www.irl.ee

Union of Serbia and Montenegro *see* **Serbia and Montenegro**.

Union of Soviet Socialist Republics (USSR) *see* **Soviet Union**.

United Nations Economic Commission for Europe (UNECE)

The UN Economic Commission for Europe was established in 1947. Representatives of European countries, the USA, Canada, Israel, Turkey and the central Asian republics study the economic, environmental and technological problems of the region and recommend courses of action. UNECE is also active in the formulation of international legal instruments and the setting of international standards.

Members: 56 countries, including **Albania**, **Bosnia and Herzegovina**, **Bulgaria**, **Croatia**, **Cyprus**, **Czech Republic**, **Estonia**, **Greece**, **Hungary**, **Latvia**, **Lithuania**, **Macedonia**, **Montenegro**, **Poland**, **Romania**, **Serbia**, **Slovakia** and **Slovenia**.

Chairman: Alex van Meeuwen.
Executive Secretary: Ján Kubiš.
Address: Palais des Nations, 1211 Geneva 10, Switzerland.
Telephone: (22) 9174444.
Fax: (22) 9170505.
E-mail: info.ece@unece.org
Internet: www.unece.org

United Nations Interim Administration Mission in Kosovo *see* **UNMIK**.

United Nations War Crimes Tribunal for the former Yugoslavia *see*
International Criminal Tribunal for the former Yugoslavia.

UNMIK
(UN Interim Administration Mission in Kosovo)

The interim legal and executive authority in **Kosovo** from June 1999, overseeing civilian administration and reconstruction as an autonomous province pending the establishment of a full domestic administration.

UNMIK was created under the terms of UN Resolution 1244 on 10 June 1999, after **Serbian** forces had withdrawn from the province. Its remit covered police and justice, civil administration, democratization and institution building, and reconstruction and economic development. Its authority was not revoked at the time of Kosovo's declaration of independence in February 2008, in the absence of a UN Security Council vote to recognize that independence (to which the Russian Federation remained opposed). However, since the deployment of **EULEX** in December 2008 UNMIK has been relieved of many of its duties, and it now retains only a small political role and a presence in the northern, ethnic **Serb**-dominated provinces of Kosovo.

Special Representative: Lamberto Zannier.
Address: PO Box 999, Pristina, Kosovo.
Telephone: (38) 504 604 4000.
Fax: (38) 504 604 4019.
Internet: www.unmikonline.org

USSR *see* **Soviet Union**.

V

Vardar Macedonia *see* **Macedonian question**.

Velvet divorce

Czechoslovakia's relatively amicable dissolution and division into the **Czech Republic** and **Slovakia**, which was formally implemented on 1 January 1993. Despite economic growth and educational improvements, many **Slovaks** regarded the united Czechoslovakia created in 1918 as advantageous only to the more numerous **Czechs**. With the collapse of communism after the 'velvet revolution' of 1989, Slovak nationalism revived. Elections in June 1992 revealed the extent of political polarization between the two republics. The Czechs elected the neo-liberal **Civic Democratic Party** led by Václav **Klaus**, while the Slovaks elected the populist, social-democratic **Movement for a Democratic Slovakia** (HZDS) led by Vladimír **Mečiar**. Although the HZDS had sought no specific mandate for independence, the Slovak National Council declared its sovereignty in July 1992, and the same month negotiations on the dissolution of the federation began. The Czechs perceived that a 'velvet divorce' would deliver them political and economic stability, and so acquiesced in the dissolution.

Velvet revolution

The near-bloodless overthrow of **Czechoslovakia**'s communist regime in November–December 1989. Despite moderate reforms in the **Soviet Union** and elsewhere in **eastern Europe**, the Communist Party of Czechoslovakia had remained highly orthodox. Tens of thousands of anti-Government demonstrators were prompted to rally in the capital, **Prague**, on 17 November 1989 by the collapse of hard-line communist regimes in **Bulgaria** and East Germany in the preceding few weeks. Violent clashes with riot police at the demonstration left 140 demonstrators injured, spurring ever greater numbers of protestors to rally on Prague's streets over the next few days. Amid the tumult, opposition forces combined to form the Czech **Civic**

Forum and the Slovak **Public Against Violence**. On 24 November communist leader Miloš **Jakeš** resigned. A demoralized Communist Party agreed to the appointment on 10 December of a Government with a non-communist majority. On 29 December 1989, the former dissident playwright Václav **Havel** became interim President.

Versailles, Treaty of

The principal treaty signed on 28 June 1919 at the Paris Peace Conference following the conclusion of the First World War. The Versailles treaty itself deals with territorial, political and other matters relating to Germany, but the term is often used for the post-1918 settlement in Europe, the dismantling of the old imperial order and the creation of successor states based broadly on the nation-state principle. Among the treaty's relevant points was the restructuring of the border between Germany and the newly independent **Poland**. Shifted significantly to the west, Poland received a land corridor to the Baltic Sea—resulting in the separation of East **Prussia** from the rest of Germany—and areas adjacent to the economically vital region of Silesia. *See also* Treaties of **Neuilly** and **Trianon**.

Vienna Awards

Decisions made by the Foreign Ministers of Nazi Germany and Italy in 1938 and 1940 in favour of **Hungary**'s irredentist territorial demands to redress the loss of '**Hungarian**' lands under the 1920 Treaty of **Trianon**. The First Vienna Award, made at the expense of **Czechoslovakia** in 1938, granted Hungary the portions of southern **Slovakia** which held significant Hungarian populations. The Second Vienna Award, in August 1940, gave Hungary northern **Transylvania**. In contrast to the first award, the lands handed over in the second had only a slim Hungarian majority. Both awards were nullified by the defeat of the Nazis and their Hungarian allies at the conclusion of the war in 1945.

Vilnius

The capital of **Lithuania** situated in the forested southern interior of the country's historic heartland. *Population*: 544,206 (2008 estimate). The city had a turbulent history throughout the 20th century. The ancient heart of the medieval Lithuanian state, it had developed as a thriving commercial and academic centre from the 14th century. From 1799 to 1938 Vilnius was the centre of eastern European **Jewish** cultural life, producing texts which are still standard and creating the first socialist and **Zionist** Jewish movements in the **Russian** sphere. Unlike other **Baltic** capitals it never came under direct Germanic or Scandinavian control, but rather served as the centre for a very much independent and powerful Lithuania—the largest country in Europe in the 15th century after its union with **Poland**. The city only came under foreign domination proper in the 18th century.

Under Russian occupation from 1795, Vilnius was occupied by Polish forces in 1919 during the Polish advance into the **Soviet Union** and became the focus of Polish–**Lithuanian** antagonism over the next decades. The Polish authorities made Vilnius the capital of their puppet Central Lithuanian state and drew it into union with Poland, prompting retaliation from Lithuanian forces and ultimately from the Soviet Union in 1939. The Nazi invasion in 1941 led to the almost total eradication of the 80,000-strong Jewish community and the destruction of much of the old city. Under renewed Soviet domination after the war the majority Lithuanian population of Vilnius was broken up and scattered throughout the Soviet Union and replaced with an influx of Russian workers. By 1959 Lithuanians constituted only 34% of its population.

As the capital of the socialist Lithuanian Soviet republic, the city was developed as an important industrial centre producing heavy machinery, electrical goods and textiles. It has retained this important role as the capital of an independent Lithuania. Its large ethnic Russian community is a source of underlying tension with the post-Soviet regime.

Vilnius Group

Association formed in May 2000 by **Albania, Bulgaria, Estonia, Latvia, Lithuania, Macedonia, Romania, Slovakia** and **Slovenia** to advance their integration into the **North Atlantic Treaty Organization** (NATO). **Croatia** joined a year later. With accession expected for seven of these countries in March 2004, the remaing three (Albania, Croatia and Macedonia) signed the **Adriatic Charter** in May 2003.

Vilnius Stock Exchange *see* **NASDAQ OMX Vilnius**.

Visegrád Group

A grouping founded in the Hungarian town of Visegrád in February 1991 by threee former communist states in **central Europe** (**Poland, Hungary** and **Czechoslovakia**) initially to persuade the West that they were better qualified for foreign investment and rapid accession to European institutions, including the **European Union** (EU), than were other former communist states of **eastern Europe**. Its member countries (increased to four from the beginning of 1993 when Czechoslovakia split into the **Czech Republic** and **Slovakia**) also shared anxiety over rising Russian nationalism. All four countries joined the EU on 1 May 2004, since when the group has focused on strengthening the identity of central Europe within the EU, promoting regional co-operation, and supporting democratization processes in Ukraine, Belarus, Moldova and the **Balkans**. The International Visegrad Fund, the group's only institution, continues to support common cultural, scientific and educational projects, youth exchanges, cross-border projects and tourism promotion.

The group's presidency rotates annually in June and is currently held by Hungary, to be followed by Slovakia (2010–11), then the Czech Republic (2011–12), then Poland (2012–13).

Address: International Visegrad Fund, Kralovske udolie 8, 81102 Bratislava.
Telephone: (259) 203811.
Fax: (259) 203805.
E-mail: visegradfund@visegradfund.org
Internet: www.visegradgroup.eu *or* www.visegradfund.org

Vlachs
(also known as Aromani)

An Indo-European people of the Romance linguistic family, spread across the southern **Balkans** and ethnically similar to modern **Romanians**/Moldovans. Vlachs proudly claim descent from Romans who established the province of Dacia in what is now **Romania**.

They are thought to have stayed in the region since the third century, adopting a nomadic and pastoral way of life. A majority of Vlachs are still shepherds in remote regions of their host countries. Spreading around the region they gave their Slavic loan name, Vlach (they are generally known to themselves as Aromani), to the **Wallachia** region north of the lower Danube, and became dominant in **Bessarabia**. Their Romance language, which is divided into regional dialects, is most similar to Romanian. Most Vlachs, like Romanians, profess **Orthodox Christianity**.

In the 12th and 13th centuries an independent Vlach state is thought to have flourished around the Greek region of Pindus. It is in **Greece** that the greatest number of Vlachs reside, and where during the Second World War they established a fascist-inspired Principality of Pindus. Estimates of their numbers vary widely up to 200,000: the Greek Government officially does not recognize any ethnic divisions. In **Macedonia**, where the Vlachs have established societies to promote their language and culture, they officially number 10,000, but estimates reach up to 100,000. Up to 50,000 Vlachs can be found in the south-east of **Albania**, living mainly from animal husbandry; around 26,500 live in Romania, around 15,000 in **Serbia** and around 11,000 in **Bulgaria**.

VMRO–DPMNE *see* **Internal Macedonian Revolutionary Organization–Democratic Party for Macedonian National Unity**.

Vojvodina

The fertile district of **Serbia** lying north of **Belgrade**, in the southern Pannonian plain, with a sizeable **Hungarian** minority of around 20%. A conglomeration of local regions unified by the Habsburgs in 1848, it was named after the immigrant **Serb** leaders, or *vojvod*. Exceptional soil lends itself to the cultivation of wheat and cash crops. A part of **Hungary** throughout most of history, including the prolonged period of Ottoman rule, the Vojvodina did not emerge as a distinct political entity until the collapse of the Habsburg Empire at the end of the First World War, and its consequent inclusion in the newly-formed Kingdom of the Serbs, Croats and Slovenes (**Yugoslavia**) in 1918.

The shift in sovereignty over the area, and the later collapse of the **Socialist Federal Republic of Yugoslavia**, led to significant shifts in the region's ethnic make-up. Thousands of ethnic Hungarians fled north and ethnic Serbs re-established their position as the dominant population. Vojvodina achieved almost total autonomy within Serbia under communist Yugoslavia's 1974 Constitution owing to its distinction as an important agricultural area and the presence of the ethnic Hungarian minority population (now around 325,000 centred around the town of Subotica and the surrounding border region). This autonomy was removed in 1989. The fall of the Serbian dictator Slobodan **Milošević** in October 2000, however, raised hopes of its restitution, and the regional administration steadily strengthened its own voice over the course of 2001, upgrading the main administrative centre, Novi Sad, to the status of Vojvodina's official capital in October. In January 2002 Serbia partially restored Vojvodina's autonomy, and financial autonomy followed in 2006. The region's provincial Assembly adopted a new statute, providing for even wider autonomy, in October 2008, which (following its eventual approval by Serbia) came into force on 1 January 2010.

Vojvodina's economic importance led to the **North Atlantic Treaty Organization** alliance targeting many of its towns, factories and bridges during the 1999 air strikes against Yugoslavia. The region also suffers from pollution from poorly-maintained factories in neighbouring **Romania**.

Voucher privatization

An innovative way of promoting a transition to free-market economics in post-communist countries, which involved moving companies from state to private ownership by 'selling' shares for vouchers which had been issued free of charge to all citizens. This had the apparent advantage that it theoretically gave everyone the opportunity of share ownership, but the disadvantage that the process brought neither capital nor management expertise into the firms concerned, many of which subsequently failed. The first voucher privatization initiative was implemented in **Czechoslovakia** in 1992, on a large scale, covering about 30% of the total value of all state-held assets scheduled to be privatized. All Czechoslovak citizens aged 18 and above received a booklet of vouchers, which they could use to bid for shares, either directly or (the more popular route) by investing in one of the Investment Privatization Funds. The two waves of Czechoslovak voucher privatization ultimately achieved the transfer into private ownership of 2,200 companies with an approximate book value of US $14,000m. In practice, however, the outcome was very rarely that ordinary citizens became long-term shareholders. Instead, they sold off their shares immediately, in many cases to foreign companies intent on asset stripping. A voucher privatization scheme was also implemented in the Russian Federation in the latter part of 1992 (with **Bosnia and Herzegovina** and **Montenegro** among those following this route later in the decade). Ostensibly the Russian scheme resulted in over 40m. individuals becoming shareholders, and the privatization of nearly 16,000 medium and large enterprises. Again, however, more than half the vouchers were either sold on, or used to buy into the investment funds, and a significant proportion were simply never used.

Vouli *see* **Parliament (Greece)**.

Vouli Antiprosópon *see* **House of Representatives (Cyprus)**.

VPN *see* **Public Against Violence**.

VTF *see* **State Property Fund**.

Vujanović, Filip

President of the Republic, **Montenegro**. Filip Vujanović is a moderate member of the centre-left **Democratic Party of Socialists of Montenegro** (DPSCG). He served in the Montenegrin Government as Justice Minister and Interior Minister before becoming Prime Minister in 1998 in succession to Milo **Đukanović**. After the October 2002 elections, when Đukanović stepped down from the presidency to retake the post of Prime Minister; Vujanović moved to become Speaker of the **Assembly**, and then, as his party's candidate for the post of President of the Republic, was eventually elected to take office from 11 May 2003.

Born on 1 September 1954 in **Belgrade**, he graduated in law from the city's university in 1978. He began work in the District Attorney's Office in Belgrade before moving to **Podgorica**, the capital of his ancestral homeland, Montenegro, in

1981. He worked in the city's District Court before being registered as the youngest lawyer in the Attorneys' Chamber in 1989. He became a well-known figure in 1992 when he represented the then President of Montenegro, Momir Bulatović, in his lawsuit against detractors. In March 1993 he was appointed to Đukanović's cabinet as Justice Minister. He moved to the Interior Ministry and remained there in the next Đukanović cabinet, inaugurated in 1995. Following Đukanović's electoral success as President, he was appointed Prime Minister of Montenegro on 5 February 1998. He was reconfirmed in the post on 2 July 2001.

Early elections in October 2002, following the collapse of the ruling coalition, gave the DPSCG a majority. On 5 November, Đukanović resigned from the presidency in order to be nominated as the new Prime Minister, while Vujanović was chosen as Speaker of the Assembly. In this capacity he was acting President until a new holder could be elected—a process in which he was also standing as the DPSCG candidate. The December poll, in which he polled 84%, was invalidated by low turnout, due to an opposition boycott. The February 2003 attempt suffered a similar fate (with Vujanović polling 82%). After this the Assembly removed the 50% turnout condition, and on 11 May Vujanović secured the presidency with 64% of the vote (facing only a partial opposition boycott). He took office immediately.

Vujanović is married with three children.

Address: Office of the President, Bulevar Blaza Jovanovica 2, 81000 Podgorica.

Telephone: (20) 242382.

Fax: (20) 242329.

E-mail: predsjednik@gov.me

Internet: www.predsjednik.gov.me

Vukovar

A town on the River Danube in the eastern **Slavonia** region of **Croatia**. *Population*: 30,126 (2001 census). The scene of the first major incidence of '**ethnic cleansing**' accompanying the break-up of the former **Yugoslavia** in the early 1990s, when the Yugoslav army, backing the ethnic **Serbs** of the **Krajina** who actively resisted Croatia's declaration of independence in 1991, mounted a particularly heavy artillery bombardment against **Croat**-held Vukovar. The town, which had a pre-war population of some 50,000, was effectively reduced to rubble. It finally fell to the Serbs after a three-month siege in November 1991. Its remaining Croat inhabitants were driven out, while over 2,000 Croat soldiers were massacred and buried in mass graves. The **Dayton Agreement** of November 1995 specified the return of Vukovar to Croatia along with the rest of eastern Slavonia.

W

Wałęsa, Lech

Leader of the **Solidarity** free trade union movement which dramatically challenged the communist regime in **Poland** in the 1980s, and the country's President in 1990–95.

Born in September 1943 near Lipno, he trained as an electrician and moved in 1967 to the Baltic port of **Gdańsk**, where he worked for nine years in the Lenin shipyard. Active in the worker protests there in December 1970, Wałęsa later won acclaim worldwide (and the 1983 Nobel Prize for Peace) as leader of the free trade union Solidarity, which was spawned by the shipyard strikes of 1980 and grew into a mass movement which rocked the communist system. He played a major role in negotiating the historic Gdańsk Accords signed at the end of August 1980, in which the Polish Government first conceded workers' demands on the right to form trade unions outside the official communist structure, and the following month he became Chairman of the National Co-ordinating Commission of the newly-formed Solidarność (Solidarity). Arrested as martial law was imposed in November 1981 and the movement was driven underground, he led its resurgence in 1988 and helped negotiate the dismantling of Poland's one-party state. When Tadeusz Mazowiecki was appointed Prime Minister, Wałęsa himself refused ministerial office and returned to trade union issues, but became increasingly critical of his erstwhile Solidarity allies as they introduced tough economic austerity measures. These differences became even more evident when Wałęsa stood against, and defeated, Mazowiecki in the 1990 presidential elections.

When the second-round result was declared in December, Wałęsa resigned as leader of Solidarity to emphasize that his new role stood above party politics. He used his international celebrity to help press his country's case for early inclusion within the **European Union** and the **North Atlantic Treaty Organization** (NATO). During his five years in office, however, his impatience, outspokenness and combative style appeared autocratic and divisive in a Head of State. Seeking to present himself as a national figure of historical significance, with echoes of the authoritarian inter-war dictator Piłsudski, he formed a Piłsudski-style Non-Party Bloc in Support of Reforms, but was unable to attract enough support for this bloc to avoid its defeat in the 1993 elections. His anti-communism made his relationship with the post-1993 Government of former communists especially problematic. He also angrily rejected allegations arising from the selective leaking of communist-era secret police records, suggesting that he had collaborated with the authorities in the early 1980s. In November 1995, seeking re-election, he was defeated in a bitterly fought campaign by the youthful former communist Aleksander **Kwaśniewski**.

Wałęsa returned to Gdańsk upon leaving office, re-emerging in the public eye at the time of the September 1997 legislative election, whose outcome gave the Solidarity Electoral Action the opportunity to return to government. He offered to broker a coalition deal between the winning parties, while denying any aspirations to the premiership himself. The following month, reflecting the extent to which the paths of different Solidarity figures had diverged, Wałęsa announced the formation of a new political party, Christian Democracy of Poland. Perhaps symbolically, the international media gave greater prominence to his subsequent announcement that he wanted his old job at the shipyard back, and stories of his apparent financial difficulties. Wałęsa was further embarrassed when, standing in the 2000 presidential elections, he finished in seventh place, with a humiliating 1.01% of the vote. He subsequently announced his retirement from politics.

Wallachia

The fertile northern bank of the eastern end of the River Danube in **Romania**, bounded by the southern Carpathians to the north and the Danube to the south. Historically a Christian principality, it came under the suzerainty of **Hungary** in 1369 before beginning a long period of domination by the Ottomans from 1389 to 1878. Since 1859 it has been an integral part of a united Romania. Its main urban centre is **Bucharest**.

Warsaw

The capital city of **Poland**, situated in the east central part of the country on the River Vistula (Wisla). *Population*: 1.7m. (2008 estimate). The city has been destroyed by invading armies several times over the last 250 years, most recently by the German forces in 1944 after the failure of the Warsaw Uprising. The entire left bank of the city was systematically razed to the ground. However, Warsaw was re-established as the capital of communist Poland and resumed the role of the country's cultural and economic centre. Its destruction allowed a complete redesigning of the city including industrial developments in its suburbs, larger parks and wider streets. Some of the older buildings were reconstructed entirely. It was not only the city's architecture which was ravaged by the war. The previously multicultural population, with large numbers of **Jews**, **Germans** and **Russians**, was transformed into one almost entirely comprising **Poles**. The local economy is dominated by the manufacture of electrical, metal and machine construction, along with lighter industries and food enterprises.

Warsaw Pact

A collective security agreement between the then communist states of **eastern Europe**, signed, and subsequently headquartered, in Warsaw on 1 May 1955 and dissolved in June 1991. Also known as the Warsaw Treaty Organization. The Pact members agreed to place the control of their armed forces under a central military command based in Moscow.

The Warsaw Pact effectively served as a Soviet-led counterweight to the **North Atlantic Treaty Organization** (NATO). The signatories were bound together to provide mutual assistance against foreign aggressors, and, in practice, to a great extent surrendered control of their foreign policies to the **Soviet Union**. The Warsaw Pact–NATO rivalry formed the basis of the **Cold War**.

The most dramatic action undertaken by the Warsaw Pact was the suppression of the 1968 Czechoslovak liberal communist experiment, the so-called **Prague Spring**. Whereas the suppression of the Hungarian Uprising 12 years earlier had been carried out by the Soviet army, the forces which entered Czechoslovakia on 20–21 August 1968, nominally at the invitation of hard-line communists there, were explicitly identified as Warsaw Pact forces (excluding **Romania** which had refused to participate). The Prague Spring movement's leaders were arrested and taken to the Soviet Union where they were compelled to resign. A 'normalizing' occupation force remained in Czechoslovakia until 1988.

Members: **Albania** (excluded from 1962 and withdrew in 1968), **Bulgaria**, **Czechoslovakia**, East Germany, **Hungary**, **Poland**, Romania and the Soviet Union.

Warsaw Stock Exchange
Giełda Papierów Wartościowych (GPW)

The exchange, originally established in 1817, was one of seven operating in **Poland** before the Second World War, and was reopened in April 1991 after the communist period. Market capitalization for the 376 companies listed in February 2010 totalled 190,204m. euros. In March 2010 there were 47 members.

President: Ludwik Sobolewski.
Address: Książęca 4, 00498 Warsaw.
Telephone: (22) 6283232.
Fax: (22) 6281754.
E-mail: wse@wse.com.pl
Internet: www.wse.com.pl

World Bank

The UN's main multilateral lending agency. Established in December 1945, the World Bank was concerned initially with financing post-war reconstruction but it has broadened its objectives to promoting the overall economic development of member nations. Its role is to make loans where private capital is not available on reasonable terms to finance productive investments. Loans are made either directly to governments, or to private enterprises with the guarantee of their governments. The World Bank comprises the International Bank for Reconstruction and Development (IBRD) and the International Development Association (IDA).

Members: 186 countries, including all **eastern European** countries.
President and Chair of Exec. Directors: Robert B. Zoellick.
Address: 1818 H St, NW, Washington, DC, 20433, USA.
Telephone: (202) 4731000.
Fax: (202) 4776391.
E-mail: pic@worldbank.org
Internet: www.worldbank.org

World Trade Organization (WTO)

The world body established on 1 January 1995 to give an institutional and legal foundation to the multilateral trading system. The successor to the General Agreement on Tariffs and Trade (GATT), it is intended to ensure that trading arrangements conform to an explicit set of rules. It provides procedures for the settlement of disputes, where WTO rulings are binding on member countries.

As of March 2010, the WTO has 153 members. Only five countries from **central** and **eastern Europe (Czech Republic, Greece, Hungary, Slovakia** and **Romania)** were members from the WTO's inception. Other member countries include **Albania** (8 September 2000), **Bulgaria** (1 December 1996), **Croatia** (30 November 2000), **Cyprus** (30 July 1995), **Estonia** (13 November 1999), **Latvia** (10 February 1999), **Lithuania** (31 May 2001), **Macedonia** (4 April 2003), **Poland** (1 July 1995) and **Slovenia** (30 July 1995). As of March 2010, there were also 29 countries in the process of applying for WTO membership. These included (with date of first establishment of a WTO working party on their application), **Bosnia and Herzegovina** (1999), **Montenegro** (2005) and **Serbia** (2005).

Director General: Pascal Lamy.
Address: Centre William Rappard, rue de Lausanne 154, 1211 Geneva 21, Switzerland.
Telephone: (22) 7395111.
Fax: (22) 7314206.
E-mail: enquiries@wto.org
Internet: www.wto.org

Y

Yalta Agreements

The conclusion of the famous summit between the leaders of the United Kingdom, the USA and the **Soviet Union** in the final stages of the Second World War. Meeting in Yalta (in modern-day Ukraine) in February 1945, the Allies unofficially parcelled up post-war Europe into spheres of influence, implicitly accepting that the Soviet Union would oversee the political future of the east. The conference also established the 1920 Curzon Line as the eastern frontier of **Poland**, granted international recognition, and support, to the Government of Marshal **Tito** in **Yugoslavia**, gave the Soviet Union its permanent seat (now Russia's) on the UN Security Council and agreed to the mass repatriation of ethnic **German** and **Russian** populations across **eastern Europe**. *See also* **Potsdam Agreements**.

Youth Party–European Greens
Stranka Mladih–Zeleni Evrope (SMS-Zeleni)

An ecologically-orientated formation in **Slovenia** contending that the established parties do not adequately represent young people. Founded in July 2000 as the Slovenian Youth Party (SMS), it unexpectedly surmounted the 4% barrier to representation in its first **National Assembly** elections in October 2000, its 4.3% of the vote earning it four seats. However, it failed to pass the election threshold in 2004, winning only 2.1% of the vote. SMS President Darko Krajnc stood in the 2007 presidential election, polling 2.2% of the vote. The SMS contested the 2008 election in alliance with the **Slovenian People's Party**, together winning five seats (with 5.2% of the vote). In July 2009 it adopted its current name, though retaining the SMS label.

Leadership: Darko Krajnc (President).
Address: Rimska cesta 8, 1000 Ljubljana.
Telephone: (1) 4211400.
Fax: (1) 4210001.
E-mail: info@sms.si
Internet: www.sms.si

Yugoslav Bank for International Economic Co-operation
Jugoslovenska Banka Za Medjunarodnu Ekonomsku Saradnju
(Jubmes Banka)

Focuses on the financing of export-orientated and development projects in **Serbia**. Founded in 1979. As of December 2007, the Bank had reserves of 362.2m. dinars.
President: Milan Stefanović.
Address: Bul. Zorana Đinđića 121, POB 219, 11070 Belgrade.
Telephone: (11) 2205500.
Fax: (11) 3110217.
E-mail: jubmes@jubmes.co.rs
Internet: www.jubmes.rs

Yugoslavia

The short-form name for a succession of 20th-century south **Slav** states in the western **Balkans**, which always included the modern republics of **Serbia**, **Montenegro** and **Kosovo**, and which until the early 1990s also included the modern republics of **Bosnia and Herzegovina**, **Croatia**, **Macedonia** and **Slovenia**

The Kingdom of Serbs, Croats and Slovenes, which had been formed in 1918, was renamed the Kingdom of Yugoslavia in 1929. At the end of the Second World War, the Yugoslav communists under **Tito** declared the Federal People's Republic of Yugoslavia on 29 November 1945. Under the 1963 Constitution this was renamed the **Socialist Federal Republic of Yugoslavia** (SFRY).

Slovenia and then Croatia seceded from the SFRY in June 1991, and Macedonia and Bosnia and Herzegovina soon followed suit, leading to the brutal regional conflict of 1992–95. The SFRY was declared non-existent in December 1991, the two remaining republics, Serbia (including Kosovo) and Montenegro, forming the rump Federal Republic of Yugoslavia (FRY) on 27 April 1992.

With Montenegro wanting its own independence a decade later, a looser union structure was agreed in 2002, and on 4 February 2003 the State Union of **Serbia and Montenegro** was formed as the successor to the FRY, finally ending the use of the name Yugoslavia.

Yugoslavism

Championed by **Tito** and the communists in the Second World War, this was intended to be a non-nationalist ideal along socialist lines which could help unify **Yugoslavia**'s various south **Slavic peoples**. However, by the 21st century the collapse of the federation left the concept of Yugoslavia as effectively the nostalgia of **Serb** nationalists for political dominance beyond the rump **Serbian** state.

Z

Zagreb

The capital of **Croatia**, situated in the middle of the country's two forks of territory. *Population*: 690,000 (2007 estimate). The city was not effectively a single entity until the construction of new buildings in the 19th century joined the ancient fortress of Gradec with the religious town of Kaptol. By the end of that century Zagreb had grown into a thriving urban centre and served as the base of **Croatian** and south **Slavic (Yugoslav)** nationalism. The declaration of Croatian independence from the Austro-Hungarian Empire was made from Zagreb in 1918 and the city remained the administrative centre of Croatia within the Kingdom of Serbs, Croats and Slovenes (later **Yugoslavia**). In this role it ensured its position as the major industrial centre for Croatia with production focusing on chemicals but also consumer goods. It also gained good transport access to the rest of the **Balkans**.

Zagreb was home to a large **Serb** community before the mass migrations engendered by the region's fierce wars in the early 1990s. During the conflict the city itself was shelled by Croat Serb forces in May 1995.

Zagreb Stock Exchange (ZSE)
Zagrebačka Burza

The securities trading exchange founded in **Croatia** in 1991 as a joint stock company by leading banks and insurance companies. The ZSE has 34 shareholders who elect a nine-member Supervisory Board. Market capitalization in March 2010 totalled 182,900m. kuna.

President of the Management Board: Roberto Motušić.
Address: Ivana Lučića 2A, 10000 Zagreb.
Telephone: (1) 4686800.
Fax: (1) 4677680.
E-mail: zeljko.kardum@zse.hr
Internet: www.zse.hr

Zares *see* **For Real—New Politics**.

Zastupnički Dom (Bosnia and Herzegovina)
(House of Representatives)

The lower house of the **Parliamentary Assembly** of **Bosnia and Herzegovina**.

Zastupnički Dom (Croatia)
(House of Representatives)

The single chamber of the **Assembly** of **Croatia**.

Zatlers, Valdis

President of **Latvia**. A medical doctor, hospital director and chair of his hospital's board in the capital, **Rīga**, Zatlers had not pursued a political career before his election as President. He was elected by **Parliament** on 31 May 2007, and inaugurated on 8 July 2007. His candidacy was supported by all four parties of the ruling coalition.

Born on 22 March 1955, he graduated from Rīga Institute of Medicine in 1979. He specialized in traumatology and orthopaedics at Rīga City Hospital No. 2, rising to head of department in 1985. During this time he spent a couple of months assisting with the consequences of the Chernobyl nuclear disaster in 1986, and six months in the USA in 1990–91 studying at Yale and Syracuse Universities. From 1994 he was Director of the State Hospital of Traumatology and Orthopaedics, and also helped to co-ordinate a Swiss Confederation Assistance Project (1995–99). From 1998 until his election as President he chaired the hospital's board, and regularly lectured on knee joint endoprosthetics and bone tissue transplantation.

Prior to Estonian independence, Zatlers had briefly been a board member of the Latvian Popular Front, but had not subsequently been active in politics.

He speaks Latvian, English and Russian.

Address: Office of the President, Pils Laukums 3, Rīga 1900.
Telephone: 67092106.
Fax: 67092157.
E-mail: chancery@president.lv
Internet: www.president.lv

ZES *see* **For a European Serbia—Boris Tadić**.

Zgromadzenie Naradowe *see* **National Assembly (Poland).**

Zhivkov, Todor

Head of Government and of the ruling party in communist-era **Bulgaria**, ousted in November 1989. Born to a peasant family in 1911, Zhivkov was apprenticed as a printer. He was a leading fighter in the communist Partisan resistance during the Second World War and helped organize the coup of September 1944 by which the Fatherland Front took power. He was brought into the top Bulgarian Communist Party leadership in 1954, and by 1962 was Prime Minister as well as the party's First Secretary. Skilled at playing off or cutting down possible rivals, he was at pains to remain always a loyal follower of the Moscow line, at least until the reform era initiated by Soviet leader Mikhail Gorbachev in the second half of the 1980s. With the Bulgarian economy deteriorating, Zhivkov clamped down on any domestic *glasnost* and launched in 1989 a fresh campaign against the **Bulgarian Turk** minority (already the target of 'Bulgarianization' in mid-decade). He was stunned when a 'palace coup' toppled him from power in November 1989 and his hope of an honourable retirement was dashed by the vehemence with which demonstrators denounced him. Zhivkov faced a wide range of charges brought in several instalments from 1992. In September 1992 he was sentenced to seven years in prison for embezzlement (a charge overturned by the Supreme Court in 1996); he faced other charges relating to the labour camps in which hundreds of detainees died amid extreme brutality, and to the anti-Turkish campaign, but was released from house arrest in September 1997 because of a limit on the length of time a defendant could be held without trial. He died on 5 August 1998.

ZSE *see* **Zagreb Stock Exchange.**

ZZS *see* **Union of Greens and Farmers.**

Country Listing

Albania

Albanian Centre for Foreign
    Investment Promotion
Albanian Independent
    News Agency
Albanian royal family
Albanian Telegraphic Agency
Albanians
Balkans
Bank of Albania
Berisha, Sali
Democratic Party of Albania
Enterprise Restructuring
    Agency
Epirus question
Greater Albania
Hoxha, Enver
Jews
Muslim peoples
National Agency
    for Privatization
People's Assembly
'Pyramid' investment schemes
Socialist Party of Albania
Tirana
Tirana Stock Exchange
Topi, Bamir
Union of Chambers
    of Commerce and
    Industry of Albania
Vlachs

Bosnia and Herzegovina

Alliance of Independent
    Social Democrats
Balkans
Banja Luka
Bosniaks
Brčko
Central Bank of Bosnia
    and Herzegovina
Chamber of Commerce of
    Bosnia and Herzegovina
Chetniks
Croatian Democratic Union
Croats
Cyrillic alphabet
Dayton Agreement
Dodik, Milorad
Ethnic cleansing
EUFOR
Federation News Agency
Foreign Investment Promotion
    Agency of Bosnia and
    Herzegovina
Goražde
Greater Croatia
Greater Serbia
Herceg-Bosna
Herzegovina
International Criminal Tribunal
    for the former Yugoslavia
Inzko, Valentin
Karadžić, Radovan
Komšić, Željko
Krišto, Borjana
Kuzmanović, Rajko
League of Communists
    of Yugoslavia
Mostar
Mrkonjič Grad
Mujezinović, Mustafa
Muslim peoples
Muslim-Croat Federation
News Agency of
    the Serb Republic
Office of the High
    Representative
Orthodox Christianity
Parliamentary Assembly

Party for Bosnia
    and Herzegovina
Party of Democratic Action
Party of Democratic Progress
Privatization Agency of the
    Federation of Bosnia
    and Herzegovina
Radmanović, Nebojša
Republika Srpska Directorate
    for Privatization
Roman Catholic Church
Sarajevo
Sarajevo Stock Exchange
Serb Republic
Serbian Democratic Party
Serbs
Silajdžić, Haris
Slavic peoples
Social Democratic Party of
    Bosnia and Herzegovina
Socialist Federal Republic
    of Yugoslavia (SFRY)
Špirić, Nikola
Srebrenica
Tito
Voucher privatization
Yugoslavism

509

510

Slovakia

Bratislava
Bratislava Stock Exchange
Charter 77
Czechoslovakia
Czechs
Direction–Social Democracy
Dubček, Alexander
Eurozone
Fico, Robert
Gabčíkovo-Nagymaros Dam
Gašparovič, Ivan
Greater Hungary
Havel, Václav
Hungarian Coalition Party
Hungarians
Husák, Gustáv
Klaus, Václav
Lustration laws
Mečiar, Vladimír
National Bank of Slovakia
National Council of the
    Republic of Slovakia
National Property Fund
News Agency of the
    Slovak Republic
People's Party–Movement for
    a Democratic Slovakia
Prague Spring
Public Against Violence
Roma
Roman Catholic Church
Slavic peoples
Slovak Chamber of Commerce
    and Industry
Slovak Democratic and
    Christian Union–
    Democratic Party
Slovak Investment and Trade
    Development Agency
Slovak National Party
Slovaks
StB
Velvet divorce
Velvet revolution
Voucher privatization

Slovenia

Agency for Reconstruction
    and Privatization
Balkans
Bank of Slovenia
Chamber of Commerce and
    Industry of Slovenia
Democratic Party of
    Slovenian Pensioners
Drnovšek, Janez
Eurozone
For Real—New Politics
Istria
League of Communists
    of Yugoslavia
Liberal Democracy of Slovenia
Ljubljana
Ljubljana Stock Exchange
National Assembly
Pahor, Borut
Roman Catholic Church
Slavic peoples
Slovene Press Agency
Slovenes
Slovenia Democratic Party
Slovenian National Party
Slovenian People's Party
Social Democrats
Socialist Federal Republic
    of Yugoslavia (SFRY)
Tito
Trieste
Türk, Danilo
Youth Party–European Greens
Yugoslavism

Other Entries

Central Europe
Cold War
Conventional Forces
    in Europe
Eastern Europe
Helsinki Final Act
Helsinki process
Islamic fundamentalism
Nomenklatura
Nuclear Suppliers' Group
Pan-Slavism
Potsdam Agreements
South-Eastern Europe
Yalta Agreements

International Organizations

Adriatic Charter
Alliance of Democrats
Baltic Council of Ministers (BCM)
Baltic Marine Environment Protection Commission
(HELCOM or Helsinki Commission)
Bank for International Settlements (BIS)
Central European Free Trade Area (CEFTA)
Central European Initiative (CEI)
Centrist Democrat International (CDI)
Conflict Prevention Centre (CPC)
Contact Group (for the former Yugoslavia)
Council for Mutual Economic Assistance (CMEA or Comecon)
Council of Europe
Council of the Baltic Sea States (CBSS)
Danube Commission
Euro-Atlantic Partnership Council (EAPC)
European Bank for Reconstruction and Development (EBRD)
European Court of Human Rights (ECHR)
European Organization for Nuclear Research (CERN)
European Stability Initiative (ESI)
European Union (EU)
International Atomic Energy Agency (IAEA)
International Bank for Reconstruction and Development (IBRD)
International Commission for the Protection of the Danube River (ICPDR)
International Court of Justice (ICJ)
International Democrat Union (IDU)
International Monetary Fund (IMF)
International Organization for Migration (IOM)
Liberal International
North Atlantic Co-operation Council (NACC)
North Atlantic Treaty Organization (NATO)
Organisation for Economic Co-operation and Development (OECD)
Organisation of the Islamic Conference (OIC)
Organization for Security and Co-operation in Europe (OSCE)
Organization of the Black Sea Economic Co-operation (BSEC)
Partnership for Peace (PfP)
Permanent Court of Arbitration (PCA)
Regional Co-operation Council (RCC)
Socialist International
Soros Foundations network
Stability Pact for South-Eastern Europe
United Nations Economic Commission for Europe (UNECE)
Vilnius Group
Visegrád Group
Warsaw Pact
World Bank
World Trade Organization (WTO)

Index of Personal Names

519

R

Račan, Ivica, 89, 102, 454
Radičová, Iveta, 185, 212, 427, 433
Radišić, Zivko, 34, 95
Radmanović, Nebojša, 12, 37, 387
Radomski, Janusz, 85
Radoš, Jozo, 102
Radu, 401
Raguž, Martin, 35, 95
Rainys, Gediminas, 470
Rajk, László, 242
Rákosi, Mátyás, 320
Rallis, George, 194, 333
Rama, Edi, 6, 460
Rasmussen, Anders Fogh, 337
Repše, Einars, 149, 267, 334
Rexhepi, Bajram, 139, 252
Rimšēvičs, Ilmārs, 24
Robinson, Patrick L., 231
Rohatinski, Željko, 99
Rologis, Vassilis, 110
Roman, Petre, 130, 394
Rop, Anton, 279, 440, 457
Rubiks, Alfreds, 203
Rugova, Ibrahim, 126, 139, 251, 252, 405, 475
Rusko, Pavel, 427, 432
Rutelli, Francesco, 11
Rüütel, Arnold, 162, 227, 449

S

Saladžienė, Arminta, 322
Salber, Herbert, 83
Salihaj, Adem, 127, 405
Samaras, Antonis, 334
Sampson, Nicos, 106
Sanader, Ivo, 90, 98, 250
Šarkinas, Reinoldijus, 25
Šarović, Mirko, 12, 36, 387, 418
Sartzetakis, Christos, 194
Saudabayev, Kanat, 344
Savisaar, Edgar, 161, 166, 167, 474
Saxecoburggotski, Simeon (Simeon II), 31, 46, 48, 52, 54, 57, 316, 385
Schuster, Rudolf, 431
Schwarzenberg, Karel, 200

Schwarz-Schilling, Christian, 38
Segliņš, Mareks, 363
Sejdiu, Fatmir, 127, 253, 254, 405
Selami, Eduard, 137
Semjén, Zsolt, 67
Šergan, Tadeja, 437
Šešelj, Vojislav, 419, 420
Shabad, George, 21
Shcharansky, Anatoly, 206
Shehu, Mehmet, 211
Shehu, Tritan, 137
Siderov, Volen, 49
Siiman, Mart, 162
Silajdžić, Haris, 34, 358, 359, 360, 422
Silenieks, Viesturs, 272
Simitis, Costas, 194, 349
Simoneti, Marko, 291
Simor, András, 324
Škele, Andris, 266, 273, 362
Skwiecinski, Piotr, 377
Slakteris, Atis, 362
Slánský, Rudolf, 79
Šleževičius, Adolfas, 282
Slota, Ján, 148, 212, 428, 429, 433
Śniadek, Janusz, 466
Sobolewski, Ludwik, 500
Sobotka, Bohuslav, 120
Sokol , Jan, 120
Soljić, Vladimir, 95
Sólyom, László, 221, 466
Somr, Zdeněk, 156
Soros, George, 467, 468
Soyer, Ferdi Sabit, 388, 389, 485
Špidla, Vladimír, 69, 115, 120
Špirić, Nikola, 12, 38, 96, 360, 469
Stalin, Joseph, 54, 79, 85, 339
Stanishev, Sergey, 49, 57, 316
Stankovski, Zvonko, 301
Stefanović, Milan, 503
Stephanopoulos, Costas, 195
Stibral, Milan, 112
Stoica, Valeriu, 328
Stolojan, Theodor, 26, 30, 131, 328, 396
Stoyanov, Petar, 47, 56, 316, 385
Stráský, Jan, 72
Strauss-Kahn, Dominique, 233

Šturanović, Željko, 143, 153, 154, 311
Suchocka, Hanna, 369
Šuškavčević, Dejana, 314
Svejnar, Jan, 73, 116, 121
Svoboda, Cyril, 69, 70
Svoboda, Jiří, 80
Svoboda, Ludvík, 79
Swing, William Lacy, 233
Szalay-Berzeviczy, Attila, 45
Szili, Katalin, 217

T

Taagepera, Rein, 166
Tadić, Boris, 136, 140, 180, 182, 258, 411, 412, 420, 472, 505
Talat, Mehmet Ali, 71, 107, 146, 159, 331, 383, 388, 473, 484
Tarand, Andres, 449
Tauscher, Ellen, 11
Terzić, Adnan, 37, 358, 360
Thaçi, Hashim, 139, 254, 257, 475
Tihić, Sulejman, 36, 358, 359, 360, 423
Tito, Marshal, 33, 66, 88, 244, 258, 275, 293, 367, 380, 408, 421, 438, 457, 477, 481, 502, 503
Tökés, László, 214
Tolkatch , Aleksandr, 123
Tomač, Zdravko, 454
Topi, Bamir, 6, 138, 460, 478
Topolánek, Mirek, 69, 73, 115, 120
Trajkovski, Boris, 228, 295
Tsatsos, Constantine, 194
Tsipras, Alexis, 77
Tsvetanov, Tsvetan, 71
Tudjman, Franjo, 88, 93, 96, 158, 189, 261, 454, 481
Tudor, Corneliu Vadim, 394
Tůma, Zdeněk, 112
Türk, Danilo, 141, 180, 440, 445, 447, 457, 482
Tusevljak, Spasoje, 35, 95
Tusk, Donald, 74, 75, 134, 242, 370, 373, 376, 485
Tzannetakis, Tzannis, 194